THE
DIVINE
COMEDY

THE
DIVINE
COMEDY

Dante Alighieri

Translated by John Ciardi

W · W · NORTON & COMPANY, INC. New York

Library of Congress Cataloging in Publication Data

Dante Alighieri, 1265–1321.
  The divine comedy.

  Translation of the Divina commedia.
I. Ciardi, John, 1916– II. Title.
PQ4315.C5 1977   851'.1   77–24225
ISBN 978-0-393-04472-0

Canto I was first published in *Italian Quarterly,* 1965.
Canto VIII was first published in *Arbor,* 1961.
Canto XXI was first published in *Hartwick Review,* 1967.
Canto XXXIII was first published in *The Rarer Action: Essays in Honor
of Francis Fergusson,* ed. Alan Cheuse and Richard Koffler, 1970.

For Archibald MacLeish

Vidi, presso di me, un veglio solo
    Degno di tant reverenza in vista,
    Che più non dee, a padre, alcun figliuolo.
                        —*Purgatorio*, I, 31–33

Contents

Introduction: The Method of *The Divine Comedy*

The traditional epic dealt with ethnic origins. It celebrated the gods and ancient heroes whose wars brought glory to the tribe that became the nation. It was sung by anonymous rhapsodes who originated around the tribal campfire.

The Divine Comedy is no such poem. It deals with the past—because it has access to the dead; it deals with the future—because Dante believed his faith gave him access to God's intention, though only in part; but it takes place in Dante's own time, and he is the main persona of the poem.

It is in its scope that the poem can be called epic. Dante travels the universe from end to end, from his personal grappling with the hairy sides of Satan to his final ecstatic vision of God. He maps the physical and moral geography of that universe. (For him physical and moral law were entwined manifestations of God's will.) He evaluates everything in the universe within a single system of values. (The universe was, for him, a sphere of which Satan was the center and God the circumference. Hence a thing is good as it occurs closer to God and evil as it occurs closer to Satan. He need only say where in that universe he saw a given thing or a given person, and that placement assigns it its value.)

In doing so much, Dante also classifies, interrelates, and assesses the good or evil of every form of human behavior. It is a standard pedagogical trick, for example, upon completing the reading of *The Inferno*, to ask the class if there is any human failing Dante has not covered. So invited, the class is likely to suggest "dope addiction" as something unknown to Dante. But addiction is, of course, a form of gluttony, and though Dante does not deal with its Platonic instance he does deal with its form. One student suggested "driving to endanger." Dante, he reasons, could not have foreseen the automobile. Nor did he. But he knew the form of that behavior. In *The Inferno*, VIII, among the Wrathful and the Sullen we find Fillippo dei Adimari, nicknamed Argenti (Silvers) because he shod his war horses with silver and rode them recklessly through the narrow alleys of Florence, insolently knocking and scattering pedestrians. He was a horseback hot-rodder, categorically no different from the reckless automobile driver. Dante deals with all that men do.

It is this inclusiveness that moved T. S. Eliot to write, "Dante and Shakespeare divide the world between them, there is no third." Eliot meant that one seems to experience a total sampling of mankind in the works of these authors.

Shakespeare's mind and mood were such that he was never moved to deal with the contemplative mystic, an important figure to Dante. To that extent, the total Shakespearean cast may be said to lack one character. It is a small omission: when we have read the collected plays we feel that we have met a total range of mankind. In *The Divine Comedy* we meet such a "total human population" within a single allegorical narrative (and angels, too, and even God). Everything it is to be a human being is brought to form and consequence within a single structure that makes *The Divine Comedy* the most massive metaphor of western culture.

The system of this metaphor is religious. The poem was conceived as a preachment, as an exhortation to godliness. Yet every specification when deepened by genius tends to become a universal. The reader who does not care to read for religious point is free to read for psychological insights. The reading remains as esthetically profound to one view as to another. The reader who cares nothing about sin has *The Inferno* available as a treatise on self-destructive behavior. It is this universality of insight that makes *The Divine Comedy* as relevant to a twentieth-century agnostic as it was to the pious man of Dante's time.

The Divine Comedy is, above all else, interesting to read. Despite the weight of social, moral, scientific, and religious commentary, the writing remains active and dramatic. It remains so because the metaphoric schema makes possible enormous economies, allowing value judgments to be made without rhetorical assertion. With his moral and religious obligations so served by the very structure of the poem, Dante is free to create dramatic incidents, to invent the memorable story of the death of Ulysses, and to work into his poem thousands of the details stored in his encyclopedic mind. For aside from his poetic genius, Dante was a scholar, and a man of great and retentive intellect. In an earlier but unfinished work he had begun to set forth in Italian prose nothing less than the whole of human knowledge. The detail and orderliness of his many-leveled intellect is in itself a marvel, especially when one recognizes that he lacked the elaborate reference works available to modern scholars. Dante had to carry his vast information in his head. He carried it with a scholastic precision beyond the normal range of our experience as readers. The reader must, therefore, adjust his attention to the exactness of Dante's.

"Midway in our life's journey," the poem begins. We are used to such phrases used for poetic resonance. We must understand that Dante uses them precisely. "Our life's journey" is the biblically allotted three score years and ten. "Midway" in it means "at age thirty-five." Dante was born in 1265. He is saying, therefore, "in the year 1300 when I was thirty-five years old."

In the first few lines we further learn that the poem opens exactly at dawn on Good Friday. From these opening lines and from later references we learn that at that beginning of the Easter season the moon was full, the sun was at the vernal equinox, and that it was in the sign of Aries (medieval legend had it that the newly created sun first shone in Aries).

Scholars have since checked Dante's detail and have shown that there was no time in the year 1300 at which all of these phenomena concurred. But Dante, too, was a scholar. He knew his details were not literally true. He so combined them in order to sound a triumphant opening theme of rebirth, the beginning of the soul's return to God. For Dante's method is not only allegorical but symphonic, the poem developing in a series of musiclike themes.

The first major theme is introduced immediately after the opening and develops throughout *The Inferno* and *The Purgatorio* to its resolution in the Terrestrial Paradise at the top of the Mount of Purgatory.

Allegorically, the knowledge that one is lost is the beginning of finding one's way. In that knowledge, Dante looks up and sees the first rays of dawn on the shoulders of a little hill.

Throughout *The Divine Comedy* the sun is a fixed symbol of God as Divine Illumination. In *The Purgatorio*, for example, the soul can ascend only when the sun is above the horizon (only in the light of God, by the grace of God); once it has set, the soul is powerless to ascend (only God can lead man to God).

Naturally, Dante yearns for that light. He races up the hill toward it. The allegorical-thematic point is that Dante's action is foolish. God will not be come by that easily. Does one simply race up to the light and say, "Here I am, God. Sorry I neglected you"? True zeal is a deeper commitment.

So it is that Dante's way is blocked by three beasts who symbolize the three divisions of Hell: a She-Wolf, the sins of incontinence, Upper Hell; a Lion, the sins of violence and ambition, Middle Hell; and a Leopard, the sins of Fraud, Lower Hell. Together they stand for all the sins of worldliness, and it is exactly his worldliness that stands between Dante and God.

Theme exfoliating from theme, Dante knows that his rebirth was in the realization that he had been paying too much attention to worldly affairs (his political involvement in Florence), and to material philosophy (his earlier scholarship), and too little attention to God.

He had been guilty of *Acedia*, or Sloth. *Acedia* is central to the seven deadly sins. It is also a central theme of *The Divine Comedy*. It is lack of zeal. It is the sin of knowing the Good while being lax in its observance. But it is more than that. If a man is truly devout, when has he prayed enough? When is it time to rise from his knees and perform good works? In the Ante-Purgatory, Henry III of England is made to wait before he may begin the pain and joy of his purification because he spent so much time in prayer that he neglected his kingdom. The fixed principle—it is another theme that intertwines throughout the symphonic structure of the poem—is Aristotle's *metron ariston*, moderation is best. Dante's aim in all things is to achieve that perfect proportion inherent in all God's works.

The Divine Comedy was conceived and executed as that precisely proportioned counteraction of zeal by which one man shapes his whole attention to God.

Forced back into the darkness by the three beasts, Dante discovers the figure of Virgil. Virgil's complex allegorical significance is best left for the text of the poem and the explanatory notes. He is most relevant here as an example of Dante's thematic structuring, as is the figure of Beatrice, at whose command Virgil comes to Dante's aid.

Virgil's first function is to show Dante the folly of trying to reach God so easily. To try to do so is as foolish as to try to catch the sun by running up a hill. Dante must go a more difficult way. He must undertake the perilous descent to the bottom of Hell, to the recognition of the true nature of sin. He must then make the arduous ascent of the Mount of Purgatory, to the total renunciation of sin. Only then, after great labor, can the soul be ready to approach God. Virgil offers the way of total experience and of total involvement.

For Dante is a man of intellect, and intellect has itself to reckon. Perhaps the simple soul, the soul so innately pure that it has no need of intellect but is free simply to obey its own inner impulse—perhaps that soul may achieve God effortlessly, but not the man of mind.

Beatrice, in one of her allegorical aspects, may be just that simple soul. In time Dante, too, must achieve that purity and simplicity: "Unless ye become as little children ye shall not enter the kingdom of Heaven." Virgil is Dante's guide from his first rebirth in the Wood of Error, to the heavenly rebirth in which Dante becomes that simple soul.

Once Virgil has introduced himself, his first words are, "He must go by another way who would escape." In the Terrestrial Paradise, as the resolution of this intricately structured theme, Virgil's last words, after which he disappears, are, "lord of yourself I crown and mitre you." Virgil is giving Dante sovereignty and holy office over his own soul, from which all evil impulse has been removed. He need no longer intellectualize. He need only obey his inner prompting and good will inevitably follow.

Morally and anagogically, Virgil's words culminate the soul's first essential evolution. Musically, they resolve what must be one of the most richly developed and sustained themes in world poetry. From the dark wood to the terrestrial paradise, this progress of the soul is a single music.

Once the reader has understood how Dante builds by thematic development rather than by rhetorical assertion, it is the poem itself that teaches the reader how it is to be read. It does so in an inexhaustible invitation to poetic pleasure.

Dante must be read attentively: mind will reveal itself only to mind. But Dante is not difficult to read. It is true that he writes in depth and on many simultaneous levels. Yet his language is usually simple and straightforward. If the gold of Dante runs deep, it also runs up to the surface. A lifetime of reading cannot mine all that gold; yet enough lies on the surface, or only an inch below, to make a first reading a bonanza in itself. All one needs are some suggestions as to what to look for. Thereafter, one need only follow the vein as it goes deeper and deeper. One must, to begin with, think allegorically. And one must be aware of Dante's intricate symphonic structure.

One must note, moreover, not only Dante's orchestration but his architectonics. *The Divine Comedy* has been compared to a Gothic cathedral. If so it is a Gothic cathedral with three floors. Just as the vistas from different points of a cathedral offer different combinations of the architectural elements, so Dante's perspectives and juxtapositions within his schema, allow him to release complex meanings that need not be said in words. Any good poem releases more meaning than can be overtly asserted. No poet achieves greater effect than Dante in his release of the unspoken insight.

Think of *The Inferno* as if it were the ground plan of a cathedral. At an equal distance in from the side walls of a cathedral one finds two rows of columns that refer to one another architecturally. At a certain distance into

The Inferno, one meets Paolo and Francesca. At an equal distance in from the end, one meets Ruggieri and Ugolino. These are the two most memorable pairs of souls in Hell. The upper two are almost the least sinful souls in Hell; the lower two, almost the most sinful.

Dante does not speak one word to suggest that we compare one and the other, yet he induces us to an inevitable comparison. Something in the phrasing and the tone of the Ruggieri-Ugolino passage echoes the phrasing and the tone of the Paolo-Francesca passage. Scholars have pointed out that the language of both passages derives in part from a single passage in the *Aeneid*—proof enough of a connection in Dante's mind, yet any careful reader will sense this connection even without the scholars' clue. Clearly, Dante wants us to compare these two passages as the subject of a pious meditation.

It becomes, I believe, a meditation on the power of love. We start with two pairs of souls who have become one another's damnation; but had either soul in either pair thought of God and of love, rather than of his or her own passions, all four might well have won salvation. So for the almost least sinful; so for the almost most sinful.

What we have is a homily of some religious and psychological substance released by juxtaposition through the assistance of overtones without the utterance of a single overt word on the subject.

In another memorable alignment Dante juxtaposes Farinata degli Uberti in Hell ("Great chest, great brow,/ he seemed to hold all Hell in disrespect."); Sordello in Purgatory ("O Lombard, soul serene,/ how nobly and deliberately you watched us!"); and his own ancestor, Cacciaguida, in Heaven ("Just so did the shade of ancient Ilium . . . greet Aeneas in Elysium."). We are not told overtly to compare these three figures. We note that they occur at corresponding points of the three levels and that they have a tonality in common. We are, therefore, induced to compare them. Having been so induced, we are left with a directed meditation on the power of great personal dignity and valor on the infernal, purgatorial, and paradisal levels.

Another element of economy, freeing Dante from the need for tedious exposition, is the simple Talmudic law of Hell: as the soul sinned, so is it punished—exactly. When souls are punished by fire, for example, each is subjected to a flame at a temperature exactly calculated to its own degree of sinfulness. One might be moved to argue that such an idea is nonsense and that a soul on the griddle could not distinguish between 450° and 451° on any scale. But Dante would likely answer, "God can and does, and he so makes the souls that they can and do. His gradations are infinite and exact."

Bertrand de Born, the Provençal poet, was an advisor of the French dauphin and moved him to oppose his father. Because he separated father from son, his head is divided from his body. He carries it around a circular trench, holding it by the hair as if it were a lantern. In order to speak to Dante, who is standing above him on the shoulder of the trench, he raises the head at arm's length, and it cries, "thus is the law of Hell observed in me" (*Inferno*, XXVIII, 143). It is the law of symbolic retribution. Dante need not discourse at length on the nature of each sin because its nature is

refigured in the punishment. Dramatic action does for rhetorical exposition
—the first rule of good narrative.

Another fixed principle of Hell is that no soul can care for another or
find comfort in another. Hell is the exclusion of others, as Heaven is the
active out-going love of others (*Caritas*), and as Purgatory, though it
includes *Caritas*, is the condition of the joyous acceptance of the pain that
purifies the soul.

Unless this principle is borne in mind, the modern reader will likely mis-
read the Paolo-Francesca episode to the conclusion that their love triumphs
even in Hell. But were they capable of love, Hell could not contain them;
they would soar toward Heaven, as all things in nature are drawn to what
they most are. Paolo and Francesca are together because they add to one
another's pain. Theirs is the condition of a marriage gone stale and hateful.
To all eternity they must be whirled about in the black wind (the whirlwind of their own mortal passions), seeing one another's bodies whirl
before them, and thinking "For that, alas, I went damned."

Another error into which the modern humanist may easily fall, is to condemn *The Inferno* as a travelogue of a trip through a concentration camp,
in which the author sympathizes with the keepers. Dante does, of course,
weep at times for the grief he sees. Yet at several points, moved by *giusto
sdegno*, righteous indignation, he adds to the pains of the sinners. And in
the *bolgia* of the Fortune Tellers and Diviners, when Dante weeps at the
distorted bodies of those souls, Virgil (The figure of Reason) scolds him
(*Inferno*, XX, 27–30):

> Still like the other fools? There is no place
> for pity here. Who is more arrogant
> within his soul, who is more impious
> than one who dares to sorrow at God's judgment?

These incidents, along with others not mentioned here, constitute a sub-
theme of the progress of the soul. The descent is the journey to the recognition of sin. At first, the experience is almost more than Dante can bear.
He swoons at the first sight of Hell. With increased recognition, however,
his soul grows, he sees sin for what it really is, and he arms himself against
it.

Dante's progress is not a matter of gloating over the evil that has befallen
others, but a much subtler recognition. To begin with, aerial bodies (as Statius explains fully in *The Purgatorio*) cannot dissemble. When the soul
passes into the eternal life, it projects on the air about it an exact image of
its inner state of being. A central image and theme of *The Divine Comedy*
is the perfection of the body of God, and of man ideally conceived in
God's image. The damned—the destroyed destroyers—are figured as distor-
tions of God's perfect body, sin being the agent of distortion. The damned
appear as they do because they appear as they truly are.

It is not Dante's purpose to take pleasure in the suffering of the damned,
but to make clear what has distorted them, as a pious warning to living
men and women. Hell is not *where* the damned are; it is *what* they are. As
all things seek what they most are, the damned *seek* Hell. The damned
have *insisted* upon their own damnation. For it is basic Catholic doctrine
(the doctrine of Ever Sufficient Grace) that God welcomes all who ask for

him. Dante makes a point of presenting to us, in Purgatory, souls whose sins were greater than those of some of the souls in Hell. They are in Purgatory (and, therefore, inevitably bound for Heaven, though only after long purification) because they repented, if only at the end, if only by whispering half the name of Mary with their last breath. The damned are beyond pity because they have what they truly want. "They yearn for what they fear," Dante says of the souls entering Acheron's ferry; a theme he develops at several points in *The Inferno*. Theirs is most nearly, perhaps, the condition of the addict: they hate the habit, but they crave the dose, and it is the dose that conquers them.

Above all, however, the humanist must bear in mind that Dante observes in each of the souls of the damned possibilities of his own soul, possibilities it is his zealous duty to recognize and to scourge from himself. He is not writing a humanist manifesto: he is constructing a thematically intricate yet ever consistent allegory of what *every* devout man must do in order to be subsumed into God as faith leads him and as Scripture and church doctrine guide him.

Because I have tried to suggest some approaches to Dante for the beginning reader, and because *The Inferno* is what comes first, I have said more of it than of *The Purgatorio* or *The Paradiso*. Most twentieth-century readers have, in fact, found *The Inferno* to be the most absorbing of the three canticles, if only because it is the most starkly dramatic. *The Paradiso*, on the contrary, has struck many readers as an abstract and pedantic work: so many having concurred in these judgments that it will not do to ignore them.

Yet these are, I have come to believe, judgments specific to a shallow reading. As one comes to know the work intimately, it is *The Paradiso* that emerges as the one work of European genius most worthy to be called miraculous.

Dante's fundamental esthetic is *il bello*, which is one more expression of the Aristotelean mean, as is his *giusto sdegno* of Fillippi Argenti, that righteous indignation which is the golden mean between wrath (which is sinful) and indifferce to evil (which is also sinful). The goal of *il bello* is to fit the form and the style exactly to the subject matter. It is ideal proportion, as the body of God and all of God's works are ideal proportion, and as the devout soul must seek ideal proportion in all its acts and thoughts.

Because *The Inferno* deals with coarseness and depravity, Dante deliberately roughens his style at times. In Cantos XXI and XXII of *The Inferno* Dante deals with the grafters. With the Cathedral metaphor in mind, many critics have referred to this passage as "the gargoyle cantos." The fiends who guard these sinners are under the command of a fell sergeant named Malacoda (Badtail). At the end of Canto XXI his squad of fiends gives a military signal asking permission to pass—they stick out their tongues—and Malacoda replies in the last line of Canto XXI: "and he had made a trumpet of his ass." The opening passage of Canto XXII is a sustained coarse comic routine on military signals and on the fact that Dante had never seen armed forces "take their direction from so low a toot."

These crudities are calculated. Too many such touches would violate the principles of *il bello*, too few would violate those principles in the opposite way. Everything is to be in exact proportion. Nor can the poet ever forget he is singing the praises of God. When he is most deeply moved among the rigors of Hell, Dante's style soars sublimely, as when he says to Brunetto Latino, "you taught me how man makes himself immortal."

The miracle of *The Paradiso* is in Dante's ability to outsoar all previous dimension of expectation. As "everywhere in Heaven is Paradise," he begins in the fullness of bliss, yet it is necessary to convey greater and greater bliss as the soul draws closer to God, level by level, through the Nine Spheres. "How speak trans-human change to human sense?" Dante asks in *Paradiso*, I, 60. He must *invent* a language for his concept. He must never forget that he does not see heaven through his own powers of observation, but that it is shown to him by God's grace. "I saw" becomes a rare form. It is generally replaced by "there appeared to me," or "it was shown to me." These subtleties are only a smallest part of the ultimate refinement of Dante's sublimest style. The total becomes an unequaled language experience.

And the language is joined to a dazzling metaphoric concept, for to greet the poet's triumphant soul, all Heaven joins in a dramatic enactment it has never before performed. Moved by limitless love, the souls of the elect descend from their blissful contemplation of God to present themselves to Dante—the first mortal ever to view all of Heaven—in a nine-leveled masque. They appear to Dante, not as they truly are, but in such forms as may be grasped by his fallible mortal understanding. It is a daring metaphor. Dante has even been accused of arrogance in having all Heaven so perform itself for his benefit. But there is no arrogance in Dante's conception. The one message of faith is that there are no limits to love, and that all Heaven does so rejoice in the triumph of every purified soul. Dante is always specifically himself, yet he is always equally the Christian pilgrim: what Heaven offers him it offers to every soul that seeks, the one difference being that the souls of the dead ascend to heaven magnified by revelation, whereas Dante comes encumbered by his mortal flesh and the limits of mortal reason. It is his limitations that make necessary this elaborate pageantry of Heaven, and it is Heavenly love that moves the heavenly souls to joy in their performance. Dante does not see Heaven through any use of his own powers: it *performs itself to him* at a level his feeble intellect can grasp; for every one of the souls that shows itself to Dante is telepathically connected to every other, because all are directly connected to the mind of God. The heavenly souls do not use language: they communicate through their common existence in the mind of God. It is for Dante's sake that they express themselves in words, in song, and in performed pageants. They do not, in fact, leave the rapture of their contemplation of God at the height of Heaven. Out of God's love, as they are joined in the body of God, they send visions down to Dante.

In the sublimity of his fullest style and within this unparalleled metaphor, Dante is left to invent means for speaking his "trans-human change." It is the inexhaustability of that invention that makes *The Paradiso* the supreme achievement of western literature. Starting with something like total bliss, total radiance, and the most dazzling of visual effects, how is the poet to invent, one by one, eight further ranges to the top of Heaven? By the time he enters the Sphere of the Sun, the fourth of the nine spheres, the souls of the blessèd are already so radiant that they stand out clearly from the background of the sun. By what poetic invention is one to express an even greater radiance in the next sphere, and again for four more increases in brilliance to the top of Heaven?

What awes the careful reader of *The Paradiso* is the unstrained and inexhaustible exfoliation of concept from concept and invention from invention. Having outsoared what seems to be the total possibility of esthetic invention, Dante constantly surmounts expectation to an even higher level. The poem soars to its conclusion with the inevitability of a symphony. It is not always easy to follow Dante's flight, but the reader who will form an attention sufficient to such conceptual music will find in *The Paradiso* the summit of all European expression.

The Inferno

Canto I

Midway in his allotted threescore years and ten, Dante comes to himself
with a start and realizes that he has strayed from the True Way into the
Dark Wood of Error (Worldliness). As soon as he has realized his loss,
Dante lifts his eyes and sees the first light of the sunrise (the Sun is the
Symbol of Divine Illumination) lighting the shoulders of a little hill (The
Mount of Joy). It is the Easter Season, the time of resurrection, and the
sun is in its equinoctial rebirth. This juxtaposition of joyous symbols fills
Dante with hope and he sets out at once to climb directly up the Mount
of Joy, but almost immediately his way is blocked by the Three Beasts of
Worldliness: *The Leopard of Malice and Fraud, The Lion of Violence and
Ambition,* and *The She-Wolf of Incontinence.* These beasts, and especially
the She-Wolf, drive him back despairing into the darkness of error. But just
as all seems lost, a figure appears to him. It is the shade of *Virgil,* Dante's
symbol of *Human Reason.*

Virgil explains that he has been sent to lead Dante from error. There
can, however, be no direct ascent past the beasts: the man who would
escape them must go a longer and harder way. First he must descend
through Hell (The Recognition of Sin), then he must ascend through Purgatory (The Renunciation of Sin), and only then may he reach the pinna-
cle of joy and come to the Light of God. Virgil offers to guide Dante, but
only as far as Human Reason can go. Another guide (*Beatrice,* symbol of
Divine Love) must take over for the final ascent, for Human Reason is
self-limited. Dante submits himself joyously to Virgil's guidance and they
move off.

Midway in our life's journey, I went astray
    from the straight road and woke to find myself
    alone in a dark wood. How shall I say   3

what wood that was! I never saw so drear,
    so rank, so arduous a wilderness!
    Its very memory gives a shape to fear.   6

Death could scarce be more bitter than that place!
    But since it came to good, I will recount
    all that I found revealed there by God's grace.   9

How I came to it I cannot rightly say,
    so drugged and loose with sleep had I become
    when I first wandered there from the True Way.   12

But at the far end of that valley of evil
    whose maze had sapped my very heart with fear
    I found myself before a little hill   15

and lifted up my eyes. Its shoulders glowed
    already with the sweet rays of that planet
    whose virtue leads men straight on every road,   18

and the shining strengthened me against the fright
   whose agony had wracked the lake of my heart
   through all the terrors of that piteous night.   21

Just as a swimmer, who with his last breath
   flounders ashore from perilous seas, might turn
   to memorize the wide water of his death—   24

so did I turn, my soul still fugitive
   from death's surviving image, to stare down
   that pass that none had ever left alive.   27

And there I lay to rest from my heart's race
   till calm and breath returned to me. Then rose
   and pushed up that dead slope at such a pace   30

each footfall rose above the last. And lo!
   almost at the beginning of the rise
   I faced a spotted Leopard, all tremor and flow   33

and gaudy pelt. And it would not pass, but stood
   so blocking my every turn that time and again
   I was on the verge of turning back to the wood.   36

This fell at the first widening of the dawn
   as the sun was climbing Aries with those stars
   that rode with him to light the new creation.   39

Thus the holy hour and the sweet season
   of commemoration did much to arm my fear
   of that bright murderous beast with their good omen.   42

Yet not so much but what I shook with dread
   at sight of a great Lion that broke upon me
   raging with hunger, its enormous head   45

held high as if to strike a mortal terror
   into the very air. And down his track,
   a She-Wolf drove upon me, a starved horror   48

ravening and wasted beyond all belief.
   She seemed a rack for avarice, gaunt and craving.
   Oh many the souls she has brought to endless grief!   51

She brought such heaviness upon my spirit
   at sight of her savagery and desperation,
   I died from every hope of that high summit.   54

And like a miser—eager in acquisition
   but desperate in self-reproach when Fortune's wheel
   turns to the hour of his loss—all tears and attrition   57

I wavered back; and still the beast pursued,
   forcing herself against me bit by bit
   till I slid back into the sunless wood.   60

And as I fell to my soul's ruin, a presence
　　gathered before me on the discolored air,
　　the figure of one who seemed hoarse from long silence.　63

At sight of him in that friendless waste I cried:
　　"Have pity on me, whatever thing you are,
　　whether shade or living man." And it replied:　66

"Not man, though man I once was, and my blood
　　was Lombard, both my parents Mantuan.
　　I was born, though late, *sub Julio*, and bred　69

in Rome under Augustus in the noon
　　of the false and lying gods. I was a poet
　　and sang of old Anchises' noble son　72

who came to Rome after the burning of Troy.
　　But you—why do *you* return to these distresses
　　instead of climbing that shining Mount of Joy　75

which is the seat and first cause of man's bliss?"
　　"And are you then that Virgil and that fountain
　　of purest speech?" My voice grew tremulous:　78

"Glory and light of poets! now may that zeal
　　and love's apprenticeship that I poured out
　　on your heroic verses serve me well!　81

For you are my true master and first author,
　　the sole maker from whom I drew the breath
　　of that sweet style whose measures have brought me honor.　84

See there, immortal sage, the beast I flee.
　　For my soul's salvation, I beg you, guard me from her,
　　for she has struck a mortal tremor through me."　87

And he replied, seeing my soul in tears:
　　"He must go by another way who would escape
　　this wilderness, for that mad beast that fleers　90

before you there, suffers no man to pass.
　　She tracks down all, kills all, and knows no glut,
　　but, feeding, she grows hungrier than she was.　93

She mates with any beast, and will mate with more
　　before the Greyhound comes to hunt her down.
　　He will not feed on lands nor loot, but honor　96

and love and wisdom will make straight his way.
　　He will rise between Feltro and Feltro, and in him
　　shall be the resurrection and new day　99

of that sad Italy for which Nisus died,
　　and Turnus, and Euryalus, and the maid Camilla.
　　He shall hunt her through every nation of sick pride　102

till she is driven back forever to Hell
whence Envy first released her on the world.
Therefore, for your own good, I think it well   105

you follow me and I will be your guide
and lead you forth through an eternal place.
There you shall see the ancient spirits tried   108

in endless pain, and hear their lamentation
as each bemoans the second death of souls.
Next you shall see upon a burning mountain   111

souls in fire and yet content in fire,
knowing that whensoever it may be
they yet will mount into the blessed choir.   114

To which, if it is still your wish to climb,
a worthier spirit shall be sent to guide you.
With her shall I leave you, for the King of Time,   117

who reigns on high, forbids me to come there
since, living, I rebelled against his law.
He rules the waters and the land and air   120

and there holds court, his city and his throne.
Oh blessed are they he chooses!" And I to him:
"Poet, by that God to you unknown,   123

lead me this way. Beyond this present ill
and worse to dread, lead me to Peter's gate
and be my guide through the sad halls of Hell."   126

And he then: "Follow." And he moved ahead
in silence, and I followed where he led.

Notes

1. *midway in our life's journey*: The Biblical life span is three-score years and ten. The action opens in Dante's thirty-fifth year, i.e., 1300 A.D.

17. *that planet*: The sun. Ptolemaic astronomers considered it a planet. It is also symbolic of God as He who lights man's way.

31. *each footfall rose above the last*: The literal rendering would be: "So that the fixed foot was ever the lower." "Fixed" has often been translated "right" and an ingenious reasoning can support that reading, but a simpler explanation offers itself and seems more competent: Dante is saying that he climbed with such zeal and haste that every footfall carried him above the last despite the steepness of the climb. At a slow pace, on the other hand, the rear foot might be brought up only as far as the forward foot. This device of selecting a minute but exactly-centered detail to convey the whole of a larger action is one of the central characteristics of Dante's style.

THE THREE BEASTS: These three beasts undoubtedly are taken from *Jeremiah* v, 6. Many additional and incidental interpretations have been advanced for them, but the central interpretation must remain as noted. They foreshadow the three divisions of Hell (incontinence, violence, and fraud) which Virgil explains at length in Canto XI, 16–111.

38–9. *Aries . . . that rode with him to light the new creation*: The medieval tradition had it that the sun was in Aries at the time of the Creation. The significance of the astronomical and religious conjunction is an important part of Dante's intended allegory. It is just before dawn of Good Friday 1300 A.D. when he awakens in the Dark Wood. Thus his new life begins under Aries, the sign of creation, at dawn (rebirth) and in the Easter season (resurrection). Moreover the moon is full and the sun is in the equinox, conditions that did not fall together on any Friday of 1300. Dante is obviously constructing poetically the perfect Easter as a symbol of his new awakening.

69. *sub Julio*: In the reign of Julius Caesar.

95. *The Greyhound . . . Feltro and Feltro*: Almost certainly refers to Can Grande della Scala (1290–1329), great Italian leader born in Verona, which lies between the towns of Feltre and Montefeltro.

100–101. *Nisus, Turnus, Euryalus, Camilla*: All were killed in the war between the Trojans and the Latians when, according to legend, Aeneas led the survivors of Troy into Italy. Nisus and Euryalus (*Aeneid* IX) were Trojan comrades-in-arms who died together. Camilla (*Aeneid* XI) was the daughter of the Latian king and one of the warrior women. She was killed in a horse charge against the Trojans after displaying great gallantry. Turnus (*Aeneid* XII) was killed by Aeneas in a duel.

110. *the second death*: Damnation. "This is the second death, even the lake of fire." (*Revelation* xx, 14)

118. *forbids me to come there since, living, etc.*: Salvation is only through Christ in Dante's theology. Virgil lived and died before the establishment of Christ's teachings in Rome, and cannot therefore enter Heaven.

125. *Peter's gate*: The gate of Purgatory. (See *Purgatorio* IX, 76 ff.) The gate is guarded by an angel with a gleaming sword. The angel is Peter's vicar (Peter, the first Pope, symbolized all Popes; i.e., Christ's vicar on earth) and is entrusted with the two great keys.

Some commentators argue that this is the gate of Paradise, but Dante mentions no gate beyond this one in his ascent to Heaven. It should be remembered, too, that those who pass the gate of Purgatory have effectively entered Heaven.

The three great gates that figure in the entire journey are: the gate of Hell (Canto III, 1–11), the gate of Dis (Canto VIII, 79–113, and Canto IX, 86–87), and the gate of Purgatory, as above.

Canto II

It is evening of the first day (Friday). Dante is following Virgil and finds himself tired and despairing. How can he be worthy of such a vision as Virgil has described? He hesitates and seems about to abandon his first purpose.

To comfort him Virgil explains how Beatrice descended to him in Limbo and told him of her concern for Dante. It is she, the symbol of Divine Love, who sends Virgil to lead Dante from error. She has come into Hell itself on this errand, for Dante cannot come to Divine Love unaided; Reason must lead him. Moreover Beatrice has been sent with the prayers of the Virgin Mary (*Compassion*), and of Saint Lucia (*Divine Light*). Rachel (*The Contemplative Life*) also figures in the heavenly scene which Virgil recounts.

Virgil explains all this and reproaches Dante: how can he hesitate longer when such heavenly powers are concerned for him, and Virgil himself has promised to lead him safely?

Dante understands at once that such forces cannot fail him, and his spirits rise in joyous anticipation.

> The light was departing. The brown air drew down
> all the earth's creatures, calling them to rest
> from their day-roving, as I, one man alone,　　　　3
>
> prepared myself to face the double war
> of the journey and the pity, which memory
> shall here set down, nor hesitate, nor err.　　　　6
>
> O Muses! O High Genius! Be my aid!
> O Memory, recorder of the vision,
> here shall your true nobility be displayed!　　　　9
>
> Thus I began: "Poet, you who must guide me,
> before you trust me to that arduous passage,
> look to me and look through me—can I be worthy?　　　　12
>
> You sang how the father of Sylvius, while still
> in corruptible flesh won to that other world,
> crossing with mortal sense the immortal sill.　　　　15
>
> But if the Adversary of all Evil
> weighing his consequence and who and what
> should issue from him, treated him so well—　　　　18
>
> that cannot seem unfitting to thinking men,
> since he was chosen father of Mother Rome
> and of her Empire by God's will and token.　　　　21

Both, to speak strictly, were founded and foreknown
    as the established Seat of Holiness
    for the successors of Great Peter's throne.   24

In that quest, which your verses celebrate,
    he learned those mysteries from which arose
    his victory and Rome's apostolate.   27

There later came the chosen vessel, Paul,
    bearing the confirmation of that Faith
    which is the one true door to life eternal.   30

But I—how should I dare? By whose permission?
    I am not Aeneas. *I* am not Paul.
    Who could believe me worthy of the vision?   33

How, then, may I presume to this high quest
    and not fear my own brashness? You are wise
    and will grasp what my poor words can but suggest."   36

As one who unwills what he wills, will stay
    strong purposes with feeble second thoughts
    until he spells all his first zeal away—   39

so I hung back and balked on that dim coast
    till thinking had worn out my enterprise,
    so stout at starting and so early lost.   42

"I understand from your words and the look in your eyes,"
    that shadow of magnificence answered me,
    "your soul is sunken in that cowardice   45

that bears down many men, turning their course
    and resolution by imagined perils,
    as his own shadow turns the frightened horse.   48

To free you of this dread I will tell you all
    of why I came to you and what I heard
    when first I pitied you. I was a soul   51

among the souls of Limbo, when a Lady
    so blessed and so beautiful, I prayed her
    to order and command my will, called to me.   54

Her eyes were kindled from the lamps of Heaven.
    Her voice reached through me, tender, sweet, and low.
    An angel's voice, a music of its own: 57

'O gracious Mantuan whose melodies
    live in earth's memory and shall live on
    till the last motion ceases in the skies,   60

my dearest friend, and fortune's foe, has strayed
    onto a friendless shore and stands beset
    by such distresses that he turns afraid   63

from the True Way, and news of him in Heaven
   rumors my dread he is already lost.
   I come, afraid that I am too-late risen.   66

Fly to him and with your high counsel, pity,
   and with whatever need be for his good
   and soul's salvation, help him, and solace me.   69

It is I, Beatrice, who send you to him.
   I come from the blessed height for which I yearn.
   Love called me here. When amid Seraphim   72

I stand again before my Lord, your praises
   shall sound in Heaven.' She paused, and I began:
   'O Lady of that only grace that raises   75

feeble mankind within its mortal cycle
   above all other works God's will has placed
   within the heaven of the smallest circle;   78

so welcome is your command that to my sense,
   were it already fulfilled, it would yet seem tardy.
   I understand, and am all obedience.   81

But tell me how you dare to venture thus
   so far from the wide heaven of your joy
   to which your thoughts yearn back from this abyss.'   84

'Since what you ask,' she answered me, 'probes near
   the root of all, I will say briefly only
   how I have come through Hell's pit without fear.   87

Know then, O waiting and compassionate soul,
   that is to fear which has the power to harm,
   and nothing else is fearful even in Hell.   90

I am so made by God's all-seeing mercy
   your anguish does not touch me, and the flame
   of this great burning has no power upon me.   93

There is a Lady in Heaven so concerned
   for him I send you to, that for her sake
   the strict decree is broken. She has turned   96

and called Lucia to her wish and mercy
   saying: 'Thy faithful one is sorely pressed;
   in his distresses I commend him to thee.'   99

Lucia, that soul of light and foe of all
   cruelty, rose and came to me at once
   where I was sitting with the ancient Rachel,   102

saying to me: 'Beatrice, true praise of God,
   why dost thou not help him who loved thee so
   that for thy sake he left the vulgar crowd?   105

Dost thou not hear his cries? Canst thou not see
the death he wrestles with beside that river
no ocean can surpass for rage and fury?'   108

No soul of earth was ever as rapt to seek
its good or flee its injury as I was—
when I had heard my sweet Lucia speak—   111

to descend from Heaven and my blessed seat
to you, laying my trust in that high speech
that honors you and all who honor it.'   114

She spoke and turned away to hide a tear
that, shining, urged me faster. So I came
and freed you from the beast that drove you there,   117

blocking the near way to the Heavenly Height.
And now what ails you? Why do you lag? Why
this heartsick hesitation and pale fright   120

when three such blessed Ladies lean from Heaven
in their concern for you and my own pledge
of the great good that waits you has been given?"   123

As flowerlets drooped and puckered in the night
turn up to the returning sun and spread
their petals wide on his new warmth and light—   126

just so my wilted spirits rose again
and such a heat of zeal surged through my veins
that I was born anew. Thus I began: 129

"Blesséd be that Lady of infinite pity,
and blesséd be thy taxed and courteous spirit
that came so promptly on the word she gave thee.   132

Thy words have moved my heart to its first purpose.
My Guide! My Lord! My Master! Now lead on:
one will shall serve the two of us in this."   135

He turned when I had spoken, and at his back
I entered on that hard and perilous track.

Notes

13–30. AENEAS AND THE FOUNDING OF ROME.
Here is a fair example of the way in which Dante absorbed pagan themes into his Catholicism.
According to Virgil, Aeneas is the son of mortal Anchises and of Venus. Venus, in her son's interest, secures a prophecy and a promise from Jove to the effect that Aeneas is to found a royal line that shall rule the world. After the burning of Troy, Aeneas is directed by various signs to sail for the Latian lands (Italy) where his destiny awaits him. After many misadventures, he is compelled (like Dante) to descend to the underworld of the dead. There he finds his father's shade, and there he is shown the shades of the great kings that are to stem from him. (*Aeneid* VI, 921 ff.) Among them are Romulus, Julius Caesar, and Augustus Caesar. The full glory of the Roman Empire is also foreshadowed to him.

Dante, however, continues the Virgilian theme and includes in the predestination not only the Roman Empire but the Holy Roman Empire and its Church. Thus what Virgil presented as an arrangement of Jove, a concession to the son of Venus, becomes part of the divine scheme of the Catholic God, and Aeneas is cast as a direct forerunner of Peter and Paul.

13. *father of Sylvius*: Aeneas.

51–52. *I was a soul among the souls in Limbo*: See Canto IV, lines 31–45, where Virgil explains his state in Hell.

78. *the heaven of the smallest circle*: The moon. "Heaven" here is used in its astronomical sense. All within that circle is the earth. According to the Ptolemaic system the earth was the center of creation and was surrounded by nine heavenly spheres (nine heavens) concentrically placed around it. The moon was the first of these, and therefore the smallest. A cross section of this universe could be represented by drawing nine concentric circles (at varying distances about the earth as a center). Going outward from the center these circles would indicate, in order, the spheres of

> The Moon
> Mercury
> Venus
> The Sun
> Mars
> Jupiter
> Saturn
> The Fixed Stars
> The Primum Mobile

Beyond the Primum Mobile lies the Empyrean.

97. *Lucia*: (Loo-TCHEE-yah) Allegorically she represents Divine Light. Her name in Italian inevitably suggests "luce" (light), and she is the patron saint of eyesight. By a process quite common in medieval religion, the special powers attributed to Lucia seem to have been suggested by her name rather than her history. (In France, by a similar process, St. Clair is the patroness of sight.)

102. *Rachel*: Represents the Contemplative Life.

A note on "thee" and "thou": except for the quotations from the souls in Heaven, and for Dante's fervent declamation to Virgil, I have insisted on "you" as the preferable pronoun form. I have used "thee" and "thou" in these cases with the idea that they might help to indicate the extraordinary elevation of the speakers and of the persons addressed.

Canto III

The Opportunists

The Poets pass the Gate of Hell and are immediately assailed by cries of anguish. Dante sees the first of the souls in torment. They are *The Opportunists*, those souls who in life were neither for good nor evil but only for themselves. Mixed with them are those outcasts who took no sides in the Rebellion of the Angels. They are neither in Hell nor out of it. Eternally unclassified, they race round and round pursuing a wavering banner that runs forever before them through the dirty air; and as they run they are pursued by swarms of wasps and hornets, who sting them and produce a constant flow of blood and putrid matter which trickles down the bodies of the sinners and is feasted upon by loathsome worms and maggots who coat the ground.

The law of Dante's Hell is the law of symbolic retribution. As they sinned so are they punished. They took no sides, therefore they are given no place. As they pursued the ever-shifting illusion of their own advantage, changing their courses with every changing wind, so they pursue eternally an elusive, ever-shifting banner. As their sin was a darkness, so they move in darkness. As their own guilty conscience pursued them, so they are pursued by swarms of wasps and hornets. And as their actions were a moral filth, so they run eternally through the filth of worms and maggots which they themselves feed.

Dante recognizes several, among them *Pope Celestine* V, but without delaying to speak to any of these souls, the Poets move on to *Acheron*, the first of the rivers of Hell. Here the newly-arrived souls of the damned gather and wait for monstrous *Charon* to ferry them over to punishment. Charon recognizes Dante as a living man and angrily refuses him passage. Virgil forces Charon to serve them, but Dante swoons with terror, and does not reawaken until he is on the other side.

> I AM THE WAY INTO THE CITY OF WOE.
> I AM THE WAY TO A FORSAKEN PEOPLE.
> I AM THE WAY INTO ETERNAL SORROW.   3
>
> SACRED JUSTICE MOVED MY ARCHITECT.
> I WAS RAISED HERE BY DIVINE OMNIPOTENCE,
> PRIMORDIAL LOVE AND ULTIMATE INTELLECT.   6
>
> ONLY THOSE ELEMENTS TIME CANNOT WEAR
> WERE MADE BEFORE ME, AND BEYOND TIME I STAND.
> ABANDON ALL HOPE YE WHO ENTER HERE.   9

These mysteries I read cut into stone
   above a gate. And turning I said: "Master,
   what is the meaning of his harsh inscription?"   12

And he then as initiate to novice:
   "Here must you put by all division of spirit
   and gather your soul against all cowardice.   15

This is the place I told you to expect.
　Here you shall pass among the fallen people,
　souls who have lost the good of intellect."　　　　18

So saying, he put forth his hand to me,
　and with a gentle and encouraging smile
　he led me through the gate of mystery.　　　　21

Here sighs and cries and wails coiled and recoiled
　on the starless air, spilling my soul to tears.
　A confusion of tongues and monstrous accents toiled　　24

in pain and anger. Voices hoarse and shrill
　and sounds of blows, all intermingled, raised
　tumult and pandemonium that still　　　　27

whirls on the air forever dirty with it
　as if a whirlwind sucked at sand. And I,
　holding my head in horror, cried: "Sweet Spirit,　　30

what souls are these who run through this black haze?"
　And he to me: "These are the nearly soulless
　whose lives concluded neither blame nor praise.　　33

They are mixed here with that despicable corps
　of angels who were neither for God nor Satan,
　but only for themselves. The High Creator　　36

scourged them from Heaven for its perfect beauty,
　and Hell will not receive them since the wicked
　might feel some glory over them." And I:　　39

"Master, what gnaws at them so hideously
　their lamentation stuns the very air?"
　"They have no hope of death," he answered me,　　42

"and in their blind and unattaining state
　their miserable lives have sunk so low
　that they must envy every other fate.　　45

No word of them survives their living season.
　Mercy and Justice deny them even a name.
　Let us not speak of them: look, and pass on."　　48

I saw a banner there upon the mist.
　Circling and circling, it seemed to scorn all pause.
　So it ran on, and still behind it pressed　　51

a never-ending rout of souls in pain.
　I had not thought death had undone so many
　as passed before me in that mournful train.　　54

And some I knew among them; last of all
　I recognized the shadow of that soul
　who, in his cowardice, made the Great Denial.　　57

At once I understood for certain: these
   were of that retrograde and faithless crew
   hateful to God and to His enemies.   60

These wretches never born and never dead
   ran naked in a swarm of wasps and hornets
   that goaded them the more the more they fled,   63

and made their faces stream with bloody gouts
   of pus and tears that dribbled to their feet
   to be swallowed there by loathsome worms and maggots. 66

Then looking onward I made out a throng
   assembled on the beach of a wide river,
   whereupon I turned to him: "Master, I long   69

to know what souls these are, and what strange usage
   makes them as eager to cross as they seem to be
   in this infected light." At which the Sage: 72

"All this shall be made known to you when we stand
   on the joyless beach of Acheron." And I
   cast down my eyes, sensing a reprimand   75

in what he said, and so walked at his side
   in silence and ashamed until we came
   through the dead cavern to that sunless tide.   78

There, steering toward us in an ancient ferry
   came an old man with a white bush of hair,
   bellowing: "Woe to you depraved souls! Bury   81

here and forever all hope of Paradise:
   I come to lead you to the other shore,
   into eternal dark, into fire and ice.   84

And you who are living yet, I say begone
   from these who are dead." But when he saw me stand
   against his violence he began again: 87

"By other windings and by other steerage
   shall you cross to that other shore. Not here! Not here!
   A lighter craft than mine must give you passage." 90

And my Guide to him: "Charon, bite back your spleen:
   this has been willed where what is willed must be,
   and is not yours to ask what it may mean."   93

The steersman of that marsh of ruined souls,
   who wore a wheel of flame around each eye,
   stifled the rage that shook his woolly jowls.   96

But those unmanned and naked spirits there
   turned pale with fear and their teeth began to chatter
   at sound of his crude bellow. In despair   99

they blasphemed God, their parents, their time on earth,
the race of Adam, and the day and the hour
and the place and the seed the womb that gave
them birth.   102

But all together they drew to that grim shore
where all must come who lose the fear of God.
Weeping and cursing they come for evermore,   105

and demon Charon with eyes like burning coals
herds them in, and with a whistling oar
flails on the stragglers to his wake of souls.   108

As leaves in autumn loosen and stream down
until the branch stands bare above its tatters
spread on the rustling ground, so one by one   111

the evil seed of Adam in its Fall
cast themselves, at his signal, from the shore
and streamed away like birds who hear their call. 114

So they are gone over that shadowy water,
and always before they reach the other shore
a new noise stirs on this, and new throngs gather. 117

"My son," the courteous Master said to me,
"all who die in the shadow of God's wrath
converge to this from every clime and country.   120

And all pass over eagerly, for here
Divine Justice transforms and spurs them so
their dread turns wish: they yearn for what they fear. 123

No soul in Grace comes ever to this crossing;
therefore if Charon rages at your presence
you will understand the reason for his cursing."   126

When he had spoken, all the twilight country
shook so violently, the terror of it
bathes me with sweat even in memory: 129

the tear-soaked ground gave out a sigh of wind
that spewed itself in flame on a red sky,
and all my shattered senses left me. Blind,   132

like one whom sleep comes over in a swoon,
I stumbled into darkness and went down.

Notes

7–8. *Only those elements time cannot wear:* The Angels, the Empyrean, and the First Matter are the elements time cannot wear, for they will last to all time. Man, however, in his mortal state, is not eternal. The Gate of Hell, therefore, was created before man. The theological point is worth attention. The doctrine of Original Sin is, of course, one familiar to many creeds. Here, however, it would seem that the preparation for damnation predates Original Sin. True, in one interpretation, Hell was created for the punishment of the Rebellious Angels and not for man. Had man not sinned, he would never have known Hell. But on the other hand, Dante's God was one who knew all, and knew therefore that man would indeed sin. The theological problem is an extremely delicate one.

It is significant, however, that having sinned, man lives out his days on the rind of Hell, and that damnation is forever below his feet. This central concept of man's sinfulness, and, opposed to it, the doctrine of Christ's ever-abounding mercy, are central to all of Dante's theology. Only as man surrenders himself to Divine Love may he hope for salvation, and salvation is open to all who will surrender themselves.

8. *and beyond time I stand*: So odious is sin to God that there can be no end to its just punishment.

9. *Abandon all hope ye who enter here*: The admonition, of course, is to the damned and not to those who come on Heaven-sent errands. The Harrowing of Hell (see Canto IV, note to l. 53) provided the only exemption from this decree, and that only through the direct intercession of Christ.

57. *who, in his cowardice, made the Great Denial*: This is almost certainly intended to be Celestine V, who became Pope in 1294. He was a man of saintly life, but allowed himself to be convinced by a priest named Benedetto that his soul was in danger since no man could live in the world without being damned. In fear for his soul he withdrew from all worldly affairs and renounced the papacy. Benedetto promptly assumed the mantle himself and became Boniface VIII, a Pope who became for Dante a symbol of all the worst corruptions of the church. Dante also blamed Boniface and his intrigues for many of the evils that befell Florence. We shall learn in Canto XIX that the fires of Hell are waiting for Boniface in the pit of the Simoniacs, and we shall be given further evidence of his corruption in Canto XXVII. Celestine's great guilt is that his cowardice (in selfish terror for his own welfare) served as the door through which so much evil entered the church.

80. *an old man*: Charon. He is the ferryman of dead souls across the Acheron in all classical mythology.

88-90. *By other windings*: Charon recognizes Dante not only as a living man but as a soul in grace, and knows, therefore, that the Infernal Ferry was not intended for him. He is probably referring to the fact that souls destined for Purgatory and Heaven assemble not at his ferry point, but on the banks of the Tiber, from which they are transported by an Angel.

100. *they blasphemed God*: The souls of the damned are not permitted to repent, for repentance is a divine grace.

123. *they yearn for what they fear*: Hell (allegorically Sin) is what the souls of the damned really wish for. Hell is their actual and deliberate choice, for divine grace is denied to none who wish for it in their hearts. The damned must, in fact, deliberately harden their hearts to God in order to become damned. Christ's grace is sufficient to save all who wish for it.

133-34 DANTE'S SWOON: This device (repeated at the end of Canto V) serves a double purpose. The first is technical: Dante uses it to cover a transition. We are never told how he crossed Acheron, for that would involve certain narrative matters he can better deal with when he crosses Styx in Canto VII. The second is to provide a point of departure for a theme that is carried through the entire descent: the theme of Dante's emotional reaction to Hell. These two swoons early in the descent show him most susceptible to the grief about him. As he descends, pity leaves him, and he even goes so far as to add to the torments of one sinner. The allegory is clear: we must harden ourselves against every sympathy for sin.

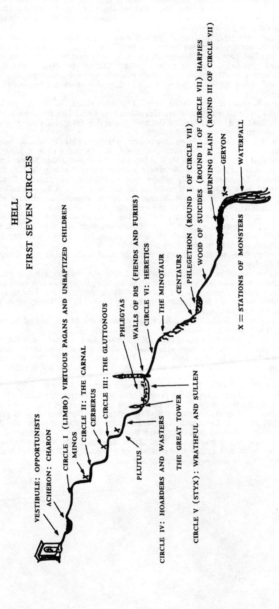

HELL
FIRST SEVEN CIRCLES

VESTIBULE: OPPORTUNISTS

ACHERON: CHARON

CIRCLE I (LIMBO) VIRTUOUS PAGANS AND UNBAPTIZED CHILDREN

MINOS

CIRCLE II: THE CARNAL

CERBERUS

CIRCLE III: THE GLUTTONOUS

PLUTUS

THE GREAT TOWER

CIRCLE IV: HOARDERS AND WASTERS

CIRCLE V (STYX): WRATHFUL AND SULLEN

PHLEGYAS

WALLS OF DIS (FIENDS AND FURIES)

CIRCLE VI: HERETICS

THE MINOTAUR

CENTAURS

PHLEGETHON (ROUND I OF CIRCLE VII)

WOOD OF SUICIDES (ROUND II OF CIRCLE VII) HARPIES

BURNING PLAIN (ROUND III OF CIRCLE VII)

GERYON

WATERFALL

X = STATIONS OF MONSTERS

Canto IV

The Virtuous Pagans

Dante wakes to find himself across Acheron. The Poets are now on the
brink of Hell itself, which Dante conceives as a great funnel-shaped cave
lying below the northern hemisphere with its bottom point at the earth's
center. Around this great circular depression runs a series of ledges, each of
which Dante calls a *Circle*. Each circle is assigned to the punishment of
one category óf sin.

As soon as Dante's strength returns, the Poets begin to cross the *First
Circle*. Here they find the *Virtuous Pagans*. They were born without the
light of Christ's revelation, and, therefore, they cannot come into the light
of God, but they are not tormented. Their only pain is that they have no
hope.

Ahead of them Dante sights a great dome of light, and a voice trumpets
through the darkness welcoming Virgil back, for this is his eternal place in
Hell. Immediately the great Poets of all time appear—*Homer, Horace,
Ovid,* and *Lucan.* They greet Virgil, and they make Dante a sixth in their
company.

With them Dante enters the Citadel of Human Reason and sees before
his eyes the Master Souls of Pagan Antiquity gathered on a green, and illuminated by the radiance of Human Reason. This is the highest state man
can achieve without God, and the glory of it dazzles Dante, but he knows
also that it is nothing compared to the glory of God.

> A monstrous clap of thunder broke apart
>   the swoon that stuffed my head; like one awakened
>   by violent hands, I leaped up with a start.   3
>
> And having risen; rested and renewed,
>   I studied out the landmarks of the gloom
>   to find my bearings there as best I could.   6
>
> And I found I stood on the very brink of the valley
>   called the Dolorous Abyss, the desolate chasm
>   where rolls the thunder of Hell's eternal cry,   9
>
> so depthless-deep and nebulous and dim
>   that stare as I might into its frightful pit
>   it gave me back no feature and no bottom.   12
>
> Death-pale, the Poet spoke: "Now let us go
>   into the blind world waiting here below us.
>   I will lead the way and you will follow."   15
>
> And I, sick with alarm at his new pallor,
>   cried out, "How can I go this way when you
>   who are my strength in doubt turn pale with terror?"   18

And he: "The pain of these below us here,
  drains the color from my face for pity,
  and leaves this pallor you mistake for fear.   21

Now let us go, for a long road awaits us."
  So he entered and so he led me in
  to the first circle and ledge of the abyss.   24

No tortured wailing rose to greet us here
  but sounds of sighing rose from every side,
  sending a tremor through the timeless air,   27

a grief breathed out of untormented sadness,
  the passive state of those who dwelled apart,
  men, women, children—a dim and endless congress.   30

And the Master said to me: "You do not question
  what souls these are that suffer here before you?
  I wish you to know before you travel on   33

that these were sinless. And still their merits fail,
  for they lacked Baptism's grace, which is the door
  of the true faith *you* were born to. Their birth fell   36

before the age of the Christian mysteries,
  and so they did not worship God's Trinity
  in fullest duty. I am one of these.   39

For such defects are we lost, though spared the fire
  and suffering Hell in one affliction only:
  that without hope we live on in desire."   42

I thought how many worthy souls there were
  suspended in that Limbo, and a weight
  closed on my heart for what the noblest suffer.   45

"Instruct me, Master and most noble Sir,"
  I prayed him then, "better to understand
  the perfect creed that conquers every error: 48

has any, by his own or another's merit,
  gone ever from this place to blessedness?"
  He sensed my inner question and answered it: 51

"I was still new to this estate of tears
  when a Mighty One descended here among us,
  crowned with the sign of His victorious years.   54

He took from us the shade of our first parent,
  of Abel, his pure son, of ancient Noah,
  of Moses, the bringer of law, the obedient.   57

Father Abraham, David the King,
  Israel with his father and his children,
  Rachel, the holy vessel of His blessing,   60

and many more He chose for elevation
   among the elect. And before these, you must know,
   no human soul had ever won salvation."   63

We had not paused as he spoke, but held our road
   and passed meanwhile beyond a press of souls
   crowded about like trees in a thick wood.   66

And we had not traveled far from where I woke
   when I made out a radiance before us
   that struck away a hemisphere of dark.   69

We were still some distance back in the long night,
   yet near enough that I half-saw, half-sensed,
   what quality of souls lived in that light.   72

"O ornament of wisdom and of art,
   what souls are these whose merit lights their way
   even in Hell. What joy sets them apart?"   75

And he to me: "The signature of honor
   they left on earth is recognized in Heaven
   and wins them ease in Hell out of God's favor."   78

And as he spoke a voice rang on the air:
   "Honor the Prince of Poets; the soul and glory
   that went from us returns. He is here! He is here!"   81

The cry ceased and the echo passed from hearing;
   I saw four mighty presences come toward us
   with neither joy nor sorrow in their bearing.   84

"Note well," my Master said as they came on,
   "that soul that leads the rest with sword in hand
   as if he were their captain and champion.   87

It is Homer, singing master of the earth.
   Next after him is Horace, the satirist,
   Ovid is third, and Lucan is the fourth.   90

Since all of these have part in the high name
   the voice proclaimed, calling me Prince of Poets,
   the honor that they do me honors them."   93

So I saw gathered at the edge of light
   the masters of that highest school whose song
   outsoars all others like an eagle's flight.   96

And after they had talked together a while,
   they turned and welcomed me most graciously,
   at which I saw my approving Master smile.   99

And they honored me far beyond courtesy,
   for they included me in their own number,
   making me sixth in that high company.   102

So we moved toward the light, and as we passed
we spoke of things as well omitted here
as it was sweet to touch on there. At last   105

we reached the base of a great Citadel
circled by seven towering battlements
and by a sweet brook flowing round them all.   108

This we passed over as if it were firm ground.
Through seven gates I entered with those sages
and came to a green meadow blooming round.   111

There with a solemn and majestic poise
stood many people gathered in the light,
speaking infrequently and with muted voice.   114

Past that enameled green we six withdrew
into a luminous and open height
from which each soul among them stood in view.   117

And there directly before me on the green
the master souls of time were shown to me.
I glory in the glory I have seen!   120

Electra stood in a great company
among whom I saw Hector and Aeneas
and Caesar in armor with his falcon's eye.   123

I saw Camilla, and the Queen Amazon
across the field. I saw the Latian King
seated there with his daughter by his throne.   126

And the good Brutus who overthrew the Tarquin:
Lucrezia, Julia, Marcia, and Cornelia;
and, by himself apart, the Saladin.   129

And raising my eyes a little I saw on high
Aristotle, the master of those who know,
ringed by the great souls of philosophy.   132

All wait upon him for their honor and his.
I saw Socrates and Plato at his side
before all others there. Democritus   135

who ascribes the world to chance, Diogenes,
and with him there Thales, Anaxagoras,
Zeno, Heraclitus, Empedocles.   138

And I saw the wise collector and analyst—
Dioscorides I mean. I saw Orpheus there,
Tully, Linus, Seneca the moralist,   141

Eculid the geometer, and Ptolemy,
Hippocrates, Galen, Avicenna,
and Averrhoës of the Great Commentary.   144

I cannot count so much nobility;
my longer theme pursues me so that often
the word falls short of the reality.   147

The company of six is reduced by four.
My Master leads me by another road
away from that serenity to the roar   150

and trembling air of Hell. I pass from light
into the kingdom of eternal night.

Notes

13 ff. *death-pale*: Virgil is most likely affected here by the return to his own place
in Hell. "The pain of these below," then (line 19), would be the pain of his own
group in Limbo (the Virtuous Pagans) rather than the total of Hell's suffering.

31 ff. *You do not question*: A master touch of characterization. Virgil's *amour
propre* is a bit piqued at Dante's lack of curiosity about the position in Hell of Virgil's own kind. And it may possibly be, by allegorical extension, that Human Reason
must urge the soul to question the place of reason. The allegorical point is conjectural, but such conjecture is certainly one of the effects inherent in the use of allegory; when well used, the central symbols of the allegory continue indenfiitely to suggest new interpretations and shades of meaning.

53. *a Mighty One*: Christ. His name is never directly uttered in Hell.

53. *descended here*: The legend of the Harrowing of Hell is Apocryphal. It is
based on I *Peter* iii, 19: "He went and preached unto the spirits in prison." The
legend is that Christ in the glory of His resurrection descended into Limbo and took
with Him to Heaven the first human souls to be saved. The event would, accordingly,
have occurred in 33 or 34 A.D. Virgil died in 19 B.C.

102. *making me sixth in that high company*: Merit and self-awareness of merit may
well be a higher thing than modesty. An additional point Dante may well have had
in mind, however, is the fact that he saw himself as one pledged to continue in his
own times the classic tradition represented by these poets.

103–105. These lines amount to a stylistic note. It is good style ('*l tacere è bello*
where *bello* equals "good style") to omit this discussion, since it would digress from
the subject and, moreover, his point is already made. Every great narrator tends to
tell his story from climax to climax. There are times on the other hand when Dante
delights in digression. (See General Note to Canto XX.)

106. A GREAT CITADEL. The most likely allegory is that the Citadel represents
philosophy (that is, human reason without the light of God) surrounded by seven
walls which represent the seven liberal arts, or the seven sciences, or the seven virtues. Note that Human Reason makes a light of its own, but that it is a light in
darkness and forever separated from the glory of God's light. The *sweet brook
flowing* round them all has been interpreted in many ways. Clearly fundamental, however, is the fact that it divides those in the Citadel (those who wish to know) from
those in the outer darkness.

109. *as if it were firm ground*: Since Dante still has his body, and since all others
in Hell are incorporeal shades, there is a recurring narrative problem in the *Inferno*
(and through the rest of the *Commedia*): how does flesh act in contact with spirit?
In the *Purgatorio* Dante attempts to embrace the spirit of Casella and his arms pass
through him as if he were empty air. In the Third Circle, below (Canto VI, 34–36),
Dante steps on some of the spirits lying in the slush and his foot passes right through
them. (The original lines offer several possible readings of which I have preferred
this one.) And at other times Virgil, also a spirit, picks Dante up and carries him
bodily.

It is clear, too, that Dante means the spirits of Hell to be weightless. When Virgil
steps into Phlegyas' bark (Canto VIII) it does not settle into the water, but it does
when Dante's living body steps aboard. There is no narrative reason why Dante
should not sink into the waters of this stream and Dante follows no fixed rule in
dealing with such phenomena, often suiting the physical action to the allegorical need.
Here, the moat probably symbolizes some requirement (The Will to Know) which he
and the other poets meet without difficulty.

THE INHABITANTS OF THE CITADEL. They fall into three main groups:

1. *The heroes and heroines*: All of these it must be noted were associated with the
Trojans and their Roman descendants. (See note on AENEAS AND THE FOUND-
ING OF ROME, Canto II.) The Electra Dante mentions here is not the sister of

Orestes (see Euripides' *Electra*) but the daughter of Atlas and the mother of Dardanus, the founder of Troy.

2. *The philosophers*: Most of this group is made up of philosophers whose teachings were, at least in part, acceptable to church scholarship. Democritus, however, "who ascribed the world to chance," would clearly be an exception. The group is best interpreted, therefore, as representing the highest achievements of Human Reason unaided by Divine Love. *Plato and Aristotle*: Through a considerable part of the Middle Ages Plato was held to be the fountainhead of all scholarship, but in Dante's time practically all learning was based on Aristotelian theory as interpreted through the many commentaries. *Linus*: the Italian is "Lino" and for it some commentators read "Livio" (Livy).

3. *The naturalists*: They are less well known today. In Dante's time their place in scholarship more or less corresponded to the role of the theoretician and historian of science in our universities. *Avicenna* (his major work was in the eleventh century) and *Avverhoës* (twelfth century) were Arabian philosophers and physicians especially famous in Dante's time for their commentaries on Aristotle. *Great Commentary*: has the force of a title, i.e., The Great Commentary as distinguished from many lesser commentaries.

The Saladin: This is the famous Saladin who was defeated by Richard the Lion-Heart, and whose divine great qualities as a ruler became a legend in medieval Europe.

Canto V

The Carnal

The Poets leave Limbo and enter the *Second Circle*. Here begin the torments of Hell proper, and here, blocking the way, sits *Minos*, the dread and semi-bestial judge of the damned who assigns to each soul its eternal torment. He orders the Poets back; but Virgil silences him as he earlier silenced Charon, and the Poets move on.

They find themselves on a dark ledge swept by a great whirlwind, which spins within it the souls of the *Carnal*, those who betrayed reason to their appetites. Their sin was to abandon themselves to the tempest of their passions: so they are swept forever in the tempest of Hell, forever denied the light of reason and of God. Virgil identifies many among them. *Semiramis* is there, and *Dido, Cleopatra, Helen, Achilles, Paris,* and *Tristan*. Dante sees *Paolo* and *Francesca* swept together, and in the name of love he calls to them to tell their sad story. They pause from their eternal flight to come to him, and Francesca tells their history while Paolo weeps at her side. Dante is so stricken by compassion at their tragic tale that he swoons once again.

So we went down to the second ledge alone;
    a smaller circle of so much greater pain
    the voice of the damned rose in a bestial moan.   3

There Minos sits, grinning, grotesque, and hale.
    He examines each lost soul as it arrives
    and delivers his verdict with his coiling tail.   6

That is to say, when the ill-fated soul
    appears before him it confesses all,
    and that grim sorter of the dark and foul   9

decides which place in Hell shall be its end,
    then wraps his twitching tail about himself
    one coil for each degree it must descend.   12

The soul descends and others take its place:
    each crowds in its turn to judgment, each confesses,
    each hears its doom and falls away through space.   15

"O you who come into this camp of woe,"
    cried Minos when he saw me turn away
    without awaiting his judgment, "watch where you go   18

once you have entered here, and to whom you turn!
    Do not be misled by that wide and easy passage!"
    And my Guide to him: "That is not your concern;   21

it is his fate to enter every door.
    This has been willed where what is willed must be,
    and is not yours to question. Say no more."   24

Now the choir of anguish, like a wound,
    strikes through the tortured air. Now I have come
    to Hell's full lamentation, sound beyond sound.   27

I came to a place stripped bare of every light
    and roaring on the naked dark like seas
    wracked by a war of winds. Their hellish flight   30

of storm and counterstorm through time foregone,
    sweeps the souls of the damned before its charge.
    Whirling and battering it drives them on,   33

and when they pass the ruined gap of Hell
    through which we had come, their shrieks begin anew.
    There they blaspheme the power of God eternal.   36

And this, I learned, was the never ending flight
    of those who sinned in the flesh, the carnal and lusty
    who betrayed reason to their appetite.   39

As the wings of wintering starlings bear them on
    in their great wheeling flights, just so the blast
    wherries these evil souls through time foregone.   42

Here, there, up, down, they whirl and, whirling, strain
    with never a hope of hope to comfort them,
    not of release, but even of less pain.   45

As cranes go over sounding their harsh cry,
    leaving the long streak of their flight in air,
    so come these spirits, wailing as they fly.   48

And watching their shadows lashed by wind, I cried:
    "Master, what souls are these the very air
    lashes with its black whips from side to side?"   51

"The first of these whose history you would know,"
    he answered me, "was Empress of many tongues.
    Mad sensuality corrupted her so   54

that to hide the guilt of her debauchery
    she licensed all depravity alike,
    and lust and law were one in her decree.   57

She is Semiramis of whom the tale is told
    how she married Ninus and succeeded him
    to the throne of that wide land the Sultans hold.   60

The other is Dido; faithless to the ashes
    of Sichaeus, she killed herself for love.
    The next whom the eternal tempest lashes   63

is sense-drugged Cleopatra. See Helen there,
    from whom such ill arose. And great Achilles,
    who fought at last with love in the house of prayer.   66

And Paris. And Tristan." As they whirled above
    he pointed out more than a thousand shades
    of those torn from the mortal life by love.   69

I stood there while my Teacher one by one
    named the great knights and ladies of dim time;
    and I was swept by pity and confusion.   72

At last I spoke: "Poet, I should be glad
    to speak a word with those two swept together
    so lightly on the wind and still so sad."   75

And he to me: "Watch them. When next they pass,
    call to them in the name of love that drives
    and damns them here. In that name they will pause."   78

Thus, as soon as the wind in its wild course
    brought them around, I called: "O wearied souls!
    if none forbid it, pause and speak to us."   81

As mating doves that love calls to their nest
    glide through the air with motionless raised wings,
    borne by the sweet desire that fills each breast—   84

Just so those spirits turned on the torn sky
    from the band where Dido whirls across the air;
    such was the power of pity in my cry.   87

"O living creature, gracious, kind, and good,
    going this pilgrimage through the sick night,
    visiting us who stained the earth with blood,   90

were the King of Time our friend, we would pray His peace
    on you who have pitied us. As long as the wind
    will let us pause, ask of us what you please.   93

The town where I was born lies by the shore
    where the Po descends into its ocean rest
    with its attendant streams in one long murmur.   96

Love, which in gentlest hearts will soonest bloom
    seized my lover with passion for that sweet body
    from which I was torn unshriven to my doom.   99

Love, which permits no loved one not to love,
    took me so strongly with delight in him
    that we are one in Hell, as we were above.   102

Love led us to one death. In the depths of Hell
    Caïna waits for him who took our lives."
    This was the piteous tale they stopped to tell.   105

And when I had heard those world-offended lovers
  I bowed my head. At last the Poet spoke:
  "What painful thoughts are these your lowered brow covers?"108

When at length I answered, I began: "Alas!
  What sweetest thoughts, what green and young desire
  led these two lovers to this sorry pass."   111

Then turning to those spirits once again,
  I said: "Francesca, what you suffer here
  melts me to tears of pity and of pain.   114

But tell me: in the time of your sweet sighs
  by what appearances found love the way
  to lure you to his perilous paradise?"   117

And she: "The double grief of a lost bliss
  is to recall its happy hour in pain.
  Your Guide and Teacher knows the truth of this.   120

But if there is indeed a soul in Hell
  to ask of the beginning of our love
  out of his pity, I will weep and tell: 123

On a day for dalliance we read the rhyme
  of Lancelot, how love had mastered him.
  We were alone with innocence and dim time.   126

Pause after pause that high old story drew
  our eyes together while we blushed and paled;
  but it was one soft passage overthrew   129

our caution and our hearts. For when we read
  how her fond smile was kissed by such a lover,
  he who is one with me alive and dead   132

breathed on my lips the tremor of his kiss.
  That book, and he who wrote it, was a pander.
  That day we read no further." As she said this,   135

the other spirit, who stood by her, wept
  so piteously, I felt my senses reel
  and faint away with anguish. I was swept   138

by such a swoon as death is, and I fell,
  as a corpse might fall, to the dead floor of Hell.

Notes

2. *a smaller circle*: The pit of Hell tapers like a funnel. The circles of ledges accordingly grow smaller as they descend.

4. *Minos*: Like all the monsters Dante assigns to the various offices of Hell, Minos is drawn from classical mythology. He was the son of Europa and of Zeus, who descended to her in the form of a bull. Minos became a mythological king of Crete, so famous for his wisdom and justice that after death his soul was made judge of the dead. Virgil presents him fulfilling the same office at Aeneas' descent to the underworld. Dante, however, transforms him into an irate and hideous monster with a tail. The transformation may have been suggested by the form Zeus assumed for the rape of Europa—the monster is certainly bullish enough here—but the obvious purpose of

the brutalization is to present a figure symbolic of the guilty conscience of the wretches who come before it to make their confessions. Dante freely reshapes his materials to his own purposes.

8. *it confesses all*: Just as the souls appeared eager to cross Acheron, so they are eager to confess even while they dread. Dante is once again making the point that sinners elect their Hell by an act of their own will.

27. *Hell's full lamentation*: It is with the second circle that the real tortures of Hell begin.

34. *the ruined gap of Hell*: See note to Canto II, 53. At the time of the Harrowing of Hell a great earthquake shook the underworld shattering rocks and cliffs. Ruins resulting from the same shock are noted in Canto XII, 34, and Canto XXI, 112 ff. At the beginning of Canto XXIV, the Poets leave the *bolgia* of the Hypocrites by climbing the ruined slabs of a bridge that was shattered by this earthquake.

THE SINNERS OF THE SECOND CIRCLE (THE CARNAL): Here begin the punishments for the various sins of Incontinence (The sins of the She-Wolf). In the second circle are punished those who sinned by excess of sexual passion. Since this is the most natural sin and the sin most nearly associated with love, its punishment is the lightest of all to be found in Hell proper. The Carnal are whirled and buffeted endlessly through the murky air (symbolic of the beclouding of their reason by passion) by a great gale (symbolic of their lust).

53. *Empress of many tongues*: Semiramis, a legendary queen of Assyria who assumed full power at the death of her husband, Ninus.

61. *Dido*: Queen and founder of Carthage. She had vowed to remain faithful to her husband, Sichaeus, but she fell in love with Aeneas. When Aeneas abandoned her she stabbed herself on a funeral pyre she had had prepared.

According to Dante's own system of punishments, she should be in the Seventh Circle (Canto XIII) with the suicides. The only clue Dante gives to the tempering of her punishment is his statement that "she killed herself for love." Dante always seems readiest to forgive in that name.

65. *Achilles*: He is placed among this company because of his passion for Polyxena, the daughter of Priam. For love of her, he agreed to desert the Greeks and to join the Trojans, but when he went to the temple for the wedding (according to the legend Dante has followed) he was killed by Paris.

74. *those two swept together*: Paolo and Francesca (PAH-oe-loe: Frahn-CHAY-ska).

Dante's treatment of these two lovers is certainly the tenderest and most sympathetic accorded any of the sinners in Hell, and legends immediately began to grow about this pair.

The facts are these. In 1275 Giovanni Malatesta (Djoe-VAH-nee Mahl-ah-TEH-stah) of Rimini, called Giovanni the Lame, a somewhat deformed but brave and powerful warrior, made a political marriage with Francesca, daughter of Guido da Polenta of Ravenna. Francesca came to Rimini and there an amour grew between her and Giovanni's younger brother Paolo. Despite the fact that Paolo had married in 1269 and had become the father of two daughters by 1275, his affair with Francesca continued for many years. It was sometime between 1283 and 1286 that Giovanni surprised them in Francesca's bedroom and killed both of them.

Around these facts the legend has grown that Paolo was sent by Giovanni as his proxy to the marriage, that Francesca thought he was her real bridegroom and accordingly gave him her heart irrevocably at first sight. The legend obviously increases the pathos, but nothing in Dante gives it support.

102. *that we are one in Hell, as we were above*: At many points of *The Inferno* Dante makes clear the principle that the souls of the damned are locked so blindly into their own guilt that none can feel sympathy for another, or find any pleasure in the presence of another. The temptation of many readers is to interpret this line romantically: *i.e.*, that the love of Paolo and Francesca survives Hell itself. The more Dantean interpretation, however, is that they add to one another's anguish (a) as mutual reminders of their sin, and (b) as insubstantial shades of the bodies for which they once felt such great passion.

104. *Caïna waits for him*: Giovanni Malatesta was still alive at the writing. His fate is already decided, however, and upon his death, his soul will fall to Caïna, the first ring of the last circle (Canto XXXII), where lie those who performed acts of treachery against their kin.

124–5. *the rhyme of Lancelot*: The story exists in many forms. The details Dante makes use of are from an Old French version.

126. *dim time*: The original simply reads "We were alone, suspecting nothing." "Dim time" is rhyme-forced, but not wholly outside the legitimate implications of the original, I hope. The old courtly romance may well be thought of as happening in the dim ancient days. The apology, of course, comes after the fact: one does the possible, then argues for justification, and there probably is none.

134. *that book, and he who wrote it, was a pander*: "Galeotto," the Italian word for "pander," is also the Italian rendering of the name of Gallehault, who in the French Romance Dante refers to here, urged Lancelot and Guinevere on to love.

Canto VI

The Gluttons

Dante recovers from his swoon and finds himself in the *Third Circle*. A great storm of putrefaction falls incessantly, a mixture of stinking snow and freezing rain, which forms into a vile slush underfoot. Everything about this Circle suggests a gigantic garbage dump. The souls of the damned lie in the icy paste, swollen and obscene, and *Cerberus*, the ravenous three-headed dog of Hell, stands guard over them, ripping and tearing them with his claws and teeth.

These are the *Gluttons*. In life they made no higher use of the gifts of God than to wallow in food and drink, producers of nothing but garbage and offal. Here they lie through all eternity, themselves like garbage, half-buried in fetid slush, while Cerberus slavers over them as they in life slavered over their food.

As the Poets pass, one of the speakers sits up and addresses Dante. He is *Ciacco, The Hog*, a citizen of Dante's own Florence. He recognizes Dante and asks eagerly for news of what is happening there. With the foreknowledge of the damned, Ciacco then utters the first of the political prophecies that are to become a recurring theme of the Inferno. The Poets then move on toward the next Circle, at the edge of which they encounter the monster Plutus.

My senses had reeled from me out of pity
   for the sorrow of those kinsmen and lost lovers.
   Now they return, and waking gradually,   3

I see new torments and new souls in pain
   about me everywhere. Wherever I turn
   away from grief I turn to grief again.   6

I am in the Third Circle of the torments.
   Here to all time with neither pause nor change
   the frozen rain of Hell descends in torrents.   9

Huge hailstones, dirty water, and black snow
   pour from the dismal air to putrefy
   the putrid slush that waits for them below.   12

Here monstrous Cerberus, the ravening beast,
   howls through his triple throats like a mad dog
   over the spirits sunk in that foul paste.   15

His eyes are red, his beard is greased with phlegm,
   his belly is swollen, and his hands are claws
   to rip the wretches and flay and mangle them.   18

And they, too, howl like dogs in the freezing storm,
   turning and turning from it as if they thought
   one naked side could keep the other warm.   21

When Cerberus discovered us in that swill
   his dragon-jaws yawed wide, his lips drew back
   in a grin of fangs. No limb of him was still.   24

My Guide bent down and seized in either fist
   a clod of the stinking dirt that festered there
   and flung them down the gullet of the beast.   27

As a hungry cur will set the echoes raving
   and then fall still when he is thrown a bone,
   all of his clamor being in his craving,   30

so the three ugly heads of Cerberus,
   whose yowling at those wretches deafened them,
   choked on their putrid sops and stopped their fuss.   33

We made our way across the sodden mess
   of souls the rain beat down, and when our steps
   fell on a body, they sank through emptiness.   36

All those illusions of being seemed to lie
   drowned in the slush; until one wraith among them
   sat up abruptly and called as I passed by: 39

"O you who are led this journey through the shade
   of Hell's abyss, do you recall this face?
   You had been made before I was unmade."   42

And I: "Perhaps the pain you suffer here
   distorts your image from my recollection.
   I do not know you as you now appear."   45

And he to me: "Your own city, so rife
   with hatred that the bitter cup flows over
   was mine too in that other, clearer life.   48

Your citizens nicknamed me Ciacco, The Hog:
   gluttony was my offense, and for it
   I lie here rotting like a swollen log.   51

Nor am I lost in this alone; all these
   you see about you in this painful death
   have wallowed in the same indecencies."   54

I answered him: "Ciacco, your agony
   weighs on my heart and calls my soul to tears;
   but tell me, if you can, what is to be   57

for the citizens of that divided state,
   and whether there are honest men among them,
   and for what reasons we are torn by hate."   60

And he then: "After many words given and taken
   it shall come to blood; White shall rise over Black
   and rout the dark lord's force, battered and shaken.   63

Then it shall come to pass within three suns
    that the fallen shall arise, and by the power
    of one now gripped by many hesitations   66

Black shall ride on White for many years,
    loading it down with burdens and oppressions
    and humbling of proud names and helpless tears.   69

Two are honest, but none will heed them. There,
    pride, avarice, and envy are the tongues
    men know and heed, a Babel of despair."   72

Here he broke off his mournful prophecy.
    And I to him: "Still let me urge you on
    to speak a little further and instruct me: 75

Farinata and Tegghiaio, men of good blood,
    Jacopo Rusticucci, Arrigo, Mosca,
    and the others who set their hearts on doing good—   78

where are they now whose high deeds might be-gem
    the crown of kings? I long to know their fate.
    Does Heaven soothe or Hell envenom them?"   81

And he: "They lie below in a blacker lair.
    A heavier guilt draws them to greater pain.
    If you descend so far you may see them there.   84

But when you move again among the living,
    oh speak my name to the memory of men!
    Having answered all, I say no more." And giving   87

his head a shake, he looked up at my face
    cross-eyed, then bowed his head and fell away
    among the other blind souls of that place.   90

And my Guide to me: "He will not wake again
    until the angel trumpet sounds the day
    on which the host shall come to judge all men.   93

Then shall each soul before the seat of Mercy
    return to its sad grave and flesh and form
    to hear the edict of Eternity."   96

So we picked our slow way among the shades
    and the filthy rain, speaking of life to come.
    "Master," I said, "when the great clarion fades   99

into the voice of thundering Omniscience,
    what of these agonies? Will they be the same,
    or more, or less, after the final sentence?"   102

And he to me: "Look to your science again
    where it is written: the more a thing is perfect
    the more it feels of pleasure and of pain.   105

As for these souls, though they can never soar
to true perfection, still in the new time
they will be nearer it than they were before."   108

And so we walked the rim of the great ledge
speaking of pain and joy, and of much more
that I will not repeat, and reached the edge   111

where the descent begins. There, suddenly,
we came on Plutus, the great enemy.

Notes

13. *Cerberus*: In classical mythology Cerberus appears as a three-headed dog. His master was Pluto, king of the Underworld. Cerberus was placed at the Gate of the Underworld to allow all to enter, but none to escape. His three heads and his ravenous disposition make him an apt symbol of gluttony.

14. *like a mad dog*: Cerberus *is* a dog in classical mythology, but Dante seems clearly to have visualized him as a half-human monster. The beard (line 16) suggests that at least one of his three heads is human, and many illuminated manuscripts so represent him.

38. *until one wraith among them*: As the Poets pass, one of the damned sits up and asks if Dante recognizes him. Dante replies that he does not, and the wraith identifies himself as a Florentine nicknamed Ciacco, *i.e.*, The Hog.

Little is known about Ciacco (TCHA-koe). Boccaccio refers to a Florentine named Ciacco (Decameron IX, 8), and several conflicting accounts of him have been offered by various commentators. All that need be known about him, however, is the nature of his sin and the fact that he is a Florentine. Whatever else he may have been does not function in the poem.

42. *You had been made before I was unmade*: That is, "you were born before I died." The further implication is that they must have seen one another in Florence, a city one can still walk across in twenty minutes, and around in a very few hours. Dante certainly would have known everyone in Florence.

61. CIACCO'S PROPHECY: This is the first of the political prophecies that are to become a recurring theme of the *Inferno*. (It is the second if we include the political symbolism in Canto I.) Dante is, of course, writing after these events have all taken place. At Easter time of 1300, however, the events were in the future.

The Whites and the Blacks of Ciacco's prophecy should not be confused with the Guelphs and the Ghibellines. The internal strife between the Guelphs and the Ghibellines ended with the total defeat of the Ghibellines. By the end of the 13th century that strife had passed. But very shortly a new feud began in Florence between White Guelphs and Black Guelphs. A rather gruesome murder perpetrated by Focaccio de' Cancellieri (Foe-KAH-tchoe day Khan-tchell-YAIR-ee) became the cause of new strife between two branches of the Cancellieri family. On May 1 of 1300 the White Guelphs (Dante's party) drove the Black Guelphs from Florence in bloody fighting. Two years later, however ("within three suns"), the Blacks, aided by Dante's detested Boniface VIII, returned and expelled most of the prominent Whites, among them Dante; for he had been a member of the Priorate (City Council) that issued a decree banishing the leaders of both sides. This was the beginning of Dante's long exile from Florence.

70. *two are honest*: In the nature of prophecies this remains vague. The two are not identified.

76-77. FARINATA will appear in Canto X among the Heretics: TEGGHIAIO and JACOPO RUSTICUCCI, in Canto XVI with the homosexuals, MOSCA in Canto XXVIII with the sowers of discord. ARRIGO does not appear again and he has not been positively identified. Dante probably refers here to Arrigo (or Oderigo) dei Fifanti, one of those who took part in the murder of Buondelmonte (Canto XXVIII, line 106, note).

86. *speak my name*: Excepting those shades in the lowest depths of Hell whose sins are so shameful that they wish only to be forgotten, all of the damned are eager to be remembered on earth. The concept of the family name and of its survival in the memories of men were matters of first importance among Italians of Dante's time, and expressions of essentially the same attitude are common in Italy today.

103. *your science*: "Science" to the man of Dante's time meant specifically "the writings of Aristotle and the commentaries upon them."

Canto VII

The Hoarders and the Wasters

The Wrathful and the Sullen

Plutus menaces the Poets, but once more Virgil shows himself more powerful than the rages of Hell's monsters. The Poets enter the *Fourth Circle*
and find what seems to be a war in progress.

The sinners are divided into two raging mobs, each soul among them
straining madly at a great boulder-like weight. The two mobs meet, clashing
their weights against one another, after which they separate, pushing the
great weights apart, and begin over again.

One mob is made up of the *Hoarders*, the other of the *Wasters*. In life,
they lacked all moderation in regulating their expenses; they destroyed the
light of God within themselves by thinking of nothing but money. Thus in
death, their souls are encumbered by dead weights (mundanity) and one
excess serves to punish the other. Their souls, moreover, have become so
dimmed and awry in their fruitless rages that there is no hope of recognizing any among them.

The Poets pass on while Virgil explains the function of *Dame Fortune* in
the Divine Scheme. As he finishes (it is past midnight now of Good
Friday) they reach the inner edge of the ledge and come to a Black Spring
which bubbles murkily over the rocks to form the *Marsh of Styx*, which is
the *Fifth Circle*, the last station of the *Upper Hell*.

Across the marsh they see countless souls attacking one another in the
foul slime. These are the *Wrathful* and the symbolism of their punishment
is obvious. Virgil also points out to Dante certain bubbles rising from the
slime and informs him that below that mud lie entombed the souls of the
Sullen. In life they refused to welcome the sweet light of the Sun (Divine
Illumination) and in death they are buried forever below the stinking
waters of the Styx, gargling the words of an endless chant in a grotesque
parody of singing a hymn.

"Papa Satán, Papa Satán, aleppy,"
    Plutus clucked and stuttered in his rage;
    and my all-knowing Guide, to comfort me: 3

"Do not be startled, for no power of his,
    however he may lord it over the damned,
    may hinder your descent through this abyss."   6

And turning to that carnival of bloat
    cried: "Peace, you wolf of Hell. Choke back your bile
    and let its venom blister your own throat.   9

Our passage through this pit is willed on high
    by that same Throne that loosed the angel wrath
    of Michael on ambition and mutiny."   12

As puffed out sails fall when the mast gives way
   and flutter to a self-convulsing heap—
   so collapsed Plutus into that dead clay.   15

Thus we descended the dark scarp of Hell
   to which all the evil of the Universe
   comes home at last, into the Fourth Great Circle   18

and ledge of the abyss. O Holy Justice,
   who could relate the agonies I saw!
   What guilt is man that he can come to this?   21

Just as the surge Charybdis hurls to sea
   crashes and breaks upon its countersurge,
   so these shades dance and crash eternally.   24

Here, too, I saw a nation of lost souls,
   far more than were above: they strained their chests
   against enormous weights, and with mad howls   27

rolled them at one another. Then in haste
   they rolled them back, one party shouting out:
   "Why do you hoard?" and the other: "Why do
                        you waste?"   30

So back around that ring they puff and blow,
   each faction to its course, until they reach
   opposite sides, and screaming as they go   33

the madmen turn and start their weights again
   to crash against the maniacs. And I,
   watching, felt my heart contract with pain.   36

"Master," I said, "what people can these be?
   And all those tonsured ones there on our left—
   is it possible they *all* were of the clergy?"   39

And he: "In the first life beneath the sun
   they were so skewed and squinteyed in their minds
   their misering or extravagance mocked all reason.   42

The voice of each clamors its own excess
   when lust meets lust at the two points of the circle
   where opposite guilts meet in their wretchedness.   45

These tonsured wraiths of greed were priests indeed,
   and popes and cardinals, for it is in these
   the weed of avarice sows its rankest seed."   48

And I to him: "Master, among this crew
   surely I should be able to make out
   the fallen image of some soul I knew."   51

And he to me: "This is a lost ambition.
   In their sordid lives they labored to be blind,
   and now their souls have dimmed past recognition.   54

All their eternity is to butt and bray:
  one crew will stand tight-fisted, the other stripped
  of its very hair at the bar of Judgment Day.   57

Hoarding and squandering wasted all their light
  and brought them screaming to this brawl of wraiths.
  You need no words of mine to grasp their plight.   60

Now may you see the fleeting vanity
  of the goods of Fortune for which men tear down
  all that they are, to build a mockery.   63

Not all the gold that is or ever was
  under the sky could buy for one of these
  exhausted souls the fraction of a pause."   66

"Master," I said, "tell me—now that you touch
  on this Dame Fortune—what *is* she, that she holds
  the good things of the world within her clutch?"   69

And he to me: "O credulous mankind,
  is there one error that has wooed and lost you?
  Now listen, and strike error from your mind: 72

That king whose perfect wisdom transcends all,
  made the heavens and posted angels on them
  to guide the eternal light that it might fall   75

from every sphere to every sphere the same.
  He made earth's splendors by a like decree
  and posted as their minister this high Dame,   78

the Lady of Permutations. All earth's gear
  she changes from nation to nation, from house to house,
  in changeless change through every turning year.   81

No mortal power may stay her spinning wheel.
  The nations rise and fall by her decree.
  None may foresee where she will set her heel: 84

she passes, and things pass. Man's mortal reason
  cannot encompass her. She rules her sphere
  as the other gods rule theirs. Season by season   87

her changes change her changes endlessly,
  and those whose turn has come press on her so,
  she must be swift by hard necessity.   90

And this is she so railed at and reviled
  that even her debtors in the joys of time
  blaspheme her name. Their oaths are bitter and wild,   93

but she in her beatitude does not hear.
  Among the Primal Beings of God's joy
  she breathes her blessedness and wheels her sphere.   96

But the stars that marked our starting fall away.
  We must go deeper into greater pain,
  for it is not permitted that we stay." 99

And crossing over to the chasm's edge
  we came to a spring that boiled and overflowed
  through a great crevice worn into the ledge. 102

By that foul water, black from its very source,
  we found a nightmare path among the rocks
  and followed the dark stream along its course. 105

Beyond its rocky race and wild descent
  the river floods and forms a marsh called Styx,
  a dreary swampland, vaporous and malignant. 108

And I, intent on all our passage touched,
  made out a swarm of spirits in that bog
  savage with anger, naked, slime-besmutched. 111

They thumped at one another in that slime
  with hands and feet, and they butted, and they bit
  as if each would tear the other limb from limb. 114

And my kind Sage: "My son, behold the souls
  of those who lived in wrath. And do you see
  the broken surfaces of those water-holes 117

on every hand, boiling as if in pain?
  There are souls beneath that water. Fixed in slime
  they speak their piece, end it, and start again: 120

'Sullen were we in the air made sweet by the Sun;
  in the glory of his shining our hearts poured
  a bitter smoke. Sullen were we begun; 123

sullen we lie forever in this ditch.'
  This litany they gargle in their throats
  as if they sang, but lacked the words and pitch." 126

Then circling on along that filthy wallow,
  we picked our way between the bank and fen,
  keeping our eyes on those foul souls that swallow 129

the slime of Hell. And so at last we came
  to the foot of a Great Tower that has no name.

Notes

1. *Papa Satán, Papa Satán, aleppy*: Virgil, the all-knowing, may understand these words, but no one familiar with merely human languages has deciphered them. In Canto XXXI the monster Nimrod utters a similar meaningless jargon, and Virgil there cites it as evidence of the dimness of his mind. Gibberish is certainly a characteristic appropriate to monsters, and since Dante takes pains to make the reference to Satan apparent in the gibberish, it is obviously infernal and debased, and that is almost certainly all he intended.

The word "papa" as used here probably means "Pope" rather than "father." "Il papa santo" is the Pope. "Papa Satán" would be his opposite number. In the original the last word is "aleppe." On the assumption that jargon translates jargon I have twisted it a bit to rhyme with "me."

2. *Plutus*: In Greek mythology, Plutus was the God of Wealth. Many commentators suggest that Dante confused him with Pluto, the son of Saturn and God of the Underworld. But in that case, Plutus would be identical with Lucifer himself and would require a central place in Hell, whereas the classical function of Plutus as God of Material Wealth makes him the ideal overseer of the miserly and the prodigal.

22. *Charybdis*: A famous whirlpool in the Straits of Sicily.

68. *Dame Fortune*: A central figure in medieval mythology. She is almost invariably represented as a female figure holding an ever-revolving wheel symbolic of Chance. Dante incorporates her into his scheme of the Universe, ranking her among the angels, and giving her a special office in the service of the Catholic God. This is the first of many passages in the *Commedia* in which Dante sets forth the details of the Divine Ordering of the universe.

84. *none may foresee where she will set her heel*: A literal translation of the original would be "She is hidden like a snake in the grass." To avoid the comic overtone of that figure in English, I have substituted another figure which I believe expresses Dante's intent without destroying his tone.

87. *the other gods*: Dante can only mean here "the other angels and ministers of God."

97. *But the stars that marked our starting fall away*: It is now past midnight of Good Friday.

101. *a spring*: All the waters of Hell derive from one source (see Canto XIV, lines 12 following). This black spring must therefore be the waters of Acheron boiling out of some subterranean passage.

THE FIFTH CIRCLE (THE WRATHFUL AND THE SULLEN)

Dante's symbolism here is self-evident, but his reaction to these sinners is different from any we have observed thus far. Up to now he has either been appalled, or overcome by pity. In his ironic description of the Sullen he ridicules the damned for the first time. And in the next Canto he is to take pleasure (if only a passing pleasure) in increasing the sufferings of Filippo Argenti.

Dante will again be moved to pity as he descends the slopes of Hell. In fact, Virgil will find it necessary to scold him for pitying those whom God in His infinite wisdom has damned. Gradually, however, Dante's heart hardens against the damned as he descends lower and lower into Hell, and this development should be followed through the *Inferno* along with many other themes Dante carries and builds upon. There is no way of grasping the genius of Dante's architectonic power without noting his careful development of such themes. Even beyond the brilliance of his details, Dante's power is structural: everything relates to everything else.

107. *Styx*: The river Styx figures variously in classic mythology, but usually (and in later myths always) as a river of the Underworld. Dante, to heighten his symbolism, makes it a filthy marsh.

This marsh marks the first great division of Hell. Between Acheron and Styx are punished the sins of Incontinence (the Sins of the She-Wolf). This is the Upper Hell. Beyond Styx rise the flaming walls of the infernal city of Dis, within which are punished Violence and Fraud (the sins of the Lion, and the Sins of the Leopard). It is symbolically fitting that the approaches to the city of Hell should be across the filthiest of marshes.

131. *a Great Tower*: No special significance need be attributed to the Tower. It serves as a signaling point for calling the ferryman from Dis.

Canto VIII

The Wrathful, Phlegyas

The Fallen Angels

The Poets stand at the edge of the swamp, and a mysterious signal flames from the great tower. It is answered from the darkness of the other side, and almost immediately the Poets see *Phlegyas*, the Boatman of Styx, racing toward them across the water, fast as a flying arrow. He comes avidly, thinking to find new souls for torment, and he howls with rage when he discovers the Poets. Once again, however, Virgil conquers wrath with a word and Phlegyas reluctantly gives them passage.

As they are crossing, a muddy soul rises before them. It is *Filippo Argenti*, one of the Wrathful. Dante recognizes him despite the filth with which he is covered, and he berates him soundly, even wishing to see him tormented further. Virgil approves Dante's disdain and, as if in answer to Dante's wrath, Argenti is suddenly set upon by all the other sinners present, who fall upon him and rip him to pieces.

The boat meanwhile has sped on, and before Argenti's screams have died away, Dante sees the flaming red towers of Dis, the Capital of Hell. The great walls of the iron city block the way to the Lower Hell. Properly speaking, all the rest of Hell lies within the city walls, which separate the Upper and the Lower Hell.

Phlegyas deposits them at a great Iron Gate which they find to be guarded by the *Rebellious Angels*. These creatures of Ultimate Evil, rebels against God Himself, refuse to let the Poets pass. Even Virgil is powerless against them, for Human Reason by itself cannot cope with the essence of Evil. Only Divine Aid can bring hope. Virgil accordingly sends up a prayer for assistance and waits anxiously for a Heavenly Messenger to appear.

> Returning to my theme, I say we came
> to the foot of a Great Tower; but long before
> we reached it through the marsh, two horns of flame   3
>
> flared from the summit, one from either side,
> and then, far off, so far we scarce could see it
> across the mist, another flame replied.   6
>
> I turned to that sea of all intelligence
> saying: "What is this signal and counter-signal?
> Who is it speaks with fire across this distance?"   9
>
> And he then: "Look across the filthy slew:
> you may already see the one they summon,
> if the swamp vapors do not hide him from you."   12
>
> No twanging bowspring ever shot an arrow
> that bored the air it rode dead to the mark
> more swiftly than the flying skiff whose prow   15

shot toward us over the polluted channel
   with a single steersman at the helm who called:
   "So, do I have you at last, you whelp of Hell?"   18

"Phlegyas, Phlegyas," said my Lord and Guide,
   "this time you waste your breath: you have us only
   for the time it takes to cross to the other side."   21

Phlegyas, the madman, blew his rage among
   those muddy marshes like a cheat deceived,
   or like a fool at some imagined wrong.   24

My Guide, whom all the fiend's noise could not nettle,
   boarded the skiff, motioning me to follow:
   and not till I stepped aboard did it seem to settle   27

into the water. At once we left the shore,
   that ancient hull riding more heavily
   than it had ridden in all of time before.   30

And as we ran on that dead swamp, the slime
   rose before me, and from it a voice cried:
   "Who are you that come here before your time?"   33

And I replied: "If I come, I do not remain.
   But you, who are *you*, so fallen and so foul?"
   And he: "I am one who weeps." And I then: 36

"May you weep and wail to all eternity,
   for I know you, hell-dog, filthy as you are."
   Then he stretched both hands to the boat, but warily   39

the Master shoved him back, crying, "Down! Down!
   with the other dogs!" Then he embraced me saying:
   "Indignant spirit, I kiss you as you frown.   42

Blessed be she who bore you. In world and time
   this one was haughtier yet. Not one unbending
   graces his memory. Here is his shadow in slime.   45

How many living now, chancellors of wrath,
   shall come to lie here yet in this pigmire,
   leaving a curse to be their aftermath!"   48

And I: "Master, it would suit my whim
   to see the wretch scrubbed down into the swill
   before we leave this stinking sink and him."   51

And he to me: "Before the other side
   shows through the mist, you shall have all you ask.
   This is a wish that should be gratified."   54

And shortly after, I saw the loathsome spirit
   so mangled by a swarm of muddy wraiths
   that to this day I praise and thank God for it.   57

"After Filippo Argenti!" all cried together.
    The maddog Florentine wheeled at their cry
    and bit himself for rage. I saw them gather.   60

And there we left him. And I say no more,
    But such a wailing beat upon my ears,
    I strained my eyes ahead to the far shore.   63

"My son," the Master said, "the City called Dis
    lies just ahead, the heavy citizens,
    the swarming crowds of Hell's metropolis."   66

And I then: "Master, I already see
    the glow of its red mosques, as if they came
    hot from the forge to smolder in this valley."   69

And my all-knowing Guide: "They are eternal
    flues to eternal fire that rages in them
    and makes them glow across this lower Hell."   72

And as he spoke we entered the vast moat
    of the sepulchre. Its wall seemed made of iron
    and towered above us in our little boat.   75

We circled through what seemed an endless distance
    before the boatman ran his prow ashore
    crying: "Out! Out! Get out! This is the entrance."   78

Above the gates more than a thousand shades
    of spirits purged from Heaven for its glory
    cried angrily: "Who is it that invades   81

Death's Kingdom in his life?" My Lord and Guide
    advanced a step before me with a sign
    that he wished to speak to some of them aside.   84

They quieted somewhat, and one called, "Come,
    but come alone. And tell that other one,
    who thought to walk so blithely through death's kingdom, 87

he may go back along the same fool's way
    he came by. Let him try his living luck.
    You who are dead can come only to stay."   90

Reader, judge for yourself, how each black word
    fell on my ears to sink into my heart:
    I lost hope of returning to the world.   93

"O my beloved Master, my Guide in peril,
    who time and time again have seen me safely
    along this way, and turned the power of evil,   96

stand by me now," I cried, "in my heart's fright.
    And if the dead forbid our journey to them,
    let us go back together toward the light."   99

My Guide then, in the greatness of his spirit:
"Take heart. Nothing can take our passage from us
when such a power has given warrant for it.   102

Wait here and feed your soul while I am gone
on comfort and good hope; I will not leave you
to wander in this underworld alone."   105

So the sweet Guide and Father leaves me here,
and I stay on in doubt with yes and no
dividing all my heart to hope and fear.   108

I could not hear my Lord's words, but the pack
that gathered round him suddenly broke away
howling and jostling and went pouring back,   111

slamming the towering gate hard in his face.
That great Soul stood alone outside the wall.
Then he came back; his pain showed in his pace.   114

His eyes were fixed upon the ground, his brow
had sagged from its assurance. He sighed aloud:
"Who has forbidden me the halls of sorrow?"   117

And to me he said: "You need not be cast down
by my vexation, for whatever plot
these fiends may lay against us, we will go on.   120

This insolence of theirs is nothing new:
they showed it once at a less secret gate
that still stands open for all that they could do—   123

the same gate where you read the dead inscription;
and through it at this moment a Great One comes.
Already he has passed it and moves down   126

ledge by dark ledge. He is one who needs no guide,
and at his touch all gates must spring aside."

Notes

1. *Returning to my theme*: There is evidence that Dante stopped writing for a longer or shorter period between the seventh and eighth Cantos. None of the evidence is conclusive but it is quite clear that the plan of the *Inferno* changes from here on. Up to this point the Circles have been described in one canto apiece. If this was Dante's original plan, Hell would have been concluded in five more Cantos, since there are only Nine Circles in all. But in the later journey the Eighth Circle alone occupies thirteen Cantos. Dante's phrase may be simply transitional, but it certainly marks a change in the plan of the poem.

19. *Phlegyas*: Mythological King of Boeotia. He was the son of Ares (Mars) by a human mother. Angry at Apollo, who had seduced his daughter (Aesculapius was born of this union), he set fire to Apollo's temple at Delphi. For this offense, the God killed him and threw his soul into Hades under sentence of eternal torment. Dante's choice of a ferryman is especially apt. Phlegyas is the link between the Wrathful (to whom his paternity relates him) and the Rebellious Angels who menaced God (as he menaced Apollo).

27. *and not till I stepped aboard did it seem to settle*: Because of his living weight.

32. *Filippo Argenti*: (Ahr-DJEN-tee) One of the Adimari family, who were bitter

political enemies of Dante. Dante's savagery toward him was probably intended in part as an insult to the family. He pays them off again in the Paradiso when he has Cacciaguida (Kah-tchah-GWEE-da) call them "The insolent gang that makes itself a dragon to chase those who run away, but is sweet as a lamb to any who show their teeth—or their purse."

43. *Blessed be she who bore you*: These were Luke's words to Christ. To have Virgil apply them to Dante after such violence seems shocking, even though the expression is reasonably common in Italian. But Dante does not use such devices lightly. The *Commedia*, it must be remembered, is a vision of the progress of man's soul toward perfection. In being contemptuous of Wrath, Dante is purging it from his soul. He is thereby growing nearer to perfection, and Virgil, who has said nothing in the past when Dante showed pity for other sinners (though Virgil will later take him to task for daring to pity those whom God has shut off from pity), welcomes this sign of relentless rejection. Only by a ruthless enmity toward evil may the soul be purified, and as Christ is the symbol of ultimate perfection by rejection of Evil, so the birth of that rejection in Dante may aptly be greeted by the words of Luke, for it is from this that the soul must be reborn. Righteous indignation, moreover (*giusto sdegno*), is one of the virtues Christ practiced (e.g., against the money changers) and is the golden mean of right action between the evil extremes of wrath and sullenness.

64. *Dis*: Pluto, King of the Underworld of ancient mythology, was sometimes called Dis. This, then, is his city, the metropolis of Satan. Within the city walls lies all the Lower Hell; within it fire is used for the first time as a torment of the damned; and at its very center Satan himself stands fixed forever in a great ice cap.

68. *mosques*: To a European of Dante's time a mosque would seem the perversion of a church, the impious counterpart of the House of God, just as Satan is God's impious counterpart. His city is therefore architecturally appropriate, a symbolism that becomes all the more terrible when the mosques are made of red-hot iron.

70-71. *they are eternal flues to eternal fire*: The fires of Hell are all within Dis.

80. *spirits purged from Heaven for its glory*: The Rebellious Angels. We have already seen, on the other side of Acheron, the Angels who sinned by refusing to take sides.

95. *time and time again*: A literal translation of the original would read "more than seven times." "Seven" is used here as an indeterminate number indicating simply "quite a number of times." Italian makes rather free use of such numbers.

106. *leaves me*: Dante shifts tenses more freely than English readers are accustomed to.

113. *That Great Soul stood alone*: Virgil's allegorical function as Human Reason is especially important to an interpretation of this passage.

122. *a less secret gate*: The Gate of Hell. According to an early medieval tradition, these demons gathered at the outer gate to oppose the descent of Christ into Limbo at the time of the Harrowing of Hell, but Christ broke the door open and it has remained so ever since. The service of the Mass for Holy Saturday still sings *Hodie portas mortis et seras pariter Salvator noster disrupit*. (On this day our Saviour broke open the door of the dead and its lock as well.)

125. *a Great One*: A Messenger of Heaven. He is described in the next Canto.

Canto IX

At the Gate of Dis the Poets wait in dread. Virgil tries to hide his anxiety
from Dante, but both realize that without Divine Aid they will surely be
lost. To add to their terrors *Three Infernal Furies*, symbols of Eternal
Remorse, appear on a near-by tower, from which they threaten the Poets
and call for *Medusa* to come and change them to stone. Virgil at once
commands Dante to turn and shut his eyes. To make doubly sure, Virgil
himself places his hands over Dante's eyes, for there is an Evil upon which
man must not look if he is to be saved.

But at the moment of greatest anxiety a storm shakes the dirty air of
Hell and the sinners in the marsh begin to scatter like frightened Frogs.
The Heavenly Messenger is approaching. He appears walking majestically
through Hell, looking neither to right nor to left. With a touch he throws
open the Gate of Dis while his words scatter the Rebellious Angels. Then
he returns as he came.

The Poets now enter the gate unopposed and find themselves in the
Sixth Circle. Here they find a countryside like a vast cemetery. Tombs of
every size stretch out before them, each with its lid lying beside it, and
each wrapped in flames. Cries of anguish sound endlessly from the
entombed dead.

This is the torment of the *Heretics* of every cult. By Heretic, Dante
means specifically those who did violence to God by denying immortality.
Since they taught that the soul dies with the body, so their punishment is
an eternal grave in the fiery morgue of God's wrath.

> My face had paled to a mask of cowardice
>   when I saw my Guide turn back. The sight of it
>   the sooner brought the color back to his.　　　　　3
>
> He stood apart like one who strains to hear
>   what he cannot see, for the eye could not reach far
>   across the vapors of that midnight air.　　　　　6
>
> "Yet surely we were meant to pass these tombs,"
>   he said aloud. "If not . . . so much was promised . . .
>   Oh how time hangs and drags till our aid comes!"　　　9
>
> I saw too well how the words with which he ended
>   covered his start, and even perhaps I drew
>   a worse conclusion from that than he intended.　　　12
>
> "Tell me, Master, does anyone ever come
>   from the first ledge, whose only punishment
>   is hope cut off, into this dreary bottom?"　　　15
>
> I put this question to him, still in fear
>   of what his broken speech might mean; and he:
>   "Rarely do any of us enter here.　　　　　18

44

Once before, it is true, I crossed through Hell
    conjured by cruel Erichtho who recalled
    the spirits to their bodies. Her dark spell   21

forced me, newly stripped of my mortal part,
    to enter through this gate and summon out
    a spirit from Judaïca. Take heart,   24

that is the last depth and the darkest lair
    and the farthest from Heaven which encircles all,
    and at that time I came back even from there.   27

The marsh from which the stinking gasses bubble
    lies all about this capital of sorrow
    whose gates we may not pass now without trouble."   30

All this and more he expounded; but the rest
    was lost on me, for suddenly my attention
    was drawn to the turret with the fiery crest   33

where all at once three hellish and inhuman
    Furies sprang to view, bloodstained and wild.
    Their limbs and gestures hinted they were women.   36

Belts of greenest hydras wound and wound
    about their waists, and snakes and horned serpents
    grew from their heads like matted hair and bound   39

their horrid brows. My Master, who well knew
    the handmaids of the Queen of Woe, cried: "Look:
    the terrible Erinyes of Hecate's crew.   42

That is Megaera to the left of the tower.
    Alecto is the one who raves on the right.
    Tisiphone stands between." And he said no more.   45

With their palms they beat their brows, with their nails they
                clawed
    their bleeding breasts. And such mad wails broke from them
    that I drew close to the Poet, overawed.   48

And all together screamed, looking down at me:
    "Call Medusa that we may change him to stone!
    Too lightly we let Theseus go free."   51

"Turn your back and keep your eyes shut tight;
    for should the Gorgon come and you look at her,
    never again would you return to the light."   54

This was my Guide's command. And he turned me about
    himself, and would not trust my hands alone,
    but, with his placed on mine, held my eyes shut.   57

Men of sound intellect and probity,
    weigh with good understanding what lies hidden
    behind the veil of my strange allegory!   60

Suddenly there broke on the dirty swell
  of the dark marsh a squall of terrible sound
  that sent a tremor through both shores of Hell;   63

a sound as if two continents of air,
  one frigid and one scorching, clashed head on
  in a war of winds that stripped the forests bare,   66

ripped off whole boughs and blew them helter skelter
  along the range of dust it raised before it
  making the beasts and shepherds run for shelter.   69

The Master freed my eyes. "Now turn," he said,
  "and fix your nerve of vision on the foam
  there where the smoke is thickest and most acrid."   72

As frogs before the snake that hunts them down
  churn up their pond in flight, until the last
  squats on the bottom as if turned to stone—   75

so I saw more than a thousand ruined souls
  scatter away from one who crossed dry-shod
  the Stygian marsh into Hell's burning bowels.   78

With his left hand he fanned away the dreary
  vapors of that sink as he approached;
  and only of that annoyance did he seem weary.   81

Clearly he was a Messenger from God's Throne,
  and I turned to my Guide; but he made me a sign
  that I should keep my silence and bow down.   84

Ah, what scorn breathed from that Angel-presence!
  He reached the gate of Dis and with a wand
  he waved it open, for there was no resistance.   87

"Outcasts of Heaven, you twice-loathsome crew,"
  he cried upon that terrible sill of Hell,
  "how does this insolence still live in you?   90

Why do you set yourselves against that Throne
  whose Will none can deny, and which, times past,
  has added to your pain for each rebellion?   93

Why do you butt against Fate's ordinance?
  Your Cerberus, if you recall, still wears
  his throat and chin peeled for such arrogance."   96

Then he turned back through the same filthy tide
  by which he had come. He did not speak to us,
    99   but went his way like one preoccupied

by other presences than those before him.
  And we moved toward the city, fearing nothing
  after his holy words. Straight through the dim   102

and open gate we entered unopposed.
    And I, eager to learn what new estate
    of Hell those burning fortress walls enclosed,   105

began to look about the very moment
    we were inside, and I saw on every hand
    a countryside of sorrow and new torment.   108

As at Arles where the Rhone sinks into stagnant marshes,
    as at Pola by the Quarnaro Gulf, whose waters
    close Italy and wash her farthest reaches,   111

the uneven tombs cover the even plain—
    such fields I saw here, spread in all directions,
    except that here the tombs were chests of pain: 114

for, in a ring around each tomb, great fires
    raised every wall to a red heat. No smith
    works hotter iron in his forge. The biers   117

stood with their lids upraised, and from their pits
    an anguished moaning rose on the dead air
    from the desolation of tormented spirits.   120

And I: "Master, what shades are these who lie
    buried in these chests and fill the air
    with such a painful and unending cry?"   123

"These are the arch-heretics of all cults,
    with all their followers," he replied, "Far more
    than you would think lie stuffed into these vaults.   126

Like lies with like in every heresy,
    and the monuments are fired, some more, some less;
    to each depravity its own degree."   129

He turned then, and I followed through that night
between the wall and the torments, bearing right.

Notes

1-15. DANTE'S FEAR AND VIRGIL'S ASSURANCE. Allegorically, this highly dramatic scene once more represents the limits of the power of Human Reason. There are occasions, Dante makes clear, in which only Divine Aid will suffice. The anxiety here is the turmoil of the mind that hungers after God and awaits His sign in fear and doubt, knowing that unless that sign is given, the final evil cannot be surmounted.

Aside from the allegorical significance the scene is both powerfully and subtly drawn. Observing Dante's fear, Virgil hides his own. Dante, however, penetrates the dissimulation, and is all the more afraid. To reassure himself (or to know the worst, perhaps) he longs to ask Virgil whether or not he really knows the way. But he cannot ask bluntly; he has too much respect for his Guide's feelings. Therefore, he generalizes the question in such a way as to make it inoffensive.

Having drawn so delicate a play of cross-motives in such brief space, Dante further seizes the scene as an opportunity for reinforcing Virgil's fitness to be his Guide. The economy of means with which Dante brings his several themes to assist one another is in the high tradition of dramatic poetry.

14. *from the first ledge*: Limbo.
20. *Erichtho*: A sorceress drawn from Lucan (*Pharsalia* VI, 508ff).

24. *a spirit from Judaïca* . . . : Judaïca (or Judecca) is the final pit of Hell. Erichtho called up the spirit in order to foretell the outcome of the campaign between Pompey and Caesar. There is no trace of the legend in which Virgil is chosen for the descent; Virgil, in fact, was still alive at the time of the battle of Pharsalia.

34ff. THE THREE FURIES: (or Erinyes) In classical mythology they were especially malignant spirits who pursued and tormented those who had violated fundamental taboos (desecration of temples, murder of kin, etc.). They are apt symbols of the guilty conscience of the damned.

41. *the Queen of Woe*: Proserpine (or Hecate) was the wife of Pluto, and therefore Queen of the Underworld.

50. *Medusa*: The Gorgon. She turned to stone whoever looked at her. Allegorically she may be said to represent Despair of ever winning the Mercy of God. The further allegory is apparent when we remember that she is summoned by the Furies, who represent Remorse.

51. *too lightly we let Theseus go free*: Theseus and Pirithous tried to kidnap Hecate. Pirithous was killed in the attempt and Theseus was punished by being chained to a great rock. He was later set free by Hercules, who descended to his rescue in defiance of all the powers of Hell. The meaning of the Furies' cry is that Dante must be made an example of. Had they punished Theseus properly, men would have acquired more respect for their powers and would not still be attempting to invade the Underworld.

59-60. *my strange allegory*: Most commentators take this to mean the allegory of the Three Furies, but the lines apply as aptly to the allegory that follows. Dante probably meant both. Almost certainly, too, "my strange allegory" refers to the whole *Commedia*.

61ff. THE APPEARANCE OF THE MESSENGER: In Hell, God is expressed only as inviolable power. His messenger is preceded by great storms, his presence sends a terror through the damned, his face is the face of scorn.

95. *Cerberus*: When Cerberus opposed the fated entrance of Hercules into Hell, Hercules threw a chain about his neck and dragged him to the upperworld. Cerberus' throat, according to Dante, is still peeled raw from it.

104. THE SIXTH CIRCLE: Once through the gate, the Poets enter the Sixth Circle and the beginning of the Lower Hell.

109ff. *Arles . . . Pola*: Situated as indicated on the Rhone and the Quarnaro Gulf respectively, these cities were the sites of great cemeteries dating back to the time of Rome. The Quarnaro Gulf is the body of water on which Fiume is situated.

114. *The Heretics*: Within the Sixth Circle are punished the Heretics. They lie in chests resembling great tombs, but the tombs are made of iron and are heated red-hot by great fires. The tombs are uncovered, and the great lids lie about on the ground. As we shall learn soon, these lids will be put into place on the Day of Judgment and sealed forever. Thus, once more the sin is refigured in the punishment, for as Heresy results in the death of the soul, so the Heretics will be sealed forever in their death within a death.

It must be noted, however, that Dante means by "heretic" specifically those skeptics who deny the soul's immortality. They stand in relation to the Lower Hell as the Pagans stood in relation to the Upper Hell. The Pagans did not know how to worship God: the Heretics denied His existence. Each group, in its degree, symbolizes a state of blindness. (Other varieties of Heretics are in Bolgia 9 of Circle VIII.) Moreover, in Dante's system, to deny God is the beginning of Violence, Bestiality, and Fraud; and it is these sins which are punished below.

131. *bearing right*: Through all of Hell the Poets bear left in their descent with only two exceptions, the first in their approach to the Heretics, the second in their approach to Geryon, the monster of fraud (see note XVII, 29, below). Note that both these exceptions occur at a major division of the *Inferno*. There is no satisfactory explanation of Dante's allegorical intent in making these exceptions.

Canto X

The Heretics

As the Poets pass on, one of the damned hears Dante speaking, recognizes him as a Tuscan, and calls to him from one of the fiery tombs. A moment later he appears. He is *Farinata degli Uberti*, a great war-chief of the Tuscan Ghibellines. The majesty and power of his bearing seem to diminish Hell itself. He asks Dante's lineage and recognizes him as an enemy. They begin to talk politics, but are interrupted by another shade, who rises from the same tomb.

This one is *Cavalcante dei Cavalcanti*, father of Guido Cavalcanti, a contemporary poet. If it is genius that leads Dante on his great journey, the shade asks, why is Guido not with him? Can Dante presume to a greater genius than Guido's? Dante replies that he comes this way only with the aid of powers Guido has not sought. His reply is a classic example of many-leveled symbolism as well as an overt criticism of a rival poet. The senior Cavalcanti mistakenly infers from Dante's reply that Guido is dead, and swoons back into the flames.

Farinata, who has not deigned to notice his fellow-sinner, continues from the exact point at which he had been interrupted. It is as if he refuses to recognize the flames in which he is shrouded. He proceeds to prophesy Dante's banishment from Florence, he defends his part in Florentine politics, and then, in answer to Dante's question, he explains how it is that the damned can foresee the future but have no knowledge of the present. He then names others who share his tomb, and Dante takes his leave with considerable respect for his great enemy, pausing only long enough to leave word for Cavalcanti that Guido is still alive.

We go by a secret path along the rim
   of the dark city, between the wall and the torments.
   My Master leads me and I follow him.   3

"Supreme Virtue, who through this impious land
   wheel me at will down these dark gyres," I said,
   "speak to me, for I wish to understand.   6

Tell me, Master, is it permitted to see
   the souls within these tombs? The lids are raised,
   and no one stands on guard." And he to me: 9

"All shall be sealed forever on the day
   these souls return here from Jehosaphat
   with the bodies they have given once to clay.   12

In this dark corner of the morgue of wrath
   lie Epicurus and his followers,
   who make the soul share in the body's death.   15

And here you shall be granted presently
   not only your spoken wish, but that other as well,
   which you had thought perhaps to hide from me."   18

And I: "Except to speak my thoughts in few
    and modest words, as I learned from your example,
    dear Guide, I do not hide my heart from you."   21

"O Tuscan, who go living through this place
    speaking so decorously, may it please you pause
    a moment on your way, for by the grace   24

of that high speech in which I hear your birth,
    I know you for a son of that noble city
    which perhaps I vexed too much in my time on earth."   27

These words broke without warning from inside
    one of the burning arks. Caught by surprise,
    I turned in fear and drew close to my Guide.   30

And he: "Turn around. What are you doing? Look there:
    it is Farinata rising from the flames.
    From the waist up his shade will be made clear."   33

My eyes were fixed on him already. Erect,
    he rose above the flame, great chest, great brow;
    he seemed to hold all Hell in disrespect.   36

My Guide's prompt hands urged me among the dim
    and smoking sepulchres to that great figure,
    and he said to me: "Mind how you speak to him."   39

And when I stood alone at the foot of the tomb,
    the great soul stared almost contemptuously,
    before he asked: "Of what line do you come?"   42

Because I wished to obey, I did not hide
    anything from him: whereupon, as he listened,
    he raised his brows a little, then replied: 45

"Bitter enemies were they to me,
    to my fathers, and to my party, so that twice
    I sent them scattering from high Italy."   48

"If they were scattered, still from every part
    they formed again and returned both times," I answered,
    "but yours have not yet wholly learned that art."   51

At this another shade rose gradually,
    visible to the chin. It had raised itself,
    I think, upon its knees, and it looked around me   54

as if it expected to find through that black air
    that blew about me, another traveler.
    And weeping when it found no other there,   57

turned back. "And if," it cried, "you travel through
    this dungeon of the blind by power of genius,
    where is my son? why is he not with you?"   60

And I to him: "Not by myself am I borne
    this terrible way. I am led by him who waits there,
    and whom perhaps your Guido held in scorn."   63

For by his words and the manner of his torment
    I knew his name already, and could, therefore,
    answer both what he asked and what he meant.   66

Instantly he rose to his full height:
    "He *held?* What is it you say? Is he dead, then?
    Do his eyes no longer fill with that sweet light?"   69

And when he saw that I delayed a bit
    in answering his question, he fell backwards
    into the flame, and rose no more from it.   72

But that majestic spirit at whose call
    I had first paused there, did not change expression,
    nor so much as turn his face to watch him fall.   75

"And if," going on from his last words, he said,
    "men of my line have yet to learn that art,
    that burns me deeper than this flaming bed.   78

But the face of her who reigns in Hell shall not
    be fifty times rekindled in its course
    before you learn what griefs attend that art.   81

And as you hope to find the world again,
    tell me: why is that populace so savage
    in the edicts they pronounce against my strain?"   84

And I to him: "The havoc and the carnage
    that dyed the Arbia red at Montaperti
    have caused these angry cries in our assemblage."   87

He sighed and shook his head. "I was not alone
    in that affair," he said, "nor certainly
    would I have joined the rest without good reason.   90

But I *was* alone at that time when every other
    consented to the death of Florence; I
    alone with open face defended her."   93

"Ah, so may your soul sometime have rest,"
    I begged him, "solve the riddle that pursues me
    through this dark place and leaves my mind perplexed: 96

you seem to see in advance all time's intent,
    if I have heard and understood correctly;
    but you seem to lack all knowledge of the present."   99

"We see asquint, like those whose twisted sight
    can make out only the far-off," he said,
    "for the King of All still grants us that much light.   102

When things draw near, or happen, we perceive
　　nothing of them. Except what others bring us
　　we have no news of those who are alive.　　　　105

So may you understand that all we know
　　will be dead forever from that day and hour
　　when the portal of the Future is swung to."　　108

Then, as if stricken by regret, I said:
　　"Now, therefore, will you tell that fallen one
　　who asked about his son, that he is not dead,　　111

and that, if I did not reply more quickly,
　　it was because my mind was occupied
　　with this confusion you have solved for me."　　114

And now my Guide was calling me. In haste,
　　therefore, I begged that mighty shade to name
　　the others who lay with him in that chest.　　117

And he: "More than a thousand cram this tomb.
　　The second Frederick is here, and the Cardinal
　　of the Ubaldini. Of the rest let us be dumb."　　120

And he disappeared without more said, and I
　　turned back and made my way to the ancient Poet,
　　pondering the words of the dark prophecy.　　123

He moved along, and then, when we had started,
　　he turned and said to me, "What troubles you?
　　Why do you look so vacant and downhearted?"　　126

And I told him. And he replied: "Well may you bear
　　those words in mind." Then, pausing, raised a finger:
　　"Now pay attention to what I tell you here:　　129

when finally you stand before the ray
　　of that Sweet Lady whose bright eye sees all,
　　from her you will learn the turnings of your way."　　132

So saying, he bore left, turning his back
　　on the flaming walls, and we passed deeper yet
　　into the city of pain, along a track　　135

that plunged down like a scar into a sink
which sickened us already with its stink.

Notes

11. *Jehosaphat:* A valley outside Jerusalem. The popular belief that it would serve
as the scene of the Last Judgment was based on *Joel* iii, 2, 12.
14. *Epicurus:* The Greek philosopher. The central aim of his philosophy was to
achieve happiness, which he defined as the absence of pain. For Dante this doctrine
meant the denial of the Eternal life, since the whole aim of the Epicurean was temporal happiness.

17. *not only your spoken wish, but that other as well*: "All knowing" Virgil is frequently presented as being able to read Dante's mind. The "other wish" is almost certainly Dante's desire to speak to someone from Florence with whom he could discuss politics. Many prominent Florentines were Epicureans.

22. *Tuscan*: Florence lies in the province of Tuscany. Italian, to an extent unknown in America, is a language of dialects, all of them readily identifiable even when they are not well understood by the hearer. Dante's native Tuscan has become the main source of modern official Italian. Two very common sayings still current in Italy are: "*Lingua toscana, lingua di Dio*" (the Tuscan tongue is the language of God) and—to express the perfection of Italian speech—"*Lingua toscana in bocca romana*" (the Tuscan tongue in a Roman mouth).

32–51. *Farinata*: Farinata degli Uberti (DEH-lyee Oob-EHR-tee) was head of the ancient noble house of the Uberti. He became leader of the Ghibellines of Florence in 1239, and played a large part in expelling the Guelphs in 1248. The Guelphs returned in 1251, but Farinata remained. His arrogant desire to rule singlehanded led to difficulties, however, and he was expelled in 1258. With the aid of the Manfredi of Siena, he gathered a large force and defeated the Guelphs at Montaperti on the River Arbia in 1260. Re-entering Florence in triumph, he again expelled the Guelphs, but at the Diet of Empoli, held by the victors after the battle of Montaperti, he alone rose in open counsel to resist the general sentiment that Florence should be razed. He died in Florence in 1264. In 1266 the Guelphs once more returned and crushed forever the power of the Uberti, destroying their palaces and issuing special decrees against persons of the Uberti line. In 1283 a decree of heresy was published against Farinata.

26. *that noble city*: Florence.

39. *"Mind how you speak to him"*: The surface interpretation is clearly that Virgil means Dante to show proper respect to so majestic a soul. (Cf. Canto XVI, 14–15.) But the allegorical level is more interesting here. Virgil (as Human Reason) is urging Dante to go forward on his own. These final words then would be an admonition to Dante to guide his speech according to the highest principles.

52. *another shade*: Cavalcante dei Cavalcanti was a famous Epicurean ("like lies with like"). He was the father of Guido Cavalcanti, a poet and friend of Dante. Guido was also Farinata's son-in-law.

61. *Not by myself*: Cavalcante assumes that the resources of human genius are all that are necessary for such a journey. (It is an assumption that well fits his character as an Epicurean.) Dante replies as a man of religion that other aid is necessary.

63. *whom perhaps your Guido held in scorn*: This reference has not been satisfactorily explained. Virgil is a symbol on many levels—of Classicism, of religiosity, of Human Reason. Guido might have scorned him on any of these levels, or on all of them. One interpretation might be that Dante wished to present Guido as an example of how skepticism acts as a limitation upon a man of genius. Guido's skepticism does not permit him to see beyond the temporal. He does not see that Virgil (Human Reason expressed as Poetic Wisdom) exists only to lead one to Divine Love, and therefore he cannot undertake the final journey on which Dante has embarked.

70. *and when he saw that I delayed*: Dante's delay is explained in lines 112–114.

79. *her who reigns in Hell*: Hecate or Proserpine. She is also the moon goddess. The sense of this prophecy, therefore, is that Dante will be exiled within fifty full moons. Dante was banished from Florence in 1302, well within the fifty months of the prophecy.

83. *that populace*: The Florentines.

97–108. THE KNOWLEDGE OF THE DAMNED: Dante notes with surprise that Farinata can foresee the future, but that Cavalcanti does not know whether his son is presently dead or alive. Farinata explains by outlining a most ingenious detail of the Divine Plan: the damned can see far into the future, but nothing of what is present or *of what has happened*. Thus, after Judgment, when there is no longer any Future, the intellects of the damned will be void.

119. *the second Frederick*: The Emperor Frederick II. In Canto XIII Dante has Pier delle Vigne speak of him as one worthy of honor, but he was commonly reputed to be an Epicurean.

119–120. *the Cardinal of the Ubaldini*: In the original Dante refers to him simply as "il Cardinale." Ottaviano degli Ubaldini (born *circa* 1209, died 1273) became a Cardinal in 1245, but his energies seem to have been directed exclusively to money and political intrigue. When he refused an important loan by the Ghibellines, he is reported by many historians as having remarked: "I may say that if I have a soul, I have lost it in the cause of the Ghibellines, and no one of them will help me now." The words "If I have a soul" would be enough to make him guilty in Dante's eyes of the charge of heresy.

131. *that Sweet Lady*: Beatrice.

Canto XI

The Heretics

The Poets reach the inner edge of the *Sixth Circle* and find a great jumble of rocks that had once been a cliff, but which has fallen into rubble as the result of the great earthquake that shook Hell when Christ died. Below them lies the *Seventh Circle*, and so fetid is the air that arises from it that the Poets cower for shelter behind a great tomb until their breaths can grow accustomed to the stench.

Dante finds an inscription on the lid of the tomb labeling it as the place in Hell of *Pope Anastasius*.

Virgil takes advantage of the delay to outline in detail *The Division of the Lower Hell*, a theological discourse based on *The Ethics* and *The Physics* of Aristotle with subsequent medieval interpretations. Virgil explains also why it is that the Incontinent are not punished within the walls of Dis, and rather ingeniously sets forth the reasons why Usury is an act of violence against Art, which is the child of Nature and hence the Grandchild of God. (By "Art," Dante means the arts and crafts by which man draws from nature, i.e., Industry.)

As he concludes he rises and urges Dante on. By means known only to Virgil, he is aware of the motion of the stars and from them he sees that it is about two hours before Sunrise of Holy Saturday.

We came to the edge of an enormous sink
　　rimmed by a circle of great broken boulders.
　　Here we found ghastlier gangs. And here the stink　　3

thrown up by the abyss so overpowered us
　　that we drew back, cowering behind the wall
　　of one of the great tombs; and standing thus,　　6

I saw an inscription in the stone, and read:
　　"I guard Anastasius, once Pope,
　　he whom Photinus led from the straight road."　　9

"Before we travel on to that blind pit
　　we must delay until our sense grows used
　　to its foul breath, and then we will not mind it,"　　12

my Master said. And I then: "Let us find
　　some compensation for the time of waiting."
　　And he: "You shall see I have just that in mind.　　15

My son," he began, "there are below this wall
　　three smaller circles, each in its degree
　　like those you are about to leave, and all　　18

are crammed with God's accurst. Accordingly,
　　that you may understand their sins at sight,
　　I will explain how each is prisoned, and why.　　21

Malice is the sin most hated by God.
   And the aim of malice is to injure others
   whether by fraud or violence. But since fraud   24

is the vice of which man alone is capable,
   God loathes it most. Therefore, the fraudulent
   are placed below, and their torment is more painful.   27

The first below are the violent. But as violence
   sins in three persons, so is that circle formed
   of three descending rounds of crueler torments.   30

Against God, self, and neighbor is violence shown.
   Against their persons and their goods, I say,
   as you shall hear set forth with open reason.   33

Murder and mayhem are the violation
   of the person of one's neighbor: and of his goods;
   harassment, plunder, arson, and extortion.   36

Therefore, homicides, and those who strike
   in malice—destroyers and plunderers—all lie
   in that first round, and like suffers with like.   39

A man may lay violent hands upon his own
   person and substance; so in that second round
   eternally in vain repentance moan   42

the suicides and all who gamble away
   and waste the good and substance of their lives
   and weep in that sweet time when they should be gay.   45

Violence may be offered the deity
   in the heart that blasphemes and refuses Him
   and scorns the gifts of Nature, her beauty and bounty.   48

Therefore, the smallest round brands with its mark
   both Sodom and Cahors, and all who rail
   at God and His commands in their hearts' dark.   51

Fraud, which is a canker to every conscience,
   may be practiced by a man on those who trust him,
   and on those who have reposed no confidence.   54

The latter mode seems only to deny
   the bond of love which all men have from Nature;
   therefore within the second circle lie   57

simoniacs, sycophants, and hypocrites,
   falsifiers, thieves, and sorcerers,
   grafters, pimps, and all such filthy cheats.   60

The former mode of fraud not only denies
   the bond of Nature, but the special trust
   added by bonds of friendship or blood-ties.   63

Hence, at the center point of all creation,
   in the smallest circle, on which Dis is founded,
   the traitors lie in endless expiation."   66

"Master," I said, "the clarity of your mind
   impresses all you touch; I see quite clearly
   the orders of this dark pit of the blind.   69

But tell me: those who lie in the swamp's bowels,
   those the wind blows about, those the rain beats,
   and those who meet and clash with such mad howls—   72

why are *they* not punished in the rust-red city
   if God's wrath be upon them? and if it is not,
   why must they grieve through all eternity?"   75

And he: "Why does your understanding stray
   so far from its own habit? or can it be
   your thoughts are turned along some other way?   78

Have you forgotten that your *Ethics* states
   the three main dispositions of the soul
   that lead to those offenses Heaven hates—   81

incontinence, malice, and bestiality?
   and how incontinence offends God least
   and earns least blame from Justice and Charity?   84

Now if you weigh this doctrine and recall
   exactly who they are whose punishment
   lies in that upper Hell outside the wall,   87

you will understand at once why they are confined
   apart from these fierce wraiths, and why less anger
   beats down on them from the Eternal Mind."   90

"O sun which clears all mists from troubled sight,
   such joy attends your rising that I feel
   as grateful to the dark as to the light.   93

Go back a little further," I said, "to where
   you spoke of usury as an offense
   against God's goodness. How is that made clear?"   96

"Philosophy makes plain by many reasons,"
   he answered me, "to those who heed her teachings,
   how all of Nature,—her laws, her fruits, her seasons,— 99

springs from the Ultimate Intellect and Its art:
   and if you read your *Physics* with due care,
   you will note, not many pages from the start,   102

that Art strives after her by imitation,
   as the disciple imitates the master;
   Art, as it were, is the Grandchild of Creation.   105

By this, recalling the Old Testament
near the beginning of Genesis, you will see
that in the will of Providence, man was meant   108

to labor and to prosper. But usurers,
by seeking their increase in other ways,
scorn Nature in herself and her followers.   111

But come, for it is my wish now to go on:
the wheel turns and the Wain lies over Caurus,
the Fish are quivering low on the horizon,   114

and there beyond us runs the road we go
down the dark scarp into the depths below."

Notes

2. *broken boulders*: These boulders were broken from the earthquake that shook Hell at the death of Christ.

3. *the stink*: The stink is, of course, symbolic of the foulness of Hell and its sins. The action of the poets in drawing back from it, and their meditations on the nature of sin, are therefore subject to allegorical as well as to literal interpretation.

8–9. ANASTASIUS and PHOTINUS: Anastasius II was Pope from 496 to 498. This was the time of schism between the Eastern (Greek) and Western (Roman) churches. Photinus, deacon of Thessalonica, was of the Greek church and held to the Acacian heresy, which denied the divine paternity of Christ. Dante follows the report that Anastasius gave communion to Photinus, thereby countenancing his heresy. Dante's sources, however, had probably confused Anastasius II, the Pope, with Anastasius I, who was Emperor from 491 to 518. It was the Emperor Anastasius who was persuaded by Photinus to accept the Acacian heresy.

17. *three smaller circles*: The Poets are now at the cliff that bounds the Sixth Circle. Below them lie Circles Seven, Eight, and Nine. They are smaller in circumference, being closer to the center, but they are all intricately subdivided, and will be treated at much greater length than were the Circles of Upper Hell. The table on page 58 sets forth the categories of the Lower Hell.

LOWER HELL: The structure of Dante's Hell is based on Aristotle (as Virgil makes clear in his exposition), but with certain Christian symbolisms, exceptions, and misconstructions of Aristotle's text. The major symbolisms are the three beasts met in Canto I. The exceptions are the two peculiarly Christian categories of sin: Paganism and Heresy. The misconstructions of Aristotle's text involve the classification of "bestiality." Aristotle classified it as a different thing from vice or malice, but medieval commentators construed the passage to mean "another sort of malice." Dante's intent is clear, however; he understood Aristotle to make three categories of sin: Incontinence, Violence and Bestiality, and Fraud and Malice. Incontinence is punished in the Upper Hell. The following table sets forth the categories of the Lower Hell.

50. *Sodom and Cahors*: Both these cities are used as symbols for the sins that are said to have flourished within them. Sodom (*Genesis* xix) is, of course, identified with unnatural sex practices. Cahors, a city in southern France, was notorious in the Middle Ages for its usurers.

64. *the center point of all creation*: In the Ptolemaic system the earth was the center of the Universe. In Dante's geography, the bottom of Hell is the center of the earth.

70. *those who lie, etc.*: These are, of course, the sinners of the Upper Hell.

73. *the rust-red city*: Dis. All of Lower Hell is within the city walls.

79. *your* Ethics: The *Ethics* of Aristotle.

101. *your* Physics: The *Physics* of Aristotle.

113. *the Wain lies over Caurus etc.*: The Wain is the constellation of the Great Bear. Caurus was the northwest wind in classical mythology. Hence the constellation of the Great Bear now lies in the northwest. The Fish is the constellation and zodiacal sign of Pisces. It is just appearing over the horizon. The next sign of the zodiac is Aries. We know from Canto I that the sun is in Aries, and since the twelve signs of the zodiac each cover two hours of the day, it must now be about two hours before dawn. It is, therefore, approximately 4:00 A.M. *of Holy Saturday*.

The stars are not visible in Hell, but throughout the *Inferno* Virgil reads them by some special power which Dante does not explain.

THE CLASSIFICATIONS OF SIN IN LOWER HELL

Heresy .... Circle VI

THE VIOLENT
AND BESTIAL
(Circle VII)
(SINS OF THE
LION)

- Round 1. Against Neighbors.
  (Murderers and war-makers)
- Round 2. Against Self.
  (Suicides and destroyers of their own substance)
- Round 3. Against God, Art, and Nature.
  (Blasphemers, perverts, and usurers)

THE FRAUDULENT
AND MALICIOUS
(SINS OF THE
LEOPARD)

(Circle VIII)
(Simple
Fraud)

- Bolgia 1. Seducers and panderers.
- Bolgia 2. Flatterers.
- Bolgia 3. Simoniacs.
- Bolgia 4. Fortune tellers and diviners.
- Bolgia 5. Grafters.
- Bolgia 6. Hypocrites.
- Bolgia 7. Thieves.
- Bolgia 8. Evil counselors.
- Bolgia 9. Sowers of discord.
- Bolgia 10. Counterfeiters and alchemists.

(Circle IX)
(Compound
Fraud)

- Caïna. Treachery against kin.
- Antenora. Treachery against country.
- Ptolemea. Treachery against guests and hosts.
- Judaïca. Treachery against lords and benefactors.

Canto XII

The Violent Against Neighbors

The Poets begin the descent of the fallen rock wall, having first to evade
the *Minotaur*, who menaces them. Virgil tricks him and the Poets hurry
by.

Below them they see the *River of Blood*, which marks the First Round
of the Seventh Circle as detailed in the previous Canto. Here are punished
the *Violent Against Their Neighbors*, great war-makers, cruel tyrants, high-
waymen—all who shed the blood of their fellowmen. As they wallowed in
blood during their lives, so they are immersed in the boiling blood forever,
each according to the degree of his guilt, while fierce Centaurs patrol the
banks, ready to shoot with their arrows any sinner who raises himself out of
the boiling blood beyond the limits permitted him. *Alexander the Great* is
here, up to his lashes in the blood, and with him *Attila, The Scourge of
God*. They are immersed in the deepest part of the river, which grows shallower as it circles to the other side of the ledge, then deepens again.

The Poets are challenged by the Centaurs, but Virgil wins a safe conduct from *Chiron*, their chief, who assigns *Nessus* to guide them and to
bear them across the shallows of the boiling blood. Nessus carries them
across at the point where it is only ankle deep and immediately leaves
them and returns to his patrol.

> The scene that opened from the edge of the pit
>   was mountainous, and such a desolation
>   that every eye would shun the sight of it: 3
>
> a ruin like the Slides of Mark near Trent
>   on the bank of the Adige, the result of an earthquake
>   or of some massive fault in the escarpment—   6
>
> for, from the point on the peak where the mountain split
>   to the plain below, the rock is so badly shattered
>   a man at the top might make a rough stair of it.   9
>
> Such was the passage down the steep, and there
>   at the very top, at the edge of the broken cleft,
>   lay spread the Infamy of Crete, the heir   12
>
> of bestiality and the lecherous queen
>   who hid in a wooden cow. And when he saw us,
>   he gnawed his own flesh in a fit of spleen.   15
>
> And my Master mocked: "How you do pump your breath!
>   Do you think, perhaps, it is the Duke of Athens,
>   who in the world above served up your death?   18
>
> Off with you, monster; this one does not come
>   instructed by your sister, but of himself
>   to observe your punishment in the lost kingdom."   21

As a bull that breaks its chains just when the knife
 has struck its death-blow, cannot stand nor run
 but leaps from side to side with its last life—   24

so danced the Minotaur, and my shrewd Guide
 cried out: "Run now! While he is blind with rage!
 Into the pass, quick, and get over the side!"   27

So we went down across the shale and slate
 of that ruined rock, which often slid and shifted
 under me at the touch of living weight.   30

I moved on, deep in thought; and my Guide to me:
 "You are wondering perhaps about this ruin
 which is guarded by that beast upon whose fury   33

I played just now. I should tell you that when last
 I came this dark way to the depths of Hell,
 this rock had not yet felt the ruinous blast.   36

But certainly, if I am not mistaken,
 it was just before the coming of Him who took
 the souls from Limbo, that all Hell was shaken   39

so that I thought the universe felt love
 and all its elements moved toward harmony,
 whereby the world of matter, as some believe,   42

has often plunged to chaos. It was then,
 that here and elsewhere in the pits of Hell,
 the ancient rock was stricken and broke open.   45

But turn your eyes to the valley; there we shall find
 the river of boiling blood in which are steeped
 all who struck down their fellow men." Oh blind!   48

Oh ignorant, self-seeking cupidity
 which spurs us so in the short mortal life
 and steeps us so through all eternity!   51

I saw an arching fosse that was the bed
 of a winding river circling through the plain
 exactly as my Guide and Lord had said.   54

A file of Centaurs galloped in the space
 between the bank and the cliff, well armed with arrows,
 riding as once on earth they rode to the chase.   57

And seeing us descend, that straggling band
 halted, and three of them moved out toward us,
 their long bows and their shafts already in hand.   60

And one of them cried out while still below:
 "To what pain are you sent down that dark coast?
 Answer from where you stand, or I draw the bow!"   63

"Chiron is standing there hard by your side;
   our answer will be to him. This wrath of yours
   was always your own worst fate," my Guide replied.   66

And to me he said: "That is Nessus, who died in the wood
   for insulting Dejanira. At his death
   he plotted his revenge in his own blood.   69

The one in the middle staring at his chest
   is the mighty Chiron, he who nursed Achilles:
   the other is Pholus, fiercer than all the rest.   72

They run by that stream in thousands, snapping their bows
   at any wraith who dares to raise himself
   out of the blood more than his guilt allows."   75

We drew near those swift beasts. In a thoughtful pause
   Chiron drew an arrow, and with its notch
   he pushed his great beard back along his jaws.   78

And when he had thus uncovered the huge pouches
   of his lips, he said to his fellows: "Have you noticed
   how the one who walks behind moves what he touches?   81

That is not how the dead go." My good Guide,
   already standing by the monstrous breast
   in which the two mixed natures joined, replied: 84

"It is true he lives; in his necessity
   I alone must lead him through this valley.
   Fate brings him here, not curisoity.   87

From singing Alleluia the sublime
   spirit who sends me came. He is no bandit.
   Nor am I one who ever stooped to crime.   90

But in the name of the Power by which I go
   this sunken way across the floor of Hell,
   assign us one of your troop whom we may follow,   93

that he may guide us to the ford, and there
   carry across on his back the one I lead,
   for he is not a spirit to move through air."   96

Chiron turned his head on his right breast
   and said to Nessus: "Go with them, and guide them,
   and turn back any others that would contest   99

their passage." So we moved beside our guide
   along the bank of the scalding purple river
   in which the shrieking wraiths were boiled and dyed.   102

Some stood up to their lashes in that torrent,
   and as we passed them the huge Centaur said:
   "These were the kings of bloodshed and despoilment.   105

Here they pay for their ferocity.
　　Here is Alexander. And Dionysius,
　　who brought long years of grief to Sicily.　　　　108

That brow you see with the hair as black as night
　　is Azzolino; and that beside him, the blonde,
　　is Opizzo da Esti, who had his mortal light　　　111

blown out by his own stepson." I turned then
　　to speak to the Poet but he raised a hand:
　　"Let him be the teacher now, and I will listen."　　114

Further on, the Centaur stopped beside
　　a group of spirits steeped as far as the throat

in the race of boiling blood, and there our guide　　117

pointed out a sinner who stood alone:
　　"That one before God's altar pierced a heart
　　still honored on the Thames." And he passed on.　　120

We came in sight of some who were allowed
　　to raise the head and all the chest from the river,
　　and I recognized many there. Thus, as we followed　　123

along the stream of blood, its level fell
　　until it cooked no more than the feet of the damned.
　　And here we crossed the ford to deeper Hell.　　126

"Just as you see the boiling stream grow shallow
　　along this side," the Centaur said to us
　　when we stood on the other bank, "I would have you know　129

that on the other, the bottom sinks anew
　　more and more, until it comes again
　　full circle to the place where the tyrants stew.　　132

It is there that Holy Justice spends its wrath
　　on Sextus and Pyrrhus through eternity,
　　and on Attila, who was a scourge on earth:　　135

and everlastingly milks out the tears
　　of Rinier da Corneto and Rinier Pazzo,
　　those two assassins who for many years　　138

stalked the highways, bloody and abhorred."
　　And with that he started back across the ford.

Notes

4. *the Slides of Mark*: *Li Slavoni di Marco* are about two miles from Rovereto (between Verona and Trent) on the left bank of the River Adige.

9. *a man at the top might, etc.*: I am defeated in all attempts to convey Dante's emphasis in any sort of a verse line. The sense of the original: "It might provide some sort of a way down for one who started at the top, but (by implication) would not be climbable from below."

12–18. *the Infamy of Crete*: This is the infamous Minotaur of classical mythology. His mother was Pasiphaë, wife of Minos, the King of Crete. She conceived an unnatural passion for a bull, and in order to mate with it, she crept into a wooden cow. From this union the Minotaur was born, half-man, half-beast. King Minos kept him in an ingenious labyrinth from which he could not escape. When Androgeos, the son of King Minos, was killed by the Athenians, Minos exacted an annual tribute of seven maidens and seven youths. These were annually turned into the labyrinth and there were devoured by the Minotaur.

The monster was finally killed by Theseus, Duke of Athens. He was aided by Ariadne, daughter of Minos (and half-sister of the monster). She gave Theseus a ball of cord to unwind as he entered the labyrinth and a sword with which to kill the Minotaur.

The Minotaur was, thus, more beast than human, he was conceived in a sodomitic union, and he was a devourer of human flesh—in all ways a fitting symbol of the souls he guards.

34 ff. THE BROKEN ROCKS OF HELL: According to *Matthew* xxvii, 51, an earthquake shook the earth at the moment of Christ's death. These stones, Dante lets us know, were broken off in that earthquake. We shall find other effects of the same shock in the Eighth Circle. It is worth noting also that both the Upper (See Canto V, 34) and the Lower Hell begin with evidences of this ruin. For details of Virgil's first descent see notes to Canto IX.

38. *the coming of Him, etc.*: For details of Christ's descent into Hell see notes to Canto IV.

40–42. *the universe felt love . . . as some believe*: The Greek philosopher, Empedocles, taught that the universe existed by the counter-balance (discord or mutual repulsion) of its elements. Should the elemental matter feel harmony (love or mutual attraction) all would fly together into chaos.

47. *the river of boiling blood*: This is Phlegethon, the river that circles through the First Round of the Seventh Circle, then sluices through the wood of the suicides (the Second Round) and the burning sands (Third Round) to spew over the Great Cliff into the Eighth Circle, and so, eventually, to the bottom of Hell (Cocytus).

The river is deepest at the point at which the Poets first approach it and grows shallower along both sides of the circle until it reaches the ford, which is at the opposite point of the First Round. The souls of the damned are placed in deeper or shallower parts of the river according to the degree of their guilt.

55. THE CENTAURS: The Centaurs were creatures of classical mythology, half-horse, half-men. They were skilled and savage hunters, creatures of passion and violence. Like the Minotaur, they are symbols of the bestial-human, and as such, are fittingly chosen as the tormentors of these sinners.

65. *Chiron*: The son of Saturn and of the nymph Philira. He was the wisest and most just of the Centaurs and reputedly was the teacher of Achilles and of other Greek heroes to whom he imparted great skill in bearing arms, medicine, astronomy, music, and augury. Dante places him far down in Hell with the others of his kind, but though he draws Chiron's coarseness, he also grants him a kind of majestic understanding.

67. *Nessus*: Nessus carried travelers across the River Evenus for hire. He was hired to ferry Dejanira, the wife of Hercules, and tried to abduct her, but Hercules killed him with a poisoned arrow. While Nessus was dying, he whispered to Dejanira that a shirt stained with his poisoned blood would act as a love charm should Hercules' affections stray. When Hercules fell in love with Iole, Dejanira sent him a shirt stained with the Centaur's blood. The shirt poisoned Hercules and he died in agony. Thus Nessus revenged himself with his own blood.

72. *Pholus*: A number of classical poets mention Pholus, but very little else is known of him.

88–89. *the sublime spirit*: Beatrice.

97. *Chiron turned his head on his right breast*: The right is the side of virtue and honor. In Chiron it probably signifies his human side as opposed to his bestial side.

107. *Alexander*: Alexander the Great. *Dionysius*: Dionysius I (died 367 B.C.) and his son, Dionysius II (died 343), were tyrants of Sicily. Both were infamous as prototypes of the bloodthirsty and exorbitant ruler. Dante may intend either or both.

110. *Azzolino* (or *Ezzelino*): Ezzelino de Romano, Count of Onora (1194–1259). The cruelest of the Ghibelline tyrants. In 1236 Frederick II appointed Ezzelino his vicar in Padua. Ezzelino became especially infamous for his bloody treatment of the Paduans, whom he slaughtered in great numbers.

111. *Opizzo da Esti*: Marquis of Ferrara (1264–1293). The account of his life is confused. One must accept Dante's facts as given.

119–120. *that one . . . a heart still honored on the Thames*: The sinner indicated is Guy de Montfort. His father, Simon de Montfort, was a leader of the barons who rebelled against Henry III and was killed at the battle of Evesham (1265) by Prince Edward (later Edward I).

In 1271, Guy (then Vicar General of Tuscany) avenged his father's death by murdering Henry's nephew (who was also named Henry). The crime was openly committed in a church at Viterbo. The murdered Henry's heart was sealed in a casket and sent to London, where it was accorded various honors.

134. *Sextus*: Probably the younger son of Pompey the Great. His piracy is mentioned in Lucan (*Pharsalia*, VI, 420–422). *Pyrrhus*: Pyrrhus, the son of Achilles, was especially bloodthirsty at the sack of Troy. Pyrrhus, King of Epirus (319–272 B.C.), waged relentless and bloody war against the Greeks and Romans. Either may be intended.

135. *Attila*: King of the Huns from 433 to 453. He was called the Scourge of God.

137. *Rinier da Corneto, Rinier Pazzo*: (Rin-YAIR PAH-tsoe) Both were especially bloodthirsty robber-barons of the thirteenth century.

Canto XIII

The Violent Against Themselves

Nessus carries the Poets across the river of boiling blood and leaves them in the Second Round of the Seventh Circle, *The Wood of the Suicides*. Here are punished those who destroyed their own lives and those who destroyed their substance.

The souls of the Suicides are encased in thorny trees whose leaves are eaten by the odious *Harpies*, the overseers of these damned. When the Harpies feed upon them, damaging their leaves and limbs, the wound bleeds. Only as long as the blood flows are the souls of the trees able to speak. Thus, they who destroyed their own bodies are denied a human form; and just as the supreme expression of their lives was self-destruction, so they are permitted to speak only through that which tears and destroys them. Only through their own blood do they find voice. And to add one more dimension to the symbolism, it is the Harpies—defilers of all they touch—who give them their eternally recurring wounds.

The Poets pause before one tree and speak with the soul of *Pier delle Vigne*. In the same wood they see *Jacomo da Sant' Andrea*, and *Lano da Siena*, two famous *Squanderers* and *Destroyers of Goods* pursued by a pack of savage hounds. The hounds overtake *Sant 'Andrea*, tear him to pieces and go off carrying his limbs in their teeth, a self-evident symbolic retribution for the violence with which these sinners destroyed their substance in the world. After this scene of horror, Dante speaks to an *Unknown Florentine Suicide* whose soul is inside the bush which was torn by the hound pack when it leaped upon Sant' Andrea.

Nessus had not yet reached the other shore
　　when we moved on into a pathless wood
　　that twisted upward from Hell's broken floor.　　　　3

Its foliage was not verdant, but nearly black.
　　The unhealthy branches, gnarled and warped and
　　　　　　　　　　　　　　　　　　　　　　tangled,
　　bore poison thorns instead of fruit. The track　　　6

of those wild beasts that shun the open spaces
　　men till between Cecina and Corneto
　　runs through no rougher nor more tangled places.　　9

Here nest the odious Harpies of whom my Master
　　wrote how they drove Aeneas and his companions
　　from the Strophades with prophecies of disaster.　　12

Their wings are wide, their feet clawed, their huge bellies
　　covered with feathers, their necks and faces human.
　　They croak eternally in the unnatural trees.　　　　15

"Before going on, I would have you understand,"
　　my Guide began, "we are in the second round
　　and shall be till we reach the burning sand.　　　　18

Therefore look carefully and you will see
    things in this wood, which, if I told them to you
    would shake the confidence you have placed in me."   21

I heard cries of lamentation rise and spill
    on every hand, but saw no souls in pain
    in all that waste; and, puzzled, I stood still.   24

I think perhaps he thought that I was thinking
    those cries rose from among the twisted roots
    through which the spirits of the damned were slinking   27

to hide from us. Therefore my Master said:
    "If you break off a twig, what you will learn
    will drive what you are thinking from your head."   30

Puzzled, I raised my hand a bit and slowly
    broke off a branchlet from an enormous thorn:
    and the great trunk of it cried: "Why do you break   33
                                            me?"

And after blood had darkened all the bowl
    of the wound, it cried again: "Why do you tear me?
    Is there no pity left in any soul?   36

Men we were, and now we are changed to sticks;
    well might your hand have been more merciful
    were we no more than souls of lice and ticks."   39

As a green branch with one end all aflame
    will hiss and sputter sap out of the other
    as the air escapes—so from that trunk there came   42

words and blood together, gout by gout.
    Startled, I dropped the branch that I was holding
    and stood transfixed by fear, half turned about   45

to my Master, who replied: "O wounded soul,
    could he have believed before what he has seen
    in my verses only, you would yet be whole,   48

for his hand would never have been raised against you.
    But knowing this truth could never be believed
    till it was seen, I urged him on to do   51

what grieves me now; and I beg to know your name,
    that to make you some amends in the sweet world
    when he returns, he may refresh your fame."   54

And the trunk: "So sweet those words to me that I
    cannot be still, and may it not annoy you
    if I seem somewhat lengthy in reply.   57

I am he who held both keys to Frederick's heart,
    locking, unlocking with so deft a touch
    that scarce another soul had any part   60

in his most secret thoughts. Through every strife
   I was so faithful to my glorious office
   that for it I gave up both sleep and life.   63

That harlot, Envy, who on Caesar's face
   keeps fixed forever her adulterous stare,
   the common plague and vice of court and palace,   66

inflamed all minds against me. These inflamed
   so inflamed him that all my happy honors
   were changed to mourning. Then, unjustly blamed,   69

my soul, in scorn, and thinking to be free
   of scorn in death, made me at last, though just,
   unjust to myself. By the new roots of this tree   72

I swear to you that never in word or spirit
   did I break faith to my lord and emperor
   who was so worthy of honor in his merit.   75

If either of you return to the world, speak for me,
   to vindicate in the memory of men
   one who lies prostrate from the blows of Envy."   78

The Poet stood. Then turned. "Since he is silent,"
   he said to me, "do not you waste this hour,
   if you wish to ask about his life or torment."   81

And I replied: "Question him for my part,
   on whatever you think I would do well to hear;
   I could not, such compassion chokes my heart."   84

The Poet began again: "That this man may
   with all his heart do for you what your words
   entreat him to, imprisoned spirit, I pray,   87

tell us how the soul is bound and bent
   into these knots, and whether any ever
   frees itself from such imprisonment."   90

At that the trunk blew powerfully, and then
   the wind became a voice that spoke these words:
   "Briefly is the answer given: when   93

out of the flesh from which it tore itself,
   the violent spirit comes to punishment,
   Minos assigns it to the seventh shelf.   96

It falls into the wood, and landing there,
   wherever fortune flings it, it strikes root,
   and there it sprouts, lusty as any tare,   99

shoots up a sapling, and becomes a tree.
   The Harpies, feeding on its leaves then, give it
   pain and pain's outlet simultaneously.   102

Like the rest, we shall go for our husks on Judgment Day,
    but not that we may wear them, for it is not just
    that a man be given what he throws away.   105

Here shall we drag them and in this mournful glade
    our bodies will dangle to the end of time,
    each on the thorns of its tormented shade."   108

We waited by the trunk, but it said no more;
    and waiting, we were startled by a noise
    that grew through all the wood. Just such a roar   111

and trembling as one feels when the boar and chase
    approach his stand, the beasts and branches crashing
    and clashing in the heat of the fierce race.   114

And there on the left, running so violently
    they broke off every twig in the dark wood,
    two torn and naked wraiths went plunging by me.   117

The leader cried, "Come now, O Death! Come now!"
    And the other, seeing that he was outrun,
    cried out: "Your legs were not so ready, Lano,   120

in the jousts at the Toppo." And suddenly in his rush,
    perhaps because his breath was failing him,
    he hid himself inside a thorny bush   123

and cowered among its leaves. Then at his back,
    the wood leaped with black bitches, swift as greyhounds
    escaping from their leash, and all the pack   126

sprang on him; with their fangs they opened him
    and tore him savagely, and then withdrew,
    carrying his body with them, limb by limb.   129

Then, taking me by the hand across the wood,
    my Master led me toward the bush. Lamenting,
    all its fractures blew out words and blood: 132

"O Jacomo da Sant' Andrea!" it said,
    "what have you gained in making me your screen?
    What part had I in the foul life you led?"   135

And when my Master had drawn up to it
    he said: "Who were you, who through all your wounds
    blow out your blood with your lament, sad spirit?"   138

And he to us: "You who have come to see
    how the outrageous mangling of these hounds
    has torn my boughs and stripped my leaves from me, 141

O heap them round my ruin! I was born
    in the city that tore down Mars and raised the Baptist.
    On that account the God of War has sworn   144

her sorrow shall not end. And were it not
that something of his image still survives
on the bridge across the Arno, some have thought   147

those citizens who of their love and pain
afterwards rebuilt it from the ashes
left by Attila, would have worked in vain.   150

I am one who has no tale to tell:
I made myself a gibbet of my own lintel."

Notes

6–10. The reference here is to the Maremma district of Tuscany which lies between the mountains and the sea. The river Cecina is the northern boundary of this district; Corneto is on the river Marta, which forms the southern boundary. It is a wild district of marsh and forest.

10–15. THE HARPIES: These hideous birds with the faces of malign women were often associated with the Erinyes (Furies). Their original function in mythology was to snatch away the souls of men at the command of the Gods. Later, they were portrayed as defilers of food, and, by extension, of everything they touched. The islands of the Strophades were their legendary abode. Aeneas and his men landed there and fought with the Harpies, who drove them back and pronounced a prophecy of unbearable famine upon them.

18. *The burning sand*: The Third Round of this Circle.

25. *I think perhaps he thought that I was thinking*: The original is "Cred' io ch'ei credette ch'io credesse."* This sort of word play was considered quite elegant by medieval rhetoricians and by the ornate Sicilian School of poetry. Dante's style is based on a rejection of all such devices in favor of a sparse and direct diction. The best explanation of this unusual instance seems to be that Dante is anticipating his talk with Pier delle Vigne, a rhetorician who, as we shall see, delights in this sort of locution. (An analogous stylistic device is common in opera, where the musical phrase identified with a given character may be sounded by the orchestra when the character is about to appear.)

48. *In my verses only*: The *Aeneid*, Book III, describes a similar bleeding plant. There, Aeneas pulls at a myrtle growing on a Thracian hillside. It bleeds where he breaks it and a voice cries out of the ground. It is the voice of Polydorus, son of Priam and friend of Aeneas. He has been treacherously murdered by the Thracian king.

58. *I am he, etc.*: Pier delle Vigne (Pee-YAIR deh-leh VEE-nyeh), 1190–1249. A famous and once-powerful minister of Emperor Frederick II. He enjoyed Frederick's whole confidence until 1247 when he was accused of treachery and was imprisoned and blinded. He committed suicide to escape further torture. (For Frederick see Canto X.) Pier delle Vigne was famous for his eloquence and for his mastery of the ornate Provençal-inspired Sicilian School of Italian Poetry, and Dante styles his speech accordingly. The double balanced construction of line 59, the repetition of key words in lines 67–69, and 70–72 are characteristic of this rhetorical fashion. It is worth noting, however, that the style changes abruptly in the middle of line 72. There, his courtly preamble finished, delle Vigne speaks from the heart, simply and passionately.

58. *who held both keys*: The phrasing unmistakably suggests the Papal keys; delle Vigne may be suggesting that he was to Frederick as the Pope is to God.

64. *Caesar*: Frederick II was of course Caesar of the Roman Empire, but in this generalized context "Caesar" seems to be used as a generic term for any great ruler, *i.e.*, "The harlot, Envy, never turns her attention from those in power."

72. *new roots*: Pier delle Vigne had only been in Hell fifty-one years, a short enough time on the scale of eternity.

98. *wherever fortune flings it*: Just as the soul of the suicide refused to accept divine regulation of its mortal life span, so eternal justice takes no special heed of where the soul falls.

102. *pain and pain's outlet simultaneously*: Suicide also gives pain and its outlet simultaneously.

117 ff. THE VIOLENT AGAINST THEIR SUBSTANCE: They are driven naked through the thorny wood pursued by ravening bitches who tear them to pieces and carry off the limbs. (Obviously the limbs must re-form at some point so that the process can be repeated. For a parallel see Canto XXVIII, the Schismatics. Boccaccio

uses an identical device in the Decameron V, vi.) The bitches may be taken as symbolizing conscience, the last besieging creditors of the damned who must satisfy their claims by dividing their wretched bodies, since nothing else is left them. It is not simply prodigality that places them here but the *violence* of their wasting. This fad of violent wasting, scandalously prevalent in Dante's Florence, is hard to imagine today.

120. *Lano*: Lano da Siena, a famous squanderer. He died at the ford of the river Toppo near Arezzo in 1287 in a battle against the Aretines. Boccaccio writes that he deliberately courted death having squandered all his great wealth and being unwilling to live on in poverty. Thus his companion's jeer probably means: "You were not so ready to run then, Lano: why are you running now?"

133. *Jacomo da Sant' Andrea* (YAH-coe-moe): A Paduan with an infamous lust for laying waste his own goods and those of his neighbors. Arson was his favorite prank. On one occasion, to celebrate the arrival of certain noble guests, he set fire to all the workers' huts and outbuildings of his estate. He was murdered in 1239, probably by assassins hired by Ezzolino (for whom see Canto XII).

131–152. AN ANONYMOUS FLORENTINE SUICIDE: All that is known of him is what he says himself.

143. *the city that tore down Mars and raised the Baptist*: Florence. Mars was the first patron of the city and when the Florentines were converted to Christianity they pulled down his equestrian statue and built a church on the site of his temple. The statue of Mars was placed on a tower beside the Arno. When Totila (see note to line 150) destroyed Florence the tower fell into the Arno and the statue with it. Legend has it that Florence could never have been rebuilt had not the mutilated statue been rescued. It was placed on the Ponte Vecchio but was carried away in the flood of 1333.

150. *Attila*: Dante confuses Attila with Totila, King of the Ostrogoths (died 552). He destroyed Florence in 542. Attila (d. 453), King of the Huns, destroyed many cities of northern Italy, but not Florence.

Canto XIV

The Violent Against God, Nature, and Art

Dante, in pity, restores the torn leaves to the soul of his countryman and
the Poets move on to the next round, a great *Plain of Burning Sand* upon
which there descends an eternal slow *Rain of Fire*. Here, scorched by fire
from above and below, are three classes of sinners suffering differing degrees
of exposure to the fire. The *Blasphemers* (The Violent against God) are
stretched supine upon the sand, the *Sodomites* (The Violent against
Nature) run in endless circles, and the *Usurers* (The Violent against Art,
which is the Grandchild of God) huddle on the sands.

The Poets find *Capaneus* stretched out on the sands, the chief sinner of
that place. He is still blaspheming God. They continue along the edge of
the Wood of the Suicides and come to a blood-red rill which flows boiling
from the Wood and crosses the burning plain. Virgil explains the miraculous power of its waters and discourses on the *Old Man of Crete* and the
origin of all the rivers of Hell.

The symbolism of the burning plain is obviously centered in sterility (the
desert image) and wrath (the fire image). Blasphemy, sodomy, and usury
are all unnatural and sterile actions: thus the unbearing desert is the eternity of these sinners; and thus the rain, which in nature should be fertile and
cool, descends as fire. Capaneus, moreover, is subjected not only to the
wrath of nature (the sands below) and the wrath of God (the fire from
above), but is tortured most by his own inner violence, which is the root of
blasphemy.

Love of that land that was our common source
   moved me to tears; I gathered up the leaves
   and gave them back. He was already hoarse.   3

We came to the edge of the forest where one goes
   from the second round to the third, and there we saw
   what fearful arts the hand of Justice knows.   6

To make these new things wholly clear, I say
   we came to a plain whose soil repels all roots.
   The wood of misery rings it the same way   9

the wood itself is ringed by the red fosse.
   We paused at its edge: the ground was burning sand,
   just such a waste as Cato marched across.   12

O endless wrath of God: how utterly
   thou shouldst become a terror to all men
   who read the frightful truths revealed to me!   15

Enormous herds of naked souls I saw,
   lamenting till their eyes were burned of tears;
   they seemed condemned by an unequal law,   18

for some were stretched supine upon the ground,
  some squatted with their arms about themselves,
  and others without pause roamed round and round.   21

Most numerous were those that roamed the plain.
  Far fewer were the souls stretched on the sand,
  but moved to louder cries by greater pain.   24

And over all that sand on which they lay
  or crouched or roamed, great flakes of flame fell slowly
  as snow falls in the Alps on a windless day.   27

Like those Alexander met in the hot regions
  of India, flames raining from the sky
  to fall still unextinguished on his legions: 30

whereat he formed his ranks, and at their head
  set the example, trampling the hot ground
  for fear the tongues of fire might join and spread—   33

just so in Hell descended the long rain
  upon the damned, kindling the sand like tinder
  under a flint and steel, doubling the pain.   36

In a never-ending fit upon those sands,
  the arms of the damned twitched all about their bodies,
  now here, now there, brushing away the brands.   39

"Poet," I said, "master of every dread
  we have encountered, other than those fiends
  who sallied from the last gate of the dead—   42

who is that wraith who lies along the rim
  and sets his face against the fire in scorn,
  so that the rain seems not to mellow him?"   45

And he himself, hearing what I had said
  to my Guide and Lord concerning him, replied:
  "What I was living, the same am I now, dead.   48

Though Jupiter wear out his sooty smith
  from whom on my last day he snatched in anger
  the jagged thunderbolt he pierced me with;   51

though he wear out the others one by one
  who labor at the forge at Mongibello
  crying again 'Help! Help! Help me, good Vulcan!'   54

as he did at Phlegra; and hurl down endlessly
  with all the power of Heaven in his arm,
  small satisfaction would he win from me."   57

At this my Guide spoke with such vehemence
  as I had not heard from him in all of Hell:
  "O Capaneus, by your insolence   60

you are made to suffer as much fire inside
   as falls upon you. Only your own rage
   could be fit torment for your sullen pride."   63

Then he turned to me more gently. "That," he said,
   "was one of the Seven who laid siege to Thebes.
   Living, he scorned God, and among the dead   66

he scorns Him yet. He thinks he may detest
   God's power too easily, but as I told him,
   his slobber is a fit badge for his breast.   69

Now follow me; and mind for your own good
   you do not step upon the burning sand,
   but keep well back along the edge of the wood."   72

We walked in silence then till we reached a rill
   that gushes from the wood; it ran so red
   the memory sends a shudder through me still.   75

As from the Bulicame springs the stream
   the sinful women keep to their own use;
   so down the sand the rill flowed out in steam.   78

The bed and both its banks were petrified,
   as were its margins; thus I knew at once
   our passage through the sand lay by its side.   81

"Among all other wonders I have shown you
   since we came through the gate denied to none,
   nothing your eyes have seen is equal to   84

the marvel of the rill by which we stand,
   for it stifles all the flames above its course
   as it flows out across the burning sand."   87

So spoke my Guide across the flickering light,
   and I begged him to bestow on me the food
   for which he had given me the appetite.   90

"In the middle of the sea, and gone to waste,
   there lies a country known as Crete," he said,
   "under whose king the ancient world was chaste.   93

Once Rhea chose it as the secret crypt
   and cradle of her son; and better to hide him,
   her Corybantes raised a din when he wept.   96

An ancient giant stands in the mountain's core.
   He keeps his shoulder turned toward Damietta,
   and looks toward Rome as if it were his mirror.   99

His head is made of gold; of silverwork
   his breast and both his arms, of polished brass
   the rest of his great torso to the fork.   102

He is of chosen iron from there down,
    except that his right foot is terra cotta;
    it is this foot he rests more weight upon.   105

Every part except the gold is split
    by a great fissure from which endless tears
    drip down and hollow out the mountain's pit.   108

Their course sinks to this pit from stone to stone,
    becoming Acheron, Phlegethon, and Styx.
    Then by this narrow sluice they hurtle down   111

to the end of all descent, and disappear
    into Cocytus. You shall see what sink that is
    with your own eyes. I pass it in silence here."   114

And I to him: "But if these waters flow
    from the world above, why is this rill met only
    along this shelf?" And he to me: "You know   117

the place is round, and though you have come deep
    into the valley through the many circles,
    always bearing left along the steep,   120

you have not traveled any circle through
    its total round; hence when new things appear
    from time to time, that hardly should surprise you."   123

And I: "Where shall we find Phlegethon's course?
    And Lethe's? One you omit, and of the other
    you only say the tear-flood is its source."   126

"In all you ask of me you please me truly,"
    he answered, "but the red and boiling water
    should answer the first question you put to me,   129

and you shall stand by Lethe, but far hence:
    there, where the spirits go to wash themselves
    when their guilt has been removed by penitence."   132

And then he said: "Now it is time to quit
    this edge of shade: follow close after me
    along the rill, and do not stray from it;   135

for the unburning margins form a lane,
    and by them we may cross the burning plain."

Notes

12. *just such a waste as Cato marched across*: In 47 B.C., Cato of Utica led an
army across the Libyan desert. Lucan described the march in *Pharsalia* IX, 587 ff.
28–33. *Like those Alexander*: This incident of Alexander the Great's campaign in
India is described in *De Meteoris* of Albertus Magnus and was taken by him with
considerable alteration from a letter reputedly sent to Aristotle by Alexander.
43. *that wraith who lies along the rim*: Capaneus, one of the seven captains who
warred on Thebes. As he scaled the walls of Thebes, Capaneus defied Jove to protect

them. Jove replied with a thunderbolt that killed the blasphemer with his blasphemy still on his lips. (Statius, *Thebiad* x, 845 ff.)

53. *Mongibello*: Mt. Etna. Vulcan was believed to have his smithy inside the volcano.

55. *as he did at Phlegra*: At the battle of Phlegra in Thessaly the Titans tried to storm Olympus. Jove drove them back with the help of the thunderbolts Vulcan forged for him. Capaneus himself is reminiscent of the Titans: like them he is a giant, and he certainly is no less impious.

73. *we reached a rill*: The rill, still blood-red and still boiling, is the overflow of Phlegethon which descends across the Wood of the Suicides and the Burning Plain to plunge over the Great Cliff into the Eighth Circle. It is clearly a water of marvels, for it not only petrifies the sands over which it flows, but its clouds of steam quench all the flames above its course. It is obvious that the Poets' course across the plain will lie along the margins of this rill.

76. *The Bulicame* (Boo-lee-KAH-meh): A hot sulphur spring near Viterbo. The choice is strikingly apt, for the waters of the Bulicame not only boil and steam but have a distinctly reddish tint as a consequence of their mineral content. A part of the Bulicame flows out through what was once a quarter reserved to prostitutes; and they were given special rights to the water, since they were not permitted to use the public baths.

94. *Rhea*: Wife of Saturn (Cronos) and mother of Jove (Zeus). It had been prophesied to Saturn that one of his own children would dethrone him. To nullify the prophecy Saturn devoured each of his children at birth. On the birth of Jove, Rhea duped Saturn by letting him bolt down a stone wrapped in baby clothes. After this tribute to her husband's appetite she hid the infant on Mount Ida in Crete. There she posted her Corybantes (or Bacchantes) as guards and instructed them to set up a great din whenever the baby cried. Thus Saturn would not hear him. The Corybantic dances of the ancient Greeks were based on the frenzied shouting and clashing of swords on shields with which the Corybantes protected the infant Jove.

97. *An ancient giant*: This is the Old Man of Crete. The original of this figure occurs in *Daniel ii*, 32–34, where it is told by Daniel as Nebuchadnezzar's dream. Dante follows the details of the original closely but adds a few of his own and a totally different interpretation. In Dante each metal represents one of the ages of man, each deteriorating from the Golden Age of Innocence. The left foot, terminating the Age of Iron, is the Holy Roman Empire. The right foot, of terra cotta, is the Roman Catholic Church, a more fragile base than the left, but the one upon which the greater weight descends. The tears of the woes of man are a Dantean detail: they flow down the great fissure that defaces all but the Golden Age. Thus, starting in woe, they flow through man's decline, into the hollow of the mountain and become the waters of all Hell. Dante's other major addition is the site and position of the figure: equidistant from the three continents, the Old Man stands at a sort of center of Time, his back turned to Damietta in Egypt (here symbolizing the East, the past, the birth of religion) and fixes his gaze upon Rome (the West, the future, the Catholic Church). It is certainly the most elaborately worked single symbol in the *Inferno*.

113. *Cocytus*: The frozen lake that lies at the bottom of Hell. (See Cantos XXXII-XXXIV.)

124–125. *Phlegethon . . . Lethe*: Dante asks about Phlegethon and is told that he has already seen it (in the First Round: it is the river of boiling blood) and, in fact, that he is standing beside a branch of it. He asks about Lethe, the river of forgetfulness, and is told it lies ahead.

Canto XV

CIRCLE SEVEN: ROUND THREE   *The Violent Against Nature*

Protected by the marvelous powers of the boiling rill, the Poets walk along its banks across the burning plain. The *Wood of the Suicides* is behind them; the *Great Cliff* at whose foot lies the *Eighth Circle* is before them.

They pass one of the roving bands of *Sodomites*. One of the sinners stops Dante, and with great difficulty the Poet recognizes him under his baked features as *Ser Brunetto Latino*. This is a reunion with a dearly loved man and writer, one who had considerably influenced Dante's own development, and Dante addresses him with great and sorrowful affection, paying him the highest tribute offered to any sinner in the *Inferno*. *Brunetto* prophesies Dante's sufferings at the hands of the Florentines, gives an account of the souls that move with him through the fire, and finally, under Divine Compulsion, races off across the plain.

We go by one of the stone margins now
    and the steam of the rivulet makes a shade above it,
    guarding the stream and banks from the flaming snow.   3

As the Flemings in the lowland between Bruges
    and Wissant, under constant threat of the sea,
    erect their great dikes to hold back the deluge;   6

as the Paduans along the shores of the Brent
    build levees to protect their towns and castles
    lest Chiarentana drown in the spring torrent—   9

to the same plan, though not so wide nor high,
    did the engineer, whoever he may have been,
    design the margin we were crossing by.   12

Already we were so far from the wood
    that even had I turned to look at it,
    I could not have made it out from where I stood,   15

when a company of shades came into sight
    walking beside the bank. They stared at us
    as men at evening by the new moon's light   18

stare at one another when they pass by
    on a dark road, pointing their eyebrows toward us
    as an old tailor squints at his needle's eye.   21

Stared at so closely by that ghostly crew,
    I was recognized by one who seized the hem
    of my skirt and said: "Wonder of wonders! You?"   24

And I, when he stretched out his arm to me,
    searched his baked features closely, till at last
    I traced his image from my memory   27

in spite of the burnt crust, and bending near
  to put my face closer to his, at last
  I answered: "Ser Brunetto, are *you* here?"   30

"O my son! may it not displease you," he cried,
  "if Brunetto Latino leave his company
  and turn and walk a little by your side."   33

And I to him: "With all my soul I ask it.
  Or let us sit together, if it please him
  who is my Guide and leads me through this pit."   36

"My son!" he said, "whoever of this train
  pauses a moment, must lie a hundred years
  forbidden to brush off the burning rain.   39

Therefore, go on; I will walk at your hem,
  and then rejoin my company, which goes
  mourning eternal loss in eternal flame."   42

I did not dare descend to his own level
  but kept my head inclined, as one who walks
  in reverence meditating good and evil.   45

"What brings you here before your own last day?
  What fortune or what destiny?" he began.
  "And who is he that leads you this dark way?"   48

"Up there in the happy life I went astray
  in a valley," I replied, "before I had reached
  the fullness of my years. Only yesterday   51

at dawn I turned from it. This spirit showed
  himself to me as I was turning back,
  and guides me home again along this road."   54

And he: "Follow your star, for if in all
  of the sweet life I saw one truth shine clearly,
  you cannot miss your glorious arrival.   57

And had I lived to do what I meant to do,
  I would have cheered and seconded your work,
  observing Heaven so well disposed toward you.   60

But that ungrateful and malignant stock
  that came down from Fiesole of old
  and still smacks of the mountain and the rock,   63

for your good works will be your enemy.
  And there is cause: the sweet fig is not meant
  to bear its fruit beside the bitter sorb-tree.   66

Even the old adage calls them blind,
  an envious, proud, and avaricious people:
  see that you root their customs from your mind.   69

It is written in your stars, and will come to pass,
  that your honours shall make both sides hunger for you:
  but the goat shall never reach to crop that grass.   72

Let the beasts of Fiesole devour their get
  like sows, but never let them touch the plant,
  if among their rankness any springs up yet,   75

in which is born again the holy seed
  of the Romans who remained among their rabble
  when Florence made a new nest for their greed."   78

"Ah, had I all my wish," I answered then,
  "you would not yet be banished from the world
  in which you were a radiance among men,   81

for that sweet image, gentle and paternal,
  you were to me in the world when hour by hour
  you taught me how man makes himself eternal,   84

lives in my mind, and now strikes to my heart;
  and while I live, the gratitude I owe it
  will speak to men out of my life and art.   87

What you have told me of my course, I write
  by another text I save to show a Lady
  who will judge these matters, if I reach her height.   90

This much I would have you know: so long, I say,
  as nothing in my conscience troubles me
  I am prepared for Fortune, come what may.   93

Twice already in the eternal shade
  I have heard this prophecy; but let Fortune turn
  her wheel as she please, and the countryman his spade."   96

My guiding spirit paused at my last word
  and, turning right about, stood eye to eye
  to say to me: "Well heeded is well heard."   99

But I did not reply to him, going on
  with Ser Brunetto to ask him who was with him
  in the hot sands, the best-born and best known.   102

And he to me: "Of some who share this walk
  it is good to know; of the rest let us say nothing,
  for the time would be too short for so much talk.   105

In brief, we all were clerks and men of worth,
  great men of letters, scholars of renown;
  all by the one same crime defiled on earth.   108

Priscian moves there along the wearisome
  sad way, and Francesco d'Accorso, and also there,
  if you had any longing for such scum,   111

you might have seen that one the Servant of Servants
sent from the Arno to the Bacchiglione
where he left his unnatural organ wrapped in cerements. 114

I would say more, but there across the sand
a new smoke rises and new people come,
and I must run to be with my own band. 117

Remember my *Treasure*, in which I still live on:
I ask no more." He turned then, and he seemed,
across that plain, like one of those who run 120

for the green cloth at Verona; and of those,
more like the one who wins, than those who lose.

Notes

4–9. Dante compares the banks of the rill of Phlegethon to the dikes built by the Flemings to hold back the sea, and to those built by the Paduans to hold back the spring floods of the river Brent. Chiarentana (Latin: Clarentana) was a Duchy of the Middle Ages. Its territory included the headwaters of the Brent (Brenta).

10. *though not so wide nor high*: Their width is never precisely specified, but we shall see when Dante walks along speaking to Ser Brunetto (line 40) that their height is about that of a man.

23–119. *Ser Brunetto Latino*: or Latini. (Born between 1210 and 1230, died 1294.) A prominent Florentine Guelph who held, among many other posts, that of notary, whence the title *Ser* (sometimes *Sere*). He was not Dante's schoolmaster as many have supposed—he was much too busy and important a man for that. Dante's use of the word "master" is to indicate spiritual indebtedness to Brunetto and his works. It is worth noting that Dante addresses him in Italian as "voi" instead of using the less respectful "tu" form. Farinata is the only other sinner so addressed in the *Inferno*. Brunetto's two principal books, both of which Dante admired, were the prose *Livre dou Tresor* (*The Book of the Treasure*) and the poetic *Tesoretta* (*The Little Treasure*). Dante learned a number of his devices from the allegorical journey which forms the *Tesoretto*.

Dante's surprise at finding Brunetto here is worth puzzling about. So too is the fact that he did not ask Ciacco about him (Canto VI) when he mentioned other prominent Florentines. One speculation is that Dante had not intended to place him in Hell, and that he found reason to believe him guilty of this sin only years after Brunetto's death (the *Inferno* was written between 1310 and 1314, in all probability). This answer is not wholly satisfactory.

40. *I will walk at your hem*: See also line 10. Dante is standing on the dike at approximately the level of Brunetto's head and he cannot descend because of the rain of fire and the burning sands.

61–67. *that ungrateful and malignant stock*: The ancient Etruscan city of Fiesole was situated on a hill about three miles north of the present site of Florence. According to legend, Fiesole had taken the side of Catiline in his war with Julius Caesar. Caesar destroyed the town and set up a new city called Florence on the Arno, peopling it with Romans and Fiesolans. The Romans were the aristocracy of the new city, but the Fiesolans were a majority. Dante ascribes the endless bloody conflicts of Florence largely to the internal strife between these two strains. His scorn of the Fiesolans is obvious in this passage. Dante proudly proclaimed his descent from the Roman strain.

66. *sorb-tree*: A species of tart apple.

67. *calls them blind*: The source of this proverbial expression, "Blind as a Florentine," can no longer be traced with any assurance, though many incidents from Florentine history suggest possible sources.

71. *shall make both sides hunger for you*: Brunetto can scarcely mean that both sides will hunger to welcome the support of a man of Dante's distinction. Rather, that both sides will hunger to destroy him. (See also lines 94–95. Dante obviously accepts this as another dark prophecy.)

73. *the beasts of Fiesole*: The Fiesolans themselves.

89. *to show a Lady*: Beatrice.

94–99. *twice already . . . I have heard*: The prophecies of Ciacco (Canto VI) and of Farinata (Canto X) are the other two places at which Dante's exile and suffering are foretold. Dante replies that come what may he will remain true to his purpose through all affliction; and Virgil turns to look proudly at his pupil uttering a proverb: *"Bene ascolta chi la nota,"* i.e., "Well heeded is well heard."

109. *Priscian*: Latin grammarian and poet of the first half of the sixth century.

110. *Francesco d'Accorso*: (Frahn-CHAY-skoe dah-KAWR-soe) A Florentine scholar. He served as a professor at Bologna and, from 1273 to 1280, at Oxford. He died in Bologna in 1294.

112–13. *that one the Servant of Servants . . . Arno to the Bacchiglione etc.*: "The Servant of Servants" was Dante's old enemy, Boniface VIII. *Servus servorum* is technically a correct papal title, but there is certainly a touch of irony in Dante's application of it in this context. In 1295 Boniface transferred Bishop Andrea de'Mozzi from the Bishopric of Florence (on the Arno) to that of Vicenza (on the Bacchiglione). The transference was reputedly brought about at the request of the Bishop's brother, Tommaso de' Mozzi of Florence, who wished to remove from his sight the spectacle of his brother's stupidity and unnatural vices.

114. *unnatural organ*: The original, *mal protesi nervi*, contains an untranslatable word-play. *Nervi* may be taken as "the male organ" and *protesi* for "erected"; thus the organ aroused to passion for unnatural purposes (*mal*). Or *nervi* may be taken as "nerves" and *mal protesi* for "dissolute." Taken in context, the first rendering strikes me as more Dantean.

121. *the green cloth*: On the first Sunday of Lent all the young men of Verona ran a race for the prize of green cloth. The last runner in was given a live rooster and was required to carry it through the town.

Canto XVI

The Violent Against Nature and Art

The Poets arrive within hearing of the waterfall that plunges over the Great Cliff into the Eighth Circle. The sound is still a distant throbbing when three wraiths, recognizing Dante's Florentine dress, detach themselves from their band and come running toward him. They are Jacopo Rusticucci, Guido Guerra, and Tegghiaio Aldobrandi, all of them Florentines whose policies and personalities Dante admired. Rusticucci and Tegghiaio have already been mentioned in a highly complimentary way in Dante's talk with Ciacco (Canto VI).

The sinners ask for news of Florence, and Dante replies with a passionate lament for her present degradation. The three wraiths return to their band and the Poets continue to the top of the falls. Here, at Virgil's command, Dante removes a Cord from about his waist and Virgil drops it over the edge of the abyss. As if in answer to a signal, a great distorted shape comes swimming up through the dirty air of the pit.

We could already hear the rumbling drive
   of the waterfall in its plunge to the next circle,
   a murmur like the throbbing of a hive,   3

when three shades turned together on the plain,
   breaking toward us from a company
   that went its way to torture in that rain.   6

They cried with one voice as they ran toward me:
   "Wait, oh wait, for by your dress you seem
   a voyager from our own tainted country."   9

Ah! what wounds I saw, some new, some old,
   branded upon their bodies! Even now
   the pain of it in memory turns me cold.   12

My Teacher heard their cries, and turning-to,
   stood face to face. "Do as they ask," he said,
   "for these are souls to whom respect is due;   15

and were it not for the darting flames that hem
   our narrow passage in, I should have said
   it were more fitting you ran after them."   18

We paused, and they began their ancient wail
   over again, and when they stood below us
   they formed themselves into a moving wheel.   21

As naked and anointed champions do
   in feeling out their grasp and their advantage
   before they close in for the thrust or blow—   24

so circling, each one stared up at my height,
  and as their feet moved left around the circle,
  their necks kept turning backward to the right.   27

"If the misery of this place, and our unkempt
  and scorched appearance," one of them began,
  "bring us and what we pray into contempt,   30

still may our earthly fame move you to tell
  who and what you are, who so securely
  set your live feet to the dead dusts of Hell.   33

This peeled and naked soul who runs before me
  around this wheel, was higher than you think
  there in the world, in honor and degree.   36

Guido Guerra was the name he bore,
  the good Gualdrada's grandson. In his life
  he won great fame in counsel and in war.   39

The other who behind me treads this sand
  was Tegghiaio Aldobrandi, whose good counsels
  the world would have done well to understand.   42

And I who share their torment, in my life
  was Jacopo Rusticucci; above all
  I owe my sorrows to a savage wife."   45

I would have thrown myself to the plain below
  had I been sheltered from the falling fire;
  and I think my Teacher would have let me go.   48

But seeing I should be burned and cooked, my fear
  overcame the first impulse of my heart
  to leap down and embrace them then and there.   51

"Not contempt," I said, "but the compassion
  that seizes on my soul and memory
  at the thought of you tormented in this fashion—   54

it was grief that choked my speech when through the
                                                scorching
  air of this pit my Lord announced to me
  that such men as you are might be approaching.   57

I am of your own land, and I have always
  heard with affection and rehearsed with honor
  your name and the good deeds of your happier days.   60

Led by my Guide and his truth, I leave the gall
  and go for the sweet apples of delight.
  But first I must descend to the center of all."   63

"So may your soul and body long continue
  together on the way you go," he answered,
  "and the honor of your days shine after you—   66

tell me if courtesy and valor raise
   their banners in our city as of old,
   or has the glory faded from its days?   69

For Borsiere, who is newly come among us
   and yonder goes with our companions in pain,
   taunts us with such reports, and his words have stung us."   72

"O Florence! your sudden wealth and your upstart
   rabble, dissolute and overweening,
   already set you weeping in your heart!"   75

I cried with face upraised, and on the sand
   those three sad spirits looked at one another
   like men who hear the truth and understand.   78

"If this be your manner of speaking, and if you can
   satisfy others with such ease and grace,"
   they said as one, "we hail a happy man.   81

Therefore, if you win through this gloomy pass
   and climb again to see the heaven of stars;
   when it rejoices you to say 'I was',   84

speak of us to the living." They parted then,
   breaking their turning wheel, and as they vanished
   over the plain, their legs seemed wings. "Amen"   87

could not have been pronounced between their start
   and their disappearance over the rim of sand.
   And then it pleased my Master to depart.   90

A little way beyond we felt the quiver
   and roar of the cascade, so close that speech
   would have been drowned in thunder. As that river—   93

the first one on the left of the Appennines
   to have a path of its own from Monte Veso
   to the Adriatic Sea—which, as it twines   96

is called the Acquacheta from its source
   until it nears Forlì, and then is known
   as the Montone in its further course—   99

resounds from the mountain in a single leap
   there above San Benedetto dell'Alpe
   where a thousand falls might fit into the steep;   102

so down from a sheer bank, in one enormous
   plunge, the tainted water roared so loud
   a little longer there would have deafened us.   105

I had a cord bound round me like a belt
   which I had once thought I might put to use
   to snare the leopard with the gaudy pelt.   108

When at my Guide's command I had unbound
its loops from about my habit, I gathered it
and held it out to him all coiled and wound.   111

He bent far back to his right, and throwing it
out from the edge, sent it in a long arc
into the bottomless darkness of the pit.   114

"Now surely some unusual event,"
I said to myself, "must follow this new signal
upon which my good Guide is so intent."   117

Ah, how cautiously a man should breathe
near those who see not only what we do,
but have the sense which reads the mind beneath!   120

He said to me: "You will soon see arise
what I await, and what you wonder at;
soon you will see the thing before your eyes."   123

To the truth which will seem falsehood every man
who would not be called a liar while speaking fact
should learn to seal his lips as best he can.   126

But here I cannot be still: Reader, I swear
by the lines of my Comedy—so may it live—
that I saw swimming up through that foul air   129

a shape to astonish the most doughty soul,
a shape like one returning through the sea
from working loose an anchor run afoul   132

of something on the bottom—so it rose,
its arms spread upward and its feet drawn close.

Notes

21 ff. *a moving wheel*: See Ser Brunetto's words (lines 37–39, Canto XV).
37. *Guido Guerra* (GHEE-doe or GWEE-doe GWEH-rah): (around 1220-1272.) A valiant leader of the Guelphs (hence his name which signifies Guido of War) despite his Ghibelline origin as one of the counts of Guidi. It is a curious fact, considering the prominence of Guido, that Dante is the only writer to label him a sodomite.
38. *the good Gualdrada* (Gwahl-DRAH-dah): The legend of "the good Gualdrada," Guido Guerra's grandmother, is a typical example of the medieval talent for embroidery. She was the daughter of Bellincione Berti de' Ravignana. The legend is that Emperor Otto IV saw her in church and, attracted by her beauty, asked who she was. Bellincione replied that she was the daughter of one whose soul would be made glad to have the Emperor salute her with a kiss. The young-lady-of-all-virtues, hearing her father's words, declared that no man might kiss her unless he were her husband. Otto was so impressed by the modesty and propriety of this remark that he married her to one of his noblemen and settled a large estate upon the couple. It was from this marriage that the counts Guidi de Modigliano (among them Guido Guerra) were said to descend.
Unfortunately for the legend, Otto's first visit to Italy was in 1209, and surviving records show that Count Guido had already had two children by his wife Gualdrada as early as 1202.
41. *Tegghiaio Aldobrandi* (Tegh-YEYE-oh Ahl-doe-BRAHN-dee): Date of birth unknown. He died shortly before 1266. A valiant knight of the family degli Adimari of the Guelph nobles. With Guido Guerra he advised the Florentines not to move

against the Sienese at the disastrous battle of Montaperti (See Farinata, Canto X), knowing that the Sienese had been heavily reinforced by mercenaries. It is probably these good counsels that "the world would have done well to understand." This is another case in which Dante is the only writer to bring the charge of sodomy.

44. *Jacopo Rusticucci* (YAH-coe-poe Roo-stee-KOO-tchee): Dates of birth and death unknown, but mention of him exists in Florentine records of 1235, 1236, 1254, and 1266. A rich and respected Florentine knight. Dante's account of his sin and of its cause is the only record and it remains unsupported: no details of his life are known.

70. *Guglielmo Borsiere* (Goo-lyELL-moe Bohrs-YEHR-eh): "Borsiere" in Italian means "pursemaker," and the legend has grown without verification or likelihood that this was his origin. He was a courtier, a peacemaker, and an arranger of marriages. Boccaccio speaks of him in highly honorable terms in the Eighth Tale of the First Day of the *Decameron*.

93ff. *that river*: The water course described by Dante and made up of the Acquacheta (Ah-kwa-KAY-tah) and the Montone flows directly into the sea without draining into the Po. The placement of it as "first on the left of the Appennines" has been shown by Casella to result from the peculiar orientation of the maps of Dante's time. The "river" has its source and course along a line running almost exactly northwest from Florence. San Benedetto dell' Alpe is a small monastery situated on that line about twenty-five miles from Florence.

106. THE CORD: As might be expected many ingenious explanations have been advanced to account for the sudden appearance of this cord. It is frequently claimed, but without proof, that Dante had been a minor friar of the Franciscans but had left without taking vows. The explanation continues that he had clung to the habit of wearing the white cord of the Franciscans, which he now produces with the information that he had once intended to use it to snare the Leopard.

One invention is probably as good as another. What seems obvious is that the narrative required some sort of device for signaling the monster, and that to meet his narrative need, Dante suddenly invented the business of the cord. Dante, as a conscientious and self-analytical craftsman, would certainly have been aware of the technical weakness of this sudden invention; but Dante the Master was sufficiently self-assured to brush aside one such detail, sure as he must have been of the strength of his total structure.

Canto XVII

The monstrous shape lands on the brink and Virgil salutes it ironically. It is *Geryon, the Monster of Fraud.* Virgil announces that they must fly down from the cliff on the back of this monster. While Virgil negotiates for their passage, Dante is sent to examine the *Usurers* (The Violent against Art).

These sinners sit in a crouch along the edge of the burning plain that approaches the cliff. Each of them has a leather purse around his neck, and each purse is blazoned with a coat of arms. Their eyes, gushing with tears, are forever fixed on these purses. Dante recognizes none of these sinners, but their coats of arms are unmistakably those of well-known Florentine families.

Having understood who they are and the reason for their present condition, Dante cuts short his excursion and returns to find Virgil mounted on the back of Geryon. Dante joins his Master and they fly down from the great cliff.

Their flight carries them from the Hell of the *Violent and the Bestial* (The Sins of the Lion) into the Hell of the *Fraudulent and Malicious* (The Sins of the Leopard).

"Now see the sharp-tailed beast that mounts the brink.
 He passes mountains, breaks through walls and
                                             weapons.
 Behold the beast that makes the whole world stink."   3

These were the words my Master spoke to me;
 then signaled the weird beast to come to ground
 close to the sheer end of our rocky levee.   6

The filthy prototype of Fraud drew near
 and settled his head and breast upon the edge
 of the dark cliff, but let his tail hang clear.   9

His face was innocent of every guile,
 benign and just in feature and expression;
 and under it his body was half reptile.   12

His two great paws were hairy to the armpits;
 all his back and breast and both his flanks
 were figured with bright knots and subtle circlets: 15

never was such a tapestry of bloom
 woven on earth by Tartar or by Turk,
 nor by Arachne at her flowering loom.   18

As a ferry sometimes lies along the strand,
 part beached and part afloat; and as the beaver,
 up yonder in the guzzling Germans' land,   21

86

squats halfway up the bank when a fight is on—
  just so lay that most ravenous of beasts
  on the rim which bounds the burning sand with stone. 24

His tail twitched in the void beyond that lip,
  thrashing, and twisting up the envenomed fork
  which, like a scorpion's stinger, armed the tip. 27

My Guide said: "It is time now we drew near
  that monster." And descending on the right
  we moved ten paces outward to be clear 30

of sand and flames. And when we were beside him,
  I saw upon the sand a bit beyond us
  some people crouching close beside the brim. 33

The Master paused. "That you may take with you
  the full experience of this round," he said,
  "go now and see the last state of that crew. 36

But let your talk be brief, and I will stay
  and reason with this beast till you return,
  that his strong back may serve us on our way." 39

So further yet along the outer edge
  of the seventh circle I moved on alone.
  And came to the sad people of the ledge. 42

Their eyes burst with their grief; their smoking hands
  jerked about their bodies, warding off
  now the flames and now the burning sands. 45

Dogs in summer bit by fleas and gadflies,
  jerking their snouts about, twitching their paws
  now here, now there, behave no otherwise. 48

I examined several faces there among
  that sooty throng, and I saw none I knew;
  but I observed that from each neck there hung 51

an enormous purse, each marked with its own beast
  and its own colors like a coat of arms.
  On these their streaming eyes appeared to feast. 54

Looking about, I saw one purse display
  azure on or, a kind of lion; another,
  on a blood red field, a goose whiter than whey. 57

And one that bore a huge and swollen sow
  azure on field argent said to me:
  "What are you doing in this pit of sorrow? 60

Leave us alone! And since you have not yet died,
  I'll have you know my neighbor Vitaliano
  has a place reserved for him here at my side. 63

A Paduan among Florentines, I sit here
  while hour by hour they nearly deafen me
  shouting: 'Send us the sovereign cavalier   66

with the purse of the three goats!' " He half arose,
  twisted his mouth, and darted out his tongue
  for all the world like an ox licking its nose.   69

And I, afraid that any longer stay
  would anger him who had warned me to be brief,
  left those exhausted souls without delay.   72

Returned, I found my Guide already mounted
  upon the rump of that monstrosity.
  He said to me: "Now must you be undaunted: 75

this beast must be our stairway to the pit:
  mount it in front, and I will ride between
  you and the tail, lest you be poisoned by it."   78

Like one so close to the quartanary chill
  that his nails are already pale and his flesh trembles
  at the very sight of shade or a cool rill—   81

so did I tremble at each frightful word.
  But his scolding filled me with that shame that makes
  the servant brave in the presence of his lord.   84

I mounted the great shoulders of that freak
  and tried to say "Now help me to hold on!"
  But my voice clicked in my throat and I could not speak.   87

But no sooner had I settled where he placed me
  than he, my stay, my comfort, and my courage
  in other perils, gathered and embraced me.   90

Then he called out: "Now, Geryon, we are ready:
  bear well in mind that his is living weight
  and make your circles wide and your flight steady."   93

As a small ship slides from a beaching or its pier,
  backward, backward—so that monster slipped
  back from the rim. And when he had drawn clear   96

he swung about, and stretching out his tail
  he worked it like an eel, and with his paws
  he gathered in the air, while I turned pale.   99

I think there was no greater fear the day
  Phaeton let loose the reins and burned the sky
  along the great scar of the Milky Way,   102

nor when Icarus, too close to the sun's track
  felt the wax melt, unfeathering his loins,
  and heard his father cry "Turn back! Turn back!"—   105

than I felt when I found myself in air,
    afloat in space with nothing visible
    but the enormous beast that bore me there.   108

Slowly, slowly, he swims on through space,
    wheels and descends, but I can sense it only
    by the way the wind blows upward past my face.   111

Already on the right I heard the swell
    and thunder of the whirlpool. Looking down
    I leaned my head out and stared into Hell.   114

I trembled again at the prospect of dismounting
    and cowered in on myself, for I saw fires
    on every hand, and I heard a long lamenting.   117

And then I saw—till then I had but felt it—
    the course of our down-spiral to the horrors
    that rose to us from all sides of the pit.   120

As a flight-worn falcon sinks down wearily
    though neither bird nor lure has signalled it,
    the falconer crying out: "What! spent already!"—   123

then turns and in a hundred spinning gyres
    sulks from her master's call, sullen and proud—
    so to that bottom lit by endless fires   126

the monster Geryon circled and fell,
    setting us down at the foot of the precipice
    of ragged rock on the eighth shelf of Hell.   129

And once freed of our weight, he shot from there
    into the dark like an arrow into air.

Notes

1. *Geryon*: A mythical king of Spain represented as a giant with three heads and three bodies. He was killed by Hercules, who coveted the king's cattle. A later tradition represents him as killing and robbing strangers whom he lured into his realm. It is probably on this account that Dante chose him as the prototype of fraud, though in a radically altered bodily form. Some of the details of Dante's Geryon may be drawn from *Revelations* ix, 9–20, but most of them are almost certainly his own invention: a monster with the general shape of a dragon but with the tail of a scorpion, hairy arms, a gaudily-marked reptilian body, and the face of a just and honest man. The careful reader will note that the gaudily-spotted body suggests the Leopard; the hairy paws, the Lion; and that the human face represents the essentially human nature of Fraud, which thus embodies corruption of the Appetite, of the Will, and of the Intellect.

17. *Tartar . . . Turk*: These were the most skilled weavers of Dante's time.

18. *Arachne*: She was so famous as a spinner and weaver that she challenged Minerva to a weaving contest. There are various accounts of what happened in the contest, but all of them end with the goddess so moved to anger that she changed Arachne into a spider.

20. *the beaver*: Dante's description of the beaver is probably drawn from some old bestiary or natural history. It may be based on the medieval belief that the beaver fished by crouching on the bank, scooping the fish out with its tail.

21. *the guzzling Germans*: The heavy drinking of the Germans was proverbial in the Middle Ages and far back into antiquity.

29. *descending on the right*: The Poets had crossed on the right bank of the rill. In the course of Geryon's flight they will be carried to the other side of the falls, thus continuing their course to the left. It should be noted that inside the walls of Dis, approaching the second great division of Hell (as here the third) they also moved to the right. No satisfactory reason can be given for these exceptions.

33. *some people*: The Usurers. Virgil explains in Canto XI why they sin against Art, which is the Grandchild of God. They are the third and final category of the Violent against God and His works.

56. *azure on or, a kind of lion*: The arms of the Gianfigliazzi (Djahn-fee-LYAH-tsee) of Florence were a lion azure on a field of gold. The sinner bearing this purse must be Catello di Rosso Gianfigliazzi, who set up as a usurer in France and was made a knight on his return to Florence.

57. *on a blood red field, a goose whiter than whey*: A white goose on a red field was the arms of the noble Ghibelline family of the Ubriachi, or Ebriachi, of Florence. The wearer is probably Ciappo Ubriachi (CHAH-poe Oob-ree-AH-kee), a notorious usurer.

58–59. *sow azure on field argent*: These are the arms of the Scrovegni (Skroe-VAY-nyee) of Padua. The bearer is probably Reginaldo Scrovegni.

62. *Vitaliano*: Vitaliano di Iacopo Vitaliani, another Paduan.

66–67. *the sovereign cavalier*: Giovanni di Buiamonte (Djoe-VAHN-ee dee Booyah-MON-teh) was esteemed in Florence as "the sovereign cavalier" and was chosen for many high offices. He was a usurer and a gambler who lost great sums at play. Dante's intent is clearly to bewail the decay of standards which permits Florence to honor so highly a man for whom Hell is waiting so dismally. Buiamonte was of the Becchi (BEH-kee) family whose arms were three black goats on a gold field. "Becchi" in Italian is the plural form of the word for "goat."

79. *quartanary chill*: Quartan fever is an ague that runs a four-day cycle with symptoms roughly like those of malaria. At the approach of the chill, Dante intends his figure to say, any thought of coolness strikes terror into the shivering victim.

101. *Phaeton*: Son of Apollo who drove the chariot of the sun. Phaeton begged his father for a chance to drive the chariot himself but he lost control of the horses and Zeus killed him with a thunderbolt for fear the whole earth would catch fire. The scar left in the sky by the runaway horses is marked by the Milky Way.

103. *Icarus*: Daedalus, the father of Icarus, made wings for himself and his son and they flew into the sky, but Icarus, ignoring his father's commands, flew too close to the sun. The heat melted the wax with which the wings were fastened and Icarus fell into the Aegean and was drowned.

121–25. *flight-worn falcon*: Falcons, when sent aloft, were trained to circle until sighting a bird, or until signaled back by the lure (a stuffed bird). Flight-weary, Dante's metaphoric falcon sinks bit by bit, rebelling against his training and sulking away from his master in wide slow circles. The weighed, slow, downward flight of Geryon is powerfully contrasted with his escaping bound into the air once he has deposited his burden.

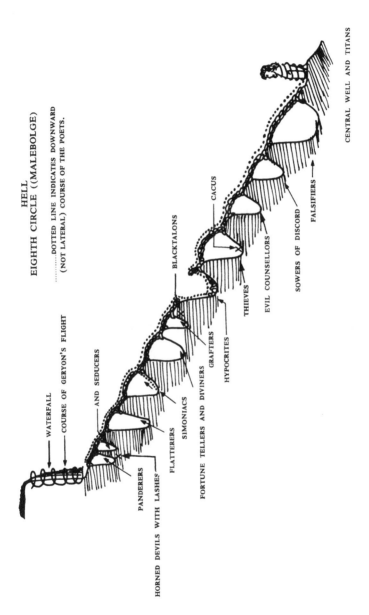

HELL
EIGHTH CIRCLE ((MALEBOLGE)
..........DOTTED LINE INDICATES DOWNWARD
(NOT LATERAL) COURSE OF THE POETS.

WATERFALL

COURSE OF GERYON'S FLIGHT

AND SEDUCERS

PANDERERS

HORNED DEVILS WITH LASHES

FLATTERERS

SIMONIACS

FORTUNE TELLERS AND DIVINERS

GRAFTERS

HYPOCRITES

BLACKTALONS

THIEVES

CACUS

EVIL COUNSELLORS

SOWERS OF DISCORD

FALSIFIERS

CENTRAL WELL AND TITANS

Canto XVIII

CIRCLE EIGHT (MALEBOLGE)   *The Fraudulent and Malicious*

BOLGIA ONE   *The Panderers and Seducers*

BOLGIA TWO   *The Flatterers*

Dismounted from Geryon, the Poets find themselves in the *Eighth Circle,*
called *Malebolge* (The Evil Ditches). This is the upper half of the *Hell of
the Fraudulent and Malicious.* Malebolge is a great circle of stone that
slopes like an amphitheater. The slopes are divided into ten concentric
ditches; and within these ditches, each with his own kind, are punished
those guilty of *Simple Fraud.*

A series of stone dikes runs like spokes from the edge of the great cliff
face to the center of the place, and these serve as bridges.

The Poets bear left toward the first ditch, and Dante observes below him
and to his right the sinners of the first bolgia, the *Panderers* and *Seducers.*
These make two files, one along either bank of the ditch, and are driven at
an endless fast walk by horned demons who hurry them along with great
lashes. In life these sinners goaded others on to serve their own foul purposes; so in Hell are they driven in their turn. The horned demons who
drive them symbolize the sinners' own vicious natures, embodiments of
their own guilty consciences. Dante may or may not have intended the
horns of the demons to symbolize cuckoldry and adultery.

The Poets see *Venedico Caccianemico* and *Jason* in the first pit, and pass
on to the second, where they find the souls of the *Flatterers* sunk in excrement, the true equivalent of their false flatteries on earth. They observe
Alessio Interminelli and *Thais,* and pass on.

There is in Hell a vast and sloping ground
   called Malebolge, a lost place of stone
   as black as the great cliff that seals it round.   3

Precisely in the center of that space
   there yawns a well extremely wide and deep.
   I shall discuss it in its proper place.   6

The border that remains between the well-pit
   and the great cliff forms an enormous circle,
   and ten descending troughs are cut in it,   9

offering a general prospect like the ground
   that lies around one of those ancient castles
   whose walls are girded many times around   12

by concentric moats. And just as, from the portal,
   the castle's bridges run from moat to moat
   to the last bank; so from the great rock wall   15

across the embankments and the ditches, high
and narrow cliffs run to the central well,
which cuts and gathers them like radii.   18

Here, shaken from the back of Geryon,
we found ourselves. My Guide kept to the left
and I walked after him. So we moved on.   21

Below, on my right, and filling the first ditch
along both banks, new souls in pain appeared,
new torments, and new devils black as pitch.   24

All of these sinners were naked; on our side
of the middle they walked toward us; on the other,
in our direction, but with swifter stride.   27

Just so the Romans, because of the great throng
in the year of the Jubilee, divide the bridge
in order that the crowds may pass along,   30

so that all face the Castle as they go
on one side toward St. Peter's, while on the other,
all move along facing toward Mount Giordano.   33

And everywhere along that hideous track
I saw horned demons with enormous lashes
move through those souls, scourging them on the back.   36

Ah, how the stragglers of that long rout stirred
their legs quick-march at the first crack of the lash!
Certainly no one waited a second, or third!   39

As we went on, one face in that procession
caught my eye and I said: "That sinner there:
It is certainly not the first time I've seen that one."   42

I stopped, therefore, to study him, and my Guide
out of his kindness waited, and even allowed me
to walk back a few steps at the sinner's side.   45

And that flayed spirit, seeing me turn around,
thought to hide his face, but I called to him:
"You there, that walk along with your eyes on the
                                          ground—   48

if those are not false features, then I know you
as Venedico Caccianemico of Bologna:
what brings you here among this pretty crew?"   51

And he replied: "I speak unwillingly,
but something in your living voice, in which
I hear the world again, stirs and compels me.   54

It was I who brought the fair Ghisola 'round
to serve the will and lust of the Marquis,
however sordid that old tale may sound.   57

There are many more from Bologna who weep away
eternity in this ditch; we fill it so
there are not as many tongues that are taught to say   60

'sipa' in all the land that lies between
the Reno and the Saveno, as you must know
from the many tales of our avarice and spleen."   63

And as he spoke, one of those lashes fell
across his back, and a demon cried, "Move on,
you pimp, there are no women here to sell."   66

Turning away then, I rejoined my Guide.
We came in a few steps to a raised ridge
that made a passage to the other side.   69

This we climbed easily, and turning right
along the jagged crest, we left behind
the eternal circling of those souls in flight.   72

And when we reached the part at which the stone
was tunneled for the passage of the scourged,
my Guide said, "Stop a minute and look down   75

on these other misbegotten wraiths of sin.
You have not seen their faces, for they moved
in the same direction we were headed in."   78

So from that bridge we looked down on the throng
that hurried toward us on the other side.
Here, too, the whiplash hurried them along.   81

And the good Master, studying that train,
said: "Look there, at that great soul that approaches
and seems to shed no tears for all his pain—   84

what kingliness moves with him even in Hell!
It is Jason, who by courage and good advice
made off with the Colchian Ram. Later it fell   87

that he passed Lemnos, where the women of wrath,
enraged by Venus' curse that drove their lovers
out of their arms, put all their males to death.   90

There with his honeyed tongue and his dishonest
lover's wiles, he gulled Hypsipyle,
who, in the slaughter, had gulled all the rest.   93

And there he left her, pregnant and forsaken.
Such guilt condemns him to such punishment;
and also for Medea is vengeance taken.   96

All seducers march here to the whip.
And let us say no more about this valley
and those it closes in its stony grip."   99

We had already come to where the walk
crosses the second bank, from which it lifts
another arch, spanning from rock to rock.   102

Here we heard people whine in the next chasm,
and knock and thump themselves with open palms,
and blubber through their snouts as if in a spasm.   105

Steaming from that pit, a vapour rose
over the banks, crusting them with a slime
that sickened my eyes and hammered at my nose.   108

That chasm sinks so deep we could not sight
its bottom anywhere until we climbed
along the rock arch to its greatest height.   111

Once there, I peered down; and I saw long lines
of people in a river of excrement
that seemed the overflow of the world's latrines.   114

I saw among the felons of that pit
one wraith who might or might not have been tonsured—
one could not tell, he was so smeared with shit.   117

He bellowed: "You there, why do you stare at me
more than at all the others in this stew?"
And I to him: "Because if memory   120

serves me, I knew you when your hair was dry.
You are Alessio Interminelli da Lucca.
That's why I pick you from this filthy fry."   123

And he then, beating himself on his clown's head:
"Down to this have the flatteries I sold
the living sunk me here among the dead."   126

And my Guide prompted then: "Lean forward a bit
and look beyond them, there—do you see that one
scratching herself with dungy nails, the strumpet   129

who fidgets to her feet, then to a crouch?
It is the whore Thaïs who told her lover
when he sent to ask her, 'Do you thank me much?'   132

'Much? Nay, past all believing!' And with this
let us turn away from the sight of this abyss."

Notes

2. *Malebolge*: *Bolgia* (BOWL-djah) in Italian equals "ditch" or "pouch." That combination of meanings is not possible in a single English word, but it is well to bear in mind that Dante intended both meanings: not only a ditch of evil, but a pouch full of it, a filthy treasure of ill-gotten souls.

5. *a well*: This is the final pit of Hell, and in it are punished the Treacherous (those Guilty of Compound Fraud). Cantos **XXIX–XXXIV** will deal with this part of Hell.

22. *below, on my right*: (See diagram.) The Poets have, as usual, borne left from the point where Geryon left them. They are walking along the outer ridge of the first *bolgia*, and the sinners are below them on the right. The Panderers are walking toward them along the near bank; the seducers are walking the other way (*i.e.*, in the same direction as the Poets) along the far bank. Dante places the Seducers closer to the center of Hell, thereby indicating that their sin is a shade worse than that of the Panderers. It is difficult to see why Dante should think so, but since both receive exactly the same punishment, the distinction is more or less academic.

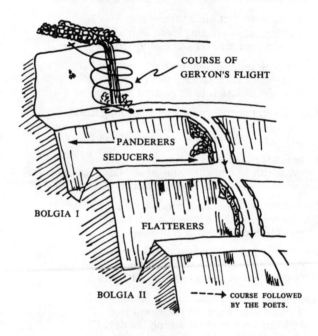

COURSE OF
GERYON'S FLIGHT

PANDERERS
SEDUCERS

BOLGIA I

FLATTERERS

BOLGIA II

- - - → COURSE FOLLOWED
BY THE POETS.

28–33. Boniface VIII had proclaimed 1300 a Jubilee Year, and consequently throngs of pilgrims had come to Rome. Since the date of the vision is also 1300, the Roman throngs are moving back and forth across the Tiber via Ponte Castello Sant' Angelo at the very time Dante is watching the sinners in Hell.

47. *thought to hide his face*: The general rule of the sinners above the great barrier cliff has been a great willingness—in fact, an eagerness—to make themselves known and to be remembered in the world. From this point to the bottom of Hell that rule is reversed, and the sinners, with a few exceptions, try to conceal their identity, asking only to be forgotten. This change should be noted as one more evidence of Dante's architectural sense of detail: this exploitation of many interrelated themes and their progression from point to point of the great journey give the poem its symphonic and many-leveled richness.

50. *Venedico Caccianemico* (Ven-AID-ee-coe Kah-tchah-neh-MEE-coe): A nobleman of Bologna. To win the favor of the Marquis Obbizo da Este of Ferrara, Caccianemico acted as the procurer of his own sister Ghisola, called "la bella" or "Ghisolabella."

61. *sipa*: Bolognese dialect for "si," *i.e.*, "yes." Bologna lies between the Savena and the Reno. This is a master taunt at Bologna as a city of panderers and seducers, for it clearly means that the Bolognese then living on earth were fewer in number than the Bolognese dead who had been assigned to this *bolgia*.

70. *turning right*: see diagram.

83–96. *Jason*: Leader of the Argonauts. He carried off the Colchian Ram (*i.e.*, The Golden Fleece). "The good advice" that helped him win the fleece was given by Medea, daughter of the King of Colchis, whom Jason took with him and later abandoned for Creusa. ("Also for Medea is vengeance taken.") In the course of his very Grecian life, Jason had previously seduced Hypsipyle and deserted her to continue his voyage after the fleece. She was one of the women of Lemnos whom Aphrodite, because they no longer worshiped her, cursed with a foul smell which made them unbearable to their husbands and lovers. The women took their epic revenge by banding together to kill all their males, but Hypsipyle managed to save her father, King Thoas, by pretending to the women that she had already killed him.

THE FLATTERERS. BOLGIA 2.

It should be noted as characteristic of Dante's style that he deliberately coarsens his language when he wishes to describe certain kinds of coarseness. The device has earned Dante the title of "master of the disgusting." It may well be added that what is disgusting in the Victorian drawing-room may be the essential landscape of Hell. Among the demons who guard the grafters (Cantos XXI–XXII), and among the sowers of discord (Canto XXVIII), Dante reinvokes the same gargoyle quality. It would be ridiculous prudery to refine Dante's diction at these points.

122. *Alessio Interminelli da Lucca* (In-ter-min-ELL-ee): One of the noble family of the Interminelli or Interminei, a prominent White family of Lucca. About all that is known of Alessio is the fact that he was still alive in 1295.

131. *Thaïs*: The flattery uttered by Thaïs is put into her mouth by Terence in his *Eunuchus* (Act III, 1:1-2). Thaïs' lover had sent her a slave, and later sent a servant to ask if she thanked him much. *Magnas vero agere gratias Thais mihi?* The servant reported her as answering *Ingentes!* Cicero later commented on the passage as an example of immoderate flattery, and Dante's conception of Thaïs probably springs from this source. (*De Amicitia*, 26.)

Canto XIX

The Simoniacs

Dante comes upon the *Simoniacs* (sellers of ecclesiastic favors and offices) and his heart overflows with the wrath he feels against those who corrupt the things of God. This *bolgia* is lined with round tube-like holes and the sinners are placed in them upside down with the soles of their feet ablaze. The heat of the blaze is proportioned to their guilt.

The holes in which these sinners are placed are debased equivalents of the baptismal fonts common in the cities of Northern Italy and the sinners' confinement in them is temporary: as new sinners arrive, the souls drop through the bottoms of their holes and disappear eternally into the crevices of the rock.

As always, the punishment is a symbolic retribution. Just as the Simoniacs made a mock of holy office, so are they turned upside down in a mockery of the baptismal font. Just as they made a mockery of the holy water of baptism, so is their hellish baptism by fire, after which they are wholly immersed in the crevices below. The oily fire that licks at their soles may also suggest a travesty on the oil used in Extreme Unction (last rites for the dying).

Virgil carries Dante down an almost sheer ledge and lets him speak to one who is the chief sinner of that place, *Pope Nicholas III*. Dante delivers himself of another stirring denunciation of those who have corrupted church office, and Virgil carries him back up the steep ledge toward the *Fourth Bolgia*.

O Simon Magus! O you wretched crew
    who follow him, pandering for silver and gold
    the things of God which should be wedded to   3

love and righteousness! O thieves for hire,
    now must the trump of judgment sound your doom
    here in the third fosse of the rim of fire!   6

We had already made our way across
    to the next grave, and to that part of the bridge
    which hangs above the mid-point of the fosse.   9

O Sovereign Wisdom, how Thine art doth shine
    in Heaven, on Earth, and in the Evil World!
    How justly doth Thy power judge and assign!   12

I saw along the walls and on the ground
    long rows of holes cut in the livid stone;
    all were cut to a size, and all were round.   15

They seemed to be exactly the same size
    as those in the font of my beautiful San Giovanni,
    built to protect the priests who come to baptize;   18

(one of which, not so long since, I broke open
to rescue a boy who was wedged and drowning in it.
Be this enough to undeceive all men.)   21

From every mouth a sinner's legs stuck out
as far as the calf. The soles were all ablaze
and the joints of the legs quivered and writhed about.   24

Withes and tethers would have snapped in their throes.
As oiled things blaze upon the surface only,
so did they burn from the heels to the points of their toes. 27

"Master," I said, "who is that one in the fire
who writhes and quivers more than all the others?
From him the ruddy flames seem to leap higher."   30

And he to me: "If you wish me to carry you down
along that lower bank, you may learn from him
who he is, and the evil he has done."   33

And I: "What you will, I will. You are my lord
and I know I depart in nothing from your wish;
and you know my mind beyond my spoken word."   36

We moved to the fourth ridge, and turning left
my Guide descended by a jagged path
into the strait and perforated cleft.   39

Thus the good Master bore me down the dim
and rocky slope, and did not put me down
till we reached the one whose legs did penance for him.   42

"Whoever you are, sad spirit," I began,
"who lie here with your head below your heels
and planted like a stake—speak if you can."   45

I stood like a friar who gives the sacrament
to a hired assassin, who, fixed in the hole,
recalls him, and delays his death a moment.   48

"Are you there already, Boniface? Are you there
already?" he cried. "By several years the writ
has lied. And all that gold, and all that care—   51

are you already sated with the treasure
for which you dared to turn on the Sweet Lady
and trick and pluck and bleed her at your pleasure?"   54

I stood like one caught in some raillery,
not understanding what is said to him,
lost for an answer to such mockery.   57

Then Virgil said, "Say to him: 'I am not he,
I am not whom you think.'" And I replied
as my good Master had instructed me.   60

The sinner's feet jerked madly; then again
   his voice rose, this time choked with sighs and tears,
   and said at last: "What do you want of me then?   63

If to know who I am drives you so fearfully
   that you descend the bank to ask it, know
   that the Great Mantle was once hung upon me.   66

And in truth I was a son of the She-Bear,
   so sly and eager to push my whelps ahead,
   that I pursed wealth above, and myself here.   69

Beneath my head are dragged all who have gone
   before me in buying and selling holy office;
   there they cower in fissures of the stone.   72

I too shall be plunged down when that great cheat
   for whom I took you comes here in his turn.
   Longer already have I baked my feet   75

and been planted upside-down, than he shall be
   before the west sends down a lawless Shepherd
   of uglier deeds to cover him and me.   78

He will be a new Jason of the Maccabees;
   and just as that king bent to his high priests' will,
   so shall the French king do as this one please."   81

Maybe—I cannot say—I grew too brash
   at this point, for when he had finished speaking
   I said: "Indeed! Now tell me how much cash   84

our Lord required of Peter in guarantee
   before he put the keys into his keeping?
   Surely he asked nothing but 'Follow me!'   87

Nor did Peter, nor the others, ask silver or gold
   of Matthew when they chose him for the place
   the despicable and damned apostle sold.   90

Therefore stay as you are; this hole well fits you—
   and keep a good guard on the ill-won wealth
   that once made you so bold toward Charles of Anjou.   93

And were it not that I am still constrained
   by the reverence I owe to the Great Keys
   you held in life, I should not have refrained   96

from using other words and sharper still;
   for this avarice of yours grieves all the world,
   tramples the virtuous, and exalts the evil.   99

Of such as you was the Evangelist's vision
   when he saw She who Sits upon the Waters
   locked with the Kings of earth in fornication.   102

She was born with seven heads, and ten enormous
and shining horns strengthened and made her glad
as long as love and virtue pleased her spouse.   105

Gold and silver are the gods you adore!
In what are you different from the idolator,
save that he worships one, and you a score?   108

Ah Constantine, what evil marked the hour—
not of your conversion, but of the fee
the first rich Father took from you in dower!"   111

And as I sang him this tune, he began to twitch
and kick both feet out wildly, as if in rage
or gnawed by conscience—little matter which.   114

And I think, indeed, it pleased my Guide: his look
was all approval as he stood beside me
intent upon each word of truth I spoke.   117

He approached, and with both arms he lifted me,
and when he had gathered me against his breast,
remounted the rocky path out of the valley,   120

nor did he tire of holding me clasped to him,
until we reached the topmost point of the arch
which crosses from the fourth to the fifth rim   123

of the pits of woe. Arrived upon the bridge,
he tenderly set down the heavy burden
he had been pleased to carry up that ledge   126

which would have been hard climbing for a goat.
Here I looked down on still another moat.

Notes

1. *Simon Magus*: Simon the Samarian magician (see *Acts* viii, 9–24) from whom
the word "Simony" derives. Upon his conversion to Christianity he offered to buy the
power to administer the Holy Ghost and was severely rebuked by Peter.
8. *the next grave*: The next *bolgia*.
8. *that part of the bridge*: The center point. The center of each span is obviously
the best observation point.
11. *Evil World*: Hell.
17–18. *the font of my beautiful San Giovanni*: It was the custom in Dante's time
to baptize only on Holy Saturday and on Pentecost. These occasions were naturally
thronged, therefore, and to protect the priests a special font was built in the Baptistry of San Giovanni with marble stands for the priests, who were thus protected from
both the crowds and the water in which they immersed those to be baptized. The
Baptistry is still standing, but the font is no longer in it. A similar font still exists,
however, in the Baptistry at Pisa.
19–21. In these lines Dante is replying to a charge of sacrilege that had been
rumored against him. One day a boy playing in the baptismal font became jammed in
the marble tube and could not be extricated. To save the boy from drowning, Dante
took it upon himself to smash the tube. This is his answer to all men on the charge of
sacrilege.
29. *more than all the others*: The fire is proportioned to the guilt of the sinner.
These are obviously the feet of the chief sinner of this *bolgia*. In a moment we shall
discover that he is Pope Nicholas III.

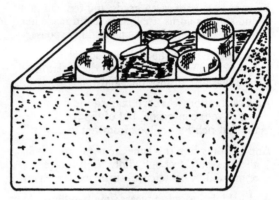

Probable detail of baptismal font.

46–47. *like a friar, etc.*: Persons convicted of murdering for hire were sometimes executed by being buried alive upside down. If the friar were called back at the last moment, he should have to bend over the hole in which the man is fixed upside down awaiting the first shovelful of earth.

POPE NICHOLAS III: Giovanni Gaetano degli Orsini, Pope from 1277–1280. His presence here is self-explanatory. He is awaiting the arrival of his successor, Boniface VIII, who will take his place in the stone tube and who will in turn be replaced by Clement V, a Pope even more corrupt than Boniface. With the foresight of the damned he had read the date of Boniface's death (1303) in the Book of Fate. Mistaking Dante for Boniface, he thinks his foresight has erred by three years, since it is now 1300.

66. *the Great Mantle*: of the Papacy.

67. *son of the She-Bear*: Nicholas' family name, degli Orsini, means in Italian "of the bear cubs."

69. *pursed*: A play on the second meaning of *bolgia* (i.e., "purse"). "Just as I put wealth in my purse when alive, so am I put in this foul purse now that I am dead."

77–79. *a lawless Shepherd . . . Jason of the Maccabees . . . the French King*: The reference is to Clement V, Pope from 1305 to 1314. He came from Gascony (the West) and was involved in many intrigues with the King of France. It was Clement V who moved the Papal See to Avignon where it remained until 1377. He is compared to Jason (see *Maccabees* iv, 7ff.) who bought an appointment as High Priest of the Jews from King Antiochus and thereupon introduced pagan and venal practices into the office in much the same way as Clement used his influence with Philip of France to secure and corrupt his high office.

Clement will succeed Boniface in Hell because Boniface's successor, Benedictus XI (1303–1304), was a good and holy man. The terms each guilty Pope must serve in this hellish baptism are:

Nicholas III 1280–1303
(four good Popes intervene)
Boniface VIII 1303–1314
(one good Pope intervenes)
Clement V 1314—not stated

88–89. *nor did Peter . . . of Matthias*: Upon the expulsion of Judas from the band of Apostles, Matthias was chosen in his place.

93. *Charles of Anjou*: The seventh son of Louis VIII of France. Charles became King of Naples and of Sicily largely through the good offices of Pope Urban IV and later of Clement IV. Nicholas III withdrew the high favor his predecessors had shown Charles, but the exact nature and extent of his opposition are open to dispute. Dante probably believed, as did many of his contemporaries, that Nicholas instigated the massacre called the Sicilian Vespers, in which the Sicilians overthrew the rule of Charles and held a general slaughter of the French who had been their masters. The Sicilian Vespers, however, was a popular and spontaneous uprising, and it did not occur until Nicholas had been dead for two years.

Dante may have erred in interpreting the Sicilian question, but his point is indisputably clear when he laments the fact that simoniacally acquired wealth had involved the Papacy in war and political intrigue, thereby perverting it from its spiritual purpose.

95. *the Great Keys*: of the Papacy.

100–105. *the Evangelist . . . She Who Sits upon the Waters*: St. John the Evangelist. His vision of She who sits upon the waters is set forth in *Revelation* xvii. The Evangelist intended it as a vision of Pagan Rome, but Dante interprets it as a vision of the Roman Church in its simoniacal corruption. The seven heads are the seven sacraments; the ten horns, the ten commandments.

109–11. *Ah Constantine, etc.*: The first rich Father was Silvester (Pope from 314 to 355). Before him the Popes possessed nothing, but when Constantine was converted and Catholicism became the official religion of the Empire, the church began to acquire wealth. Dante and the scholars of his time believed, according to a document called "The Donation of Constantine," that the Emperor had moved his Empire to the East in order to leave sovereignty of the West to the Church. The document was not shown to be a forgery until the fifteenth century. Knowledge of the forgery would not, however, have altered Dante's view; he was unwavering in his belief that wealth was the greatest disaster that had befallen the Church, for in wealth lay the root of the corruption which Dante denounced so passionately.

Canto XX

The Fortune Tellers and Diviners

Dante stands in the middle of the bridge over the *Fourth Bolgia* and looks down at the souls of the *Fortune Tellers* and *Diviners*. Here are the souls of all those who attempted by forbidden arts to look into the future. Among these damned are: *Amphiareus, Tiresias, Aruns, Manto, Eurypylus, Michael Scott, Guido Bonatti,* and *Asdente.*

Characteristically, the sin of these wretches is reversed upon them: their punishment is to have their heads turned backwards on their bodies and to be compelled to walk backwards through all eternity, their eyes blinded with tears. Thus, those who sought to penetrate the future cannot even see in front of themselves; they attempted to move themselves forward in time, so must they go backwards through all eternity; and as the arts of sorcery are a distortion of God's law, so are their bodies distorted in Hell.

No more need be said of them: Dante names them, and passes on to fill the Canto with a lengthy account of the founding of Virgil's native city of Mantua.

Now must I sing new griefs, and my verses strain
    to form the matter of the Twentieth Canto
    of Canticle One, the Canticle of Pain.   3

My vantage point permitted a clear view
    of the depths of the pit below: a desolation
    bathed with the tears of its tormented crew,   6

who moved about the circle of the pit
    at about the pace of a litany procession.
    Silent and weeping, they wound round and round it.   9

And when I looked down from their faces, I saw
    that each of them was hideously distorted
    between the top of the chest and the lines of the jaw;   12

for the face was reversed on the neck, and they came on
    backwards, staring backwards at their loins,
    for to look before them was forbidden. Someone,   15

sometime, in the grip of a palsy may have been
    distorted so, but never to my knowledge;
    nor do I believe the like was ever seen.   18

Reader, so may God grant you to understand
    my poem and profit from it, ask yourself
    how I could check my tears, when near at hand   21

I saw the image of our humanity
    distorted so that the tears that burst from their eyes
    ran down the cleft of their buttocks. Certainly   24

I wept. I leaned against the jagged face
of a rock and wept so that my Guide said: "Still?
Still like the other fools? There is no place   27

for pity here. Who is more arrogant
within his soul, who is more impious
than one who dares to sorrow at God's judgment?   30

Lift up your eyes, lift up your eyes and see
him the earth swallowed before all the Thebans,
at which they cried out: 'Whither do you flee,   33

Amphiareus? Who do you leave the field?'
And he fell headlong through the gaping earth
to the feet of Minos, where all sin must yield.   36

Observe how he has made a breast of his back.
In life he wished to see too far before him,
and now he must crab backwards round this track.   39

And see Tiresias, who by his arts
succeeded in changing himself from man to woman,
transforming all his limbs and all his parts;   42

later he had to strike the two twined serpents
once again with his conjurer's wand before
he could resume his manly lineaments.   45

And there is Aruns, his back to that one's belly,
the same who in the mountains of the Luni
tilled by the people of Carrara's valley,   48

made a white marble cave his den, and there
with unobstructed view observed the sea
and the turning constellations year by year.   51

And she whose unbound hair flows back to hide
her breasts—which you cannot see—and who also wears
all of her hairy parts on that other side,   54

was Manto, who searched countries far and near,
then settled where I was born. In that connection
there is a story I would have you hear.   57

Tiresias was her sire. After his death,
Thebes, the city of Bacchus, became enslaved,
and for many years she roamed about the earth.   60

High in sweet Italy, under the Alps that shut
the Tyrolean gate of Germany, there lies
a lake known as Benacus roundabout.   63

Through endless falls, more than a thousand and one,
Mount Appennine from Garda to Val Cammonica
is freshened by the waters that flow down   66

into that lake. At its center is a place
  where the Bishops of Brescia, Trentine, and Verona
  might all give benediction with equal grace.   69

Peschiera, the beautiful fortress, strong in war
  against the Brescians and the Bergamese,
  sits at the lowest point along that shore.   72

There, the waters Benacus cannot hold
  within its bosom, spill and form a river
  that winds away through pastures green and gold.   75

But once the water gathers its full flow,
  it is called Mincius rather than Benacus
  from there to Governo, where it joins the Po.   78

Still near its source, it strikes a plain, and there
  it slows and spreads, forming an ancient marsh
  which in the summer heats pollutes the air.   81

The terrible virgin, passing there by chance,
  saw dry land at the center of the mire,
  untilled, devoid of all inhabitants.   84

There, shunning all communion with mankind,
  she settled with the ministers of her arts,
  and there she lived, and there she left behind   87

her vacant corpse. Later the scattered men
  who lived nearby assembled on that spot
  since it was well defended by the fen.   90

Over those whited bones they raised the city,
  and for her who had chosen the place before all others
  they named it—with no further augury—   93

Mantua. Far more people lived there once—
  before sheer madness prompted Casalodi
  to let Pinamonte play him for a dunce.   96

Therefore, I charge you, should you ever hear
  other accounts of this, to let no falsehood
  confuse the truth which I have just made clear."   99

And I to him: "Master, within my soul
  your word is certainty, and any other
  would seem like the dead lumps of burned out coal.   102

But tell me of those people moving down
  to join the rest. Are any worth my noting?
  For my mind keeps coming back to that alone."   101

And he: "That one whose beard spreads like a fleece
  over his swarthy shoulders, was an augur
  in the days when so few males remained in Greece   108

that even the cradles were all but empty of sons.
He chose the time for cutting the cable at Aulis,
and Calchas joined him in those divinations.   111

He is Eurypylus. I sing him somewhere
in my High Tragedy; you will know the place
who know the whole of it. The other there,   114

the one beside him with the skinny shanks
was Michael Scott, who mastered every trick
of magic fraud, a prince of mountebanks.   117

See Guido Bonatti there; and see Asdente,
who now would be wishing he had stuck to his last,
but repents too late, though he repents aplenty.   120

And see on every hand the wretched hags
who left their spinning and sewing for soothsaying
and casting of spells with herbs, and dolls, and rags.   123

But come: Cain with his bush of thorns appears
already on the wave below Seville,
above the boundary of the hemispheres;   126

and the moon was full already yesternight,
as you must well remember from the wood,
for it certainly did not harm you when its light   129

shone down upon your way before the dawn."
And as he spoke to me, we traveled on.

Notes

A GENERAL NOTE

The rather long account of the origin of Mantua with which Dante fills up this Canto often prompts students to ask why he does not delete this "irrelevant account" in order to spend more time on the diviners. The answer to that question (it could be asked in connection with many other passages in the *Commedia*) points to the core of Dante's allegorical style. The fact is that once he has placed the diviners in their proper pit and assigned them an appropriate punishment, his essential allegorical function has been fulfilled: nothing more need be said.

Thus, the structure carries all. Once the poem is under way, it is enough simply to name a man as being in a certain place in Hell suffering a certain punishment, and that man is not only located as precisely as an x drawn on a map locates the point it marks, but the sin which that man typifies is located on the scale of value which is constructed into the whole nature of the Universe as Dante saw it.

The Poet is thereby left free to pass on to the discussion of all those matters of theology, history, politics, and "science" which fascinate him. But there is nothing "irrelevant" about these multiple interests. Dante's journey is "to experience all." He is not simply taking a long walk: he is constructing a Universe. As part of that construction, he reaches out to draw data from a variety of sources. These are not "data" in the scientific sense. Rather they are "typical" data: *i.e.*, each of Dante's side discussions considers data that are central to its type: the history of Mantua relates to the history of Troy, to the history of Virgil, to the history of Rome, to the history of Florence. Moreover, the history of Mantua is excerpted as typical from the whole range of history (as if Dante were saying: "Thus are the States of man begun") to advance one of the great themes of the *Commedia*—the backgrounds of civilization as Dante knew it.

3. *Canticle One: The Inferno*. The other Canticles are, of course, *The Purgatorio* and *The Paradiso*.

4. *my vantage point*: Virgil, it will be recalled, had set Dante down on the bridge across the Fourth Bolgia.

8. *at about the pace of a litany procession*: The litanies are chanted not only in church (before the mass), but sometimes in procession, the priest chanting the prayers and the marchers the response. As one might gather from the context, the processions move very slowly.

10. *And when I looked down from their faces*: A typically Dantean conception. Dante often writes as if the eye pin-pointed on one feature of a figure seen at a distance. The pin-point must then be deliberately shifted before the next feature can be observed. As far as I know, this stylistic device is peculiar to Dante.

14. *loins*: General usage seems to have lost sight of the fact that the first meaning of "loin" is "that part of a human being or quadruped on either side of the spinal column between the hipbone and the false ribs." (Webster.)

23-24. *tears . . . ran down the cleft of the buttocks*: Since the heads of these sinners are backwards on their necks, their tears would run down their backs, and this is the obvious track they must follow. But what a debasement of sorrow! This is the sort of detail Dante knew how to use with maximum effect.

26-30. VIRGIL SCOLDS DANTE FOR SHOWING PITY. It is worth noting that Virgil has not scolded Dante for showing pity in earlier cases, though he might easily have done so and for exactly the same reason. One interpretation may be that Dante was not yet ready to recognize the true nature of evil. Another may be that Human Reason (despite Dante's earlier reference to his "all-knowing Master") is essentially fallible. Beatrice, a higher creature, is so made that she is incapable of being moved by the creatures of Hell (see Canto II), as is the Divine Messenger who springs open the Gates of Dis (Canto IX).

34. *Amphiareus*: Another of the seven Captains who fought against Thebes (v. Capaneus, Canto XIV). Statius (*Thebaid* VII, 690 ff. and VIII, 8 ff.) tells how he foresaw his own death in this war, and attempted to run away from it, but was swallowed in his flight by an earthquake. I have Romanized his name from "Amphiaraus."

40. *Tiresias*: A Theban diviner and magician. Ovid (*Metamorphoses* III) tells how he came on two twined serpents, struck them apart with his stick, and was thereupon transformed into a woman. Seven years later he came on two serpents similarly entwined, struck them apart, and was changed back.

46-48. *Aruns*: An Etruscan soothsayer (see Lucan, *Pharsalia*, I, 580 ff.). He foretold the war between Pompey and Julius Caesar, and also that it would end with Caesar's victory and Pompey's death. *Luni*: Also *Luna*. An ancient Eruscan city, *Carrara's valley*: The Carrarese valley is famous for its white (Carrara) marble.

46. *that one's*: Tiresias.

55. *Manto*: The text is self-explanatory. Dante's version of the founding of Mantua is based on a reference in the *Aeneid* X, 198-200.

63 ff. *Benacus*: The ancient name for the famous Lago di Garda, which lies a short distance north of Mantua. The other places named in this passage lie around Lago di Garda. On an island in the lake the three dioceses mentioned in line 68 conjoined. All three bishops, therefore, had jurisdiction on the island.

95-96. *Casalodi . . . Pinamonte*: Albert, Count of Casalodi and Lord of Mantua, let himself be persuaded by Pinamonte de Buonaccorsi to banish the nobles from Mantua as a source of danger to his rule. Once the nobles had departed, Pinamonte headed a rebellion against the weakened lord and took over the city himself.

106. *That one whose beard*: Eurypylus, Greek augur. According to Greek custom an augur was summoned before each voyage to choose the exact propitious moment for departure (cutting the cables). Dante has Virgil imply that Eurypylus and Calchas were selected to choose the moment for Agamemnon's departure from Aulis to Troy. Actually, according to the *Aeneid*, Eurypylus was not at Aulis. The *Aeneid* (II, 110 ff.) tells how Eurypylus and Calchas were both consulted in choosing the moment for the departure from Troy. Dante seems to have confused the two incidents.

109. *even the cradles were all but empty of sons*: At the time of the Trojan Wars, Greece was said to be so empty of males that scarcely any were to be found even in the cradles.

116. *Michael Scott*: An Irish scholar of the first half of the thirteenth century. His studies were largely in the occult. Sir Walter Scott refers to him in *The Lay of the Last Minstrel*.

118. *Guido Bonatti*: A thirteenth-century astrologer of Forli. He was court astrologer to Guido da Montefeltro (see Canto XXVII) advising him in his wars. *Asdente*: A shoemaker of Parma who turned diviner and won wide fame for his forecasting in the last half of the thirteenth century.

124 ff. *Cain with his bush of thorns*: The Moon. Cain with a bush of thorns was the medieval equivalent of our Man in the Moon. Dante seems to mean by "Seville" the whole area of Spain and the Straits of Gibralter (Pillars of Hercules), which were believed to be the western limit of the world. The moon is setting (*i.e.*, it appears on the western waves) on the morning of Holy Saturday, 1300.

Canto XXI

The Grafters

The Poets move on, talking as they go, and arrive at the *Fifth Bolgia*. Here the *Grafters* are sunk in boiling pitch and guarded by *Demons*, who tear them to pieces with claws and grappling hooks if they catch them above the surface of the pitch.

The sticky pitch is symbolic of the sticky fingers of the Grafters. It serves also to hide them from sight, as their sinful dealings on earth were hidden from men's eyes. The demons, too, suggest symbolic possibilities, for they are armed with grappling hooks and are forever ready to rend and tear all they can get their hands on.

The Poets watch a demon arrive with a grafting *Senator* of *Lucca* and fling him into the pitch where the demons set upon him.

To protect Dante from their wrath, Virgil hides him behind some jagged rocks and goes ahead alone to negotiate with the demons. They set upon him like a pack of mastiffs, but Virgil secures a safe-conduct from their leader, *Malacoda*. Thereupon Virgil calls Dante from hiding, and they are about to set off when they discover that the *Bridge Across the Sixth Bolgia* lies shattered. Malacoda tells them there is another further on and sends a squad of demons to escort them. Their adventures with the demons continue through the next Canto.

These two Cantos may conveniently be remembered as the *Gargoyle Cantos*. If the total *Commedia* is built like a cathedral (as so many critics have suggested), it is here certainly that Dante attaches his grotesqueries. At no other point in the *Commedia* does Dante give such free rein to his coarsest style.

> Thus talking of things which my Comedy does not care
>   to sing, we passed from one arch to the next
>   until we stood upon its summit. There   3
>
> we checked our steps to study the next fosse
>   and the next vain lamentations of Malebolge;
>   awesomely dark and desolate it was.   6
>
> As in the Venetian arsenal, the winter through
>   there boils the sticky pitch to caulk the seams
>   of the sea-battered bottoms when no crew   9
>
> can put to sea—instead of which, one starts
>   to build its ship anew, one plugs the planks
>   which have been sprung in many foreign parts;   12
>
> some hammer at a mast, some at a rib;
>   some make new oars, some braid and coil new lines;
>   one patches up the mainsail, one the jib—   15
>
> so, but by Art Divine and not by fire,
>   a viscid pitch boiled in the fosse below
>   and coated all the bank with gluey mire.   18

I saw the pitch; but I saw nothing in it
   except the enormous bubbles of its boiling,
   which swelled and sank, like breathing, through all the pit.   21

And as I stood and stared into that sink,
   my Master cried, "Take care!" and drew me back
   from my exposed position on the brink.   24

I turned like one who cannot wait to see
   the thing he dreads, and who, in sudden fright,
   runs while he looks, his curiosity   27

competing with his terror—and at my back
   I saw a figure that came running toward us
   across the ridge, a Demon huge and black.   30

Ah what a face he had, all hate and wildness!
   Galloping so, with his great wings outspread
   he seemed the embodiment of all bitterness.   33

across each high-hunched shoulder he had thrown
   one haunch of a sinner, whom he held in place
   with a great talon round each ankle bone.   36

"Blacktalons of our bridge," he began to roar,
   "I bring you one of Santa Zita's Elders!
   Scrub him down while I go back for more: 39

I planted a harvest of them in that city:
   everyone there is a grafter except Bonturo.
   There 'Yes' is 'No' and 'No' is 'Yes' for a fee."   42

Down the sinner plunged, and at once the Demon
   spun from the cliff; no mastiff ever sprang
   more eager from the leash to chase a felon.   45

Down plunged the sinner and sank to reappear
   with his backside arched and his face and both his feet
   glued to the pitch, almost as if in prayer.   48

But the Demons under the bridge, who guard that place
   and the sinners who are thrown to them, bawled out:
   "You're out of bounds here for the Sacred Face: 51

this is no dip in the Serchio: take your look
   and then get down in the pitch. And stay below
   unless you want a taste of a grappling hook."   54

Then they raked him with more than a hundred hooks
   bellowing: "Here you dance below the covers.
   Graft all you can there: no one checks your books."   57

They dipped him down into that pitch exactly
   as a chef makes scullery boys dip meat in a boiler,
   holding it with their hooks from floating free.   60

And the Master said: "You had best not be seen
   by these Fiends till I am ready. Crouch down here.
   One of these rocks will serve you as a screen.   63

And whatever violence you see done to me,
   you have no cause to fear. I know these matters:
   I have been though this once and come back safely."   66

With that, he walked on past the end of the bridge;
   and it wanted all his courage to look calm
   from the moment he arrived on the sixth ridge.   69

With that same storm and fury that arouses
   all the house when the hounds leap at a tramp
   who suddenly falls to pleading where he pauses—   72

so rushed those Fiends from below, and all the pack
   pointed their gleaming pitchforks at my Guide.
   But he stood fast and cried to them: "Stand back!   75

Before those hooks and grapples make too free,
   send up one of your crew to hear me out,
   then ask yourselves if you still care to rip me."   78

All cried as one: "Let Malacoda go."
   So the pack stood and one of them came forward,
   saying: "What good does he think *this* will do?"   81

"Do you think, Malacoda," my good Master said,
   "you would see me here, having arrived this far
   already, safe from you and every dread,   84

without Divine Will and propitious Fate?
   Let me pass on, for it is willed in Heaven
   that I must show another this dread state."   87

The Demon stood there on the flinty brim,
   so taken aback he let his pitchfork drop;
   then said to the others: "Take care not to harm him!"   90

"O you crouched like a cat," my Guide called to me,
   "among the jagged rock piles of the bridge,
   come down to me, for now you may come safely."   93

Hearing him, I hurried down the ledge;
   and the Demons all pressed forward when I appeared,
   so that I feared they might not keep their pledge.   96

So once I saw the Pisan infantry
   march out under truce from the fortress at Caprona,
   staring in fright at the ranks of the enemy.   99

I pressed the whole of my body against my Guide,
   and not for an instant did I take my eyes
   from those black fiends who scowled on every side.   102

They swung their forks saying to one another:
"Shall I give him a touch in the rump?" and answering:
"Sure, give him a taste to pay him for his bother."   105

But the Demon who was talking to my Guide
turned round and cried to him: "At ease there, Snatcher!"
And then to us: "There's no road on this side: 108

the arch lies all in pieces in the pit.
If you *must* go on, follow along this ridge;
there's another cliff to cross by just beyond it.   111

In just five hours it will be, since the bridge fell,
a thousand two hundred sixty-six years and a day;
that was the time the big quake shook all Hell.   114

I'll send a squad of my boys along that way
to see if anyone's airing himself below:
you can go with them: there will be no foul play.   117

Front and center here, Grizzly and Hellken,"
he began to order them. "You too, Deaddog.
Curlybeard, take charge of a squad of ten.   120

Take Grafter and Dragontooth along with you.
Pigtusk, Catclaw, Cramper, and Crazyred.
Keep a sharp lookout on the boiling glue   123

as you move along, and see that these gentlemen
are not molested until they reach the crag
where they can find a way across the den."   126

"In the name of heaven, Master," I cried, "what sort
of guides are these? Let us go on alone
if you know the way. Who can trust such an escort!   129

If you are as wary as you used to be
you surely see them grind their teeth at us,
and knot their beetle brows so threateningly."   132

And he: "I do not like this fear in you.
Let them gnash and knot as they please; they menace only
the sticky wretches simmering in that stew."   135

They turned along the left bank in a line;
but not before they had formed a single rank
and stuck their pointed tongues out as a sign   138

to their Captain that they wished permission to pass;
and he had made a trumpet of his ass.

Notes

A GENERAL NOTE ON DANTE'S TREATMENT OF THE
GRAFTERS AND THEIR GUARDS
(Cantos XXI and XXII)

Dante has been called "The Master of the Disgusting" with the stress at times on
the mastery and at times on the disgust. The occasional coarseness of details in other
Cantos (especially in Cantos XVIII and XXVIII) has offended certain delicate readers. It is worth pointing out that the mention of bodily function is likely to be more

shocking in a Protestant than in a Catholic culture. It has often seemed to me that the offensive language of Protestantism is obscenity; the offensive language of Catholicism is profanity or blasphemy: one offends on a scale of unmentionable words for bodily function, the other on a scale of disrespect for the sacred. Dante places the Blasphemous in Hell as the worst of the Violent against God and His Works, but he has no category for punishing those who use four-letter words.

The difference is not, I think, national, but religious. Chaucer, as a man of Catholic England, took exactly Dante's view in the matter of what was and what was not shocking language. In "The Pardoner's Tale," Chaucer sermonized with great feeling against the rioters for their profanity and blasphemy (for the way they rend Christ's body with their oaths) but he is quite free himself with "obscenity." Modern English readers tend to find nothing whatever startling in his profanity, but the schoolboys faithfully continue to underline the marvels of his Anglo-Saxon monosyllables and to make marginal notes on them.

7. *the Venetian arsenal*: The arsenal was not only an arms manufactory but a great center of shipbuilding and repairing.

37. *Blacktalons*: The original is Malebranche, i.e., "Evil Claws."

38. *Santa Zita*: The patron saint of the city of Lucca. "One of Santa Zita's Elders" would therefore equal "one of Lucca's Senators" (ie., Alderman). Commentators have searched the records of Luccan Aldermen who died on Holy Saturday of 1300, and one Martino Bottaio has been suggested as the newcomer, but there is no evidence that Dante had a specific man in mind. More probably he meant simply to underscore the fact that Lucca was a city of grafters, just as Bologna was represented as a city of panderers and seducers.

41. *Bonturo*: Bonturo Dati, a politician of Lucca. The phrase is ironic: Bonturo was the most avid grafter of them all.

51. *Sacred Face*: *Il volto santo* was an ancient wooden image of Christ venerated by the Luccanese. These ironies and the grotesqueness of the Elder's appearance mark the beginning of the gargoyle dance that swells and rolls through this Canto and the next.

52. *Serchio*: A river near Lucca.

61. *You had best not been seen*: It is only in the passage through this Bolgia, out of the total journey, that Dante presents himself as being in physical danger. Since his dismissal from office and his exile from Florence (on pain of death if he return) was based on a false charge of grafting, the reference is pointedly autobiographical. Such an autobiographical interpretation is certainly consistent with the method of Dante's allegory.

79. *Malacoda*: The name equals "Bad Tail," or "Evil Tail." He is the captain of these grim and semi-military police. I have not translated his name as I have those of the other fiends, since I cannot see that it offers any real difficulty to an English reader.

97-99. *Pisan infantry . . . Caprona, etc.*: A Tuscan army attacked the fortress of Caprona near Pisa in 1289 and after fierce fighting the Pisan defenders were promised a safe-conduct if they would surrender. Dante was probably serving with the Tuscans (the opening lines of the next Canto certainly suggest that he had seen military service) and places the hours of Christ's death at exactly noon. According some accounts it is reported that the Tuscans massacred the Pisans despite their promised safe-conduct—an ominous analogy if true. In any case the emerging Pisans would be sufficiently familiar with the treacheries of Italian politics to feel profoundly uneasy at being surrounded by their enemies under such conditions.

110-111. *If you must go on, etc.*: Malacoda is lying, as the Poets will discover: all the bridges across the Sixth Bolgia have fallen as a result of the earthquake that shook Hell at the death of Christ. The great rock fall between the Sixth and Seventh Circle (see Canto IX) was caused by the same shock, as was the ruin at the entrance to the Second Circle (see Canto V).

112-14. *In just five hours . . . a thousand two hundred sixty-six years and a day*: Christ died on Good Friday of the year 34, and it is now Holy Saturday of the year 1300, five hours before the hour of his death. Many commentators (and Dante himself in the *Convivio*) place the hours of Christ's death at exactly noon. Accordingly, it would now be 7:00 A.M. of Holy Saturday—exactly eight minutes since the Poets left the bridge over the Fourth Bolgia (at moonset).

In the gospels of Matthew, Mark, and Luke, however, the hour of Christ's death is precisely stated as 3:00 P.M. Dante would certainly be familiar with the Synoptic Gospels, and on that authority it would now be 10:00 A.M.

As far as the action of the poem is concerned the only question of consequence is the time-lapse from the bridge over the Fourth Bolgia to the talk with Malacoda, a matter of eight minutes or of three hours and eight minutes. One certainly seems too short, the other needlessly long, and while either answer can be supported with good arguments, this may be another case of literal worrying of "poetic" accuracy.

138-40. *tongues . . . trumpet*: The fiends obviously constitute a kind of debased military organization and these grotesqueries are their sign and countersign. Dante, himself, in his present satyr-like humor, finds them quite remarkable signals, as he goes on to note in the next Canto.

Canto XXII

The Grafters

The poets set off with their escorts of demons. Dante sees the *Grafters* lying in the pitch like frogs in water with only their muzzles out. They disappear as soon as they sight the demons and only a ripple on the surface betrays their presence.

One of the Grafters, *An Unidentified Navarrese*, ducks too late and is seized by the demons who are about to claw him, but *Curlybeard* holds them back while Virgil questions him. The wretch speaks of his fellow sinners, *Friar Gomita* and *Michel Zanche*, while the uncontrollable demons rake him from time to time with their hooks.

The Navarrese offers to lure some of his fellow sufferers into the hands of the demons, and when his plan is accepted he plunges into the pitch and escapes. *Hellken* and *Grizzly* fly after him, but too late. They start a brawl in mid-air and fall into the pitch themselves. Curlybeard immediately organizes a rescue party and the Poets, fearing the bad temper of the frustrated demons, take advantage of the confusion to slip away.

I have seen horsemen breaking camp. I have seen
    the beginning of the assult, the march and muster,
    and at times the retreat and riot. I have been   3

where chargers trampled your land, O Aretines!
    I have seen columns of foragers, shocks of tourney,
    and running of tilts. I have seen the endless lines   6

march to bells, drums, trumpets, from far and near.
    I have seen them march on signals from a castle.
    I have seen them march with native and foreign gear.   9

But never yet have I seen horse or foot,
    nor ship in range of land nor sight of star,
    take its direction from so low a toot.   12

We went with the ten Fiends—ah, savage crew!—
    but "In church with saints; with stewpots in the
                           tavern,"
    as the old proverb wisely bids us do.   15

All my attention was fixed upon the pitch:
    to observe the people who were boiling in it,
    and the customs and the punishments of that ditch.   18

As dolphins surface and begin to flip
    their arched backs from the sea, warning the sailors
    to fall-to and begin to secure ship—   21

So now and then, some soul, to ease his pain,
    showed us a glimpse of his back above the pitch
    and quick as lightning disappeared again.   24

And as, at the edge of a ditch, frogs squat about
hiding their feet and bodies in the water,
leaving only their muzzles sticking out—   27

so stood the sinners in that dismal ditch;
but as Curlybeard approached, only a ripple
showed where they had ducked back into the
                                        pitch.   30

I saw—the dread of it haunts me to this day—
one linger a bit too long, as it sometimes happens
one frog remains when another spurts away;   33

and Catclaw, who was nearest, ran a hook
through the sinner's pitchy hair and hauled him in.
He looked like an otter dripping from the brook.   36

I knew the names of all the Fiends by then;
I had made a note of them at the first muster,
and, marching, had listened and checked them over
                                        again.   39

"Hey, Crazyred," the crew of Demons cried
all together, "give him a taste of your claws.
Dig him open a little. Off with his hide."   42

And I then: "Master, can you find out, please,
the name and history of that luckless one
who has fallen into the hands of his enemies?"   45

My Guide approached that wraith from the hot tar
and asked him whence he came. The wretch replied:
"I was born and raised in the Kingdom of Navarre.   48

My mother placed me in service to a knight;
for she had borne me to a squanderer
who killed himself when he ran through his birthright.   51

Then I became a domestic in the service
of good King Thibault. There I began to graft,
and I account for it in this hot crevice."   54

And Pigtusk, who at the ends of his lower lip
shot forth two teeth more terrible than a boar's,
made the wretch feel how one of them could rip.   57

The mouse had come among bad cats, but here
Curlybeard locked arms around him crying:
"While I've got hold of him the rest stand clear!"   60

And turning his face to my Guide: "If you want to ask
                                        him
anything else," he added, "ask away
before the others tear him limb from limb."   63

And my Guide to the sinner: "I should like to know
    if among the other souls beneath the pitch
    are any Italians?" And the wretch: "Just now   66

I left a shade who came from parts near by.
    Would I were still in the pitch with him, for then
    these hooks would not be giving me cause to cry."   69

And suddenly Grafter bellowed in great heat:
    "We've stood enough!" And he hooked the sinner's arm
    and, raking it, ripped off a chunk of meat.   72

Then Dragontooth wanted to play, too, reaching down
    for a catch at the sinner's legs; but Curlybeard
    wheeled round and round with a terrifying frown,   75

and when the Fiends had somewhat given ground
    and calmed a little, my Guide, without delay,
    asked the wretch, who was staring at his wound: 78

"Who was the sinner from whom you say you made
    your evil-starred departure to come ashore
    among these Fiends?" And the wretch: "It was the shade 81

of Friar Gomita of Gallura, the crooked stem
    of every Fraud: when his master's enemies
    were in his hands, he won high praise from them.   84

He took their money without case or docket,
    and let them go. He was in all his dealings
    no petty bursar, but a kingly pocket.   87

With him, his endless crony in the fosse,
    is Don Michel Zanche of Logodoro;
    they babble about Sardinia without pause.   90

But look! See that fiend grinning at your side!
    There is much more that I should like to tell you,
    but oh, I think he means to grate my hide!"   93

But their grim sergeant wheeled, sensing foul play,
    and turning on Cramper, who seemed set to strike,
    ordered: "Clear off, you buzzard. Clear off, I say!"   96

"If either of you would like to see and hear
    Tuscans or Lombards," the pale sinner said,
    "I can lure them out of hiding if you'll stand clear   99

and let me sit here at the edge of the ditch,
    and get all these Blacktalons out of sight;
    for while they're here, no one will leave the pitch.   102

In exchange for myself, I can fish you up as pretty
    a mess of souls as you like. I have only to whistle
    the way we do when one of us gets free."   105

Deaddog raised his snout as he listened to him;
    then, shaking his head, said, "Listen to the grafter
    spinning his tricks so he can jump from the brim!"   111

And the sticky wretch, who was all treachery:
    "Oh I am more than tricky when there's a chance
    to see my friends in greater misery."   114

Hellken, against the will of all the crew,
    could hold no longer. "If you jump," he said
    to the scheming wretch, "I won't come after you   117

at a gallop, but like a hawk after a mouse.
    We'll clear the edge and hide behind the bank:
    let's see if you're trickster enough for all of us."   120

Reader, here is new game! The Fiends withdrew
    from the bank's edge, and Deaddog, who at first
    was most against it, led the savage crew.   123

The Navarrese chose his moment carefully:
    and planting both his feet against the ground,
    he leaped, and in an instant he was free.   126

The Fiends were stung with shame, and of the lot
    Hellken most, who had been the cause of it.
    He leaped out madly bellowing: "You're caught!"   129

but little good it did him; terror pressed
    harder than wings; the sinner dove from sight
    and the fiend in full flight had to raise his breast.   132

A duck, when the falcon dives, will disappear
    exactly so, all in a flash, while he
    returns defeated and weary up the air.   135

Grizzly, in a rage at the sinner's flight,
    flew after Hellken, hoping the wraith would escape,
    so he might find an excuse to start a fight.   138

And as soon as the grafter sank below the pitch,
    Grizzly turned his talons against Hellken,
    locked with him claw to claw above the ditch.   141

But Hellken was sparrowhawk enough for two
    and clawed him well; and ripping one another,
    they plunged together into the hot stew.   144

The heat broke up the brawl immediately,
    but their wings were smeared with pitch and they
                          could not rise.
    Curlybeard, upset as his company,   147

commanded four to fly to the other coast
    at once with all their grapples. At top speed
    the Fiends divided, each one to his post.   150

Some on the near edge, some along the far,
they stretched their hooks out to the clotted pair
who were already cooked deep through the scar   153

of their first burn. And turning to one side
we slipped off, leaving them thus occupied.

Notes

4. *Aretines*: The people of Arezzo. In 1289 the Guelphs of Florence and Lucca defeated the Ghibellines of Arrezo at Campaldino. Dante was present with the Guelphs, though probably as an observer and not as a warrior.

5–6. *tourney . . . tilts*: A tourney was contested by groups of knights in a field; a tilt by individuals who tried to unhorse one another across a barrier.

7. *bells*: The army of each town was equipped with a chariot on which bells were mounted. Signals could be given by the bells and special decorations made the chariot stand out in battle. It served therefore as a rallying point.

8. *signals from a castle*: When troops were in sight of their castle their movements could be directed from the towers—by banners in daytime and by fires at night, much as some naval signals are still given today.

19–21. *dolphins, etc.*: It was a common belief that when dolphins began to leap around a ship they were warning the sailors of an approaching storm.

31 ff. *The Navarrese grafter*: His own speech tells all that is known about him. The recital could serve as a description of many a courtier. Thibault II was King of Navarre, a realm that lay in what is now northern Spain.

54. *and I account*: Dante's irony is certainly intentional: the accounts of the Grafters can not be concealed from God's Justice.

66. *Italians*: Dante uses the term *Latino* strictly speaking, a person from the area of ancient Latium, now (roughly) Lazio, the province in which Rome is located. It was against the Latians that Aeneas fought on coming to Italy. More generally, Dante uses the term for any southern Italian. Here, however, the usage seems precise, since the sinner refers to "points near by" and means Sardinia. Rome is the point in Italy closest to Sardinia.

82. *Friar Gomita of Gallura* (GHAW-mee-ta): In 1300 Sardinia was a Pisan possession, and was divided into four districts, of which Galluria was the northeast. Friar Gomita administered Gallura for his own considerable profit. He was hanged by the Pisan governor when he was found guilty of taking bribes to let prisoners escape.

89. *Michel Zanche of Logodoro* (Mee-KELL ZAHN-keh): He was made Vicar of Logodoro when the King of Sardinia went off to war. The King was captured and did not return. Michel maneuvered a divorce for the Queen and married her himself. About 1290 he was murdered by his son-in-law, Branca d'Oria (see Canto XXXIII).

Canto XXIII

The Hypocrites

The Poets are pursued by the Fiends and escape them by sliding down the sloping bank of the next pit. They are now in the *Sixth Bolgia*. Here the *Hypocrites*, weighted down by great leaden robes, walk eternally round and round a narrow track. The robes are brilliantly gilded on the outside and are shaped like a monk's habit, for the hypocrite's outward appearance shines brightly and passes for holiness, but under that show lies the terrible weight of his deceit which the soul must bear through all eternity.

The Poets talk to *Two Jovial Friars* and come upon *Caiaphas*, the chief sinner of that place. Caiaphas was the High Priest of the Jews who counseled the Pharisees to crucify Jesus in the name of public expedience. He is punished by being himself crucified to the floor of Hell by three great stakes, and in such a position that every passing sinner must walk upon him. Thus he must suffer upon his own body the weight of all the world's hypocrisy, as Christ suffered upon his body the pain of all the world's sins.

The Jovial Friars tell Virgil how he may climb from the pit, and Virgil discovers that Malacoda lied to him about the bridges over the Sixth Bolgia.

Silent, apart, and unattended we went
    as Minor Friars go when they walk abroad,
    one following the other. The incident   3

recalled the fable of the Mouse and the Frog
    that Aesop tells. For compared attentively
    point by point, "pig" is no closer to "hog"   6

than the one case to the other. And as one thought
    springs from another, so the comparison
    gave birth to a new concern, at which I caught   9

my breath in fear. This thought ran through my mind:
    "These Fiends, through us, have been made ridiculous,
    and have suffered insult and injury of a kind   12

to make them smart. Unless we take good care—
    now rage is added to their natural spleen—
    they will hunt us down as greyhounds hunt the
                        hare."   15

Already I felt my scalp grow tight with fear.
    I was staring back in terror as I said:
    "Master, unless we find concealment here   18

and soon, I dread the rage of the Fiends: already
    they are yelping on our trail: I imagine them
    so vividly I can hear them now." And he: 21

"Were I a pane of leaded glass, I could not
summon your outward look more instantly
into myself, than I do your inner thought.   24

Your fears were mixed already with my own
with the same suggestion and the same dark look;
so that of both I form one resolution: 27

the right bank may be sloping: in that case
we may find some way down to the next pit
and so escape from the imagined chase."   30

He had not finished answering me thus
when, not far off, their giant wings outspread,
I saw the Fiends come charging after us.   33

Seizing me instantly in his arms, my Guide—
like a mother wakened by a midnight noise
to find a wall of flame at her bedside   36

(who takes her child and runs, and more concerned
for him than for herself, does not pause even
to throw a wrap about her) raised me, turned,   39

and down the rugged bank from the high summit
flung himself down supine onto the slope
which walls the upper side of the next pit.   42

Water that turns the great wheel of a land-mill
never ran faster through the end of a sluice
at the point nearest the paddles—as down that hill   45

my Guide and Master bore me on his breast,
as if I were not a companion, but a son.
And the soles of his feet had hardly come to rest   48

on the bed of the depth below, when on the height
we had just left, the Fiends beat their great wings.
But now they gave my Guide no cause for fright;   51

for the Providence that gave them the fifth pit
to govern as the ministers of Its will,
takes from their souls the power of leaving it.   54

About us now in the depth of the pit we found
a painted people, weary and defeated.
Slowly, in pain, they paced it round and round.   57

All wore great cloaks cut to as ample a size
as those worn by the Benedictines of Cluny.
The enormous hoods were drawn over their eyes.   60

The outside is all dazzle, golden and fair;
the inside, lead, so heavy that Frederick's capes,
compared to these, would seem as light as air.   63

O weary mantle for eternity!
  We turned to the left again along their course,
  listening to their moans of misery, 66

but they moved so slowly down that barren strip,
  tired by their burden, that our company
  was changed at every movement of the hip. 69

And walking thus, I said: "As we go on,
  may it please you to look about among these people
  for any whose name or history may be known." 72

And one who understood Tuscan cried to us there
  as we hurried past: "I pray you check your speed,
  you who run so fast through the sick air: 75

it may be I am one who will fit your case."
  And at his words my Master turned and said:
  "Wait now, then go with him at his own pace." 78

I waited there, and saw along that track
  two souls who seemed in haste to be with me;
  but the narrow way and their burden held them back. 81

When they had reached me down that narrow way
  they stared at me in silence and amazement,
  then turned to one another, I heard one say: 84

"This one seems, by the motion of his throat,
  to be alive; and if they are dead, how is it
  they are allowed to shed the leaden coat?" 87

And then to me "O Tuscan, come so far
  to the college of the sorry hypocrites,
  do not disdain to tell us who you are." 90

And I: "I was born and raised a Florentine
  on the green and lovely banks of Arno's waters,
  I go with the body that was always mine. 93

But who are *you*, who sighing as you go
  distill in floods of tears that drown your cheeks?
  What punishment is this that glitters so?" 96

"These burnished robes are of thick lead," said one,
  "and are hung on us like counterweights, so heavy
  that we, their weary fulcrums, creak and groan. 99

Jovial Friars and Bolognese were we.
  We were chosen jointly by your Florentines
  to keep the peace, an office usually 102

held by a single man; near the Gardingo
  one still may see the sort of peace we kept.
  I was called Catalano, he, Loderingo." 105

I began: "O Friars, your evil . . ."—and then I saw
a figure crucified upon the ground
by three great stakes, and I fell still in awe.   108

When he saw me there, he began to puff great sighs
into his beard, convulsing all his body;
and Friar Catalano, following my eyes,   111

said to me: "That one nailed across the road
counselled the Pharisees that it was fitting
one man be tortured for the public good.   114

Naked he lies fixed there, as you see,
in the path of all who pass; there he must feel
the weight of all through all eternity.   117

His father-in-law and the others of the Council
which was a seed of wrath to all the Jews,
are similarly staked for the same evil."   120

Then I saw Virgil marvel for a while
over that soul so ignominiously
stretched on the cross in Hell's eternal exile.   123

Then, turning, he asked the Friar: "If your law permit,
can you tell us if somewhere along the right
there is some gap in the stone wall of the pit   126

through which we two may climb to the next brink
without the need of summoning the Black Angels
and forcing them to raise us from this sink?"   129

He: "Nearer than you hope, there is a bridge
that runs from the great circle of the scarp
and crosses every ditch from ridge to ridge,   132

except that in this it is broken; but with care
you can mount the ruins which lie along the slope
and make a heap on the bottom." My Guide stood there 135

motionless for a while with a dark look.
At last he said: "He lied about this business,
who spears the sinners yonder with his hook."   138

And the Friar: "Once at Bologna I heard the wise
discussing the Devil's sins; among them I heard
that he is a liar and the father of lies."   141

When the sinner had finished speaking, I saw the face
of my sweet Master darken a bit with anger:
he set off at a great stride from that place,   144

and I turned from that weighted hypocrite
to follow in the prints of his dear feet.

Notes

4. *the fable of the Mouse and the Frog*: The fable was not by Aesop, but was attributed to him in Dante's time: A mouse comes to a body of water and wonders how to cross. A frog, thinking to drown the mouse, offers to ferry him, but the mouse is afraid he will fall off. The frog thereupon suggests that the mouse tie himself to one of the frog's feet. In this way they start across, but in the middle the frog dives from under the mouse, who struggles desperately to stay afloat while the frog tries to pull him under. A hawk sees the mouse struggling and swoops down and seizes him; but since the frog is tied to the mouse, it too is carried away, and so both of them are devoured.

6. *point by point*: The mouse would be the Navarrese Grafter. The frog would be the two fiends, Grizzly and Hellken. By seeking to harm the Navarrese they came to grief themselves.

22. *a pane of leaded glass*: A mirror. Mirrors were backed with lead in Dante's time.

43. *land-mill*: As distinguished from the floating mills common in Dante's time and up to the advent of the steam engine. These were built on rafts that were anchored in the swift-flowing rivers of Northern Italy.

44–45. *ran faster . . . at the point nearest the paddles*: The sharp drop of the sluice makes the water run fastest at the point at which it hits the wheel.

59. *the Benedictines of Cluny*: The habit of these monks was especially ample and elegant. St. Bernard once wrote ironically to a nephew who had entered this monastery: "If length of sleeves and amplitude of hood made for holiness, what could hold me back from following [your lead]."

62. *Frederick's capes*: Frederick II executed persons found guilty of treason by fastening them into a sort of leaden shell. The doomed man was then placed in a cauldron over a fire and the lead was melted around him.

68–9. *our company was changed, etc.*: Another tremendous Dantean figure. Sense: "They moved so slowly that at every step (movement of the hip) we found ourselves beside new sinners."

100. *Jovial Friars*: A nickname given to the military monks of the order of the Glorious Virgin Mary founded at Bologna in 1261. Their original aim was to serve as peacemakers, enforcers of order, and protectors of the weak, but their observance of their rules became so scandalously lax, and their management of worldly affairs so self-seeking, that the order was disbanded by Papal decree.

101–2. *We were chosen jointly . . . to keep the peace*: Catalano dei Malavoti (c. 1210–1285), a Guelph, and Loderingo degli Andolo (c. 1210–1293), a Ghibelline, were both Bolognese and, as brothers of the Jovial Friars, both had served as *podestà* (the chief officer charged with keeping the peace) of many cities for varying terms. In 1266 they were jointly appointed to the office of *podestà* of Florence on the theory that a bipartisan administration by men of God would bring peace to the city. Their tenure of office was marked by great violence, however; and they were forced to leave in a matter of months. Modern scholarship has established the fact that they served as instruments of Clement IV's policy in Florence, working at his orders to overthrow the Ghibellines under the guise of an impartial administration.

103. *Gardingo*: The site of the palace of the Ghibelline family degli Uberti. In the riots resulting from the maladministration of the two Jovial Friars, the Ghibellines were forced out of the city and the Uberti palace was razed.

107 ff. *a figure crucified upon the ground*: Caiaphas. His words were: "It is expedient that one man shall die for the people and that the whole nation perish not." (*John* xi, 50).

118. *his father-in-law and the others*: Annas, father-in-law of Caiaphas, was the first before whom Jesus was led upon his arrest. (*John* xviii, 13). He had Jesus bound and delivered to Caiaphas.

121. *I saw Virgil marvel*: Caiaphas had not been there on Virgil's first descent into Hell.

137–38. *he lied . . . who spears the sinners yonder*: Malacoda.

143. *darken a bit*: The original is *turbatao un poco d'ira*. A bit of anger befits the righteous indignation of Human Reason, but immoderate anger would be out of character. One of the sublimities of Dante's writing is the way in which even the smallest details reinforce the great concepts.

Canto XXIV

The Poets climb the right bank laboriously, cross the bridge of the *Seventh Bolgia* and descend the far bank to observe the Thieves. They find the pit full of monstrous reptiles who curl themselves about the sinners like living coils of rope, binding each sinner's hands behind his back, and knotting themselves through the loins. Other reptiles dart about the place, and the Poets see one of them fly through the air and pierce the jugular vein of one sinner who immediately bursts into flames until only ashes remain. From the ashes the sinner reforms painfully.

These are Dante's first observations of the Thieves and will be carried further in the next Canto, but the first allegorical retribution is immediately apparent. Thievery is reptilian in its secrecy; therefore it is punished by reptiles. The hands of the thieves are the agents of their crimes; therefore they are bound forever. And as the thief destroys his fellowmen by making their substance disappear, so is he painfully destroyed and made to disappear, not once but over and over again.

The sinner who has risen from his own ashes reluctantly identifies himself as *Vanni Fucci.* He tells his story, and to revenge himself for having been forced to reveal his identity he utters a dark prophecy against Dante.

> In the turning season of the youthful year,
>   when the sun is warming his rays beneath Aquarius
>   and the days and nights already begin to near   3
>
> their perfect balance; the hoar-frost copies then
>   the image of his white sister on the ground,
>   but the first sun wipes away the work of his pen.   6
>
> The peasants who lack fodder then arise
>   and look about and see the fields all white,
>   and hear their lambs bleat; then they smite their
>   thighs,   9
>
> go back into the house, walk here and there,
>   pacing, fretting, wondering what to do,
>   then come out doors again, and there, despair   12
>
> falls from them when they see how the earth's face
>   has changed in so little time, and they take their staffs
>   and drive their lambs to feed—so in that place   15
>
> when I saw my Guide and Master's eyebrows lower,
>   my spirits fell and I was sorely vexed;
>   and as quickly came the plaster to the sore: 18
>
> for when he had reached the ruined bridge, he stood
>   and turned on me that sweet and open look
>   with which he had greeted me in the dark wood.   21

When he had paused and studied carefully
    the heap of stones, he seemed to reach some plan,   24
    for he turned and opened his arms and lifted me.

Like one who works and calculates ahead,
    and is always ready for what happens next—
    so, raising me above that dismal bed   27

to the top of one great slab of the fallen slate,
    he chose another saying: "Climb here, but first
    test it to see if it will hold your weight."   30

It was no climb for a lead-hung hypocrite:
    for scarcely we—he light and I assisted—
    could crawl handhold by handhold from the pit;   33

and were it not that the bank along this side
    was lower than the one down which we had slid,
    I at least—I will not speak for my Guide—   36

would have turned back. But as all of the vast rim
    of Malebolge leans toward the lowest well,
    so each succeeding valley and each brim   39

is lower than the last. We climbed the face
    and arrived by great exertion to the point
    where the last rock had fallen from its place.   42

My lungs were pumping as if they could not stop;
    I thought I could not go on, and I sat exhausted
    the instant I had clambered to the top.   45

"Up on your feet! This is no time to tire!"
    my Master cried. "The man who lies asleep
    will never waken fame, and his desire   48

and all his life drift past him like a dream,
    and the traces of his memory fade from time
    like smoke in air, or ripples on a stream.   51

Now, therefore, rise. Control your breath, and call
    upon the strength of soul that wins all battles
    unless it sink in the gross body's fall.   54

There is a longer ladder yet to climb:
    this much is not enough. If you understand me,
    show that you mean to profit from your time."   57

I rose and made my breath appear more steady
    than it really was, and I replied: "Lead on
    as it pleases you to go: I am strong and ready."   60

We picked our way up the cliff, a painful climb,
    for it was narrower, steeper, and more jagged
    than any we had crossed up to that time.   63

I moved along, talking to hide my faintness,
 when a voice that seemed unable to form words
 rose from the depths of the next chasm's darkness.   66

I do not know what it said, though by then the Sage
 had led me to the top of the next arch;
 but the speaker seemed in a tremendous rage.   69

I was bending over the brim, but living eyes
 could not plumb to the bottom of that dark;
 therefore I said, "Master, let me advise   72

that we cross over and climb down the wall:
 for just as I hear the voice without understanding,
 so I look down and make out nothing at all."   75

"I make no other answer than the act,"
 the Master said: "the only fit reply
 to a fit request is silence and the fact."   78

So we moved down the bridge to the stone pier
 that shores the end of the arch on the eighth bank,
 and there I saw the chasm's depths made clear;   81

and there great coils of serpents met my sight,
 so hideous a mass that even now
 the memory makes my blood run cold with fright.   84

Let Libya boast no longer, for though its sands
 breed chelidrids, jaculi, and phareans,
 cenchriads, and two-headed amphisbands,   87

it never bred such a variety
 of vipers, no, not with all Ethiopia
 and all the lands that lie by the Red Sea.   90

Amid that swarm, naked and without hope,
 people ran terrified, not even dreaming
 of a hole to hide in, or of heliotrope.   93

Their hands were bound behind by coils of serpents
 which thrust their heads and tails between the loins
 and bunched in front, a mass of knotted torments.   96

One of the damned came racing round a boulder,
 and as he passed us, a great snake shot up
 and bit him where the neck joins with the shoulder.   99

No mortal pen—however fast it flash
 over the page—could write down *o* or *i*
 as quickly as he flamed and fell in ash;   102

and when he was dissolved into a heap
 upon the ground, the dust rose of itself
 and immediately resumed its former shape.   105

Precisely so, philosophers declare,
  the Phoenix dies and then is born again
  when it approaches its five hundredth year.   108

It lives on tears of balsam and of incense;
  in all its life it eats no herb or grain,
  and nard and precious myrrh sweeten its cerements.   111

And as a person fallen in a fit,
  possessed by a Demon or some other seizure
  that fetters him without his knowing it,   114

struggles up to his feet and blinks his eyes
  (still stupefied by the great agony
  he has just passed), and, looking round him, sighs—   117

such was the sinner when at last he rose.
  O Power of God! How dreadful is Thy will
  which in its vengeance rains such fearful blows.   120

Then my Guide asked him who he was. And he
  answered reluctantly: "Not long ago
  I rained into this gullet from Tuscany.   123

I am Vanni Fucci, the beast. A mule among men,
  I chose the bestial life above the human.
  Savage Pistoia was my fitting den."   126

And I to my Guide: "Detain him a bit longer
  and ask what crime it was that sent him here;
  I knew him as a man of blood and anger."   129

The sinner, hearing me, seemed discomforted,
  but he turned and fixed his eyes upon my face
  with a look of dismal shame; at length he said: 132

"That you have found me out among the strife
  and misery of this place, grieves my heart more
  than did the day that cut me from my life.   135

But I am forced to answer truthfully:
  I am put down so low because it was I
  who stole the treasure from the Sacristy,   138

for which others once were blamed. But that you may
  find less to gloat about if you escape here,
  prick up your ears and listen to what I say: 141

First Pistoia is emptied of the Black,
  then Florence changes her party and her laws.
  From Valdimagra the God of War brings back   144

a fiery vapor wrapped in turbid air:
  then in a storm of battle at Piceno
  the vapor breaks apart the mist, and there   147

every White shall feel his wounds anew.
  And I have told you this that it may grieve you."

Notes

2. *Aquarius*: The zodiacal sign for the period from January 21 to February 21. The sun is moving north then to approach the vernal equinox (March 21), at which point the days and the nights are equal. The Italian spring comes early, and the first warm days would normally occur under Aquarius.

4. *hoar-frost copies then*: The hoar-frost looks like snow but melts away as soon as the sun strikes it.

7–15. *the peasants, etc.*: A fine example of Dante's ability to build dramatic equivalents for the emotion he wishes to convey.

9. *they smite their thighs*: A common Italian gesture of vexation, about equivalent to smiting the forehead with the palm of the hand.

34–5. *the bank along this side was lower*: See diagram, Canto XIX.

55. *there is a longer ladder yet to climb*: Many allegorical possibilities are obvious here. The whole ascent of Purgatory lies ahead, Virgil points out, and here Dante seems exhausted simply in climbing away from (renouncing) hypocrisy. Further, the descent into Hell is symbolic of the recognition of sin, and the ascent of purgatory of the purification from sin. The ascent is by far the more arduous task.

61. *a painful climb*: The "top" Dante mentions in line 45 must obviously have been the top of the fallen stone that was once the bridge. There remains the difficult climb up the remainder of the cliff.

85–90. *Libya . . . Ethiopia . . . lands that lie by the Red Sea*: The desert areas of the Mediterranean shores. Lucan's *Pharsalia* describes the assortment of monsters listed here by Dante. I have rendered their names from Latin to English jabberwocky to avoid problems of pronunciation. In Lucan *chelydri* make their trails smoke and burn, they are amphibious; *jaculi* fly through the air like darts piercing what they hit; *pharese* plow the ground with their tails; *cenchri* waver from side to side when they move; and *amphisboenae* have a head at each end.

93. *heliotrope*: Not the flower, but the bloodstone, a spotted chalcedony. It was believed to make the wearer invisible.

107. *the Phoenix*: The fabulous Phoenix of Arabia was the only one of its kind in the world. Every five hundred years it built a nest of spices and incense which took fire from the heat of the sun and the beating of the Phoenix's wings. The Phoenix was thereupon cremated and was then reborn from its ashes.

123. *this gullet*: Dante often gives an animate force to the ledges of Hell. The place in which the sinner is punished possesses him as if it were a living force. It should be remembered that, on one level of the allegory, Hell is every sinner's own guilty conscience.

124. *Vanni Fucci* (VAH-nee FOO-tchee): The bastard son of Fuccio de Lazzeri, a nobleman (Black) of Pistoia. In 1293 with two accomplices he stole the treasure of San Jacopo in the Duomo of San Zeno. Others were accused, and one man spent a year in jail on this charge before the guilty persons were discovered. Vanni Fucci had escaped from Pistoia by then, but his accomplices were convicted.

129. *a man of blood and anger*: Dante (the traveler within the narrative rather than Dante the author) claims that he did not know Fucci was a thief, but only that he was a man of blood and violence. He should therefore be punished in the Seventh Circle.

142 ff. *Vanni Fucci's prophecy*: In May of 1301 the Whites of Florence joined with the Whites of Pistoia to expel the Pistoian Blacks and destroy their houses. The ejected Blacks fled to Florence and joined forces with the Florentine Blacks. On November 1st of the same year, Charles of Valois took Florence and helped the Blacks drive out the Whites. Piceno was the scene of a battle in which the Blacks of Florence and Lucca combined in 1302 to capture Serravalle, a White strong point near Pistoia.

Dante's meteorological figure is based on the contemporary belief that electric storms were caused by a conflict between "fiery vapors" and the preponderant "watery vapors." By their contraries the watery vapors (mist) surround the fiery vapors, seeking to extinguish them, and the fiery vapors combat to shatter the mist. Here the fiery vapor is the Blacks and the shattered mist is the Whites.

Canto XXV

The Thieves

Vanni's rage mounts to the point where he hurls an ultimate obscenity at God, and the serpents immediately swarm over him, driving him off in great pain. The Centaur, *Cacus*, his back covered with serpents and a fire-eating dragon, also gives chase to punish the wretch.

Dante then meets *Five Noble Thieves of Florence* and sees the further retribution visited upon the sinners. Some of the thieves appear first in human form, others as reptiles. All but one of them suffer a painful trans-formation before Dante's eyes. Agnello appears in human form and is merged with *Cianfa*, who appears as a six-legged lizard. *Buoso* appears as a man and changes form with *Francesco*, who first appears as a tiny reptile. Only *Puccio Sciancato* remains unchanged, though we are made to under-stand that his turn will come.

For endless and painful transformation is the final state of the thieves. In life they took the substance of others, transforming it into their own. So in Hell their very bodies are constantly being taken from them, and they are left to steal back a human form from some other sinner. Thus they waver constantly between man and reptile, and no sinner knows what to call his own.

> When he had finished, the thief—to his disgrace—
> raised his hands with both fists making figs,
> and cried: "Here, God! I throw them in your face!"　　3
>
> Thereat the snakes became my friends, for one
> coiled itself about the wretch's neck
> as if it were saying: "You shall not go on!"　　6
>
> and another tied his arms behind him again,
> knotting its head and tail between his loins
> so tight he could not move a finger in pain.　　9
>
> Pistoia! Pistoia! why have you not decreed
> to turn yourself to ashes and end your days,
> rather than spread the evil of your seed!　　12
>
> In all of Hell's corrupt and sunken halls
> I found no shade so arrogant toward God,
> not even him who fell from the Theban walls!　　15
>
> Without another word, he fled; and there
> I saw a furious Centaur race up, roaring:
> "Where is the insolent blasphemer? Where?"　　18
>
> I do not think as many serpents swarm
> in all the Maremma as he bore on his back
> from the haunch to the first sign of our human form.　　21
>
> Upon his shoulders, just behind his head
> a snorting dragon whose hot breath set fire
> to all it touched, lay with its wings outspread.　　24

My Guide said: "That is Cacus. Time and again
in the shadow of Mount Aventine he made
a lake of blood upon the Roman plain.   27

He does not go with his kin by the blood-red fosse
because of the cunning fraud with which he stole
the cattle of Hercules. And thus it was   30

his thieving stopped, for Hercules found his den
and gave him perhaps a hundred blows with his club,
and of them he did not feel the first ten."   33

Meanwhile, the Centaur passed along his way,
and three wraiths came. Neither my Guide nor I
knew they were there until we heard them say: 36

"You there—who are you?" There our talk fell still
and we turned to stare at them. I did not know them,
but by chance it happened, as it often will,   39

one named another. "Where is Cianfa?" he cried;
"Why has he fallen back?" I placed a finger
across my lips as a signal to my Guide.   42

Reader, should you doubt what next I tell,
it will be no wonder, for though I saw it happen,
I can scarce believe it possible, even in Hell.   45

For suddenly, as I watched, I saw a lizard
come darting forward on six great taloned feet
and fasten itself to a sinner from crotch to gizzard.   48

Its middle feet sank in the sweat and grime
of the wretch's paunch, its forefeet clamped his arms,
its teeth bit through both cheeks. At the same time   51

its hind feet fastened on the sinner's thighs:
its tail thrust through his legs and closed its coil
over his loins. I saw it with my own eyes!   54

No ivy ever grew about a tree
as tightly as that monster wove itself
limb by limb about the sinner's body;   57

they fused like hot wax, and their colors ran
together until neither wretch nor monster
appeared what he had been when he began: 60

just so, before the running edge of the heat
on a burning page, a brown discoloration
changes to black as the white dies from the sheet.   63

The other two cried out as they looked on:
"Alas! Alas! Agnello, how you change!
Already you are neither two nor one!"   66

The two heads had already blurred and blended;
  now two new semblances appeared and faded,
  one face where neither face began nor ended.   69

From the four upper limbs of man and beast
  two arms were made, then members never seen
  grew from the thighs and legs, belly and breast.   72

Their former likenesses mottled and sank
  to something that was both of them and neither;
  and so transformed, it slowly left our bank.   75

As lizards at high noon of a hot day
  dart out from hedge to hedge, from shade to shade,
  and flash like lightning when they cross the way,   78

so toward the bowels of the other two,
  shot a small monster; livid, furious,
  and black as a pepper corn. Its lunge bit through   81

that part of one of them from which man receives
  his earliest nourishment; then it fell back
  and lay sprawled out in front of the two thieves.   84

Its victim stared at it but did not speak:
  indeed, he stood there like a post, and yawned
  as if lack of sleep, or a fever, had left him weak.   87

The reptile stared at him, he at the reptile;
  from the wound of one and from the other's mouth
  two smokes poured out and mingled, dark and vile.   90

Now let Lucan be still with his history
  of poor Sabellus and Nassidius,
  and wait to hear what next appeared to me.   93

Of Cadmus and Arethusa be Ovid silent.
  I have no need to envy him those verses
  where he makes one a fountain, and one a serpent: 96

for he never transformed two beings face to face
  in such a way that both their natures yielded
  their elements each to each, as in this case.   99

Responding sympathetically to each other,
  the reptile cleft his tail into a fork,
  and the wounded sinner drew his feet together.   102

The sinner's legs and thighs began to join:
  they grew together so, that soon no trace
  of juncture could be seen from toe to loin.   105

Point by point the reptile's cloven tail
  grew to the form of what the sinner lost;
  one skin began to soften, one to scale.   108

The armpits swallowed the arms, and the short shank
  of the reptile's forefeet simultaneously
  lengthened by as much as the man's arms shrank.   111

Its hind feet twisted round themselves and grew
  the member man conceals; meanwhile the wretch
  from his one member generated two.   114

The smoke swelled up about them all the while:
  it tanned one skin and bleached the other; it stripped
  the hair from the man and grew it on the reptile.   117

While one fell to his belly, the other rose
  without once shifting the locked evil eyes
  below which they changed snouts as they changed pose.   120

The face of the standing one drew up and in
  toward the temples, and from the excess matter
  that gathered there, ears grew from the smooth skin;   123

while of the matter left below the eyes
  the excess became a nose, at the same time
  forming the lips to an appropriate size.   126

Here the face of the prostrate felon slips,
  sharpens into a snout, and withdraws its ears
  as a snail pulls in its horns. Between its lips   129

the tongue, once formed for speech, thrusts out a fork;
  the forked tongue of the other heals and draws
  into his mouth. The smoke has done its work.   132

The soul that had become a beast went flitting
  and hissing over the stones, and after it
  the other walked along talking and spitting.   135

Then turning his new shoulders, said to the one
  that still remained: "It is Buoso's turn to go
  crawling along this road as I have done."   138

Thus did the ballast of the seventh hold
  shift and reshift; and may the strangeness of it
  excuse my pen if the tale is strangely told.   141

And though all this confused me, they did not flee
  so cunningly but what I was aware
  that it was Puccio Sciancato alone of the three   144

that first appeared, who kept his old form still.
  The other was he for whom you weep, Gaville.

Notes

THE FIVE NOBLE THIEVES OF FLORENCE

Dante's concise treatment and the various transformations which the thieves undergo may lead to some confusion. It is worth noting that none of these thieves is important as an individual, and, in fact, that very little is known of the lives of these sinners beyond the sufficient fact that they were thieves.

The first three appear in line 35 and hail the Poets rather insolently. They are Agnello Brunelleschi (Ah-NYELL-oh Broo-nell-AY-skee), Buoso (BWOE-soe) degli Abati, and Puccio Sciancato. They have been walking along with Cianfa de' Donati (TCHAHN-fa day Don-AH-tee), but they suddenly miss him and ask about him with some concern. The careful reader will sense that a sudden disappearance is cause for very special concern in this *bolgia*, and sure enough, Cianfa suddenly reappears in the form of a six-legged lizard. His body has been taken from him and he is driven by a consuming desire to be rid of his reptilian form as fast as possible. He immediately fixes himself upon Agnello and merges his lizard body with Agnello's human form. (A possible symbolic interpretation is that Cianfa is dividing the pains of Hell with a fellow thief, as on earth he might have divided the loot.)

Immediately after Cianfa and Agnello go off together, a tiny reptile bites Buoso degli Abati and exchanges forms with him. The reptile is Francesco dei Cavalcanti. (Here the symbolism is obvious: the thieves must steal from one another the very shapes in which they appear.)

Thus only Puccio Sciancato (POO-tchoe Shahn-KAH-toe) is left unchanged for the time being.

2. *figs*: An obscene gesture made by closing the hand into a fist with the thumb protruding between the first and second fingers. The fig is an ancient symbol for the vulva, and the protruding thumb is an obvious phallic symbol. The gesture is still current in Italy and has lost none of its obscene significance since Dante's time.

25. *Cacus*: The son of Vulcan. He lived in a cave at the foot of Mount Aventine, from which he raided the herds of the cattle of Hercules, which pastured on the Roman plain. Hercules clubbed him to death for this thievery, beating him in rage long after he was dead. Cacus is condemned to the lower pit for his greater crime, instead of guarding Phlegethon with his brother centaurs. Virgil, however, did not describe him as a Centaur (V. *Aeneid* VIII, 193–267). Dante's interpretation of him is probably based on the fact that Virgil referred to him as "half-human."

82. *that part*: The navel.

91 ff. *let Lucan be still, etc.*: In *Pharsalia* (IX, 761 ff.) Lucan relates how Sabellus and Nassidius, two soldiers of the army Cato led across the Libyan desert, were bitten by monsters. Sabellus melted into a puddle and Nassidius swelled until he popped his coat of mail. In his *Metamorphoses*, Ovid wrote how Cadmus was changed into a serpent (IV, 562–603) and how Arethusa was changed into a fountain (V, 572–661).

Dante cites these cases, obviously, that he may boast of how much better he is going to handle the whole matter of transformation. The master knows his own mastery and sees no real point in being modest about it.

146. *he for whom you weep, Gaville*: Francesco dei Cavalcanti. He was killed by the people of Gaville (a village in the Valley of the Arno). His kinsmen rallied immediately to avenge his death, and many of the townsmen of Gaville were killed in the resulting feud.

Canto XXVI

The Evil Counselors

Dante turns from the Thieves toward the Evil Counselors of the next
Bolgia, and between the two he addresses a passionate lament to Florence
prophesying the griefs that will befall her from these two sins. At the purported time of the Vision, it will be recalled, Dante was a Chief Magistrate
of Florence and was forced into exile by men he had reason to consider
both thieves and evil counselors. He seems prompted, in fact, to say much
more on this score, but he restrains himself when he comes in sight of the
sinners of the next Bolgia, for they are a moral symbolism, all men of gift
who abused their genius, perverting it to wiles and stratagems. Seeing them
in Hell he knows his must be another road: his way shall not be by decep-
tion.

So the Poets move on and Dante observes the *Eighth Bolgia* in detail.
Here the *Evil Counselors* move about endlessly, hidden from view inside
great flames. Their sin was to abuse the gifts of the Almighty, to steal his
virtues for low purposes. And as they stole from God in their lives and
worked by hidden ways, so are they stolen from sight and hidden in the
great flames which are their own guilty consciences. And as, in most
instances at least, they sinned by glibness of tongue, so are the flames made
into a fiery travesty of tongues.

Among the others, the Poets see a great doubleheaded flame, and discover that *Ulysses* and *Diomede* are punished together within it. Virgil
addresses the flame, and through its wavering tongue Ulysses narrates an
unforgettable tale of his last voyage and death.

Joy to you, Florence, that your banners swell,
  beating their proud wings over land and sea,
  and that your name expands through all of Hell!   3

Among the thieves I found five who had been
  your citizens, to my shame; nor yet shall you
  mount to great honor peopling such a den!   6

But if the truth is dreamed of toward the morning,
  you soon shall feel what Prato and the others
  wish for you. And were that day of mourning   9

already come it would not be too soon.
  So may it come, since it must! for it will weigh
  more heavily on me as I pass my noon.   12

We left that place. My Guide climbed stone by stone
  the natural stair by which we had descended
  and drew me after him. So we passed on,   15

and going our lonely way through that dead land
  among the crags and crevices of the cliff,
  the foot could make no way without the hand.   18

I mourned among those rocks, and I mourn again
   when memory returns to what I saw:
   and more than usually I curb the strain   21

of my genius, lest it stray from Virtue's course;
   so if some star, or a better thing, grant me merit,
   may I not find the gift cause for remorse.   24

As many fireflies as the peasant sees
   when he rests on a hill and looks into the valley
   (where he tills or gathers grapes or prunes his trees)   27

in that sweet season when the face of him
   who lights the world rides north, and at the hour
   when the fly yields to the gnat and the air grows
                            dim—   30

such myriads of flames I saw shine through
   the gloom of the eighth abyss when I arrived
   at the rim from which its bed comes into view.   33

As he the bears avenged so fearfully
   beheld Elijah's chariot depart—
   the horses rise toward heaven—but could not see   36

more than the flame, a cloudlet in the sky,
   once it had risen—so within the fosse
   only those flames, forever passing by   39

were visible, ahead, to right, to left;
   for though each steals a sinner's soul from view
   not one among them leaves a trace of the theft.   42

I stood on the bridge, and leaned out from the edge;
   so far, that but for a jut of rock I held to
   I should have been sent hurtling from the ledge   45

without being pushed. And seeing me so intent,
   my Guide said: "There are souls within those flames;
   each sinner swathes himself in his own torment."   48

"Master," I said, "your words make me more sure,
   but I had seen already that it was so
   and meant to ask what spirit must endure   51

the pains of that great flame which splits away
   in two great horns, as if it rose from the pyre
   where Eteocles and Polynices lay?"   54

He answered me: "Forever round this path
   Ulysses and Diomede move in such dress,
   united in pain as once they were in wrath;   57

there they lament the ambush of the Horse
   which was the door through which the noble seed
   of the Romans issued from its holy source;   60

there they mourn that for Achilles slain
sweet Deidamia weeps even in death;
there they recall the Palladium in their pain." 63

"Master," I cried, "I pray you and repray
till my prayer becomes a thousand—if these souls
can still speak from the fire, oh let me stay 66

until the flame draws near! Do not deny me:
You see how fervently I long for it!"
And he to me: "Since what you ask is worthy, 69

it shall be. But be still and let me speak;
for I know your mind already, and they perhaps
might scorn your manner of speaking, since they were
Greek." 72

And when the flame had come where time and place
seemed fitting to my Guide, I heard him say
these words to it: "O you two souls who pace 75

together in one flame!—if my days above
won favor in your eyes, if I have earned
however much or little of your love 78

in writing my High Verses, do not pass by,
but let one of you be pleased to tell where he,
having disappeared from the known world, went to die." 81

As if it fought the wind, the greater prong
of the ancient flame began to quiver and hum;
then moving its tip as if it were the tongue 84

that spoke, gave out a voice above the roar.
"When I left Circe," it said, "who more than a year
detained me near Gaeta long before 87

Aeneas came and gave the place that name,
not fondness for my son, nor reverence
for my aged father, nor Penelope's claim 90

to the joys of love, could drive out of my mind
the lust to experience the far-flung world
and the failings and felicities of mankind. 93

I put out on the high and open sea
with a single ship and only those few souls
who stayed true when the rest deserted me. 96

As far as Morocco and as far as Spain
I saw both shores; and I saw Sardinia
and the other islands of the open main. 99

I and my men were stiff and slow with age
when we sailed at last into the narrow pass
where, warning all men back from further voyage, 102

Hercules' Pillars rose upon our sight.
Already I had left Ceuta on the left;
Seville now sank behind me on the right.   105

'Shipmates,' I said, 'who through a hundred thousand
perils have reached the West, do not deny
to the brief remaining watch our senses stand   108

experience of the world beyond the sun.
Greeks! You were not born to live like brutes,
but to press on toward manhood and recognition!   111

With this brief exhortation I made my crew
so eager for the voyage I could hardly
have held them back from it when I was through;   114

and turning our stern toward morning, our bow toward night,
we bore southwest out of the world of man;
we made wings of our oars for our fool's flight.   117

That night we raised the other pole ahead
with all its stars, and ours had so declined
it did not rise out of its ocean bed.   120

Five times since we had dipped our bending oars
beyond the world, the light beneath the moon
had waxed and waned, when dead upon our course   123

we sighted, dark in space, a peak so tall
I doubted any man had seen the like.
Our cheers were hardly sounded, when a squall   126

broke hard upon our bow from the new land:
three times is sucked the ship and the sea about
as it pleased Another to order and command.   129

At the fourth, the poop rose and the bow went down
till the sea closed over us and the light was gone."

Notes

7. *if the truth is dreamed of toward the morning*: A semi-proverbial expression. It was a common belief that those dreams that occur just before waking foretell the future. "Morning" here would equal both "the rude awakening" and the potential "dawn of a new day."

8. *Prato*: Not the neighboring town (which was on good terms with Florence) but Cardinal Niccolò da Prato, papal legate from Benedict XI to Florence. In 1304 he tried to reconcile the warring factions, but found that neither side would accept mediation. Since none would be blessed, he cursed all impartially and laid the city under an interdict (i.e., forbade the offering of the sacraments). Shortly after this rejection by the Church, a bridge collapsed in Florence, and later a great fire broke out. Both disasters cost many lives, and both were promptly attributed to the Papal curse.

34. *he the bears avenged*: Elisha saw Elijah translated to Heaven in a fiery chariot. Later he was mocked by some children, who called out tauntingly that he should "Go up" as Elijah had. Elisha cursed the children in the name of the Lord, and bears came suddenly upon the children and devoured them. (2 *Kings* ii, 11–24.)

53-54. *the pyre where Eteocles and Polynices lay*: Eteocles and Polynices, sons of Oedipus, succeeded jointly to the throne of Thebes, and came to an agreement whereby each one would rule separately for a year at a time. Eteocles ruled the first year and when he refused to surrender the throne at the appointed time, Polynices led the Seven against Thebes in a bloody war. In single combat the two brothers killed one another. Statius (*Thebaid* XII, 429 ff.) wrote that their mutual hatred was so great that when they were placed on the same funeral pyre the very flame of their burning drew apart in two great raging horns.

56-63. *Ulysses and Diomede, etc.*: They suffer here for their joint guilt in counseling and carrying out many stratagems which Dante considered evil, though a narrator who was less passionately a partisan of the Trojans might have thought their actions justifiable methods of warfare. They are in one flame for their joint guilt, but the flame is divided, perhaps to symbolize the moral that men of evil must sooner or later come to a falling out, for there can be no lasting union except by virtue.

Their first sin was the stratagem of the Wooden Horse, as a result of which Troy fell and Aeneas went forth to found the Roman line. The second evil occurred at Scyros. There Ulysses discovered Achilles in female disguise, hidden by his mother, Thetis, so that he would not be taken off to the war. Deidamia was in love with Achilles and had borne him a son. When Ulysses persuaded her lover to sail for Troy, she died of grief. The third count is Ulysses' theft of the sacred statue of Pallas from the Palladium. Upon the statue, it was believed, depended the fate of Troy. Its theft, therefore, would result in Troy's downfall.

72. *since they were Greek*: Dante knew no Greek, and these sinners might scorn him, first, because he spoke what to them would seem a barbarous tongue, and second, because as an Italian he would seem a descendant of Aeneas and the defeated Trojans. Virgil, on the other hand, appeals to them as a man of virtuous life (who therefore has a power over sin) and as a poet who celebrated their earthly fame. (Prof. MacAllister suggests another meaning as well: that Dante [and his world] had no direct knowledge of the Greeks, knowing their works through Latin intermediaries. Thus Virgil stood between Homer and Dante.)

80-81. *one of you*: Ulysses. He is the figure in the larger horn of the flame (which symbolizes that his guilt, as leader, is greater than that of Diomede). His memorable account of his last voyage and death is purely Dante's invention.

86. *Circe*: Changed Ulysses' men to swine and kept him a prisoner, though with rather exceptional accommodations.

87. *Gaeta*: Southeastern Italian coastal town. According to Virgil (*Aeneid*, VII, 1 ff.) it was earlier named Caieta by Aeneas in honor of his aged nurse.

90. *Penelope*: Ulysses' wife.

98. *both shores*: Of the Mediterranean.

101. *narrow pass*: The Straits of Gibraltar, formerly called the Pillars of Hercules. They were presumed to be the Western limit beyond which no man could navigate.

104. *Ceuta*: In Africa, opposite Gibraltar.

105. *Seville*: In Dante's time this was the name given to the general region of Spain. Having passed through the Straits, the men are now in the Atlantic.

115. *morning . . . night*: East and West.

118. *we raised the other pole ahead*: i.e., They drove south across the equator, observed the southern stars, and found that the North Star had sunk below the horizon. The altitude of the North Star is the easiest approximation of latitude. Except for a small correction, it is directly overhead at the North Pole, shows an altitude of 45° at North latitude 45, and is on the horizon at the equator.

124. *a peak*: Purgatory. They sight it after five months of passage. According to Dante's geography, the Northern hemisphere is land and the Southern is all water except for the Mountain of Purgatory which rises above the surface at a point directly opposite Jerusalem.

Canto XXVII

The Evil Counselors

The double flame departs at a word from Virgil and behind it appears
another which contains the soul of *Count Guido da Montefeltro,* a Lord of
Romagna. He had overheard Virgil speaking Italian, and the entire flame in
which his soul is wrapped quivers with his eagerness to hear recent news of
his wartorn country. (As Farinata has already explained, the spirits of the
damned have prophetic powers, but lose all track of events as they
approach.)

Dante replies with a stately and tragic summary of how things stand in
the cities of Romagna. When he has finished, he asked Guido for his story,
and Guido recounts his life, and how Boniface VIII persuaded him to sin.

When it had finished speaking, the great flame
  stood tall and shook no more. Now, as it left us
  with the sweet Poet's license, another came   3

along that track and our attention turned
  to the new flame: a strange and muffled roar
  rose from the single tip to which it burned.   6

As the Sicilian bull—that brazen spit
  which bellowed first (and properly enough)
  with the lament of him whose file had tuned it—   9

was made to bellow by its victim's cries
  in such a way, that though it was of brass,
  it seemed itself to howl and agonize: 12

so lacking any way through or around
  the fire that sealed them in, the mournful words
  were changed into its language. When they found   15

their way up to the tip, imparting to it
  the same vibration given them in their passage
  over the tongue of the concealed sad spirit,   18

we heard it say: "O you at whom I aim
  my voice, and who were speaking Lombard, saying:
  'Go now, I ask no more,' just as I came—   21

though I may come a bit late to my turn,
  may it not annoy you to pause and speak a while:
  you see it does not annoy me—and I burn.   24

If you have fallen only recently
  to this blind world from that sweet Italy
  where I acquired my guilt, I pray you, tell me: 27

is there peace or war in Romagna? for on earth
   I too was of those hills between Urbino
   and the fold from which the Tiber springs to birth."   30

I was still staring at it from the dim
   edge of the pit when my Guide nudged me, saying:
   "This one is Italian: *you* speak to him."   33

My answer was framed already; without pause
   I spoke these words to it: "O hidden soul,
   your sad Romagna is not and never was   36

without war in her tyrants' raging blood;
   but none flared openly when I left just now.
   Ravenna's fortunes stand as they have stood   39

these many years: Polenta's eagles brood
   over her walls, and their pinions cover Cervia.
   The city that so valiantly withstood   42

the French, and raised a mountain of their dead,
   feels the Green Claws again. Still in Verrucchio
   the Aged Mastiff and his Pup, who shed   45

Montagna's blood, raven in their old ranges.
   The cities of Lamone and Santerno
   are led by the white den's Lion, he who changes   48

his politics with the compass. And as the city
   the Savio washes lies between plain and mountain,
   so it lives between freedom and tyranny.   51

Now, I beg you, let us know your name;
   do not be harder than one has been to you;
   so, too, you will preserve your earthly fame."   54

And when the flame had roared a while beneath
   the ledge on which we stood, it swayed its tip
   to and fro, and then gave forth this breath: 57

"If I believed that my reply were made
   to one who could ever climb to the world again,
   this flame would shake no more. But since no shade   60

ever returned—if what I am told is true—
   from this blind world into the living light,
   without fear of dishonor I answer you.   63

I was a man of arms: then took the rope
   of the Franciscans, hoping to make amends:
   and surely I should have won to all my hope   66

but for the Great Priest—may he rot in Hell!—
   who brought me back to all my earlier sins;
   and how and why it happened I wish to tell   69

in my own words: while I was still encased
    in the pulp and bone my mother bore, my deeds
    were not of the lion but of the fox: I raced   72

through tangled ways; all wiles were mine from birth,
    and I won to such advantage with my arts
    that rumor of me reached the ends of the earth.   75

But when I saw before me all the signs
    of the time of life that cautions every man
    to lower his sail and gather in his lines,   78

that which had pleased me once, troubled my spirit,
    and penitent and confessed, I became a monk.
    Alas! What joy I might have had of it!   81

It was then the Prince of the New Pharisees drew
    his sword and marched upon the Lateran—
    and not against the Saracen or the Jew,   84

for every man that stood against his hand
    was a Christian soul: not one had warred on Acre,
    nor been a trader in the Sultan's land.   87

It was he abused his sacred vows and mine:
    his Office and the Cord I wore, which once
    made those it girded leaner. As Constantine   90

sent for Silvestro to cure his leprosy,
    seeking him out among Soracte's cells;
    so this one from his great throne sent for me   93

to cure the fever of pride that burned his blood.
    He demanded my advice, and I kept silent
    for his words seemed drunken to me. So it stood   96

until he said: 'Your soul need fear no wound;
    I absolve your guilt beforehand; and now teach me
    how to smash Penestrino to the ground.   99

The Gates of Heaven, as you know, are mine
    to open and shut, for I hold the two Great Keys
    so easily let go by Celestine.'   102

His weighty arguments led me to fear
    silence was worse than sin. Therefore, I said:
    'Holy Father, since you clean me here   105

of the guilt into which I fall, let it be done:
    long promise and short observance is the road
    that leads to the sure triumph of your throne.'   108

Later, when I was dead, St. Francis came
    to claim my soul, but one of the Black Angels
    said: 'Leave him. Do not wrong me. This one's name   111

went into my book the moment he resolved
to give false counsel. Since then he has been mine,
for who does not repent cannot be absolved;   114

nor can we admit the possibility
of repenting a thing at the same time it is willed,
for the two acts are contradictory.'   117

Miserable me! with what contrition
I shuddered when he lifted me, saying: 'Perhaps
you hadn't heard that I was a logician.'   120

He carried me to Minos: eight times round
his scabby back the monster coiled his tail,
then biting it in rage he pawed the ground   123

and cried: 'This one is for the thievish fire!'
And, as you see, I am lost accordingly,
grieving in heart as I go in this attire."   126

His story told, the flame began to toss
and writhe its horn. And so it left, and we
crossed over to the arch of the next fosse   129

where from the iron treasury of the Lord
the fee of wrath is paid the Sowers of Discord.

Notes

3. *by the sweet Poet's license*: The legend of Virgil as a magician and sorcerer was widespread through the Middle Ages and was probably based on the common belief that his Fourth Eclogue was a specific prophecy of the birth of Christ and of the Christian Era. Some commentators have argued as an extension of this legend that Dante assigns Virgil a magical power of conjuration over the damned, a power of white rather than black magic—that distinction being necessary to save him from damnation. Despite the fact that Dante nowhere makes that distinction himself, this interpretation can be made plausible, but only in the most incidental way. The whole idea of Virgil as a magician is trivial beside Dante's total concept. Virgil's power is divinely given him by Beatrice. That is, it represents Human Reason informed and commanded by Divine Love, a reassertion of a fundamental medieval theme that reason is God's will. His power is most clearly expressed in his words to Minos: "This has been willed where what is willed must be." Only with this light within it, can reason exert its power over evil.

3. *another came*: Guido da Montefeltro (1223–1298). As head of the Ghibellines of Romangna, he was reputed the wisest and cunningest man in Italy.

7. *the Sicilian bull*: In the sixth century B.C. Perillus of Athens constructed for Phalaris, Tyrant of Sicily, a metal bull to be used as an instrument of torture. When victims were placed inside it and roasted to death, their screams passed through certain tuned pipes and emerged as a burlesque bellowing of the bull. Phalaris accepted delivery and showed his gratitude by appointing the inventor the bull's first victim. Later Phalaris was overthrown, and he, too, took his turn inside the bull.

21. *Go now, I ask no more*: These are the words with which Virgil dismisses Ulysses and Diomede, his "license."

29–30. *Urbino and the fold from which the Tiber, etc.*: Romagna is the district that runs south from the Po along the east side of the Apennines. Urbino is due east of Florence and roughly south of Rimini. Between Urbino and Florence rise the Coronaro Mountains which contain the headwaters of the Tiber.

39–41. *Ravenna . . . Polenta's eagles . . . Cervia*: In 1300 Ravenna was ruled by Guido Vecchio da Polenta, father of Francesca da Rimini. His arms bore an eagle and his domain included the small city of Cervia about twelve miles south of Ravenna.

42–44. *The city . . . the Green Claws*: The city is Forli. In 1282 Guido da Monte-feltro defended Forli from the French, but in 1300 it was under the despotic rule of Sinibaldo degli Ordelaffi, whose arms were a green lion.

44–45. *Verrucchio . . . the Aged Mastiff and his Pup . . . Montagna*: Verrucchio (Vehr-OO-Kyoe) was the castle of Malatesta and his son Malatestino, Lords of Rimini, whom Dante calls dogs for their cruelty. Montagna de' Parcitati (Mon-TAH-nyah day Pahr-tchit-AH-tee), the leader of Rimini's Ghibellines, was captured by Malatesta in 1295 and murdered in captivity by Malatestino.

47–48. *Lamone and Santerno . . . the white den's Lion*: Maginardo (Mah-djin-AHR-doe) de' Pagani (died 1302) ruled Faenza, on the River Lamone, and Imola, close by the River Santerno. His arms were a blue lion on a white field (hence "the Lion from the white den"). He supported the Ghibellines in the north, but the Guelphs in the south (Florence), changing his politics according to the direction in which he was facing.

49–50. *the city the Savio washes*: Cesena. It ruled itself for a number of years, but was taken over by Malatestino in 1314. It lies between Forli and Rimini.

67. *the Great Priest*: Boniface VIII, so called as Pope.

82. *the Prince of the New Pharisees*: Also Boniface.

83. *marched upon the Lateran*: Boniface had had a long-standing feud with the Colonna family. In 1297 the Colonna walled themselves in a castle twenty-five miles east of Rome at Penestrino (now called Palestrina) in the Lateran. On Guido's advice the Pope offered a fair-sounding amnesty which he had no intention of observing. When the Colonna accepted the terms and left the castle, the Pope destroyed it, leaving the Colonna without a refuge.

86–87. *Acre . . . trader in the Sultan's land*: It was the Saracens who opposed the crusaders at Acre, the Jews who traded in the Sultan's land.

90–92. *Constantine . . . Silvestro . . . Soracte*: In the persecutions of the Christians by the Emperor Constantine, Pope Sylvester I took refuge in the caves of Mount Sor-acte near Rome. (It is now called Santo Oreste.) Later, according to legend, Con-stantine was stricken by leprosy and sent for Sylvester, who cured him and converted him to Christianity, in return for which the Emperor was believed to have made the famous "Donation of Constantine." (See Canto XIX.)

102. *so easily let go by Celestine*: Celestine V under the persuasion of Boniface abdicated the Papacy. (See Canto III notes.)

107. *long promise and short observance*: This is the advice upon which Boniface acted in trapping the Colonna with his hypocritical amnesty.

109. *St. Francis came*: To gather in the soul of one of his monks.

110. *Black Angel*: A devil.

130–31. I have taken liberties with these lines in the hope of achieving a reasonably tonic final couplet. The literal reading is: "In which the fee is paid to those who, sowing discord, acquire weight (of guilt and pain)."

Canto XXVIII

CIRCLE EIGHT: BOLGIA NINE   *The Sowers of Discord*

The Poets come to the edge of the *Ninth Bolgia* and look down at a parade of hideously mutilated souls. These are the *Sowers of Discord*, and just as their sin was to rend asunder what God had meant to be united, so are they hacked and torn through all eternity by a great demon with a bloody sword. After each mutilation the souls are compelled to drag their broken bodies around the pit and to return to the demon, for in the course of the circuit their wounds knit in time to be inflicted anew. Thus is the law of retribution observed, each sinner suffering according to his degree.

Among them Dante distinguishes three classes with varying degrees of guilt within each class. First come the *Sowers of Religious Discord*. Mahomet is chief among them, and appears first, cleft from crotch to chin, with his internal organs dangling between his legs. His son-in-law, Ali, drags on ahead of him, cleft from topknot to chin. These reciprocal wounds symbolize Dante's judgment that, between them, these two sum up the total schism between Christianity and Mohammedanism. The revolting details of Mahomet's condition clearly imply Dante's opinion of that doctrine. Mahomet issues an ironic warning to another schismatic, *Fra Dolcino*.

Next come the *Sowers of Political Discord*, among them *Pier da Medicina*, the Tribune *Curio*, and *Mosca dei Lamberti*, each mutilated according to the nature of his sin.

Last of all is *Bertrand de Born, Sower of Discord Between Kinsmen*. He separated father from son, and for that offense carries his head separated from his body, holding it with one hand by the hair, and swinging it as if it were a lantern to light his dark and endless way. The image of Bertrand raising his head at arm's length in order that it might speak more clearly to the Poets on the ridge is one of the most memorable in the *Inferno*. For some reason that cannot be ascertained, Dante makes these sinners quite eager to be remembered in the world, despite the fact that many who lie above them in Hell were unwilling to be recognized.

> Who could describe, even in words set free
>   of metric and rhyme and a thousand times retold,
>   the blood and wounds that now were shown to me!   3
>
> At grief so deep the tongue must wag in vain;
>   the language of our sense and memory
>   lacks the vocabulary of such pain.   6
>
> If one could gather all those who have stood
>   through all of time on Puglia's fateful soil
>   and wept for the red running of their blood   9
>
> in the war of the Trojans; and in that long war
>   which left so vast a spoil of golden rings,
>   as we find written in Livy, who does not err;   12

along with those whose bodies felt the wet
   and gaping wounds of Robert Guiscard's lances;
   with all the rest whose bones are gathered yet   15

at Ceperano where every last Pugliese
   turned traitor; and with those from Tagliacozzo
   where Alardo won without weapons—if all these   18

were gathered, and one showed his limbs run through,
   another his lopped off, that could not equal
   the mutilations of the ninth pit's crew.   21

A wine tun when a stave or cant-bar starts
   does not split open as wide as one I saw
   split from his chin to the mouth with which man farts.   24

Between his legs all of his red guts hung
   with the heart, the lungs, the liver, the gall bladder,
   and the shriveled sac that passes shit to the bung.   27

I stood and stared at him from the stone shelf;
   he noticed me and opening his own breast
   with both hands cried: "See how I rip myself!   30

See how Mahomet's mangled and split open!
   Ahead of me walks Ali in his tears,
   his head cleft from the top-knot to the chin.   33

And all the other souls that bleed and mourn
   along this ditch were sowers of scandal and schism:
   as they tore others apart, so are they torn.   36

Behind us, warden of our mangled horde,
   the devil who butchers us and sends us marching
   waits to renew our wounds with his long sword   39

when we have made the circuit of the pit;
   for by the time we stand again before him
   all the wounds he gave us last have knit.   42

But who are you that gawk down from that sill—
   probably to put off your own descent
   to the pit you are sentenced to for your own evil?"   45

"Death has not come for him, guilt does not drive
   his soul to torment," my sweet Guide replied.
   "That he may experience all while yet alive   48

I, who am dead, must lead him through the drear
   and darkened halls of Hell, from round to round:
   and this is true as my own standing here."   51

More than a hundred wraiths who were marching under
   the sill on which we stood, paused at his words
   and stared at me, forgetting pain in wonder.   54

"And if you do indeed return to see
    the sun again, and soon, tell Fra Dolcino
    unless he longs to come and march with me   57

he would do well to check his groceries
    before the winter drives him from the hills
    and gives the victory to the Novarese."   60

Mahomet, one foot raised, had paused to say
    these words to me. When he had finished speaking
    he stretched it out and down, and moved away.   63

Another—he had his throat slit, and his nose
    slashed off as far as the eyebrows, and a wound
    where one of his ears had been—standing with those   66

who stared at me in wonder from the pit,
    opened the grinning wound of his red gullet
    as if it were a mouth, and said through it: 69

"O soul unforfeited to misery
    and whom—unless I take you for another—
    I have seen above in our sweet Italy;   72

if ever again you see the gentle plain
    that slopes down from Vercelli to Marcabò,
    remember Pier da Medicina in pain,   75

and announce this warning to the noblest two
    of Fano, Messers Guido and Angiolello:
    that unless our foresight sees what is not true   78

they shall be thrown from their ships into the sea
    and drown in the raging tides near La Cattolica
    to satisfy a tyrant's treachery.   81

Neptune never saw so gross a crime
    in all the seas from Cyprus to Majorca,
    not even in pirate raids, nor the Argive time.   84

The one-eyed traitor, lord of the demesne
    whose hill and streams one who walks here beside me
    will wish eternally he had never seen,   87

will call them to a parley, but behind
    sweet invitations he will work it so
    they need not pray against Focara's wind."   90

And I to him: "If you would have me bear
    your name to time, show me the one who found
    the sight of that land so harsh, and let me hear   93

his story and his name." He touched the cheek
    of one nearby, forcing the jaws apart,
    and said: "This is the one; he cannot speak.   96

This outcast settled Caesar's doubts that day
   beside the Rubicon by telling him:
   'A man prepared is a man hurt by delay.'"   99

Ah, how wretched Curio seemed to me
   with a bloody stump in his throat in place of the tongue
   which once had dared to speak so recklessly!   102

And one among them with both arms hacked through
   cried out, raising his stumps on the foul air
   while the blood bedaubed his face: "Remember, too,   105

Mosca dei Lamberti, alas, who said
   'A thing done has an end!' and with those words
   planted the fields of war with Tuscan dead."   108

"And brought about the death of all your clan!"
   I said, and he, stung by new pain on pain,
   ran off; and in his grief he seemed a madman.   111

I stayed to watch those broken instruments,
   and I saw a thing so strange I should not dare
   to mention it without more evidence   114

but that my own clear conscience strengthens me,
   that good companion that upholds a man
   within the armor of his purity.   117

I saw it there; I seem to see it still—
   a body without a head, that moved along
   like all the others in that spew and spill.   120

It held the severed head by its own hair,
   swinging it like a lantern in its hand;
   and the head looked at us and wept in its despair.   123

It made itself a lamp of its own head,
   and they were two in one and one in two;
   how this can be, He knows who so commanded.   126

And when it stood directly under us
   it raised the head at arm's length toward our bridge
   the better to be heard, and swaying thus   129

it cried: "O living soul in this abyss,
   see what a sentence has been passed upon me,
   and search all Hell for one to equal this!   132

When you return to the world, remember me:
   I am Bernard de Born, and it was I
   who set the young king on to mutiny,   135

son against father, father against son
   as Achitophel set Absalom and David;
   and since I parted those who should be one   138

in duty and in love, I bear my brain
divided from its source within this trunk;
and walk here where my evil turns to pain,   141

an eye for an eye to all eternity:
thus is the law of Hell observed in me."

Notes

8. *Puglia* (POO-lyah): I have used the modern name but some of the events Dante narrates took place in the ancient province of Apulia. The southeastern area of Italy is the scene of all the fighting Dante mentions in the following passage. It is certainly a bloody total of slaughter that Dante calls upon to illustrate his scene.

10. *the war of the Trojans*: The Romans (descended from the Trojans) fought the native Samnites in a long series of raids and skirmishes from 343–290 B.C.

10–12. *and in that long war . . . Livy*: The Punic Wars (264–146 B.C.). Livy writes that in the battle of Cannae (216 B.C.) so many Romans fell that Hannibal gathered three bushels of gold rings from the fingers of the dead and produced them before the Senate at Carthage.

14. *Robert Guiscard*: Dante places Guiscard (1015–1085) in the *Paradiso* among the Warriors of God. He fought the Greeks and Saracens in their attempted invasion of Italy.

16. *Ceperano* (Tcheh-peh-RAH-noe): In 1266 the Pugliese under Manfred, King of Sicily, were charged with holding the pass at Ceperano against Charles of Anjou. The Pugliese, probably under Papal pressure, allowed the French free passage, and Charles went on to defeat Manfred at Benevento. Manfred himself was killed in that battle.

17–18. *Tagliacozzo . . . Alardo*: At Tagliacozzo (Tah-lyah-KAW-tsoe) (1268) in a continuation of the same strife, Charles of Anjou used a stratagem suggested to him by Alard de Valéry and defeated Conradin, nephew of Manfred. "Won without weapons" is certainly an overstatement: what Alardo suggested was a simple but effective concealment of reserve troops. When Conradin seemed to have carried the day and was driving his foes before him, the reserve troops broke on his flank and rear, and defeated Conradin's outpositioned forces.

32. *Ali*: Ali succeeded Mahomet to the Caliphate, but not until three of the disciples had preceded him. Mahomet died in 632, and Ali did not assume the Caliphate until 656.

56. *Fra Dolcino*: (Dohl-TCHEE-noe) In 1300 Fra Dolcino took over the reformist order called the Apostolic Brothers, who preached, among other things, the community of property and of women. Clement V declared them heretical and ordered a crusade against them. The brotherhood retired with its women to an impregnable position in the hills between Novara and Vercelli, but their supplies gave out in the course of a year-long siege, and they were finally starved out in March of 1307. Dolcino and Margaret of Trent, his "Sister in Christ," were burned at the stake at Vercelli the following June.

74. *Vercelli . . . Marcabò*: Vercelli is the most western town in Lombardy. Marcabò stands near the mouth of the Po.

76–90. *this warning*: Malatestino da Rimini (see preceding Canto), in a move to annex the city of Fano, invited Guido del Cassero and Angioletto da Carignano (Ahn-djoe-LEH-toe dah Kahr-ee-NYAH-noe), leading citizens of Fano, to a conference at La Cattolica, a point on the Adriatic midway between Fano and Rimini. At Malatestino's orders the two were thrown overboard off Focara, a headland swept by such dangerous currents that approaching sailors used to offer prayers for a safe crossing.

83. *Cyprus . . . Majorca*: These islands are at apposite ends of the Mediterranean.

84. *nor the Argive time*: The Greeks were raiders and pirates.

85. *the one-eyed traitor*: Malatestino.

86. *one who walks here beside me*: This is the Roman Tribune Curio, who was banished from Rome by Pompey and joined Caesar's forces, advising him to cross the Rubicon, which was then the boundary between Gaul and the Roman Republic. The crossing constituted invasion, and thus began the Roman Civil War. The Rubicon flows near Rimini.

106. *Mosca dei Lamberti*: Dante had asked Ciacco (Canto VI) for news of Mosca as a man of good works. Now he finds him, his merit canceled by his greater sin. Buondelmonte dei Buondelmonti had insulted the honor of the Amidei by breaking off his engagement to a daughter of that line in favor of a girl of the Donati. When the Amidei met to discuss what should be done, Mosca spoke for the death of Buon-

delmonte. The Amidei acted upon his advice and from that murder sprang the bloody feud between the Guelphs and Ghibellines of Florence.

119. *a body without a head*: Bertrand de Born (1140-1215), a great knight and master of the troubadours of Provence. He is said to have instigated a quarrel between Henry II of England and his son Prince Henry, called "The Young King" because he was crowned within his father's lifetime.

137. *Achitophel*: One of David's counselors, who deserted him to assist the rebellious Absalom. (II *Samuel*, xv–xvii.)

Canto XXIX

The Falsifiers
(Class I, Alchemists)

Dante lingers on the edge of the Ninth Bolgia expecting to see one of his
kinsmen, *Geri del Bello*, among the Sowers of Discord. Virgil, however,
hurries him on, since time is short, and as they cross the bridge over the
Tenth Bolgia, Virgil explains that he had a glimpse of Geri among the
crowd near the bridge and that he had been making threatening gestures at
Dante.

The Poets now look into the last *Bolgia* of the Eighth Circle and see
The Falsifiers. They are punished by afflictions of every sense: by darkness,
stench, thirst, filfth, loathsome diseases, and a shrieking din. Some of them,
moreover, run ravening through the pit, tearing others to pieces. Just as in
life they corrupted society by their falsifications, so in death these sinners
are subjected to a sum of corruptions. In one sense they figure forth what
society would be if all falsifiers succeeded—a place where the senses are an
affliction (since falsification deceives the senses) rather than a guide, where
even the body has no honesty, and where some lie prostrate while others
run ravening to prey upon them.

Not all of these details are made clear until the next Canto, for Dante
distinguishes four classes of Falsifiers, and in the present Canto we meet
only the first class, *The Alchemists*, the Falsifiers of Things. Of this class
are *Griffolino D'Arezzo* and *Capocchio*, with both of whom Dante speaks.

> The sight of that parade of broken dead
>   had left my eyes so sotted with their tears
>   I longed to stay and weep, but Virgil said: 3
>
> "What are you waiting for? Why do you stare
>   as if you could not tear your eyes away
>   from the mutilated shadows passing there?   6
>
> You did not act so in the other pits.
>   Consider—if you mean perhaps to count them—
>   this valley and its train of dismal spirits   9
>
> winds twenty-two miles round. The moon already
>   is under our feet; the time we have is short,
>   and there is much that you have yet to see."   12
>
> "Had you known what I was seeking," I replied,
>   "you might perhaps have given me permission
>   to stay on longer." (As I spoke, my Guide   15
>
> had started off already, and I in turn
>   had moved along behind him; thus, I answered
>   as we moved along the cliff.) "Within that cavern   18
>
> upon whose brim I stood so long to stare,
>   I think a spirit of my own blood mourns
>   the guilt that sinners find so costly there."   21

And the Master then: "Hereafter let your mind
   turn its attention to more worthy matters
   and leave him to his fate among the blind;   24

for by the bridge and among that shapeless crew
   I saw him point to you with threatening gestures,
   and I heard him called Geri del Bello. You   27

were occupied at the time with that headless one
   who in his life was master of Altaforte,
   and did not look that way; so he moved on."   30

"O my sweet Guide," I answered, "his death came
   by violence and is not yet avenged
   by those who share his blood, and, thus, his shame.   33

For this he surely hates his kin, and, therefore,
   as I suppose, he would not speak to me;
   and in that he makes me pity him the more."   36

We spoke of this until we reached the edge
   from which, had there been light, we could have seen
   the floor of the next pit. Out from that ledge   39

Malebolge's final cloister lay outspread,
   and all of its lay brethren might have been
   in sight but for the murk; and from those dead   42

such shrieks and strangled agonies shrilled through me
   like shafts, but barbed with pity, that my hands
   flew to my ears. If all the misery   45

that crams the hospitals of pestilence
   in Maremma, Valdichiano, and Sardinia
   in the summer months when death sits like a presence   48

on the marsh air, were dumped into one trench—
   that might suggest their pain. And through the screams,
   putrid flesh spread up its sickening stench.   51

Still bearing left we passed from the long sill
   to the last bridge of Malebolge. There
   the reeking bottom was more visible.   54

There, High Justice, sacred ministress
   of the First Father, reigns eternally
   over the falsifiers in their distress.   57

I doubt it could have been such pain to bear
   the sight of the Aeginian people dying
   that time when such malignance rode the air   60

that every beast down to the smallest worm
   shriveled and died (it was after that great plague
   that the Ancient People, as the poets affirm,   63

were reborn from the ants)—as it was to see
   the spirits lying heaped on one another
   in the dank bottom of that fetid valley.   66

One lay gasping on another's shoulder,
   one on another's belly; and some were crawling
   on hands and knees among the broken boulders.   69

Silent, slow step by step, we moved ahead
   looking at and listening to those souls
   too weak to raise themselves from their stone bed.   72

I saw two there like two pans that are put
   one against the other to hold their warmth.
   They were covered with great scabs from head to foot.   75

No stable boy in a hurry to go home,
   or for whom his master waits impatiently,
   ever scrubbed harder with his currycomb   78

than those two spirits of the stinking ditch
   scrubbed at themselves with their own bloody claws
   to ease the furious burning of the itch.   81

And as they scrubbed and clawed themselves, their nails
   drew down the scabs the way a knife scrapes bream
   or some other fish with even larger scales.   84

"O you," my Guide called out to one, "you there
   who rip your scabby mail as if your fingers
   were claws and pincers; tell us if this lair   87

counts any Italians among those who lurk
   in its dark depths; so may your busy nails
   eternally suffice you for your work."   90

"We both are Italian whose unending loss
   you see before you," he replied in tears.
   "But who are you who come to question us?"   93

"I am a shade," my Guide and Master said,
   "who leads this living man from pit to pit
   to show him Hell as I have been commanded."   96

The sinners broke apart as he replied
   and turned convulsively to look at me,
   as others did who overheard my Guide.   99

My Master, then, ever concerned for me,
   turned and said: "Ask them whatever you wish."
   And I said to those two wraiths of misery: 102

"So may the memory of your names and actions
   not die forever from the minds of men
   in that first world, but live for many suns,   105

tell me who you are and of what city;
do not be shamed by your nauseous punishment
into concealing your identity."   108

"I was a man of Arezzo," one replied,
"and Albert of Siena had me burned;
but I am not here for the deed for which I died.   111

It is true that jokingly I said to him once:
'I know how to raise myself and fly through air';
and he—with all the eagerness of a dunce—   114

wanted to learn. Because I could not make
a Daedalus of him—for no other reason—
he had his father burn me at the stake.   117

But Minos, the infallible, had me hurled
here to the final bolgia of the ten
for the alchemy I practiced in the world."   120

And I to the Poet: "Was there ever a race
more vain than the Sienese? Even the French,
compared to them, seem full of modest grace."   123

And the other leper answered mockingly:
"Excepting Stricca, who by careful planning
managed to live and spend so moderately;   126

and Niccolò, who in his time above
was first of all the shoots in that rank garden
to discover the costly uses of the clove;   129

and excepting the brilliant company of talents
in which Caccia squandered his vineyards and his woods,
and Abbagliato displayed his intelligence.   132

But if you wish to know who joins your cry
against the Sienese, study my face
with care and let it make its own reply.   135

So you will see I am the suffering shadow
of Capocchio, who, by practicing alchemy,
falsified the metals, and you must know,   138

unless my mortal recollection strays
how good an ape I was of Nature's ways."

Notes

10. *twenty-two miles*: Another instance of "poetic" rather than "literal" detail.
Dante's measurements cannot be made to fit together on any scale map.
10–11. *the moon . . . is under our feet*: If the moon, nearly at full, is under their
feet, the sun must be overhead. It is therefore approximately noon of Holy Saturday.
18. *cavern*: Dante's use of this word is not literally accurate, but its intent and its
poetic force are obvious.

27. *Geri del Bello* (DJEH-ree): A cousin of Dante's father. He became embroiled in a quarrel with the Sacchetti of Florence and was murdered. At the time of the writing he had not been avenged by his kinsmen in accord with the clan code of a life for a life.

29. *Altaforte*: (Ahl-tah-FAWR-teh) Bertrand de Born was Lord of Hautefort.

40–41. *cloister . . . lay brethren*: A Dantean irony. This is the first suggestion of a sardonic mood reminiscent of the Gargoyle Cantos that will grow and swell in this Canto until even Virgil resorts to mocking irony.

47. *Maremma, Valdichiano, and Sardinia*: Malarial plague areas. Valdichiano and Maremma were swamp areas of eastern and western Tuscany.

59. *the Aeginian people dying*: Juno, incensed that the nymph Aegina let Jove possess her, set a plague upon the island that bore her name. Every animal and every human died until only Aeacus, the son born to Aegina of Jove, was left. He prayed to his father for aid and Jove repopulated the island by transforming the ants at his son's feet into men. The Aeginians have since been called Myrmidons, from the Greek word for ant. Ovid (*Metamorphoses* VII, 523–660).

76. *in a hurry to go home*: The literal text would be confusing here. I have translated one possible interpretation of it as offered by Giuseppe Vandelli. The original line is *"ne da colui che mal volentier vegghia"* ("nor by one who unwillingly stays awake," or less literally, but with better force: "nor by one who fights off sleep").

85. *my Guide called out to one*: The sinner spoken to is Griffolino D'arezzo (Ah-RAY-tsoe), an alchemist who extracted large sums of money from Alberto da Siena on the promise of teaching him to fly like Daedalus. When the Sienese oaf finally discovered he had been tricked, he had his "uncle," the Bishop of Siena, burn Griffolino as a sorcerer. Griffolino, however, is not punished for sorcery, but for falsification of silver and gold through alchemy.

125–132. *Stricca . . . Niccolò . . . Caccia . . . Abbagliato*: (STREE-kah, Nee-koe-LAW, KAH-tchah, Ahb-ah-LYAH-toe) All of these Sienese noblemen were members of the Spendthrift Brigade and wasted their substance in competitions of riotous living. Lano (Canto XIII) was also of this company. Niccolò dei Salimbeni discovered some recipe (details unknown) prepared with fabulously expensive spices. "Excepting" is ironical. (cf. the similar usage in XXI, 41.)

137. *Capocchio*: (Kah-PAW-kyoe) Reputedly a Florentine friend of Dante's student days. For practicing alchemy he was burned at the stake at Siena in 1293.

Canto XXX

The Falsifiers (The Remaining Three Classes:
Evil Impersonators, Counterfeiters, False Witnesses)

Just as Capocchio finishes speaking, two ravenous spirits come racing
through the pit; and one of them, sinking his tusks into Capocchio's neck,
drags him away like prey. Capocchio's companion, Griffolino, identifies the
two as *Gianni Schicchi* and *Myrrha*, who run ravening through the pit
through all eternity, snatching at other souls and rending them. These are
the *Evil Impersonators*, Falsifiers of Persons. In life they seized upon the
appearance of others, and in death they must run with never a pause, seizing upon the infernal apparition of these souls, while they in turn are
preyed upon by their own furies.

Next the Poets encounter *Master Adam*, a sinner of the third class, a
Falsifier of Money, i.e., a *Counterfeiter*. Like the alchemists, he is punished
by a loathsome disease and he cannot move from where he lies, but his disease is compounded by other afflictions, including an eternity of unbearable
thirst. Master Adam identifies two spirits lying beside him as *Potiphar's
Wife* and *Sinon the Greek*, sinners of the fourth class, *The False Witnesses*,
i.e., Falsifiers of Words.

Sinon, angered by Master Adam's identification of him, strikes him across
the belly with the one arm he is able to move. Master Adam replies in
kind; and Dante, fascinated by their continuing exchange of abuse, stands
staring at them until Virgil turns on him in great anger, for "The wish to
hear such baseness is degrading." Dante burns with shame, and Virgil
immediately forgives him because of his great and genuine repentance.

At the time when Juno took her furious
  revenge for Semele, striking in rage
  again and again at the Theban royal house,   3

King Athamas, by her contrivance, grew
  so mad, that seeing his wife out for an airing
  with his two sons, he cried to his retinue: 6

"Out with the nets there! Nets across the pass!
  for I will take this lioness and her cubs!"
  And spread his talons, mad and merciless,   9

and seizing his son Learchus, whirled him round
  and brained him on a rock; at which the mother
  leaped into the sea with her other son and drowned.   12

And when the Wheel of Fortune spun about
  to humble the all-daring Trojan's pride
  so that both king and kingdom were wiped out;   15

Hecuba—mourning, wretched, and a slave—
  having seen Polyxena sacrificed,
  and Polydorus dead without a grave;   18

lost and alone, beside an alien sea,
   began to bark and growl like a dog
   in the mad seizure of her misery.   21

But never in Thebes nor Troy were Furies seen
   to strike at man or beast in such mad rage
   as two I saw, pale, naked, and unclean,   24

who suddenly came running toward us then,
   snapping their teeth as they ran, like hungry swine
   let out to feed after a night in the pen.   27

One of them sank his tusks so savagely
   into Capocchio's neck, that when he dragged him,
   the ditch's rocky bottom tore his belly.   30

And the Aretine, left trembling by me, said:
   "That incubus, in life, was Gianni Schicchi;
   here he runs rabid, mangling the other dead."   33

"So!" I answered, "and so may the other one
   not sink its teeth in you, be pleased to tell us
   what shade it is before it races on."   36

And he: "That ancient shade in time above
   was Myrrha, vicious daughter of Cinyras
   who loved her father with more than rightful love. 39

She falsified another's form and came
   disguised to sin with him just as that other
   who runs with her, in order that he might claim   42

the fabulous lead-mare, lay under disguise
   on Buoso Donati's death bed and dictated
   a spurious testament to the notaries."   45

And when the rabid pair had passed from sight,
   I turned to observe the other misbegotten
   spirits that lay about to left and right.   48

And there I saw another husk of sin,
   who, had his legs been trimmed away at the groin,
   would have looked for all the world like a mandolin. 51

The dropsy's heavy humors, which so bunch
   and spread the limbs, had disproportioned him
   till his face seemed much too small for his swollen paunch. 54

He strained his lips apart and thrust them forward
   the way a sick man, feverish with thirst,
   curls one lip toward the chin and the other upward. 57

"O you exempt from every punishment
   of this grim world (I know not why)," he cried,
   "look well upon the misery and debasement   60

of him who was Master Adam. In my first
    life's time, I had enough to please me; here,
    I lack a drop of water for my thirst.   63

The rivulets that run from the green flanks
    of Casentino to the Arno's flood,
    spreading their cool sweet moisture through their banks,   66

run constantly before me, and their plash
    and ripple in imagination dries me
    more than the disease that eats my flesh.   69

Inflexible Justice that has forked and spread
    my soul like hay, to search it the more closely,
    finds in the country where my guilt was bred   72

this increase of my grief; for there I learned,
    there in Romena, to stamp the Baptist's image
    on alloyed gold—till I was bound and burned.   75

But could I see the soul of Guido here,
    or of Alessandro, or of their filthy brother,
    I would not trade that sight for all the clear   78

cool flow of Branda's fountain. One of the three—
    if those wild wraiths who run here are not lying—
    is here already. But small good it does me   81

when my legs are useless! Were I light enough
    to move as much as an inch in a hundred years,
    long before this I would have started off   84

to cull him from the freaks that fill this fosse,
    although it winds on for eleven miles
    and is no less than half a mile across.   87

Because of them I lie here in this pig-pen;
    it was they persuaded me to stamp the florins
    with three carats of alloy." And I then: 90

"Who are those wretched two sprawled alongside
    your right-hand borders, and who seem to smoke
    as a washed hand smokes in winter?" He replied: 93

"They were here when I first rained into this gully,
    and have not changed position since, nor may they,
    as I believe, to all eternity.   96

One is the liar who charged young Joseph wrongly:
    the other, Sinon, the false Greek from Troy.
    A burning fever makes them reek so strongly."   99

And one of the false pair, perhaps offended
    by the manner of Master Adam's presentation,
    punched him in the rigid and distended   102

belly—it thundered like a drum—and he
  retorted with an arm blow to the face
  that seemed delivered no whit less politely,   105

saying to him: "Although I cannot stir
  my swollen legs, I still have a free arm
  to use at times when nothing else will answer."   108

And the other wretch said: "It was not so free
  on your last walk to the stake, free as it was
  when you were coining." And he of the dropsy: 111

"That's true enough, but there was less truth in you
  when they questioned you at Troy." And Sinon then:
  "For every word I uttered that was not true   114

you uttered enough false coins to fill a bushel:
  I am put down here for a single crime,
  but you for more than any Fiend in Hell."   117

"Think of the Horse," replied the swollen shade,
  "and may it torture you, perjurer, to recall
  that all the world knows the foul part you played."   120

"And to you the torture of the thirst that fries
  and cracks your tongue," said the Greek, "and of the water
  that swells your gut like a hedge before your eyes."   123

And the coiner: "So is your own mouth clogged
  with the filth that stuffs and sickens it as always;
  if I am parched while my paunch is waterlogged,   126

you have the fever and your cankered brain;
  and were you asked to lap Narcissus' mirror
  you would not wait to be invited again."   129

I was still standing, fixed upon those two
  when the Master said to me: "Now keep on looking
  a little longer and I quarrel with you."   132

When I heard my Master raise his voice to me,
  I wheeled about with such a start of shame
  that I grow pale yet at the memory.   135

As one trapped in a nightmare that has caught
  his sleeping mind, wishes within the dream
  that it were all a dream, as if it were not—   138

such I became: my voice could not win through
  my shame to ask his pardon; while my shame
  already won more pardon than I knew.   141

"Less shame," my Guide said, ever just and kind,
  "would wash away a greater fault than yours.
  Therefore, put back all sorrow from your mind;   144

And never forget that I am always by you
should it occur again, as we walk on,
that we find ourselves where others of this crew   147

fall to such petty wrangling and upbraiding.
The wish to hear such baseness is degrading."

Notes

1–2. *Juno took her furious revenge*: As in the case of the Aeginians, Jove begot a
son (Bacchus) upon a mortal (Semele, daughter of the King Cadmus of Thebes);
and Juno, who obviously could not cope with her husband's excursions directly,
turned her fury upon the mortals in a number of godlike ways, among them inducing
the madness of King Athamas (Semele's brother-in-law) which Ovid recounts in
Metamorphoses IV, 512 ff.

16. *Hecuba*: Wife of King Priam. When Troy fell she was taken to Greece as a
slave. En route she was forced to witness the sacrifice of her daughter and to look
upon her son lying murdered and unburied. She went mad in her affliction and fell to
howling like a dog. Ovid (*Metamorphoses* XIII, 568 ff.) describes her anguish but
does not say she was changed into a dog.

31. *the Aretine*: Capocchio's companion, Griffolino.

32. *Gianni Schicchi*: (DJAHN-ee SKEE-kee) Of the Cavalcanti of Florence. When
Buoso di Donati (see Canto XXV) died, his son, Simone, persuaded Schicchi to
impersonate the dead man and to dictate a will in Simone's favor. Buoso was
removed from the death bed, Schicchi took his place in disguise, and the will was
dictated to a notary as if Buoso were still alive. Schicchi took advantage of the occasion to make several bequests to himself, including one of a famous and highly-prized
mare.

38. *Myrrha*: The second figure that runs rabid through the pit was the daughter of
Cinyras, King of Cyprus. Moved by an incestuous passion for her father, she disguised herself and slipped into his bed. After he had mated with her, the king discovered who she was and threatened to kill her but she ran away and was changed into
a myrtle. Adonis was born from her trunk. (Ovid. *Metamorphoses* X, 298 ff.)

61. *Master Adam*: Of Brescia. Under the orders of the Counts Guidi of Romena,
he counterfeited Florentine florins of twenty-one rather than twenty-four carat gold,
and on such a scale that a currency crisis arose in Northern Italy. He was burned at
the stake by the Florentines in 1281.

65. *Casentino*: A mountainous district in which the Arno rises.

74. *the Baptist's image*: John the Baptist's. As patron of Florence, his image was
stamped on the florins.

76–77. *Guido . . . Alessandro . . . their filthy brother*: The Counts Guidi.

79. *Branda*: A spring near Romena. The famous fountain of Branda is in Siena,
but Adam is speaking of his home country and must mean the spring.

79–81. *One of the three . . . is here already*: Guido died before 1300.

92. *your right-hand borders*: Master Adam's right side. Dante uses *confini* (borders) for "side," suggesting ironically that Master Adam in his swollen state is more
like a territory than a man.

97. *the liar who charged young Joseph*: Potiphar's wife bore false witness against
Joseph. (*Genesis* xxxix, 6–23.)

98. *Sinon*: The Greek who glibly talked the Trojans into taking the Horse inside
the city walls. (*Aeneid* II, 57–194.)

115–117. *a single crime*: Dante must reckon each false florin as a separate sin.

128. *Narcissus' mirror*: A pool of water. Ovid (*Metamorpheses* III, 407–510) tells
how the young Narcissus fell in love with his own reflection in a pool. He remained
bent over the reflection till he wasted away and was changed into a flower.

Canto XXXI

Dante's spirits rise again as the Poets approach the Central Pit, a great well, at the bottom of which lies Cocytus, the Ninth and final circle of Hell. Through the darkness Dante sees what appears to be a city of great towers, but as he draws near he discovers that the great shapes he has seen are the Giants and Titans who stand perpetual guard inside the well-pit with the upper halves of their bodies rising above the rim.

Among the Giants, Virgil identifies *Nimrod,* builder of the Tower of Babel; *Ephialtes* and *Briareus,* who warred against the Gods; and *Tityos* and *Typhon,* who insulted Jupiter. Also here, but for no specific offense, is *Antaeus,* and his presence makes it clear that the Giants are placed here less for their particular sins than for their general natures.

These are the sons of earth, embodiments of elemental forces unbalanced by love, desire without restraint and without acknowledgment of moral and theological law. They are symbols of the earth-trace that every devout man must clear from his soul, the unchecked passions of the beast. Raised from the earth, they make the very gods tremble. Now they are returned to the darkness of their origins, guardians of earth's last depth.

At Virgil's persuasion, Antaeus takes the Poets in his huge palm and lowers them gently to the final floor of Hell.

> One and the same tongue had first wounded me
> so that the blood came rushing to my cheeks,
> and then supplied the soothing remedy.   3
>
> Just so, as I have heard, the magic steel
> of the lance that was Achilles' and his father's
> could wound at a touch, and, at another, heal.   6
>
> We turned our backs on the valley and climbed from it
> to the top of the stony bank that walls it round,
> crossing in silence to the central pit.   9
>
> Here it was less than night and less than day;
> my eyes could make out little through the gloom,
> but I heard the shrill note of a trumpet bray   12
>
> louder than any thunder. As if by force,
> it drew my eyes; I stared into the gloom
> along the path of the sound back to its source.   15
>
> After the bloody rout when Charlemagne
> had lost the band of Holy Knights, Roland
> blew no more terribly for all his pain.   18
>
> And as I stared through that obscurity,
> I saw what seemed a cluster of great towers,
> whereat I cried: "Master, what is this city?"   21

160

And he: "You are still too far back in the dark
to make out clearly what you think you see;
it is natural that you should miss the mark: 24

you will see clearly when you reach that place
how much your eyes mislead you at a distance;
I urge you, therefore, to increase your pace." 27

Then taking my hand in his, my Master said:
"The better to prepare you for strange truth,
let me explain those shapes you see ahead: 30

they are not towers but giants. They stand in the well
from the navel down; and stationed round its bank
they mount guard on the final pit of Hell." 33

Just as a man in a fog that starts to clear
begins little by little to piece together
the shapes the vapor crowded from the air— 36

so, when those shapes grew clearer as I drew
across the darkness to the central brink,
error fled from me; and my terror grew. 39

For just as at Montereggione the great towers
crown the encircling wall; so the grim giants
whom Jove still threatens when the thunder roars 42

raised from the rim of stone about that well
the upper halves of their bodies, which loomed up
like turrets through the murky air of Hell. 45

I had drawn close enough to one already
to make out the great arms along his sides,
the face, the shoulders, the breast, and most of the belly. 48

Nature, when she destroyed the last exemplars
on which she formed those beasts, surely did well
to take such executioners from Mars. 51

And if she has not repented the creation
of whales and elephants, the thinking man
will see in that her justice and discretion: 54

for where the instrument of intelligence
is added to brute power and evil will,
mankind is powerless in its own defense. 57

His face, it seemed to me, was quite as high
and wide as the bronze pine cone in St. Peter's
with the rest of him proportioned accordingly: 60

so that the bank, which made an apron for him
from the waist down, still left so much exposed
that three Frieslanders standing on the rim, 63

one on another, could not have reached his hair;
  for to that point at which men's capes are buckled,
  thirty good hand-spans of brute bulk rose clear.   66

"Rafel mahee amek zabi almit,"
  began a bellowed chant from the brute mouth
  for which no sweeter psalmody was fit.   69

And my Guide in his direction: "Babbling fool,
  stick to your horn and vent yourself with it
  when rage or passion stir your stupid soul.   72

Feel there around your neck, you muddle-head,
  and find the cord; and there's the horn itself,
  there on your overgrown chest." To me he said: 75

"His very babbling testifies the wrong
  he did on earth: he is Nimrod, through whose evil
  mankind no longer speaks a common tongue.   78

Waste no words on him: it would be foolish.
  To him all speech is meaningless; as his own,
  which no one understands, is simply gibberish."   81

We moved on, bearing left along the pit,
  and a crossbow-shot away we found the next one,
  an even huger and more savage spirit.   84

What master could have bound so gross a beast
  I cannot say, but he had his right arm pinned
  behind his back, and the left across his breast   87

by an enormous chain that wound about him
  from the neck down, completing five great turns
  before it spiraled down below the rim.   90

"This piece of arrogance," said my Guide to me,
  "dared try his strength against the power of Jove;
  for which he is rewarded as you see.   93

He is Ephialtes, who made the great endeavour
  with the other giants who alarmed the Gods;
  the arms he raised then, now are bound forever."   96

"Were it possible, I should like to take with me,"
  I said to him, "the memory of seeing
  the immeasurable Briareus." And he: 99

"Nearer to hand, you may observe Antaeus
  who is able to speak to us, and is not bound.
  It is he will set us down in Cocytus,   102

the bottom of all guilt. The other hulk
  stands far beyond our road. He too, is bound
  and looks like this one, but with a fiercer sulk."   105

No earthquake in the fury of its shock
  has ever seized a tower more violently,
  than Ephialtes, hearing, began to rock.   108

Then I dreaded death as never before;
  and I think I could have died for very fear
  had I not seen what manacles he wore.   111

We left the monster, and not far from him
  we reached Antaeus, who to his shoulders alone
  soared up a good five ells above the rim.   114

"O soul who once in Zama's fateful vale—
  where Scipio became the heir of glory
  when Hannibal and all his troops turned tail—   117

took more than a thousand lions for your prey;
  and in whose memory many still believe
  the sons of earth would yet have won the day   120

had you joined with them against High Olympus—
  do not disdain to do us a small service,
  but set us down where the cold grips Cocytus.   123

Would you have us go to Tityos or Typhon?—
  this man can give you what is longed for here:
  therefore do not refuse him, but bend down.   126

For he can still make new your memory:
  he lives, and awaits long life, unless Grace call him
  before his time to his felicity."   129

Thus my Master to that Tower of Pride;
  and the giant without delay reached out the hands
  which Hercules had felt, and raised my Guide.   132

Virgil, when he felt himself so grasped,
  called to me: "Come, and I will hold you safe."
  And he took me in his arms and held me clasped.   135

The way the Carisenda seems to one
  who looks up from the leaning side when clouds
  are going over it from that direction,   138

making the whole tower seem to topple—so
  Antaeus seemed to me in the fraught moment
  when I stood clinging, watching from below   141

as he bent down; while I with heart and soul
  wished we had gone some other way, but gently
  he set us down inside the final hole   144

whose ice holds Judas and Lucifer in its grip.
  Then straightened like a mast above a ship.

Notes

5. *Achilles' lance*: Peleus, father of Achilles, left this magic lance to his son. (Ovid, *Metamorphoses* XIII, 171 ff.) Sonneteers of Dante's time made frequent metaphoric use of this lance: just as the lance could cure and then heal, so could the lady's look destroy with love and her kiss make whole.

14–15. *stared . . . along the path of the sound*: Another of Dante's peculiar reports of how the senses work. He treats his eyes here as if they were radio-compasses tracking a beam. There is not another man in literature who would anatomize this reaction in this way. Compare with this the opening of Canto XX and the note on Dante's peculiar treatment of his vision.

17. *Roland*: Nephew of Charlemagne, hero of the French epic poem, the *Chanson de Roland*. He protected the rear of Charlemagne's column on the return march through the Pyrenees from a war against the Saracens. When he was attacked he was too proud to blow his horn as a signal for help, but as he was dying he blew so prodigious a blast that it was heard by Charlemagne eight miles away. *Band of Holy Knights*: The original is *"la santa gesta,"* which may be interpreted as "the holy undertaking." *"Gesta,"* however, can also mean "a sworn band or fellowship of men at arms" (such as the Knights of the Round Table), and since it was his Knights, rather than his undertaking, that Charlemagne lost, the second rendering seems more apt in context.

40. *Montereggione*: (Mon-teh-reh-DJOE-neh) A castle in Val d'Elsa near Siena built in 1213. Its walls had a circumference of more than half a kilometer and were crowned by fourteen great towers, most of which are now destroyed.

59. *the bronze pine cone in St. Peter's*: Originally a part of a fountain. In Dante's time it stood in front of the Basilica of St. Peter. It is now inside the Vatican. It stands about thirteen feet high (Scartazzini-Vandelli give the height as four meters) but shows signs of mutilation that indicate it was once higher. Many translations incorrectly render the original "la pina" as pine tree. In Italian "pino" is "pine tree" and "pina" is "pine cone." Like most of Dante's measurements it is a poetical rather than a literal assistance in determining the height of the giants. How tall is a man whose face is thirteen feet long? If the face represents one-sixth of a man's height, a minimum figure will be seventy-eight feet; but other interpretations of Dante's details will yield figures ranging from forty to one hundred feet. Lines 65–66, for example, would yield a figure between 300 and 474 inches for the measurement from the waist to (roughly) the collarbone.

63. *Frieslanders*: The men of Friesland were reputed to be the tallest in Europe.

66. *thirty good hand-spans*: Dante uses the word "palma," which in Italian signifies the spread of the open hand, a considerably larger measure than the English "hand" which equals four inches. The Dante Society edition of the *Comedy* equates ten palms to four meters or 158 inches, but 15.8 inches seems excessive. Ten inches would seem closer to a "good hand-span."

67. *Rafel mahee, etc.*: This line, as Virgil explains below, is Nimrod's gibberish.

77. *Nimrod*: The first king of Babylon, supposed to have built the Tower of Babel, for which he is punished, in part, by the confusion of his own tongue and understanding. Nothing in the Biblical reference portrays him as one of the earth-giants.

94. *Ephialtes*: Son of Neptune (the sea) and Iphimedia. With his brother, Otus, he warred against the Gods striving to pile Mt. Ossa on Mt. Olympus, and Mt. Pelion on Mt. Ossa. Apollo restored good order by killing the two brothers.

99. *Briareus*: Another of the giants who rose against the Olympian Gods. Virgil speaks of him as having a hundred arms and fifty hands (*Aeneid* X, 565–568), but Dante needs only of his size, and of his sin, which he seems to view as a kind of revolt of the angels, just as the action of Ephialtes and Otus may be read as a pagan distortion of the Tower of Babel legend. He was the son of Uranus and Tellus.

100. *Antaeus*: The son of Neptune and Tellus (the earth). In battle, his strength grew every time he touched the earth, his mother. He was accordingly invincible until Hercules killed him by lifting him over his head and strangling him in midair. Lucan (*Pharsalia* IV, 595–660) describes Antaeus' great lion-hunting feat in the valley of Zama where, in a later era, Scipio defeated Hannibal. Antaeus did not join in the rebellion against the Gods and therefore he is not chained.

123. *Cocytus*: The final pit of Hell. See the remaining Cantos.

124. *Tityos or Typhon*: Also sons of Tellus. They offended Jupiter, who had them hurled into the crater of Etna, below which the Lake Tartarus was supposed to lie.

136. *the Carisenda*: A leaning tower of Bologna.

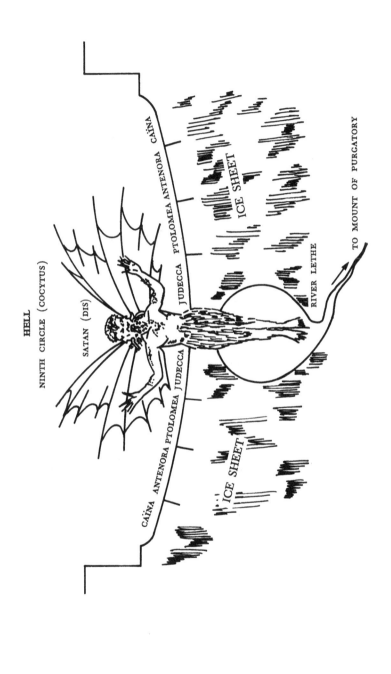

HELL
NINTH CIRCLE (COCYTUS)

SATAN (DIS)

CAÏNA ANTENORA PTOLOMEA JUDECCA

JUDECCA PTOLOMEA ANTENORA CAÏNA

ICE SHEET

ICE SHEET

RIVER LETHE

TO MOUNT OF PURGATORY

Canto XXXII

CIRCLE NINE: COCYTUS   *Compound Fraud*

ROUND ONE: CAÏNA   *The Treacherous to Kin*

ROUND TWO: ANTENORA   *The Treacherous to Country*

At the bottom of the well Dante finds himself on a huge frozen lake. This is *Cocytus*, the *Ninth Circle*, the fourth and last great water of Hell, and here, fixed in the ice, each according to his guilt, are punished sinners guilty of *Treachery Against Those to Whom They Were Bound by Special Ties*. The ice is divided into four concentric rings marked only by the different positions of the damned within the ice.

This is Dante's symbolic equivalent of the final guilt. The treacheries of these souls were denials of love (which is God) and of all human warmth. Only the remorseless dead center of the ice will serve to express their natures. As they denied God's love, so are they furthest removed from the light and warmth of His Sun. As they denied all human ties, so are they bound only by the unyielding ice.

The first round is *Caïna*, named for Cain. Here lie those who were treacherous against blood ties. They have their necks and heads out of the ice and are permitted to bow their heads—a double boon since it allows them some protection from the freezing gale and, further, allows their tears to fall without freezing their eyes shut. Here Dante sees *Alessandro* and *Napoleone degli Alberti*, and he speaks to *Camicion*, who identifies other sinners of this round.

The second round is *Antenora*, named for Antenor, the Trojan who was believed to have betrayed his city to the Greeks. Here lie those guilty of *Treachery to Country*. They, too, have their heads above the ice, but they cannot bend their necks, which are gripped by the ice. Here Dante accidentally kicks the head of *Bocca degli Abbati* and then proceeds to treat him with a savagery he has shown to no other soul in Hell. Bocca names some of his fellow traitors, and the Poets pass on to discover two heads frozen together in one hole. One of them is gnawing the nape of the other's neck.

If I had rhymes as harsh and horrible
　　as the hard fact of that final dismal hole
　　which bears the weight of all the steeps of Hell,　　　3

I might more fully press the sap and substance
　　from my conception; but since I must do
　　without them, I begin with some reluctance.　　　6

For it is no easy undertaking, I say,
　　to describe the bottom of the Universe;
　　nor is it for tongues that only babble child's play.　　　9

But may those Ladies of the Heavenly Spring
　　who helped Amphion wall Thebes, assist my verse,
　　that the word may be the mirror of the thing.　　　12

O most miscreant rabble, you who keep
   the stations of that place whose name is pain,
   better had you been born as goats or sheep!   15

We stood now in the dark pit of the well,
   far down the slope below the Giant's feet,
   and while I still stared up at the great wall,   18

I heard a voice cry: "Watch which way you turn:
   take care you do not trample on the heads
   of the forworn and miserable brethren."   21

Whereat I turned and saw beneath my feet
   and stretching out ahead, a lake so frozen
   it seemed to be made of glass. So thick a sheet   24

never yet hid the Danube's winter course,
   nor, far away beneath the frigid sky,
   locked the Don up in its frozen source: 27

for were Tanbernick and the enormous peak
   of Pietrapana to crash down on it,
   not even the edges would so much as creak.   30

The way frogs sit to croak, their muzzles leaning
   out of the water, at the time and season
   when the peasant woman dreams of her day's gleaning—   33

just so the livid dead are sealed in place
   up to the part at which they blushed for shame,
   and they beat their teeth like storks. Each holds his face   36

bowed toward the ice, each of them testifies
   to the cold with his chattering mouth, to his heart's grief
   with tears that flood forever from his eyes.   39

When I had stared about me, I looked down
   and at my feet I saw two clamped together
   so tightly that the hair of their heads had grown   42

together. "Who are you," I said, "who lie
   so tightly breast to breast?" They strained their necks,
   and when they had raised their heads as if to reply,   45

the tears their eyes had managed to contain
   up to that time gushed out, and the cold froze them
   between the lids, sealing them shut again   48

tighter than any clamp grips wood to wood,
   and mad with pain, they fell to butting heads
   like billy-goats in a sudden savage mood.   51

And a wraith who lay to one side and below,
   and who had lost both ears to frostbite, said,
   his head still bowed: "Why do you watch us so?   54

If you wish to know who they are who share one doom,
   they owned the Bisenzio's valley with their father,
   whose name was Albert. They sprang from one womb,   57

and you may search through all Caïna's crew
   without discovering in all this waste
   a squab more fit for the aspic than these two;   60

not him whose breast and shadow a single blow
   of the great lance of King Arthur pierced with light;
   nor yet Focaccia; nor this one fastened so   63

into the ice that his head is all I see,
   and whom, if you are Tuscan, you know well—
   his name on the earth was Sassol Mascheroni.   66

And I—to tell you all and so be through—
   was Camicion de' Pazzi. I wait for Carlin
   beside whose guilt my sins will shine like virtue."   69

And leaving him, I saw a thousand faces
   discolored so by cold, I shudder yet
   and always will when I think of those frozen places.   72

As we approached the center of all weight,
   where I went shivering in eternal shade,
   whether it was my will, or chance, or fate,   75

I cannot say, but as I trailed my Guide
   among those heads, my foot struck violently
   against the face of one. Weeping, it cried: 78

"Why do you kick me? If you were not sent
   to wreak a further vengeance for Montaperti,
   why do you add this to my other torment?"   81

"Master," I said, "grant me a moment's pause
   to rid myself of a doubt concerning this one,
   then you may hurry me at your own pace."   84

The Master stopped at once, and through the volley
   of foul abuse the wretch poured out, I said:
   "Who are you who curse others so?" And he: 87

"And who are *you* who go through the dead larder
   of Antenora kicking the cheeks of others
   so hard, that were you alive, you could not kick harder?"   90

"I *am* alive," I said, "and if you seek fame,
   it may be precious to you above all else
   that my notes on this descent include your name."   93

"Exactly the opposite is my wish and hope,"
   he answered. "Let me be; for it's little you know
   of how to flatter on this icy slope."   96

I grabbed the hair of his dog's-ruff and I said:
"Either you tell me truly who you are,
or you won't have a hair left on your head."   99

And he: "Not though you snatch me bald. I swear
I will not tell my name nor show my face.
Not though you rip until my brain lies bare."   102

I had a good grip on his hair; already
I had yanked out more than one fistful of it,
while the wretch yelped, but kept his face turned from me;   105

when another said: "Bocca, what is it ails you?
What the Hell's wrong? Isn't it bad enough
to hear you bang your jaws? Must you bark too?"   108

"Now filthy traitor, say no more!" I cried,
"for to your shame, be sure I shall bear back
a true report of you." The wretch replied: 111

"Say anything you please but go away.
And if you *do* get back, don't overlook
that pretty one who had so much to say   114

just now. Here he laments the Frenchman's price.
'I saw Buoso da Duera,' you can report,
'where the bad salad is kept crisp on ice.'   117

And if you're asked who else was wintering here,
Beccheria, whose throat was slit by Florence,
is there beside you. Gianni de' Soldanier   120

is further down, I think, with Ganelon,
and Tebaldello, who opened the gates of Faenza
and let Bologna steal in with the dawn."   123

Leaving him then, I saw two souls together
in a single hole, and so pinched in by the ice
that one head made a helmet for the other.   126

As a famished man chews crusts—so the one sinner
sank his teeth into the other's nape
at the base of the skull, gnawing his loathsome dinner.   129

Tydeus in his final raging hour
gnawed Menalippus' head with no more fury
than this one gnawed at skull and dripping gore.   132

"You there," I said, "who show so odiously
your hatred for that other, tell me why
on this condition: that if in what you tell me   135

you seem to have a reasonable complaint
against him you devour with such foul relish,
I, knowing who you are, and his soul's taint,   138

may speak your cause to living memory,
God willing the power of speech be left to me."

Notes

3. *which bears the weight of all the steeps of Hell*: Literally, it is the base from which all the steeps rise; symbolically, it is the total and finality of all guilt.

10. *those Ladies of the Heavenly Spring, etc*: The Muses. They so inspired Amphion's hand upon the lyre that the music charmed blocks of stone out of Mount Cithaeron, and the blocks formed themselves into the walls of Thebes.

28–29. *Tanbernick . . . Pietrapana*: There is no agreement on the location of the mountain Dante called Tanbernick. Pietrapana, today known as *la Pania*, is in Tuscany.

32–33. *season . . . gleaning*: The summer.

35. *the part at which they blushed*: The cheeks. By extension, the whole face.

41–61. *two clamped together*: Alessandro and Napoleone, Counts of Mangona. Among other holdings, they inherited a castle in the Val di Bisenzio. They seemed to have been at odds on all things and finally killed one another in a squabble over their inheritance and their politics (Alessandro was a Guelph and Napoleone a Ghibelline).

61. *him whose breast and shadow, etc.*: Modred, King Arthur's traitorous nephew. He tried to kill Arthur, but the king struck him a single blow of his lance, and when it was withdrawn, a shaft of light passed through the gaping wound and split the shadow of the falling traitor.

63. *Focaccia*: (Foh-KAH-tcha) Of the Cancellieri of Pistoia. He murdered his cousin (among others) and may have been the principal cause of a great feud that divided the Cancellieri, and split the Guelphs into the White and Black parties.

66. *Sassol Mascheroni*: Of the Toschi of Florence. He was appointed guardian of one of his nephews and murdered him to get the inheritance for himself.

68. *Camicion de' Pazzi*: (Kah-mih-TCHONE day PAH-tsee) Alberto Camicion de' Pazzi of Valdarno. He murdered a kinsman. *Carlin*: Carlino de' Pazzi, relative of Alberto. He was charged with defending for the Whites the castle of Piantravigne (Pyahn-trah-VEE-nyeh) in Valdarno but surrendered it for a bribe. He belongs therefore in the next lower circle, Antenora, as a traitor to his country, and when he arrives there his greater sin will make Alberto seem almost virtuous by comparison.

70. *And leaving him*: These words mark the departure from Caïna to Antenora.

73. *the center of all weight*: In Dante's cosmology the bottom of Hell is at the center of the earth, which is in turn the center of the universe; it is therefore the center of all gravity. Symbolically, it is the focal point of all guilt. Gravity, weight, and evil are equivalent symbols on one level; they are what ties man to the earth, what draws him down. At the center of all, Satan is fixed forever in the eternal ice. The journey to salvation, however, is up from that center, once the soul has realized the hideousness of sin.

78. *against the face of one*: Bocca degli Abbati, a traitorous Florentine. At the battle of Montaperti (cf. Farinata, Canto X) he hacked off the hand of the Florentine standard bearer. The cavalry, lacking a standard around which it could rally, was soon routed.

107. *What the Hell's wrong?*: In the circumstances, a monstrous pun. The original is *"qual diavolo ti tocca?"* (what devil touches, or molests, you?) a standard colloquialism for "what's the matter with you?" A similar pun occurs in line 117 "kept crisp (cool) on ice." Colloquially *"stare fresco"* (to be or to remain cool) equals "to be left out in the cold," i.e., to be out of luck.

116. *Buoso da Duera*: Of Cremona. In 1265 Charles of Anjou marched against Manfred and Naples (see Canto XIX), and Buoso da Duera was sent out in charge of a Ghibelline army to oppose the passage of one of Charles' armies, but accepted a bribe and let the French pass unopposed. The event took place near Parma.

119. *Beccheria*: Tesauro dei Beccheria of Pavia, Abbot of Vallombrosa and Papal Legate (of Alexander IV) in Tuscany. The Florentine Guelphs cut off his head in 1258 for plotting with the expelled Ghibellines.

120. *Gianni de' Soldanier*: A Florentine Ghibelline of ancient and noble family. In 1265, however, during the riots that occurred under the Two Jovial Friars, he deserted his party and became a leader of the commoners (Guelphs). In placing him in Antenora, Dante makes no distinction between turning on one's country and turning on one's political party, not at least if the end is simply for power.

121. *Ganelon*: It was Ganelon who betrayed Roland to the Saracens. (See Canto XXXI.)

122. *Tebaldello*: Tebaldello de' Zambrasi of Faenza. At dawn on November 13, 1280, he opened the city gates and delivered Faenza to the Bolognese Guelphs in order to revenge himself on the Ghibelline family of the Lambertazzi who, in 1274, had fled from Bologna to take refuge in Faenza.

130–1. *Tydeus . . . Menalippus*: Statius recounts in the *Thebaid* that Tydeus killed Menalippus in battle but fell himself mortally wounded. As he lay dying he had Menalippus' head brought to him and fell to gnawing it in his dying rage.

Canto XXXIII

CIRCLE NINE: COCYTUS   *Compound Fraud*

ROUND TWO: ANTENORA   *The Treacherous to Country*

ROUND THREE: PTOLOMEA   *The Treacherous to Guests and Hosts*

In reply to Dante's exhortation, the sinner who is gnawing his companion's head looks up, wipes his bloody mouth on his victim's hair, and tells his harrowing story. He is *Count Ugolino* and the wretch he gnaws is *Archbishop Ruggieri*. Both are in Antenora for treason. In life they had once plotted together. Then Ruggieri betrayed his fellow-plotter and caused his death, by starvation, along with his four "sons.' In the most pathetic and dramatic passage of the *Inferno*, Ugolino details how their prison was sealed and how his "sons" dropped dead before him one by one, weeping for food. His terrible tale serves only to renew his grief and hatred, and he has hardly finished it before he begins to gnaw Ruggieri again with renewed fury. In the immutable Law of Hell, the killer-by-starvation becomes the food of his victim.

The Poets leave Ugolino and enter *Ptolomea*, so named for the Ptolomaeus of *Maccabees*, who murdered his father-in-law at a banquet. Here are punished those who were *Treacherous Against the Ties of Hospitality*. They lie with only half their faces above the ice and their tears freeze in their eye sockets, sealing them with little crystal visors. Thus even the comfort of tears is denied them. Here Dante finds *Friar Alberigo* and *Branca d'Oria*, and discovers the terrible power of Ptolomea: so great is its sin that the souls of the guilty fall to its torments even before they die, leaving their bodies still on earth, inhabited by Demons.

The sinner raised his mouth from his grim repast
    and wiped it on the hair of the bloody head
    whose nape he had all but eaten away. At last   3

he began to speak: "You ask me to renew
    a grief so desperate that the very thought
    of speaking of it tears my heart in two.   6

But if my words may be a seed that bears
    the fruit of infamy for him I gnaw,
    I shall weep, but tell my story through my tears.   9

Who you may be, and by what powers you reach
    into this underworld, I cannot guess,
    but you seem to me a Florentine by your speech.   12

I was Count Ugolino, I must explain;
    this reverend grace is the Archbishop Ruggieri:
    now I will tell you why I gnaw his brain.   15

That I, who trusted him, had to undergo
    imprisonment and death through his treachery,
    you will know already. What you cannot know—   18

that is, the lingering inhumanity
of the death I suffered—you shall hear in full:
then judge for yourself if he has injured me.   21

A narrow window in that coop of stone
now called the Tower of Hunger for my sake
(within which others yet must pace alone)   24

had shown me several waning moons already
between its bars, when I slept the evil sleep
in which the veil of the future parted for me.   27

This beast appeared as master of a hunt
chasing the wolf and his whelps across the mountain
that hides Lucca from Pisa. Out in front   30

of the starved and shrewd and avid pack he had placed
Gualandi and Sismondi and Lanfranchi
to point his prey. The father and sons had raced   33

a brief course only when they failed of breath
and seemed to weaken; then I thought I saw
their flanks ripped open by the hounds' fierce teeth.   36

Before the dawn, the dream still in my head,
I woke and heard my sons, who were there with me,
cry from their troubled sleep, asking for bread.   39

You are cruelty itself if you can keep
your tears back at the thought of what foreboding
stirred in my heart; and if you do not weep,   42

at what are you used to weeping?—The hour when food
used to be brought, drew near. They were now awake,
and each was anxious from his dream's dark mood.   45

And from the base of that horrible tower I heard
the sound of hammers nailing up the gates:
I stared at my sons' faces without a word.   48

I did not weep: I had turned stone inside.
They wept. 'What ails you, Father, you look so strange,'
my little Anselm, youngest of them, cried.   51

But I did not speak a word nor shed a tear:
not all that day nor all that endless night,
until I saw another sun appear.   54

When a tiny ray leaked into that dark prison
and I saw staring back from their four faces
the terror and the wasting of my own,   57

I bit my hands in helpless grief. And they,
thinking I chewed myself for hunger, rose
suddenly together. I heard them say: 60

'Father, it would give us much less pain
   if you ate us: it was you who put upon us
   this sorry flesh; now strip it off again.'   63

I calmed myself to spare them. Ah! hard earth,
   why did you not yawn open? All that day
   and the next we sat in silence. On the fourth,   66

Gaddo, the eldest, fell before me and cried,
   stretched at my feet upon that prison floor:
   'Father, why don't you help me?' There he died.   69

And just as you see me, I saw them fall
   one by one on the fifth day and the sixth.
   Then, already blind, I began to crawl   72

from body to body shaking them frantically.
   Two days I called their names, and they were dead.
   Then fasting overcame my grief and me."   75

His eyes narrowed to slits when he was done,
   and he seized the skull again between his teeth
   grinding it as a mastiff grinds a bone.   78

Ah, Pisa! foulest blemish on the land
   where "si" sounds sweet and clear, since those nearby you
   are slow to blast the ground on which you stand,   81

may Caprara and Gorgona drift from place
   and dam the flooding Arno at its mouth
   until it drowns the last of your foul race!   84

For if to Ugolino falls the censure
   for having betrayed your castles, you for your part
   should not have put his sons to such a torture: 87

you modern Thebes! those tender lives you spilt—
   Brigata, Uguccione, and the others
   I mentioned earlier—were too young for guilt!   90

We passed on further, where the frozen mine
   entombs another crew in greater pain;
   these wraiths are not bent over, but lie supine.   93

Their very weeping closes up their eyes;
   and the grief that finds no outlet for its tears
   turns inward to increase their agonies: 96

for the first tears that they shed knot instantly
   in their eye-sockets, and as they freeze they form
   a crystal visor above the cavity.   99

And despite the fact that standing in that place
   I had become as numb as any callus,
   and all sensation had faded from my face,   102

somehow I felt a wind begin to blow,
   whereat I said: "Master, what stirs this wind?
   Is not all heat extinguished here below?"   105

And the Master said to me: "Soon you will be
   where your own eyes will see the source and cause
   and give you their own answer to the mystery."   108

And one of those locked in that icy mall
   cried out to us as we passed: "O souls so cruel
   that you are sent to the last post of all,   111

relieve me for a little from the pain
   of this hard veil; let my heart weep a while
   before the weeping freeze my eyes again."   114

And I to him: "If you would have my service,
   tell me your name; then if I do not help you
   may I descend to the last rim of the ice."   117

"I am Friar Alberigo," he answered therefore,
   "the same who called for the fruits from the bad garden.
   Here I am given dates for figs full store."   120

"What! Are you dead already?" I said to him.
   And he then: "How my body stands in the world
   I do not know. So privileged is this rim   123

of Ptolomea, that often souls fall to it
   before dark Atropos has cut their thread.
   And that you may more willingly free my spirit   126

of this glaze of frozen tears that shrouds my face,
   I will tell you this: when a soul betrays as I did,
   it falls from flesh, and a demon takes its place,   129

ruling the body till its time is spent.
   The ruined soul rains down into this cistern.
   So, I believe, there is still evident   132

in the world above, all that is fair and mortal
   of this black shade who winters here behind me.
   If you have only recently crossed the portal   135

from that sweet world, you surely must have known
   his body: Branca D'Oria is its name,
   and many years have passed since he rained down."   138

"I think you are trying to take me in," I said,
   "Ser Branca D'Oria is a living man;
   he eats, he drinks, he fills his clothes and his bed."   141

"Michel Zanche had not yet reached the ditch
   of the Black Talons," the frozen wraith replied,
   "there where the sinners thicken in hot pitch,   144

when this one left his body to a devil,
as did his nephew and second in treachery,
and plumbed like lead through space to this dead level.   147

But now reach out your hand, and let me cry."
And I did not keep the promise I had made,
for to be rude to him was courtesy.   150

Ah, men of Genoa! souls of little worth,
corrupted from all custom of righteousness,
why have you not been driven from the earth?   153

For there beside the blackest soul of all
Romagna's evil plain, lies one of yours
bathing his filthy soul in the eternal   156

glacier of Cocytus for his foul crime,
while he seems yet alive in world and time!

Notes

1-90. *Ugolino and Ruggieri*: (Oog-oh-LEE-noe: Roo-DJAIR-ee) Ugolino, Count of Donoratico and a member of the Guelph family della Gherardesca. He and his nephew, Nino de' Visconti, led the two Guelph factions of Pisa. In 1288 Ugolino intrigued with Archbishop Ruggieri degli Ubaldini, leader of the Ghibellines, to get rid of Visconti and to take over the command of all the Pisan Guelphs. The plan worked, but in the consequent weakening of the Guelphs, Ruggieri saw his chance and betrayed Ugolino, throwing him into prison with his sons and his grandsons. In the following year the prison was sealed up and they were left to starve to death. The law of retribution is clearly evident: in life Ruggieri sinned against Ugolino by denying him food; in Hell he himself becomes food for his victim.

18. *you will know already*: News of Ugolino's imprisonment and death would certainly have reached Florence, *what you cannot know*: No living man could know what happened after Ugolino and his sons were sealed in the prison and abandoned.

22. *coop*: Dante uses the word *muda*, in Italian signifying a stone tower in which falcons were kept in the dark to moult. From the time of Ugolino's death it became known as The Tower of Hunger.

25. *several waning moons*: Ugolino was jailed late in 1288. He was sealed in to starve early in 1289.

28. *This beast*: Ruggieri.

29-30. *the mountain that hides Lucca from Pisa*: These two cities would be in view of one another were it not for Monte San Giuliano.

32. *Gualandi and Sismondi and Lanfranchi*: (Gwah-LAHN-dee . . . Lahn-FRAHN-kee) Three Pisan nobles, Ghibellines and friends of the Archbishop.

51-71. UGOLINO'S "SONS": Actually two of the boys were grandsons and all were considerably older than one would gather from Dante's account. Anselm, the younger grandson, was fifteen. The others were really young men and were certainly old enough for guilt despite Dante's charge in line 90.

75. *Then fasting overcame my grief and me*: i.e., He died. Some interpret the line to mean that Ugolino's hunger drove him to cannibalism. Ugolino's present occupation in Hell would certainly support that interpretation but the fact is that cannibalism is the one major sin Dante does not assign a place to in Hell. So monstrous would it have seemed to him that he must certainly have established a special punishment for it. Certainly he could hardly have relegated it to an ambiguity. Moreover, it would be a sin of bestiality rather than of fraud, and as such it would be punished in the Seventh Circle.

79-80. *the land where "sì" sounds sweet and clear*: Italy.

82. *Caprara and Gorgona*: These two islands near the mouth of the Arno were Pisan possessions in 1300.

86. *betrayed your castles*: In 1284, Ugolino gave up certain castles to Lucca and Florence. He was at war with Genoa at the time and it is quite likely that he ceded the castles to buy the neutrality of these two cities, for they were technically allied with Genoa. Dante, however, must certainly consider the action as treasonable, for otherwise Ugolino would be in Caïna for his treachery to Visconti.

88. *you modern Thebes*: Thebes, as a number of the foregoing notes will already have made clear, was the site of some of the most hideous crimes of antiquity.

91. *we passed on further*: Marks the passage into Ptolomea.

105. *is not all heat extinguished*: Dante believed (rather accurately, by chance) that all winds resulted from "exhalations of heat." Cocytus, however, is conceived as wholly devoid of heat, a metaphysical absolute zero. The source of the wind, as we discover in the next Canto, is Satan himself.

117. *may I descend to the last rim of the ice*: Dante is not taking any chances; he has to go on to the last rim in any case. The sinner, however, believes him to be another damned soul and would interpret the oath quite otherwise than as Dante meant it.

118. *Friar Alberigo*: (Ahl-beh-REE-ghoe) Of the Manfredi of Faenza. He was another Jovial Friar. In 1284 his brother Manfred struck him in the course of an argument. Alberigo pretended to let it pass, but in 1285 he invited Manfred and his son to a banquet and had them murdered. The signal to the assassins was the words: "Bring in the fruit." "Friar Alberigo's bad fruit," became a proverbial saying.

125. *Atropos*: The Fate who cuts the thread of life.

137. *Branca d'Oria*: (DAW-ree-yah) A Genoese Ghilbelline. His sin is identical in kind to that of Friar Alberigo. In 1275 he invited his father-in-law, Michel Zanche (see Canto XXII), to a banquet and had him and his companions cut to pieces. He was assisted in the butchery by his nephew.

Canto XXXIV

NINTH CIRCLE: COCYTUS   *Compound Fraud*

ROUND FOUR: JUDECCA   *The Treacherous to Their Masters*

THE CENTER   *Satan*

"On march the banners of the King," Virgil begins as the Poets face the last depth. He is quoting a medieval hymn, and to it he adds the distortion and perversion of all that lies about him. "On march the banners of the King—of Hell." And there before them, in an infernal parody of Godhead, they see Satan in the distance, his great wings beating like a windmill. It is their beating that is the source of the icy wind of Cocytus, the exhalation of all evil.

All about him in the ice are strewn the sinners of the last round, *Judecca*, named for Judas Iscariot. These are the *Treacherous to Their Masters*. They lie completely sealed in the ice, twisted and distorted into every conceivable posture. It is impossible to speak to them, and the Poets move on to observe Satan.

He is fixed into the ice at the center to which flow all the rivers of guilt; and as he beats his great wings as if to escape, their icy wind only freezes him more surely into the polluted ice. In a grotesque parody of the Trinity, he has three faces, each a different color, and in each mouth he clamps a sinner whom he rips eternally with his teeth. *Judas Iscariot* is in the central mouth: *Brutus* and *Cassius* in the mouths on either side.

Having seen all, the Poets now climb through the center, grappling hand over hand down the hairy flank of Satan himself—a last supremely symbolic action—and at last, when they have passed the center of all gravity, they emerge from Hell. A long climb from the earth's center to the Mount of Purgatory awaits them, and they push on without rest, ascending along the sides of the river Lethe, till they emerge once more to see the stars of Heaven, just before dawn on Easter Sunday.

> "On march the banners of the King of Hell,"
> my Master said. "Toward us. Look straight ahead:
> can you make him out at the core of the frozen shell?"   3
>
> Like a whirling windmill seen afar at twilight,
> or when a mist has risen from the ground—
> just such an engine rose upon my sight   6
>
> stirring up such a wild and bitter wind
> I cowered for shelter at my Master's back,
> there being no other windbreak I could find.   9
>
> I stood now where the souls of the last class
> (with fear my verses tell it) were covered wholly;
> they shone below the ice like straws in glass.   12

Some lie stretched out; others are fixed in place
   upright, some on their heads, some on their soles;
   another, like a bow, bends foot to face.   15

When we had gone so far across the ice
   that it pleased my Guide to show me the foul creature
   that once had worn the grace of Paradise,   18

he made me stop, and, stepping aside, he said:
   "Now see the face of Dis! This is the place
   where you must arm your soul against all dread."   21

Do not ask, Reader, how my blood ran cold
   and my voice choked up with fear. I cannot write it:
   this is a terror that cannot be told.   24

I did not die, and yet I lost life's breath:
   imagine for yourself what I became,
   deprived at once of both my life and death.   27

The Emperor of the Universe of Pain
   jutted his upper chest above the ice;
   and I am closer in size to the great mountain   30

the Titans make around the central pit,
   than they to his arms. Now, starting from this part,
   imagine the whole that corresponds to it!   33

If he was once as beautiful as now
   he is hideous, and still turned on his Maker,
   well may he be the source of every woe!   36

With what a sense of awe I saw his head
   towering above me! for it had three faces:
   one was in front, and it was fiery red;   39

the other two, as weirdly wonderful,
   merged with it from the middle of each shoulder
   to the point where all converged at the top of the skull; 42

the right was something between white and bile;
   the left was about the color one observes
   on those who live along the banks of the Nile.   45

Under each head two wings rose terribly,
   their span proportioned to so gross a bird:
   I never saw such sails upon the sea.   48

They were not feathers—their texture and their form
   were like a bat's wings—and he beat them so
   that three winds blew from him in one great storm: 51

it is these winds that freeze all Cocytus.
   He wept from his six eyes, and down three chins
   the tears ran mixed with bloody froth and pus.   54

In every mouth he worked a broken sinner
between his rake-like teeth. Thus he kept three
in eternal pain at his eternal dinner.   57

For the one in front the biting seemed to play
no part at all compared to the ripping: at times
the whole skin of his back was flayed away.   60

"That soul that suffers most," explained my Guide,
"is Judas Iscariot, he who kicks his legs
on the fiery chin and has his head inside.   63

Of the other two, who have their heads thrust forward,
the one who dangles down from the black face
is Brutus: note how he writhes without a word.   66

And there, with the huge and sinewy arms, is the soul
of Cassius.—But the night is coming on
and we must go, for we have seen the whole."   69

Then, as he bade, I clasped his neck, and he,
watching for a moment when the wings
were opened wide, reached over dexterously   72

and seized the shaggy coat of the king demon;
then grappling matted hair and frozen crusts
from one tuft to another, clambered down.   75

When we had reached the joint where the great thigh
merges into the swelling of the haunch,
my Guide and Master, straining terribly,   78

turned his head to where his feet had been
and began to grip the hair as if he were climbing;
so that I thought we moved toward Hell again.   81

"Hold fast!" my Guide said, and his breath came shrill
with labor and exhaustion. "There is no way
but by such stairs to rise above such evil."   84

At last he climbed out through an opening
in the central rock, and he seated me on the rim;
then joined me with a nimble backward spring.   87

I looked up, thinking to see Lucifer
as I had left him, and I saw instead
his legs projecting high into the air.   90

Now let all those whose dull minds are still vexed
by failure to understand what point it was
I had passed through, judge if I was perplexed.   93

"Get up. Up on your feet," my Master said.
"The sun already mounts to middle tierce,
and a long road and hard climbing lie ahead."   96

It was no hall of state we had found there,
   but a natural animal pit hollowed from rock
   with a broken floor and a close and sunless air.   99

"Before I tear myself from the Abyss,"
   I said when I had risen, "O my Master,
   explain to me my error in all this: 102

where is the ice? and Lucifer—how has he
   been turned from top to bottom: and how can the sun
   have gone from night to day so suddenly?"   105

And he to me: "You imagine you are still
   on the other side of the center where I grasped
   the shaggy flank of the Great Worm of Evil   108

which bores through the world—you *were* while I climbed
                                                          down,
   but when I turned myself about, you passed
   the point to which all gravities are drawn.   111

You are under the other hemisphere where you stand;
   the sky above us is the half opposed
   to that which canopies the great dry land.   114

Under the midpoint of that other sky
   the Man who was born sinless and who lived
   beyond all blemish, came to suffer and die.   117

You have your feet upon a little sphere
   which forms the other face of the Judecca.
   There it is evening when it is morning here.   120

And this gross Fiend and Image of all Evil
   who made a stairway for us with his hide
   is pinched and prisoned in the ice-pack still.   123

On this side he plunged down from heaven's height,
   and the land that spread here once hid in the sea
   and fled North to our hemisphere for fright;   126

and it may be that moved by that same fear,
   the one peak that still rises on this side
   fled upward leaving this great cavern here."   129

Down there, beginning at the further bound
   of Beelzebub's dim tomb, there is a space
   not known by sight, but only by the sound   132

of a little stream descending through the hollow
   it has eroded from the massive stone
   in its endlessly entwining lazy flow."   135

My Guide and I crossed over and began
   to mount that little known and lightless road
   to ascend into the shining world again.   138

He first, I second, without thought of rest
   we climbed the dark until we reached the point
   where a round opening brought in sight the blest   141

and beauteous shining of the Heavenly cars.
   And we walked out once more beneath the Stars.

Notes

1. *On march the banners of the King*: The hymn (*Vexilla regis prodeunt*) was written in the sixth century by Venantius Fortunatus, Bishop of Poitiers. The original celebrates the Holy Cross, and is part of the service for Good Friday to be sung at the moment of uncovering the cross.

17. *the foul creature*: Satan.

38. *three faces*: Numerous interpretations of these three faces exist. What is essential to all explanation is that they be seen as perversions of the qualities of the Trinity.

54. *bloody froth and pus*: The gore of the sinners he chews which is mixed with his slaver.

62. *Judas*: Note how closely his punishment is patterned on that of the Simoniacs (Canto XIX).

67. *huge and sinewy arms*: The Cassius who betrayed Caesar was more generally described in terms of Shakespeare's "lean and hungry look." Another Cassius is described by Cicero (*Catiline* III) as huge and sinewy. Dante probably confused the two.

68. *the night is coming on*: It is now Saturday evening.

82. *his breath came shrill*: Cf. Canto XXIII, 85, where the fact that Dante breathes indicates to the Hypocrites that he is alive. Virgil's breathing is certainly a contradiction.

95. *middle tierce*: In the canonical day tierce is the period from about six to nine A.M. Middle tierce, therefore, is seven-thirty. In going through the center point, they have gone from night to day. They have moved ahead twelve hours.

128. *the one peak*: The Mount of Purgatory.

129. *this great cavern*: The natural animal pit of line 98. It is also "Beelzebub's dim tomb," line 131.

133. *a little stream*: Lethe. In classical mythology, the river of forgetfulness, from which souls drank before being born. In Dante's symbolism it flows down from the top of Purgatory, where it washes away the memory of sin from the souls that have achieved purity. That memory it delivers to Hell, which drawn all sin to itself.

143. *Stars*: As part of his total symbolism Dante ends each of the three divisions of the *Commedia* with this word. Every conclusion of the upward soul is toward the stars. God's shining symbols of hope and virtue. It is just before dawn of Easter Sunday that the Poets emerge—a further symbolism.

The Purgatorio

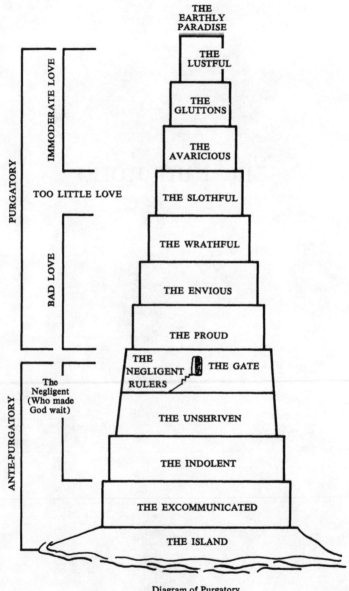

Diagram of Purgatory

Canto I

The Poets emerge from Hell just before dawn of Easter Sunday (April 10, 1300), and Dante revels in the sight of the rediscovered heavens. As he looks eagerly about at the stars, he sees nearby an old man of impressive bearing. The ancient is *Cato of Utica*, guardian of the shores of Purgatory. Cato challenges the Poets as fugitives from Hell, but Virgil, after first instructing Dante to kneel in reverence, explains Dante's mission and Beatrice's command. Cato then gives them instructions for proceeding.

The Poets have emerged at a point a short way up the slope of Purgatory. It is essential, therefore, that they descend to the lowest point and begin from there, an allegory of Humility. Cato, accordingly, orders Virgil to lead Dante to the shore, to wet his hands in the dew of the new morning, and to wash the stains of Hell from Dante's face and the film of Hell's vapors from Dante's eyes. Virgil is then to bind about Dante's waist one of the pliant reeds (symbolizing Humility) that grow in the soft mud of the shore.

Having so commanded, Cato disappears. Dante arises in silence and stands waiting, eager to begin. His look is all the communication that is necessary. Virgil leads him to the shore and performs all that Cato has commanded. Dante's first purification is marked by a miracle: when Virgil breaks off a reed, the stalk immediately regenerates a new reed, restoring itself exactly as it had been.

> For better waters now the little bark
>   of my indwelling powers raises her sails,
>   and leaves behind that sea so cruel and dark.   3
>
> Now shall I sing that second kingdom given
>   the soul of man wherein to purge its guilt
>   and so grow worthy to ascend to Heaven.   6
>
> Yours am I, sacred Muses! To you I pray.
>   Here let dead poetry rise once more to life,
>   and here let sweet Calliope rise and play   9
>
> some far accompaniment in that high strain
>   whose power the wretched Pierides once felt
>   so terribly they dared not hope again.   12
>
> Sweet azure of the sapphire of the east
>   was gathering on the serene horizon
>   its pure and perfect radiance—a feast   15
>
> to my glad eyes, reborn to their delight,
>   as soon as I had passed from the dead air
>   which had oppressed my soul and dimmed my sight.   18

The planet whose sweet influence strengthens love
was making all the east laugh with her rays,
veiling the Fishes, which she swam above.   21

I turned then to my right and set my mind
on the other pole, and there I saw four stars
unseen by mortals since the first mankind.   24

The heavens seemed to revel in their light.
O widowed Northern Hemisphere, bereft
forever of the glory of that sight!   27

As I broke off my gazing, my eyes veered
a little to the left, to the other pole
from which, by then, the Wain had disappeared.   30

I saw, nearby, an ancient man, alone.
His bearing filled me with such reverence,
no father has had more from any son.   33

His beard was long and touched with strands of white,
as was his hair, of which two tresses fell
over his breast. Rays of the holy light   36

that fell from the four stars made his face glow
with such a radiance that he looked to me
as if he faced the sun. And standing so,   39

he moved his venerable plumes and said:
"Who are you two who climb by the dark stream
to escape the eternal prison of the dead?   42

Who led you? or what served you as a light
in your dark flight from the eternal valley,
which lies forever blind in darkest night?   45

Are the laws of the pit so broken? Or is new counsel
published in Heaven that the damned may wander
onto my rocks from the abyss of Hell?"   48

At that my Master laid his hands upon me,
instructing me by word and touch and gesture
to show my reverence in brow and knee,   51

then answered him: "I do not come this way
of my own will or powers. A Heavenly Lady
sent me to this man's aid in his dark day.   54

But since your will is to know more, my will
cannot deny you; I will tell you truly
why we have come and how. This man has still   57

to see his final hour, though in the burning
of his own madness he had drawn so near it
his time was perilously short for turning.   60

As I have told you, I was sent to show
　the way his soul must take for its salvation;
　and there is none but this by which I go.　　　63

I have shown him the guilty people. Now I mean
　to lead him through the spirits in your keeping,
　to show him those whose suffering makes them clean.　66

By what means I have led him to this strand
　to see and hear you, takes too long to tell:
　from Heaven is the power and the command.　　　69

Now may his coming please you, for he goes
　to win his freedom; and how dear that is
　the man who gives his life for it best knows.　　　72

You know it, who in that cause found death sweet
　in Utica where you put off that flesh
　which shall rise radiant at the Judgment Seat.　　　75

We do not break the Laws: this man lives yet,
　and I am of that Round not ruled by Minos,
　with your own Marcia, whose chaste eyes seem set　　78

in endless prayers to you. O blessed breast
　to hold her yet your own! for love of her
　grant us permission to pursue our quest　　　81

across your seven kingdoms. When I go
　back to her side I shall bear thanks of you,
　if you will let me speak your name below."　　　84

"Marcia was so pleasing in my eyes
　there on the other side," he answered then
　"that all she asked, I did. Now that she lies　　　87

beyond the evil river, no word or prayer
　of hers may move me. Such was the Decree
　pronounced upon us when I rose from there.　　　90

But if, as you have said, a Heavenly Dame
　orders your way, there is no need to flatter:
　you need but ask it of me in her name.　　　93

Go then, and lead this man, but first see to it
　you bind a smooth green reed about his waist
　and clean his face of all trace of the pit.　　　96

For it would not be right that one with eyes
　still filmed by mist should go before the angel
　who guards the gate: he is from Paradise.　　　99

All round the wave-wracked shore-line, there below,
　reeds grow in the soft mud. Along that edge
　no foliate nor woody plant could grow.　　　102

for what lives in that buffeting must bend.
Do not come back this way: the rising sun
will light an easier way you may ascend."   105

With that he disappeared; and silently
I rose and moved back till I faced my Guide,
my eyes upon him, waiting. He said to me: 108

"Follow my steps and let us turn again:
along this side there is a gentle slope
that leads to the low boundaries of the plain."   111

The dawn, in triumph, made the day-breeze flee
before its coming, so that from afar
I recognized the trembling of the sea.   114

We strode across that lonely plain like men
who seek the road they strayed from and who count
the time lost till they find it once again.   117

When we had reached a place along the way
where the cool morning breeze shielded the dew
against the first heat of the gathering day,   120

with gentle graces my Sweet Master bent
and laid both outspread palms upon the grass.
Then I, being well aware of his intent,   123

lifted my tear-stained cheeks to him, and there
he made me clean, revealing my true color
under the residues of Hell's black air.   126

We moved on then to the deserted strand
which never yet has seen upon its waters
a man who found his way back to dry land.   129

There, as it pleased another, he girded me.
Wonder of wonders! when he plucked a reed
another took its place there instantly,   132

arising from the humble stalk he tore
so that it grew exactly as before.

Notes

4. *that second kingdom*: Purgatory.
5. *to purge its guilt*: (See also line 66: *those whose suffering makes them clean.*)
There is suffering in Purgatory but no torment. The torment of the damned is endless, produces no change in the soul that endures it, and is imposed from without.
The suffering of the souls in Purgatory, on the other hand, is temporary, is a means
of purification, and is eagerly embraced as an act of the soul's own will. Demons
guard the damned to inflict punishment and to prevent escape. In Purgatory, the sinners are free to leave off their sufferings: nothing but their own desire to be made
clean moves them to accept their pains, and nothing more is needed. In fact, it is left
to the suffering soul itself (no doubt informed by Divine Illumination) to decide at
what point it has achieved purification and is ready to move on.
8. *dead poetry*: The verses that sang of Hell. Dante may equally have meant that

poetry as an art has long been surpassed by history as the medium for great subjects. Here poetry will return to its classic state.

7-12. THE INVOCATION. Dante invokes all the Muses, as he did in *Inferno*, II, 7, but there the exhortation was to his own powers, to High Genius, and to Memory. Here he addresses his specific exhortation to Calliope, who, as the Muse of Epic Poetry, is foremost of the Nine. In *Paradiso* (I, 13) he exhorts Apollo himself to come to the aid of the poem.

Dante exhorts Calliope to fill him with the strains of the music she played in the defeat of the Pierides, the nine daughters of Pierius, King of Thessaly. They presumed to challenge the Muses to a contest of song. After their defeat they were changed into magpies for their presumption. Ovid (*Metamorphoses*, V, 294-340 and 662-678) retells the myth in detail.

Note that Dante not only calls upon Calliope to fill him with the strains of highest song, but that he calls for that very song that overthrew the arrogant pretensions of the Pierides, the strains that humbled false pride. The invocation is especially apt, therefore, as a first sounding of the theme of Humility.

17. *the dead air*: Of Hell.

19-21. *The planet whose sweet influence strengthens love*: Venus. Here, as morning star, Venus is described as rising in Pisces, the Fishes, the zodiacal sign immediately preceding Aries. In Canto I of the *Inferno* Dante has made it clear that the Sun is in Aries. Hence it is about to rise.

Allegorically, the fact that Venus represents love is, of course, indispensable to the mood of the *Purgatory*. At no time in April of 1300 was Venus the morning star. Rather, it rose after the sun. Dante's description of the first dawn in Canto I of the *Inferno* similarly violates the exact detail of things. But Dante is no bookkeeper of the literal. In the *Inferno* he violated fact in order to compile a perfect symbol of rebirth. Here, he similarly violates the literal in order to describe an ideal sunrise, and simultaneously to make the allegorical point that Love (Venus) leads the way and that Divine Illumination (the Sun) follows upon it.

23. *four stars*: Modern readers are always tempted to identify these four stars as the Southern Cross, but it is almost certain that Dante did not know about that formation. In VIII, 89, Dante mentions three other stars as emphatically as he does these four and no one has been tempted to identify them on the star-chart. Both constellations are best taken as allegorical. The four stars represent the Four Cardinal Virtues: Prudence, Justice, Fortitude, and Temperance. Dante will encounter them again in the form of nymphs when he achieves the Earthly Paradise.

24. *the first mankind*: Adam and Eve. In Dante's geography, the Garden of Eden (the Earthly Paradise) was at the top of the Mount of Purgatory, which was the only land in the Southern Hemisphere. All of what were called "the southern continents" were believed to lie north of the equator. When Adam and Eve were driven from the Garden, therefore, they were driven into the Northern Hemisphere, and no living soul since had been far enough south to see those stars.

Ulysses and his men (*Inferno*, XXVII) had come within sight of the Mount of Purgatory, but Ulysses mentioned nothing of having seen these stars.

29. *the other pole*: The North Pole. The Wain (Ursa Major, *i.e.*, the Big Dipper) is below the horizon.

31 ff. CATO OF UTICA. Marcus Porcius Cato, the younger, 95-46 B.C. In the name of freedom, Cato opposed the policies of both Caesar and Pompey, but because he saw Caesar as the greater evil joined forces with Pompey. After the defeat of his cause at the Battle of Thapsus, Cato killed himself with his own sword rather than lose his freedom. Virgil lauds him in the *Aeneid* as a symbol of perfect devotion to liberty, and all writers of Roman antiquity have given Cato a similar high place. Dante spends the highest praises on him both in *De Monarchia* and *Il Convivio*.

Why Cato should be so signally chosen by God as the special guardian of Purgatory has been much disputed. Despite his suicide (and certainly one could argue that he had less excuse for it than had Pier delle Vigne-see *Inferno*, XIII-for his) he was sent to Limbo as a Virtuous Pagan. From Limbo he was especially summoned to his present office. It is clear, moreover, that he will find a special triumph on Judgment Day, though he will probably not be received into Heaven.

The key to Dante's intent seems to lie in the four stars, the Four Cardinal Virtues, that shine so brightly on Cato's face when Dante first sees him. Once Cato is forgiven his suicide (and a partisan could argue that it was a positive act, a death for freedom), he may certainly be taken as a figure of Prudence, Justice, Fortitude, and Temperance. He does very well, moreover, as a symbol of the natural love of freedom; and Purgatory, it must be remembered, is the road to Ultimate Freedom. Cato may be taken, therefore, as representative of supreme virtue short of godliness. He has accomplished everything but the purifying total surrender of his will to God. As such he serves as an apt transitional symbol, being the highest rung on the ladder of natural virtue, but the lowest on the ladder of those godly virtues to which Purgatory is the ascent. Above all, the fact that he took Marcia (see line 78, note) back to his love, makes him an especially apt symbol of God's forgiveness in allowing the strayed soul to return to him through Purgatory.

53. *A Heavenly Lady*: Beatrice.

77. *Minos*: The Judge of the Damned. The round in Hell not ruled by Minos is Limbo, the final resting place of the Virtuous Pagans. Minos (see *Inferno,* V) is stationed at the entrance to the second circle of Hell. The souls in Limbo (the first circle) have never had to pass before him to be judged.

78. *Marcia.* The story of Marcia and of Cato is an extraordinary one. She was the daughter of the consul Philippus and became Cato's second wife, bearing his three children. In 56 B.C., in an unusual transaction approved by her father, Cato released her in order that she might marry his friend Hortensius. (Hence line 87: "that all she asked I did.") After the death of Hortensius, Cato took her back.

In *Il Convivio*, IV, 28, Dante presents the newly widowed Marcia praying to be taken back in order that she may die the wife of Cato, and that it may be said of her that she was not cast forth from his love. Dante treats that return as an allegory of the return of the strayed soul to God (that it may die "married" to God, and that God's love for it be made manifest to all time). Virgil describes Marcia as still praying to Cato.

89. *the Decree*: May be taken as that law that makes an absolute separation between the damned and the saved. Cato cannot be referring here to *Mark,* xii, 25 ("when they shall rise from the dead, they neither marry, nor are given in marriage") for that "decree" was not pronounced upon his ascent from Limbo.

98. *filmed by mist*: Of Hell.

100 ff. THE REED. The pliant reed clearly symbolizes humility, but other allegorical meanings suggest themselves at once. First, the Reed takes the place of the Cord that Dante took from about his waist in order to signal Geryon. The Cord had been intended to snare and defeat the Leopard with the Gaudy Pelt, a direct assault upon sin. It is now superseded by the Reed of submission to God's will. Second, the reeds are eternal and undiminishable. As such they must immediately suggest the redemption purchased by Christ's sufferings (ever-abounding grace), for the quantity of grace available to mankind through Christ's passion is, in Christian creed, also eternal and undiminishable. The importance of the fact that the reeds grow at the lowest point of the Island and that the Poets must descend to them before they can begin, has already been mentioned. Curiously, the reed is never again mentioned, though it must remain around Dante's waist. See also *Matthew,* xxvii, 29.

119. *breeze shielded the dew*: The dew is a natural symbol of God's grace. The morning breeze shields it in the sense that, being cool, it retards evaporation.

Even more naturally, being bathed in the dew may be taken to signify baptism. The structure of Purgatory certainly suggests a parable of the soul's stages of sacred development: the dew, baptism; the gate of Purgatory, above, first communion; Virgil's certification of Dante as lord of himself (XXVII, 143), confirmation; and Dante's swoon and awakening (XXXI, 89), as extreme unction and the reception into the company of the blessed.

Canto II

ANTE-PURGATORY: THE SHORE OF THE ISLAND

The Angel Boatman · *Casella* · *Cato of Utica*

It is dawn. Dante, washed, and girded by the reed, is standing by the shore when he sees a light approaching at enormous speed across the sea. The light grows and becomes visible as *The Angel Boatman* who ferries the souls of the elect from their gathering place at *The Mouth of the Tiber* to the shore of Purgatory.

The newly arrived souls debark and, taking the Poets as familiars of the place, ask directions. Virgil explains that he and Dante are new arrivals but that they have come by the dark road through Hell. The newly arrived souls see by his breathing that Dante is alive and crowd about him. One of the new souls is *Casella*, a musician who seems to have been a dear friend of Dante's. Dante tries three times to clasp him to his bosom, but each time his arms pass through empty air. Casella explains the function of the Angel Boatman and then, at Dante's request, strikes up a song, one of Dante's own *canzone* that Casella had set to music. Instantly, *Cato* descends upon the group, berating them, and they break like startled pigeons up the slope toward the mountain.

> The sun already burned at the horizon,
>   while the high point of its meridian circle
>   covered Jerusalem, and in opposition   3
>
> equal Night revolved above the Ganges
>   bearing the Scales that fall out of her hand
>   as she grows longer with the season's changes: 6
>
> thus, where I was, Aurora in her passage
>   was losing the pale blushes from her cheeks
>   which turned to orange with increasing age.   9
>
> We were still standing by the sea's new day
>   like travelers pondering the road ahead
>   who send their souls on while their bones delay;   12
>
> when low above the ocean's western rim,
>   as Mars, at times, observed through the thick vapors
>   that form before the dawn, burns red and slim;   15
>
> just so—so may I hope to see it again!—
>   a light appeared, moving above the sea
>   faster than any flight. A moment then   18
>
> I turned my eyes to question my sweet Guide,
>   and when I looked back to that unknown body
>   I found its mass and brightness magnified.   21

Then from each side of it came into view
    an unknown something-white; and from beneath it,
    bit by bit, another whiteness grew.   24

We watched till the white objects at each side
    took shape as wings, and Virgil spoke no word.
    But when he saw what wings they were, he cried: 27

"Down on your knees! It is God's angel comes!
    Down! Fold your hands! From now on you shall see
    many such ministers in the high kingdoms.   30

See how he scorns man's tools: he needs no oars
    nor any other sail than his own wings
    to carry him between such distant shores.   33

See how his pinions tower upon the air,
    pointing to Heaven: they are eternal plumes
    and do not moult like feathers or human hair."   36

Then as that bird of heaven closed the distance
    between us, he grew brighter and yet brighter
    until I could no longer bear the radiance,   39

and bowed my head. He steered straight for the shore,
    his ship so light and swift it drew no water;
    it did not seem to sail so much as soar.   42

Astern stood the great pilot of the Lord,
    so fair his blessedness seemed written on him;
    and more than a hundred souls were seated forward,   45

singing as if they raised a single voice
    in exitu Israel de Aegypto.
    Verse after verse they made the air rejoice.   48

The angel made the sign of the cross, and they
    cast themselves, at his signal, to the shore.
    Then, swiftly as he had come, he went away.   51

The throng he left seemed not to understand
    what place it was, but stood and stared about
    like men who see the first of a new land.   54

The Sun, who with an arrow in each ray
    had chased the Goat out of the height of Heaven,
    on every hand was shooting forth the day,   57

when those new souls looked up to where my Guide
    and I stood, saying to us, "If you know it,
    show us the road that climbs the mountainside."   60

Virgil replied: "You think perhaps we two
    have had some long experience of this place,
    but we are also pilgrims, come before you   63

only by very little, though by a way
   so steep, so broken, and so tortuous
   the climb ahead of us will seem like play."   66

The throng of souls, observing by my breath
   I was still in the body I was born to,
   stared in amazement and grew pale as death.   69

As a crowd, eager for news, will all but smother
   a messenger who bears the olive branch,
   and not care how they trample one another—   72

so these, each one of them a soul elect,
   pushed close to stare at me, well-nigh forgetting
   the way to go to make their beauty perfect.   75

One came forward to embrace me, and his face
   shone with such joyous love that, seeing it,
   I moved to greet him with a like embrace.   78

O solid seeming shadows! Three times there
   I clasped my hands behind him, and three times
   I drew them to my breast through empty air.   81

Amazed, I must have lost all color then,
   for he smiled tenderly and drew away,
   and I lunged forward as if to try again.   84

In a voice as gentle as a melody
   he bade me pause; and by his voice I knew him,
   and begged him stay a while and speak to me.   87

He answered: "As I loved you in the clay
   of my mortal body, so do I love you freed:
   therefore I pause. But what brings you this way?"   90

"Casella mine, I go the way I do
   in the hope I may return here," I replied.
   "But why has so much time been taken from you?"   93

And he: "I am not wronged if he whose usage
   accepts the soul at his own time and pleasure
   has many times refused to give me passage: 96

his will moves in the image and perfection
   of a Just Will; indeed, for three months now
   he has taken all who asked, without exception.   99

And so it was that in my turn I stood
   upon that shore where Tiber's stream grows salt,
   and there was gathered to my present good.   102

It is back to the Tiber's mouth he has just flown,
   for there forever is the gathering place
   of all who do not sink to Acheron."   105

"If no new law has stripped you of your skill
or of the memory of those songs of love
that once could calm all passion from my will,"   108

I said to him, "Oh sound a verse once more
to soothe my soul which, with its weight of flesh
and the long journey, sinks distressed and sore."   111

"Love that speaks its reasons in my heart,"
he sang then, and such grace flowed on the air
that even now I hear that music start.   114

My Guide and I and all those souls of bliss
stood tranced in song; when suddenly we heard
the Noble Elder cry: "What's this! What's this!   117

Negligence! Loitering! O laggard crew
run to the mountain and strip off the scurf
that lets not God be manifest in you!"   120

Exactly as a flock of pigeons gleaning
a field of stubble, pecking busily,
forgetting all their primping and their preening,   123

will rise as one and scatter through the air,
leaving their feast without another thought
when they are taken by a sudden scare—   126

so that new band, all thought of pleasure gone,
broke from the feast of music with a start
and scattered for the mountainside like one   129

who leaps and does not look where he will land.
Nor were my Guide and I inclined to stand.

Notes

1–9. The bit of erudite affectation in which Dante indulges here means simply, "It was dawn." To understand the total figure, one must recall the following essentials of Dante's geography: (1) Jerusalem is antipodal to the Mount of Purgatory. Thus it is sunset at Jerusalem when it is sunrise on the mountain. (2) All the land of the earth is contained in one half of the Northern Hemisphere. That is to say, there is no land (except the Mount of Purgatory) anywhere in the Southern Hemisphere and of the total circle of the Northern Hemisphere (360°) only half (180°) is land. Jerusalem is at the exact center of this 180° arc of land. Spain, 90° to one side, is the West, and India (Ganges), 90° to the other, is the East.

Every fifteen degrees of longitude equals one hour of time. That is to say, it takes the Sun an hour to travel fifteen degrees. Thus at sunset over Jerusalem it is midnight (six hours later) over India, and noon (six hours earlier) over Spain. The journey, moreover, is conceived as taking place during the venal equinox, when the days and nights are of the same length. Thus it is "equal Night" (line 4).

Finally, when the Sun is in Aries, midnight is in Libra (the Scales). Thus the night bears the Scales in her hand (*i.e.*, that constellation is visible), but Libra will no longer be the sign of the night as the season changes, and thus it may be said that the Scales will fall from her hand (*i.e.*, will no longer be visible).

47. *in exitu Israel de Aegypto*: When Israel out of Egypt came. Psalm CXIII.

50. *cast themselves, at his signal, to the shore*: Note that this is exactly what Dante says of the sinners leaving Charon's ferry in *Inferno*, III, 113. In Dante there

is no accident in such correspondence. Such parallels between the *Purgatorio* and the *Inferno* are essential parts of the poem's total structure.

56. *the Goat*: Capricorn.

71. *who bears the olive branch*: In Dante's time couriers bore the olive branch to indicate not only peace but good news in general.

79–84. *O solid seeming shadows*: As always, Dante treats the substance of the souls to suit his own dramatic convenience, at times giving them attributes of fleshly bodies, at others treating them as mirages.

91. *Casella*: Practically all that is known about Casella has been drawn from the text itself. He seems to have died several months before Dante began his journey, hence early in 1300 or late in 1299. There is no explanation of his delay in reaching Purgatory (the time that has been taken from him). Dante later meets several classes of sinners who must spend a certain period of waiting before they can begin their purification. Clearly it is Dante's conception that the souls bound for Purgatory do not always proceed instantly to their destination, but may be required to expiate by a delay at their gathering point by the mouth of the Tiber (line 101).

Casella was a musician and is known to have set some of Dante's *canzone* to music. The song he strikes up (line 112) is such a *canzone*.

99. *he has taken all who asked*: Boniface VIII decreed a Jubilee Year from Christmas 1299 to Christmas 1300. (*See Inferno*, XVIII, 28–33 and note.) His decree extended special indulgences even to the dead. Hence the Angel's permissiveness.

Note, however, that he has taken all who wished to go, all who asked. It follows that some souls did not express such a wish, almost certainly because they did not feel themselves to be ready. As in note to I, 5, the souls of Purgatory decide for themselves when they are ready to progress from one stage to the next.

Canto III

The souls scatter for the mountain, and Dante draws close to Virgil as they both race ahead. The newly risen sun is at Dante's back. He runs, therefore, with his shadow stretched long and directly before him. Suddenly he becomes aware that there is only one shadow on the ground and he turns in panic, thinking Virgil is no longer at his side. Virgil reassures him, explaining that souls are so made as to cast no shadow. His remarks on the nature of souls give him occasion to define *The Limits of Reason in the Scheme of Creation.*

The poets reach *The Base of the Cliff* and are dismayed to find that it rises sheer, offering no way by which they may climb. While Virgil is pondering this new difficulty, Dante looks about and sees a band of souls approaching so slowly that they seem scarcely to move. These are the first of *The Late Repentant* souls the Poets will encounter. In life they put off the desire for grace: now, as they were laggard in life, so must they wait before they may begin their purification. The souls in this band are all souls of *The Contumacious:* they died excommunicated, but surrendered their souls to God when they were at the point of death. Their punishment is that they must wait here at the Base of the Cliff for thirty times the period of their contumacy.

One soul among them identifies himself as *Manfred* and begs Dante to bear a message to his daughter Constance in order that she may offer prayers for Manfred's soul and thereby shorten his period of waiting. Manfred explains that prayer can greatly assist the souls in Purgatory. He also explains how it is that though contumacy is punished, no act of priest or pope may keep from salvation a soul that has truly given itself to God.

> Those routed souls scattered across the scene,
> their faces once again turned toward the mountain
> where Reason spurs and Justice picks us clean;   3
>
> but I drew ever closer to my Guide:
> and how could I have run my course without him?
> who would have led me up the mountainside?   6
>
> He seemed gnawed by remorse for his offense:
> O noble conscience without stain! how sharp
> the sting of a small fault is to your sense!   9
>
> When he had checked that haste that urges men
> to mar the dignity of every act,
> my mind, forced in upon itself till then,   12
>
> broke free, and eager to see all before me,
> I raised my eyes in wonder to that mountain
> that soars highest to Heaven from the sea.   15

Low at my back, the sun was a red blaze;
  its light fell on the ground before me broken
  in the form in which my body blocked its rays.   18

I gave a start of fear and whirled around
  seized by the thought that I had been abandoned,
  for I saw one shadow only on the ground.   21

And my Comfort turned full to me then to say:
  "Why are you still uncertain? Why do you doubt
  that I am here and guide you on your way?   24

Vespers have rung already on the tomb
  of the body in which I used to cast a shadow.
  It was taken to Naples from Brindisium.   27

If now I cast no shadow, should that fact
  amaze you more than the heavens which pass the light
  undimmed from one to another? We react   30

within these bodies to pain and heat and cold
  according to the workings of That Will
  which does not will that all Its ways be told.   33

He is insane who dreams that he may learn
  by mortal reasoning the boundless orbit
  Three Persons in One Substance fill and turn.   36

Be satisfied with the *quia* of cause unknown,
  O humankind! for could you have seen All,
  Mary need not have suffered to bear a son.   39

You saw how some yearn endlessly in vain:
  such as would, else, have surely had their wish,
  but have, instead, its hunger as their pain.   42

I speak of Aristotle and Plato," he said.
  "—Of them and many more." And here he paused,
  and sorrowing and silent, bowed his head.   45

Meanwhile we reached the mountain's foot; and there
  we found so sheer a cliff, the nimblest legs
  would not have served, unless they walked on air.   48

The most forsaken and most broken goat-trace
  in the mountains between Lerici and Turbia
  compared to this would seem a gracious staircase.   51

My Guide exclaimed: "Now who is there to say
  in which direction we may find some slope
  up which one without wings may pick his way!"   54

While he was standing, head bowed to his shoulders,
  and pondering which direction we might take,
  I stood there looking up among the boulders,   57

and saw upon my left beside that cliff-face
   a throng that moved its feet in our direction,
   and yet seemed not to, so slow was its pace.   60

"Master," I said, "look up and you will find
   some people coming who may solve the problem,
   if you have not yet solved it in your mind."   63

He looked up then and, openly relieved,
   said: "Let us go to them, since they lag so.
   And you, dear son, believe as you have believed."   66

We were as far off yet from that slow flock
   (I mean when we had gone a thousand paces)
   as a strong slingsman could have thrown a rock,   69

when they drew in against the cliff and stood there
   like men who fear what they see coming toward them
   and, waiting for it, huddle close and stare.   72

"O well-concluded lives! O souls thus met
   already among the chosen!" Virgil said,
   "By that sweet crown of peace that shall be set   75

on each of you in time, tell us which way
   leads to some slope by which we two may climb.
   Who best knows time is most grieved by delay."   78

As sheep come through a gate—by ones, by twos,
   by threes, and all the others trail behind,
   timidly, nose to ground, and what the first does   81

the others do, and if the first one pauses,
   the others huddle up against his back,
   silly and mute, not knowing their own causes—   84

just so, I stood there watching with my Guide,
   the first row of that happy flock come on,
   their look meek and their movements dignified.   87

And when the souls that came first in that flock
   saw the light broken on the ground to my right
   so that my shadow fell upon the rock,   90

they halted and inched back as if to shy,
   and all the others who came after them
   did as the first did without knowing why.   93

"Let me confirm the thought you leave unspoken:
   it is a living body you see before you
   by which the sunlight on the ground is broken.   96

Do not be astonished: you may rest assured
   he does not seek the way to climb this wall
   without a power from Heaven."—Thus my Lord   99

addressed them, and those worthy spirits said,
  waving the backs of their hands in our direction:
  "First turn around, and then go straight ahead."   102

And one soul said to me: "Whoever you are,
  as you move on, look back and ask yourself
  if you have ever seen me over there."   105

I studied him with care, my head turned round:
  gold-blond he was, and handsomely patrician,
  although one brow was split by a sword wound.   108

When I, in all humility, confessed
  I never before had seen him, he said, "Look"
  —and showed me a great slash above his breast.   111

Then, smiling, added: "I am Manfred, grandson
  of the blessed Empress Constance, and I beg you,
  when you return there over the horizon,   114

go to my sweet daughter, noble mother
  of the honor of Sicily and of Aragon
  and speak the truth, if men speak any other.   117

My flesh had been twice hacked, and each wound mortal,
  when, tearfully, I yielded up my soul
  to Him whose pardon gladly waits for all.   120

Horrible were my sins, but infinite
  is the abiding Goodness which holds out
  its open arms to all who turn to It.   123

If the pastor of Cosenza, by the rage
  of Clement sent to hunt me down, had first
  studied the book of God at this bright page,   126

my body's bones would still be in the ground
  there by the bridgehead outside Benevento,
  under the heavy guard of the stone mound.   129

Now, rattled by the wind, by the rain drenched,
  they lie outside the kingdom, by the Verde,
  where he transported them with tapers quenched.   132

No man may be so cursed by priest or pope
  but what the Eternal Love may still return
  while any thread of green lives on in hope.   135

Those who die contumacious, it is true,
  though they repent their feud with Holy Church,
  must wait outside here on the bank, as we do,   138

for thirty times as long as they refused
  to be obedient, though by good prayers
  in their behalf, that time may be reduced.   141

See, then, how great a service you may do me
    when you return, by telling my good Constance
    of my condition and of this decree   144

that still forbids our entrance to the kingdom.
    For here, from those beyond, great good may come."

Notes

1–3. The original lines are in Dante's densest style, and every commentator has felt the need to discuss this passage at length. *once again turned*: Dante's intent here seems clear enough. On their arrival the souls had looked straight ahead at the mountain. The distraction for which Cato chastised them had led them to look away. *where Reason spurs and Justice picks us clean*: The original phrasing is *ove ragion ne fruga*. If *ragion* is taken to mean "reason" and *fruga* in one of its senses to mean "to prick on," then one meaning follows clearly enough. If, however, *ragion* is taken in context to mean Divine Justice—and many commentators have argued that it must so be taken—and if *fruga* (a very complex word) is taken in its first sense of "to probe, to search minutely, to pick clean"—then a second meaning follows. I am inclined to think that Dante always means both possibilities in such cases and I have therefore rendered both.

10–11. *that haste that urges men to mar the dignity of every act*: There can be no doubt that Dante cherished his dignity. Even in moving toward salvation he preferred a slow and stately manner. On his own premises, there is obviously a taint of pride in such a disposition. When he reaches the Cornice of the Proud, he makes it clear that Pride is the sin that most weighs upon him. Dignity, of course, is closely related to Moderation, one of the Cardinal Virtues.

21 ff. *for I saw one shadow only on the ground*: The fact that Dante was still in his mortal body was evidenced in Hell by his breathing, by the way his weight made a boat settle in the water, by the fact that his foot dislodged a stone, and by the force with which he inadvertently kicked one of the damned. Now that he is once more in the light, his shadow becomes the principal means of identifying him as a living man, for souls cast no shadows. Dante is to use this device often in the Cantos that follow.

27. *It was taken to Naples from Brindisium*: Virgil died in Brindisium in 19 B.C. His bones were later exhumed and reinterred in Naples by order of the Emperor Augustus.

29–30. *the heavens which pass the light*: The heavens are the spheres of the Ptolemaic system. They are conceived as crystalline and as so clear that light passes from one to the other undiminished. Dante's figure, literally rendered, is: "whose rays do not block one another."

40–45. *You saw how some yearn*: Dante saw them in Limbo. As Virgil goes on to explain, he means "the masters of those who know." His clear implication is that if such monuments of human intellect could never penetrate the mystery of the All, it is folly for mankind to seek to explain the reasons for God's ways. *Of them and many more*: Part of Virgil's sorrow is due to the fact that he is one of the "many more."

50. *Lerici and Turbia*: Lerici lies on the shores of the Mediterranean near the river Magra, and Turbia stands a bit inland from the Mediterranean on the other side of Liguria. The tract of mountains between them is one of the most rugged in all Europe.

52. *Now who is there to say*: Virgil had traveled through Hell once before (see *Inferno*, IX, 24, note) and knew that way, but the road of Purgatory is unknown to him.

58 ff. THE CONTUMACIOUS. The section of the Mount of Purgatory that lies below the Gate (the Ante-Purgatory) is occupied by the Late Repentant who put off their surrender to God until the end of their lives. As they made God wait, so must they now wait before they may begin their purification. These souls suffer no pain but the burning of their own frustrated desire to mount to God. They may well be compared with the souls in Limbo, except that they are all assured that they will one day rise, whereas there is no hope in Limbo.

The Contumacious, therefore, are the first class of the Late Repentant. (Hence the slowness of their motions now. Note that such slowness, in constraining souls whose most ardent wish is to race forward to God, is a moral allegory. Purgatory, one must recall, is the way to the renunciation of sin. The soul so long curbed cannot fail to root out of itself the last laggard impulse. Such, at least, is clearly Dante's moral intention.) The present band must expiate not only personal negligence and tardiness in turning to God but disobedience to the Church from which they were excommuni-

cated. Before they can mount to the next phase of their purification they must delay
here for a period thirty times as long as the period of their disobedience.

66. *believe as you have believed*: Virgil's remark here is best taken to mean, in an
extended paraphrase: "Continue as you have done [to submit yourself and your
reason to the revealed fact of God without seeking to probe too deeply], for unlike
these souls who put off their repentance to the moment of their deaths, you have
repented early and strained every resource to win to Grace."

74. *already among the chosen*: The souls in Purgatory must suffer their purification
but they are already, in effect, saved and will eventually enter Heaven.

78. *Who best knows time is most grieved by delay*: A home thrust. Who knows
time better than these souls who must suffer their most grievious delay?

89–90. *to my right . . . my shadow fell upon the rock*: The sun has only recently
risen. It is still, therefore, in the east. Since it threw Dante's shadow directly before
him as he approached the mountain, and now throws his shadow to the right, the
Poets must have moved more or less due west toward the cliff and must then have
borne south.

101. *waving the backs of their hands in our direction*: To indicate the way. The
gesture is Italian. We should be inclined to point.

104. *as you move on, look back*: Note that the speaker does not ask Dante to
delay his journey even an instant, but only to look back while continuing on his way.

105. *over there*: In Purgatory "over there" always means "back in the world."

108. *one brow was split by a sword wound*: See also line 111: *a great slash above
his breast*: Dante obviously intends the souls to be immaterial replicas of the last
appearance of the mortal flesh. In future Cantos, however, he does not pursue this
idea. See XXV, 34–108, note, for a discourse on the nature of aerial bodies.

112. *I am Manfred*: Manfred, King of Sicily, was the legitimized natural son of
Frederick II. He was born in Sicily in 1231 and was killed at the battle of Benevento
after a defeat by Charles of Anjou in 1266. (See *Inferno*, XXVIII, 16, note.) He was
famous as an Epicurean (see *Inferno*, X, 14, note) and for his taste for physical
pleasures rather than for godliness. In the everlasting internal wars of Italy, Manfred
often opposed the Papal States, but was too powerful to be excommunicated while
alive. He was nevertheless disobedient to Mother Church and therefore must pass
thirty times the period of his disobedience outside the cliff. He has served 24 years to
date. Assuming that he was contumacious for half his life (17½ years), his total
delay would amount to 525 years, if not shortened by prayer.

112–113. *grandson of the blessed Empress Constance*: Constance was the mother of
Frederick II. Since Manfred was not a legitimate son, he identifies himself by his
grandmother as a delicate way of avoiding any reference to his illegitimacy.

115. *my sweet daughter*: Also named Constance. She married Peter of Aragon and
bore him three sons. One died before full manhood. Of the remaining two, Frederick
became King of Sicily, and Iacopo succeeded his father to the throne of Aragon.

118. *My flesh had been twice hacked*: At the battle of Benevento. After Manfred's
defeat and death, Charles of Anjou ordered that every soldier in his army file past
the body of the dead Manfred and place a stone upon it. Thus a great cairn was
erected to the memory of a fallen warrior.

124. *the pastor of Cosenza*: Bartolommeo Pignatelli, cardinal and archbishop of
Cosenza from 1254 to 1266. On orders from Pope Clement IV, he disinterred the
body of Manfred and had it carried without honors (with quenched tapers) outside
the kingdom of Naples, which was then a Papal State. Thus, Clement expelled from
Church territory the body of the man he could not expel in life.

131. *the Verde*: Various streams may be identified as the Verde. Dante clearly
enough implies that Manfred's body was carried out of the kingdom of Naples and
deposited on the other side of a boundary-river.

139. *thirty times*: There seems to be no identifiable significance to Dante's choice
of thirty (instead, say, of fifty, or a hundred, or any other multiple).

Canto IV

ANTE-PURGATORY: THE FIRST LEDGE

The Late-Repentant · Class Two: The Indolent · Belacqua

Listening to Manfred's discourse, Dante has lost track of time. Now, at midmorning, the Poets reach the opening in the cliff-face and begin the laborious climb. Dante soon tires and cries that he can go no farther, but Virgil urges him to pull himself a little higher yet—significantly—to the *Ledge of the Indolent*, those souls whose sin was their delay in pulling themselves up the same hard path.

Seated on the ledge, Virgil explains that in the nature of the mountain, the beginning of the ascent (the First Turning from Sin to True Repentance) is always hardest. The higher one climbs from sin to repentance, the easier it becomes to climb still higher until, in the Perfection of Grace, the climb becomes effortless. But to that ultimate height, as Virgil knows, Human Reason cannot reach. It is Beatrice (Divine Love) who must guide him there.

As Virgil finishes speaking, an ironic reply comes from behind a boulder. The speaker is *Belacqua*, an old friend of Dante's, and the laziest man in Florence. Because of his indolence, he put off good works and the active desire for grace until he lay dying. In life he made God wait. Now God makes him wait an equal period before he may pass through the Gate into Purgatory and begin his purification. Unless, as Belacqua adds, the prayers of the devout intercede for him.

But now Virgil points out that the sun is already at its noon-height and that Dante, unlike the Indolent, must not delay.

When any sense of ours records intense
    pleasure or pain, then the whole soul is drawn
    by such impressions into that one sense,   3

and seems to lose all other powers. And thus
    do I refute the error that asserts
    that one soul on another burns in us.   6

And, for this reason, when we see or hear
    whatever seizes strongly on the soul,
    time passes, and we lose it unaware.   9

For that which senses is one faculty;
    and that which keeps the soul intact, another:
    the first, as it were, bound; the second, free.   12

To this, my own experience bears witness,
    for while I listened to that soul and marveled,
    the sun had climbed—without my least awareness—   15

to fifty full degrees of its noon peak
    when, at one point along the way, that band
    cried out in chorus: "Here is what you seek."   18

Often when grapes hang full on slope and ledge
  the peasant, with one forkful of his thorns,
  seals up a wider opening in his hedge   21

than the gap we found there in that wall of stone;
  up which—leaving that band of souls behind—
  my Guide led and I followed: we two alone.   24

Go up to San Leo or go down to Noli;
  go climb Bismantova—two legs suffice:
  here nothing but swift wings will answer wholly.   27

The swift wings and the feathers, I mean to say,
  of great desire led onward by that Guide
  who was my hope and light along the way.   30

Squeezed in between two walls that almost meet
  we labor upward through the riven rock:
  a climb that calls for both our hands and feet.   33

Above the cliff's last rise we reached in time
  an open slope. "Do we go right or left?"
  I asked my Master, "or do we still climb?"   36

And he: "Take not one step to either side,
  but follow yet, and make way up the mountain
  till we meet someone who may serve as guide."   39

Higher than sight the peak soared to the sky:
  much steeper than a line drawn from mid-quadrant
  to the center, was the slope that met my eye.   42

The climb had sapped my last strength when I cried:
  "Sweet Father, turn to me: unless you pause
  I shall be left here on the mountainside!"   45

He pointed to a ledge a little ahead
  that wound around the whole face of the slope.
  "Pull yourself that much higher, my son," he said. 48

His words so spurred me that I forced myself
  to push on after him on hands and knees
  until at last my feet were on that shelf.   51

There we sat, facing eastward, to survey
  the trail we had just climbed; for oftentimes
  a backward look comforts one on the way.   54

I looked down first to the low-lying shore,
  then upward to the sun—and stopped amazed,
  for it was from the left its arrows bore.   57

Virgil was quick to note the start I gave
  when I beheld the Chariot of the Sun
  driven between me and the North Wind's cave.   60

"Were Castor and Pollux," he said, "in company
of that bright mirror which sends forth its rays
equally up and down, then you would see   63

the twelve-toothed cogwheel of the Zodiac
turned till it blazed still closer to the Bears
—unless it were to stray from its fixed track.   66

If you wish to understand why this is so,
imagine Zion and this Mount so placed
on earth, the one above, the other below,   69

that the two have one horizon though they lie
in different hemispheres. Therefore, the path
that Phaëthon could not follow in the sky   72

must necessarily, in passing here
on the one side, pass there upon the other,
as your own reasoning will have made clear."   75

And I then: "Master, I may truly vow
I never grasped so well the very point
on which my wits were most astray just now: 78

that the mid-circle of the highest Heaven,
called the Equator, always lies between
the sun and winter, and, for the reason given,   81

lies as far north of this place at all times
as the Hebrews, when they held Jerusalem,
were wont to see it toward the warmer climes.   84

But—if you please—I should be glad to know
how far we have yet to climb, for the peak soars
higher to Heaven than my eye can go."   87

And he: "Such is this Mount that when a soul
begins the lower slopes it most must labor;
then less and less the more it nears its goal.   90

Thus when we reach the point where the slopes seem
so smooth and gentle that the climb becomes
as easy as to float a skiff downstream,   93

then will this road be run, and not before
that journey's end will your repose be found.
I know this much for truth and say no more."   96

His words were hardly out when, from nearby,
we heard a voice say: "Maybe by that time
you'll find you need to sit before you fly!"   99

We turned together at the sound, and there,
close on our left, we saw a massive boulder
of which, till then, we had not been aware.   102

To it we dragged ourselves, and there we found
  stretched in the shade, the way a slovenly man
  lies down to rest, some people on the ground.   105

The weariest of them, judging by his pose,
  sat hugging both knees while his head, abandoned,
  dropped down between them halfway to his toes.   108

"Master," I said, "look at that sorry one
  who seems so all-let-down. Were Sloth herself
  his sister, he could not be so far gone!"   111

That heap took heed, and even turned his head
  upon his thigh—enough to look at us.
  "You climb it if you're such a flash," he said.   114

I knew him then, and all the agony
  that still burned in my lungs and raced my pulse
  did not prevent my going to him. He   117

raising his head—just barely—when I stood by,
  drawled: "So you really know now why the sun
  steers to the left of you across the sky?"   120

His short words and his shorter acts, combined,
  made me half smile as I replied: "Belacqua,
  your fate need never again trouble my mind.   123

Praise be for that. But why do you remain
  crouched here? Are you waiting for a guide, perhaps?
  Or are you up to your old tricks again?"   126

"Old friend," he said, "what good is it to climb?—
  God's Bird above the Gate would never let me
  pass through to start my trials before my time.   129

I must wait here until the heavens wheel past
  as many times as they passed me in my life,
  for I delayed the good sighs till the last.   132

Prayer could help me, if a heart God's love
  has filled with Grace should offer it. All other
  is worthless, for it is not heard above."   135

But now the Poet already led the way
  to the slope above, saying to me: "Come now:
  the sun has touched the very peak of day   138

above the sea, and night already stands
  with one black foot upon Morocco's sands."

Notes

1–12. THE DOCTRINE OF MULTIPLE SOULS. The original doctrine (the "error" of line 5) was set forth by Plato, who claimed that we have three souls within us, each with its specific function: the Vegetative Soul (roughly corresponding to what we might call the Somatic) which is seated in the liver, the Sensitive (*i.e.*, the Emotional) Soul which is seated in the heart, and the Intellectual Soul which is seated in the brain. Dante's emphatic concern over this point is easy enough to understand. Plato was, for him, one of the fundamental sources of the truth. Yet here, Plato was putting forth a doctrine impossible to reconcile with the Christian doctrine of the unity of the soul. (If there are several souls in a man, how shall one judgment fit them all?) Aristotle (see XXV, 52 ff.), the Church Fathers, Aquinas, and many others also found it necessary to repudiate or to modify this Platonic doctrine. The fact that Dante had seen himself as a follower of Plato in the *Vita Nuova* is one more evidence that the *Purgatorio* is intended, among other things, as a progress of the soul. Dante is correcting his earlier errors and turning his mind to greater sources.

16. *to fifty full degrees of its noon peak*: Since one degree of arc equals four minutes of time, the sun, therefore, traverses fifteen degrees an hour. It is, therefore, three hours and twenty minutes since sunrise, at which time (Canto II) Dante saw the Angel Pilot bring in his cargo of souls. On Easter in the year 1300 the sun rose a little before 6:00. It is now, therefore, a little after 9:00 A.M.

25–26. *San Leo*: An almost inaccessible town on a mountaintop near San Marino. *Noli*: a seacoast town accessible (in Dante's time) only from the sea or by treacherously steep steps cut into the cliffs behind the town. *Bismantova*: a village on a mountain of the same name about twenty miles south of Reggio Emilia. Dante selects three places that his contemporaries would recognize as most difficult to get to, and then says in effect that the climb to them is nothing as compared to the labor of climbing Purgatory.

30. *light*: The narrowness of the fissure would make it dark. Virgil's allegorical character as Human Reason is especially important in this context.

33. *a climb that calls for both our hands and feet*: Dante uses this same figure in describing the path that led up from the Bolgia of the Thieves (*Inferno*, XXVI, 18): "the foot could make no way without the hand."

37 ff. *Take not one step to either side*: The original contains an ambiguity that has led many commentators to understand Virgil as saying "Take not one backward step," that being the law of the mountain. In context, however, such a rendering seems doubtful. Dante had no least thought of taking a backward step. He has asked, "Do we go right or left," and Virgil replies, logically, "no least step to either side but upward only." See also *Isaiah*, xxx, 21, and *Joshua*, i, 7.

41–42. *a line drawn from mid-quadrant to the center*: of an astrolabe. Hence 45°. Note, however, that the slope is "much steeper" than 45°.

50–51. *my feet were on that shelf*: (Literally: "the shelf was under my feet.") Dante says nothing to explain why a man climbing on "hands and knees" (Italian: *carpando*) to a ledge above him would not simple crawl onto it (especially if near exhaustion) instead of first standing on it and then sitting down. He might, perhaps, have meant that he crawled onto the ledge, then sat with his knees drawn up so that the ledge was under his feet. Perhaps.

55–75. THE POSITION OF THE SUN: Dante, habituated to the phenomena of the Northern Hemisphere, is astonished to find that the sun is on his left (*i.e.*, north) when he faces east. Virgil points out that there is nothing surprising in that, and that as the sun moves toward the summer solstice it will move even further north (toward "the Bears" of line 65, *i.e.*, Ursa Major and Ursa Minor, the Big and the Little Dipper) into the zodiacal sign of Gemini, the Twins (*i.e.*, Castor and Pollux). Unless, he adds with something like humor, it should depart from its fixed track.

Virgil then goes on to a more detailed statement of the case. He asks Dante to visualize the globe with the Mount of Zion and the Mount of Purgatory so placed that they are in different hemispheres but share the same celestial horizon. They are, therefore, antipodal, and since the sun must pass between them, it follows that when it is on one side of one it must be on the other side of the other, *i.e.*, Zion must always be north of the sun and Purgatory must always be south of it. Since the two places are antipodal, moreover, the celestial equator is always as far south of one as it is north of the other.

60. *the North Wind's cave*: Aquilon, the North Wind, rules the compass from NW to NE, *i.e.*, for 45° on either side of the North Pole.

62–63. *that bright mirror*: The Sun, reflector of God's Love. *up and down*: in two senses: first, to the upper (Northern) and lower (Southern) Hemispheres; second, up to Heaven and down to Earth.

71–72. *the path that Phaëthon could not follow*: Apollo was the charioteer of the Sun. One day Phaëthon, son of Apollo, tried to drive the chariot of his father, but lost control and the four great horses dragged the Sun out of its course, threatening both Heaven and Earth until Zeus killed Phaëthon with a thunderbolt and saved Creation. The Milky Way is the scar left on the sky by Phaëthon's mad course.

76–84. THE CELESTIAL EQUATOR: The passage is in Dante's most pedantic style and has given rise to several varying interpretations. I take the soundest of them

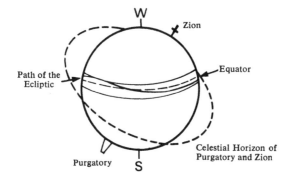

to be based on Dante's *Il Convivio*, II, iv, 50–58: "And it is to be understood that each heaven below the Crystalline [*i.e.*, the *Sphere of the Fixed Stars*] has two poles that are constant in relation to that heaven itself; and the ninth [the Crystalline] has two poles that are firm and fixed and immovable in every respect; and each, the ninth like all the others, has a circle which may be called the equator of its proper heaven; the which is equally distant from one pole and the other, as one may clearly understand if he revolves an apple or some other round thing."

Hence the following extended paraphrase of lines 79–84: "The mid-circle of the Crystalline Sphere, which is called the Celestial Equator, always lies between the Sun and that hemisphere in which it is winter, and, for the reason you have just given [*i.e.*, that Purgatory and Zion are antipodal] the Celestial Equator must always lie as far to the north of this place [Purgatory] as the Hebrews [when, before the dispersion of the Jews, they looked at it from Jerusalem] were accustomed to seeing it toward the south [warmer climes]."

96. *I know this much for truth and say no more*: At that journey's end, Virgil (Human Reason) will vanish and Beatrice (Divine Love, a compound of Mercy, Light, and Contemplation) will lead Dante. Virgil has spoken as much as Reason can know to be true.

97–135. Belacqua: He was a Florentine who manufactured parts for musical instruments. Of him the Anonimo Fiorentino says: "He was the most indolent man who ever lived. . . . Dante was very intimate with him and used often to take him to task for his laziness." Dante's own treatment of him would certainly indicate that he is dealing with an old friend about whose indolence he has often worried.

119–120. *So you really know now . . .* : Belacqua's words are sarcastic, perhaps by way of taking revenge for Dante's description of him to Virgil, but it is the easy and fond sarcasm of a friend, and Dante accepts Belacqua's way of speaking with a half-smile.

128. *God's Bird above The Gate*: God's Angel above the Gate Dante will come to in Canto IX. Dante refers to Angels as God's Birds in a number of passages. The gate is the entrance to Purgatory proper. There is no gate between Purgatory and Heaven as there is between Earth and Hell. Those who pass the Gate of Purgatory are already effectively in Heaven, though they must first undergo their purification.

130–132. *I must wait here*: Because Belacqua indolently put off his repentance (the good sighs) until his last breath, he in effect refused God during the days of his life. Now God makes Belacqua wait, before he may begin his approach to Heaven, for as long a period as Belacqua made Him wait.

133–135. *Prayer could help me*: See VI, 30–45.

136–140. THE TIME: It is now noon at Purgatory. It must therefore be midnight in Jerusalem. Dante believed Morocco to lie exactly 90° west of Jerusalem (in the same longitude as Spain) and 90° west of midnight is six hours earlier. Hence, it is six o'clock there and night would just be beginning.

Canto V

ANTE-PURGATORY: THE SECOND LEDGE   *The Late-Repentant* ·

Class Three: Those Who Died by Violence Without Last Rites

The Poets continue up the mountain and Dante's shadow once more creates excitement among the waiting souls. These are the souls of *Those Who Died by Violence Without Last Rites.* Since their lives were cut off, they did not have full opportunity to repent, and therefore they are placed a step higher than the simply Indolent.

These souls crowd about Dante, eager to have him bear news of them back to the world and so to win prayers that will shorten their delay. Virgil instructs Dante to listen to these souls, but warns him not to interrupt his own climb to Grace. The Poets, therefore, continue to press on while the souls cluster about and follow them, each of them eager to tell his story and to beg that Dante speak of them when he returns to the world.

> I was following the footsteps of my Guide,
>   having already parted from those shades,
>   when someone at my back pointed and cried: 3
>
> "Look there! see how the sun's shafts do not drive
>   through to the left of that one lower down,
>   and how he walks as if he were alive!"   6
>
> I looked behind me to see who had spoken,
>   and I saw them gazing up at me alone,
>   at me, and at the light, that it was broken.   9
>
> At which my Master said: "Why do you lag?
>   What has so turned your mind that you look back?
>   What is it to you that idle tongues will wag?   12
>
> Follow my steps, though all such whisper of you:
>   be as a tower of stone, its lofty crown
>   unswayed by anything the winds may do.   15
>
> For when a man lets his attention range
>   toward every wisp, he loses true direction,
>   sapping his mind's force with continual change."   18
>
> What could I say except "I come"? I said it
>   flushed with that hue that sometimes asks forgiveness
>   for which it shows the asker to be fit.   21
>
> Meanwhile across the slope a little before us
>   people approached chanting the *Miserere*
>   verse by verse in alternating chorus.   24

But when they noticed that I blocked the course
   of the Sun's arrows when they struck my body,
   their song changed to an "Oh! . . ." prolonged and hoarse.   27

Out of that silenced choir two spirits ran
   like messengers and, reaching us, they said:
   "We beg to know—are you a living man?"   30

My Guide replied: "You may be on your way.
   And bear back word to those who sent you here
   he does indeed still walk in mortal clay.   33

If, as I think, it was his shadow drew them
   to stand and stare, they know already. Tell them
   to honor him: that may be precious to them."   36

I never saw hot vapors flashing through
   the first sweet air of night, or through the clouds
   of August sunsets, faster than those two   39

ran up to join their band, wheeled round again,
   and, with the whole band following, came toward us,
   like cavalry sent forward with a loose rein.   42

"There are hundreds in that troop that charges so,"
   my Guide said, "and all come to beg a favor.
   Hear them, but press on, listening as you go."   45

"Pure spirit," they came crying, "you who thus
   while still inside the body you were born to
   climb to your bliss—oh pause and speak to us.   48

Is there no one here you recognize? Not one
   of whom you may bear tidings to the world?
   Wait! Won't you pause? Oh please! Why do you run?   51

We all are souls who died by violence,
   all sinners to our final hour, in which
   the lamp of Heaven shed its radiance   54

into our hearts. Thus from the brink of death,
   repenting all our sins, forgiving those
   who sinned against us, with our final breath   57

we offered up our souls at peace with Him
   who saddens us with longing to behold
   His glory on the throne of Seraphim."   60

"Oh well-born souls," I said, "I can discover
   no one among you that I recognize
   however much I search your faces over;   63

but if you wish some service of me, speak,
   and if the office is within my power
   I will perform it, by that peace I seek   66

in following the footsteps of this Guide,
  that peace that draws me on from world to world
  to my own good." I paused, and one replied: 69

"No soul among us doubts you will fulfill
  all you declare, without your need to swear it,
  if lack of power does not defeat your will. 72

I, then, who am no more than first to plead,
  beg that if ever you see that land that lies
  between Romagna and Naples, you speak my need 75

most graciously in Fano, that they to Heaven
  send holy prayers to intercede for me;
  so may my great offenses be forgiven. 78

I was of Fano, but the wounds that spilled
  my life's blood and my soul at once, were dealt me
  among the Antenori. I was killed 81

where I believed I had the least to fear.
  Azzo of Este, being incensed against me
  beyond all reason, had me waylaid there. 84

Had I turned toward La Mira when they set
  upon me first outside of Oriaco,
  I should be drawing breath among men yet. 87

I ran into the swamp, and reeds and mud
  tangled and trapped me. There I fell. And there
  I watched my veins let out a pool of blood." 90

Another spoke: "So may the Love Divine
  fulfill the wish that draws you up the mountain,
  for sweet compassion, lend your aid to mine. 93

I am Bonconte, once of Montefeltro.
  Because Giovanna and the rest forget me,
  I go among these souls with head bowed low." 96

And I: "What force or chance led you to stray
  so far from Campaldino that your grave
  remains to be discovered to this day?" 99

And he: "There flows below the Casentino
  a stream, the Archiana, which arises
  above the hermitage in Appennino. 102

There where its name ends in the Arno's flood
  I came, my throat pierced through, fleeing on foot
  and staining all my course with my life's blood. 105

There my sight failed. There with a final moan
  which was the name of Mary, speech went from me.
  I fell, and there my body lay alone. 108

I speak the truth. Oh speak it in my name
　to living men! God's angel took me up,
　and Hell's cried out: 'Why do you steal my game?　111

If his immortal part is your catch, brother,
　for one squeezed tear that makes me turn it loose,
　I've got another treatment for the other!'　114

You are familiar with the way immense
　watery vapors gather on the air,
　then burst as rain, as soon as they condense.　117

To ill will that seeks only ill, his mind
　added intelligence, and by the powers
　his nature gives, he stirred the mist and wind.　120

From Pratomagno to the spine, he spread
　a mist that filled the valley by day's end;
　then turned the skies above it dark as lead.　123

The saturated air changed into rain
　and down it crashed, flooding the rivulets
　with what the sodden earth could not retain;　126

the rills merged into torrents, and a flood
　swept irresistibly to the royal river.
　The Archiana, raging froth and mud,　129

found my remains in their last frozen rest
　just at its mouth, swept them into the Arno,
　and broke the cross I had formed upon my breast　132

in my last agony of pain and guilt.
　Along its banks and down its bed it rolled me,
　and then it bound and buried me in silt."　135

A third spoke when that second soul had done:
　"When you have found your way back to the world,
　and found your rest from this long road you run,　138

oh speak my name again with living breath
　to living memory. Pia am I.
　Siena gave me birth; Maremma, death.　141

As he well knows who took me as his wife
　with jeweled ring before he took my life."

Notes

3. *when someone at my back pointed and cried*: Dante does not explain how he could see a gesture made behind his back.

8–9. *at me alone, at me*: Dante feels a moment of pride at attracting so much attention. He will have more to say later about Pride as his most dangerous spiritual fault.

20. *that hue that sometimes asks forgiveness*: A typically Dantean figure. The hue,

of course, is red, i.e., the blush. But one may flush red with anger as well as blush with shame. Hence, the hue only "sometimes" asks forgiveness.

22. *across*: The souls are not climbing the slope but are circling it in their long delay. *before us*: Since the poets are facing uphill, "before" must equal "above."

23. *Miserere*: The souls are singing the Fiftieth Psalm: "Have mercy upon us." Each band of souls on the mountain has its particular prayer—all, that is, but the Contumacious (who have been cut off from the offices of ritual).

24. *verse by verse in alternating chorus*: They are singing, that is to say, antiphonally, but with two choruses rather than with a single voice and a chorus as is more usual in the litany.

37-39. *hot vapors*: Dante's meteorology was built largely on a theory of the opposition of hot and wet vapors. (See *Inferno*, XXIV, 142 ff., note.) Here he describes, first, falling stars (flashing through the first sweet air of night) and, second, heat lightning (flashing through the clouds of August sunsets). He attributes both phenomena to hot or "fiery" vapors.

37-42. The figure certainly goes from the instantaneous to the merely rapid with an interesting flourish of anticlimax. One may guess that Dante set out to indicate great speed, established that in the meteorological part of the figure, and then, needing time for Virgil to make the remarks that establish the following scene, slowed down the charge from the speed of lightning to the speed of horses.

52. THE LATE-REPENTANT WHO DIED BY VIOLENCE: Like the Indolent, these souls put off repentance to their last breath, but with the partially extenuating circumstance that their lives were cut short. Had they lived out their full lives, they might have repented before the end. The benefit of the doubt is at least possible. They are, therefore, a step above the merely Indolent and a step below the Negligent Princes who, powerfully occupied by worldly affairs (with the exception of Henry III of England), had a special excuse for not turning their thoughts to Heaven sooner.

69-90. *one replied*: Jacopo del Cassero. Of a leading family of Fano, a city located in the district that lay between Romagna and the kingdom of Naples, he served as chief magistrate of Bologna from 1296 to 1297 in a manner that offended the powerful Azzo VIII of Este. In 1298, Jacopo was called to Milan to serve as chief magistrate (podesta) of that city. On his way there he was set upon outside the town of Oriaco (or Oriago) and killed by Azzo's hirelings after a chase in which he foundered among the reeds and mud of a nearby swamp area. Had he turned instead toward La Mira, a Paduan city, he would have found refuge. *among the Antenori*: Among the Paduans. According to legend, Padua was founded by Antenor of Troy.

incensed . . . beyond all reason: Theologically, of course, murder is beyond all reason, but Jacopo's constant slurring references to Azzo as a traitor, and worse, would have passed as reason enough among the proud lords of that day.

94-135. *Bonconte*: Son of Guido da Montefeltro who is in Hell as an evil counselor (*Inferno*, XXVII). Bonconte was a leader of the Ghibellines at the battle of Campaldino, a battle in which it has been reported that Dante took part. The Florentine Guelphs defeated the Ghibellines in this battle and Bonconte was killed (June 11, 1289). The Archiana is a nearby river that rises in the Apennines and flows into the Arno (the point at which "its name ends"). Giovanna (line 95) was his wife, and neither she nor anyone else has offered prayers to shorten his time of waiting.

The nicely functioning ambiguity of line 96 must not be missed: (1) I go among these whose heads are bowed low; (2) with head bowed low in shame for such neglect I go among these.

110-114. The incident is very similar to the one Bonconte's father describes in *Inferno*, XXVII, but with opposite results. Such parallel scenes, as noted before, are very much a part of Dante's structural sense and are certainly intended to suggest moral reflection on the parallelism.

120. *his nature gives*: The demons are fallen but they still retain many of the powers given them by their angelic origins. Note that Dante implies the existence of no such power in those Angels found in the vestibule of Hell (those who took no sides in the Wars of Heaven).

121. *From Pratomagno to the spine*: The Casentino, or upper valley of the Arno, is closed in on the east by the spine of the Apennines, and on the west by the Pratomagno range.

128. *the royal river*: The Arno.

132. *the cross I had formed upon my breast*: His arms crossed in contrition and as a symbol of surrender to God.

140. *Pia*: She has been traditionally identified as Pia de' Tolomei (Tall-oh-MAYyee) of Siena, who married a Guelph leader and was murdered by him. The identification is doubtful, however. The text itself must say all that is certain about her. Nor can there be much doubt that Dante's principal interest in her is poetic rather than historical. After Bonconte's fulsome account of his own dramatic importance, Pia's gracious and courteous voice enters as a moving example of how effortlessly Dante can change and contrast tone. Note especially Pia's graciousness (despite her ardent desire to win the help of prayers) in asking nothing of Dante until he has returned and rested from his great journey.

Canto VI

The Late-Repentant ·

Class Three: Those Who Died by Violence · Sordello

The Poets move along with the souls still crowding about them. Dante
promises all of them that he will bear word of them back to the world, but
he never pauses in his climb. Among that press of souls, Dante specifically
mentions seeing *Benincasa di Laterino, Guccio de' Tarlati, Federico Novello, Count Orso,* and *Pierre de la Brosse.*

Finally free of that crowd, Dante asks Virgil how it is that prayer may
sway God's will. Virgil explains in part but once more finishes by declaring
that the whole truth is beyond him and that Dante must refer the question
to Beatrice when he meets her.

The sun passes behind the mountain as they climb (midafternoon of
Easter Sunday). The Poets press on, and there on the shady slope they
encounter the majestic spirit of Sordello who, like Virgil, is a Mantuan.
Dante watches Sordello and Virgil embrace in a transport of love for their
common birthplace and is moved to denounce Italy for setting brothers to
war on one another, to denounce the *Emperor Albert* for his failure to
bring unity and peace to Italy, and finally to utter an invective against Florence as the type of the war-torn and corrupt state.

> The loser, when a game of dice is done,
>   remains behind reviewing every roll
>   sadly, and sadly wiser, and alone.   3
>
> The crowd leaves with the winner: one behind
>   tugs at him, one ahead, one at his side—
>   all calling their long loyalty to his mind.   6
>
> Not stopping, he hands out a coin or two
>   and those he has rewarded let him be.
>   So he fights off the crowd and pushes through.   9
>
> Such was I then, turning my face now here,
>   now there, among that rout, and promising
>   on every hand, till I at last fought clear.   12
>
> There was the Aretine who came to woe
>   at the murderous hand of Tacco; and the other
>   who drowned while he was hunting down his foe.   15
>
> There, hands outstretched to me as I pushed through,
>   was Federico Novello; and the Pisan
>   who made the good Marzucco shine so true.   18
>
> I saw Count Orso; and the shade of one
>   torn from its flesh, it said, by hate and envy,
>   and not for any evil it had done—   21

Pierre de la Brosse, I mean: and of this word
 may the Lady of Brabant take heed while here,
 lest, there, she find herself in a worse herd.   24

When I had won my way free of that press
 of shades whose one prayer was that others pray,
 and so advance them toward their blessedness,   27

I said: "O my Soul's Light, it seems to me
 one of your verses most expressly states
 prayer may not alter Heaven's fixed decree: 30

yet all these souls pray only for a prayer.
 Can all their hope be vain? Or have I missed
 your true intent and read some other there?"   33

And he: "The sense of what I wrote is plain,
 if you bring all your wits to bear upon it.
 Nor is the hope of all these spirits vain.   36

The towering crag of Justice is not bent,
 nor is the rigor of its edict softened
 because the supplications of the fervent   39

and pure in heart cancel the debt of time
 decreed on all these souls who linger here,
 consumed with yearning to begin the climb.   42

The souls I wrote about were in that place
 where sin is not atoned for, and their prayers—
 they being pagan—were cut off from Grace.   45

But save all questions of such consequence
 till you meet her who will become your lamp
 between the truth and mere intelligence.   48

Do you understand me? I mean Beatrice.
 She will appear above here, at the summit
 of this same mountain, smiling in her bliss."   51

"My Lord," I said, "let us go faster now:
 I find the climb less tiring than at first,
 and see, the slope already throws a shadow."   54

"The day leads on," he said, "and we shall press
 as far as we yet may while the light holds,
 but the ascent is harder than you guess: 57

before it ends, the Sun must come around
 from its present hiding place behind the mountain
 and once more cast your shadow on the ground.   60

But see that spirit stationed all alone
 and looking down at us: he will point out
 the best road for us as we travel on."   63

We climbed on then. O Lombard, soul serene,
  how nobly and deliberately you watched us!
  how distant and majestic was your mien!   66

He did not speak to us as on we pressed
  but held us fixed in his unblinking eyes
  as if he were a lion at its rest.   69

Virgil, nonetheless, climbed to his side
  and begged him to point out the best ascent.
  The shade ignored the question and replied   72

by asking in what country we were born
  and who we were. My gentle Guide began:
  "Mantua . . ." And that shade, till then withdrawn,   75

leaped to his feet like one in sudden haste
  crying: "O Mantuan, I am Sordello
  of your own country!" And the two embraced.   78

Ah servile Italy, grief's hostelry,
  ah ship unpiloted in the storm's rage,
  no mother of provinces but of harlotry!   81

That noble spirit leaped up with a start
  at the mere sound of his own city's name,
  and took his fellow citizen to his heart: 84

while still, within you, brother wars on brother,
  and though one wall and moat surrounds them all,
  your living sons still gnaw at one another!   87

O wretched land, search all your coasts, your seas,
  the bosom of your hills—where will you find
  a single part that knows the joys of peace?   90

What does it matter that Justinian came
  to trim the bit, if no one sits the saddle?
  Without him you would have less cause for shame!   93

You priests who, if you heed what God decreed,
  should most seek after holiness and leave
  to Caesar Caesar's saddle and his steed—   96

see how the beast grows wild now none restrains
  its temper, nor corrects it with the spur,
  since you set meddling hands upon its reins!   99

O German Albert, you who turn away
  while she grows vicious, being masterless;
  you should have forked her long before today!   102

May a just judgment from the stars descend
  upon your house, a blow so weirdly clear
  that your line tremble at it to the end.   105

For you, sir, and your father, in your greed
   for the cold conquests of your northern lands,
   have let the Empire's Garden go to seed.   108

Come see the Montagues and Capulets,
   the Monaldi and Filippeschi, reckless man!
   those ruined already, these whom ruin besets.   111

Come, cruel Emperor, come and see your lords
   hunted and holed; come tend their wounds and see
   what fine security Santafior affords.   114

Come see your stricken Rome that weeps alone,
   widowed and miserable, and day and night
   laments: "O Caesar mine, why are you gone?"   117

Come see your people—everywhere the same—
   united in love; and if no pity for us
   can move you, come and blush for your good name.   120

O Supreme Jove, for mankind crucified,
   if you permit the question, I must ask it:
   are the eyes of your clear Justice turned aside?   123

Or is this the unfolding of a plan
   shaped in your fathomless counsels toward some good
   beyond all reckoning of mortal man?   126

For the land is a tyrant's roost, and any clod
   who comes along playing the partisan
   passes for a Marcellus with the crowd.   129

Florence, my Florence, may you not resent
   the fact that my digression has not touched you—
   thanks to your people's sober management.   132

Others have Justice at heart but a bow strung
   by careful counsels and not quickly drawn:
   yours shoot the word forever—from the tongue.   135

Others, offered public office, shun
   the cares of service. Yours cry out unasked:
   "I will! I'll take it on! I am the one!"   138

Rejoice, I say, that your great gifts endure:
   your wealth, your peacefulness, and your good sense.
   What truth I speak, the facts will not obscure.   141

Athens and Sparta when of old they drew
   the codes of law that civilized the world,
   gave only merest hints, compared to you,   144

of man's advance. But all time shall remember
   the subtlety with which the thread you spin
   in mid-October breaks before November.   147

How often within living recollection
   have you changed coinage, custom, law, and office,
   and hacked your own limbs off and sewed them on?   150

But if your wits and memory are not dead
   you yet will see yourself as that sick woman
   who cannot rest, though on a feather bed,   153

but flails as if she fenced with pain and grief.
Ah, Florence, may your cure or course be brief.

Notes

13-14. *the Aretine*: Benincasa di Laterino, a justice of the city of Arezzo. ("Aretine" means "of Arezzo.") On the charge of highway robbery and brigandage, he passed the death sentence on the brother of Ghino (GHEE-no) di Tacco. Soon thereafter Benincasa was called to Rome to a Papal Judgeship. Ghino, a fierce robberbaron, followed him there, burst in upon him in open court, cut off his head, and escaped safely. *the other* (Aretine): *Guccio* (GHOO-tchoe) or Ciacco (TCHA-coe) de' Tarlati (day Tahr-LAH-tee). He drowned in the Arno after the battle of Montaperti, or perhaps of Campaldino. There is some doubt as to whether he was hunter or hunted at the time.

17. *Federico Novello*: Little is known about him except that he was the son of Guido Novello and that he was killed in a skirmish with a band of Aretines.

17-18. *the Pisan . . . Marzucco*: Farinata, son of Marzucco degli Scornigiani (Score-nih-JAH-nee) of Pisa. Farinata was killed in Pisa and Marzucco, who had become a minor friar, went to bury his body. In one account, he preached a funeral sermon of forgiveness and ended by kissing the hand that had murdered his son, thus "shining so true" in Christian charity. In another account, Count Ugolino ordered that the body be left unburied, and Marzucco went boldly before his enemy and won permission to bury his son, thus "shining so true" in courage.

19. *Count Orso*: Alessandro and Napoleone degli Alberti are two of the most infamous sinners in Hell. They lie together in the ice of Caïna among those who were treacherous against their own kin. Count Orso, son of Napoleone, was murdered by his cousin, the son of Alessandro.

19-22. *Pierre de la Brosse*: Court physician and favorite of Louis IX and later of Philip III of France. Philip had Pierre hanged in 1278. The accounts of Pierre's downfall vary. Dante clearly believes him to have been the innocent victim of the intrigues of Queen Mary of Brabant, "the Lady" he calls upon to repent while still on earth, for fear she may find herself in a worse herd (*i.e.,* in Hell) than that in which Pierre finds himself.

29. *one of your verses*: Dante must be referring to the *Aeneid*, VI, 376: Palinurus begs Aeneas to get him out of Hell, but the reply comes from the Sibyl: *Desine fata deum flecti sperare precando* (Do not hope to bend the fixed decree of the Gods by prayer).

54. *the slope already throws a shadow*: The sun had declined to the west of the mountain and the Poets, on the east slope, are now in shadow. Because of the enormous height of the mountain, however, the sun would decline behind it relatively early. It is probably about 3:00 P.M. (or a bit later) on Easter Sunday.

60. *and once more cast your shadow on the ground*: Virgil is chiding Dante for having been so proud of the attention his shadow attracted, and Dante has earned the gentle reproof (which, in one sense of course, he is giving himself). When Virgil mentioned Beatrice (line 49) Dante was suddenly afire to run up the rest of the mountain to the top. (As he was ready to climb the Mount of Joy in *Inferno*, I.) Virgil tells him that the climb is longer and harder than he supposes, for purification does not happen in a day. It is as if Virgil were saying: "Don't sound so suddenly zealous so soon after your proud strutting: you will still have a chance to astonish the souls here with that shadow of yours." Allegorically, if the Sun is taken as Divine Illumination, it will return to make Dante see the error of Pride—as it will indeed when Dante comes upon the souls of the Proud.

77. *Sordello*: A troubadour poet of the first three-quarters of the thirteenth century. He was born in Mantua, which was also Virgil's birthplace. His life is only sketchily known, but he seems to have been a person of some political consequence. Such accounts as survive also seem to indicate his considerable accomplishments as a climber into assorted bedroom windows.

Dante has given Sordello the same relative position in Purgatory and the same majestic dignity he assigns to Farinata in Hell (*Inferno*, X). There is no entirely satisfactory explanation of Dante's reasons in assigning such greatness of character to Sordello. Aside from his love poems, Sordello did write several impassioned political pieces, and Dante probably honors him for their integrity and sincerity. Great political integrity would make Sordello an especially apt guide to the souls of the Negligent Princes, the next group above, and in lines 91–137 of Canto VII, Sordello repeats exactly the sort of charges he made against the rulers of his day in *Complaint (Planh)* on the death of Baron Blacas, whom he represented as the figure of high chivalry dying from the world.

These correspondences may serve to explain his selection as guide to what follows, but why is he drawn so majestically? High indignation such as Sordello had shown in his *Complaint* seems always to have had a special attraction for Dante, who had his own gift for indignation. It would, moreover, honor Virgil to honor his noble fellow Mantuan. I am tempted to guess, however, that it was Dante's structural sense that ruled. Sordello is one of three majestic figures that occur at roughly equivalent points of the three kingdoms: Farinata in Hell, Sordello in Purgatory, and Cacciaguida (Dante's own ancestor) in Paradise. Since all three are political figures, it follows, too, that it is for Sordello's politics rather than for his poetry or for his amours that Dante has so ennobled him. Note too, as evidence of Dante's own character, the traits of slow dignity and hauteur for which Dante admires Sordello (*cf.* III: 10–11, and note).

91. *Justinian*: The Emperor Justinian. His reorganization and codification of Roman law trimmed the bit and adjusted the bridle of the horse (the Empire), making a unified Italy possible, but his work has gone for nothing.

94–99. *You priests . . . set meddling hands upon its reins*: Dante has already (*Inferno*, XIX, 109–111, and see note) asserted that the corruption of the Church began when it acquired wealth and power. He now charges the priests with having helped create the bloody chaos of Italian politics by meddling in temporal affairs. Thus by disregarding the Biblical injunction to render unto Caesar what is Caesar's and unto God what is God's, they have brought corruption upon the Church and destruction upon the State.

100. *German Albert*: Albert of Austria, born 1248, Emperor 1298, assassinated 1308. He was, therefore, Emperor at the purported time of Dante's journey.

At that time Italy was a part of the Holy Roman Empire though torn by internal strife between the Ghibellines (nominally the party of the Emperor though the party lines were blurred by local urgencies) and the Guelphs (nominally for independence and more often for anarchy). Many of the warring lords were, moreover, lieges of the Emperor. Dante's lament for Italy is always for her bloody internal wars, which he attributed, logically enough, to the lack of a central authority. The Emperor had that authority and could easily have brought unification and peace to Italy. But Albert and his father Rudolph (see VII, 91–96, and note) concerned themselves with affairs to the north and neither ever so much as visited Italy. Because of their negligence, Italy had all but slipped out of the Empire and the many Italian robber-barons warred on unceasingly at the very time that the northern kingdoms of the Empire were enjoying a long era of peace.

Dante goes on to specify the charges against Albert and his father more fully. They have allowed the Ghibelline lords to fall into ruinous feuds which could have been stopped by a word from the Emperor since the feuding parties were all lieges of the Emperor. Dante cites two such feuding Ghibelline pairs. The Montagues and the Capulets are the same Veronese family made familiar by *Romeo and Juliet*. The Monaldi and the Filippeschi were of Orvieto. All should have served as pillars of Empire in Italy, and all ruined themselves in their feuds.

The Emperor has, moreover, allowed robber barons to destroy the peace of the land. Dante's reference to the district of Santafiora in the Sienese Maremma is ironic: Santafiora was a robber's roost that afforded no security whatever.

The Emperor has, further, allowed Rome, the seat and glory of his Empire, to fall into decay by withholding his authority (the strong hand of Caesar).

By such neglect (lines 118–120) he has destroyed his own people ("united in love" is a bitter irony) and his own good name.

121. *Supreme Jove*: The usage must seem strange to modern ears, but there can be no doubt that Dante is referring here to God. In Dante's view the pagan names Zeus and Jove referred always to the Christian God as (dimly) perceived by the ancients who lacked Christ's clarifying word.

129. *Marcellus*: Marcellus opposed Caesar and was forgiven by him. Dante may, therefore, mean that anyone who calls himself a local partisan may safely oppose Caesar-Emperor and win support by doing so.

130–155. INVECTIVE AGAINST FLORENCE. (Cf. *Inferno*, XXVI, 1–12.) Having bewailed the anarchy of Italy under Imperial neglect, Dante now turns to another of his invectives against his own city as the type of the bloodily self-divided and corrupt state. His praises are, of course, ironic and every semblance of a good quality ascribed to Florence should be understood to imply the opposite.

133. *Others have Justice at heart* . . . : Sense: Others have justice sincerely at heart and are ready to defend the right by arms, but they deliberate carefully, as wise men should, and are slow to draw the bow. You, Florence, have the word "justice" forever on your tongue and are forever ready to fire, but it is only the word you shoot, and from the tongue only, the deed never fulfilling the word.

136–137. *Others, offered public office, shun the cares of service*: They refuse out of conscientious misgivings because they take duty seriously, or perhaps because they are lazy, but your greedy politicians, Florence, are forever exclaiming their pious readiness to sacrifice themselves, even before they are asked—but they have no other aim than to raid the till.

140. *your wealth, your peacefulness, and your good sense*: The last two have already expired from Florence, and Dante seems to imply that the first will not last long as things are going.

145–146. *But all time shall remember the subtlety*: A mocking comparison between the stability of Athenian and Spartan law, one of the foundations of Western civilization, and the "more advanced" Florentine way of doing things in which nothing—not coinage, nor custom, nor law, nor office, nor pledged word—lives out the month.

152. *that sick woman*: Though she lies in luxury (on a feather bed) she can find no relief from what is wrong with her but flails about as if she were fencing with her pain and grief, seeking to overcome it by outmaneuvering it. The last line (154) is not in the original. It is my own addition, forced upon me by the need to rhyme.

Canto VII

Sordello, discovering Virgil's identity, pays homage to him and offers to guide the Poets as far as Peter's Gate. It is nearly sunset, however, and Sordello explains that by *The Law of the Ascent* no one may go upward after sundown. He suggests that they spend the night in the nearby *Flowering Valley* in which the souls of *The Negligent Rulers* wait to begin their purification. The three together climb in the failing light to the edge of the valley. In it, they observe, among others: *Rudolph of Hapsburg, Ottocar of Bohemia, Philip the Bold of France, Henry of Navarre, Pedro III of Aragon, Charles I of Anjou, Henry III of England,* and *William VII, Marquis of Monferrato.*

All of the rulers, except Henry of England, were in one way or another connected with the Holy Roman Empire. Thus they were specially sanctified by the Divine Right of Kings and again sanctified for their place in the temporal hierarchy of Christ's Empire. Dante signalizes this elevation by the beauty of the valley in which he places them, a flower-strewn green hollow of unearthly beauty and fragrance. The valley is certainly a counterpart of the Citadel of the Virtuous Pagans in Limbo, but it outshines that lower splendor by as much as Divine Love outshines Human Reason.

> Three or four times in brotherhood the two
>   embraced and re-embraced, and then Sordello
>   drew back and said: "Countryman, who are *you?*"   3

> "Before those spirits worthy to be blessed
>   had yet been given leave to climb this mountain,
>   Octavian had laid my bones to rest.   6

> I am Virgil, and I am lost to Heaven
>   for no sin, but because I lacked the faith."
>   In these words was my Master's answer given.   9

> Just as a man who suddenly confronts
>   something too marvelous either to believe
>   or disbelieve, and so does both at once—   12

> so did Sordello. Then his great head lowered,
>   and, turning, he once more embraced my Master,
>   but round the knees, as a menial does his lord.   15

> "Eternal Glory of the Latin race,
>   through whom our tongue made all its greatness clear!
>   Of my own land the deathless pride and praise!   18

> What grace or merit lets me see you plain?"
>   he said. "And oh, if I am worthy, tell me
>   if you come here from Hell, and from what pain."   21

"Through every valley of the painful kingdom
I passed," my Lord replied. "A power from Heaven
marked me this road, and in that power I come.   24

Not what I did but what I left undone,
who learned too late, denies my right to share
your hope of seeing the Eternal Sun.   27

There is a place below where sorrow lies
in untormented gloom. Its lamentations
are not the shrieks of pain, but hopeless sighs.   30

There do I dwell with souls of babes whom death
bit off in their first innocence, before
baptism washed them of their taint of earth.   33

There do I dwell with those who were not dressed
in the Three Sacred Virtues but, unstained,
recognized and practiced all the rest.   36

But if you know and are allowed to say,
show us how we may reach the true beginning
of Purgatory by the shortest way."   39

"We are not fixed in once place," he replied,
"but roam at will up and around this slope
far as the Gate, and I will be your guide.   42

But the day is fading fast, and in no case
may one ascend at night: we will do well
to give some thought to a good resting place.   45

Some souls are camped apart here on the right.
If you permit, I will conduct you to them:
I think you will find pleasure in the sight."   48

"What is it you say?" my Guide asked. "If one sought
to climb at night, would others block his way?
Or would he simply find that he could not?"   51

"Once the sun sets," that noble soul replied,
"you would not cross this line"—and ran his finger
across the ground between him and my Guide.   54

"Nor is there anything to block the ascent
except the shades of night: they of themselves
suffice to sap the will of the most fervent.   57

One might, indeed, go down during the night
and wander the whole slope, were he inclined to,
while the horizon locks the day from sight."   60

I heard my Lord's voice, touched with wonder, say:
"lead us to the place of which you spoke
where we may win some pleasure from delay."   63

We had not traveled very far from there
   before I saw a hollow in the slope
   such as one often finds in mountains here.   66

"There," said that spirit, "where the mountain makes
   a lap among its folds: that is the place
   where we may wait until the new day breaks."   69

The dell's rim sank away from left to right.
   A winding path, half-level and half-steep,
   led us to where the rim stood at mid-height.   72

Indigo, phosphorescent wood self-lit,
   gold, fine silver, white-lead, cochineal,
   fresh emerald the moment it is split—   75

all colors would seem lusterless as shade
   if placed beside the flowers and grassy banks
   that made a shining of that little glade.   78

Nor has glad Nature only colored there,
   but of a thousand sweet scents made a single
   earthless, nameless fragrance of the air.   81

Salve Regina!—from that green the hymn
   was raised to Heaven by a choir of souls
   hidden from outer view by the glade's rim.   84

"Sirs," said that Mantuan, "do not request
   that I conduct you there while any light
   remains before the Sun sinks to its nest.   87

You can observe them from this rise and follow
   their actions better, singly and en masse,
   than if you moved among them in the hollow.   90

He who sits highest with the look of one
   ashamed to move his lips when others praise,
   in life left undone what he should have done.   93

He was the Emperor Rudolph whose high state
   could once have stayed the death of Italy.
   Now, though another try, 't will be too late.   96

That one who comforts him ruled formerly
   the land where rise the waters that flow down
   the Moldau to the Elbe to the sea.   99

He was Ottocar, and more respected and feared
   while still in diapers than his dissipated
   son Wenceslaus is now with a full beard.   102

That Snubnose there who talks with head close-pressed
   to the kindly looking one, died while in flight,
   dishonoring the Lily on his crest.   105

Observe the way he beats his breast and cries.
And how the other one has made his palm
a bed to rest his cheek on while he sighs.   108

They are father and father-in-law of The Plague of France.
They know his dissolute and vicious ways,
and hence their grief among these holy chants.   111

The heavy-sinewed one beside that spirit
with the manly nose, singing in harmony,
bore in his life the seal of every merit.   114

And if that younger one who sits in place
behind him, had remained king after him,
true merit would have passed from vase to vase.   117

As it has not, alas, in their successors.
Frederick and James possess the kingdoms now.
Their father's better heritage none possesses.   120

Rare is the tree that lifts to every limb
the sap of merit—He who gives, so wills
that men may learn to beg their best from Him.   123

And what I say goes for that bignosed one
no less than for the other who sings with him.
On his account Provence and Puglia mourn.   126

By as much as Margaret and Beatrice
must yield when Constance speaks her husband's worth,
that much less than the tree the seedling is.   129

See Henry of England seated there alone,
the monarch of the simple life: his branches
came to good issue in a noble son.   132

The other lone one seated on the ground
below the rest and looking up to them
was the Marquis William Longsword, he who found   135

such grief in Allesandria, for whose pride
both Monferrato and Canavese cried."

Notes

General Note: THE NEGLIGENT RULERS. The Negligent Rulers are the fourth and final class of the Late-Repentant. All of the Late-Repentant made God wait by putting off their surrender to His will until the end. Accordingly God now makes them wait before they may begin their ascent to Him through the purifying pains of Purgatory-proper. The Negligent Rulers, however, had special cause to be preoccupied by worldly affairs. Their responsbility for their subjects was not only a duty but a duty in some measure imposed upon them by God's Will since kings were believed to be divinely selected. Just as those who died by violence are elevated a step above the merely indolent, so the Negligent Rulers are elevated above their negligent subjects because their special duties made it difficult for them to think about the welfare of their own souls.

4–6. THE FIRST SALVATION. Before Christ's redemption, the souls of the virtuous went to Limbo. In *Inferno*, IV, Dante refers to Christ's apocryphal descent into Limbo in 33 A.D. The incident is known as The Harrowing of Hell, and in it Christ was said to have taken with him to Heaven the first souls to win salvation. (Adam and Eve were among those so elevated.) From the time of the Fall until 33 A.D., therefore, Purgatory existed but was not in use. Virgil died in 19 A.D. under the Emperor Octavian.

19. *What grace or merit*: I.e., what special grace granted me by Heaven, or what merit of my own I know not of?

33. *taint of earth*: Original sin. Unbaptized infants have not yet been taken to Christ and have not, accordingly, been cleaned of their part in Adam's guilt. They must, therefore, share the fate of the virtuous pagans (*Inferno*, IV) whom they resemble in being sinless but lacking Christ's sacrament. Infant damnation is one of the most vexed and least attractive tenets of dogmatic Christianity.

35-36. *The Three Sacred Virtues*: Faith, Hope, and Charity. These are the "revealed" or "theological" virtues. *the rest*: The Four Cardinal Virtues. They are Justice, Prudence, Temperance, and Fortitude. (See I, 23, and 31 ff., notes.)

40-60. THE LAW OF THE ASCENT. No allegory, by its nature, is containable within a paraphrase. The center of the allegory here is clearly in the fact that the Sun symbolizes Divine Illumination. Note that Dante underlines this idea by referring to God in line 27 above as "the Eternal Sun." Thus the primary meanings of the allegory may be clearly enough stated: first, that one cannot achieve true repentance and purification except in the sight of God (light of the Sun); second, that one has no difficulty in backsliding (going down the mountain) once he is out of God's sight (darkness); and third, that once out of sight of God/Sun one simply cannot find within himself the will to climb. See also note to lines 85–87, below.

Once in Heaven, it should be noted, there is no night: one is constantly in the presence and light of God, the Sun. Here is another of those harmonies of concept that mark Dante's structural power: in Heaven there is no darkness; in Hell there is no light (except the dimness of Human Reason unaided); in Purgatory—the Kingdom between—there is both light and darkness.

70-72. THE SHAPE OF THE VALLEY. The point is much disputed. I conceive the valley to lie in a U-shaped fold with the mouth of the U facing East and the sides inclining upward into the mass of the Mountain. The incline would seem to be regular. Hence, when the Poets come to the point at which the rim stands at mid-height, they are halfway up what I understand to be the southern side of the U, a position from which they can best observe the whole valley, being as it were at the fifty-yard line.

82. *Salve Regina!*: The beginning of the Compline Hymn in the Roman Catholic Breviary. It is an especially apt choice as the hymn of these souls: "Hail Queen, mother of Mercy . . . to thee we sigh . . . in this valley of tears."

85-87. *"Sirs," said that Mantuan*: This is the first time Sordello's form of address includes both the poets. Dante has not yet even been presented to him. *do not request that I conduct you there while any light remains*: See note on The Law of the Ascent. Sordello here carries it a step further: one may descend into the valley after dark (as they will in the next Canto), but no downward step may be taken while any of the Sun's light remains. Characteristically, the detail is sound both as allegory and as narrative, for the valley is in fact best observed from the rim.

91-95. *the Emperor Rudolph*: Rudolph of Hapsburg, 1218–1291, crowned Emperor, 1273. He is the Father of "German Albert" (VI, 100, note) and with him shared the blame for failing to unify Italy. Dante's dream of a unified Italy was not realized until the mid-nineteenth century.

96. *Now, though another try, 't will be too late*: The other is Henry VII of Luxemburg, Emperor from 1308 to 1313. Henry, as Emperor, tried to accomplish, under circumstances that had by then made it impossible, what Rudolph and Albert had neglected to do under circumstances that assured success.

This line contains another of Dante's political "prophecies," the accuracy of which (see *Inferno*, VI, 61, note) was made possible by the fact that he was writing *as if* in 1300 but actually *as of* ten to fifteen years later. The exact dates of the composition of the *Commedia* cannot be fixed, though likely dates would be from 1308 to 1321. Clearly *Purgatory* must have been written after Henry had attempted to unify Italy and had failed, hence, after 1310.

97. *That one who comforts him*: Ottocar II, King of Bohemia (the land whose waters drain into the Moldau, to the Elbe, to the sea) from 1253 to 1278. In life he was Rudolph's enemy and a tyrant whose acts might well have reserved for him a bath in Phlegethon (*Inferno*, XII) with the Violent against their Neighbors. Dante may have known him only as a valiant warrior. His object in placing him here seems to be to show the reconciliation of enemies after true repentance and forgiveness.

102. *Wenceslaus*: Wenceslaus IV (the Good), born in 1270, succeeded his father as King of Bohemia in 1278. He was elected King of Poland in 1300, and died 1305. Despite a promising beginning as king, Wenceslaus was forced to cede many territories for which his warrior father would have fought to the death. Wenceslaus preferred piety to warfare, habitually hearing several masses daily. With his spirits thus restored, he seems to have found the strength for scouting various bedrooms, for he had begotten numerous illegitimate children by the time he was twenty-five. Hence Dante's charge that he was dissipated.

103. *That Snubnose*: Philip III of France (the Bold, also The Snubnose), 1245–1285, succeeded his father, Louis IX, in 1270. He did not die while actually in flight from the field of battle, but at Perpignan, to which he had retired after the French navy had been annihilated by Pedro III of Aragon.

104. *the kindly looking one*: Henry (the Fat) of Navarre, reigned 1270–1274. He died reportedly "suffocated by the fat of his own body." In life he was quite other than kindly, and might have made excellent Hell-bait, but Dante obviously credits him with having breathed a true repentance from somewhere among the folds of his "suffocating fat."

109. *The Plague of France*: Philip IV (the Fair) of France, born 1268, crowned 1285, died 1314. Second son of Philip III, he married Juana, daughter of Henry of Navarre. It is his misrule and his vicious life that unite (line 103: their heads "close pressed") his father and father-in-law.

Philip IV was for Dante the archetype of the evil ruler, in much the same way that Boniface VIII (whom Philip humiliated and drove to an early death) was the archetype of the evil Pope. Internally, Philip ruined whole provinces by his extortions and currency frauds. He systematically jailed Italian merchants (for ransom) on false charges, cruelly robbed the Jews, and suppressed the Knights Templars in order to confiscate their properties. Externally, he played a disastrous hand in Italian politics. Soon after he had eliminated Boniface VIII, he succeeded in placing one of his puppet cardinals on the Papal Throne as Clement V. Under Clement V the Papal Seat was transferred to Avignon. (*Inferno*, XIX, refers to Clement's intrigue with Philip and makes clear that a place in Hell is awaiting Clement.) In XX and XXXII, below, Dante inveighs against Philip, and again in *Paradiso*, XIX.

112–113. *The heavy-sinewed one . . . that spirit with the manly nose*: Another pair of former enemies reconciled. The first is Pedro III of Aragon, 1236–1285, King of Aragon, 1276, and (after the bloody Sicilian Vespers of 1282 in which all the French were massacred) King of Sicily. He married Manfred's "good Constance" (III, 143). Dante's phrasing in these lines obviously suggests that the first spirit is virile, whereas the second is virile only in the nose.

That second spirit, Pedro's equal only in the nose, is Charles I of Anjou, 1220–1285, crowned King of Sicily and Puglia (Apulia) in 1265. It was Charles who destroyed Manfred at Benevento in 1265 and who was overthrown in the Sicilian Vespers. Dante inveighs against his misrule in XX and again in *Paradiso*, VIII, 73 ff. Once again Dante's intent in presenting the soul of such a man in Purgatory must have been to show that no amount of wickedness will damn a man if he achieves true repentance.

115. *that younger one*: Alfonso III (the Magnificent), 1271–1291, crowned King of Aragon, 1286. He left no heirs and his rule passed to his degenerate younger brothers, the throne of Aragon to James, and that of Sicily to Frederick, both of whom were ruling in 1300, hence the "now" of line 120. Thus the meaning of lines 119–120 is that the younger sons have the material heritage of their father, Pedro, but that no one (now that Alfonso is dead) possesses his better heritage (*i.e.*, his merit).

124–129. A difficult passage. Dante refers again to Charles and Pedro, still developing the theme of the degeneracy of sons. The theme applies not only to Pedro in the degeneracy of James and of Frederick, but to Charles as well. Dante's meaning is that the son, Charles the Lame, is as inferior to Charles I, as Charles I is to Pedro. Hence their kingdoms mourn. But Dante carries the figure through a very complicated comparison, which may be read: "The seedling [Charles II] is inferior to the tree [Charles I] by as much as Constance [widow of Pedro III] may praise her husband above the husband of Margaret and Beatrice [they were the two wives of Chares I]."

130. *Henry of England*: Henry III, 1216–1278. A pious but pallid king. His son, Edward I, however (who was ruling in 1300), crowned a glorious reign with an enduring reform of English law. Hence Henry's "branches came to a good issue in a noble son."

Henry is seated alone in part, perhaps, because he had no connection with the Holy Roman Empire, but much more importantly because he is unique in this company. Henry attended so many masses daily that he never got around to governing his kingdom. His sin, therefore, could not have been neglect of God, but rather neglect of his divinely imposed duties to rule his kingdom well. His presence in this company adds an interesting dimension to Dante's concept, for Henry's sin is the reverse of the general pattern here. Dante's Aristotelian mind could not cherish any excess: the Good is the Golden Mean, to wander from the mean in either direction is equally culpable.

133–137. *The Marquis William*: William VII (Longsword), Marquis of Monferrato, 1245–1292. A lesser prince than the others, hence he sits below and looks up to them. As Imperial Vicar to Italy he headed a coalition of Ghibelline towns. In 1290 the Republic of Asti formented a rebellion in Alessandria, a town held by William. William, attempting to put down the rebellion, was captured, locked in an iron cage, and exposed to public ridicule. He died in the cage, and even in death his body was shockingly abused by the Alessandrians. William's son moved against Alessandria to avenge his father, but the Alessandrians defeated him and invaded Monferrato and Canavese, the two districts of William's fief. Their invasion left the citizens with ample reasons for tears.

Canto VIII

Nightfall, Easter Sunday · The Guardian Angels · The Serpent

As the light fades, Dante, Virgil, and Sordello stand on the bank and watch the souls below gather and sing the *Compline Hymn*, asking for protection in the night. In response to the hymn *Two Green Angels* descend from Heaven and take their posts, one on each side of the valley. Full darkness now settles, and the Poets may make their *Descent into the Valley*.

Dante immediately finds a soul he knows, *Judge Nino de' Visconti*, and has a long conversation with him in which both bemoan the infidelity of widows who remarry.

When Judge Nino has finished speaking, Dante looks at the South Pole and sees that *Three Stars* (the Three Theological Virtues) have replaced *The Four Stars* (The Four Cardinal Virtues) he had seen at dawn.

As he is discussing them with Virgil *The Serpent* appears and is immediately routed by the Angels, who return to their posts. Dante then has a conversation with *Conrad Malaspina*, whom Judge Nino had summoned when he found out Dante was a living man. Dante owes a debt of gratitude to the Malaspina House for its hospitality to him in his exile, and he takes this opportunity to praise the house and to have Conrad prophesy that Dante shall live to know more about it.

> It was the hour that turns the memories
> of sailing men their first day out, to home,
> and friends they sailed from on that morning's breeze;   3
>
> that thrills the traveler newly on his way
> with love and yearning when he hears afar
> the bell that seems to mourn the dying day—   6
>
> when I began, for lack of any sound,
> to count my hearing vain: and watched a spirit
> who signaled for attention all around.   9
>
> Raising his hands, he joined his palms in prayer
> and turned his rapt eyes east, as if to say:
> "I have no thought except that Thou art there."   12
>
> "*Te lucis ante*" swelled from him so sweetly,
> with such devotion and so pure a tone,
> my senses lost the sense of self completely.   15
>
> Then all the others with a golden peal
> joined in the hymn and sang it to the end,
> their eyes devoutly raised to Heaven's wheel.   18
>
> Reader, if you seek truth, sharpen your eyes,
> for here the veil of allegory thins
> and may be pierced by any man who tries.   21

I saw that host of kings, its supplication
    sung to a close, stand still and pale and humble,
    eyes raised to Heaven as if in expectation.   24

I saw two angels issue and descend
    from Heaven's height, bearing two flaming swords
    without a point, snapped off to a stub end.   27

Green as a leaf is at its first unfurling,
    their robes; and green the wings that beat and blew
    the flowing folds back, fluttering and whirling.   30

One landed just above me, and one flew
    to the other bank. Thus, in the silent valley,
    the people were contained between the two.   33

I could see clearly that their hair was gold,
    but my eyes drew back bedazzled from their faces,
    defeated by more light than they could hold.   36

"They are from Mary's bosom," Sordello said,
    "and come to guard the valley from the Serpent
    that in a moment now will show its head."   39

And I, not knowing where it would appear,
    turned so I stood behind those trusted shoulders
    and pressed against them icy-cold with fear.   42

Once more Sordello spoke: "Now let us go
    to where the great souls are, and speak to them.
    The sight of you will please them much, I know."   45

It was, I think, but three steps to the base
    of the little bank; and there I saw a shade
    who stared at me as if he knew my face.   48

The air was closing on its darkling hour,
    yet not so fast but what it let me see,
    at that close range, what it had veiled before.   51

I took a step toward him; he, one toward me—
    Noble Judge Nin! how it rejoiced my soul
    to see you safe for all eternity!   54

No welcome was left unsaid on either side.
    Then he inquired: "How long since did you come
    to the mountain's foot over that widest tide?"   57

"Oh," I replied, "I came by the pits of woe—
    this morning. I am still in my first life,
    though I gain the other on the road I go."   60

He and Sordello, when they heard me thus
    answer the question, suddenly drew back
    as if surprised by something marvelous.   63

One turned to Virgil and one turned aside
    to a shade who sat nearby. "Conrad! Get up!
    See what the grace of God has willed!" he cried.   66

And then to me: "By all the thankful praise
    you owe to Him who hides His primal cause
    so deep that none may ever know His ways—   69

when you have once more crossed the enormous tide,
    tell my Giovanna to cry out my name
    there where the innocent are gratified.   72

I do not think her mother cares for me
    since she put off the weeds and the white veil
    that she will once more long for presently.   75

She shows all men how long love's fire will burn
    within a woman's heart when sight and touch
    do not rekindle it at every turn.   78

Nor will the Milanese viper she must bear
    upon her tomb do her such honor in it
    as would Gallura's cock emblazoned there."   81

So spoke he; and his features bore the seal
    of that considered anger a good man
    reaches in reason and may rightly feel.   84

I looked up at the Heavens next, and eyed
    that center point at which the stars are slowest,
    as a wheel is next the axle. And my Guide: 87

"My son, what is it that you stare at so?"
    And I: "At those three stars there in whose light
    the polar regions here are all aglow."   90

And he to me: "Below the rim of space
    now ride the four bright stars you saw this morning,
    and these three have arisen in their place."   93

Sordello started as my Guide said this;
    and clutching him, he pointed arm and finger,
    crying: "Our Adversary! There he is!"   96

Straight through the valley's unprotected side
    a serpent came, perhaps the very one
    that gave the bitter food for which Eve cried.   99

Through the sweet grass and flowers the long sneak drew,
    turning its head around from time to time
    to lick itself as preening beasts will do.   102

I did not see and cannot tell you here
    how the celestial falcons took to flight;
    but I did see that both were in the air.   105

Hearing their green wings beating through the night,
   the serpent fled. The angels wheeled and climbed
   back to their posts again in equal flight. 108

The shade the Judge had summoned with his cry
   had not moved from his side; through all that fray
   he stared at me without blinking an eye. 111

"So may the lamp that leads to what you seek
   find oil enough," he said, "in your own will
   to light your way to the enameled peak; 114

if you can say for certain how things stand
   in Val di Magra or those parts, please do,
   for I was once a great lord in that land. 117

Conrad Malaspina I was—the grandson
   and not the Elder. Here I purify
   the love I bore for those who were my own." 120

"Oh," I replied, "I never have been near
   the lands you held; but is there in all Europe
   a hamlet ignorant of the name you bear? 123

The glories of your noble house proclaim
   its lords abroad, proclaim the lands that bear them;
   and he who does not know them knows their fame. 126

I swear to you—so may my present course
   lead me on high—your honored house has never
   put by its strict sword and its easy purse. 129

Usage and nature have so formed your race
   that, though the Guilty Head pervert all else,
   it still shuns ill to walk the path of grace." 132

And he: "Go now, for the Sun shall not complete
   its seventh rest in that great bed the Ram
   bestrides and covers with its four spread feet, 135

before this testimony you have given
   shall be nailed to the center of your head
   with stouter nails, and more securely driven, 138

than ever hearsay was. And this shall be
   certain as fate is in its fixed decree."

Notes

7–9. The original passage is hard to interpret. I think it is best taken as another of Dante's extraordinary accounts of how his senses work. (*Cf. Inferno,* XX, 10, and XXXI, 14–15, and notes thereto.) Dante's descriptions of how his senses work seem ever to call forth his pedantry. His basic idea here seems to be most nearly related to that with which he opens Canto IV—that the soul, under intense stimulus, is absorbed into one sense at a time. Up to this point he has been absorbed in listening to the spirits sing *Salve Regina!* and to Sordello's account of the spirits. Now both have fallen still, and Dante gives what amounts to a sort of physiological report of his reactions, stating that bit by bit he emerges from his absorption in the sense of hearing, now useless for lack of anything to hear, and re-settles his attention in his sense of sight. (*Cf.* also lines 13–15, below.)

13. *Te lucis ante*: The beginning of the Compline Hymn, *Te lucis ante terminum* ("To Thee before the light is done"). The hymn is a prayer for protection against the evils that walk the dark. Like all of Dante's hymn choices, it is fitted to the situation, the vision that follows being precisely in answer to the hymn's plea.

15. *my senses lost the sense of self completely*: (Lit.: "It made me from myself pass from all awareness.") Here, too, I think the key to the proper interpretation lies in the opening lines of Canto IV.

26–27. THE BROKEN SWORDS. Symbols, well used, can seldom be narrowed to a single meaning that excludes other possibilities. The swords may symbolize God's Justice, and the broken points that it is tempered with Mercy. They may equally symbolize that the Angel Guardians are for defense only and not for offense. There is also a possible reference to the legend that the guardian angels broke their swords when Christ entered Paradise, thereby symbolizing that they would no longer exclude with the whole sword, *i.e.*, completely.

34–36. In line 36, Dante clearly meant one of his characteristic comments on the behavior of *all* of our senses. A more literal rendering of this tercet would be:

> I could distinctly see their golden hair,
> but my eyes drew back defeated from their faces,
> like a sense perceiving more than it can bear.

I have preferred the less literal rendering because it seems to manage a better effect as English poetry.

46. *three steps*: I am inclined to think Dante intended only to show that the bank was not very high, but three is an important number and any of its symbolic possibilities could be argued here.

51. *before*: Then Dante was standing on the bank.

53. *Judge Nin*: Nino de' Visconti da Pisa, nephew of Count Ugolino (see *Inferno*, XXXIII) was Justiciary of Gallura in Sardinia, then a Pisan possession. It was he who ordered the hanging of Friar Gomita (see *Inferno*, XXII, 82, note). He should be thought of as more nearly a viceroy for his uncle than as a judge in the modern sense. Dante knew him intimately. Lines 53–54 should be taken not as an implication that Dante knew of any great sin for which Nino should have been damned, but rather as a simple rejoicing that a man so deeply involved in worldly affairs had yet managed not to lose his soul to worldliness. Nino died in 1296.

68–69. *Cf.* III, 34–39.

70. *enormous tide*: Figuratively, the enormous tide between life and death. Literally, the sea between the mouth of the Tiber and the shores of Purgatory, the longest sea-route on earth as Dante conceived it.

71. *my Giovanna*: his daughter.

72–81. JUDGE NINO'S REPROACH OF HIS WIFE BEATRICE: Nino Visconti's widow was Beatrice, daugher of Opizzo da Este (*Inferno*, XII, 111). She put off the weeds and white veil (the mourning costume of Dante's time) first in being betrothed to Alberto Scotti, Lord of Piacenza, and then in jilting him to marry Galeazzo Visconti of Milan, all under the pressure of her family's insistence and for political motives. Nino makes no allowance for the pressures that must have been brought to bear upon Beatrice, and Dante (see below) endorses his sentiments with the same lack of reservation.

Nino proceeds to prophesy (it had already happened between 1300 and the time of the writing) that Beatrice will one day wish she had remained a widow, for the jilted Scotti took his revenge by ruining Visconti, and Beatrice had to share his poverty. Nino carries his reproach to eternity in saying that even her burial will be less honorable than it would have been had she remained true. (It was the custom for the tombs of ladies to be marked with their husbands' coats of arms.) "The Milanese is Galeazzo Visconti, whose arms contained a viper eating a child. That viper on her tomb, says Nino, will do her less honor than would the cock of Gallura from Nino's arms. A piece of family pride: the arms of Gallura were more ancient than those of the Visconti of Milan and Nino looks upon Galeazzo as an upstart.

In 1328 Beatrice's son (she was then a widow for the second time) was made Lord of Milan and her fortunes thereafter (she died in 1334) rode high once again—a turn of events Dante could not have prophesied at the time of the writing, and which, in fact, he did not live to see.

73. *her mother*: Nino's wife. But note that he refers to her not as "my wife" but as "her mother."

83. *considered anger*: *Cf. Inferno*, VIII, 43, and note.

85–87. *I looked up . . . next*: Students regularly take this line to mean that Dante is avoiding Nino's eyes. It is simply one of Dante's fast transitions. Nino's remarks are closed, Dante has emphatically approved them, and with no time wasted, he passes on to the next thing of interest—the South Pole, whose stars he has never before seen except for a glimpse at dawn.

90. *the polar regions here*: "Here," equals "on this side of the Equator." The stars are important symbols and will recur. At dawn, on the shore (at the beginning of the Ante-Purgatory) Dante had seen Four Stars representing the Four Cardinal Virtues. Now, just before beginning the True Purgatory, he sees three evening stars which may be taken as the Three Theological Virtues. In Canto XXIX, just before the appearance of Beatrice in the Earthly Paradise, Dante sees all seven together in the form of Heavenly Nymphs.

106. *hearing their green wings*: How even the Serpent can register with his hearing the color of the wings remains an unanswered question. This sort of figure is one of Dante's mannerisms. *Cf.* his first description of Virgil in *Inferno*, I, where Virgil is described as appearing (visual) hoarse (auditory) with long silence. Some critics have labeled both these passages as master ambiguities. Perhaps so.

107-108. *climbed back to their posts again*: Dante does not specify whether to the bank (their watch posts) or to Heaven (their original posts). I think he meant watch posts, for the souls' prayer (which the Angels answer) is for night-long protection. In Purgatory, only the souls below the Gate (Ante-Purgatory) are subject to temptation, and that, it would seem, of only the most perfunctory sort. In any case it is certain that they will not yield to temptation, for they are saved. The Serpent, therefore, is best taken as a formal masque-like allegory, like the Heavenly Pageant Dante will encounter at the top of the mountain.

109-111. *The shade the Judge had summoned with his cry*: Conrad. See line 65. *stared at me without blinking an eye*: Another Dantean peculiarity. If Dante was staring at the Angels and the Serpent, he could not know this detail.

112-113. *the lamp*: the light of Divine Grace must be merited (*i.e.*, find oil within the soul). The summit of Purgatory (the Earthly Paradise) is an "enameled" plateau. Dante uses the same word to describe the Citadel of Limbo (*Inferno*, IV, 115). Sense: "So may you find within your soul all the merit you need to win to the summit. . . ."

118. *Conrad Malaspina*: Very little is known about this Conrad except that he was the son of Frederick I, Marchese di Villafranca, and the grandson of Conrad I. The house of Malaspina, on the other hand, was honorably known, though scarcely as well as Dante declares below. In his praise of the Malaspina family, Dante is paying a debt of gratitude for the honor and hospitality with which it received him after his exile from Florence.

119-120. *Here I purify . . .* : Various interpretations of these lines have been offered. I think Conrad means that for love of friends and kin he remained so occupied in worldly affairs that he neglected God. Now in Purgatory he purifies and offers to God the love that formerly led him to be negligent.

129. *strict sword . . . easy purse*: valor . . . liberality.

131. *the Guilty Head*: Certainly the primary meaning is the Devil. The corrupt Papacy and the negligent Emperor may be secondary meanings.

133-134. *the Sun shall not complete its seventh rest*: The sun will not have completed its seventh transit of Aries (the Ram), *i.e.*, the seven years will not pass, before Dante will know from his own experience the truth of what he has here uttered as hearsay (of the virtue and liberality of the Malaspina family). *the great bed the Ram bestrides*: That portion of the zodiac which falls under the sign of Aries. Aries is often depicted with his four feet spread wide.

Canto IX

The Angel Guardian

Dawn is approaching. Dante has a dream of A *Golden Eagle* that descends from the height of Heaven and carries him up to the Sphere of Fire. He wakes to find he has been transported in his sleep, that it was *Lucia* who bore him, laying him down beside an enormous wall, through an opening in which he and Virgil may approach *The Gate of Purgatory*.

Having explained these matters, Virgil leads Dante to the Gate and its *Angel Guardian*. The Angel is seated on the topmost of *Three Steps* that symbolize the three parts of a perfect *Act of Confession*. Dante prostrates himself at the feet of the Angel, who cuts *Seven P's* in Dante's forehead with the point of a blazing sword. He then allows the Poets to enter. As the Gates open with a sound of thunder, the mountain resounds with a great *Hymn of Praise*.

Now pale upon the balcony of the East
    ancient Tithonus' concubine appeared,
    but lately from her lover's arms released.   3

Across her brow, their radiance like a veil,
    a scroll of gems was set, worked in the shape
    of the cold beast whose sting is in his tail.   6

And now already, where we were, the night
    had taken two steps upward, while the third
    thrust down its wings in the first stroke of flight;   9

when I, by Adam's weight of flesh defeated,
    was overcome by sleep, and sank to rest
    across the grass on which we five were seated.   12

At that new hour when the first light grows
    and the little swallow starts her mournful cry,
    perhaps in memory of her former woes;   15

and when the mind, escaped from its submission
    to flesh and to the chains of waking thought,
    becomes almost prophetic in its vision;   18

in a dream I saw a soaring eagle hold
    the shining height of heaven, poised to strike,
    yet motionless on widespread wings of gold.   21

He seemed to hover where old history
    records that Ganymede rose from his friends,
    borne off to the supreme consistory.   24

I thought to myself: "Perhaps his habit is
    to strike at this one spot; perhaps he scorns
    to take his prey from any place but this."   27

Then from his easy wheel in Heaven's spire,
   terrible as a lightning bolt, he struck
   and snatched me up high as the Sphere of Fire.   30

It seemed that we were swept in a great blaze,
   and the imaginary fire so scorched me
   my sleep broke and I wakened in a daze.   33

Achilles must have roused exactly thus—
   glancing about with unadjusted eyes,
   now here, now there, not knowing where he was—   36

when Thetis stole him sleeping, still a boy,
   and fled with him from Chiron's care to Scyros,
   whence the Greeks later lured him off to Troy.   39

I sat up with a start; and as sleep fled
   out of my face, I turned the deathly white
   of one whose blood is turned to ice by dread.   42

There at my side my comfort sat—alone.
   The sun stood two hours high, and more. I sat
   facing the sea. The flowering glen was gone.   45

"Don't be afraid," he said. "From here our course
   leads us to joy, you may be sure. Now, therefore,
   hold nothing back, but strive with all your force.   48

You are now at Purgatory. See the great
   encircling rampart there ahead. And see
   that opening—it contains the Golden Gate.   51

A while back, in the dawn before the day,
   while still your soul was locked in sleep inside you,
   across the flowers that made the valley gay,   54

a Lady came. 'I am Lucia,' she said.
   'Let me take up this sleeping man and bear him
   that he may wake to see his hope ahead.'   57

Sordello and the others stayed. She bent
   and took you up. And as the light grew full,
   she led, I followed, up the sweet ascent.   60

Here she put you down. Then with a sweep
   of her sweet eyes she marked that open entrance.
   Then she was gone; and with her went your sleep."   63

As one who finds his doubt dispelled, sheds fear
   and feels it change into new confidence
   as bit by bit he sees the truth shine clear—   66

so did I change; and seeing my face brim
   with happiness, my Guide set off at once
   to climb the slope, and I moved after him.   69

Reader, you know to what exalted height
   I raised my theme. Small wonder if I now
   summon still greater art to what I write.   72

As we drew near the height, we reached a place
   from which—inside what I had first believed
   to be an open breach in the rock face—   75

I saw a great gate fixed in place above
   three steps, each its own color; and a guard
   who did not say a word and did not move.   78

Slow bit by bit, raising my lids with care,
   I made him out seated on the top step,
   his face more radiant than my eyes could bear.   81

He held a drawn sword, and the eye of day
   beat such a fire back from it, that each time
   I tried to look, I had to look away.   84

I heard him call: "What is your business here?
   Answer from where you stand. Where is your Guide?
   Take care you do not find your coming dear."   87

"A little while ago," my Teacher said,
   "A Heavenly Lady, well versed in these matters,
   told us 'Go there. That is the Gate ahead.' "   90

"And may she still assist you, once inside,
   to your soul's good! Come forward to our three steps,"
   the courteous keeper of the gate replied.   93

We came to the first step: white marble gleaming
   so polished and so smooth that in its mirror
   I saw my true reflection past all seeming.   96

The second was stained darker than blue-black
   and of a rough-grained and a fire-flaked stone,
   its length and breadth crisscrossed by many a crack.   99

The third and topmost was of porphyry,
   or so it seemed, but of a red as flaming
   as blood that spurts out of an artery.   102

The Angel of the Lord had both feet on
   this final step and sat upon the sill
   which seemed made of some adamantine stone.   105

With great good will my Master guided me
   up the three steps and whispered in my ear:
   "Now beg him humbly that he turn the key."   108

Devoutly prostrate at his holy feet,
   I begged in mercy's name to be let in,
   but first three times upon my breast I beat.   111

Seven *P*'s, the seven scars of sin,
   his sword point cut into my brow. He said:
   "Scrub off these wounds when you have passed within."   114

Color of ashes, of parched earth one sees
   deep in an excavation, were his vestments,
   and from beneath them he drew out two keys.   117

One was of gold, one silver. He applied
   the white one to the gate first, then the yellow,
   and did with them what left me satisfied.   120

"Whenever either of these keys is put
   improperly in the lock and fails to turn it,"
   the Angel said to us, "the door stays shut.   123

One is more precious. The other is so wrought
   as to require the greater skill and genius,
   for it is that one which unties the knot.   126

They are from Peter, and he bade me be
   more eager to let in than to keep out
   whoever cast himself prostrate before me."   129

Then opening the sacred portals wide:
   "Enter. But first be warned: do not look back
   or you will find yourself once more outside."   132

The Tarpeian rock-face, in that fatal hour
   that robbed it of Metellus, and then the treasure,
   did not give off so loud and harsh a roar   135

as did the pivots of the holy gate—
   which were of resonant and hard-forged metal—
   when they turned under their enormous weight.   138

At the first thunderous roll I turned half-round,
   for it seemed to me I heard a chorus singing
   Te deum laudamus mixed with that sweet sound.   141

I stood there and the strains that reached my ears
   left on my soul exactly that impression
   a man receives who goes to church and hears   144

the choir and organ ringing out their chords
   and now does, now does not, make out the words.

Notes

1-9. There is no wholly satisfactory explanation of this complex opening description. Dante seems to be saying that the third hour of darkness is beginning (hence, if sunset occurred at 6:00 it is now a bit after 8:00 P.M.) and that the aurora of the rising moon is appearing above the horizon.

He describes the moon as the concubine of Tithonus. Tithonus, however, married the daughter of the sun, Aurora (dawn), and it was she who begged Jove to give her husband immortality while forgetting to ask perpetual youth for him. Thus Tithonus lived but grew older and older beside his ageless bride. (In one legend he was later changed into a grasshopper.) Despite his advanced years, however, he seems here to be philandering with the moon as his concubine. Dante describes the moon as rising from Tithonus' bed and standing on the balcony of the East (the horizon) with the constellation Scorpio gemmed on her forehead, that "cold [blooded] beast whose sting is in his tail" being the scorpion.

Having given Tithonus a double life, Dante now adds a mixed metaphor in which the "steps" of the night have "wings." Two of the steps (hours) have flown, and the third has just completed the first downstroke of its wings (*i.e.*, has just begun its flight).

15. *former woes*: Tereus, the husband of Procne, raped her sister Philomela, and cut out her tongue so that she could not accuse him. Philomela managed to communicate the truth to Procne by means of her weaving. The two sisters thereupon took revenge by killing Itys, son of Procne and Tereus, and serving up his flesh to his father. Tereus, learning the truth, was about to kill the sisters when all were turned into birds. Ovid (*Metamorphoses*, VI, 424 ff.) has Tereus changed into a hoopoe, and probably (though the text leaves some doubt) Procne into a swallow and Philomela into a nightingale. Dante clearly takes the swallow to be Philomela.

18. *prophetic in its vision*: (Cf. *Inferno*, XXVI, 7.) It was an ancient belief that the dreams that came toward dawn were prophetic.

19–33. DANTE'S DREAM. Each of Dante's three nights on the Mount of Purgatory ends with a dream that comes just before dawn. The present dream is relatively simple in its symbolism, and as we learn shortly after Dante's awakening, it parallels his ascent of the mountain in the arms of Lucia. The dream is told, however, with such complexities of allusion that every reference must be carefully weighed.

To summarize the symbolism in the simplest terms, the Golden Eagle may best be rendered in its attributes. It comes from highest Heaven (from God), its feathers are pure gold (Love? God's splendor?), its wings are outspread (the open arms of Divine Love?), and it appears poised to descend in an instant (as is Divine Grace). The Eagle snatches Dante up to the Sphere of Fire (the presence of God? the beginning of Purgatorial purification? both?), and both are so consumed by the fire that Dante, in his unpurified state, cannot bear it.

On another level, of course, the Eagle is Lucia (Divine Light), who has descended from Heaven, and who bears the sleeping Dante from the Flowering Valley to the beginning of the true Purgatory. Note that Lucia is an anagram for *acuila*, "eagle."

On a third level, the dream simultaneously connects with the earlier reference to Ganymede, also snatched up by the eagle of God, but the two experiences are contrasted as much as they are compared. Ganymede was carried up by Jove's eagle, Dante by Lucia. Ganymede was out hunting in the company of his worldly associates; Dante was laboring for grace, had renounced worldliness, and was in the company of great souls who were themselves awaiting purification. Ganymede was carried to Olympus; Dante to the beginning of a purification which, though he was still too unworthy to endure it, would in time make him a perfect servant of the true God. Thus, his experience is in the same pattern as Ganymede's, but surpasses it as Faith surpasses Human Reason, and as Beatrice surpasses Virgil.

23. *Ganymede*: Son of Tros, the mythical founder of Troy, was reputedly the most beautiful of mortals, so beautiful that Jove sent an eagle (or perhaps went himself in the form of an eagle) to snatch up the boy and bring him to Heaven, where he became cupbearer to the gods. The fact that Dante himself is about to begin the ascent of Purgatory proper (and hence to Heaven) inevitably suggests an allegory of the soul in the history of Ganymede. God calls to Himself what is most beautiful in man.

The fact that Dante always thought of the Trojans as an especially chosen people is also relevant (*Cf. Inferno*, II, 13–30 and note). Ganymede was the son of the founder of Troy; Troy, in Dante's Virgilian view, founded Rome. And through the Church of Rome men's souls were enabled to mount to Heaven.

24. *consistory*: Here, the council of the gods on Olympus. Dante uses the same term to describe Paradise (*Paradiso*, XXIX, 67).

30. *Sphere of Fire*: The four elemental substances are earth, water, fire, and air. In Dante's cosmography, the Sphere of Fire was located above the Sphere of Air and just under the Sphere of the Moon. Hence the eagle bore him to the top of the atmosphere. The Sphere of Fire, however, may also be taken as another symbol for God.

34–39. ACHILLES' WAKING. It had been prophesied that Achilles would be killed at Troy. Upon the outbreak of the Trojan War, his mother, Thetis, stole him while he was sleeping, from the care of the centaur Chiron who was his tutor (see *Inferno*, XII, 71 ff.) and fled with him to Scyros, where she hid him disguised as a girl. He was found there and lured away by Ulysses and Diomede, who burn for that sin (among others) in Malebolge (see *Inferno*, XXVI, 56–63, and note). Thus Achilles, like Dante, was borne off in his sleep and awoke to find himself in a strange place.

51. *that opening*: The Gate, as the Poets will find, is closed and guarded. Dante (here and in line 62, below) can only mean "the opening in which the gate was set" and not "an open entrance." At this distance, they do not see the Gate itself but only the gap in the otherwise solid wall.

55. *Lucia* (Loo-TCHEE-ya): Symbolizes Divine Light, Divine Grace. (See *Inferno*, II, 97, and note.)

77. *three steps*: (See also lines 94–102, below.) The entrance into Purgatory involves the ritual of the Roman Catholic confessional with the Angel serving as the confessor. The three steps are the three acts of the perfect confession: candid confession (mirroring the whole man), mournful contrition, and burning gratitude for God's mercy. The Angel Guardian, as the priestly confessor, does not move or speak as the Poets approach, because he can admit to purification only those who ask for admission.

86. *Where is your Guide?* It must follow from the Angel's question that souls ready to enter Purgatory are led up the mountain by another Angel. Dante and Virgil are arriving in an irregular way, as they did to the shore below, where they were asked essentially the same question by Cato. Note, too, that Virgil answers for the Poets, as he did to Cato. The allegory may be that right thinking answers for a man, at least to start with, though the actual entrance into the state of Grace requires an act of Faith and of Submission.

90. *told us*: Lucia spoke only with her eyes, and what Virgil is quoting is her look. What he is quoting is, in essence, correct, but it does seem he could have been a bit more accurate in his first actual conversation with an Angel.

94–96. *the first step*: Contrition of the heart. White for purity, shining for hope, and flawless for perfection. It is not only the mirror of the soul, but it is that mirror in which the soul sees itself as it truly is and not in its outward seeming.

97–99. *the second*: Contrition of the mouth, *i.e.*, confession. The color of a bruise for the shame that envelops the soul as it confesses, rough-grained and fire-flaked for the pain the confessant must endure, and cracked for the imperfection (sin) the soul confesses.

100–102. *the third*: Satisfaction by works. Red for the ardor that leads to good works. Porphyry is, of course, a purple stone, but Dante does not say the stone was porphyry; only that it resembled it, though red in color.

"Artery" here is, of course, an anachronism, the circulation of the blood having yet to be discovered in Dante's time. Dante uses the word *vena* (vein), but it seems to me the anachronism will be less confusing to a modern reader than would be the idea of bright red and spurting venous blood.

103–105. The Angel, as noted, represents the confessor, and, more exactly, the Church Confessant. Thus the Church is founded on adamant and rests its feet on Good Works.

112. *Seven P's*: P is for the Latin *peccatum*. Thus there is one *P* for each of the Seven Deadly Sins for which the sinners suffer on the seven ledges above: Pride, Envy, Wrath, Acedia (Sloth), Avarice (Hoarding and Prodigality), Gluttony, and Lust.

Dante has just completed the act of confession and the Angel confessor marks him to indicate that even in a shriven soul there remain traces of the seven sins which can be removed only by suffering.

115–117. *Color of ashes, of parched earth*: The colors of humility which befit the office of the confessor. *two keys*: (*Cf.* the Papal Seal, which is a crown above two crossed keys, and also *Inferno*, XXVII, 99–102). The keys symbolize the power of the confessor (the Church, and hence the Pope) to grant or withhold absolution. In the present context they may further be interpreted as the two parts of the confessor's office of admission: the gold key may be taken to represent his ordained authority, the silver key as the learning and reflection with which he must weigh the guilt before assigning penance and offering absolution.

126. *unties the knot*: Another mixed metaphor. The soul-searched judgment of the confessor (the silver key) decides who may and who may not receive absolution, and in resolving that problem the door is opened, provided that the gold key of ordained authority has already been turned.

133–138. *The Tarpeian rock-face*: The public treasury of Rome was kept in the great scarp of Tarpeia on the Campidoglio. The tribune Metellus was its custodian when Caesar, returned to Rome after crossing the Rubicon, moved to seize the treasury. Metellus opposed him but was driven away and the great gates were opened. Lucan (*Pharsalia*, III, 154–156 and 165–168) describes the scene and the roar that echoed from the rock face as the gates were forced open.

139–141. The thunder of the opening of the Gates notifies the souls within that a new soul has entered, and they burst into the hymn "We Praise Thee, O God." (Contrast these first sounds of Purgatory with the first sounds of Hell—*Inferno*, III, 22–24.) Despite the thunderous roar right next to him, Dante seems to hear with his "allegorical ear" what certainly could not have registered upon his physical ear.

This seeming incongruity has long troubled me. I owe Professor MacAllister a glad thanks for what is certainly the essential clarification. The whole *Purgatorio*, he points out, is built upon the structure of a Mass. The Mass moreover is happening not on the mountain but in church with Dante devoutly following its well-known steps. I have not yet had time to digest Professor MacAllister's suggestion, but it strikes me immediately as a true insight and promises another illuminating way of reading the *Purgatorio*.

Canto X

The Whip of Pride

The gate closes behind them and the Poets begin the ascent to The First Cornice through a tortuous passage that Dante describes as a Needle's Eye. They reach the Cornice about 9:00 or 10:00 of Monday morning.

At first the Cornice seems deserted. Dante's eye is caught by a series of three marvelously wrought bas-reliefs in the marble of the inner cliff face. Three panels depict three scenes that serve as The Whip of Pride, exemplifying to each sinner as he enters how far greater souls have put by far greater reasons for pride in order to pursue the grace of humility.

As Dante stands in admiration before the carvings, Virgil calls his attention to a band of souls approaching from the left, and Dante turns for his first sight of the souls of The Proud, who crawl agonizingly round and round the Cornice under the crushing weight of enormous slabs of rock. Their punishment is so simple and so terrible that Dante can scarcely bear to describe it. He cries out in anguish to the proud of this world to take heed of the nature of their sin and of its unbearable punishment.

When we had crossed the threshold of that gate
   so seldom used because man's perverse love
   so often makes the crooked path seem straight,   3

I knew by the sound that it had closed again;
   and had I looked back, to what water ever
   could I have gone to wash away that stain?   6

We climbed the rock along a narrow crack
   through which a zigzag pathway pitched and slid
   just as a wave swells full and then falls back.   9

"This calls for careful judgment," said my guide.
   "Avoid the places where the rock swells up
   and weave among the troughs from side to side."   12

Our steps became so difficult and few,
   the waning moon had reached its western bed
   and sunk to rest before we could work through   15

that needle's eye. But when we had won clear
   to an open space above, at which the mountain
   steps back to form a ledge, we halted there;   18

I tired, and both of us confused for lack
   of any sign or guide. The ledge was level,
   and lonelier even than a desert track.   21

From brink to cliff-face measured three men's height,
    and the Cornice did not vary in its width
    as far as I could see to left or right.   24

Our feet had not yet moved a step up there,
    when I made out that all the inner cliff
    which rose without a foothold anywhere   27

was white and flawless marble and adorned
    with sculptured scenes beside which Polyclitus',
    and even Nature's, best works would be scorned.   30

The Angel who came down from God to man
    with the decree of peace the centuries wept for,
    which opened Heaven, ending the long ban,   33

stood carved before us with such force and love,
    with such a living grace in his whole pose,
    the image seemed about to speak and move.   36

One could have sworn an *Ave!* sounded clear,
    for she who turned the key that opened to us
    the Perfect Love, was also figured there;   39

and all her flowing gesture seemed to say—
    impressed there as distinctly as a seal
    impresses wax—*Ecce ancilla Dei.*   42

"Do not give all your thoughts to this one part,"
    my gentle Master said. (I was then standing
    on that side of him where man has his heart.)   45

I turned my eyes a little to the right
    (the side on which he stood who had thus urged me)
    and there, at Mary's back, carved in that white   48

and flawless wall, I saw another scene,
    and I crossed in front of Virgil and drew near it
    the better to make out what it might mean.   51

Emerging from the marble were portrayed
    the cart, the oxen, and the Ark from which
    the sacrilegious learned to be afraid.   54

Seven choirs moved there before it, bringing
    confusion to my senses; with my hearing
    I thought "No," with my sight, "Yes, they are singing."   57

In the same way, the smokes the censers poured
    were shown so faithfully that eyes and nose
    disputed yes and no in happy discord.   60

And there before the Holy Vessel, dancing
    with girt-up robes, the humble Psalmist moved,
    less than a king, and more, in his wild prancing.   63

Facing him, portrayed with a vexed frown
  of mingled sadness and contempt, Michal
  stood at a palace window looking down.   66

I moved a little further to the right,
  the better to observe another panel
  that shone at Michal's back, dazzling and white.   69

Here was portrayed from glorious history
  that Roman Prince whose passion to do justice
  moved Gregory to his great victory.   72

I speak of Trajan, blessed Emperor.
  And at his bridle was portrayed a widow
  in tears wept from the long grief of the poor.   75

Filling the space on both sides and behind
  were mounted knights on whose great golden banners
  the eagles seemed to flutter in the wind.   78

The widow knelt and by consummate art
  appeared to say: "My Lord, avenge my son
  for he is slain and I am sick at heart."   81

And he to answer: "Justice shall be done;
  wait only my return." And she: "My Lord"—
  speaking from the great grief that urged her on—   84

"If you do not?" And he: "Who wears my crown
  will right your wrong." And she: "Can the good deed
  another does grace him who shuns his own?"   87

And he, then: "Be assured. For it is clear
  this duty is to do before I go.
  Justice halts me, pity binds me here."   90

The Maker who can never see or know
  anything new, produced that "visible speaking":
  new to us, because not found below.   93

As I stood relishing the art and thought
  of those high images—dear in themselves,
  and dearer yet as works His hand had wrought—   96

the poet said: "Look there: they seem to crawl
  but those are people coming on our left:
  they can tell us where to climb the wall."   99

My eyes, always intent to look ahead
  to some new thing, finding delight in learning,
  lost little time in doing as he said.   102

Reader, I would not have you be afraid,
  nor turn from your intention to repent
  through hearing how God wills the debt be paid.   105

Do not think of the torments: think, I say,
of what comes after them: think that at worst
they cannot last beyond the Judgment Day.   108

"Master," I said, "those do not seem to me
people approaching us; nor do I know—
they so confuse my sight—what they may be."   111

And he to me: "Their painful circumstance
doubles them to the very earth: my own eyes
debated what they saw there at first glance.   114

Look hard and you will see the people pressed
under the moving boulders there. Already
you can make out how each one beats his breast."   117

O you proud Christians, wretched souls and small,
who by the dim lights of your twisted minds
believe you prosper even as you fall—   120

can you not see that we are worms, each one
born to become the Angelic butterfly
that flies defenseless to the Judgment Throne?   123

What have your souls to boast of and be proud?
You are no more than insects, incomplete
as any grub until it burst the shroud.   126

Sometimes at roof or ceiling-beam one sees
a human figure set there as a corbel,
carved with its chest crushed in by its own knees,   129

so cramped that what one sees imagined there
makes his bones ache in fact—just such a sense
grew on me as I watched those souls with care.   132

True, those who crawled along that painful track
were more or less distorted, each one bent
according to the burden on his back;   135

yet even the most patient, wracked and sore,
seemed to be groaning: "I can bear no more!"

Notes

2. *perverse love*: All human actions, in Dante's view, are motivated by love: right love produces good actions and perverse love produces bad. Virgil discusses this concept in detail in XVII, 103 ff.

7–12. THE NEEDLE'S EYE: "It is easier for a camel to pass through the eye of a needle than for a rich man to enter into the kingdom of God." (*Matthew*, xix, 24, and *Mark*, xx, 25. See also *Luke*, xvii, 25.) I understand Dante to mean here that there shall be no passage to purification without the ardor of the spirit that strips a man of worldliness. Once again, as in the first climb at the very foot of the mountain, the beginning is the most difficult part of the ascent.

14. *waning moon*: The moon had been full on the night before Good Friday (*Inferno*, XX, 127). It is now four and a half days later. In two and a half more days it will be a half moon.

15. *sunk to rest*: The moon rose sometime after 8:00 P.M., perhaps closer to 9:00, as described at the beginning of Canto X. It would set about twelve hours later. But Dante says it has *already* set. It is, therefore, sometime after 8:00 A.M. But to assume that it has just set, would make it only two hours after sunrise, and would mark the hour of Dante's awakening outside the Gate. The passage, moreover, was a slow one. Something between 9:00 and 10:00 A.M. would, therefore, seem to be a reasonable time for Dante's emergence on the first ledge. See XII, 80–81, note.

22–24. The turns of Dante's style and the natural tendency of Italian to use more syllables than does English in stating a similar thought, sometimes make it desirable to render six lines of Dante into three of English. I have so rendered it here. A literal translation of the original would read: "From its edge where it borders the void, to the foot of the high bank which rises again, would measure three times a human body; and as far as my eyes could extend their flight either to the left or to the right side, this Cornice seemed to me to be that [wide]."

26 ff. THE WHIP AND THE REIN. At the entrance to each Cornice, Dante presents high examples of the virtue opposite the sin punished on that Cornice. Their purpose is clearly to whip the souls on to emulation. The form in which these examples are presented varies from Cornice to Cornice, but the examples are usually three, and the first of them is always taken from the life of the Virgin.

At the end of the passage of each Cornice, also in various forms, Dante presents examples of the terrible price one must pay for succumbing to each particular sin. The opening exhortations designed to drive the souls on to emulation may be called the Whip of each sin; the closing examples, or admonitions, may be called the Rein, serving to check the impulse toward that sin. See XIII, 39–40.

29. *Polyclitus*: Greek sculptor of the late fifth century B.C., contemporary with Phidias. His name seems to have been the word for artistic perfection during the late Middle Ages and early Renaissance, probably because he is often mentioned by Aristotle.

31–90. THE WHIP OF PRIDE. It consists of three bas-relief panels carved on the inner cliff-face, each panel portraying a scene of great humility, humility being, of course, the virtue opposite pride.

The first panel (lines 31–42) depicts the Annunciation. The angel Gabriel appears to Mary, bringing the word of her great election, and Mary, untouched by pride, answers in her great hour, *Ecce ancilla Dei*, "Behold the handmaiden of God." (*Luke*, i, 38). *the key*: Christ.

The second panel (lines 49–66) depicts King David putting aside all the offices of majesty to dance in humility and total abandonment before the Lord (see *II Samuel*, vi, 14) on bringing the Ark to Jerusalem from the house of the Gittite, Obed-edom. Dante has confused, or deliberately blended, two scenes into one. The first journey of the Ark began with an ox-drawn cart and it was then that Uzzah (an example of overweening pride) was struck dead for laying unsanctified hands upon the Ark, a sacrilegious act. (See *II Samuel*, vi, 6–7.) David laid up the Ark in the house of the Gittite and returned for it three months later, on which occasion it was carried to Jerusalem by the Levites. It was on the second journey that David put by his majesty to dance before the Lord. Michal, daughter of King Saul, and David's first wife, looked on scornfully and was punished for her arrogance by sterility: "therefore Michal the daughter of Saul had no child unto the day of her death." (*II Samuel*, vi, 23.)

The third panel (lines 70–90) depicts the Emperor Trajan halting his royal cavalry en route to battle and dismounting in order to secure justice for a poor woman. Dante places Trajan in *Paradiso*, XX, his soul according to legend having been summoned back to earth and baptized by St. Gregory.

100 ff. THE PUNISHMENT OF THE PROUD. The simple and terrible penance of these souls is that each must crawl round and round the Cornice bearing enormous slabs of rock that press him down, each according to the degree of his sin. The higher a soul tried to raise itself in its pride, the more it is crushed to earth. For pride is a weight of worldliness and bears down the spirit, and therefore it is crushed under the rock of the earth. It is, moreover, the primal sin and the father of all other sins, for the proud man seeks to set himself up as God, and therefore his soul, here, is crushed agonizingly into the very dust until it has suffered itself clean and may rise free of the weight it has placed upon itself.

Canto XI

The Proud

As the souls of the Proud creep near, the Poets hear them recite a long and humble prayer based on the Paternoster. When the prayer is ended, Virgil asks one of the souls, hidden from view under its enormous burden, the way to the ascent. The sinner, who identifies himself as *Omberto Aldobrandesco*, instructs the Poets to follow along in the direction the souls are crawling. He recites his history in brief, and it becomes clear that Dante means him to exemplify *Pride of Birth*. The conversation between Dante and Omberto is overheard by *Oderisi d'Agobbio*, who turns in pain and speaks to Dante, explaining his sin of *Pride of Talent*, the avidity of the artist for pre-eminence. Oderisi also points out the soul that struggles along just ahead of him as *Provenzano Salvani*, once war lord of Siena, who is being punished for *Pride of Temporal Power*, though he has been advanced toward his purification in recognition of a single *Act of Great Humility* performed in order to save the life of a friend.

Oderisi concludes with a *Dark Prophecy of Dante's Exile* from Florence.

> *Our Father in Heaven, not by Heaven bounded*
> *but there indwelling for the greater love*
> *Thou bear'st Thy first works in the realm first-founded,*   3
>
> *hallowed be Thy name, hallowed Thy Power*
> *by every creature as its nature grants it*
> *to praise Thy quickening breath in its brief hour.*   6
>
> *Let come to us the sweet peace of Thy reign,*
> *for if it come not we cannot ourselves*
> *attain to it however much we strain.*   9
>
> *And as Thine Angels kneeling at the throne*
> *offer their wills to Thee, singing Hosannah,*
> *so teach all men to offer up their own.*   12
>
> *Give us this day Thy manna, Lord we pray,*
> *for if he have it not, though man most strive*
> *through these harsh wastes, his speed is his delay.*   15
>
> *As we forgive our trespassers the ill*
> *we have endured, do Thou forgive, not weighing*
> *our merits, but the mercy of Thy will.*   18
>
> *Our strength is as a reed bent to the ground:*
> *do not Thou test us with the Adversary,*
> *but deliver us from him who sets us round.*   21

This last petition, Lord, with grateful mind,
  we pray not for ourselves who have no need,
  but for the souls of those we left behind.   24

—So praying godspeed for themselves and us,
  those souls were crawling by under such burdens
  as we at times may dream of. Laden thus,   27

unequally tormented, weary, bent,
  they circled the First Cornice round and round,
  purging away the world's foul sediment.   30

If they forever speak our good above,
  what can be done for their good here below
  by those whose will is rooted in God's love?   33

Surely, we should help those souls grow clear
  of time's deep stain, that each at last may issue
  spotless and weightless to his starry sphere.   36

"Ah, so may Justice and pity soon remove
  the load you bear, that you may spread your wings
  and rise rejoicing to the Perfect Love—   39

help us to reach the stairs the shortest way,
  and should there be more than one passage, show us
  the one least difficult to climb, I pray;   42

for my companion, who is burdened still
  with Adam's flesh, grows weak in the ascent,
  though to climb ever higher is all his will."   45

I heard some words in answer to my Lord's,
  but could not tell which of those souls had spoken,
  nor from beneath which stone. These were the words: 48

"Your way is to the right, along with ours.
  If you will come with us, you will discover
  a pass within a living person's powers.   51

And were I not prevented by the stone
  that masters my stiff neck and makes me keep
  my head bowed to the dust as I move on,   54

I would look up, hoping to recognize
  this living and still nameless man with you,
  and pray to find compassion in his eyes.   57

I was Italian. A Tuscan of great fame—
  Guglielmo Aldobrandesco—was my father.
  I do not know if you have heard the name.   60

My ancient lineage and the hardihood
  my forebears showed in war, went to my head.
  With no thought that we all share the one blood   63

of Mother Eve, I scorned all others so
I died for it; as all Siena knows,
and every child in Campagnatico. 66

I am Omberto, and my haughty ways
were not my ruin alone, but brought my house
and all my followers to evil days. 69

Here until God be pleased to raise my head
I bear this weight. Because I did not do so
among the living, I must among the dead." 72

I had bowed low, better to know his state,
when one among them—not he who was speaking—
twisted around beneath his crushing weight, 75

saw me, knew me, and cried out. And so
he kept his eyes upon me with great effort
as I moved with those souls, my head bowed low. 78

"Aren't you Od'risi?" I said. "He who was known
as the honor of Agobbio, and of that art
Parisians call *illumination?*" 81

"Brother," he said, "what pages truly shine
are Franco Bolognese's. The real honor
is all his now, and only partly mine. 84

While I was living, I know very well,
I never would have granted him first place,
so great was my heart's yearning to excel. 87

Here pride is paid for. Nor would I have been
among these souls, had I not turned to God
while I still had in me the power to sin. 90

O gifted men, vainglorious for first place,
how short a time the laurel crown stays green
unless the age that follows lacks all grace! 93

Once Cimabue thought to hold the field
in painting, and now Giotto has the cry
so that the other's fame, grown dim, must yield. 96

So from one Guido has another shorn
poetic glory, and perhaps the man
who will un-nest both is already born. 99

A breath of wind is all there is to fame
here upon earth: it blows this way and that,
and when it changes quarter it changes name. 102

Though loosed from flesh in old age, will you have
in, say, a thousand years, more reputation
than if you went from child's play to the grave? 105

What, to eternity, is a thousand years?
Not so much as the blinking of an eye
to the turning of the slowest of the spheres.   108

All Tuscany once sounded with the fame
of this one who goes hobbling on before me;
now, one hears scarce a whisper of his name,   111

even in Siena, where he was in power
when he destroyed the rage of Florence (then,
as much a shrew as she is now a whore).   114

The fame of man is like the green of grass:
it comes, it goes; and He by whom it springs
bright from earth's plenty makes it fade and pass."   117

And I to him: "These truths bend my soul low
from swollen pride to sweet humility.
But who is he of whom you spoke just now?"   120

"That's Provenzan Salvani, and the stone
is on him," he replied, "for his presumption
in making all Siena his alone.   123

So he goes on and has gone since his death,
without a pause. Such coin must one pay here
for being too presumptuous on earth."   126

And I: "But if the souls that do not mend
their sinful ways until the brink of life,
must wait below before they can ascend   129

(unless the prayers of those whom God holds dear
come to their aid) the period of their lives—
how was he given license to be here?"   132

"At the peak of his life's glory," said the ghost,
"in the Campo of Siena, willingly,
and putting by all pride, he took his post;   135

and there, to free his dear friend from the pains
he suffered in the dungeons of King Charles,
stood firm, although he trembled in his veins.   138

I say no more; and though you well may feel
I speak in riddles, it will not be long
before your neighbors' actions will reveal   141

all you need know to fathom what I say.
—It was this good work spared him his delay."

Notes

1–24. THE PRAYER OF THE PROUD. The sinners on each cornice of Purgatory recite a prayer appropriate to their particular penance. The prayer spoken by the souls under the stones is, of course, an extended form of the Lord's Prayer, and Dante's choice of it must be understood by its relevance to the sin of Pride.

The Lord's Prayer is so basic to Christian practice, and so much the possession of every Christian child, that its very nature as a primer of the creed must explain its first relevance here. If Pride is seen as a blind and arrogant assertion of secondary things (self, power, family name, talent, etc.), it follows that such a wrong emphasis on what is secondary can only be arrived at by ignoring what is primary. It is in these terms, I believe, that Dante's intent can be best grasped. The proud must begin over again as children, learning the first expression of the first principles of faith. It is exactly relevant that the first child's prayer is also the most central to Christian belief. Note, moreover, that every petition of the prayer is for the grace of humility and subservience to God's will, and that the last petition is for the good of others.

1-3. *Our Father . . . not by Heaven bounded*: God lives in Heaven by choice, not in confinement. He is drawn to Heaven by the greater love (greater than His love for man) he bears his first works (the Angels) in His first realm (Heaven).

6. *Thy quickening breath*: The breath of life.

21. *but deliver us from him*: In the original form, the Lord's Prayer reads "Deliver us from the Evil One."

22-24. *This last petition*: The last petition is for deliverance from the Evil One. It is obviously not needed by the souls in Purgatory proper, since they are no longer subject to temptation, but is offered up (a happy instance of concern for others) for the souls of those left behind on earth, and perhaps also in Ante-Purgatory.

25. *us*: Refers not to the Poets but to all mankind.

28. *unequally tormented*: As Dante has already indicated (X, 134–135) the burdens of the sinners varied according to the degree of their sin.

30. *the world's foul sediment*: The traces of pride and worldliness surviving in each soul.

33. *by those . . . God's love*: No other prayer helps. *Cf.* Belacqua, IV, 130–135.

43. *for my companion, who is burdened still*: Virgil's famous tact hardly shines brilliantly in begging these souls, bowed as they are under their enormous loads, to help Dante so heavily burdened with his own flesh.

47. *could not tell which of those souls had spoken*: It must be remembered that Dante and Virgil are standing above the souls, who are bent to the ground under slabs of stone that must, in some cases at least, completely hide them from sight.

53. *stiff neck*: A recurring Biblical figure for pride and obstinacy. *Cf. Acts.* vii, 51: "Ye stiffnecked and uncircumcised in heart and ears." (An interesting piece of language.) See also *Exodus*, xxxii, 9, and xxxiii, 3, 5.

58-72. THE ALDOBRANDESCHI. Guglielmo Aldobrandesco (Gool-YELL-mo Ahl-doe-brahnd-ESS-coe) was a powerful Ghibelline of the Sienese Maremma, and Count of Santafiora, the district Dante has already cited as a lawless robber-barony. Little is known of Omberto, and such accounts as there are contradict one another, though all agree that he was excessively proud of his lineage. The Aldobrandeschi were in constant conflict with Siena. In 1259, according to varying accounts, the Sienese either besieged the Aldobrandeschi castle in Campagnatico (Cahm-pahn-YAH-tee-coe), killing Omberto in battle, or their agents crept in and strangled Omberto in bed. Since Dante refers to it (line 66) as an event known to every child, he was probably following the account in which Omberto, though with very few men at his disposal, scorned his enemies, refused to surrender, killed many Sienese, and even made a mad charge into the thick of the enemy's forces, where he was killed after giving a bloody account of himself. Omberto's words seem to indicate that his main motive in this action was utter contempt for those who opposed him. Thus (lines 64–65) his scorn was so great that he died for it.

Omberto's death broke the power of the Aldobrandeschi, their rule passing to the Sienese. Thus (lines 67–69) his pride destroyed not only Omberto but all of his line and its adherents.

60. *I do not know if you have heard the name*: One of those Dantean touches that must not be missed. As Omberto goes on to say, he was, while alive, overweeningly proud of his father's fame. The proud mention of him may, thus, be taken as a relapse into his besetting sin. He immediately covers it with a deliberate act of modesty, as if to say, "You probably never heard of him." The fact is that everyone in Italy would have known of Guglielmo Aldobrandesco.

73. *I had bowed low, better to know his state*: I think Dante intends an ambiguity here. He had bowed low physically better to hear Omberto, and he had bowed low in the spirit of humility better to experience the state of those who purify themselves of pride by making themselves humble. Line 78 reinforces this second meaning.

79. *Od'risi*: Oderisi d'Agobbio. Agobbio or Gubbio is a small city in Umbria, and was known to the Romans as Eugubium. Oderisi was a famous illuminator of manuscripts and a miniaturist. He is reputed to have illuminated many Vatican manuscripts on Papal commission. He probably died in Rome in 1299, though the record is not certain.

As Omberto typifies pride of lineage, Oderisi typifies the pride of the artist avid for reputation. Dante's praise of him may be a test to see how a Proud-one so recently dead (within the year) would respond.

83. *Franco Bolognese* (Bo-lo-NYEA-zeh): Oderisi's student. He was alive in 1300 (hence the "now" of line 84). A few mentions of his name and some disputed traces of his work still exist, but the words Dante puts into Oderisi's mouth will have to explain themselves, there being no other record.

Note especially that Dante cites little-known artists working in what is generally considered to be a minor art. He could, of course, have demonstrated artistic pride in artists of much greater stature, but his point is certainly the more strongly made when he presents great pride swelling in little men.

86–87. *I never would have granted him first place*: Oderisi may mean that in his lifetime he so desired to excel that he would have labored for greater mastery and so have wrested first place from his student. In context, however, the far more likely meaning is that he was then too proud to admit what he now, in his new-found humility, well knows.

88–90. *Nor would I have been among these souls*: Oderisi would still have been in Ante-Purgatory enduring his delay had he waited for a deathbed repentence. *while I still had in me the power to sin*: While I was yet alive.

91–93. The difficulty of Dante's condensed way of speaking is here compounded by his easy way with mixed metaphors. Sense: "O talented men [of arts, crafts, government, and every human attainment], what a vanity it is to seek to be known as foremost in your field! How short a while the laurel crown stays green, unless the age that succeeds you is graceless [*i.e.*, lacks the talent to produce rivals who will excel you]."

94. *Cimabue*: Giovanni dei Cimabui (Joe-VAH-nee day Tcheem-ah-BOO-ee), 1240?–1308. He was esteemed by his Florentine contemporaries as the master painter. His particular innovation was in liberating painting from strict Byzantine domination in favor of a more natural style. If he is no longer hailed as a supreme master, succeeding ages have generally been aware of his genius.

95. *Giotto* (DJAW-toe): A shepherd boy who became Cimabue's pupil and who went on to excel his teacher, becoming the true father of the Renaissance tradition of painting from nature. He was probably a friend of Dante's. The most familiar portrait of Dante is one commonly, but uncertainly, attributed to Giotto.

97–99. THE TWO GUIDOS. The first is Guido (GWEE-doe) Cavalcanti (1250?–1300), a fellow poet whom Dante saluted in the *Vita Nuova* as "he whom I call first among my friends." (See also *Inferno*, X, 52 ff. for a different feeling toward him.) The other Guido, whose poetic glory was shorn by Cavalcanti, is generally taken to be Guido Guinizelli (Gwee-nee-TZELL-ee) of Bologna (died approx. 1275–1276).

Dante may mean himself by "the man who will un-nest them both," or he may be making a general statement. Good arguments can support either interpretation. If it is argued that Dante, his head bowed in humility and observing the terrible penance of the proud, would not be praising himself, it can as forcibly be shown that Dante has already (*Inferno*, X, 52 ff.) asserted his poetical supremacy to Guido, ascribing it modestly to the fact that Guido did not give his whole devotion to the high models Dante took for his own.

108. *the turning of the slowest of the spheres*: The Ptolemaic cosmography attributed to the Sphere of the Fixed Stars a west-to-east rotation of 1 degree per 100 years, hence 36,000 years for one revolution. (See *Il Convivio*, II, 6, lines 140–143.)

110. *this one*: Provenzano Salvani, the Ghibelline chief of Siena at the battle of Montaperti (see *Inferno*, X, 85–87, 91–93, and note to 32–51). After the defeat of the Florentine forces, he led the cry for the destruction of Florence. In 1269 the Florentines defeated the Sienese at Colle di Val d'Elsa, and Salvani, taken prisoner, was beheaded on the field of battle.

116. *He*: God is constantly identified with the Sun in Dante. Here the identification is especially apt.

127–132. *But . . . how was he given license to be here?*: Salvani died, as noted, in 1269. He has, therefore, been dead thirty-one years. Dante assumes that he put off repentance till the end. Normally, therefore, he would have had to wait in Ante-Purgatory for a period equal to his lifetime, and though his exact age at death is not known, his normal delay would still have years to run. Dante asks the cause of this exception and Oderisi tells of an incident of great self-abasement that won special grace for Salvani. See below.

133–138. The incident here referred to is variously told, but the gist of it remains the same in all accounts. A friend of Salvani's was captured, probably by Charles of Anjou at Tagliacozza, and held for a great ransom to be paid within a month, failing which the friend would be executed. Salvani, despite his great pride, posted himself in the Piazza del Campo in Siena and begged alms to raise his friend's ransom. Whether beggars do especially well in Siena, or whether Salvani's action was the sort of thing we now call a "promotional campaign," the sum was made up and the friend freed.

Note how the law is still, as in Hell, an eye for an eye and a tooth for a tooth, but now in reverse: as ye merited, so shall ye be rewarded—with the additional boons that may be procured by the prayers of the pure in heart.

139–142. *I say no more*: Still another of the dark prophecies of impending exile Dante hears throughout his journey. (His "neighbors" are, of course, the Florentines. Their "actions" will be to exile him, thus forcing him to beg as did Salvani. Then only will he understand what it means to tremble in his veins.) Dante left Florence in 1301 and a decree of banishment was read against him in 1302. He never returned.

It is especially appropriate that Dante should be reminded of his banishment to beggary at just this point. Dante, as he makes clear later, was especially concerned about Pride as his own besetting sin. The reminder of his banishment serves aptly to humble him.

Canto XII

The Rein of Pride · The Angel of Humility

Virgil instructs Dante to arise from where he has been walking bent beside Oderisi and to move on. Dante follows obediently, and soon Virgil points out to him *The Rein of Pride* carved in thirteen scenes into the stone beneath their feet. The scenes portray dreadful examples of the destruction that follows upon great pride.

The Poets pass on and find *The Angel of Humility* approaching to welcome them. The Angel strikes Dante's forehead with his wings and, though Dante does not discover it till later, *The First P* instantly disappears without a trace, symbolizing the purification from the sin of Pride. The Poets pass on, up a narrow *Ascent to the Second Cornice*, but though the way is narrow, Dante finds it much easier than the first, since steps have been cut into it, and since he is lighter by the weight of the first *P*. As they climb they hear the first beatitude, *Beati pauperes spiritu*, ring out behind them, sung by the Angel of Humility.

As oxen go in yoke—step matched, head bowed—
    I moved along beside that laden soul
    as long as the sweet pedagogue allowed.   3

But when he said: "Leave him his weary trail:
    here each must speed his boat as best he can
    urging it onward with both oars and sail"—   6

I drew myself again to the position
    required for walking: thus my body rose,
    but my thoughts were still bent double in contrition.   9

I was following my Guide, and we had put
    those laden souls behind us far enough
    to make it clear that we were light of foot,   12

when he said, without turning back his head:
    "Look down. You will find solace on the way
    in studying what pavement your feet tread."   15

In order that some memory survive
    of those who die, their slabs are often carved
    to show us how they looked while yet alive.   18

And often at the sight a thought will stir
    the passer-by to weep for what has been—
    though only the compassionate feel that spur.   21

Just so, but with a far more lifelike grace—
  they being divinely wrought—stone figures covered
  the track that jutted from the mountain's face.   24

Mark there, on one side, him who had been given
  a nobler form than any other creature.
  He plunged like lightning from the peak of Heaven.   27

Mark, on the other, lying on the earth,
  stricken by the celestial thunderbolt,
  Briareus, heavy with the chill of death.   30

Mark there, still armed, ranged at their father's side,
  Thymbraeus, Mars, and Pallas looking down
  at the Giants' severed limbs stewn far and wide.   33

Mark Nimrod at the foot of his great tower,
  bemused, confounded, staring at his people
  who shared at Shinar his mad dream of power.   36

Ah, Niobe! with what eyes wrung with pain
  I saw your likeness sculptured on that road
  between your seven and seven children slain!   39

Ah, Saul! how still you seemed to me, run through
  with your own sword, dead upon Mount Gilboa,
  which never after that felt rain nor dew.   42

Ah mad Arachne! so I saw you there—
  already half turned spider—on the shreds
  of what you wove to be your own despair.   45

Ah Rehoboam! your image in that place
  no longer menaces; a chariot bears it
  in panic flight, though no one gives it chase.   48

Now see Alcmaeon, there on the hard pavement,
  standing above her mother when she learned
  the full cost of the fatal ornament.   51

Now see there how his own sons fell upon
  Sennacherib at prayer within the temple,
  and how they left him dead when they were done.   54

Now see Tomyris bloody with her kill
  after the ruin she wrought, saying to Cyrus:
  "Your thirst was all for blood. Now drink your fill."   57

Now see how the Assyrians broke and ran
  from Israel after Holofernes' murder;
  and showed the slaughtered remnants of the man.   60

Mark Troy there in its ashes overthrown.
  Ah, Ilion! how lowly and how lost!
  Now see your hollow shell upon that stone!   63

What brush could paint, or etching-stylus draw
such lineaments and shadings? At such skill
the subtlest genius would have stared in awe.   66

The dead seemed dead, the living alive. A witness
to the event itself saw it no better
than I did, looking down there at its likeness.   69

Now swell with pride and cut your reckless swath
with head held high, you sons of Eve, and never
bow down to see the evil in your path!   72

We had, I found, gone round more of the mount,
and the sun had run more of its daily course,
than my bound soul had taken into account;   75

when Virgil, ever watchful, ever leading,
commanded: "Lift your head. This is no time
to be shut up in your own thoughts, unheeding.   78

Look there and see an Angel on his way
to welcome us; and see—the sixth handmaiden
returns now from her service to the day.   81

That he may gladly send us up the mountain,
let reverence grace your gestures and your look.
Remember, this day will not dawn again."   84

I was well used to his warnings to abjure
all that delayed me from my good: on that point
nothing he said to me could be obscure.   87

Toward us, dressed in white, and with a face
serenely tremulous as the Morning Star,
the glorious being came, radiant with Grace.   90

First his arms and then his wings spread wide.
"Come," he said, "the stars are near, and now
the way is easy up the mountainside.   93

Few, all too few, come answering to this call.
O sons of man, born to ascend on high,
how can so slight a wind-puff make you fall?"   96

Straight to where the rock was cut he led.
There he struck my forehead with his wings,
then promised us safe journeying ahead.   99

When a man has climbed the first slope toward the crown
on which is built the church that overhangs
at the Rubaconte, the well-managed town,   102

the abrupt ascent is softened on his right
by steps cut in the rock in other days,
before the stave and ledger had grown light—   105

just so the bank here, plunging like a slide
from the Round above, has been made easier,
though towering cliffs squeeze us from either side.   108

We set out on the climb, and on the way
Beati pauperes spiritu rang out,
more sweetly sung than any words could say.   111

Ah, what a difference between these trails
and those of Hell: here every entrance fills
with joyous song, and there with savage wails!   114

We were going up the holy steps, and though
the climb was steep, I seemed to feel much lighter
than I had felt on level ground below.   117

"Master," I said, tell me what heaviness
has been removed from me that I can climb
yet seem to feel almost no weariness."   120

He answered: "When the *P*'s that still remain,
though fading, on your brow, are wiped away
as the first was, without a trace of stain—   123

then will your feet be filled with good desire:
not only will they feel no more fatigue
but all their joy will be in mounting higher."   126

A man with some strange thing lodged on his hat
will stroll, not knowing, till the stares of others
set him to wonder what they're staring at: 129

whereat his hand seeks out and verifies
what he suspected, thus performing for him
the office he could not serve with his eyes—   132

just so, I put my right hand to my brow,
fingers outspread, and found six letters only
of those that had been carved there down below   135

by the Angel with the keys to every grace;
at which a smile shone on my Master's face.

Notes

3. *the sweet pedagogue*: Virgil.
5–6. *boat . . . oars and sail*: Virgil may simply be saying something equivalent to
"every man must do his utmost." More likely, however, each item mentioned had
some allegorical significance in Dante's mind. Thus *boat* might equal "the will to
grace"; *oars*, "the individual's own efforts"; and *sail*, "assistance from the prayers of
others."
12. *light of foot*: Dante intends eagerness, of course. But one must remember that
weight is always equated to sin. (See *Inferno*, XXXII, 73, note.) Every step toward
purification makes the soul lighter.
17. *slabs*: Dante specifically means a kind of gravestone rare in the United States
but common in Europe and usually found in churches where the dead are sometimes
buried under the pavement, their gravestones being set flush with the pavement and
forming part of it.

25-63. THE REIN OF PRIDE. The Whip of Pride consisted of examples of great humility designed to whip the soul on to emulation. Now as the Poets leave the First Cornice, their souls made humble, they find set before them as a final lesson, examples of great Pride and of the downfall to which it brings men. Their thoughts are reined in and brought under God's control by a final reminder of what disasters they have escaped.

The present rein is elaborately conceived and consists of thirteen bas-reliefs cut into the pavement over which the souls pass. Dante's description of the first four panels begins with "I saw," of the next four, with "Oh!" and of the next four, with "It showed." In Italian these phrases are: *Vedea . . . O! . . . Mostrava*. Acrostically (*V* being equal to *U* in Latin), this combination reads *UOM*, *i.e.*, "Man." The tercet describing the thirteenth panel repeats the three phrases in order at the beginning of each of the three lines. The pattern in the original reads, therefore: *UUUU, OOOO, MMMM, UOM*.

This elaborate structure is clearly intended to show not only that Pride is the first and heaviest of man's sins, but that it is so characteristic of him that PRIDE and MAN are practically synonymous.

25. *him*: Satan.

30. *Briareus*: One of the Titans (Giants) who now guard the central well of Hell. (See *Inferno*, XXXI, 97-99, and note.) He stormed Olympus and tried to unseat Jupiter (as Satan tried to unseat God) but was felled by a thunderbolt.

31-33. *their father*: Jupiter. *Thymbraeus*: Apollo, so called after his temple at Thymbra. *Pallas*: Minerva. The scene portrays another repulse of the Titans in their effort to storm heaven, this time at Phlegra in Thessaly.

34-36. *Nimrod*: (See *Inferno*, XXXI, 77, note.) The first king of Babylon and builder of the Tower of Babel at Shinar. ". . . the Lord scattered them abroad from thence upon the face of all the earth; and they left off to build the city. Therefore is the name of it called Babel; because the Lord did there confound the language of all the earth." (*Genesis*, xi, 8-9.)

37-39. *Niobe*: Had seven sons and seven daughters. In her pride, she mocked Latona, concubine of Jupiter, for having only one son (Apollo) and one daughter (Diana). Thereupon, Apollo took his bow and killed all the sons; Diana, hers and killed all the daughters. Dante follows Ovid's version of this happy little legend on the solaces of religion (*Metamorphoses*, VI, 146-312).

40. *Saul*: The proud first king of Israel. Defeated by the Philistines on Mount Gilboa, he fell on his own sword to avoid capture (*I Samuel*, xxxi, 4-5). David, mourning the death of Saul, cursed Mount Gilboa: "Ye mountains of Gilboa, let there be no dew, neither let there be rain upon you, nor fields of offerings." (*II Samuel*, i, 21.)

43. *Arachne*: Her story runs much like that of the Pierides (I, 11, note). So proud was Arachne of her weaving that she boasted that it was superior to Minerva's. Minerva in disguise challenged her to a contest. Arachne presumed to disparage the gods in her tapestry and was changed into a spider by Minerva, who had portrayed the glory of the gods.

46-48. *Rehoboam*: The arrogant king of Israel who would not lighten the taxes of the ten tribes. He sent Adoram to collect the taxes, and when Adoram was stoned to death, Rehoboam fled in panic from Jerusalem, though no one pursued him (see *I Kings*, xii, 1-18).

49-51. *Alcmaeon*: Son of Amphiareus, the Soothsayer (*Inferno*, XX, 34, note). Through his arts, Amphiareus foresaw that he would die at Thebes, and to avoid having to go there he hid in a place known only to Eriphyle, his wife. Eriphyle accepted a gold necklace as a bribe for revealing his hiding place, whereupon Amphiareus instructed his son, Alcmaeon, to avenge him. The panel, therefore, would represent Alcmaeon killing his mother, her downfall being the result of vanity, which is, of course, a form of pride. The ornament (certainly a further moral) was, moreover, predestined to be fatal. It had been made by Vulcan and it bore a charm that brought to grief whoever owned it. (Dante would certainly have thought of Vanity as precisely such an ornament.)

52-54. *Sennacherib*: King of Assyria. He was defeated by the inferior forces of Hezekiah of Judah. Praying to his gods after his defeat, he was murdered by two of his sons. (See *Isaiah*, xxxvii, 37-38, and *II Kings*, xix, 37.)

Dante's moral seems to be that Sennacherib's downfall was the result of his arrogant faith in a false god. Sennacherib with a mighty host blasphemed God. Hezekiah, with an inferior force, prayed humbly to the God of Israel and won the battle. Sennacherib, not yet sufficiently humbled, went back to his false god and met death in the act of prayer, but the true God made Hezekiah rejoice.

55-57. *Tomyris . . . Cyrus*: Cyrus (560-529) B.C., Emperor of the Persians, showed his contempt for Tomyris, the Scythian queen, by killing her son. Tomyris gathered her armies and defeated Cyrus in a battle in which he was killed. She then had Cyrus' head cut off and threw it into an urn full of human blood, commanding the head of the bloodthirsty tyrant to drink his fill. (History does not record where Tomyris got an urnful of human blood.)

58–60. *Holofernes*: He laid siege to Bethulia as general of the army of Nebuchadnezzar. The city, cut off from water, was about to surrender when Judith, a beautiful widow, made her way to Holofernes' tent to spend the night with him. While he slept, she cut off his head and took it back to the city, where it was mounted on the wall. Holofernes' fate threw the Assyrians into a panic and they fled, pursued by the Jews.

75. *bound soul*: See IV, 1–18, and especially 10–12.

80–81. *the sixth handmaiden*: The figure here conceives of the twelve hours of the light as twelve handmaidens serving the day. The sixth handmaiden is, therefore, the sixth hour of light, hence, noon, sunrise being at six o'clock. If the Poets emerged from the Needle's Eye about 10:00 A.M. or a bit before, they have been on the First Cornice about two hours.

89. *the Morning Star*: Venus. Note that the Angel Boatman of Canto II was first seen as a ruddy glow and compared to Mars.

90. *the glorious being*: The Angel of Humility.

92. *now*: Now that the soul has been purged of the heaviness of Pride. The Angel is about to remove the first *P*.

96. *so slight a wind-puff*: The Angel of Humility is specifically concerned with Pride. In that context, the feeble wind seems best interpreted as the vanity of earthly ambition as compared to the eternal good of the soul.

100–105. The church is San Miniato, built on a rise across the Arno from Florence. The Rubaconte (now Ponte alle Grazie) is the bridge that leads most directly to San Miniato. An old account explains: "Issuing from the gate [in the city walls] to go to San Miniato, one finds at first, only one road by which to climb. Then the road forks. And the one on the climber's right hand has the stairs."

"Well managed" is, of course, ironic when applied to Florentine affairs. The "stave" was formerly an official measure, primarily for salt, which was taxed. One of the Chiaramontesi family, as head of the Salt Tax Department, had given rise to a famous scandal by auditing the salt in with a full stave and auditing it out with a lightened one, thus shaving a certain quantity from each transaction. The "ledger" had grown light when two officials ripped out a page to remove evidence of graft. The exact date of these events are disputed, but both took place in Dante's time and both were widely known. The matter of the lightened stave even became the subject for a mocking popular ditty.

110. *Beati pauperes spiritu*: "Blessed are the poor in spirit: for theirs is the kingdom of heaven." (*Matthew*, v, 3.) Each time Dante leaves one of the Cornices, he hears sung one of the beatitudes from the Sermon on the Mount. Dante does not specify in this instance that it is the Angel who sings. At each subsequent ascent, however, the beatitude is sung by the Angel who has allowed the Poets to pass. It should be clear that Dante is not likely to break so firm a part of his pattern without special reason. One must conclude, therefore, that it is the Angel who sings.

Canto XIII

The Envious

The Whip of Envy

The Poets reach *The Second Cornice* and find the blue-black rock
unadorned by carvings. There are no souls in sight to guide them
and Virgil, therefore, turns toward the Sun as his Guide, *Bearing
Right* around the Cornice.

As they walk on, Dante hears voices crying out examples of great
love of others (*Caritas*), the virtue opposed to Envy. These voices
are *The Whip of Envy.*

A short way beyond, Dante comes upon the souls of *The Envious*
and describes *Their Punishment.* The Cornice on which they sit is
the color of a bruise, for every other man's good fortune bruised the
souls of the Envious. They offended with their eyes, envying all the
good they saw of others, and therefore their eyes are wired shut. So
blinded, they sit supporting one another, as they never did in life,
and all of them lean for support against the blue-black cliff (God's
Decree). They are dressed in haircloth, the further to subdue their
souls, and they intone endlessly *The Litany of the Saints.*

Among them Dante encounters *Sapìa of Siena* and has her relate
her story. When she questions him in turn, Dante confesses his fear
of *His Own Besetting Sin,* which is Pride.

> We climbed the stairs and stood, now, on the track
>   where, for a second time, the mount that heals
>   all who ascend it, had been terraced back.   3
>
> The terrace circles the entire ascent
>   in much the same way as the one below,
>   save that the arc it cuts is sooner bent.   6
>
> There were no spirits and no carvings there.
>   Bare was the cliff-face, bare the level path.
>   The rock of both was livid, dark and bare.   9
>
> "Were we to wait till someone came this way
>   who might direct us," Virgil said to me,
>   "I fear that would involve a long delay."   12
>
> Then he looked up and stared straight at the sun;
>   and then, using his right side as a pivot,
>   he swung his left around; then he moved on.   15
>
> "O Blessed Lamp, we face the road ahead
>   placing our faith in you: lead us the way
>   that we should go in this new place," he said.   18

"You are the warmth of the world, you are its light;
    if other cause do not urge otherwise,
    your rays alone should serve to lead us right."   21

We moved on with a will, and in a while
    we had already gone so far up there
    as would be reckoned, here on earth, a mile;   24

when we began to hear in the air above
    invisible spirits who flew toward us speaking
    sweet invitations to the feast of love.   27

The first voice that flew past rang to the sky
    "*Vinum non habent.*" And from far behind us
    we heard it fade repeating the same cry.   30

Even before we heard it cry its last
    far round the slope, another voice rang out:
    "I am Orestes!"—and it, too, sped past.   33

"Sweet Father," I began, "what are these cries?"—
    and even as I asked, I heard a third
    bodiless voice say: "Love your enemies."   36

And my good Master then: "This circle purges
    the guilt of Envious spirits, and for these
    who failed in Love, Love is the lash that scourges.   39

The Rein must cry the opposite of Love:
    you will hear it, I expect, before you reach
    the pass of absolution that leads above.   42

But now look carefully across the air
    ahead of us, and you will see some people
    seated against the inner cliff up there."   45

I opened my eyes wider: further on
    I saw a group of spirits dressed in cloaks
    exactly the same color as the stone.   48

As we drew nearer I heard prayers and plaints.
    "O Mary, pray for us," I heard them cry;
    and to Michael, and to Peter, and all Saints.   51

I cannot think there walks the earth today
    a man so hard that he would not be moved
    by what I saw next on that ashen way.   54

For when I drew near and could see the whole
    penance imposed upon those praying people,
    my eyes milked a great anguish from my soul.   57

Their cloaks were made of haircloth, coarse and stiff.
    Each soul supported another with his shoulder,
    and all leaned for support against the cliff.   60

The impoverished blind who sit all in a row
　　during Indulgences to beg their bread
　　lean with their heads together exactly so,　　　　　63

the better to win the pity they beseech,
　　not only with their cries, but with their look
　　of fainting grief, which pleads as loud as speech.　　66

Just as the sun does not reach to their sight,
　　so to those shades of which I spoke just now
　　God's rays refuse to offer their delight;　　　　　69

for each soul has its eyelids pierced and sewn
　　with iron wires, as men sew new-caught falcons,
　　sealing their eyes to make them settle down.　　　　72

Somehow it seemed to me a shameful act
　　to stare at others and remain unseen.
　　I turned to Virgil. He, with perfect tact,　　　　　75

knew what the mute was laboring to say
　　and did not wait my question. "Speak," he said,
　　"but count your words and see they do not stray."　　78

Virgil was walking by me down the ledge
　　on the side from which—because no parapet
　　circled the cliff—one might plunge off the edge.　　81

On the other side those spirits kept their places
　　absorbed in prayer, while through the ghastly stitches
　　tears forced their way and flowed down from their faces.　84

I turned to them and said: "O souls afire
　　with hope of seeing Heaven's Light, and thus
　　already certain of your heart's desire—　　　　　87

so may High Grace soon wash away the scum
　　that clogs your consciousness, that memory's stream
　　may flow without a stain in joys to come—　　　　　90

tell me if there is any Latin soul
　　among you here: I dearly wish to know,
　　and telling me may help him to his goal."　　　　　93

—"We are all citizens of one sublime
　　and final city, brother; you mean to ask
　　who lived in Italy in his pilgrim-time."　　　　　96

These are the words I heard a spirit say
　　from somewhere further on. I moved up, therefore,
　　in order to direct my voice that way.　　　　　99

I saw one shade who seemed to have in mind
　　what I had said.—How could I tell? She sat
　　chin raised, the waiting gesture of the blind.　　　102

"O soul self-humbled for the climb to Grace,"
I said, "if it was you who spoke, I beg you,
make yourself known either by name or place."   105

"I was Sienese," she answered. "On this shelf
I weep away my world-guilt with these others
in prayers to Him that he vouchsafe Himself.   108

Sapìa was I, though sapient I was not;
I found more joy in the bad luck of others
than in the good that fell to my own lot.   111

If this confession rings false to your ears,
hear my tale out; then see if I was mad.
—In the descending arc of my own years,   114

the blood of my own land was being spilled
in battle outside Colle's walls, and I
prayed God to do what He already willed.   117

So were they turned—their forces overthrown—
to the bitter paths of flight; and as I watched
I felt such joy as I had never known;   120

such that I raised my face, flushed with false power,
and screamed to God: 'Now I no longer fear you'—
like a blackbird when the sun comes out an hour.   123

Not till my final hour had all but set
did I turn back to God, longing for peace.
Penance would not yet have reduced my debt   126

had not Pier Pettinaio in saintly love
grieved for my soul and offered holy prayers
that interceded for me there above.   129

But who are you that you come here to seek
such news of us; and have your eyes unsewn,
as I believe; and breathe yet when you speak?"   132

"My eyes," I said, "will yet be taken from me
upon this ledge, but not for very long:
little they sinned through being turned in envy.   135

My soul is gripped by a far greater fear
of the torment here below, for even now
I seem to feel the burden those souls bear."   138

And she: "Then who has led you to this Round,
if you think to go below again?" And I:
"He who is with me and who makes no sound.   141

And I still live: if you would have me move
my mortal feet down there in your behalf,
ask what you will, O soul blessed by God's love."   144

"Oh," she replied, "this is a thing so rare
it surely means that God has loved you greatly;
from time to time, then, help me with a prayer.   147

I beg by all you most desire to win
that if you walk again on Tuscan soil
you will restore my name among my kin.   150

You will find them in that foolish mob whose dream
is Talamone now, and who will lose there
more than they did once in their silly scheme   153

to find the lost Diana. Though on that coast
it is the admirals who will lose the most."

Notes

6. *the arc it cuts is sooner bent*: As the mountain tapers, the circumference of each succeeding circle shrinks; its arc, therefore, is "sooner bent."

9. *livid*: I have found this word to be so frequently misunderstood that it seems well to remind readers that Latin *livious* means "ashen blue-black, the color of a bruise." The color is symbolic of Envy, the fortune of all others bruising the souls of the Envious. There are no carvings on this ledge, only the first ledge is so carved, and carvings would in any case be lost on these blind shades.

13–15. Having contemplated the Divine Light for a while, Virgil executes a sort of military right-face, swinging his left side around on the pivot of his right heel, and then moves toward the sun. He has learned the rule of the Mountain, which is. to follow the Light of God. In the first twenty-seven Cantos of the *Purgatorio* (up to the time Virgil disappears), there are two pilgrims. In the *Inferno*, only Dante was the pilgrim. There, Virgil was an experienced guide. Dante's rather strange way of describing Virgil's action is almost certainly meant to indicate how utterly Virgil gives himself to the Sun's (God's) guidance.
It is shortly after noon (see XII, 80–81); the Sun is a little beyond the mid-point from east to west, and, of course, to the north of the Poets. They have, therefore, entered the second Cornice at a point just a bit north of east.

19–21. VIRGIL'S ADDRESS TO THE SUN. Virgil seems to be confusing the allegorical and the literal function of the Sun in this apostrophe. How could the Sun as Divine Illumination fail to lead men right? Virgil can only mean, "Since no other guide is available to us, let us walk toward the [literal] Sun." Yet his words seem clearly to take the Sun in more than its literal significance.

25 ff. THE WHIP OF ENVY. Since the Envious have their eyes wired shut, it is appropriate that the Whip of Envy be oral rather than visual. The Whip, accordingly, consists of three disembodied voices that cry out the key lines from scenes that exemplify great Charity (*i.e.*, *Caritas*, the love of others). Thus "sweet invitations to the feast of love" (line 27) may be read in two senses. The feast may be in contemplating these high examples, and it may as readily be taken to mean the feast of Divine Love these sinners will share in the sight of God when they have been purified.

29. *Vinum non habent*: "They have no wine." These words were spoken by Mary at the Wedding Feast in Cana of Galilee (*John*, ii, 1–10). Mary, instead of envying those about her, thought only of their happiness, and noting that there was not enough wine, she turned to Jesus and spoke her loving dismay. Thereupon Jesus turned the water into wine, his first miracle. Note that it was in response to an act of *Caritas* that the first miracle took place.
Structurally, it may be well to note again, that the first incident in each Whip is drawn from the life of Mary.

33. *I am Orestes*: The second lesson in love of others clearly reflects *John*, xv, 13: "Greater love hath no man than this, that a man lay down his life for his friends."
Orestes and Pylades were famous for the depth of their friendship. Cicero (*De Amicitia*, VII, 24) relates the incident in which, Orestes having been condemned to death, Pylades pretended to be Orestes in order to die in his friend's place. Orestes then came forward asserting his own identity, and thereupon both friends argued "I am Orestes," each trying to save the other.

36. *Love your enemies*: These words were spoken by Jesus in the Sermon on the Mount (*cf.* the Mount of Purgatory). "Love your enemies, bless them that curse you,

do good to them that hate you, and pray for them which despitefully use you, and persecute you." (*Matthew*, v, 44.) Dante specifies that the first two voices were loud, but in their special dignity the words of Christ are not rung out; they are "said."

So the third lesson in love: not only to love others, and to love friends, but to love those who offer injury. When the Envious have suffered their souls to this understanding, they will be free to ascend to the next ledge.

37–42. It must be remembered that Virgil is not speaking here from experience. His earlier journey (see *Inferno*, IX, 19–24) was only as far as Judaïca. Virgil, in his capacity as Human Reason, is deducing what probably lies ahead by analogy to what has gone before, and from his understanding of the nature of Envy.

46. *I opened my eyes wider*: Another example of Dante's characteristically strange way of describing how his senses work.

50. *I heard them cry*: They are chanting the Litany of the Saints, hence invoking those who were most free of Envy. Note, moreover, that they are chanting "pray for *us*" rather than "pray for *me*," as they might have prayed on earth in their Envy.

57. *my eyes milked a great anguish from my soul*: The line literally rendered would be: "Through my eyes: I was milked of heavy grief," a strange and daring figure.

58. *haircloth*: A coarse, heavy fabric made of goat hair. Even today peasants wear haircloth capes in heavy weather, but in the Middle Ages, and beyond, haircloth was worn against the skin as a penance, and to discipline the flesh. Such hair shirts were not only intolerably itchy; they actually rubbed the flesh open, causing running sores. In an age, moreover, that was very slightly given to soap and water, such hair shirts offered an attractive habitat to all sorts of bodily vermin that were certain to increase the odor of sanctity, even to the point of the gangrenous. I am told, and have no wish to verify, that hair shirts are still worn today by some penitential and unventilated souls.

59–60. *each soul supported another*: As they had failed to do in life. *and all leaned for support against the cliff*: The cliff is probably best taken as God's Decree: their punishment, which is also their purification, sustains them.

61–66. The figure here is based on the behavior of blind beggars at church doors, and particularly at the doors of those churches which offer special Indulgences (Pardons for Sin) during certain feast days. English readers, long devoted to the illustrations of Doré, will do well to visualize Dante's scenes in terms of Dante's own details rather than in terms of Doré's romantic misconceptions.

71–72. *sew new-caught falcons*: Since diurnal birds sit still in the dark, the eyelids of newly caught falcons were sewn shut by their trainers to make them sit still, partly, as I understand it, to keep them from battering themselves against the cage, and partly to break them for their later training. In hunting, the birds were normally carried hooded to the point of release.

76. *the mute*: Dante himself.

81. *one might plunge off the edge*: Allegorically, therefore, Dante places Human Reason between him and a fall.

86. *Heaven's Light*: God.

88–90. Dante is alluding here to the River Lethe, the same stream along whose banks he climbed from Hell. At the top of Purgatory, the finally purified souls are washed in Lethe, and it removes from them the very memory of sin. Thus Dante is uttering a wish for the more rapid advancement of these souls, a sentiment all of them would take in good part.

93. *and telling me may help him to his goal*: Dante is making use here of one of those narrator's devices in which the reader will understand the remark made, more fully than will the characters to whom it is addressed. We know that Dante is alive and that he may therefore win prayers for these souls on earth. The souls addressed, however, know only that an unknown voice is making a vague but attractive offer.

94 ff. SAPIA OF SIENA. Dante speaks briefly and to the point, as Virgil instructed him, but Sapìa responds with a long and rambling narrative, to understand which one must recall the story of Provenzano Salvani (Canto XI). Sapìa was Salvani's paternal aunt. As the wife of another nobleman, she resented Salvani's rise to great power. When Salvani attacked the Florentines at Colle in 1269, she stationed herself at a palace window to watch the battle, and when she saw Salvani defeated and beheaded on the field, she is reported to have cried: "Now God, do what you will with me, and do me any harm you can, for after this I shall live happily and die content."

According to another account, she had been exiled from Siena (hence her resentment) and was living at Colle at the time of the battle.

The dates of her birth and death are unknown, but she seems to have been about sixty at the time of the Battle of Colle, and Dante makes clear that she died before Pier Pettinaio, whose death occurred in 1289.

94–95. *one sublime and final city*: Heaven, The New Jerusalem.

96. *his pilgrim-time*: His time on earth. As any concordance to the Bible will

show, "pilgrim" for "wayfarer through life" and "pilgrimage" for "man's time on earth" are common Biblical usages.

103. *self-humbled for the climb to Grace*: A poor compromise rendering of *che per salir ti dome* (literally: "who master yourself in order to ascend.") The idea not to be missed here touches upon *the* essence of Purgatory: that the souls purify themselves. Just as Hell is the state of things the damned truly desire (see *Inferno*, III, 123, note), so the souls in Purgatory *will* their purifying pains upon themselves, and nothing but their own will keeps them from ascending, for they themselves decide when they are worthy to move up.

105. *either by name or place*: I.e., "Let me know who you are or from what city you came."

109. *Sapìa was I, though sapient I was not*: The pun is based, of course, upon the fact that the name "Sapìa" is derived from Latin *sapiens*.

114. *the descending arc of my own years*: The figure seems to envision life as a semicircle. Since Dante has already made clear (*Inferno*, I, 1) that thirty-five is the midpoint, the arc would rise on one side of thirty-five and descend on the other. Since Sapìa was actually about sixty at the time she refers to, the figure may be taken to mean simply "my declining years."

117. *prayed God to do what He already willed*: Sapìa's prayer that the Sienese be defeated was granted, and at the time she took the defeat as the answer to her prayer. Now, however, she sees that her prayer was answered by accident: she had simply happened to pray for what God had already willed should happen.

123. *like a blackbird*: The occasional warm, sunny days that occur in Italy in January and February are called in Tuscany and Lombardy "the days of the blackbird." The European blackbird is reputed by Italians to dread cold. When the winter sun shines brightly, however, it immediately perks up and acts as if it owned the world. But as soon as the cold returns, it huddles shivering and miserable.

126. *Penance would not yet have reduced my debt*: As one of the Negligent who put off repentance till her final hour, Sapìa would still be waiting below but for the prayers of Pier Pettinaio. Her presently accomplished penance, therefore, would not yet have begun to reduce her debt of pain.

127. *Pier Pettinaio* (Peh-tin-EYE-oh): Literally, Peter Combseller. He came to Siena as a boy from the country, became a Sienese citizen, and grew into a local legend of piety, later being honored by an annual feast day such as is normally reserved for saints. He operated a small shop in which he sold combs, hence his name. The legend of his piety is general among Sienese writers, but the incidents they cite from his life seem at least as daft as they are saintly. He was, however, much given to public prayer and to elaborate ideas of honesty, and as Dante might say, either tendency would be more than enough to distinguish him from the rest of the Sienese.

131-132. *and have your eyes unsewn*: Sapìa could certainly tell from Dante's words that he was not one of the Envious, but his very freedom in walking around would have been enough to tell her he was not blind. *and breathe yet when you speak*: The blind are well known for the sharpness of their hearing; even a slight aspiration on Dante's part would reveal him to Sapìa. How the spirits managed to talk without breathing is a matter Dante would, of course, refer to God's Will.

Throughout this Cornice, Dante's description of the behavior of the blind is marvelously acute: the way they turn their heads, the way they talk (in the next Canto) about a man who is standing in front of them as if he were not there, the way they put their heads together to speak to one another—all bear evidence to Dante's powers of observation.

142-143. *if you would have me move*: If you would like me to bestir myself to solicit prayers for you when I return to Earth.

150. *restore my name*: In her final years Sapìa performed a number of good works for Siena, but there are several reports that she was generally condemned as a traitor.

151-155. A complicated passage of local reference certainly put into Sapìa's mouth by Dante as a Florentine jibe at the Sienese ("that foolish mob"). Dante (who fears the Ledge of Pride just below him) may have to carry his stone a bit further for his addiction to such touches, but his poem is certainly the livelier for them.

Talamone is a point on Italy's west coast about eighty miles almost due south of Siena. The Sienese, lacking a port, and wanting to compete with Genoa, bought the site in 1303 and invested heavily in building and dredging operations. The scheme, not nearly as unreasonable as Dante would have it seem, failed because of malarial conditions and because the hoped-for port silted in almost as fast as it could be dredged.

The Diana was another project intermittently undertaken by the Sienese over a long period. Siena was water-poor, but the magnificent flow at certain wells suggested to the Sienese the presence of an underground river which they christened the Diana, and which they dug for at great expense. All efforts had failed up to Dante's time and the failures were used as a standing joke against the Sienese as overambitious crackpots trying to make themselves better than they were. The Sienese, however (and largely out of hard necessity), continued their expensive digging and did, sometime later, locate a substantial underground flow. There is still a Well of Diana in a convent in Siena.

A third difficulty in this passage is in the meaning of "admirals." Some of the old commentators report "admiral" was the term for what we should call "contractor" or "engineer in charge of construction." (*Cf.* British-English "navvy," derived from "navigator.") Or it may be that Dante meant that "port-admirals" (*i.e.*, "port-masters" or "harbor-masters") supervised the work. If these are proper interpretations, then the "admirals" would "lose the most" because they would die of malaria. If, however, Dante means "admirals" as "ships' captains," they would lose the most if they tried to use the port, or if they waited until the Sienese finished it. Dante may, of course, have intended all three possibilities at once.

Canto XIV

The Rein of Envy

Dante's conversation with Sapìa of Siena is overheard by two spirits
who sit side by side against the inner cliff-face. They are *Guido del
Duca* and *Rinieri da Calboli.*

Dante enters into conversation with them, and Guido denounces
the inhabitants of the cities of the Valley of the Arno. He then prophesies the slaughter that Rinieri's grandson, *Fulcieri,* shall visit upon
Florence. And he prophesies also that Fulcieri's actions will have a bearing on Dante's approaching exile from Florence. Guido concludes with a
lament for the past glories of Romagna as compared to its present
degeneracy.

Leaving the two spirits in tears, Dante and Virgil move on, and
they have hardly left when Dante is struck with terror by two bodiless voices that break upon them like thunder. The voices are *The
Rein of Envy.* The first is *The Voice of Cain* lamenting that he is
forever cut off from mankind. The second is *The Voice of Aglauros,*
who was changed to stone as a consequence of her envy of her
sister.

Virgil concludes the Canto with a denunciation of mankind's
stubborn refusal to heed the glory of the Heavens and to prepare
for eternal Grace.

"Who do you think that is? He roams our hill
    before death gives him wings, and he's left free
    to shut his eyes or open them at will."   3

"I don't know, but I know he's not alone.
    Ask him—you're nearer—but put in a way
    that won't offend him. Take a careful tone."   6

Thus, on my right, and leaning head to head,
    two of those spirits were discussing me.
    Then they turned up their faces, and one said: 9

"O soul that though locked fast within the flesh
    still makes its way toward Heaven's blessedness,
    in charity, give comfort to our wish: 12

tell us your name and city, for your climb
    fills us with awe at such a gift of grace
    as never has been seen up to this time."   15

And I: "In Falterona lies the source
    of a brook that grows and winds through Tuscany
    till a hundred miles will not contain its course.   18

From its banks I bring this flesh. As for my name—
to tell you who I am would serve no purpose:
I have as yet won very little fame."   21

And the first spirit: "If I rightly weigh
your words upon the balance of my mind,
it is the Arno you intend to say."   24

And the other to him: "Why is he so careful
to avoid the river's name? He speaks as men do
when they refer to things too foul or fearful."   27

To which the shade he had addressed replied:
"That I don't know; but it would be a mercy
if even the name of such a valley died.   30

From its source high in the great range that outsoars
almost all others (from whose chain Pelorus
was cut away), to the point where it restores   33

in endless soft surrender what the sun
draws from the deep to fall again as rain,
that every rill and river may flow on,   36

men run from virtue as if from a foe
or poisonous snake. Either the land is cursed,
or long corrupted custom drives them so.   39

And curse or custom so transform all men
who live there in that miserable valley,
one would believe they fed in Circe's pen.   42

It sets its first weak course among sour swine,
indecent beasts more fit to grub and grunt
for acorns than to sit to bread and wine.   45

It finds next, as it flows down and fills out,
a pack of curs, their snarl worse than their bite;
and in contempt it turns aside its snout.   48

Down, down it flows, and as the dogs grow fewer
the wolves grow thicker on the widening banks
of that accursed and God-forsaken sewer.   51

It drops through darkened gorges, then, to find
the foxes in their lairs, so full of fraud
they fear no trap set by a mortal mind.   54

Nor will I, though this man hear what I say,
hold back the prophecy revealed to me;
for well may he recall it on his way.   57

I see your grandson riding to the chase.
He hunts the wolves that prowl by the fierce river.
He has become the terror of that place.   60

He sells their living flesh, then—shame on shame—
    the old beast slaughters them himself, for sport.
    Many will die, and with them, his good name.   63

He comes from that sad wood covered with gore,
    and leaves it in such ruin, a thousand years
    will not serve to restock its groves once more."   66

Just as a man to whom bad chance announces
    a dreadful ill, distorts his face in grief,
    no matter from what quarter the hurt pounces—   69

just so that shade, who had half turned his head
    better to listen, showed his shock and pain
    when he had registered what the other said.   72

So moved by one's words and the other's face,
    I longed to know their names, I asked them, therefore,
    phrasing my plea with prayers to win their grace;   75

at which the spokesman of the two replied:
    "You beg me of my good grace that I grant you
    what I have asked of you and been denied;   78

but God has willed His favor to shine forth
    so greatly in you, I cannot be meager:
    Guido del Duca was my name on earth.   81

The fires of envy raged so in my blood
    that I turned livid if I chanced to see
    another man rejoice in his own good.   84

This seed I sowed; this sad straw I reap here.
    O humankind, why do you set your hearts
    on what it is forbidden you to share?   87

This is Rinier, the honor and the pride
    of the house of the Calboli, of which no one
    inherited his merit when he died.   90

Nor in that war-torn land whose boundary-lines
    the sea and the Reno draw to the east and west;
    and, north and south, the Po and the Apennines,   93

in his the only house that seems to be
    bred bare of those accomplishments and merits
    which are the good and truth of chivalry.   96

For the land has lost the good of hoe and plow,
    and poisonous thorns so choke it that long years
    of cultivation would scarce clear it now.   99

Where is Mainardi? Have you lost the seed
    of Lizio? Traversaro? di Carpigna?
    O Romagnoles changed to a bastard breed!   102

When will a Fabbro evermore take root
in all Bologna? or in Faenza, a Fosco?—
who was his little plant's most noble shoot.   105

O Tuscan, can I speak without a tear
of Ugolino d'Azzo and Guido da Prata,
who shared our time on earth? and with them there   108

Federico di Tignoso and his train?
the house of the Traversari and the Anastagi,
both heirless now? or, dry-eyed, think again   111

of knights and ladies, of the court and field
that bonded us in love and courtesy
where now all hearts are savagely self-sealed?   114

O Brettinoro, why do you delay?
Your lords and many more have fled your guilt;
and why, like them, will you not melt away?   117

Bagnacaval does well to have no heirs;
and Castrocaro badly, and Conio worse
in bothering to breed such Counts as theirs.   120

The Pagani will do well enough, all told,
when once their fiend is gone, but not so well
their name will ever again shine as pure gold.   123

O Ugolin de' Fantolini, your name
remains secure, since you have none to bear it
and, in degeneracy, bring it to shame.   126

But leave me Tuscan, I am more inclined
to spell my grief in tears now than in words;
for speaking thus has wrung my heart and mind."   129

We knew those dear souls heard us go away.
Their silence, therefore, served as our assurance
that, leaving them, we had not gone astray.   132

We had scarce left those spirits to their prayer,
when suddenly a voice that ripped like lightning
struck at us with a cry that split the air: 135

"All men are my destroyers!" It rolled past
as thunder rolls away into the sky
if the cloud bursts to rain in the first blast.   138

Our ears were scarcely settled from that burst
when lo, the second broke, with such a crash
it seemed the following thunder of the first: 141

"I am Aglauros who was turned to stone!"
Whereat, to cower in Virgil's arms, I took
a step to my right instead of going on.   144

The air had fallen still on every hand
when Virgil said: "That was the iron bit
that ought to hold men hard to God's command.   147

But still you gulp the Hellbait hook and all
and the Old Adversary reels you in.
Small good to you is either curb or call.   150

The Heavens cry to you, and all around
your stubborn souls, wheel their eternal glory,
and yet you keep your eyes fixed on the ground.   153

And for each turning from the joys of Love
the All-Discerning flails you from above."

Notes

16. *Falterona*: One of the major peaks of the Tuscan Apennines. It is northeast of Florence and both the Arno and the Tiber spring from its sides.

18. *a hundred miles*: "Hundred" is used here as a large round number; the Arno with all its windings has a course of at least a hundred and fifty miles.

22–24. *If I rightly weigh*: The first spirit is Guido (see below). He does most of the talking here and hereafter. Dante has answered in words that run like a riddle, and Guido, knowing that Falterona gives rise to both the Arno and the Tiber, has to weigh out his own conclusion. He would have decided that Dante meant the Arno because the Tiber is so much longer that "a hundred miles" would be out of all reason for its length.

31–36. The gist of these lines may be stated as: "From the Arno's source to the point at which it enters the sea." *the great range*: The Apennines. *Pelorus*: A mountain in Sicily, part of the Apennine system, but cut off from the rest of the chain by the Straits of Messina.

42. *they fed in Circe's pen*: Circe changed men into beasts of various kinds. Guido goes on to specify four species of beasts into which the Arno transforms the people along its course: the swine of the Casentine, the curs of Arezzo, the wolves of Florence, and the foxes of Pisa.

Dante's riddle-like answer to a simple question, though it appears to be mere ornamentation at first, serves to introduce the whole discussion of the degeneracy of the city-states of the Arno Valley.

43. *its first weak course*: In the Upper Casentine the Arno is not yet swollen by any tributaries.

46–48. *a pack of curs*: The Aretines. *turns aside its snout*: The Arno flows from the Upper Casentine straight toward Arezzo but at a point a few miles north of the town it swings east without entering the town proper. Note how Dante's phrasing gives the river itself bestial characteristics, beast scorning beast.

53–57. For the sense of this difficult passage one must remember that Guido (not yet identified) is speaking to Rinieri (not yet identified) and not to Dante. Guido is about to reveal a prophecy concerning the evil actions of Rinieri's grandson, and further concerning Dante's banishment from Florence. The prophecy will grieve Rinieri, but it will be well for Dante to hear it and ponder it. The sense then: "Though it grieve you to hear me say this, especially in front of others, I still must say it, and it will in fact be well for this man to think about it as he moves on." Note that Guido obviously knows who Dante is, though Dante has refused to identify himself by name.

These lines imply strongly, and lines 67 ff. confirm, that Rinieri does not share Guido's prophetic powers, at least at this point. I know of nothing in Dante that will explain why one soul in a given category should be more prophetic than another, but it can certainly be assumed that the prophetic vision comes in flashes now to one soul, now to another.

58–66. *your grandson*: Rinieri's grandson (Dante calls him *nipote*, which may mean either "nephew" or "grandson") was Fulcieri da Calboli (Ful-CHYEH-ree dah KAHL-boe-lee), who in 1302 became podesta (chief magistrate) of Florence.

In Dante's time many of the city-states of Italy were so torn by internal strife that they could not hope to agree on one of their own citizens as podesta. The practice grew, therefore, of electing a (presumably neutral) outsider to administer impartial justice for a given term. Fulcieri (either bribed by the Black Guelphs, or put into office in the first place as part of their plot) arrested and put to painful death many leaders of the White Guelphs (Dante's party) as well as some of the few remaining and powerless Ghibellines. The leaders disposed of, he proceeded murderously against the Whites in general. The "wolves" he hunts (line 59) are, of course, the White Florentines; the "sad wood" (line 64) is, of course, Florence. "The old beast" is Fulcieri, who, after selling them alive, piles shame on shame by killing them himself for sport.

69. *no matter from what quarter the hurt pounces:* I have no satisfactory explanation of this line. Dante seems to stress the unexpectedness of the news. "Pounces" in the original is *l'assanni* (*i.e.*, "seizes him by the teeth"). But what the source of the bad news has to do with the man's reaction to it, in this case at least, remains unexplained, though one may, of course, conjecture at will.

81. *Guido del Duca:* Little is known about him. He was a Ghibelline of Brettinoro, a member of the prominent Onesti family of Ravenna. He served in various judicial posts in Romagna from 1195 on, and is known to have been alive in 1229.

85. *This seed:* Envy. *this sad straw:* His present pains. "Be not deceived; God is not mocked: for whatsoever a man soweth, that shall he also reap" (*Galatians,* vi, 7).

87. *on what it is forbidden you to share:* These words puzzle Dante and remain in his mind. In the next Canto he asks Virgil what they mean. For Virgil's reply see XV, 46–57, and 64–81. See also note on Dante's Doctrine of Wealth (p. 167), and *Inferno,* VII, 68, note on Dame Fortune.

88. *Rinier:* Rinieri dei Paolucci da Calboli di Forlì. (Rih-NYEH-ree DAY-ee Pah-oh-LOO-tchee da KAHL-boe-lee dee For-LEE.) A Guelph leader, podesta of Faenza in 1247, and later of other cities. In 1292 he was re-elected podesta of Faenza, but he and his supporters were expelled by the Ghibellines in 1294. In 1296 Rinieri seized Faenza while the Ghibellines were away paying a social war on Bologna. Those courtesies concluded, they returned in force, and Rinieri was killed in the homecoming festivities.

91–96. To avoid a tangle of scholarly references and disputes I have simplified the text here and taken six lines to render three of Dante's, into what I hope is a reasonably clear exposition. The war-torn land is Romagna. The Reno is a river that bounds Romagna on the west. The sea on the east is the Adriatic.

100–102. All the persons mentioned here were leaders of Romagna during the last decades of the twelfth century and into the first three quarters of the thirteenth. All are cited as examples of knightly grace, bravery, largesse, and sound counsel. *Romagnoles:* People of Romagna (Roe-MAH-nyah). Dante's phrasing unmistakably suggests here the opening lines of Ariosto's *Orlando Furioso.*

103–105. Dante is carrying out the agricultural metaphor begun in lines 97–99. *Fabbro:* Fabbro de' Lambertazzi, leader of all Romagna's Ghibellines, died in 1259. *Fosco:* Bernardin di Fosco, son of a small landholder (hence his family tree was "a little plant"), rose to high estate through great merit and served as podesta of Pisa in 1248 and of Siena in 1249. Both men are cited for the same virtues exemplified by Mainardi and the others listed in lines 100–114.

The first part of Guido's denunciation of Romagna cites the glories of its past. All those mentioned here by Duca were prominent leaders of Romagna, and all were alive during some part of Guido's lifetime. He laments their passing as the passing of chavalric virtue.

110. *the house of the Traversari:* Guido has cited Pier Traversaro among the best lords of the land. Here he extends his praise to the whole house, along with his lament that it is an expiring line. *the Anastagi:* (Ah-nah-STAH-djee) of Ravenna. Another great house left without heirs.

115–117. *Brettinoro:* (Now Bertinoro) A small town between Forlì and Cesena, it was Guido's birthplace. Some of the details of this passage may be variously interpreted, but the general sense is clear enough: "Since the best of your people have fled you to escape the contagion of your guilt, why don't you just do away with yourself?" *Your lords:* Your ruling house. *and many more:* and many more of your citizens.

118–120. The towns here mentioned are small fortified towns of Romagna. In Guido's view, their ruling houses have bred down to degenerate stock. In 1300 the Malvacini di Bagnacavallo (Mahl-vah-TCHEE-nee dee Bah-nya-kah-VAH-loe) had no male heirs and the line was doomed to extinction.

121–123. The Pagani ruled over various holdings in Romagna, Faenza and Imola among them. The "fiend" of the Pagani was Count Maginardo (see *Inferno,* XXVII, 47–49, and note). Maginardo died in 1302, and after him his sons ruled well, but never well enough to remove the stain left on the family name by Maginardo's misrule.

124. *Ugolin de' Fantolini:* Of Faenza. A lord of great good reputation. He died in 1278 leaving two sons and two daughters, but both sons had died without issue by 1286.

130-132. *We knew those dear souls heard us* . . . : A good example of Dante's characteristic sparseness and precision. The souls, well disposed toward the Poets, could hear in which direction they walked away. Had the Poets turned the wrong way (left), the souls would have spoken up. Since nothing was said, the Poets knew they were headed the right way—and each pair knew that the other knew.

134-141. Dante's theory of electric storms (see *Inferno*, XXIV, 145-149, and note at end of that Canto) is likely to confuse modern readers. His basic theory is that fiery vapors (lightning) try to shatter watery vapors (clouds), bringing them down as rain. (So line 138, *if the cloud bursts* . . .)

136-144. THE REIN OF ENVY. Like the Whip, the Rein consists of bodiless voices racing through the air.

The first voice is that of Cain crying to God at his punishment: "Everyone that findeth me shall slay me." (*Genesis*, iv, 14.) Thus the first crash resounds with the cry of the first man punished for envy.

The second voice is of Aglauros, daughter of Cecrops, King of Athens. Her sisters were Herse and Pandrace. Mercury fell in love with the beautiful Herse and bribed Aglauros to arrange for him an assignation with her sister. Aglauros took the bribe, but in envy that her sister should lie with a god, she turned Mercury away when he arrived for his appointment. Mercury, enraged, turned her to stone.

Thus the doom brought on by envy cries in the voice of brother sinning against brother and sister sinning against sister.

146-150. VIRGIL'S REPLY. As mixed metaphors go, this one ranks high even for Dante. "You [mankind] ought to be bridled [like a horse] but instead you swallow the hook [like a fish] and are not saved by either curb [bridle] or call [the original word is *richiamo*, signifying the whistle used to call a falcon back from the hunt]."

Canto XV

THE SECOND CORNICE   *The Envious*

THE ASCENT   *The Angel of Caritas*

THE THIRD CORNICE   *The Wrathful*

The Whip of Wrath

It is 3:00 P.M. and the Poets are walking straight into the sun when an even greater radiance blinds Dante and he finds himself in the presence of *The Angel of Caritas* who passes the Poets on to the ledge above. As they ascend, they hear the Angel sing *The Fifth Beatitude*.

As soon as the Poets enter *The Third Cornice*, Dante is entranced by *Three Visions* which constitute *The Whip of Wrath*, extolling the virtue of *Meekness* toward kin, toward friends, and toward enemies.

These events consume three hours. It is, therefore, 6:00 P.M. of *The Second Day in Purgatory* when the Poets, moving forward, observe an enormous *Cloud of Smoke* ahead of them.

> Of that bright Sphere that, like a child at play,
> skips endlessly, as much as lies between
> the third hour's end and the first light of day   3
>
> remained yet of the Sun's course toward the night.
> Thus, it was Vespers there upon the mountain
> and midnight here in Italy, where I write.   6
>
> The Sun's late rays struck us full in the face,
> for in our circling course around the mountain
> we now were heading toward his resting place.   9
>
> Suddenly, then, I felt my brow weighed down
> by a much greater splendor than the first.
> I was left dazzled by some cause unknown   12
>
> and raised my hands and joined them in the air
> above my brows, making a sunshade of them
> which, so to speak, blunted the piercing glare.   15
>
> When a ray strikes glass or water, its reflection
> leaps upward from the surface once again
> at the same angle but opposite direction   18
>
> from which it strikes, and in an equal space
> spreads equally from a plumb-line to mid-point,
> as trial and theory show to be the case.   21

Just so, it seemed to me, reflected light
   struck me from up ahead, so dazzlingly
   I had to shut my eyes to spare my sight.   24

"Dear Father, what is that great blaze ahead
   from which I cannot shade my eyes enough,
   and which is still approaching us?" I said.   27

"Do not be astonished," answered my sweet Friend
   "if those of the Heavenly Family still blind you.
   He has been sent to bid us to ascend.   30

Soon now, such sights will not aggrieve your sense
   but fill you with a joy as great as any
   Nature has fitted you to experience."   33

We stand before the Blessed Angel now.
   With joyous voice he cries: "Enter. The stair
   is far less steep than were the two below."   36

We had gone past him and were climbing on
   when *Blessed are the merciful* hymned out
   behind us, and *Rejoice you who have won*.   39

My Guide and I were going up the stair—
   we two alone—and I, thinking to profit
   from his wise words as we were climbing there,   42

questioned him thus: "What deep intent lay hidden
   in what the spirit from Romagna said?
   He spoke of 'sharing' and said it was 'forbidden.' "   45

And he: "He knows the sad cost of his own
   besetting sin: small wonder he reviles it
   in hope that you may have less to atone.   48

It is because you focus on the prize
   of wordly goods, which every sharing lessens
   that Envy pumps the bellows for your sighs.   51

But if, in true love for the Highest Sphere,
   your longing were turned upward, then your hearts
   would never be consumed by such a fear;   54

for the more there are there, who say 'ours'—not 'mine'—
   by that much is each richer, and the brighter
   within that cloister burns the Love Divine."   57

"I am left hungrier being thus fed,
   and my mind is more in doubt being thus answered,
   than if I had not asked at all," I said.   60

"How can each one of many who divide
   a single good have more of it, so shared,
   than if a few had kept it?" He replied: 63

"Because within the habit of mankind
  you set your whole intent on earthly things,
  the true light falls as darkness on your mind.   66

The infinite and inexpressible Grace
  which is in Heaven, gives itself to Love
  as a sunbeam gives itself to a bright surface.   69

As much light as it finds there, it bestows;
  thus, as the blaze of Love is spread more widely,
  the greater the Eternal Glory grows.   72

As mirror reflects mirror, so, above,
  the more there are who join their souls, the more
  Love learns perfection, and the more they love.   75

And if this answer does not yet appease
  your hunger, you will soon see Beatrice,
  and this, and every wish, shall find surcease.   78

Only strive hard that soon no trace may show
  of the five scars which true contrition heals—
  as the first two have faded from your brow."   81

I was about to say, "I am satisfied,"
  when suddenly we came to the next Round,
  and my eyes' avidity left me tongue-tied.   84

Here suddenly, in an ecstatic trance,
  I find myself caught up into a vision.
  I see a crowded temple, and in the entrance   87

a lady by herself, her eyes aglow
  with the sweet grace of a mother, saying gently:
  "My son, my son, why do you treat us so?   90

Your father and I were seeking you in tears."
  So saying, she falls silent, and as quickly
  as it first came, the vision disappears.   93

Another lady now appears, her cheeks
  bathed in those waters that are born of grief
  when grief is born of anger. Now she speaks: 96

"O Pisistratus, if you are true Lord
  of the city for whose name the Gods debated,
  and whence all learning shone forth afterward,   99

avenge yourself on the presumptuous one
  who dared embrace our daughter." And her master,
  sweetly forbearing, in a placid tone,   102

and smiling gently at her, answers thus:
  "What shall we do to those that wish us harm
  if we take vengeance upon those that love us?"   105

Then there appears a wild and murderous spill
    of people hate-incensed, stoning a boy,
    and roaring to each other's wrath: "Kill! Kill!"   108

I see the boy sink to the ground, his death
    already heavy on him, but his eyes,
    like gates of Heaven, open through such wrath;   111

and even in his last extremity
    he prays God to forgive his murderers,
    turning to Him the look that unlocks pity.   114

When finally my soul could see and feel
    things which were true outside it, I understood
    my not-false errors had been dreams, though real.   117

My Guide, who watched me as I moved along
    like one just wakened and still sleep-stunned, said:
    "You barely seem to keep your feet—what's wrong?   120

You've stumbled on now for a good half-league
    with eyes half-shut and legs too-wide, like one
    groggy with wine or dropping with fatigue."   123

"O my sweet Father, if you wish to know,
    listen, and I shall tell you what I saw,"
    I answered, "when my legs were stricken so."   126

"Were you to wear a hundred masks," he said,
    "to hide your face, it would lie open to me
    so that your slightest thought might yet be read.   129

These visions warn your soul on no account
    still to refuse the water of that peace
    which flows to man from the Eternal Fount.   132

I did not ask 'what's wrong' as a man might
    who sees with eyes alone, and when the body
    is lying senseless has no other sight;   135

but rather to put strength into your stride:
    for so must laggards be spurred on to use
    their reawakening senses as a guide."   138

Through the last vesper-hour we traveled on,
    looking ahead as far as eye could see
    against the level rays of the late sun.   141

And there ahead of us against the light
    we saw come billowing in our direction
    by slow degrees, a smoke as black as night.   144

Nor was there refuge from it anywhere.
    It took our sight from us, and the pure air.

Notes

1-6. *that bright Sphere that . . . skips endlessly:* Despite the fact that Dante says "Sphere" rather than "great circle" or "zone," the reference here is best taken to be to the Zodiac, which dips above and below the horizon and may, therefore, be said to "skip endlessly." Dante uses the word *scherza*, which may signify any kind of play. *as much as lies between:* Three full hours (from the end of the third hour of the day, *i.e.,* 9:00 A.M., back to the dawn, *i.e.,* 6:00 A.M.). Since one hour equals 15°, "as much as" must equal 45°. If the sun has 45° remaining of its daily course, it is three hours short of sunset, hence 3:00 P.M. *it was Vespers there . . . and midnight here:* Purgatory is antipodal to Jerusalem. If it is 3:00 P.M. in Purgatory, it is 3:00 A.M. in Jerusalem. But by Dante's reckoning, Italy is taken as lying exactly 45° west of Jerusalem. As above, 45° converts to three hours, and since Italy is to the west (hence in an earlier time zone), it must be midnight there.

16-21. *a ray . . . . its reflection:* In the old didactic tradition, Dante is describing the reflection of a beam of light.

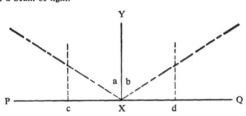

Angle *a* equals angle *b*. *YX* is a "plumb-line to mid-point." If from any two points on line *PQ* equally distant from *X* (*c* and *d*, for example) perpendiculars are raised to intersect that ray of light and its reflection, they will intersect an amount of reflection equal to the amount of ray.

Allegorically, this process of reflection may best be taken for the perfection of outgoing love, which the Angel—as the true opposite of the Envious—represents.

34. *the Blessed Angel:* Since the Angel of each Cornice represents the virtue opposite the sin there punished, this would be the Angel of *Caritas, i.e.,* of Love of Others.

38-39. *Blessed are the merciful:* The fifth beatitude. See *Matthew,* v. 7. It is probably the Angel who sings this beatitude and the spirits of the Envious who reply: *Rejoice you who have won.* The words are chosen from no particular text, but their sentiment is that which concludes the beatitudes, a rejoicing in the triumph over sin. See *Matthew,* v. 12.

48. *you:* You living men. Mankind in general.

51. *that Envy pumps the bellows for your sighs:* a Dantean figure. Envy seems to change the breast into a bellows which does nothing but pump out sighs of envious desire.

52-57. *the Highest Sphere:* The Empyrean. *such a fear:* that someone else will get the material good one cherishes. *that cloister:* Heaven.

DANTE'S DOCTRINE OF WEALTH. Virgil is propounding a favorite Dantean doctrine. Since there is a limit to material wealth, everything that one man possesses lessens what others may possess. Those, therefore, who are avid for the goods of the world must live in fear that it will be taken by others, and therefore Envy drives them to lament everyone else's material gains. The treasure of Heaven, however, grows greater in being shared.

67. *The infinite and inexpressible Grace:* God's love. It shines forth to the souls of those who love Him as a sunbeam shines upon a bright surface, dazzling it full of light without in any way diminishing the source but rather, by giving, increasing the total of light.

76-77. *appease your hunger:* The phrasing here responds to the phrasing of line 58: "I am left hungrier being thus fed."

84. *my eyes' avidity left me tongue-tied:* The avidity of my eyes [to observe new sights] left me [so busy staring at all about me that I was] tongue-tied. *Cf.,* the opening lines of Canto IV, and Dante's discussion of how one sense may so absorb the soul that all others fail.

85-114. THE WHIP OF WRATH. Consists of three visions that seize upon the souls on their way to enter the cloud of smoke.

The first (lines 85-93) is, as always, from the life of Mary. It is based on *Luke,* ii, 41-52. When the Nazarenes started back from Jerusalem after Passover, Jesus did not leave with them, but stayed behind without informing either Joseph or Mary. They, thinking he must be in some other part of the caravan, had traveled a whole day before they learned the truth. They turned back to search for him and spent three days combing Jerusalem before they found him in the Temple disputing with the learned men. Mary, despite the anxieties and exertions to which Jesus had put her, remonstrates without wrath.

The second (lines 94–105) is of an incident from the life of Pisistratus, Tyrant of Athens from 560–527 B.C., the usurper who ruled so wisely and gently that the Athenians forgave his usurpation. A young man who loved the daughter of Pisistratus and wished to marry her, but who had not won the parents' consent, embraced her in public in a moment of high spirits. The wife of Pisistratus, seething with wrath, demands a bloody vengeance for what she takes to be an act of dishonor, but Pisistratus turns away wrath with a soft answer. (Valerius Maximus, *Facta et Dicta*, VI, i.)

The third (lines 106–114) is of the martyrdom of St. Stephen. (*Acts*, vii, 58.) Dante is in error in making Stephen a boy at the time of his death.

Thus the Whip once more presents three degrees of the virtue opposed to the sin being punished, and thus the Wrathful are whipped on by high examples of Meekness toward kin, toward friends, and toward enemies.

98. *for whose name the Gods debated*: The legend is that Neptune and Athena both wished the new city to bear their names. Ovid (*Metamorphoses*, VI, 70–82) describes the resultant contest, which Athena won.

131. *still to refuse*: Dante has already recognized that his own besetting sin is Pride, and Pride is clearly related to Wrath. He seems to have had so strong a sense of his own rightness that any indignity or error could arouse his anger. Boccaccio says that everyone in Romagna was sure Dante would throw stones even at women and children if he heard them insult his principles. His mistreatment by the Florentines, moreover, must have left him with some substantial hunger for revenge. Thus these examples of high meekness have special point for him, and Virgil (his own reason) tells him so.

132. *the Eternal Fount*: Jeremiah, ii, 13, and xvii, 13, refers to God as "the fountain of living waters."

133–138. *lying senseless*: Virgil means "so caught up in a trance that the soul is beyond the reach of the senses." In extension, he is saying: "I do not ask in a material way, seeing things only with the physical senses, but rather in terms of your newly awakened spiritual understanding of your faults, and to urge you to act upon that new understanding."

In a second sense, of course, Dante is analyzing himself. If he is to move higher up the mountain he must put by all his Wrath, all his sense of outraged righteousness, all his desire for vindication and vengeance. But he knows it will not be easy for him truly to forgive his enemies, for he knows how deeply Wrath is rooted in his nature. It requires, therefore, a special urging to act truly upon the three visions he has seen. (Contrast, for example, how lightly Dante was able to dismiss Envy as a personal concern of his soul.)

139–141. It is nearing 6:00 P.M., the last hour of Vespers. Note that about three hours ago (lines 1–6 above), the Poets were on the ledge below and were walking straight into the sun. Now, having climbed the stairway and having walked half a league (about a mile and a half) and a bit more, at a very slow pace (lines 121–123), they are still walking straight into the sun. The fact that they could walk so far without a turning that would leave the sun on their right, certainly indicates that these first Cornices circle very slowly, being conceived on an enormous scale.

Canto XVI

The Wrathful

Marco Lombardo

The Poets enter the acrid and blinding smoke in which *The Wrath-ful* suffer their purification. As Wrath is a corrosive state of the spirit, so the smoke stings and smarts. As Wrath obscures the true light of God, so the smoke plunges all into darkness. Within it, Dante hears souls singing *The Litany of the Lamb of God*. The Lamb, of course, is the symbol of the *Meekness of Divine Love*. As such, it is the opposite of Wrath. A further purification is implicit in the fact that the souls all sing as if with one voice, for Wrath is the sin that soonest breeds division among men, and only Spiritual Concord can reunite them.

Marco Lombardo hears Dante speak and calls to him. Invited by Dante, Marco accompanies the Poets to the edge of the smoke, discoursing on the causes of the modern world's corruption, which he locates in the usurpation of temporal power and wealth by the church. As Marco concludes, a light begins to appear through the smoke. Marco explains that it is the radiance of the Angel who waits ahead. He then turns back, for he is not yet fit to show himself to the Angel of the Lord.

No gloom of Hell, nor of a night allowed
    no planet under its impoverished sky,
    the deepest dark that may be drawn by cloud;   3

ever drew such a veil across my face,
    nor one whose texture rasped my senses so,
    as did the smoke that wrapped us in that place.   6

The sting was more than open eyes could stand.
    My wise and faithful Guide drew near me, therefore,
    and let me grasp his shoulder with my hand.   9

Just as a blindman—lest he lose his road
    or tumble headlong and be hurt or killed—
    walks at his guide's back when he goes abroad;   12

so moved I through that foul and acrid air,
    led by my sweet Friend's voice, which kept repeating:
    "Take care. Do not let go of me. Take care."   15

And I heard other voices. They seemed to pray
    for peace and pardon to the Lamb of God
    which, of Its mercy, takes our sins away.   18

They offered up three prayers, and every one
    began with *Agnus Dei*, and each word
    and measure rose in perfect unison.   21

"Master, do I hear spirits on this path?"
I said. And he to me: "You do indeed,
and they are loosening the knot of Wrath."   24

"And who are you, then, that you cleave our smoke,
yet speak of us as if you still kept time
by kalends?"—without warning, someone spoke   27

these words to me; at which my Lord and Guide
said: "Answer. And inquire respectfully
if one may find a way-up on this side."   30

And I: "O spirit growing pure and free
to go once more in beauty to your Maker—
you will hear wonders if you follow me."   33

"As far as is permitted me," he said,
"I will. And if the smoke divide our eyes,
our ears shall serve to join us in their stead."   36

So I began: "I make my way above
still in these swathings death dissolves. I came here
through the Infernal grief. Now, since God's love   39

incloses me in Grace so bounteous
that he permits me to behold His court
by means wholly unknown to modern use—   42

pray tell me who you were before you died,
and if I go the right way to the pass
that leads above. Your words shall be our guide."   45

"I was a Lombard. Marco was my name.
I knew the ways of the world, and loved that good
at which the bows of men no longer aim.   48

You are headed the right way to reach the stair
that leads above," he added. And: "I pray you
to pray for me when you have mounted there."   51

And I: "On my faith I vow it. But a doubt
has formed within me and has swelled so large
I shall explode unless I speak it out.   54

It was a simple doubt at first, but now
it doubles and grows sure as I compare
your words with what was said to me below.   57

The world, as you have said, is truly bare
of every trace of good; swollen with evil;
by evil overshadowed everywhere.   60

But wherein lies the fault? I beg to know
that I may see the truth and so teach others.
Some see it in the stars; some, here below."   63

A deep sigh wrung by grief, almost a moan
escaped as a long "Ah!" Then he said: "Brother,
the world is blind and you are its true son.   66

Mankind sees in the heavens alone the source
of all things, good and evil; as if by Law
they shaped all mortal actions in their course.   69

If that were truly so, then all Free Will
would be destroyed, and there would be no justice
in giving bliss for virtue, pain for evil.   72

The spheres *do* start your impulses along.
I do not say *all*, but suppose I did—
the light of reason still tells right from wrong;   75

and Free Will also, which, though it be strained
in the first battles with the heavens, still
can conquer all if it is well sustained.   78

You are free subjects of a more immense
nature and power which grants you intellect
to free you from the heavens' influence.   81

If, therefore, men today turn from God's laws,
the fault is in yourselves to seek and find;
and I shall truly explicate the cause: 84

From the hand of God, whose love shines like a ray
upon it, even before birth, comes forth
the simple soul which, like a child at play,   87

cries, laughs, and ignorant of every measure
but the glad impulse of its joyous Maker,
turns eagerly to all that gives it pleasure.   90

It tastes small pleasures first. To these it clings,
deceived, and seeks no others, unless someone
curb it, or guide its love to higher things.   93

Men, therefore, need restraint by law, and need
a monarch over them who sees at least
the towers of The True City. Laws, indeed,   96

there are, but who puts nations to their proof?
No one. The shepherd who now leads mankind
can chew the cud, but lacks the cloven hoof.   99

The people, then, seeing their guide devour
those wordly things to which their hunger turns
graze where he grazes, and ask nothing more.   102

The bad state of the modern world is due—
as you may see, then—to bad leadership;
and not to natural corruption in you.   105

Rome used to shine in two suns when her rod
  made the world good, and each showed her its way:
  one to the ordered world, and one to God.   108

Now one declining sun puts out the other.
  The sword and crook are one, and only evil
  can follow from them when they are together;   111

for neither fears the other, being one.
  Look closely at the ear, if still you doubt me,
  for by the seed it bears is the plant known.   114

Honor and Courtesy once made their home
  in the land the Adige and the Po water
  till Frederick came to loggerheads with Rome.   117

Now any man who has good cause to fear
  the sound of truth or honest company
  may cross it safely—he will find none there.   120

True, three old men are left in whom the past
  reproves the present. How time drags for them
  till God remove them to their joy at last—   123

Conrad da Palazzo, the good Gherard',
  and Guido da Castel, who is better named,
  in the fashion of the French, 'The Honest Lombard.'   126

Say, then, that since the Church has sought to be
  two governments at once, she sinks in muck,
  befouling both her power and ministry."   129

"O Marco mine," I said, "you reason well!
  And now I know why Levi's sons alone
  could not inherit wealth in Israel.   132

But who is this Gherard' in whom you say
  the past survives untarnished to reprove
  the savage breed of this degenerate day?"   135

"Your question seeks to test me," said Lombardo,
  "or else to trick me. How can you speak Tuscan
  and still seem to know nothing of Gherardo?   138

Just what his surname is, I do not know—
  unless he might be known as Gaia's father.
  Godspeed: this is as far as I may go.   141

See there across the smoke, like dawn's first rays,
  the light swell like a glory and a guide.
  The Angel of this place gives forth that blaze,   144

and it is not fit he see me." Thus he spoke,
and said no more, but turned back through the smoke.

Notes

2. *no planet*: Dante, it must be remembered, considered the Moon (like the Sun) to be a planet.

١ 15. *Take care. Do not let go of me. Take care*: Virgil's warning is especially apt at this point. Wrath is a bitter and a smoky passion that blinds the wrathful soul to reason. The Italian idiom *a perso i lumi degli occhii* (literally, "he has lost the lamps of his eyes") means that a man has lost his reason. Thus Virgil is warning Dante, allegorically, not to lose his Guiding Reason in the blind immoderations of Wrath.

19-20. *Agnus Dei*: The Litany of the Mass includes three prayers, each of which begins with *Agnus Dei*—"Lamb of God which taketh away the sins of the world." The first two add "have mercy upon us." The third adds "give us peace."

21. *in perfect unison*: Wrath is a discord that divides men. So, as part of their purification, these souls learn to unite in perfect concord.

27. *kalends*: The kalends were the first day of each Roman month. To reckon time by kalends, therefore, is to use mortal measures which are meaningless in the eternity of the dead.

27. *someone spoke*: Marco Lombardo, or Marco the Lombard. Nothing is definitely known of him, not even his exact name, for his own identification of himself may mean either "I am a man of Lombardy named Marco," or "I am Marco of the Lombardi family."

38. *these swathings death dissolves*: mortal flesh. That Dante is alive and that he came by way of Hell are the wonders he promised to reveal to Marco in line 33. (Here, too, one may argue that he is comparing his eternal journey with the voyages of Marco Polo.)

51. *mounted there*: To Heaven, not to the next Cornice.

57. *what was said to me below*: Dante must surely mean what was said by Guido del Duca. Lombardo's theme certainly continues from what Guido had said.

63. *Some see it in the stars; some, here below*: The movements of the stars and planets, as surviving astrologists still believe, determine man's fate and compel his actions. *here below*: Despite the fact that Dante is in Purgatory, his words here must mean "in the world."

66. *and you are its true son*: I.e., "you have inherited its blindness."

70-72. The problem of Free Will is one of the knottiest in Christian theology. Dante is arguing that if a man's actions were entirely determined by the stars, he would have no control over what he does, and that he could not, therefore, justly be given eternal rewards for his virtues nor punishment for his sins.

98-99. *The shepherd who now leads mankind*: The Pope. In 1300 the Pope was Boniface VIII, Dante's supreme symbol of clerical corruption. *can chew the cud, but lacks the cloven hoof . . .* : Another mixed metaphor: the shepherd is presented as himself a sheep. Almost all commentators agree that chewing the cud signified spiritual reflection, and that the cloven hoof signifies the ability to distinguish between good and evil. Cf. Aquinas: *discrezionem boni et mali.*

105. *in you*: In mankind.

116. *the land the Adige and the Po water*: Lombardy.

117. *till Frederick came to loggerheads with Rome*: Frederick II engaged in a long and disastrous conflict with, successively, Popes Honorious III, Gregory IX, and Innocent IV.

121-122. *in whom the past reproves the present*: Their merit as survivors from a better age of honor and courtesy is a living reproof to the debased new age.

124. *Conrad* (Corrado) *da Palazzo*: A nobleman of Brescia (BRESH-ah). He held various high offices in Florence, Siena, and Piacenza between 1276 and 1289. According to one old commentator, there was a report that during a battle in which Conrad served as standard-bearer, both his arms were hacked off, but that he held the standard up by hugging it with his stumps until he died. The report is unconfirmed.

124. *Gherard'*: Gherardo da Cammino, Captain-General of Treviso from 1283 till his death in 1306. Dante cites him as the type of the true noble in *Il Convivio*, IV, 16, 114-123.

125. *Guido da Castel* (Castello): A nobleman of Reggio, famous for his graciousness and liberality. Dante himself had been received by Guido with great honor.

126. *in the fashion of the French, "The Honest Lombard"*: The French called all Italians "Lombards" and believed all of them to be shrewd and unscrupulous usurers. To be thus called "honest" by them would be to win praise from the least likely source. (Dante's word is "simple"—*i.e.*, not shrewd and unscrupulous—but "honest" is closer in English to what Dante intended.)

127. *Say, then*: Dante has asked to be shown the truth that he may teach it to others. Here, Marco is summing up with Dante's request in mind. "Say [to them] then [to sum up the whole thing]."

131. *why Levi's sons alone*: The Levites, the priests of Israel, were forbidden to inherit wealth, for the Lord was their inheritance, and except for their houses, they

were commanded to depend on the tithes and offerings of the people. (See *Numbers*, xviii, 20; *Joshua*, xiii, 14; and *D·uteronomy*, xviii, 2.) Dante has returned once more to his basic charge against the C·urch—that in massing wealth and power it lost spirituality and grew corrupt. (See *).ferno*, XIX, 109–111).

139. *Just what his surname is, I do not know*: Whoever Marco may be, it seems unlikely that he, in his turn, could speak Tuscan, know so much about Gherardo, and not know him as one of the famous da Cammino family. Dante probably has Marco phrase things in this way in order to bring in a reference to the daughter, Gaia (GUY-yah). Gaia seems to have left two reputations behind her, one for chastity, and one for sexual abandon. Dante has been developing the theme of the degeneration of the descendants of great and good men. It seems likely, therefore, that he thought of Gaia as a wanton, hence, as one more example of the degenerate age in which the daughter of great virtue flits through easy beds.

Canto XVII

The Wrathful

The Angel of Meekness

The Poets emerge from the smoke and Dante is immediately enrapt
by the visions that make up *The Rein of Wrath*. In succession he
beholds *The Destruction Caused by Wrath* to Procne, to Haman,
and to *Queen Amata. Dante* emerges from his trance to hear *The
Angel of Meekness* calling to him to show him the ascent, and the
Poets mount at once as the Beatitude, *Blessed are the Peacemakers*,
is sounded behind them.
    They reach the top of the Ascent just as night falls, and though
they might normally continue along the level way Dante feels his
body so weighed down that he has to pause and rest.
    As the Poets rest, Virgil gives Dante a *Discourse on Love*, dem-
onstrating to him that all actions spring from either *Natural* or *Spiritual Love*, and that it is the various *Perversions of Love* that lead
to the sins that are punished in Purgatory.

Reader, if you have ever been closed in
    by mountain mist that left you with no eyes
    to see with, save as moles do, through the skin;   3

think how those dense damp vapors thinned away
    slow bit by bit till through them the sun's ball
    was once more dimly visible—thus you may,   6

and without strain, image from your own
    recalled experience how I came again
    to see the sun, which now was almost down.   9

Thus, matching steps with my true Guide once more,
    I passed beyond the cloud into those rays
    which lay already dead on the low shore.   12

O Fantasy, which can entrance us so
    that we at times stand and are not aware
    though in our ears a thousand trumpets blow!—   15

what moves you since our senses lie dead then?
    —A light that forms in Heaven of itself,
    or of His will who sends its rays to men.   18

A vision grew within me of the wrong
    she did who for her cruelty was changed
    into that bird which most delights in song;   21

and my imagination was so shut
into itself that what I saw revealed
could never have come to me from without.　　24

Next, down like rain, a figure crucified
fell into my high fantasy, his face
fierce and contemptuous even as he died.　　27

Nearby him great Ahasuerus stood,
Esther his wife, and the just Mordecai
whose word and deed were always one in good.　　30

And as soap bubbles rise in air and seem
full-bodied things, then rupture of themselves
when the film about them breaks, just so that dream　　33

vanished, and through my vision rose an image
in which a maid cried: "O Queen! Queen no more!
Your very being canceled by your rage!　　36

All not to lose Lavinia? Ah, mother,
now have you truly lost her. I am she,
and mourn your death before I mourn another."　　39

When strong light beats against a man's closed eyes
his sleep is broken in him; yet, though broken,
gives a last twitch before it wholly dies:　　42

my vision fell from me exactly so
the instant a new light beat on my face,
a light outshining any that men know.　　45

I was looking all about, as if to find
where I might be, when a new voice that cried,
"Here is the ascent" drove all else from my mind;　　48

and kindled in my spirit such a fire
to see who spoke, as cannot ever rest
till it stand face to face with its desire.　　51

But, as in looking at the sun, whose rays
keep his form hidden from our stricken eyes—
so I lacked power to look into that blaze.　　54

"A spirit of Heaven guides us toward the height:
he shows us the ascent before we ask,
and hides himself in his own holy light.　　57

He does for us what men in the world's uses
do only for themselves; for who sees need
and waits a plea, already half refuses.　　60

To such sweet bidding let our feet reply
by striving as they may before night fall;
for then they may not, till day light the sky."　　63

So spoke my Guide, and he and I as one
    moved toward the ascent; and soon as I had mounted
    the first step cut into that ramp of stone,   66

I felt what seemed to be a great wing fan
    my face and heard: "Blessèd are the peacemakers,
    who feel no evil wrath toward any man."   69

The last rays, after which night rules the air,
    were now so far above us that already
    the stars began to shine through, here and there.   72

"O strength, why do you melt away?" I said
    several times over to myself, for now
    it seemed my legs were turning into lead.   75

We had come to where the stair ascends no more
    and we were stuck fast on the topmost step
    like a vessel half drawn up upon the shore.   78

I waited with my head cocked to one side
    for any sound that might reveal the nature
    of the new ledge. Then, turning to my Guide,   81

I said: "Dear Father, what impurity
    is washed in pain here? Though our feet must stay,
    I beg you not to stay your speech." And he: 84

"That love of good which in the life before
    lay idle in the soul is paid for now.
    Here Sloth strains at the once-neglected oar.   87

But that you may more clearly know The Way,
    give your entire attention to my words;
    thus shall you gather good fruit from delay.   90

Neither Creator nor his creatures move,
    as you well know," he said, "but in the action
    of animal or of mind-directed love.   93

Natural love may never fall to error.
    The other may, by striving to bad ends,
    or by too little, or by too much fervor.   96

While it desires the Eternal Good and measures
    its wish for secondary goods in reason,
    this love cannot give rise to sinful pleasures.   99

But when it turns to evil, or shows more
    or less zeal than it ought for what is good,
    then the creature turns on its Creator.   102

Thus you may understand that love alone
    is the true seed of every merit in you,
    and of all acts for which you must atone.   105

Now inasmuch as love cannot abate
   its good wish for the self that loves, all things
   are guarded by their nature from self-hate.   108

And since no being may exist alone
   and apart from the First Being, by their nature,
   all beings lack the power to hate That One.   111

Therefore, if I have parsed the truth of things,
   the evil that man loves must be his neighbor's.
   In mortal clay such bad love has three springs: 114

some think they see their own hope to advance
   tied to their neighbor's fall, and thus they long
   to see him cast down from his eminence;   117

some fear their power, preferment, honor, fame
   will suffer by another's rise, and thus,
   irked by his good, desire his ruin and shame;   120

and some at the least injury catch fire
   and are consumed by thoughts of vengeance; thus,
   their neighbor's harm becomes their chief desire.   123

Such threefold love those just below us here
   purge from their souls. The other, which seeks good,
   but without measure, I shall now make clear.—   126

All men, though in a vague way, apprehend
   a good their souls may rest in, and desire it;
   each, therefore, strives to reach his chosen end.   129

If you are moved to see good or pursue it,
   but with a lax love, it is on this ledge—
   after a proper penance—you will rue it.   132

There is another good which bears bad fruit:
   it is not happiness, nor the true essence
   of the Eternal Good, its flower and root.   135

The love that yields too much to this false good
   is mourned on the three Cornices above us;
   but in what way it may be understood   138

as a tripartite thing, I shall not say.
   That, you may learn yourself upon our way."

Notes

1–3. *as moles do, through the skin*: Dante follows a medieval belief that the eyes of moles were completely sealed by a membranous covering through which they could see a diffused foggy light only. Here the fog does for Dante what the skin covering was supposed to do for the eyes of moles.

9. *the sun, which now was almost down*: It is near sunset of Easter Monday, the second day on the mountain.

10. *matching steps . . . once more*: Through the smoke, Dante has stumbled along holding on to Virgil's shoulder. Now, once more in the light, he is able to match Virgil's pace.

12. *already dead on the low shore*: Dante, it must be remembered, conceives Purgatory to be on a scale unmatched by any earthly mountain. The sun, as seen from the mountain's base, would already have set. At the poet's altitude, however, the sun is still in sight. Since sunset would be at six o'clock on the earth's surface, it must be a bit later than six now.

13–18. THE POWER OF FANTASY: Dante is about to describe the Rein of Wrath, which consists of another set of visions. Typically, he introduces the visions with a question on the nature of the imagination, and in developing his discussion makes clear, first, that the visions are from Heaven, and second, that he is utterly enrapt by them.

19–39. THE REIN OF WRATH: The three visions of the ruinous results of wrath may be taken as exemplifying wrath against kin, against neighbor, and against God (and self).

The first vision (lines 19–21) shows Procne killing her own son in wrath. The bird that most delights in song is the nightingale. Dante probably intends Procne as "she . . . who was changed." See IX, 15, note; which will also explain her act of great wrath.

The second vision (lines 25–30) is of the crucifixion of Haman, the powerful minister of Ahasuerus, King of Persia. Enraged against Mordecai, Haman persuaded Ahasuerus to decree the death of all the Jews in Persia. A cross (as Dante envisions it, though more likely it was a stake or a gibbet) was especially prepared for Mordecai. Queen Esther, however, persuaded Ahasuerus of Haman's iniquity and the decree was canceled. Not to waste a perfectly good cross, or perhaps because he was confused by the number of people who were making up his mind for him, Ahasuerus had Haman crucified in Mordecai's place. The basic story is told in *The Book of Esther*.

The third vision (lines 34–39) is of Amata killing herself for wrath. The incident is from the *Aeneid*, XII, 595 ff. Lavinia, daughter of the Latian king, was betrothed to Turnus, a neighboring king. War broke out between Turnus and Aeneas, and Queen Amata, mother of Lavinia, hoped Turnus would kill the invader and marry Lavinia. When a false rumor of Turnus' death reached Amata, she hanged herself for rage at the thought that she had lost Lavinia beyond all hope. Aeneas did later kill Turnus in a duel. Lavinia's words in line 39—"and mourn your death before I mourn another"—are prophetic of the death of Turnus. Lavinia later married Aeneas.

The incident itself will not, however, explain Dante's full intent in citing it unless one remembers Dante's partisan identification with the Trojans. (See especially *Inferno*, II, 13–30, and XXVI, 56–63 and notes.) Aeneas was God's chosen and was sent to Italy by Divine Will to found the Roman Empire as the seat of the True Church. It was God's will, therefore, that Aeneas marry Lavinia, daughter of Italy, and thus bring together God's two chosen races. Amata's wrath, therefore, was not only against herself but against God's decree.

47. *a new voice*: The Angel of Meekness.

49–51. Dante's phrasing should be understood in two senses (and both at once). The first: "I was filled with that yearning that allows a man no rest till he have his wish." The second: "I was filled with such yearning that I shall never rest until, this life ended, I rise to stand once more before the Angel."

64–66. *as one*: Virgil leading and Dante a step behind, as they have been going. Thus when Dante switches from the "he and I" of line 64, to the "I" of line 65, he is not being careless but, rather, precise. He mounts the steps a pace behind Virgil. (Reason goes first.)

69. *evil wrath*: One might think wrath inherently evil, and the adjective, therefore, redundant. Dante distinguishes here between Wrath as an evil thing, and Righteous Indignation as a just thing. (See *Inferno*, VIII, 43, note.)

70–72. To read Dante is to educate the eye. The observation here is both subtle and exact. At high altitudes the setting sun's rays shoot up so steeply that the first stars begin to appear before the last light of the sun is gone. I do not know whether the phenomenon is observable from any earthly mountain, but it is easily observable in an airplane at high altitude.

77. *and we were stuck fast*: The Poets cannot ascend after darkness, but they have already finished the ascent to the Fourth Cornice. They are, therefore, free to continue on the level of the ledge. It is not darkness that stops them, but the contagion of Sloth that takes away their wills, though briefly. (See also XVIII, 87–90, and note to 87. And compare the pause they make in *Inferno*, XI, where the stench of Lower Hell is so great the Poets must wait till their nostrils adjust to it.)

85–87. SLOTH: The central sin (there are three deadly sins below it and three above it) is Acedia (from L. *accidia*, from Gr. roots meaning "not caring") or Sloth. Sloth, however, must not be understood as physical laziness or slovenliness but as torpor of the soul which, loving the good, does not pursue it actively enough.

Dante's condition in the Dark Wood of Error, from which he embarked on his long journey, is best conceived as a recognition of the slothful worldliness of his soul up to that time. The entire journey, in fact, is Dante's active pursuit of the true good, his own purgation from Acedia.

Acedia, however, is not simply the failure to perform good works for others, though it readily involves that failure. It is, more specifically, the failure to pay enough attention to the good, to make enough demands upon oneself. Were one to give all of his energy and attention to the pursuit of God's truth, good works would follow automatically. Acedia may consist in being too torpid to arrive at a vision of the good, or in achieving that vision but neglecting to pursue it.

90. *from delay*: Since Dante finds himself temporarily deprived of strength to continue, he seeks to win advantage from delay, thus showing a zeal of which the Slothful failed in their lives. (Here, also, compare *Inferno*, XI.)

93. *animal love*: Blind instinct. *mind-directed love*: Those desires shared by the God-given light of reason.

95–96. Free will may err in three ways. First, by seeking bad goals (the self-love of Pride, which seeks to rise above others; of Envy, which resents the rise of others; and of Wrath, which seeks revenge at the cost of others). Second, by too little zeal for the known good (Sloth). And third, by too much love for the good things of this world (Avarice, Gluttony, and Lust).

97–98. *the Eternal Good*: God. *secondary goods*: The pleasures of the earth given to man for his delight. To deny these is to reject God's bounty; to seek them immoderately is to abandon God for His gifts.

106–108. *love cannot abate*: The doctrine here is Aquinian. Nothing in creation seeks anything but what it takes to be the good of love. Even suicide is an act motivated by self-love, the suicide believing he does himself more good in escaping life than in enduring it.

124. *those just below . . . purge*. Those on the first three Cornices.

125. *The other*: The other kind of love.

132. *after a proper penance*: After a penitent turning to God, and after the delay in Purgatory for the period of time they made God wait. After due penance, due punishment.

Canto XVIII

The Slothful

The Whip of Sloth · The Rein of Sloth

Virgil continues his *Discourse on Love*, explaining *The Relation of Love and Free Will*, but warns Dante that Reason is limited. Dante must seek the final answer from Beatrice, for the question involves one of the mysteries of faith.

It is near midnight when Virgil concludes, and Dante is starting to drowse, when he is suddenly brought awake by a long train of souls who come running and shouting from around the mountain. They are *The Slothful*, the souls of those who recognized The Good but were not diligent in pursuit of it. As once they delayed, so now they are all hurry and zeal, and will not even pause to speak to the Poets.

Two souls run before the rest shouting aloud *The Whip of Sloth*, one citing Mary as an example of holy zeal, the other citing Caesar as an example of temporal zeal.

Virgil hails the racing souls to ask the nearer way to the ascent, but not even the news that Dante is still alive slows them. One soul, a former *Abbot of San Zeno*, shouts back an answer while still running.

Behind the train come two more souls shouting *The Rein of Sloth*, citing as examples of the downfall of the laggard, the Israelites in the desert, and those followers of Aeneas who remained in ʾSicily.

The souls pass from sight and hearing. Dante, his head full of confused thoughts, sinks into sleep. Instantly, his thoughts are transformed into *A Dream*.

> His explanation at an end, My Guide,
> that lofty scholar, scrutinized my face
> as if to see if I seemed satisfied.   3

> And I, my thirst already sprung anew,
> said nothing, thinking "He may well be tired
> of all this questioning I put him through."   6

> But that true Father, sensing both my thirst
> and that I was too timid to reveal it,
> encouraged me to speak by speaking first.   9

> I, therefore: "Master, in the light you shed
> my sight grows so acute that I see clearly
> all that your argument implied or said.   12

> But, dear and gentle Father, please discourse
> more fully on that love in which you say
> all good and evil actions have their source."   15

And he: "Focus the keen eyes of your mind
  on what I say, and you will see made clear
  the error of the blind who lead the blind.   18

The soul, being created prone to Love,
  is drawn at once to all that pleases it,
  as soon as pleasure summons it to move.   21

From that which really is, your apprehension
  extracts a form which it unfolds within you;
  that form thereby attracts the mind's attention,   24

then if the mind, so drawn, is drawn to it,
  that summoning force is Love; and thus within you,
  through pleasure, a new natural bond is knit.   27

Then, just as fire yearns upward through the air,
  being so formed that it aspires by nature
  to be in its own element up there;   30

so love, which is a spiritual motion,
  fills the trapped soul, and it can never rest
  short of the thing that fills it with devotion.   33

By now you will, of course, have understood
  how little of the truth they see who claim
  that every love is, in itself, a good;   36

for though love's substance always will appear
  to be a good, not every impress made,
  even in finest wax, is good and clear."   39

"Your words and my own eager mind reveal
  exactly what Love is," I said, "but now
  there is an even greater doubt I feel: 42

if love springs from outside the soul's own will,
  it being made to love, what merit is there
  in loving good, or blame in loving ill?"   45

And he to me: "As far as reason sees,
  I can reply. The rest you must ask Beatrice.
  The answer lies within faith's mysteries.   48

Every substantial form distinct from matter
  and yet united with it in some way,
  has a specific power in it. This latter   51

is not perceivable save as it gives
  evidence of its workings and effects—
  as the green foliage tells us a plant lives.   54

Therefore, no man can know whence springs the light
  of his first cognizance, nor of the bent
  of such innate primordial appetite   57

as springs within you, as within the bee
the instinct to make honey; and such instincts
are, in themselves, not blamable nor worthy.   60

Now, that all later wills and this first bent
may thrive, the innate counsel of your Reason
must surely guard the threshold of consent.   63

This is the principle from which accrue
your just desserts, according as it reaps
and winnows good or evil love in you.   66

Those masters who best reasoned nature's plan
discerned this innate liberty, and therefore
they left their moral science to guide Man.   69

Or put it this way: all love, let us say,
that burns in you, springs from necessity;
but you still have the power to check its sway.   72

These noble powers Beatrice will comprehend
as 'The Free Will.' Keep that term well in mind
if she should speak of it when you ascend."   75

It was near midnight. The late-risen moon,
like a brass bucket polished bright as fire,
thinned out the lesser stars, which seemed to drown.   78

It traveled retrograde across that sign
the sun burns when the Romans look between
the Sards and Corsicans to its decline.   81

And he who made Piètola shine above
all other Mantuan towns, had discharged fully
the burden I had laid on him for love;   84

because of which I, being pleased to find
such clear and open answers to my questions,
was rambling drowsily within my mind.   87

I wakened in an instant to a pack
of people running toward us, a great mob
that broke around the mountain at my back: 90

as once, of old, wild hordes ran through the night
along Ismenus' and Asopus' banks
when Thebes invoked no more than Bacchus' might;   93

in such a frenzy, far as I could see,
those who were spurred by good will and high love
ran bent like scythes along that Cornice toward me.   96

They were upon us soon, for all that rout
was running furiously, and out in front
two spirits streaming tears were calling out: 99

"Mary *ran* to the hills"—so one refrain;
 and the other: "Caesar, to subdue Ilerda
 struck at Marseilles, and then *swooped* down on Spain." 102

"Faster! Faster! To be slow in love
 is to lose time," cried those who came behind;
 "Strive on that grace may bloom again above." 105

"O souls in whom the great zeal you now show
 no doubt redeems the negligence and delay
 that marred your will to do good, there below; 108

this man lives—truly—and the instant day
 appears again, he means to climb. Please show him
 how he may reach the pass the nearer way." 111

So spoke my Master, and one running soul
 without so much as breaking step replied:
 "Come after us, and you will find the hole. 114

The will to move on with all speed so fills us
 we cannot stop; we humbly beg your pardon
 if duty makes us seem discourteous. 117

I was abbot of San Zeno in the reign
 of the good emperor Frederick Barbarossa,
 of whom the Milanese still speak with pain. 120

And another with one foot now in the grave
 will shed tears for the monastery soon,
 and rue the evil orders he once gave. 123

For he has set his son up as the head—
 a man deformed in body, worse in mind,
 and bastard born—in its true Pastor's stead." 126

He had by then left us so far behind
 that if he said more, it was lost to me:
 but I was pleased to keep this much in mind. 129

My aid on all occasion, the prompt Master,
 said: "Look, for here come two who cry aloud
 the Scourge of Sloth, that souls may flee it faster." 132

At the tail end one runner cried: "They died
 before the Jordan saw its heirs, those people
 for whom the Red Sea's waters stood aside." 135

The other: "Those who found it too laborious
 to go the whole way with Anchises' son
 cut from their lives all that was glorious." 138

Then when those shades had drawn so far ahead
 that I could not make out a trace of them,
 a new thought seized upon me, and it bred 141

so many more, so various, and so scrambled,
that turning round and round inside itself
so many ways at once, my reason rambled;   144

I closed my eyes and all that tangled theme
was instantly transformed into a dream.

Notes

18. *the blind who lead the blind*: Virgil means here the teachers of Epicurean philosophy and their students, both spiritually blind in Dante's view in that they teach that all desire (*i.e.*, all love, as Virgil calls it) is a good thing and should be gratified.

19 ff. VIRGIL'S DISCOURSE ON LOVE: The doctrine Dante puts into Virgil's mouth is typically medieval both in content and in the manner of its statement. The soul, Virgil posits, is made with a potential for love, *i.e.*, it is naturally drawn to that which pleases it. Such love passes to action in three stages.

Lines 22-24 describe the first stage. The apprehensive faculty (the senses plus the intellect) observes *that which really is* (any object that has real existence) and extracts from it a *form* (not the thing, but what the mind conceives the thing to be). This *form* is registered upon the soul.

Lines 25-27 describe the second stage. If the soul is drawn to that form, it yields to it with a natural tie of love. It is in this way that the soul has contact with creation.

Lines 28-33 describe the third stage. Just as fire is so conceived and made by Nature that it naturally yearns to rise "up there" (*i.e.*, to the Sphere of Fire) so the soul, by its very nature (its natural disposition to love) yearns for that which attracts it.

37-39. *love's substance*: Dante uses the philosophical term *matera*, *i.e.*, matter, which may be taken to mean either "the thing loved" (which will always appear as a good to one who loves it), or "the natural substance of love," *i.e.*, the soul's naturally created aptitude to love.

The Epicureans, according to Dante, err in not seeing that appearances may beguile the soul into loving a bad object (the Epicureans, of course, would reply that nothing that gives pleasure can be bad) and thus, that a force that is good in its potential may be exercised in such a way as to be evil in its action.

43-45. I have taken liberties here for the sake of clarity. The passage literally rendered would read: "If love is offered to us from outside, and the soul does not go with another foot (*i.e.*, has no other way of choosing its course), then whether it goes rightly or wrongly is not a matter of its own merit."

49. *substantial form*: A scholastic term for "the essence of a thing." The substantial form of man is his soul, which is distinct from matter, yet united with it. Each substantial form has its specific tendencies, characteristics, and capacities which are visible only in its working and effects. Before what the Catholic Church declares to be the age of reason (approximately age seven) these powers are simply innate and neutral. Thereafter, there develops within the soul a capacity to reason, and in order to gather the soul into a harmonious unit, innate reason must decide what may and what may not pass the threshold of the soul and be gathered into its love. With reason as the principle of conduct, the soul is then responsible for its actions.

67. *those masters*: Aristotle and Plato. Both based their moral philosophy upon free will.

75. *if she should speak of it*: Beatrice discusses Free Will in the Sphere of the Moon, *Paradiso*, V, 19 ff.

76-81. Note that Dante does not say that the moon rose at midnight, but only that it was near midnight and that the moon was late-risen.

He then appends an astronomical figure too complicated to explain here in detail. In brief, the moon in its monthly retrograde motion is in the sign of the Zodiac (commentators dispute whether Dante means Scorpio or Sagittarius) in which the sun is when a Roman feast is set in a position between Sardinia and Corsica.

82. *Piètola*: A village near Mantua. One legend—and Dante obviously follows it— has it that Virgil was born in Piètola rather than in Mantua proper. Thus Piètola outshines all other Mantuan towns because it was Virgil's birthplace.

83-84. *had discharged fully*: The burden of all the doubts Dante has laid upon him.

87. *was rambling drowsily*: Mental laxness seems to be contagious on this Cornice. Dante, satisfied with what he has learned, does not answer with his usual eagerness, but lets his mind wander off. The appearance of the band of the Slothful, however,

awakens him instantly, their presence and the nature of their sin reproaching Dante for his self-indulgence.

91-93. Ismenus and Asopus: Boetian rivers. The ancient Thebans ran on their banks at night invoking the aid of Bacchus when they needed rain for their vines. Dante makes a careful point in his phrasing: the Thebans exerted themselves for no more than such a pagan and earthly deity as Bacchus could give, but here the sinners strain for the Supreme Good.

96. bent like scythes: Bent so in the speed of their race.

97-102. THE WHIP OF SLOTH: The examples here are shouted by two of the sinners who run before the others. The first example of zeal (spiritual) is Mary's haste, after the Annunciation, to go visit Elizabeth in the hill country of Juda (*Luke*, i, 39). The second (temporal) is Caesar's diligence in the conquest of Ilerda (the modern Spanish town of Lérida). He laid siege to Marseilles, left an army there under Brutus, and pushed by forced marches to take Ilerda.

Since all zeal must be either spiritual or temporal, two examples are enough to cover all possible categories.

109. this man lives—truly: Virgil is announcing the news that has amazed all other souls in Purgatory, but these souls are so intent on pursuing their purification that they pay no attention. Their attention is focused on the Supreme Good, and they shun the distraction of lesser things.

111. the nearer way: There is one ascent from each Cornice. Virgil's object on each ledge is to learn the short rather than the long way round the circle to it. As it has been on every other ledge, the nearer way is to the right.

118. San Zeno: There are three churches of San Zeno in Verona, one of which has a monastery attached. The speaker has not been positively identified, but the Abbot of San Zeno through most of Barbarossa's reign was Gherardo II, who died in 1187.

119. Frederick Barbarossa: Frederick Redbeard. Frederick I, Emperor from 1152-1190. Dante calls him "good" because he pursued the good of the Empire. Frederick quarreled with Pope Alexander III and was excommmunicated by him. Frederick then warred on the Pope's adherents in Lombardy. He took Milan in 1163, pulled down its walls, burned the city, ploughed the ruins, and sowed the ground with salt that nothing might grow there. After other bloody successes, his fortunes turned, and he had to kneel to Alexander for pardon. He drowned while crusading in the Holy Land.

121-126. another with one foot now in the grave: Alberto della Scala, Lord of Verona, who died in September of 1301. Thus, in 1300 he already had one foot in the grave. He had three natural sons, among them the famous Can Grande della Scala, who was Dante's host and protector in exile. Another was Giuseppe, and it was this son Alberto forced upon the monks as Abbot of San Zeno, a post he held from 1292 to 1313. The speaker, as former abbot, is especially indignant that an unworthy man should hold so high an office. Giuseppe was triply disqualified, being mentally incapable, physically deformed, and a bastard. Except by special dispensation, the Catholic Church does not grant ordination to the illegitimate; the candidate for ordination must of course be mentally qualified, and he must be free of physical deformities that would interfere with the performance of his duties. (A priest with a mutilated hand, for example, might not be able to celebrate the mass properly. Nor could a deaf priest hear confessions.)

127. left us so far behind: The sinner never slackened pace as he spoke.

129. but I was pleased to keep this much in mind: Dante seems to relish his chance to fire a shot at Alberto della Scala, certainly not as a personal attack on the father of his great protector, but generally against all the temporal lords of Italy who used their power to corrupt the church by imposing their will and politics upon its offices.

131-138. THE REIN OF SLOTH. As two of the sinners ran ahead to shout the examples of the Whip, so two more run behind the train shouting the examples that constitute the Rein.

As usual, the first example of the destruction of the laggard is from sacred history. It reminds the sinners that though the Lord delivered Israel from Egyptian bondage, opening the Red Sea for their passage, the people still muttered and would not follow Moses (*i.e.*, would not diligently pursue good); and that, therefore, the Lord doomed them to die in the wilderness. Of all Israel that crossed the Red Sea, only Joshua and Caleb reached the Promised Land of Jordan's waters. (*Numbers*, xiv 26-34; *Exodus*, xiv, 10-20; *Deuteronomy*, i, 26-36.)

The second example, from secular history, reminds the sinners of those followers of Aeneas who chose to live at ease in Sicily rather than follow him to the great end that had been promised. Thus they did not share in the glory of founding Rome.

Note that both incidents provide a parable of a promised joy (Heaven) lost by lack of zeal in following the clearly indicated road.

Canto XIX

The Slothful

Dante's Dream of Sirena

THE ASCENT   *The Angel of Zeal*

THE FIFTH CORNICE   *The Hoarders and Wasters (The Avaricious)*

Just before morning (when the truth is dreamed) Dante dreams of
The Siren that lures the souls of men to incontinent worldliness.
Hideous in her true form, the Siren grows irresistible in men's eyes
as they look upon her. A *Heavenly Lady* races in upon the dream
and calls to Virgil who, thus summoned, strips the Siren, exposing
her filthy body. Such a stench rises from her, so exposed, that
Dante wakens shuddering, to find Virgil calling him to resume the
journey.

The *Angel of Zeal* shows them the passage, and when his wings
have fanned the Poets, Dante casts off his depression and lethargy,
and rushes up the remaining length of the passage.

Arrived at *The Fifth Cornice,* Virgil inquires the way of one of
the souls of *The Hoarders and Wasters,* who lie motionless and
outstretched, bound hand and foot, with their faces in the dust.

The soul of *Pope Adrian V* replies that, if they have incurred no
guilt by Hoarding or Wasting, they may pass on to the right. Dante
kneels in reverence to Adrian and is scolded for doing so. Adrian
then dismisses Dante in order to resume his purification. Adrian's
last request is that his niece, *Alagia,* be asked to pray for his soul.

> At the hour when the heat of the day is overcome
>   by Earth or at times by Saturn, and can no longer
>   temper the cold of the moon; when on the dome   3
>
> of the eastern sky the geomancers sight
>   Fortuna Major rising on a course
>   on which, and soon, it will be drowned in light;   6
>
> there came to me in a dream a stuttering crone,
>   squint-eyed, clubfooted, both her hands deformed,
>   and her complexion like a whitewashed stone.   9
>
> I stared at her; and just as the new sun
>   breathed life to night-chilled limbs, just so my look
>   began to free her tongue, and one by one   12
>
> drew straight all her deformities, and warmed
>   her dead face, till it bloomed as love would wish it
>   for its delight. When she was thus transformed,   15

295

her tongue thus loosened, she began to sing
in such a voice that only with great pain
could I have turned from her soliciting.   18

"I am," she sang, "Sirena. I am she
whose voice is honeyed with such sweet enticements
it trances sailing men far out to sea.   21

I turned Ulysses from his wanderer's way
with my charmed song, and few indeed who taste
how well I satisfy would think to stray."   24

Her mouth had not yet shut when at my side
appeared a saintly lady, poised and eager
to heap confusion on the Siren's pride.   27

"O Virgil, Virgil! Who," she cried, "is this?"
Roused by her indignation, Virgil came:
his eyes did not once leave that soul of bliss.   30

He seized the witch, and with one rip laid bare
all of her front, her loins and her foul belly:
I woke sick with the stench that rose from there.   33

I turned then, and my Virgil said to me:
"I have called at least three times now. Rise and come
and let us find your entrance." Willingly   36

I rose to my feet. Already the high day
lit all the circles of the holy mountain.
The sun was at our backs as we took our way.   39

I followed in his steps, my brow as drawn
as is a man's so bowed with thought he bends
like half an arch of a bridge. And moving on,   42

I heard the words: "Come. This is where you climb."
pronounced in such a soft and loving voice
as is not heard here in our mortal time.   45

With swanlike wings outspread, he who had spoken
summoned us up between the walls of rock.
He fanned us with his shining pinions then,   48

affirming over us as we went by
"Blessed are they that mourn"—for they shall have
their consolation given them on high."   51

"What ails you?" said my Guide. "What heavy mood
makes you stare at the ground?" (We were by then
above the point at which the Angel stood.)   54

And I: "An apparition clouds my spirit,
a vision from a dream so strange and dreadful
I cannot seem to leave off thinking of it."   57

"Did you see that ageless witch," he said, "for whom
——and for no other——those above us weep?
And did you see how men escape her doom?   60

Let it teach your heels to scorn the earth, your eyes
to turn to the high lure the Eternal King
spins with his mighty spheres across the skies."   63

As falcons stare at their feet until they hear
the wished-for call, then leap with wings outspread
in eagerness for the meat that waits them there;   66

so did I move: filled with desire, I ran
up the remaining length of the rock passage
to the point at which the next great Round began.   69

When I stood on the fifth ledge and looked around,
I saw a weeping people everywhere
lying outstretched and face-down on the ground.   72

"My soul cleaves to the dust," I heard them cry
over and over as we stood among them;
and every word was swallowed by a sigh.   75

"O Chosen of God, spirits whose mournful rites
both Hope and Justice make less hard to bear,
show us the passage to the further heights."   78

"If you have not been sentenced to lie prone
in the bitter dust, and seek the nearest way,
keep the rim to your right as you go on."   81

So spoke the Poet, and so a voice replied
from the ground in front of us. I took good note
of what its way of speaking did not hide.   84

I turned my eyes to Virgil then, and he
gave me a happy sign of his permission
to do what my eyes asked. Being thus free   87

to act according to my own intention,
I moved ahead and stood above that soul
whose speaking had attracted my attention,   90

saying: "O Soul in whom these tears prepare
that without which no soul can turn to God,
put off a while, I beg, your greater care,   93

to tell me who you were, why you lie prone,
and if there is some way that I may serve you
in the world I left while still in flesh and bone."   96

"Why Heaven makes us turn our backs shall be
made known to you," the spirit said, "but first
scias quod ego fui successor Petri.   99

Between Sestri and Chiaveri, flowing on
    through a fair land, there is a pleasant river
    from which the title of my line is drawn.   102

A single month, a month and some few days
    I came to know on my own weary body
    how heavily the Papal Mantle weighs   105

upon the wearer who would take good care
    to keep it from the mire; compared to that
    all other burdens are as light as air.   108

My conversion, alas, came late; for only when
    I had been chosen Pastor of Holy Rome
    did I see the falseness in the lives of men.   111

I saw no heart's rest there, nor ease from strife,
    nor any height the flesh-bound soul might climb,
    and so I came to love this other life.   114

My soul was lost to God until that moment,
    and wholly given over to avarice;
    such was my sin, such is my punishment.   117

The nature of avarice is here made plain
    in the nature of its penalty; there is not
    a harsher forfeit paid on the whole mountain.   120

We would not raise our eyes to the shining spheres
    but kept them turned to mundane things: so Justice
    bends them to earth here in this place of tears.   123

As Avarice, there, quenched all our souls' delight
    in the good without which all our works are lost,
    so, here, the hand of Justice clamps us tight.   126

Taken and bound here hand and foot, we lie
    outstretched and motionless; and here we stay
    at the just pleasure of the Father on High."   129

I had knelt to him. Now I spoke once more.
    That spirit sensed at once my voice was nearer
    and guessed my reverence. "Why do you lower   132

your knees into the dust?" he said to me.
    And I: "My conscience troubled me for standing
    in the presence of your rank and dignity."   135

"Straighten your legs, my brother! Rise from error!"
    he said. "I am, like you and all the others,
    a fellow servant of one Emperor.   138

It is written in holy scripture *Neque nubent*;
    if ever you understood that sacred text,
    my reason for speaking will be evident.   141

Now go your way. I wish to be alone.
Your presence here distracts me from the tears
that make me ready. And to your last question:

I have a niece, Alagia, still on earth.
If she can but avoid the bad example
those of our line have set, her native worth

will lead her yet the way the blessed go.
And she alone remains to me below."

Notes

1–3. An intricate passage based on the medieval belief that sunlight reflected from earth to the moon produced warmth on the moon, whereas sunlight reflected from the moon to the earth produced cold on the earth. *At the hour:* Before dawn. The accumulated heat of the day would have been dissipated through the long night and could no longer temper the cold of the moon. *overcome by Earth:* The last heat of the day is overcome by the night-chilled earth, *or at times by Saturn:* The times would be those in which Saturn draws close to the horizon. Saturn was believed to be a cold planet, as opposed to Mars, a hot planet.

5. *Fortuna Major:* A conjunction of the last stars of Aquarius and the first of Pisces, supposed to signify great good fortune. In this season these stars would be rising just before dawn, hence the sun is coming up behind them and their course will soon be drowned in light.

7 ff. DANTE'S DREAM. The Sirens were mythological creatures, usually of great beauty, and with the power of singing so entrancingly that they charmed the souls of men. They were usually presented as luring sailors at sea to their destruction.

Dante's Sirena is a Christian adaptation. She symbolizes the three remaining sins (Greed, Gluttony, and Lust), which is to say, the abandonment to physical appetites. So in lines 58–60 Dante calls her "the ageless witch, for whom—and for no other—those above us [on the three remaining ledges] weep." Dante's description of her tells all the rest: she is deformed and hideous in herself but grows beautiful in the eyes of men, and few of those she lures to her pleasures ever stray from the kind of satisfaction she gives them. Only when a Heavenly Voice (the unidentified Saintly Lady of lines 26–30) summons Reason to strip Sensual Abandon of its false trappings, does man waken from his dream to realize what abomination has entranced him.

Note that she cannot be taken to symbolize the Pleasures of the Appetite (for those were given by God for man's joy in His creation), but the Abandonment of the Soul to Excessive Physical Appetite.

22. *I turned Ulysses:* In the Homeric version Ulysses escapes the Siren's blandishments by stuffing his ears with wax and having himself lashed to the mast of his ship. Dante may, perhaps, be following another version of the myth, but more probably he means to portray the Siren as a liar, an allegorically significant point.

26. *a saintly lady:* She may be Beatrice, or she may be Provenient Grace, but any identification is speculative.

43. *I heard the words:* They are spoken by the Angel of Zeal. Note that Dante is moving along bowed in thought and rather slowly, his spirit still weighed by the vision of the Siren, until they pass the Angel. Once the Angel of Zeal has fanned them with his wings, however (and by now the reader knows, without being told, that the fourth P has disappeared from Dante's brow), Virgil, as Dante's own Reason, tells him what he should do, and Dante immediately loses his heaviness, and hurries eagerly up the remaining passage to the next Cornice.

50. *blessed are they that mourn:* The Fourth Beatitude. "Blessed are they that mourn: for they shall be comforted." (*Matthew,* iv, 5).

73. *My soul cleaves to the dust:* Psalm CXIX.

76 ff. THE HOARDERS AND WASTERS. The sinfulness of Avarice is in the fact that it turns the soul away from God to an inordinate concern for material things. Since such immoderation can express itself in either getting or spending, the Hoarders and Wasters are here punished together and in the same way for the two extremes of the same excess, as in Hell.

84. *what its way of speaking did not hide:* The soul has said, "If you have not been sentenced to lie prone in the bitter dust." The implication is—and it is the first time the point has emerged clearly—that souls may pass through some of the Cornices without delay, if they are free of the taint of sin there punished. The speaker,

his face in the dust, cannot know that Dante is a living man. He must have assumed, therefore, that Virgil's request for directions is that of a soul that has completed its purification on one of the lower Cornices, and that has no penance to do for Avarice. Dante, ever eager to grasp the nature of things, seizes upon the implication. In XIII, 133 ff., Dante makes it clear that he has penance to do for Pride, and some, though very little, for Envy. It is clear, therefore, that souls may be required to undergo penance on successive Cornices, and in XXI and XXII Statius confirms that fact. Now we know that souls may pass through some of the Cornices without delay.

99. *scias quod ego fui successor Petri*: "Know that I was Peter's successor." The speaker is Pope Adrian V. He died in 1276 after having been Pope for thirty-eight days.

101. *a pleasant river*: The river is the Lavagna. It flows between Sestri and Chiaveri, small coastal towns near Genoa. Adrian, born Ottobuono de' Fieschi, was of the line of the Counts of Lavagna.

139. *Neque nubent*: ". . . they neither marry [nor are given in marriage but are as the angels of God in heaven]" (*Matthew*, xxii, 30). These were Christ's words when asked to which husband a remarried widow would belong in Heaven. Adrian obviously extends the meaning to include the cancellation of all earthly contracts, fealties, and honors. *Cf.* Cato's attitude toward Marcia in Canto I. It is well to remember, too, that the passing of the Christian marriage vow is "till death do us part."

145. *Alagia* (Ah-LAH-djah): Daughter of Niccolò di Tedisio di Ugone de' Fieschi (Oo-GO-ne day Fee-YEH-ski) and wife of Moroello (Moh-roh-ELL-oh) Malaspina, Marquis of Giovagallo (Djoe-vah-GAH-lo). Dante had been well received by Malaspina and knew and admired his wife for her good works.

Canto XX

The Hoarders and Wasters (The Avaricious)

The Whip of Avarice · The Rein of Avarice

Dante walks on after Adrian has dismissed him, wishing he might have continued the conversation, but bowing to Adrian's wish to resume his purification.

The Poets find the ledge so crowded with the souls of the Avaricious that only one narrow passage is left open to them. Dante hears a soul cry out *The Whip of Avarice*, a litany in praise of *Mary, Fabricius,* and *St. Nicholas.* The sinner identifies himself as *Hugh Capet* and proceeds to a *Denunciation of The Capetian Kings*, the dynasty he himself founded, but which has degenerated into a succession of kings distinguished only for their bloodthirsty avarice.

Hugh Capet then explains *The Rein of Avarice*, citing seven examples of the downfall of the Avaricious.

Dante has hardly left Capet when he feels the mountain shake as if stricken by *An Earthquake*, and he hears *A Shout of Triumph*. Dante is frightened but Virgil reassures him. The Poets move on at top speed, but Dante remains deep in thought, his mind pondering these new phenomena.

What's willed must bow to what is stronger willed:
    against my pleasure, to please him, I drew
    my sponge back from the water still unfilled.   3

I turned: my Guide set off along the space
    left clear next to the rock; for they who drain,
    slow tear by tear, the sin that eats the race   6

left little room along the outer edge.
    Thus, as one hugs the battlements in walking
    atop a wall, we moved along the ledge.   9

Hell take you, She-Wolf, who in the sick feast
    of your ungluttable appetite have taken
    more prey on earth than any other beast!   12

You Heavens, in whose turnings, as some say,
    things here below are changed—when will he come
    whose power shall drive her from the light of day?   15

We moved along with measured step and slow,
    and all my thoughts were centered on those shades,
    their tears and lamentations moved me so.   18

And walking thus, I heard rise from the earth
    before us: "Blessed Mary!—with a wail
    such as is wrung from women giving birth.   21

"How poor you were," the stricken voice went on,
"is testified to all men by the stable
in which you laid your sacred burden down."   24

And then: "O good Fabricius, you twice
refused great wealth that would have stained your honor,
and chose to live in poverty, free of vice."   27

These words had pleased me so that I drew near
the place from which they seemed to have been spoken,
eager to know what soul was lying there.   30

The voice was speaking now of the largesse
St. Nicholas bestowed on the three virgins
to guide their youth to virtuous steadiness.   33

"O soul," I said, "whose words recite such good,
let me know who you were, and why no other
joins in your praises of such rectitude.   36

If I return to finish the short race
remaining of that life that ends so soon,
your words will not lack some reward of grace."   39

"Not for such comfort as the world may give
do I reply," he said, "but that such light
of grace should shine on you while yet you live.   42

I was the root of that malignant tree
which cast its shadow on all Christendom
so that the soil bears good fruit only rarely.   45

But if Douay and Lille and Bruges and Ghent
were strong again, their vengeance would be swift;
and that it may, I pray the King of Judgment.   48

I was Hugh Capet in my mortal state.
From me stem all the Philips and the Louis'
who have occupied the throne of France of late.   51

I was born in Paris as a butcher's son.
When the old line of kings had petered out
to one last heir, who wore a monk's gray gown,   54

I found that I held tight in my own hand
the reins of state, and that my new wealth gave me
such power and such allies at my command,   57

that my son's head, with pomp and sacrament
rose to the widowed crown of France. From him
those consecrated bones took their descent.   60

Till the great dowry of Provence increased
my race so that it lost its sense of shame,
it came to little, but did no harm at least.   63

That was the birth of its rapacity,
    its power, its lies. Later—to make amends—
    it took Normandy, Ponthieu, and Gascony.   66

Charles came to Italy, and—to make amends—
    he victimized Conradin. Then he sent
    Saint Thomas back to Heaven—to make amends.   69

I see a time, not far off, that brings forth
    another Charles from France. It shall make clear
    to many what both he and his are worth.   72

He comes alone, unarmed but for the lance
    of Judas, which he drives so hard he bursts
    the guts of Florence with the blow he plants.   75

He wins no land there; only sin and shame.
    And what is worse for him is that he holds
    such crimes too lightly to repent his blame.   78

The third, once hauled from his own ship, I see
    selling his daughter, haggling like a pirate
    over a girl sold into slavery.   81

O Avarice, what more harm can you do?
    You have taken such a hold on my descendants
    they sell off their own flesh and blood for you!   84

But dwarfing all crimes, past or yet to be,
    I see Alagna entered, and, in His Vicar,
    Christ Himself dragged in captivity.   87

I see Him mocked again and crucified,
    the gall and vinegar once more sent up.
    He dies again—with *live* thieves at His side.   90

I see another Pilate, so full of spite
    not even that suffices: his swollen sails
    enter the very Temple without right.   93

O God, my Lord, when shall my soul rejoice
    to see Thy retribution, which, lying hidden,
    sweetens Thine anger in Thy secret choice?   96

What you first heard me cry in adoration
    of that one only Bride of the Holy Ghost,
    which made you turn and ask an explanation.   99

is the litany we add to every prayer
    as long as it is day. When the sun sets
    we raise the counter-cry on the night air.   102

We cry then how Pygmalion of old
    was made a traitor, thief, and parricide
    by his insatiable sick lust for gold;   105

how Midas suffered when his miser's prayer
    was answered, and became forever after
    the legend of a ludicrous despair;   108

and then we tell how Achan, covetous,
    stole from the booty, for which Joshua's rage
    still falls upon him—so it seems to us.   111

We cry Sapphira's and her husband's blame;
    we praise the hooves that battered Heliodorus;
    then round the ledge runs Polymnestor's name,   114

foul to all time with Polydorus' blood.
    Then we conclude the litany crying: 'Crassus,
    you supped on gold—tell us, did it taste good?'   117

We wail or mutter in our long remorse
    according to the inner spur that drives us,
    at times with more, at others with less force: 120

thus I was not the only one who praised
    the good we tell by day; but, as it happened,
    the only one nearby whose voice was raised."   123

We had already left him to his prayers
    and were expending every ounce of strength
    on the remaining distance to the stairs,   126

when suddenly I felt the mountain shake
    as if it tottered. Such a numb dread seized me
    as a man feels when marching to the stake.   129

Not even Delos, in that long ago
    before Latona went there to give birth
    to Heaven's eyes, was ever shaken so.   132

Then there went up a cry on every side,
    so loud that the sweet Master, bending close
    said: "Do not fear, for I am still your Guide."   135

"Glory to God in the Highest!" rang a shout
    from every throat—as I could understand
    from those nearby, whose words I could make out.   138

We stood there motionless, our souls suspended—
    as had the shepherds who first heard that hymn—
    until the ground grew still and the hymn ended.   141

Then we pushed on our holy way once more,
    studying those prostrate souls who had already
    resumed their lamentation, as before.   144

I never felt my soul assaulted so—
    unless my memory err—as in that war
    between my ignorance and desire to know   147

the explanation of that shock and shout;
nor dared I ask, considering our haste;
nor could I of myself, looking about,   150

find anywhere the key to what I sought.
So I moved on, timid and sunk in thought.

Notes

2. *him*: Adrian. Dante's wish to know more had to bow to Adrian's greater wish
to resume his purification. Thus, Dante had to withdraw the sponge of his desire to
know, from the water of Adrian's presence, before he had absorbed all he wished for.

4–9. THE CROWDING OF THE LEDGE. The point, of course, is that Avarice is
so common a sin that the ledge is jammed full of sinners, so many in fact that the
space between their shades and the open side of the ledge is too narrow for safe passage. Virgil leads Dante, therefore, along the narrow space between the bodies and
the inner cliff-face.

10–15. *She-Wolf*: See the three beasts encountered by Dante in *Inferno*, I, 33 ff.
have taken more prey: As in lines 4–9, above, Avarice has infected more souls than
has any other sin. *when will he come*: Another reference to the mysterious Greyhound who will come to make the world pure again and who will drive the She-Wolf
from the light of day, back into Hell. (See *Inferno*, I, 95–104, and note.)

20–33. THE WHIP OF AVARICE. Once more the examples that make up the
Whip are cried aloud by the sinners themselves. On this Cornice, however, all the
sinners cry out the examples as impulse moves them, adding them as a litany to each
prayer they recite as part of their penance. The prayer of this Cornice is, of course,
from Psalm CXIX, "My soul cleaves to the dust." (See Canto XIX, 73.)

A further peculiarity of the Whip and the Rein on this ledge is that the sinners
recite the Whip by day and the Rein by night.

The first example of the Whip (lines 20–24) praises the blessed poverty of Mary.
So great was it that she gave birth to Jesus in a manger. Yet in such poverty she
achieved blessedness in comparison with which all the possessions of the world are as
baubles.

The second example (lines 25–27) praises the honorable poverty of Fabricius Caius
Luscinus, Roman Consul in 282 B.C. and Censor in 275. He refused to deal in the
bribes and gifts which were normally assumed to be perquisites of such high offices,
and he died so poor that the state had to bury him, and had also to provide dowries
for his daughters.

The third example (lines 31–33) cites Saint Nicholas, Bishop of Myra in Lycia,
who was born rich and gave all his riches to the poor. A local minor nobleman
found himself so poor that he could not provide dowries for his daughters. He was
about to turn them over to a life of sin in order that they might make a living, when
Nicholas heard of their plight and threw three bags of gold through the nobleman's
window, one on each of three successive nights. Thus the father was able to buy husbands for the girls, and thus Nicholas guided their youth to "virtuous steadiness."

34–96. *Hugh Capet*: Dante seems to confuse Hugh, Duke of the Franks (died
956), and his son, Hugh Capet (King of France 987–996), into one person. Hugh
Capet founded the Capetian dynasty of French kings, succeeding Louis V, the last of
the Carlovingian line founded by Charlemagne.

Hugh Capet begins by replying to Dante's customary promise of earthly recollection, that he has little interest in any good the world can do him. Since he has been
in Purgatory 344 years (by 1300), it seems reasonable enough to assume that he is
well advanced in other worldliness.

He then laments the degeneracy of the line he himself founded and prays God's
vengeance upon it soon, as it would already have fallen had Flanders the power to
avenge itself. Douay, Lille, Bruges, and Ghent are the four principal cities of Flanders. Philip the Fair, King of France, and his brother, Charles of Valois, warred on
Flanders. In 1299 Charles negotiated the surrender of Ghent by making liberal promises, which he later ignored, dealing harshly with the conquered. The vengeance Hugh
Capet prayed for as of 1300 had already taken place by the time Dante wrote these
lines, the Flemish having inflicted a major defeat upon the French at the Battle of
Courtrai in 1302.

50. *all the Philips and the Louis'*: From 1060 to 1300 all the Kings of France bore
one or another of these names.

52. *a butcher's son*: Dante follows here a popular but erroneous legend: the meat
business was not that good in tenth-century France. King Hugh Capet, as noted, was
the son of Hugh Capet, Duke of France, of Burgundy, and of Aquitaine, and Count

of Paris and of Orleans. The history that follows is full of similar confusions, some of which may best be left to scholars, but some of which must be explained for a basic understanding of the text.

53. *the old line of kings*: The Carlovingian dynasty.

54. *one last heir, who wore a monk's gray gown*: There is no evidence that Charles of Lorraine, the last of the Carlovingians, took holy orders. He died in prison, put there by Hugh Capet. Two sons born to him while he was in prison were hustled away to Germany, where they disappeared.

58. *my son's head*: The son of King Hugh Capet was Robert I, but Dante is clearly having King Hugh speak now as if he were Duke Hugh.

60. *those consecrated bones*: The Capetian kings. By the sacramental anointment which was part of the coronation, the King's person became sacred.

61–63. *the great dowry of Provence*: Raymond Berengar was Count of Provence. After the Count's death, Louis IX (St. Louis) married the eldest of the Count's four daughters and Louis' brother, Charles of Anjou, married one of the younger daughters. The brothers then seized all of Provence, claiming it as their wives' dowry. *lost its sense of shame*: Dante may have meant that in seizing Provence they acquired a title so ancient that it wiped out the taint of low origin Dante ascribes to the Capets. The more obvious meaning is that in waxing great on so much wealth, they lost all sense of just reckoning.

65. *to make amends*: The triple repetition is meant as bitter irony; after each bad action the French kings "make amends" by doing something worse.

66. *Normandy, Ponthieu, and Gascony*: Philip II took Normandy from England in 1202. Philip the Fair took Ponthieu and Gascony from England in 1295.

67. *Charles*: Charles of Anjou, brother of Louis IX. When Clement IV excommunicated Manfred (see III, 103 ff., note), he summoned Charles to Italy and crowned him King of Sicily. In 1266 Charles defeated Manfred at Benevento. In 1268 he defeated Conradin, Manfred's nephew, at Tagliacozzo, and had him beheaded.

68–69. *sent Saint Thomas back to Heaven*: Dante is following an unfounded popular legend that Charles had Thomas Aquinas poisoned.

71. *another Charles*: Charles of Valois, brother of Philip the Fair. He was called Charles Sans Terre. Boniface VIII called him to Florence in 1301, presumably as peacemaker, but actually to destroy all who opposed Papal policy.

76. *He wins no land there*: A taunt at the fact that Charles had inherited no land. He will not improve his temporal state, says Hugh, and will only blacken his honor and his soul.

79. *The third*: The third Charles is Charles II of Anjou (Charles the Lame), King of Naples and of Apulia. He was born in 1243 and died in 1309. *once hauled from his own ship*: In June of 1284 the admiral of Peter III of Aragon sailed into the Bay of Naples. Charles, against express orders left by his father, allowed himself to be lured out to meet the Aragonese and was easily taken prisoner. Two hundred of his court were taken with him and were executed by the Aragonese to avenge the death of Conradin. Charles escaped with his life but remained a prisoner in Sicily until 1288.

80. *selling his daughter*: In 1305 Charles concluded a marriage contract between his very young daughter and Azzo (or Ezzo) VIII of Este, then 42. For the honor of marrying the king's daughter, Azzo settled for practically no dowry, and made very valuable gifts to his father-in-law.

85–93. *But dwarfing all crimes, past or yet to be*: The crime was the capture and humiliation of Pope Boniface VIII at the instigation of Philip the Fair. Philip had charged Boniface with heresy, and Boniface had prepared a bull excommunicating Philip. On September 7, 1303, before the bull could be published, Philip sent a large force to Alagna (now Anagni) under Guillaume de Nogaret and Sciarra (SHAH-rah) Colonna. They ransacked the palace and the cathedral treasury, and subjected Boniface to great indignities, threatening to haul him off in chains to execution. Boniface, then eighty-six, was released in a few days but his mind seems to have cracked, and he died of "hysterical seizures" in Rome within a few weeks, on October 12, 1303. Dante's attitude in this matter is characteristic. Much as he loathed Boniface for his corruption of the Papacy, Dante saw the office itself as sacred, for Boniface was officially Christ's Vicar on Earth. Thus to offend his person was to offend the person of Christ Himself. King Philip's all-dwarfing crime, therefore, was against the very body of Christ.

90. *He dies again—with* live *thieves at His side*: Christ died between dead thieves who had been crucified with Him. In the person of Boniface, He "died" again, but with live thieves (de Nogaret and Colonna) at His side.

91. *another Pilate*: Philip. As Pilate turned Christ over to His tormentors, so Philip turned Him over—in the person of His Vicar—to de Nogaret and Colonna.

93. *enter the very Temple*: Philip out-Pilated Pilate by breaking into the Temple. The reference here is to Philip's suppression of the Knights Templars and the seizure

of their lands and treasuries in 1314. He tortured those he captured and forced Pope Clement V to legalize the action (see VII, 109, note).

95–96. *which, lying hidden*: God's retribution. It lies hidden from men, but is known to God in His omniscient prevision, and will take place at His pleasure. His anger, therefore, is sweetened by the fact that His vengeance is already calculated and certain.

97–120. THE REIN OF AVARICE. The Rein of Avarice consists of seven examples of the downfall caused by Avarice. Note that although Dante divides Avarice into its two extremes of Hoarding and Wasting, the examples of the downfall of the Avaricious are all of what might be called Acquisitive Avarice.

(103–105) *Pygmalion*: Brother of Queen Dido. He killed King Sichaeus in the temple, stole his gold, and drove Dido into exile. Dante calls him a parricide because Sichaeus was not only his brother-in-law but his uncle. (He is not to be confused with the Pygmalion of Greek legend who fell in love with a statue.) Thus Avarice led him to damnation. If Pygmalion's crime is taken to be Treachery to his Host or Master, there is a strong probability (see *Inferno*, XXXIII, 128–147) that his soul instantly descended to Ptolomea or Judaïca, while his body still lived.

(106–108) *Midas*: The famous King of Phrygia who did a favor for Bacchus and was promised the fulfillment of a wish. Midas wished for the power to change all things to gold at his touch. Bacchus granted the wish, but Midas began to starve since even his food turned to gold, and he had to beg Bacchus to take the power from him. The best-known version of the story is in Ovid's *Metamorphoses*. XI, 85–145.

(109–111) *Achan*: After the fall of Jericho, Joshua commanded that all the booty should go into the Temple as the Lord's. Achan pilfered some treasures for himself and Joshua had him and his family stoned to death (*Joshua*, vii, 1–26).

(112) *Sapphira and her husband*: They were entrusted to sell some property held in common by the apostles, but they returned only part of the sale price, representing it as the whole sum. When St. Peter reproved them for their fraud, they fell dead at his feet (*Acts*, v, 1–11).

(113) *Heliodorus*: He was sent to Jerusalem by the King of Syria with orders to steal the Treasury but was driven from the Temple by the apparition of a great horse that battered him with its forefeet. "And it seemed that he that sat upon the horse had complete harness of gold." (*II Maccabees*, iii, 25).

(114) *Polymnestor*: King of Thrace and a friend of King Priam. During the siege of Troy, Priam sent his youngest son, Polydorus, into Thrace for Polymnestor's protection. A considerable treasure accompanied the boy, and Polymnestor killed him for it as soon as Troy fell. Hecuba, mother of Polydorus, later avenged her son by blinding Polymnestor and killing him. *Aeneid*, III, 19–68; *Metamorphoses*, XIII, 429–575; and Euripides' *Hecuba*, all recount part of the story. (See also *Inferno*, XXX, 16, note.)

(116) *Crassus*: Marcus Licinus Crassus (114–53 B.C.) Triumvir of Rome with Julius Caesar and Pompey, and infamous for his avarice, bribe taking, and plundering. He was taken in battle by the Parthians and his head was brought to King Hyrodes, who had molten gold poured into its mouth, thus mocking the memory of Crassus' bloody avarice by serving his severed head a last feast of gold.

130–132. *Not even Delos . . . Latona . . . Heaven's eyes*: Latona was pregnant by Jupiter and was chased from place to place by the jealous Juno. According to one legend, Jupiter caused an earthquake to raise the island of Delos from the bottom of the sea as a place of refuge for Latona. According to another, Delos was a floating island left over from the original division of the sea and the land and tossed about by waves until Jupiter fixed it in place for Latona. On Delos, Latona gave birth to Apollo (the Sun) and Diana (the Moon), hence, the twin eyes of Heaven. Dante regularly draws parallel-and-contrasting examples from both the Classical and the Judeo-Christian worlds. Note that in this example and the next he cites divine birth in both of those worlds.

140. *who first heard that hymn*: The shepherds of Bethlehem. It was first sung, according to *Luke*, ii, 14, to announce the birth of Christ.

145–152. I have taken substantial liberties with these lines in trying to make Dante's intent clear. A literal rendering might read: "No ignorance ever with so much war [within me] made me so desirous to know—if my memory does not err in this—as I seemed to be at this time, pondering [the explanation of the earthquake and the shout]; nor, since we were hurrying so, did I dare ask; nor could I by myself see anything (that would explain them) there: thus I moved on, timid and deep in thought."

Canto XXI

Statius

Burning with desire to know the cause of the "shock and shout," Dante hurries after Virgil along the narrow way. Suddenly they are overtaken by a figure that salutes them. Virgil answers, and the new soul, taking the Poets to be souls who may not enter Heaven, expresses astonishment at finding them in this place.

Virgil explains his and Dante's state and asks the explanation of the earthquake and of the great cry. The new soul explains that these phenomena occur only when a soul arises from its final purification and begins its final ascent to Heaven. The newcomer then reveals that he is *Statius* and recites his earthly history, ending with a glowing statement of his love for the works of Virgil. To have lived in Virgil's time, says Statius, he would have endured another year of the pains he has just ended.

Virgil warns Dante, with a glance, to be silent, but Dante cannot suppress a half smile, which Statius notices, and asks Dante to explain. He thus learns that he is, in fact, standing in the presence of Virgil. Immediately he kneels to embrace Virgil's knees, but Virgil tells him to arise at once, for such earthly vanities are out of place between shades.

> The natural thirst that nothing satisfies
> except that water the Samaritan woman
> begged of Our Lord, as St. John testifies,　　　　　3
>
> burned me; haste drove me on the encumbered way
> behind my Guide, and I was full of grief
> at the just price of pain those spirits pay;　　　　　6
>
> when suddenly—just as Luke lets us know
> that Christ, new risen from the tomb, appeared
> to the two travelers on the road—just so　　　　　9
>
> as we moved there with bowed heads lest we tread
> upon some soul, a shade appeared behind us;
> nor did we guess its presence till it said:　　　　　12
>
> "Brothers, God give you peace." My Guide and I
> turned quickly toward his voice, and with a sign
> my master gave the words their due reply.　　　　　15
>
> Then he began: "May the True Court's behest,
> which relegates me to eternal exile,
> establish you in peace among the blest."　　　　　18
>
> "But how, if you are souls denied God's bliss,"
> he said—and we forged onward as he spoke—
> "have you climbed up the stairs as far as this?"　　　　　21

My Teacher then: "You cannot fail to see,
   if you observe the Angel's mark upon him,
   that he will reign among the just. But she   24

whose wheel turns day and night has not yet spun
   the full length of the thread that Clotho winds
   into a hank for him and everyone.   27

Therefore, his soul, sister to yours and mine,
   since it cannot see as we do, could not
   climb by itself. And, therefore, Will Divine   30

has drawn me out of the great Throat of Woe
   to guide him on his way, and I shall lead him
   far as my knowledge gives me power to go.   33

But tell me, if you can, what was the shock
   we felt just now? And why did all the mountain
   cry with one voice down to its last moist rock?"   36

He struck the needle's eye of my desire
   so surely with his question, that my thirst,
   by hope alone, lost something of its fire.   39

The shade began: "The holy rules that ring
   the mountain round do not permit upon it
   any disordered or unusual thing,   42

nor any change. Only What Heaven draws
   out of itself into itself again—
   that and nothing else—can be a cause.   45

Therefore, there never can be rain nor snow,
   nor hail, nor dew, nor hoarfrost higher up
   than the little three-step stairway there below.   48

Neither dense clouds nor films of mist appear,
   nor lightning's flash, nor Thaumas' glowing daughter,
   who shifts about from place to place back there;   51

nor can dry vapors raise their shattering heat
   above the top of these three steps I mentioned
   upon which Peter's vicar plants his feet.   54

Shocks may occur below, severe or slight,
   but tremors caused by winds locked in the earth
   —I know not how—do not reach to this height.   57

It trembles here whenever a soul feels
   so healed and purified that it gets up
   or moves to climb; and then the great hymn peals.   60

The soul, surprised, becomes entirely free
   to change its cloister, moved by its own will,
   which is its only proof of purity.   63

Before purgation it does wish to climb,
  but the will High Justice sets against that wish
  moves it to will pain as it once willed crime.   66

And I, who in my torments have lain here
  five hundred years and more, have only now
  felt my will free to seek a better sphere.   69

It was for that you felt the mountain move
  and heard the pious spirits praise the Lord—
  ah may He call them soon to go above!"   72

These were the spirit's words to us, and mine
  cannot express how they refreshed my soul,
  but as the thirst is greater, the sweeter the wine. 75

And my wise Leader: "Now I see what snare
  holds you, how you slip free, why the mount trembles,
  and why your joint rejoicing fills the air.   78

Now it would please me greatly, if you please,
  to know your name and hear in your own words
  why you have lain so many centuries."   81

"In the days when the good Titus, with the aid
  of the Almighty King, avenged the wounds
  that poured the blood Iscariot betrayed,   84

I lived renowned back there," replied that soul,
  "in the most honored and enduring name,
  but still without the faith that makes us whole.   87

My verses swelled with such melodious breath
  that, from Toulouse, Rome called me to herself,
  and there I merited a laurel wreath.   90

Statius my name, and it still lives back there.
  I sang of Thebes, then of the great Achilles,
  but found the second weight too great to bear.   93

The sparks that were my seeds of passion came
  from that celestial fire which has enkindled
  more than a thousand poets; I mean the flame   96

of the *Aeneid*, the mother that brought forth,
  the nurse that gave suck to my song. Without it
  I could not have weighed half a penny's worth.   99

And to have lived back there in Virgil's time
  I would agree to pass another year
  in the same banishment from which I climb."   102

Virgil, at these last words, shot me a glance
  that said in silence, "Silence!" But man's will
  is not supreme in every circumstance: 105

for tears and laughter come so close behind
the passions they arise from, that they least
obey the will of the most honest mind.   108

I did no more than half smile, but that shade
fell still and looked me in the eye—for there
the secrets of the soul are most betrayed.   111

"So may the road you travel lead to grace,"
he said, "what was the meaning of the smile
that I saw flash, just now, across your face?"   114

Now am I really trapped on either side:
one tells me to be still, one begs me speak.
So torn I heave a sigh, and my sweet Guide   117

understands all its meaning. "Never fear,"
he says to me, "speak up, and let him know
what he has asked so movingly to hear."   120

At which I said: "Perhaps my smiling thus
has made you marvel, Ancient Soul; but now
listen to something truly marvelous: 123

this one who guides my eyes aloft is he,
Virgil, from whom you drew the strength to sing
the deeds of men and gods in poetry.   126

The only motive for my smiling lay
in your own words. If you conceived another,
as you love truth, pray put the thought away."   129

He was bending to embrace my Teacher's knee,
but Virgil said: "No, brother. Shade you are,
and shade am I. You must not kneel to me."   132

And Statius, rising, said: "So may you find
the measure of the love that warms me to you
when for it I lose all else from my mind,   135

forgetting we are empty semblances
and taking shadows to be substances."

Notes

1. *The natural thirst*: "All men naturally desire knowledge." (Aristotle, *Metaphysics*, I, 1.) *that nothing satisfies*: "In acquiring knowledge, there always grows the thirst for more." (*Il Convivio*, IV, 12.)

2–3. *that water the Samaritan woman begged*: At Jacob's Well, Jesus asked the Samaritan woman for a drink, and she showed surprise that a Jew should make such a request of her, but Jesus replied that had she known who he was, she would have asked him for a drink and he would have given her the living water of the truth. "The woman saith unto him, Sir, give me this water that I thirst not. . . ." (*John*, iv, 6–15).

7. *as Luke lets us know*: "And behold two of them [James and John] went that same day to a village called Emmaus. . . . And it came to pass that, while they com-

muned together and reasoned, Jesus himself drew near, and went with them." (Luke, xxiv, 13–15.)

11. a shade appeared: The shade is Statius, for whom see note to lines 82 ff.

14–15. with a sign . . . due reply: There were regular formulas for greeting and reply among monks of the Middle Ages. Most commonly, "God give you peace" or "God's peace be with you," would be answered. "And with thy spirit." Virgil's answer is not verbal. He replies with what must have been a gesture of benediction.

23. the Angel's mark: The three remaining P's on Dante's brow, which identify him as a saved soul, i.e., as one who will enter Heaven when he has completed his purification.

24–27. she: Lachesis. She is the Fate (or Parca) who spins the Thread of Life. Her sister Clotho winds each man's thread about her distaff, forming it into a hank begun at each man's birth. The third sister, Atropos, cuts the thread at the end of the man's life. Virgil means simply that Dante is not yet dead, i.e., his thread has not been cut. (The Poets are on the western side of the mountain with the sun in the east, and Dante casts no identifying shadow.)

36. cry with one voice down to its last moist rock: I.e., "Down to the shore where the reeds grow." "Rock" is rhyme-forced. Dante says, literally, "down to its moist feet," and the shore is described not as rocky but as muddy.

40 ff. STATIUS' REPLY. Virgil has asked the reason for the earthquake and the shout. Statius begins his elaborate reply in good scholastic form by explaining the principles on which the answer must be based, and having stated them in brief, he goes on to develop each in detail.

The first principle is that nothing on the mountain is subject to change except within itself, for nothing there is subject to external forces. Every soul in Purgatory is effectively in Heaven, and beyond the Gate evil does not exist.

The second principle follows from the first. The soul issues from the hand of God. When the soul goes from Purgatory to Heaven, therefore, it is not entering from outside. Heaven is simply receiving its own again. Only that motion of Heaven's receiving its own from itself to itself can, therefore, be a cause on the mountain, "cause" being "that which gives rise to an effect."

48. the little three-step stairway: The three steps that lead to the Gate of Purgatory mark the highest point to which the weathers of the world (literally and in every extended sense) can reach. Above them, all that is, is from God.

50. Thaumas' glowing daughter: Iris, the rainbow. Daughter of the Centaur Thaumas and of Electra. Her sisters were the Harpies. Like her sisters, she was a messenger of the Gods and came and went by way of the rainbow, with which she became identified.

The rainbow is an especially apt symbol of mutability. Note, too, that it always appears away from the sun, never between the sun and the observer. Taking Iris to represent changeableness and the sun to represent God, one may pursue a number of interesting allegories.

52. dry vapors: For Dante's theory of wet and dry vapors as the origin of storms see Inferno, XXIV, last note. The theory is from Aristotle. Wet vapors cause rain, hail, dew, and hoarfrost, as specified in lines 46–47. Dry vapors, if they are free, produce lightning and thunder. If, however, they enter the earth as winds and are locked inside, they cause earthquakes. But such terrestrial earthquakes (lines 55–60) cannot be felt above the three steps at the Gate.

58. whenever a soul feels: Once again the point is made that the Purgatorial souls are free of external restraints. Each decides within itself when it is free to move up.

59. that it gets up: If the soul has been crawling with the Proud, seated with the Envious, or lying with the Avaricious, its moment of purity is achieved when it feels the will to get up.

60. or moves to climb: If the soul has been circling with the Wrathful, the Slothful, the Gluttonous, or the Lustful, it would not need to get up: its moment of purity would be achieved when it feels moved to stop circling and to move toward the ascent. to climb: Statius must mean "to climb to Paradise" rather than merely to a higher ledge. As Dante has already hinted, and as Statius soon demonstrates, a soul may pass unchecked through those ledges that punish sins of which it is not guilty. Thus on completing a given penance, a soul may move on to another, or directly to Paradise. There is no conclusive evidence that the mountain shakes and the hymn peals only when souls achieve their final purification, but the very scale of the celebration suggests that it is reserved for graduation exercises only. If the shock and shout occurred every time a soul moved from one ledge to another, there is every likelihood that Dante would have touched things off every time he passed up one of the stairways, or every time an Angel removed one of his P's.

62. cloister: An especially apt choice in that "cloister" implies (a) confinement, (b) confinement of one's own free will, and (c) a life ordered by strict rules of worship and discipline. Dante, because "soul" is feminine in Italian, uses "convent."

64–66. wish . . . will: I am not happy about these terms, but they are the only ones I could make work within prosodic necessity. The intended distinction is between "impulse" (the *relative will* of scholastic philosophy) and what might be called "innate desire" (the *absolute will* of scholastic philosophy). Thus the passage in extended paraphrase: "Before purification it does have a relative will to climb, but the absolute will that High Justice sets against that relative will, gives the soul the same sort of will to suffer penitential pain that it once had [in life] toward the crime it now expiates." (Compare the state of the Infernal souls who cross Acheron driven by their own absolute will to yearn for what they fear.)

82 ff. *Statius*: Publius Papinius Statius (c. 45–96 A.D.) is a central figure of the *Purgatorio* and an especially complex one. He remains with Dante till the very end of the ascent. Thus Dante completes his climb to the presence of Beatrice (Divine Love) in the company of Virgil as Human Reason, and of Statius, who must be taken as a symbol of the soul's triumphant redemption.

Thus Statius has a major role, though his known history hardly serves to explain it. In life he was a Latin poet much admired by Dante, though it is difficult to see why Dante, himself so stylistically sparse, should admire a writer as prolix as was Statius. Statius' main work was the *Thebaid*, an epic of the Seven against Thebes (so line 92: "I sang of Thebes"). He was engaged in an epic of the Trojan War, the *Achilleid*, at his death (so line 93, "but found the second weight too great to bear," *i.e.*, he died bearing it). An earlier collection of poems, the *Silvae*, came to light after Dante's time.

Statius was born in Naples and lived in Rome. Dante confused him in part with Lucius Statius Ursulus, a rhetorician of Toulouse, and has Statius give his birthplace accordingly in line 89.

Why Dante should have chosen Statius to represent the triumph of the purified soul is a matter open to any careful reader's speculation. The very fact that so little is known of Statius' life may be a point in favor, for it leaves Dante free to attribute qualities to Statius without embarrassment from history. (There is, for example, no slightest historical evidence that Statius turned Christian.)

If, as seems likely, Dante himself invented this legend, its own elements best explain it, for so interpreted, Statius becomes a symbolic figure joining the Roman, and the Christian past, a theme always dear to Dante. Thus Statius may be seen as a lesser Virgil and a greater; a less perfect writer, but a greater soul in the gift of Christ's redemption. Thus he may be taken as springing from that cardinal point in Church history at which the greatness of the Roman past and the glory of the Christian present are joined. So Dante may now climb guided not only by Virgil (as Human Reason, Philosophy, and the Classic Virtues of Ancient Rome) but by Statius (these same qualities transformed by faith and thus nearer to God.) Between Virgil and Statius, that is, Dante now climbs in the company of the total Roman tradition.

Dramatically, of course, the possibilities inherent in presenting Statius to Virgil must have been especially inviting.

82. *the good Titus*: Roman Emperor 79–81 A.D. In 70 A.D. in the reign of his father, Vespasian, Titus besieged and took Jerusalem. Thus, with God's help, Rome avenged the death (the wounds) of Christ. So Dante, within his inevitable parochialism, chose to take that passage of history. The Jews, one may be sure, found less cause for rejoicing in the goodness of Titus.

86. *in the most honored and enduring name*: Of poet.

Canto XXII

THE ASCENT TO THE SIXTH CORNICE

THE SIXTH CORNICE   *The Gluttons*

The Tree · The Whip of Gluttony

The Poets have passed the Angel who guards the ascent, and Dante has
had one more *P* removed from his forehead. So lightened, he walks easily
behind Virgil and Statius despite their rapid ascent, listening eagerly to
their conversation.

Virgil declares his great regard for Statius, and Statius explains that he
was on the Fifth Cornice for Wasting rather than for Hoarding. He adds
that he would certainly have been damned, had Virgil's poetry not led him
to see his error. For Virgil, he acknowledges, not only inspired his song, but
showed him the road to faith, whereby he was baptized, though secretly,
for fear of the persecutions—a lukewarmness for which he spent four
hundred years on the Fourth Cornice.

Statius then names his favorite poets of antiquity and asks where they
are. Virgil replies that they are with him in Limbo. He then cites many
who have not been mentioned before as being among his eternal companions.

At this point the Poets arrive at *The Sixth Cornice* and, moving to the
right, come upon *An Enormous Tree* laden with fruits. From its foliage a
voice cries out the examples of abstinence that constitute *The Whip of
Gluttony*.

> We had already left behind by now
>   the Angel who directs to the Sixth Round.
>   He had erased a stigma from my brow,   3
>
> and said that they who thirst for rectitude
>   are blessèd, but he did not say "who hunger"
>   when he recited that Beatitude.   6
>
> I, lighter than on any earlier stairs,
>   followed those rapid spirits, and I found it
>   no strain at all to match my pace to theirs.   9
>
> Virgil began: "When virtue lights in us
>   a fire of love, that love ignites another
>   within the soul that sees its burning. Thus,   12
>
> ever since Juvenal came down to be
>   one of our court in the Infernal Limbo,
>   and told me of your great regard for me,   15
>
> my good will toward you has been of a sort
>   I had not felt for any unseen person;
>   such as will make the climb ahead seem short.   18

314

But tell me—and if I presume too much
   in slackening the rein this way, forgive me
   as a friend would and answer me as such: 21

how, amid all the wisdom you possessed—
   and which you won to by such diligence—
   could Avarice find a place within your breast?"   24

At these words Statius let a brief smile play
   across his lips, and fade. Then he replied:
   "I hear love's voice in every word you say.   27

Often, indeed, appearances give rise
   to groundless doubts in us, and false conclusions,
   the true cause being hidden from our eyes.   30

Seeing me on the ledge from which I rose,
   you have inferred my sin was Avarice;
   an inference your question clearly shows.   33

Know then that my particular offense
   was all too far from Avarice: I wept
   thousands of months for riotous expense.   36

Had I not turned from prodigality
   in pondering those lines in which you cry,
   as if you raged against humanity: 39

'To what do you not drive man's appetite
   O cursèd gold-lust!'—I should now be straining
   in the grim jousts of the Infernal night.   42

I understood then that our hands could spread
   their wings too wide in spending, and repented
   of that, and all my sins, in grief and dread.   45

How many shall rise bald to Judgment Day
   because they did not know this sin to grieve it
   in life, or as their last breaths slipped away!   48

For when the opposite of a sin, as here,
   is as blameworthy as the sin itself,
   both lose their growth together and turn sere.   51

If, then, I lay so long in my distress
   among the Avaricious where they weep,
   it was to purge the opposite excess."   54

"But when you sang of the fierce warfare bred
   between the twin afflictions of Jocasta,"
   the singer of the sweet *Bucolics* said,   57

"from what you said when Clio tuned your strain,
   it would not seem that you had found the faith
   without the grace of which good works are vain.   60

If that be so, what sun or beacon shone
 into your mist that you set sail to follow
 the Fisherman?" And that long-waiting one: 63

"You were the lamp that led me from that night.
 You led me forth to drink Parnassian waters;
 then on the road to God you shed your light.   66

When you declared, 'A new birth has been given.
 Justice returns, and the first age of man.
 And a new progeny descends from Heaven'—   69

you were as one who leads through a dark track
 holding the light behind—useless to you,
 precious to those who followed at your back.   72

Through you I flowered to song and to belief.
 That you may know all, let me stretch my hand
 to paint in full what I have sketched in brief.   75

The world, by then, was swollen with the birth
 of True Belief sown by those messengers
 the Everlasting Kingdom had sent forth.   78

Those words of yours I quoted, so agreed
 with the new preachers', that I took to going
 to where they gathered to expound the Creed.   81

In time, they grew so holy in my eyes
 that in the persecutions of Domitian
 the tears burst from me when I heard their cries.   84

And long as I remained upon the vexed
 shores of that life, I helped them, and they taught me,
 by their strict ways, to scorn all other sects.   87

Before my poem sang how the Greeks drew near
 the Theban rivers, I had been baptized,
 but kept my faith a secret, out of fear,   90

pretending to be pagan as before;
 for which lukewarmness I was made to circle
 the Ledge of Sloth four hundred years and more.   93

Now may you please to tell me—you who rent
 the veil that hid me from this good I praise—
 while we have time to spare in the ascent,   96

where is our ancient Terence now? and where
 Caecilius, Varro, Plautus?—are they damned?
 and if they are, what torments must they bear?"   99

—"All these are there with Persius and the rest,
 myself among them, who surround that Greek
 who outsucked all men at the Muses' breast.   102

All walk the first ledge of the dark of Hell;
and we speak often of the glorious mountain
on which the Nine who suckled us still dwell.   105

Euripides is with us, Antiphon,
Athenian Agathon, Simonides,
and many more who wore the laurel crown.   108

And there, of your own people, one may see
Ismene, mournful as she was before,
Deiphyle, Argia, Antigone,   111

Hypsipyle, who led to Langia's water,
Thetis, Deidamia with her sisters,
and there, too, one may see Tiresias' daughter."   114

We stepped from the walled stairs to level ground,
and both the Poets now had fallen still,
attentive once again to look around.   117

Of the day's handmaids, four had fallen back,
and now the fifth stood at the chariot's pole,
pointing the bright tip on its upward track,   120

when Virgil said: "I think we ought to go
with our right shoulders to the outer edge,
circling the slope as we have done below."   123

So custom served to guide us, and we went
as Virgil said, with all the more assurance
since Statius' silence gave us his consent.   126

They walked ahead and I came on behind
treasuring their talk, which was of poetry,
and every word of which enriched my mind.   129

But soon, in mid-road, there appeared a tree
laden with fragrant and delicious fruit,
and at that sight the talk stopped instantly.   132

As fir trees taper up from limb to limb,
so this tree tapered down; so shaped, I think,
that it should be impossible to climb.   135

From that side where the cliff closed-off our way
a clear cascade fell from the towering rock
and broke upon the upper leaves as spray.   138

The poets drew nearer, reverent and mute,
and from a center of the towering tree
a voice cried: "You shall not eat of the fruit!"   141

Then said: "Mary thought more of what was due
the joy and honor of the wedding feast
than of her mouth, which still speaks prayers for you.   144

Of old, the mothers of Rome's noble blood
found joy in water. And great wisdom came
to holy Daniel in despising food.   147

Bright as pure gold was mankind's state at first:
then, hunger seasoned acorns with delight,
and every rill ran sweet to honest thirst.   150

No wine nor meat were in the wilderness.
Honey and locusts—that and nothing more
nourished the Baptist in his holiness;   153

and to that fact is his great glory due,
as the Gospel clearly testifies to you."

Notes

1–6. *We had already . . .* : The Poets, now three, are climbing the stairway to the
Sixth Cornice, having passed the Angel posted at the entrance to the Ascent. Since
this Angel must represent the virtue opposite both Avarice and Prodigality, he may
best be called the Angel of Moderation.

The Angel has lightened Dante's soul by striking away one more *P*, and has
speeded the Poets on their way by reciting a Beatitude, but with an interesting variation. The whole Beatitude would be *Beati qui esuriunt et sitiunt justitiam*—"Blessed
are they who hunger and thirst after righteousness." But the Angel left out *esuriunt*
("they hunger") and said only "Blessed are they who thirst after righteousness." The
"who hunger" will be spoken by the next Angel; appropriately, for the Gluttons.
Dante was forced into some such device if he was to make six Beatitudes do for
seven Cornices. Certainly, the aptness of his invention under such pressures is the
mark of his structural genius.

11. *that love ignites another*: *Cf. Inferno*, V, 103: "Love which permits no loved
one not to love. . . ."

13. *Juvenal*: Decius Junius Juvenal, satiric poet born about 47 A.D., died about 130
A.D. His long life almost entirely overlapped that of Statius. Since both lived in
Rome, and both were poets (Juvenal mentions Statius in his *Seventh Satire*), he
would be a natural choice as the bearer of tidings of Statius.

17. *for any unseen person*: For any person one has not met.

18. *such as will make the climb ahead seem short*: Since it will be passed in such
happy company.

27 ff. STATIUS' REPLY. Statius smiles briefly at Virgil's error in forgetting that
Avarice and Prodigality are twin sins, both of which absorb the soul into an immoderate concern for material matters. (*Cf.* Wordsworth, "Getting and spending we lay
waste our powers.") Statius then explains that he was not a miser but a waster, and
that his sin was riotous expense.

He then pays tribute to Virgil, explaining that it was a passage from the *Aeneid*
(as he quotes in lines 40–41) that led him to correct his ways, else he would at that
moment be in Hell rolling the enormous weights that the Hoarders and Wasters send
crashing against one another there. There is no historic evidence either that Statius
was a wasteful spender or that he turned Christian. On the contrary, Juvenal's *Seventh Satire* mentions Statius as being so poor that he would have starved without a
patron.

Dante's reasons for both these inventions will have to be inferred from the text
itself. Obviously, in making Statius' sin wasteful spending, Dante makes an opportunity to discuss Wasting along with Hoarding as related extremes of Avarice. Even
more obviously, Statius could not be in Purgatory at all unless Dante established him
as a Christian.

40–41. *To what do you not drive . . .* : These lines are from the *Aeneid* (III, 56–
57)—*quid non mortalia pectora cogis Auri sacra fames* ("to what do you not drive
mortal appetites, o sacred [godlike] hunger for gold?") In the Italian, Dante seems
to have rendered these lines: "Why do you not control mortal appetites, O sacred
hunger for gold?" rendering Virgil's *quid* as "why" instead of as "to what" and
thereby not only praising gold-hunger, but making it responsible for the control of
avarice. The hunger could, of course, be called "sacred" in that it is God-given,
whereby only its excesses would be evil.

No lines in the *Divine Comedy* have called forth more critical argument. Did

Dante make a ludicrous mistake? Was he so familiar with the text that he rendered it carelessly in a sleepy moment? Has the text been corrupted? Was he indulging in a sermonizer's license to twist the text to some obscure purpose? Was he using "sacred" in a special reverse way meaning "cursed," a usage still current in some parts of Italy? All these are puzzles for scholars. Dante is probably reading into Virgil an idea of Aristotelian moderation.

42. *the grim jousts*: Of the Hoarders and Wasters in the Fourth Circle of Hell (*Inferno*, VII).

46. *rise bald to Judgment Day*: Cf. *Inferno*, VII, 56–57, where Dante says of the Hoarders and Wasters:

> one crew will stand tight-fisted, the other stripped
> of its very hair at the bar of Judgment Day.

49–51. *when the opposite of a sin . . . is as blameworthy*: On this Cornice, as noted, Hoarding and Wasting are the two opposite faces of Avarice and are equally blameworthy. The opposites of Pride, Envy, and Anger, on the other hand, are the virtues of Humility, Caritas, and Meekness. The force of "when" is exactly in the fact that not every opposite is blameworthy.

55–57. *the twin afflictions of Jocasta*: Eteocles and Polynices, the twin sons of Oedipus by his own mother, Jocasta. When they succeeded to the throne of Thebes they agreed to rule in alternating years, the nonruling brother to pass the year in exile. Eteocles occupied the throne the first year and then refused to surrender it when Polynices came to claim it. Thereupon there broke out the war of the Seven against Thebes which Statius celebrated in his *Thebaid*. *the singer of the sweet Bucolics*: Virgil. So identified in preparation for the reference to *Eclogue* IV in line 67. This is the first time Virgil has been cited as the author of any work but the *Aenid*.

58. *when Clio tuned your strain*: I.e., in the *Thebaid*, which Statius began with an invocation to Clio, the Muse of History. Virgil is saying that there is no sign in Statius' work to indicate that he had turned Catholic (as, in fact, he almost certainly had not).

59–60. *the faith without the grace of which good works are vain*: Virgil is citing the doctrine that there can be no salvation except through the Catholic Church. The doctrine has only very recently been modified and was the object of some controversy in the United States in the late 1940's.

61. *what sun*: Divine Illumination. *or beacon*: Power of Reason. (Probable interpretations only.)

63. *the Fisherman*: St. Peter.

64. *You were the lamp*: Allegorically, Statius was guided by Human Reason.

67. *A new birth . . .* : These are the words of the Sybil in Virgil's *Eclogue* IV, 5–7, from his *Bucolics*. Virgil, as a courtier, was celebrating the birth of a son to the well-placed Asinius Pollio. Medieval readers were quick to interpret the lines as a prophecy of the birth of Christ, thus giving rise to the legend of Virgil as a powerful soothsayer and magician.

77. *those messengers*: The Apostles.

88–90. *drew near the Theban rivers*: The ninth book of the *Thebaid* relates the arrival of the Greeks under Adrastus to the Theban rivers, the Ismenus and the Asopus. The *Thebaid* consists of twelve books in all. Thus Statius would have had to write something more than three books (plus his work on the *Achilleid*) without letting slip any slightest indication that he was a Christian. Such a lack is sufficiently explained historically by the fact that there is no slightest evidere that Statius was converted. Within Dante's legend, however, that lack is further evidence of the Sloth of Statius, for which he spent more than four hundred years on the Fourth Cornice.

Statius must also have spent a considerable time in Ante-Purgatory or at the Mouth of the Tiber, or both, for he had been dead for 1,204 years by 1300. If "over four hundred years" plus "over five hundred years" is taken to equal as much as "about a thousand" there are still two centuries unaccounted for. Statius died at fifty-four. If he had been made to wait in Ante-Purgatory for as long as his entire life, there would still remain a century and a half unaccounted for. Some of that time may have been spent in doing minor penances on the other ledges, but he probably spent most of it at the Mouth of the Tiber waiting for the Angel Ferryman's approval.

95. *this good I praise*: The True Faith.

97–99. *Terrace . . . Caecilius, Varro, Plautus*: All those here mentioned were Latin poets of the third and second centuries B.C. Since all of them died before Christ, none could have won to salvation.

100. *Persius*: Latin poet, 34–62 A.D.

101. *that Greek*: Homer.

104. *the glorious mountain*: Parnassus.

105. *the Nine*: The Muses. Here, as in line 102, they are conceived as the mothers at whose breasts poets sucked the milk of inspiration. Homer, who outsucked all others, is, therefore, the foremost poet.

106–108. *Euripides . . . Antiphon . . . Agathon, Simonides*: All those here mentioned were Greek poets of the Golden Age.

109 ff. *of your own people*: Virgil means "of the people you wrote about in *Thebaid*." All those listed may be taken as characters of the poem, only two of whom here require further explanation: *Ismene, mournful as she was*: Daughter of Oedipus and Jocasta, sister of Antigone and of Eteocles and Polynices. She had good reason to mourn, having witnessed the death of all her family and of her betrothed, and having been sentenced to death by Creon. *who led to Langia's water*: When the Seven Heroes who fought against Thebes were dying of thirst on their march through Boetia, Hypsipyle showed them the way to a spring called Langia. For the rest of her story see XXVI, 94–96, note.

118–120. THE TIME. In Canto XII Dante has established the fact that he means the hours when he speaks of the "handmaids of the day." Here he presents them as directing the chariot of the sun in turn, each handing over her position at the chariot's pole to her successor. Four have already fallen back. It is, therefore, at least four hours since dawn (which was at 6:00 A.M.). The fifth hour is now pointing the bright tip of the chariot's pole (bright because it is approaching noon) toward the zenith. It is therefore, between 10:00 and 11:00 A.M.

133 ff. THE TREE. The description of this tree has led to many strange speculations. A number of the early commentators thought of it as growing upside down and it is so illustrated in some old manuscripts. I take Dante's central idea to be of an unclimbable tree with a great spreading top.

140 ff. THE WHIP OF GLUTTONY. It is prefaced (line 141) by a voice that cries from amid the luscious fruits, denying them to the sinners. Note how much the phrasing suggests God's first command prohibiting the Fruit of Knowledge.

The voice then cites great examples of abstinence and moderation. It cites first (lines 142–144) the example of Mary at the marriage feast at Cana in Galilee (*cf.* XIII, 28–30) and how she thought only of the good of others, not of her own appetite.

The voice then cites (lines 145–146) the matrons of ancient Rome. It was the custom during the Republic for noble matrons not to drink wine. Thus they "found joy in water."

The third example (lines 146–147) is based on *Daniel*, i, 8 and 17. Daniel determined not to defile himself with the king's wine and meat . . . "and Daniel had understanding in all visions and dreams."

The fourth example (lines 148–150) cites mankind's earliest and most natural state, when men lived in accord with nature and had not developed the cookery that leads men to gluttonous feasting, nor the wine (distilled spirits were not developed till the eighteenth century) that leads to drunkenness. Then, according to the voice, acorns and water were enough to delight men.

The final example (lines 151–155) cites John the Baptist, who ate only honey and locusts in the desert (*Matthew*, iii, 4) and won thereby to the glory the Gospel attests (*Matthew*, xi, 11, and *Luke*, vii, 28).

Canto XXIII

The Gluttons

Dante stares up into the tree to see who has spoken but he is called away by Virgil who leads on, talking to Statius, while Dante walks behind, drinking in their conversation. Suddenly, from behind him, Dante hears a psalm, and turning, he sees a band of *Gluttons* overtaking them, souls so emaciated that one can read in their sunken eyes and in the lines of the cheeks and nose the word "*Omo.*"

After some difficulty Dante recognizes one of the hideously wasted souls as his old friend *Forese* who had died only five years before, but who had been advanced into Purgatory and directly to this Cornice by the prayers of his widow, Nella.

In praising Nella for her devotion, Forese takes occasion to deliver a rather salty *Invective Against the Women of Florence* for their immodest dress and behavior.

In answer to Forese's plea (for the souls have all seen Dante's shadow), Dante explains how he has mounted into Purgatory and with whom he is traveling.

In hope of seeing who had cried those words
   I drew near and peered up at the green boughs
   like one who wastes his lifetime stalking birds.   3

At that, my more-than-father said: "My son,
   come now, for we must portion out more wisely
   the time allotted us." And he moved on.   6

I looked down and turned round to join those sages
   in the same instant. And their talk was such
   that every step I took paid double wages.   9

Then suddenly at my back I heard the strain
   of *Labia mea, Domine,* so sung
   that it was both a hymn and cry of pain.   12

"Father," I said, "What is this sound?" And he:
   "Spirits who, circling so, loosen perhaps
   the knot of debt they owe Eternity."   15

As pilgrims wrapped in holy meditation,
   when they encounter strangers on the way,
   look, but do not pause for conversation;   18

so from behind us, turning half about
   to stare as they went by, a band of souls
   came up and passed us, silent and devout.   21

The sockets of their eyes were caves agape;
   their faces death-pale, and their skin so wasted
   that nothing but the gnarled bones gave it shape.   24

I doubt that even Erysichthon's skin,
   even when he most feared that he would starve,
   had drawn so tight to bone, or worn so thin.   27

"Behold," I thought, although I did not speak,
   "the face of those who lost Jerusalem
   when Miriam ripped her son with her own beak."   30

Their eye pits looked like gem-rims minus gem.
   Those who read OMO in the face of man
   would easily have recognized the M.   33

Who could imagine, without knowing how,
   craving could waste souls so at the mere smell
   of water and of fruit upon the bough?   36

I was still wondering how they could have grown
   so thin and scabby (since what famished them
   had not yet been made clear to me), when one   39

turning his eyes from deep inside his skull,
   stared at me fixedly, then cried aloud:
   "How have I earned a grace so bountiful?"   42

I never would have recognized his face,
   but in his voice I found that which his features
   had eaten from themselves without a trace.   45

That spark relit my memory and, in awe,
   I understood beneath those altered features
   it was Forese's very self I saw.   48

"Ah, do not stare," he pleaded, "at my hide,
   bleached like a leper's by these flaming scabs,
   nor at the fleshless bones I bear inside;   51

but tell me all about yourself, and who
   these two souls are that bear you company;
   and tell me with all haste, I beg of you."   54

"I wept to see your face once when it lay
   in death," I said, "and I weep no less now
   to see what pain has wasted it away;   57

in God's name tell me how. Do not demand
   I speak while still bemused, for he speaks badly
   whose mind is too full to be at command."   60

And he: "From the Eternal Counsel flow
   the powers whereby the water and the tree
   we have just passed, emaciate us so.   63

All those who sing while weeping in their pain
   once loved their stomach-sacs beyond all measure.
   Here, thirst and hunger wring them clean again.   66

Hunger and thirst that nothing can assuage
  grow in us from the fragrance of the fruit
  and of the spray upon the foliage.   69

And not once only as we round this place
  do we endure renewal of our pain.
  —Did I say 'pain'? I should say 'gift of grace.'   72

For the same will that drives us to the Tree
  drove Christ on gladly to cry 'Eli! Eli!'
  when he paid with his blood to set us free."   75

And I to him: "Forese, from the day
  in which you changed worlds for the better life,
  less than five years, as yet, have passed away.   78

If your ability to sin had fled
  before the hour of that sublime sweet sorrow
  that weds us back to God, among his blessèd,   81

how have you reached so high in the great climb?
  I thought to find you still below, with those
  who sit and wait, repaying time for time."   84

"My Nella's flood of tears," he answered me,
  "Have borne me up so soon to let me drink
  the blessed wormwood of my agony.   87

Her sighs and prayers were heard where Love abounds:
  they raised me from the slope where I lay waiting
  and set me free of all the other Rounds.   90

The dearer and more pleasing in God's sight
  is the poor widow of my love, as she
  is most alone in doing what is right.   93

For the Barbagia of Sardinia breeds
  chaste women as compared to that Barbagia
  in which I left her to her widow's weeds.   96

O my dear brother, what is there to say?
  In vision I already see a time—
  and it is not far distant from this day—   99

in which the pulpit shall denounce by writ
  the shameless jades that Florentines call ladies,
  who go about with breasts bare to the tit.   102

What Moslem woman ever has required
  a priestly discipline, or any other,
  before she would go decently attired?   105

But if the chippies only could foresee
  swift Heaven's punishment, they'd have their mouths
  already open to howl misery.   108

For if what we foresee here does not lie,
  they shall be sad before those sons grow beards
  who can be soothed now with a lullaby.   111

Now, brother, answer in your turn. You see
  your shadow there, and how these other souls
  are staring at the spot along with me."   114

I then: "If you call back to mind from here
  my past life in your company, yours in mine,
  memory will seem too great a load to bear.   117

I was recalled from such ways by that one
  who leads me here, and just the other day
  when that one's sister (pointing to the Sun)   120

was at the full. Through the profoundest night
  of final death he led me in this flesh
  which follows him to find the final Right.   123

From there with many a sweet encouragement
  he led me upward and around the mountain
  which straightens in you what the world has bent.   126

And he has pledged himself to go with me
  until I stand by Beatrice, above.
  Then I must do without his company.   129

The one who pledges this (and as I spoke
  I pointed to him standing there) is Virgil.
  The other is the shade of him who woke   132

to blessedness just now when every rim,
  the mountain round, shook in releasing him."

Notes

11. *Labia mea, Domines*: "O Lord, open Thou my Lips, and my mouth shall pour forth Thy praise." From the Fifty-first Psalm of the Vulgate. The psalm is part of the service of Lauds for Tuesdays, and the time is now Easter Tuesday. A second aptness is in the mention of lips being opened for praise, rather than for eating and drinking.

21. *silent and devout*: Virgil (lines 14–15) seems to have implied that the souls go circling the ledge endlessly uttering their mixed hymn and lament. Here they are presented as silent and devout. The only possible inference seems to be that they circle the ledge in devout and silent meditation until they reach the tree, and then cry aloud.

25. *Erysichthon*: Erysichthon mocked the goddess Ceres by felling an oak in her sacred grove, and Ceres visited an insatiable hunger upon him. He ate up all his own substance, sold his daughter in order to buy more food, consumed that, and finally devoured his own limbs. (*Metamorphoses*, VIII, 726–881.) He does admirably as the archetype of gluttony, for the glutton consumes his soul just as Erysichthon consumed his body.

29–30. *who lost Jerusalem . . . Miriam*: Josephus (Jewish Wars, VI, 3) relates that when Titus was besieging Jerusalem in 70 A.D. (see XXI, 82, note), the people were so reduced by hunger that a woman named Mary or Miriam, the daugher of Eleazar, killed her son, cooked him, and ate half his body. *with her own beak*: As if she were a bird of prey, a creature reduced from all humanity. So gluttony reduces the soul.

32. *Those who read OMO in the face of man*: A medieval notion held that the

Creator had signed His creation (thoughtfully anticipating the Latin alphabet) *OMO DEI*, "Man [is] of God"; the eyes forming the two *O*'s the brows, nose, and cheekbones forming the *M*, the ears the *D*, the nostrils the *E*, and the mouth the *I*. Dante mentions only the *OMO*, making the point that these souls were so emaciated that one could readily see the *M*.

34. *without knowing how*: Dante's wonderment here concerns the nature of souls. How can insubstantial spirits become so hideously wasted by the craving aroused by the mere smell of food and water? (One need only inhale the moist air near a fountain or waterfall to know what Dante means by the "smell" of water.) In XXV the question arises again and is answered in detail.

42. *How have I earned a grace so bountiful*: The grace of seeing Dante again.

46. *That spark*: The soul's voice.

48. *Forese*: Forese Donati (For-RAY-zeh) died 28 July 1296. Gemma Donati, Dante's wife, was Forese's kinswoman. Forese was the brother of Corso Donati, head of the Black Guelphs, and Dante was a passionate White, but before politics separated them they had been warm friends. Forese had been something of a poet, and he and Dante had exchanged rhymed lampoons in one of which Dante had accused him of Gluttony; and of Pride and Prodigality as well.

70. *And not once only*: In XXIV, 104, Dante sights a second tree, and in XXIV, 115–117 we are told that this second tree sprawled from yet a third, which is the original Tree of Knowledge from which Eve and then Adam ate. (The third tree is not described here except as growing "further up the slope." Dante finds it in the Terrestrial Paradise, Canto XXXII, 37–60.)

74. *drove Christ on gladly to cry 'Eli! Eli'!*: At the ninth hour of his agony Christ cried, *Eli, Eli, lama sabachthani?*—"My God, my God, why hast thou forsaken me?" (*Matthew*, xxvii, 46). Dante does not mean that Christ rejoiced in his final despair but, rather, that foreseeing it, he still went gladly toward it. The desire of these sinners to endure their terrible suffering is thus compared to Christ's eagerness to endure the pain that would redeem the souls of mankind.

76–84. DANTE'S QUESTION. Dante's phrasing is difficult here. It must be understood to be Dante's personal knowledge that Forese did not give up gluttony until he was too weak to eat any more, *i.e.*, in his final hour. Then only did he achieve the sweet sublime sorrow of repentance. But since he died in 1295, only five years before the present meeting, Dante would have expected to find him outside The Gate, his purifying pains delayed for as long as he made God wait. So line 84, "repaying time for time."

85. *Nella*: Forese's wife Giovanna, a name whose affectionate diminutive is Giovanella, whence Nella. Dante clearly offers her as the type of the good Christian wife. Her virtue puts all the more to shame the decadence of the other women of Florence.

90. *set me free of all the other Rounds*: Nella's prayers have not only moved Forese out of Ante-Purgatory, but have freed him of all the pains of the Rounds below, on which he might have suffered (if Dante's charge in his rhymed lampoons had any substance) for Pride and Prodigality.

94. the *Barbagia of Sardinia*: Barbagia, a wild region in the Sardinian mountains, was dominated by the Barbacini, a bandit clan said to have been landed by the Vandals. They were reputed to be savages and idolaters. St. Gregory speaks of them as living like animals. Other medieval sources report their women as going half-naked; and inevitably some later sources (Dante's son Pietro among them) drop the "half" and report the Barbagian women to be naked savages. Thus, Forese is saying that the naked savages of the Sardinian Barbagia are chaste as compared to the women of that other Barbagia, *i.e.*, Florence, Barbagia-on-the-Arno.

109. *For if what we foresee here does not lie*: As usual, it does not, the calamities here foreseen, as of 1300, having already befallen Florence by the time Dante wrote this prophecy. In November of 1301 (see XX, 70–78) Charles de Valois entered Florence and sowed disaster. In 1302 Rinier da Calboli introduced his reign of terror

(XIV, 58 ff.), and a great famine occurred in the same year. In 1303 Florence was interdicted, and shortly thereafter a bridge collapsed, killing many people. (See also *Inferno*, XVI, 7–12) It would take about fifteen years for male children to progress from lullabies to beards, and by 1315 Florence had more than enough to mourn.

120. *that one's sister (pointing to the Sun)*: The Moon. As Diana, she was said to be the sister of Apollo, the Sun. (See note to XX, 130–132.) Dante is, of course, referring to the moon of the night of Holy Thursday when he was in the Dark Wood of Error (*Inferno*, I).

121–122. *the profoundest night of final death*: Hell.

Canto XXIV

The Gluttons

The Tree of Knowledge · The Rein of Gluttony

The Poets move on as Dante continues his talk with Forese, who identifies
many of the souls of the Gluttons, among them *Bonagiunta of Lucca.* Bonagiunta mutters a prophecy concerning Dante's future meeting with *Gentucca.* He then questions Dante about *The Sweet New Style* and ends by
concluding that had he and the others of his school of poetry grasped the
principle of natural expression, they would have written as well as do the
poets of Dante's school.

All the other souls speed ahead, but Forese remains to prophesy the
death of his brother, *Corso Donati,* leader of the Black Guelphs. Then he
speeds away and soon disappears.

The Poets move on and come to *The Tree of Knowledge* from which a
voice cries *The Rein of Gluttony,* citing *Eve, The Centaurs,* and *The Army
of Gideon.* Having skirted the tree carefully, warned away by the voice, the
Poets move ahead and meet *The Angel of Abstinence,* who shows them to
the ascent.

Talk did not slow our steps, nor they in turn
　　our talk, but still conversing we moved on
　　like ships at sea with a brisk wind astern.　　　　　　3

And all those shades, looking like things twice dead,
　　were drinking in through their sepulchral eyes
　　the awe of seeing me as I had been bred.　　　　　　6

And I, continuing as I had begun,
　　said: "His ascent, I think, is somewhat slower
　　than it would be but for that other one.　　　　　　9

—But where now is Piccarda? Do you know?
　　And is there anyone of special note
　　among these people who stare at me so?"　　　　　　12

"My sister, who was good as she was fair,
　　and fair as good, sits crowned on High Olympus,
　　rejoicing in eternal triumph there."　　　　　　15

Thus he began. Then: "To identify
　　anyone here is certainly permitted,
　　for abstinence has milked our features dry.　　　　　　18

This" (and he pointed to him) "dearest brother,
　　was Bonagiunta of Lucca. That behind him,
　　his face more sunken in than any other,　　　　　　21

once fathered Holy Church. Of Tours his line;
    and here in the long fast he expiates
    Bolsena's eels and the Vernaccia wine."   24

Then he named many others, one by one,
    at which I saw not one black look among them,
    but all seemed pleased at being thus made known.   27

Ubaldino della Pila hungered there,
    and Boniface, shepherd to all those bellies—
    they were so starved they used their teeth on air.   30

I saw my Lord Marchese. Before he died
    he drank with somewhat less thirst at Forlì,
    yet no man ever saw him satisfied.   33

As one who notes one face especially
    among a crowd, I noted him of Lucca
    who seemed most to desire a word with me.   36

He muttered something, and I seemed to hear
    the word "Gentucca" issue from the wound
    where most he felt High Justice pluck him bare.   39

"Spirit," I said, "since you seem so intent
    on talking to me, do so audibly,
    and speaking so, make both of us content."   42

"Through men may mock my city," he replied,
    "she who will teach you how to treasure it
    is born there, though she is not yet a bride.   45

This presage you shall take with you from here,
    and if you misconstrued what I first muttered
    the facts themselves, in time, will make it clear.   48

But is this really the creator of
    those new *canzoni,* one of which begins
    'Ladies who have the intellect of Love'?"   51

And I: "When Love inspires me with delight,
    or pain, or longing, I take careful note,
    and as he dictates in my soul, I write."   54

And he: "Ah, brother, now I see the thong
    that held Guittone, and the Judge, and me
    short of that sweet new style of purest song.   57

I see well how your pens attained such powers
    by following exactly Love's dictation,
    which certainly could not be said of ours.   60

And if one scan the two styles side by side,
    that is the only difference he will find."
    With that he fell still, as if satisfied.   63

Just as the cranes that winter by the Nile
  form close-bunched flights at times, then, gathering speed,
  streak off across the air in single file;   66

so all the people there faced straight ahead,
  and being lightened by both will and wasting,
  quickened their paces, and away they sped.   69

And as a runner who must take a rest
  lets his companions pull ahead and walks
  till he has eased the panting in his chest;   72

just so Forese let that blessed train
  outdistance him, and held his pace to mine,
  and said to me: "When shall we meet again?"   75

"I do not know how long my life will be,"
  I said, "but I cannot return so soon
  but what my wish will reach the shore before me;   78

for from that city where I came to life
  goodness is disappearing day by day;
  a place foredoomed to ruin by bloody strife."   81

"Take heart," he said, "for I see him whose crime
  exceeds all other's dragged at a beast's tail
  to where sin lasts beyond the end of time.   84

At every stride the beast goes faster, faster,
  until its flashing hooves lash out, and leave
  the foul ruin of what was once its master.   87

Those Spheres (and he looked toward the Heavens here)
  will not turn far before what I have said,
  and may not add to now, shall be made clear.   90

Now I must leave you far behind: your pace
  has cost me a considerable delay;
  and time is precious to us in this place."   93

At times during a horse charge, one brave knight
  will spur ahead, burning to claim the honor
  of having struck the first blow in the fight;   96

just so his lengthened stride left us behind,
  and I trailed on, accompanied by those two
  who were such mighty marshals of mankind.   99

And when, in such haste, he had pulled ahead
  so far that I could only make him out
  as I could understand what he had said;   102

we turned a corner and there came in sight,
  not far ahead, a second tree, its boughs
  laden with fruit its foliage bursting bright.   105

Sometimes when greedy children beg and screech
   for what they may not have, the one they cry to
   holds it in plain sight but beyond their reach   108

to whet their appetites: so, round that tree,
   with arms raised to the boughs, a pack of souls
   begged and was given nothing. Finally   111

they gave up and moved on unsatisfied,
   and we drew close in our turn to that plant
   at which such tears and pleadings were denied.   114

"Pass on. Do not draw near. The tree whose fruit
   Eve took and ate grows further up the slope,
   and this plant sprouted from that evil root."   117

—Thus, from the boughs, an unknown voice called down.
   And thus warned, Virgil, Statius, and myself
   drew close, and hugged the cliff, and hurried on.   120

"Recall," the voice went on, "those cursed beasts
   born of a cloud. When they had swilled the wine,
   Theseus had to slash their double breasts.   123

Recall those Jews who once showed Gideon
   how to abandon all to thirst, whereat
   he would not lead them down the hills to Midian."   126

So we strode on along the inner way
   while the voice cried the sins of Gluttony
   which earn, as we had seen, such fearful pay.   129

Then the road cleared, and with more room for walking
   we spread out, and had gone a thousand paces
   in meditation, with no thought of talking;   132

when suddenly a voice cried, startling me
   as if I were a panic-stricken colt:
   "What are you thinking of alone, you three?"   135

I looked up to see who had spoken so:
   no man has ever seen in any furnace,
   metal or glass raised to so red a glow.   138

"If your wish is to ascend," I heard one say,
   "this is the place where you must turn aside.
   All you who search for Peace—this is the way."   141

His glory blinded me. I groped and found
   my Teacher's back and followed in his steps
   as blind men do who guide themselves by sound.   144

Soft on my brow I felt a zephyr pass,
   soft as those airs of May that herald dawn
   with breathing fragrances of flowers and grass;   147

and unmistakably I felt the brush
of the soft wing releasing to my senses
ambrosial fragrances in a soft rush.   150

And soft I heard the Angel voice recite:
"Blessèd are they whom Grace so lights within
that love of food in them does not excite   153

excessive appetite, but who take pleasure
in keeping every hunger within measure."

Notes

6. *as I had been bred*: In the flesh of the first life.

8. *His ascent, I think, is somewhat slower*: Dante is speaking of Statius, continuing his answer to Forese's question from the last Canto. Statius is now free to ascend to the top of the Mount, and thence to Heaven, but is slowing his ascent in order to be with Virgil that much longer. Were Statius to climb with the speed of the almost-weightless (for, barring last rites, his soul is now purified and free) he would have to leave Virgil, who is still slowed by his need to keep pace with Dante, who is still slowed by his flesh.

Clearly, however, Dante is making an exception to the rule of his own great concept, for Statius is delaying his ascent to God (making God wait) in favor of Virgil. Such a choice would certainly emerge as sinful were Dante to apply his own rule impartially, and in Canto XXX Dante himself receives a substantial tongue-lashing from Beatrice when he mourns the disappearance of Virgil.

10. *Piccarda*: Sister of Forese. She took vows as a nun but was later forced by her other brother, Corso, into a political marriage in violation of her vows. Dante will meet her in the lowest sphere of Paradise.

14. *High Olympus*: Heaven. Another of Dante's easy adaptations of pagan themes and concepts to Christian belief.

16. *Thus he began. Then*: As at many other points in *The Divine Comedy*, Dante has asked two questions. "Thus he began" signifies that the preceding speech was in answer to the first question (line 10). "Then" begins the answer to the second (lines 11–12).

17. *is certainly permitted*: Their emaciation being such that they could never be recognized by their appearances.

19. *(and he pointed to him)*: Dante seems to have discovered this device at the end of the last Canto, and to have become so taken by it that he uses it three times in thirty-one lines.

20. *Bonagiunta of Lucca*: See below, note to line 35.

20–21. *That [one] behind him . . .* : Simon de Brie, of Tours, Pope from 1281–1285 as Martin IV. Italians, with their normal proprietary arrogance toward Vatican matters, frowned at the thought of a French Pope, but generally granted him to be a good one, though gluttonous. Since in Dante the punishment is always meant to fit the crime, the fact that his face is more sunken-in than any other, would indicate that he was, in life, the most gluttonous of all. Or it may indicate that his exalted position as Pope made his gluttony that much more sinful.

24. *Bolsena's eels and the Vernaccia wine*: The eels of Lake Bolsena, near Viterbo, are still especially prized. Vernaccia is a rich, sweet white wine of the mountains near Genoa. Eels were prepared by dropping them alive into a vat of wine. The eels, thus pickled alive, died and were roasted. Martin IV gorged incessantly on such eels and died of an attack brought on by overindulgence.

28. *Ubaldino della Pila*: A knight of the Ubaldini. Brother of the Cardinal of the Ubaldini who is roasting in Hell with Farinata, among the Epicureans (*Inferno, X*). Another brother was Ugolino d'Azzo, who is mentioned with great honor in XIV. Ubaldino was the father of Archbishop Ruggieri who is serving as lunch for Ugolino in the cooler of Hell (*Inferno, XXXII–XXXIII*). He was a great feaster and entertainer, once playing host for several months—in necessarily lavish style—to the Pope and his whole court.

29. *Boniface*: Archbishop of Ravenna, 1274–1294. He was rather more drawn to political than to spiritual affairs. Dante's charge against him involves a word play I could not render without taking considerable liberties. Literally: "Who pastured so many people with his crozier [*i.e.*, shepherd's staff]." But there is the spiritual pasturage the archbishop should provide for his flock of souls, and there is the material pasturage that filled the bellies of all the retainers Boniface kept about him as political boss of his district and its patronage. Thus the essential sarcasm of Dante's charge is that Boniface was shepherd to the bellies rather than to the souls of his archdiocese. There is no evidence outside of Dante that Boniface was a glutton.

31. *my lord Marchese*: Messer Marchese of Forlì, Podestà of Faenza in 1296. He once asked what the people thought of him. When told they spoke of nothing but his incessant drinking, he replied that they should remember he was always thirsty.

35. *him of Lucca*: Bonagiunta (Bon-ah-DJOON-tah) degli Overardi. Poet and orator of some repute in Lucca, but one whose language Dante condemns in *De Vulgari Eloquentia*, I, xiii. He was a famous glutton and tippler. Died 1297.

38. *Gentucca*: Is probably best taken as the name of a lady Dante met when he went to live with a friend at Lucca, probably about 1314–1316.

38–39. *the wound where most he felt High Justice pluck him bare*: Another of Dante's mixed metaphors. "Pluck him bare" can only be understood as "waste him away." "The wound" where he would most feel his wasting is his mouth, now reduced to a wound in his ruined face, but originally the part of him through which he sinned.

43. *Though men may mock my city*: Dante is certainly not more scornful of Lucca then of the other cities of Tuscany. Throughout the *Comedy* he enjoys taking pot shots at all of them.

44. *she*: Gentucca. In 1300 she had been born and was living in Lucca but as a girl not yet married.

49–51. Literally: "But tell me if I truly behold him who brought forth the new rhymes beginning . . ." The line quoted is the first line of a *canzone* of the *Vita Nuova* (XIX).

Bonagiunta already knows who Dante is. His phrasing is not, therefore, for identification. He has just prophesied a Platonic love into which Dante will enter with Gentucca. His thoughts turn naturally to the past Platonic love that Dante celebrated in his *Vita Nuova*. As a poet himself, Bonagiunta would be interested in discussing the "sweet new style" with its foremost practitioner.

49–62. BONAGIUNTA AND THE SWEET NEW STYLE. Bonagiunta, Guittone d'Arezzo (who first perfected the form of the Italian sonnet), and Jacopo da Lentino (known as "Il Notaro," *i.e.*, The Judge)—a Sicilian poet to whom Dante gives some qualified praise in *De Vulgari Eloquentia* (I, xxi)—were all practitioners of a kind of conventionalized verse modeled after the most decadent phase of Provençal poetry. They flourished in the first half of the thirteenth century. Dante was a prime mover in the later "sweet new style" of more natural expression. In lines 55–57 Bonagiunta regrets that his school failed to discover the principle of the sweet new style, for only the adherence to that principle of natural expression, he adds (lines 61–62), distinguishes the one style from the other. His implication is that, had his school observed that principle, he and his fellows would have written as well as the new poets, being their equals in all else. And with this final wishful assertion, Bonagiunta seems satisfied, and says no more.

It is possible to interpret Bonagiunta's remarks as a lament over his failure to discover the new style and thereby to write better, but the first interpretation seems firmer.

64–66. Compare Dante's description of the Carnal, *Inferno*, V, 46–47.

68. *being lightened by both will and wasting*: Sin is equated to heaviness and purity to lightness throughout the *Comedy*. These souls are made lighter both by their own will to endure the purifying penance and by the wasting that resulted from it. Dante seems to imply that an emaciated incorporeal essence weighs less than a normal one. If so, the explanation must lie in one of the mysteries of faith.

76–81. DANTE'S ANSWER TO FORESE. Forese, moved by love, has expressed his longing to see Dante again, but obviously he cannot until Dante is dead. To a soul in Purgatory, to be sure, death is not a tragedy but an arrival. Yet Forese phrases his question delicately, aware that he is speaking to a living man. Dante, on the other hand, understands Forese's intent, and answers without circumlocution: however soon his return to the second life, his wish will be there before him.

78. *the shore*: Of Purgatory. Dante will have some time to spend on the Cornice of Pride (and perhaps of Wrath), but he may yet overtake Forese in the final ascent.

79. *that city*: Florence.

82. *him*: Corso Donati. Forese's brother and head of the Black Guelphs. It was Corso who persuaded Boniface VIII to send Charles of Valois to Florence in 1300. Thus the crimes of Charles are indirectly his. In 1309 Corso tried a coalition that would make him the supreme authority in Florence, but the Blacks, whom he had done so much so bloodily to put into power, discovered his plot and condemned him to death. He fled but was pursued and killed. Dante follows an account (line 83) that has him dragged to death by his horse.

84. *where sin lasts beyond the end of time*: Hell.

88. *Those Spheres*: Of Heaven, as indicated by the parenthetical stage direction.

90. *and may not add to now*: Forese has already overstayed and must rejoin his band.

92. *a considerable delay*: In matching his pace to Dante's when he should be speeding toward his expiation with the other spirits.

100–105. These two tercets present fairly typical problems of Dantean interpretation. In 100–102 Dante says he can follow Forese with his eyes only as he could follow in his mind (*i.e.*, understand) what Forese had said. Hence if Forese was still remotely in sight, it would follow that Dante had some glimmer of the meaning of his prophecy. If, on the other hand, Dante meant he could not grasp the prophecy at all, Forese must have disappeared.

At that very instant, however (103–105) the Poets round a bend in the cliff. If they are that close to a turning (and the circles at this altitude would turn on a shortened radius), Forese must have long since disappeared around the bend. It must follow, therefore, that Dante means he had no idea whatever of the meaning of Forese's prophecy—as, in fact, he could not have known in 1300 how Corso would die in 1309.

104. *a second tree*: Various attempts have been made to relate this tree to the first, as they must, indeed, be related since from one the Whip of Gluttony is spoken, and from the other, the Rein. This one, we are told by the voice, is sprung from the same root as the Tree of Knowledge from which Eve ate. Among other things, therefore, it is the Tree of Death. By simple opposites the other may be argued to be the Tree of Life. Or the two may be seen as the Tree of Mortal Woe (death included) and the Tree of Eternal Life, the former containing the voice of the ruin brought on by sin, the latter the voice of the eternal joy that arises from obedience.

115–126. THE REIN OF GLUTTONY. (115–117) The first admonition cites the downfall of Eve (aptly cited from an offshoot of the original tree). Gluttony, in Dante's view, is sinful because it rejects God in favor of appetite: the Glutton thinks of his belly rather than of his soul. Eve's act is, therefore, the supreme Gluttony in that it lost God to all mankind until the coming of Christ. In Dante's geography, the Garden of Eden stands at the top of the Mount of Purgatory. Thus the tree from which Eve ate, and from whose roots this tree springs, must stand above it.

(121–123) The second admonition cites the drunkenness of the Centaurs and the grief to which it brought them. Invited to a wedding feast by the neighboring Lapithae, the Centaurs became so drunk they tried to make off with the bride, whereupon Theseus and the Lapithae seized arms and killed great numbers of the Centaurs. The Centaurs are spoken of as "born of a cloud" (line 122) because they were supposed to have been sired by Ixion upon the cloud Nephele whom Jupiter had formed into the likeness of Juno, beloved of Ixion. They are said to have double breasts (line 123) because of their two natures, half-horse and half-human.

(124–126) The third admonition is based on *Judges*, vii, 5–6. When Gideon was leading the army of the Jews against Midian, he was instructed by the Lord to lead his men to the river and to watch how they drank. Those who threw aside all caution at the sight of water and plunged their faces into the river, were to be set aside. Those who stayed alert despite their thirst, drinking cautiously by scooping the water up in their hands and remaining watchful, were to be chosen. Three hundred were so chosen, and with them alone Gideon moved down to victory.

127. *the inner way*: Along the cliff-face.

130–131. *the road cleared, and with more room . . .* : One must remember that the tree grows in the middle of the ledge. The Voice had warned the Poets not to draw near. Since the ledge is narrow and the tree spreads wide, the Poets had to draw far to one side along the inner cliff-face, naturally drawing close together. Now, with the road cleared, they once more draw apart for better walking.

135. *alone*: As Dante has made clear, the souls in Purgatory go normally in great bands. Three alone is an exception the Angel could not fail to note.

135–155. THE ANGEL OF ABSTINENCE. The combined fieriness and softness of the Angel of Abstinence makes him an especially memorable figure, and an especially appropriate one, his office considered. The fieriness of his aura may be taken to symbolize raging appetite, perhaps prefiguring the Fire of *Luxuria* (lust) of the next Canto; his softness to symbolize the sweetness of abstinence in its conquest of such fire.

His blessing to the Poets is based on the second half of the Fifth Beatitude, the first half of which was recited by the Angel of Moderation on the ledge just below. (See opening lines of XXII.) That Angel had left out "who hunger" in his version of the Beatitude. The Angel leaves out "who thirst" but puts in "who hunger."

Canto XXV

It is 2:00 P.M. as the Three Poets leave the Cornice of the Gluttonous and begin their hurried *Ascent to the Seventh Cornice.*

Dante, burning with eagerness to ask how the Gluttons could give the appearance of advanced starvation despite the fact that they are airy bodies and do not need food, fears to speak but is finally encouraged to do so by Virgil. Dante immediately offers his question, and Virgil, as an act of courtesy, invites Statius to answer it. The rest of the rapid ascent is then occupied by *The Discourse of Statius on the Nature of the Generative Principle, The Birth of the Human Soul,* and *The Nature of Aerial Bodies.*

By the time Statius is finished, the Poets have reached the Seventh Cornice. There, enwrapped in sheets of flame, in the souls of *The Lustful* sing over and over the hymn *Summae Deus Clementiae.* At each conclusion of the hymn, they cry out in praise of an example of High Chastity. These examples form *The Whip of Lust.* It is in this way, singing and praising as they move through the flames, that the Lustful perform their purification.

> It was an hour to climb without delay.
>   Taurus succeeded to the Sun's meridian,
>   and Scorpio to Night's—a world away;   3
>
> thus, as a man spurred on by urgent cause
>   will push ahead, no matter what appears
>   along the way inviting him to pause—   6
>
> just so we filed, one of us at a time,
>   into the gap, and started up those stairs
>   whose narrowness divides all those who climb.   9
>
> And as a little stork, eager to fly
>   but afraid to leave the nest, will raise a wing
>   then let it fall again—just such was I,   12
>
> the will within me now strong and now weak,
>   eager to ask, but going only so far
>   as to make me clear my throat, and then not speak.   15
>
> The pace was swift: nor did my Sweet Lord slow
>   his stride, but said: "I see the bow of speech
>   drawn back to the very iron. Let it go."   18

My doubts resolved, I did not hesitate
  to use my mouth. "How can they grow so thin,"
  I said, "who need no food in their new state?"   21

"Recall Meleager wasting as the brand
  wasted in fire," he said, "and you will find
  the matter not so hard to understand.   24

Or think how your least move before a glass
  is answered by your image, and what seemed hard
  is bound to grow much clearer than it was.   27

But this wish burns you, I know, and to put out
  all of its flames, I shall beg Statius now
  to be the one to heal the wounds of doubt."   30

"If, in your presence," Statius first replied,
  "I explain eternal things, let my excuse
  be only that your wish be not denied."   33

And then to me: "Son, let it be your task
  to hear and heed my words, and they will be
  a light upon the 'how' of what you ask.   36

Perfect blood—that pure blood that remains
  as one might say, like food upon the table,
  and never goes to slake the thirsty veins—   39

acquires, within the heart, formative power
  over all human organs; as that which flows
  into the veins forms *them*. It is once more   42

changed in the heart, then flows down to that place
  the better left unmentioned. Thence, it drips
  over another blood in its natural vase.   45

There, the two commingle; and one blood shows
  a passive bent, while the other blood is active,
  due to the perfect place from which it flows.   48

So joined, the active force within the latter
  first clots, then quickens what it has made firm
  of the former blood to serve as working matter.   51

The active force has now become a soul
  like that of a plant, but with the difference
  that this begins where that achieves its goal.   54

Soon, like some sea-thing, half-beast and half-weed,
  it moves and feels. It then begins to form
  those powers of sense of which it is the seed.   57

Now, my son, the formative power expands
  and elongates within, till every member
  takes form and place as nature's plan commands.   60

But how this animal-thing grows human powers
 you do not yet see; and this very point
 has led astray a wiser head than yours.   63

By him, the *possible intellect* was thought
 (since it occupied no organ) to be disjoined
 from the *vegetative soul*—and so he taught.   66

Open your heart to the truth I shall explain,
 and know that at the instant articulation
 has been perfected in the foetal brain,   69

that instant the First Mover turns to it.
 And there, rejoicing at such art in nature,
 breathes into it a new and powerful spirit.   72

All that is active there, this spirit draws
 into itself, forming a single soul
 that lives, and feels, and measures its own cause.   75

(Consider, if you find these words of mine
 too strange to understand, how the sun's heat
 joined to the sap of the vine turns into wine.)   78

Then when Lachesis' flax is drawn, it frees
 itself from flesh, but takes with it the essence
 of its divine and human faculties—   81

its lower powers grown passive now and mute;
 but memory, intelligence, and will
 more active than they were, and more acute.   84

Miraculously then, by its own will,
 it falls at once to one or the other shore.
 There it first learns its way, for good or ill.   87

And once inclosed in that new atmosphere,
 the *formative power* rays out, as it did first
 in shaping the bodily parts it left back there.   90

Then, as the air after a rain will glow
 inside itself, reflecting an outer ray,
 and clothe itself in many colors—so   93

wherever the soul may stop in its new hour,
 the air about it takes on that soul's image.
 Such is the virtue of the *formative power*.   96

Thereafter, in the same way one may see
 flame follow fire wherever it may shift,
 the new form follows the soul eternally.   99

From air it draws its visibility. Hence,
 it is called a *shade*. And out of air it forms
 the organs of sight, speech, and every sense.   102

Thus are we able to speak and laugh. And thus
  are we able to weep such tears and breathe such sighs
  as you have seen and heard, passing among us.   105

As desire, or other feelings move us, so
  our shades change their appearances. And that
  is the cause of what amazed you just below."   108

—We had come, by then, to the last turn of the stairs
  from which we bore to the right along the cornice,
  and our minds were drawn already to other cares.   111

Here, from the inner wall, flames blast the ledge,
  while from the floor an air-blast bends them back,
  leaving one narrow path along the edge.   114

This path we were forced to take as best we might,
  in single file. And there I was—the flames
  to the left of me, and the abyss to the right.   117

My Leader said: "In this place, it is clear,
  we all must keep a tight rein on our eyes.
  To take a false step would be easy here."   120

"*Summae Deus clementiae*," sang a choir
  inside that furnace, and despite my road
  I could not help but look into the fire.   123

Then I saw spirits moving through the flames,
  and my eyes turned now to them, now to my feet,
  as if divided between equal claims.   126

When they had sung the hymn, those souls in pain
  cried out in full voice: "*Virum non cognosco*."
  Then, softly, they began the hymn again.   129

That done, they cried: "Diana kept to the wood,
  and drove Helicé from her when that nymph
  had felt Venus's poison in her blood."   132

Then, once again, the hymn swelled from their choir;
  and after it they praised husbands and wives
  who were chaste as virtue and marriage vows require.   135

And in this way, I think, they sing their prayer
  and cry their praise for as long as they must stay
  within the holy fire that burns them there.   138

Such physic and such diet has been thought fit
before the last wound of them all may knit.

Notes

1. *It was an hour to climb without delay*: Afternoon. Hence there was no time to waste, for darkness will come soon.
2–3. *Taurus succeeded to the Sun's meridian*: The sun is in the sign of Aries,

which is succeeded by the sign of Taurus. If Taurus has replaced the sun at the meridian, the sun must have moved lower toward the west. And since the signs of the Zodiac each represent two hours (twelve of them for twenty-four hours), it must be two hours past noon. *and Scorpio to Night's—a world away*: Night is personified here. A world away (above Jerusalem). Night would have reached its meridian point (midnight) in the sign of Libra, but has now passed on and Scorpio is the ruling sign. It is, therefore, 2:00 A.M. in Jerusalem.

7. *one of us at a time*: The probable order is: Virgil, Statius, Dante. (*Cf.*, XXVI, 1.)

9. *whose narrowness divides all those who climb*: A clear allegorical meaning not to be overlooked here, is that each soul must ultimately climb to salvation alone, inside itself, no matter how much assistance it may receive from others. Another would be the soul's loneliness in meeting sexual temptation.

10-15. *eager . . . afraid*: Dante is burning to ask how such insubstantial entities as shades, who need no physical nourishment, could have every appearance of advanced starvation, as is the case with the souls of the Gluttonous. This eagerness to ask, along with the need to hurry on, is implicit in all of Dante's phrasing in lines 1-6.

17-18. *the bow of speech . . .* : Dante's speech is conceived to be a bow that he has bent back to the very iron (the head) of the arrow, in his eagerness to let fly, but which he has been afraid to release.

22. *Meleager*: Son of Oeneus, King of Calydon, and of Althaea. When he was born, the Fates threw a branch into the fire and decreed that he should live until fire had consumed it. Althaea pulled it out of the fire and hid it.

When he had grown, Meleager fell in love with Atalanta, famous for the story of the golden apples. He slew a great bear for her and gave her the skin. His own brothers stole the skin from Atalanta and Meleager, in his rage, killed them. Althaea thereupon brought the fatal branch out of hiding and threw it into the fire. As the flames consumed it, Meleager's life was consumed.

29. *I shall beg Statius now*: Some commentators see Virgil's action in calling upon Statius as signifying that Human Reason has begun to surrender its function to the redeemed soul. Certainly, however, there is nothing in what Statius goes on to say, that lies beyond the province of Virgil as Human Reason. Statius's long reply, in fact, would have been taken as a scientific disquisition in Dante's time.

Virgil's action is better taken, I believe, as a courtesy to Statius. Rather than have Statius stand by while Virgil lectures on matters that Statius knows perfectly well, Virgil invites Statius to take over the lecture—a courtesy to a visiting professor. Statius returns the courtesy by pointing out that he can say nothing not known to Virgil, but undertakes the lecture because Virgil has been so gracious in requesting that he do so.

36. *the 'how'*: Dante had asked (line 20): "How can they grow so thin?"

34-108. THE DISCOURSE OF STATIUS. The long discourse into which Statius launches cannot fail to present unusual difficulties to modern readers, yet it is worth special attention as an illustration of what Dante meant by "Science," as a series of outdated but interesting theories, and especially as an example of how carefully Dante led up to and then introduced his inquiries into the nature of things as an important part of the total scheme of the *Commedia*.

The discourse may be divided into three parts: I. The Nature of the Generative Principle; II. The Birth of the Human Soul; and III. The Nature of Aerial Bodies. An extended paraphrase is perhaps the best way to deal with the complexities of the discourse.

I. *The Nature of the Generative Principle*:

31-39. Dante's concept of blood includes not only blood as we understand it, but a pre-substance (perfect blood) some of which flows into the veins (*i.e.*, the arteries), but some of which remains apart (like food left untouched and in its original state).

40-42. This perfect blood enters the heart (without entering into the general circulation of the bloodstream) and acquires the power (which we now associate with the genes) to determine the development of the bodily organs and members. Similarly, the blood that flows into the "veins" has the power to determine *their* form and function. *formative power*: a technical term from Scholastic philosophy. It may be thought of as "the generative principle." It is derived entirely from the male parent.

43-45. Within the heart of the father, this "perfect blood" undergoes a change into sperm. It then flows down to the male organs ("better left unmentioned") and, in the act of conception, drips over the blood of the female in the womb ("another blood in its natural vase").

46-48. These two bloods commingle. One of them (the female blood) is passive, *i.e.*, it is menstrual, tending to flow away rather than to take form. The other (the male blood), because of the perfect place from which it flows (the heart), is active, *i.e.*, it seeks to generate form.

49-51. The active blood then causes the passive blood to clot. It thus forms it into solid and workable matter, which it then quickens into life. Conception has taken place.

II. *The Birth of the Human Soul.*

52–54. With conception the soul is born, not as a coinheritance from the mother and father, but from the active force (the formative power) of the father-blood alone, the maternal blood providing only the matter for the formative power to work on. (Dante's views here are pure Aquinian doctrine.)

This newly formed soul is like that of a plant (vegetative only), but with the difference that the plant soul is fully formed at this stage, whereas the human soul is only beginning.

55–57. From this plantlike state (possessing only "vegetative faculties") the soul grows capable of elementary motion and sensation (the "sensitive faculties"). It has achieved the state of some "sea-thing." Dante says not "sea-thing" but "sea-fungus." He probably meant some coelenterate, such as the hydra, sea anemone, or jellyfish. In Dante's time such life-forms were believed to be single living masses without differentiated organs of any sort.

58–60. From this "sea-thing" stage, the *formative power* of the soul (from the father) moves within the maternal material shaping each organ and member into its form and place in human anatomy, according to nature's plan.

61–63. One must still ask how this animal foetus acquires the power of human reason (in Scholastic phrasing, "the possible intellect"). And here, before propounding the true doctrine as he sees it, Statius pauses to refute the teaching of Averroës ("a wiser head than yours"), who erred on this point.

64–66. The grasp the importance to Dante's doctrine of the error of Averroës, one must understand that in Scholastic teaching the soul possesses (1) the *vegetative faculty,* which is to say it lives, (2) the *sensitive or perceiving faculty,* which is to say it feels and receives impressions, and (3) the *reflective faculty,* called the *possible intellect,* which is to say it has the power of reasoning from the known to the unknown, and of extracting forms and concepts from nature.

The vegetative and sensitive faculties receive particular impressions only. The organ of those faculties, common to both man and beast, is the brain. Where then was the organ of the higher intellectual faculty, the possible intellect?

Since he could find no such organ, Averroës postulated a generalized universal rationality from which all men could draw rational faculties during their lives, but which was lost to them at death. It must follow, therefore, that no individual and rational soul could be summoned to eternal judgment, since the soul would have lost its possible intellect (rationality) at death. Church scholars would necessarily be required to reject such a doctrine since it denied the very basis of free will and of just reward and punishment.

67–75. Having refuted error, Statius then explains the truth: the instant the brain is fully formed in the human foetus, God turns to it in his joy at the art of nature in forming so perfect a thing, and breathes into it a powerful spirit peculiar to man. This God-infused spirit draws all the life forces (vegetative, sensitive, and rational) into a single soul. Note especially, in reply to Averroës, that the soul so formed is individualized, self-measuring, and, therefore, self-responsible.

76–78. Statius then compares the change wrought by the new spirit with the way the heat of the sun is transformed into the quickened wine when joined to the relatively inert sap of the vine.

III. *The Nature of Aerial Bodies:*

79–81. Then when Lachesis (the Fate who draws out the flaxen thread of life–see XXI, 24–27, note) measures the end of the mortal life, the soul goes free of the flesh but takes with it, by virtue of that essence God breathed into it, all of its faculties both human (vegetative and sensitive) and divine (rational).

82–84. These lower (vegetative and sensitive) faculties grow passive and mute after death, since they have left behind the organs whereby they functioned. The higher faculties, however, since they are God-inspired and now free of their mortal involvement in materiality, become more active and acute.

85–87. At the instant of death the soul miraculously falls, by an act of its own will, either to the shore of Hell for damnation, or to the mouth of the Tiber to await transport to Purgatory.

88–90. As soon as the soul feels itself inclosed in the new atmosphere of the afterlife, the *formative power* from the heart of the father (line 40) sends out its rays, as it first did through the matter of the maternal blood to shape the living organs of the body.

91–93. The process is compared to the way the sun's rays (a force from without) work upon moist air to form a rainbow (within the air). Note that the power of the Sun's rays is, allegorically, from God the Father, just as the formative power of the soul is from the mortal father, and that both work upon passive matter to give it form.

94–96. Wherever (*i.e.*, on whichever shore, as in line 86) the soul lights, the inclosing air takes on the image of that soul by virtue of the soul's indwelling formative power.

97–99. Then, ever after, and just as flame follows fire, the new form follows the soul, wherever it may move.

100–102. This new form is called a *shade* because it is made of insubstantial air, and because out of air it forms all the organs of sense.

103–105. Not only is the shade able to receive sensory impressions, but to produce sounds and appearances that can be registered by mortal senses. (As well as by other shades, as the narrative has made clear at many points.)

106–108. The appearance of the shade, moreover, conforms in detail to the inner feelings of the soul. Thus, if God fills the souls of the gluttonous with a craving for food which is then denied them, their shades appear to wither and starve, their outward appearance conforming to their inner state. It is this phenomenon that amazed Dante on the ledge below. (Note, too, the difference made clear here between men and shades. Men may appear virtuous by hiding their inner evil desires, and thus practice fraud. But shades cannot hide their inner workings: as they are within themselves, so must they appear. This doctrine applied retrospectively, especially to the souls in Hell, will immediately suggest another dimension to be considered when reading Dante's descriptions of the souls he meets there.)

119. *we all must keep a tight rein on our eyes*: On the narrative level, Virgil means simply, we must watch our dangerous path with great care. On the allegorical level, however, he can certainly be read to mean that lust (the excess of love) is the most readily inviting sin, but that it is as dangerous as a fall off the cliff, and that all men must guard against it and refuse, like the souls of the Carnal now in Hell, to "abandon reason to their appetites." It was a convention of the "sweet new style," moreover, that love always enters through the eyes.

121. *"Summae Deus clementiae"*: God of clemency supreme. These words are the beginning of the old hymn (now revised) which was sung at Matins on Saturday. The hymn is a prayer for chastity, begging God, of his supreme clemency, to burn lust from the soul and to leave the suppliant chaste.

128 ff. THE WHIP OF LUST. The Whip of Lust consists of examples of chastity which are called forth in praises by the sinners themselves, one example being cried forth at each completion of the Hymn they sing endlessly. The first example (Holy chastity) is, as always, from the life of Mary. The second (Natural chastity) cites Diana. In subsequent intervals between the hymn-singing, the sinners cry out the praise of various husbands and wives (not specified by Dante) who were chaste as required by natural virtue and the sacramental vows of matrimony. They might be called examples of Catholic chastity.

128. *"Virum non cognosco"*: "I know not a man." These words were spoken by Mary at the Annunciation. Gabriel had said, "Behold, thou shalt conceive in thy womb, and bring forth a son." Mary replied, "How shall this be, seeing I know not a man?" (*Luke,* i, 26–38.)

130 ff. *"Diana kept to the wood . . ."*: In order to preserve her virginity, Diana lived in the woods and became a huntress. One of her attendant nymphs, Helicé, felt the urging of lust (the *poison of Venus,* as opposed to love itself, which would also be from Venus, but not as poison) and gave herself to Jove. After she had been driven away by Diana, Helicé was changed into a bear by Juno. Jove, who seemed systematically incapable of keeping his wife under control where his philandering was concerned, made his new she-bear a questionable sort of recompense by placing her in the sky as Ursa Major, the Big Dipper. (Ovid, *Metamorphoses,* II, 401-530.)

Canto XXVI

The Lustful

The Rein of Lust

Dante's shadow falls on the wall of flame and it is noticed by the souls of the Lustful who approach (without leaving the flames) to question him. Dante's answer, however, is interrupted by the approach of a second band of souls from the opposite direction. These are The Sodomites. *The two bands of souls exchange brief embraces and then cry out* The Rein of Lust *as they move on, drawing rapidly apart.*

The first group again approaches Dante and the soul of Guido Guinizelli *speaks to him. Dante pays high homage to Guinizelli and discusses with him the growth of the Sweet New Style.*

With a final request for a prayer for his soul, Guido withdraws and Dante then addresses Arnaut Daniel, *who answers in the* langue d'oc, *and also begs that Dante say a prayer for him. His petition made, Daniel disappears into the purifying flame.*

> So, one before the other, we moved there
> along the edge, and my Sweet Guide kept saying:
> "Walk only where you see me walk. Take care."   3
>
> The Sun, already changing from blue to white
> the face of the western sky, struck at my shoulder,
> its rays now almost level on my right;   6
>
> and my shadow made the flames a darker red.
> Even so slight an evidence, I noticed,
> made many shades that walk there turn their head.   9
>
> And when they saw my shadow, these began
> to speak of me, saying to one another:
> "He seems to be no shade, but a living man!"   12
>
> And some of them drew near me then—as near
> as they could come, for they were ever careful
> to stay within the fire that burned them there.   15
>
> "O you who trail the others—with no desire
> to lag, I think, but out of deference—
> speak to me who am burned by thirst and fire.   18
>
> Not I alone need what your lips can tell:
> all these thirst for it more than Ethiopes
> or Indians for a drink from a cold well: 21
>
> how is it that you cast a shadow yet,
> making yourself a barrier to the Sun,
> as if death had not caught you in its net?"   24

—So one addressed me. And I should have been
explaining myself already, but for a new
surprising sight that caught my eye just then;   27

for down the center of that fiery way
came new souls from the opposite direction,
and I forgot what I had meant to say.   30

I saw them hurrying from either side,
and each shade kissed another, without pausing,
each by the briefest greeting satisfied.   33

(Ants, in their dark ranks, meet exactly so,
rubbing each other's noses, to ask perhaps
what luck they've had, or which way they should go.)   36

As soon as they break off their friendly greeting,
before they take the first step to pass on,
each shade outshouts the other at that meeting.   39

"Sodom and Gomorrah," the new souls cry.
And the others: "Pasiphaë enters the cow
to call the young bull to her lechery."   42

As if cranes split into two flocks, and one
flew to the Rhipheans, one to the sands,
these to escape the ice, and those the Sun—   45

so, then, those shades went their opposing ways;
and all returned in tears to their first song,
and each to crying an appropriate praise.   48

Then those who came my way drew close once more—
the same shades that had first entreated me.
They seemed as eager to hear me as before.   51

I, having had their wish presented twice,
replied without delay: "O souls assured—
whenever it may be—of Paradise,   54

I did not leave my limbs beyond the flood,
not green nor ripe, but bear them with me here
in their own jointure and in their own blood.   57

I go to be no longer blind. Above
there is a lady wins us grace, and I,
still mortal, cross your world led by her love.   60

But now I pray—so may it soon befall
you have your greater wish to be called home
into that heaven of love that circles all—   63

tell me, that I may write down what you say
for all to read, who are you? and those others
who move away behind you—who are they?"   66

Just as our mountaineers, their first time down,
  half-wild and shaggy, gape about the streets
  and stare in dumb amazement at the town—   69

just such a look I saw upon those shades;
  but when they had recovered from their stupor
  (which from a lofty heart the sooner fades),   72

the first shade spoke again: "Blessèd are you
  who for a better life, store in your soul
  experience of these realms you travel through!   75

Those souls you saw going the other way
  grew stained in that for which triumphant Caesar
  heard his own legions call him "Queen" one day.   78

Therefore their band, at parting from us, cries
  'Sodom!'—as you have heard—that by their shame
  they aid the fire that makes them fit to rise.   81

We were hermaphroditic in our offenses,
  but since we did not honor human laws,
  yielding like animals to our lusting senses,   84

we, when we leave the other band, repent
  by crying to our shame the name of her
  who crouched in the mock-beast with beast's intent.   87

And now you know our actions and our crime.
  But if you wish our names, we are so many
  I do not know them all, nor is there time.   90

Your wish to know mine shall be satisfied:
  I am Guido Guinizelli, here so soon
  because I repented fully before I died."   93

In King Lycurgus' darkest hour, two sons
  discovered their lost mother: I was moved
  as they had been (but could not match their actions)   96

when I heard his name, for he had fathered me
  and all the rest, my betters, who have sung
  sweet lilting rhymes of love and courtesy.   99

Enraptured, I can neither speak nor hear
  but only stare at him as we move on,
  although the flames prevent my drawing near.   102

When at last my eyes had fed, I spoke anew;
  and in such terms as win belief, I offered
  to serve him in whatever I could do.   105

And he to me then: "What you say has made
  such a profound impression on my mind
  as Lethe cannot wash away, nor fade.   108

But if the words you swore just now are true,
　　let me know why you show by word and look
　　such love as I believe I see in you?"　　　　111

And I to him: "Your songs so sweet and clear
　　which, for as long as modern usage lives,
　　shall make the very ink that writes them dear."　　114

"Brother," he said, "that one who moves along
　　ahead there," (and he pointed) "was in life
　　a greater craftsman of the mother tongue.　　117

He, in his love songs and his tales in prose,
　　was without peer—and if fools claim Limoges
　　produced a better, there are always those　　120

who measure worth by popular acclaim,
　　ignoring principles of art and reason
　　to base their judgments on the author's name.　　123

So, once, our fathers sent Guittone's praise,
　　and his alone, bounding from cry to cry,
　　though truth prevails with most men nowadays.　　126

And now, if you enjoy such privilege
　　that you are free to go up to that cloister
　　within which Christ is abbot of the college,　　129

say an Our Father for me in that host,
　　as far as it may serve us in this world
　　in which the very power to sin is lost."　　132

With that, perhaps to yield his place with me
　　to someone else he vanished through the fire
　　as a fish does to the dark depths of the sea.　　135

I drew ahead till I was by that shade
　　he had pointed to, and said that in my heart
　　a grateful place to feast his name was laid.　　138

And he replied at once and willingly:
　　"Such pleasaunce have I of thy gentilesse,
　　that I ne can, ne will I hide from thee.　　141

Arnaut, am I, and weepe and sing my faring.
　　In grievousnesse I see my follies past;
　　in joie, the blistful daie of my preparing.　　144

And by the eke virtue, I thee implour,
　　that redeth thee, that thou amount the staire,
　　be mindful in thy time of my dolour."　　147

Then he, too, hid himself within the fire
　　that makes those spirits ready to go higher.

Notes

4–8. changing from blue to white . . . the western sky: It is now 4:00 P.M., or a bit later, of the third day on the mountain. At that hour of a clear day Dante sees the sun as washing the blue out of the western sky and turning it whiter and brighter than the east. *struck at my shoulder . . . now almost level on my right*: If the circumference of the mountain is taken as a compass rose, the Poets have moved beyond WNW and are moving toward W. The sun is in about the same position in the sky and getting low (perhaps a bit less than 30°), and Dante says its rays are almost level. In point of fact, the mean distance of the sun from the earth is approximately 93,000,000 miles and to be level with it at one-third of its altitude, Dante would have to be about 30,000,000 miles up: an altitude that makes it a considerable mountain even as hyperbole goes. In any case, the shadow of Dante's body falls on the wall of flame to his left, where it is noticed by many of the shades within the fire. This fact, too, is certainly impossible: Dante is treating the wall of flame as if it were a fog bank.

20–21. all these: All these others who walk with me here. *Ethiopes or Indians*: Dante thought of Ethiopia and India as nothing but parched and burning wastes.

29 ff. THE SODOMITES. The first shades Dante met on this Cornice walked along bearing to the right (from east to west, the direction of the sun, and the natural way of going on the mountain). These new souls, to Dante's surprise, walk in the opposite direction, *i.e.*, against the natural way. They are The Sodomites. (See further note to 37–42, below.)

31. them: Both bands of sinners.

32. and each shade kissed another: In accordance with the Apostolic admonition: "Salute one another with a holy kiss." (*Romans*, xvi, 16.) These holy kisses not only remind them of the libidinous kisses of their sin, but help expiate it. *without pausing*: Throughout, Dante is moving behind Virgil and Statius as rapidly as possible along that dangerous path. Thus, all his exchanges with these sinners are carried on at a fast walk, the Sodomites walking the opposite way and soon passing from view, the other shades retaining their same relative positions to Dante in their course along the ledge.

37–42. THE REIN OF LUST. The Rein consists here of a single admonition against *unnatural lust*, and of another against *natural lust*.

(40) Sodom and Gomorrah: Ancient cities destroyed in a rain of fire from Heaven as punishment for the fact that homosexuality was a general practice in them.

(41–42) Pasiphaë: Daughter of Apollo by the nymph Perseis. Wife of King Minos of Crete. Poseidon sent Minos a black bull to be offered as a sacrifice, but Minos put it in his herd. For revenge, Poseidon made Pasiphaë fall in love with the bull. She had Daedalus make a cunning effigy of a cow with wicker or wooden ribs, over which a cowhide was spread. She then crouched inside in order to be possessed by the bull. The Minotaur (see *Inferno*, XII, 12–18, note) was born of the union. Thus, lust gave birth to a monster.

Note that Dante reserves "sodomy" specifically for "homosexuality." In modern usage "sodomy" includes "sexual relations with animals." Parsiphaë's example, though it may seem unnatural enough to us, does not violate natural law, but only human law. See 82–84, note, below.

43–45. the Rhipheans: The Rhiphean Mountains, a mythical range that occurs "somewhere in the north" on some old maps. Dante's phrasing is best understood to mean north in a generic sense. *the sands*: Of the African desert. Note that Dante does not say cranes actually behave in this way (he could not fail to know that cranes do not migrate both north and south in the same season), but only that it is *as if* cranes did so behave. Clearly the figure relates to the cranes of *Inferno*, V, 46–47, thereby suggesting both a parallelism and a contrast.

46–48. their opposing ways: The Sodomites go away from Dante. The others continue along in his direction. *their first song: Summae Deus clementiae. each . . . an appropriate praise*: The appropriate praises are the miscellaneous exhortations from The Whip of Lust. The sinners sing their hymn, then shout a praise, then sing again. After the first hymn they praise Mary. After the second, Diana. After the third, and before starting the cycle over, each cites his own example of chastity, probably an example that stands directly opposite his particular sin.

55. beyond the flood: Across the sea. Hence, in the world.

59. a lady: Dante could mean either Beatrice or the Virgin Mary.

63. that heaven . . . that circles all: The Empyrean. *of love*: Note the special aptness of "holy love" to the state of these sinners whose crime was unholy love.

77–78. Caesar . . . "Queen": Suetonius (*Caesar*, 49) reports Caesar's homosexual relation with Nicomedes, the conquered King of Bithynia, and that he was called "The Queen of Bithynia" for it, his soldiers singing a lampoon that ran:

> *Gallias Caesar subegit, Nicomedes Caesarem;*
> *Ecce Caesar nunc triumphat, qui subegit Gallias;*
> *Nicomedes non triumphat, quit subegit Caesarem.*

The point of the lampoon lies in a pun on the word *subegit*—"put under" or "conquered." Thus:

Caesar put Gaul under; Nicomedes, Caesar.
Now behold Caesar triumphant who put Gaul under,
But not Nicomedes who put Caesar under.

80–81. *by their shame they aid the fire*: To do its purifying work. The pains of Purgatory are willed joyously by those who endure them. Both the flame and the shame therefore are a gladly offered penance. In Dante's view, the fire itself would be meaningless (and Infernal rather than Purgatorial) without the shame (a true act of contrition).

82–84. *hermaphroditic*: Heterosexual. These sinners were guilty of abandoning themselves to lust, but not of mating with their own sex. *human law*: Those restraints that govern human but not animal behavior, and which are the functions of intelligence and of a moral sense. To lose those restraints is to be bestial, and therefore the example of Pasiphaë in the Rein of Lust.

87. *the mock-beast*: The "cow" in which Pasaphaë crouched, and which consisted of a hide stretched over a framework.

92. *Guido Guinizelli*: Guido di Guinizelli de' Principi (GWEE-doh dee Gwee-nee-TZEH-lee day PREEN-chee-pee). Vernacular poet of the mid-thirteenth century, esteemed as a forerunner of the sweet new style. Died 1276. *here so soon*: Since Guido had been dead only twenty-four years by 1300, his full repentance spared him a long delay.

94–96. *Lycurgus' darkest hour*: Hypsipyle, wife of Jason, to whom she had borne twin sons, Thoas and Euneus, was captured by pirates and sold to Lycurgus, King of Nemea. She was appointed nurse of the king's infant son.

When she met the parched heroes who fought against Thebes (XXII, 112, note) she put the baby down on the grass long enough to point out the spring called Langia. While she was gone, the infant was bitten by a poisonous snake. Lycurgus condemned her to death for negligence, and she was on the point of being executed when her sons (they had been sent to Nemea by Dionysus) discovered her, rushed to embrace her, and won her release.

Dante's point is that he felt upon discovering the identity of Guinizelli as the twins had felt on discovering their lost mother. He adds, however, that he could not match their actions in racing to embrace her, for he was prevented by the fire. (Note, also, that in basing his figure on an incident narrated in the *Thebaid*, Dante is once more registering the presence of Statius.) Statius' earlier feeling for Virgil forms another parallel.

98. *my betters*: There is some disagreement as to whether or not Dante meant to rate himself among the six greatest poets of all time in narrating his reception in Limbo. Considering his confessed pride, and his willingness to point out how well he can accomplish certain poetic feats that no other has equaled (see *Inferno*, XXV, 91–99, and XXXII, 7–9), I believe Dante knew very well how good he was, and that he had few betters. This phrasing, therefore, is best taken as a compliment to the generation of poets that preceded him, its tone set by his wish to honor Guido Guinizelli. One must also recognize, however, that Dante distinguished between *poeti* (poets) and *rimatori* (versifiers). Here, "betters" could mean "as versifiers."

113. *modern usage*: Of writing about love in the spoken tongue rather than in Latin or in elaborate euphuisms. The Sweet New Style.

169-A

119–120. *Limoges produced a better*: Girault de Bornelh, of Limoges, a rival poet.

121–123. I have all but abandoned Dante's phrasing here in attempting to convey his meaning. Literally rendered, the passage reads: "They turn their faces to rumor (*i.e.*, to what is being said, *i.e.*, to reputation) more than to the truth (of merit in the writing) and so they fix their opinions before they have heeded art or reason."

124. *Guittone*: See XXIV, 56, and note. *our fathers*: Dante says *antichi*, the primary meaning of which is "the ancients" but which can also mean simply "gone by." Guittone died in 1294, and Guinizelli, though only thirty-two years old, in 1276.

131. *as far as it may serve*: The souls in Purgatory cannot yield to temptation, for their power to sin has been taken from them. Thus the supplication "and lead us not into temptation but deliver us from evil" could not apply to them. One could argue, too, that Purgatorial souls do not need their "daily bread," but "bread" can, of course, be taken to mean "spiritual sustenance." In any case, the point is that not all of the Lord's Prayer is apt to the state of the Purgatorial souls.

136–139. *that shade he had pointed to*: Arnaut Daniel, Provençal poet of the second half of the twelfth century. He was especially given to intricate rhyme structures and elaborate phrasing and is generally credited with having invented the sestina. Many commentators have wondered why Dante held him up for such high praise, for his work seems rather more elaborate than compelling to most readers. Perhaps it was Dante's particular passion for elaborate structural relations and for such devices as the *UOM* of Canto XII that drew him to Daniel.

140–147. DANIEL'S REPLY. Daniel replies, in the original, not in Italian, but in the *langue d'oc*, the Provençal tongue in which he wrote. Since some obvious shift of language is necessary here, and since Daniel's would seem an antique and a courtly tongue to Dante, I have rendered his lines into what can best be called a desperate attempt at bastard Spenserian. *faring*: going. *blistful*: blissful. *redeth*: leads. *amount*: mount.

Canto XXVII

A little before sunset of the third day on the Mountain the Poets come to
the further limit of the Seventh Cornice and are greeted by *The Angel of
Chastity*, who tells them they must pass through the wall of fire. Dante
recoils in terror, but Virgil persuades him to enter in Beatrice's name.

They are guided through the fire by a chant they hear coming from the
other side. Emerging, they find it is sung by *The Angel Guardian* of the
Earthly Paradise, who stands in a light so brilliant that Dante cannot see
him. (It is probably here that *The Last P* is stricken from Dante's brow.
Or perhaps it was consumed by the fire.)

The Angel hurries them toward the ascent, but night overtakes them,
and the Poets lie down to sleep, each on the step on which he finds himself. (For Statius it will be the last sleep, since there is no night in
Heaven.) There, just before Dawn, Dante has a prophetic *Dream of Leah
and Rachel*, which foreshadows the appearance, above, of Matilda and Beatrice.

Day arrives; the Poets rise and race up the rest of the ascent until they
come in sight of *The Earthly Paradise*. Here *Virgil Speaks His Last Words*,
for the Poets have now come to the limit of Reason, and Dante is now free
to follow his every impulse, since all motion of sin in him has been purged
away.

As the day stands when the Sun begins to glow
   over the land where his Maker's blood was shed,
   and the scales of Libra ride above the Ebro,   3

while Ganges' waters steam in the noonday glare—
   so it stood, the light being nearly faded,
   when we met God's glad Angel standing there   6

on the rocky ledge beyond the reach of the fire,
   and caroling *"Beati mundo corde"*
   in a voice to which no mortal could aspire.   9

Then: "Blessèd ones, till by flame purified
   no soul may pass this point. Enter the fire
   and heed the singing from the other side."   12

These were his words to us when we had come
   near as we could, and hearing them, I froze
   as motionless as one laid in his tomb.   15

I lean forward over my clasped hands and stare
   into the fire, thinking of human bodies
   I once saw burned, and once more see them there.   18

My kindly escorts heard me catch my breath
and turned, and Virgil said: "Within that flame
there may be torment, but there is no death.   21

Think well, my son, what dark ways we have trod . . .
I guided you unharmed on Geryon:
shall I do less now we are nearer God?   24

Believe this past all doubt: were you to stay
within that womb of flame a thousand years,
it would not burn a single hair away.   27

And if you still doubt my sincerity,
but reach the hem of your robe into the flame:
your hands and eyes will be your guarantee.   30

My son, my son, turn here with whole assurance.
Put by your fears and enter to your peace."
And I stood fixed, at war with my own conscience.   33

And seeing me still stubborn, rooted fast,
he said, a little troubled: "Think, my son,
you shall see Beatrice when this wall is past."   36

As Pyramus, but one breath from the dead,
opened his eyes when he heard Thisbe's name,
and looked at her, when the mulberry turned red—   39

just so my hard paralysis melted from me,
and I turned to my Leader at that name
which wells forever in my memory;   42

at which he wagged his head, as at a child
won over by an apple. Then he said:
"Well, then, what are we waiting for?" and smiled.   45

He turned then and went first into the fire,
requesting Statius, who for some time now
had walked between us, to bring up the rear.   48

Once in the flame, I gladly would have cast
my body into boiling glass to cool it
against the measureless fury of the blast.   51

My gentle father, ever kind and wise,
strengthened me in my dread with talk of Beatrice,
saying: "I seem already to see her eyes."   54

From the other side, to guide us, rose a paean,
and moving toward it, mindless of all else,
we emerged at last where the ascent began.   57

There I beheld a light that burned so brightly
I had to look away; and from it rang:
"*Venite benedicti patris mei.*"   60

"Night falls," it added, "the sun sinks to rest;
    do not delay but hurry toward the height
    while the last brightness lingers in the west."   63

Straight up through the great rock-wall lay the way
    on such a line that, as I followed it,
    my body blocked the sun's last level ray.   66

We had only climbed the first few stairs as yet
    when I and my two sages saw my shadow
    fade from me; and we knew the sun had set.   69

Before the vast sweep of the limned horizon
    could fade into one hue and night win all
    the immeasurable air to its dominion,   72

each made the step on which he stood his bed,
    for the nature of the Mount not only stopped us
    but killed our wish to climb, once day had fled.   75

As goats on a rocky hill will dance and leap,
    nimble and gay, till they find grass, and then,
    while they are grazing, grow as tame as sheep   78

at ease in the green shade when the sun is high
    and the shepherd stands by, leaning on his staff,
    and at his ease covers them with his eye—   81

and as the herdsman beds down on the ground,
    keeping his quiet night watch by his flock
    lest it be scattered by a wolf or hound;   84

just so we lay there, each on his stone block,
    I as the goat, they as my guardians,
    shut in on either side by walls of rock.   87

I could see little ahead—rock blocked the way—
    but through that little I saw the stars grow larger,
    brighter than mankind sees them. And as I lay,   90

staring and lost in thought, a sleep came on me—
    the sleep that oftentimes presents the fact
    before the event, a sleep of prophecy.   93

At the hour, I think, when Venus, first returning
    out of the east, shone down upon the mountain—
    she who with fires of love comes ever-burning—   96

I dreamed I saw a maiden innocent
    and beautiful, who walked a sunny field
    gathering flowers, and caroling as she went: 99

"Say I am Leah if any ask my name,
    and my white hands weave garlands wreath on wreath
    to please me when I stand before the frame   102

of my bright glass. For this my fingers play
  among these blooms. But my sweet sister Rachel
  sits at her mirror motionless all day.   105

To stare into her own eyes endlessly
  is all her joy, as mine is in my weaving.
  She looks, I do. Thus live we joyously."   108

Now eastward the new day rayed Heaven's dome
  (the sweeter to the returning wanderer
  who wakes from each night's lodging nearer home),   111

and the shadows fled on every side as I
  stirred from my sleep and leaped upon my feet,
  seeing my Lords already standing by.   114

"This is the day your hungry soul shall be
  fed on the golden apples men have sought
  on many different boughs so ardently."   117

These were the very words which, at the start,
  my Virgil spoke to me, and there have never
  been gifts as dear as these were to my heart.   120

Such waves of yearning to achieve the height
  swept through my soul, that at each step I took
  I felt my feathers growing for the flight.   123

When we had climbed the stairway to the rise
  of the topmost step, there with a father's love
  Virgil turned and fixed me with his eyes.   126

"My son," he said, "you now have seen the torment
  of the temporary and the eternal fires;
  here, now, is the limit of my discernment.   129

I have led you here by grace of mind and art;
  now let your own good pleasure be your guide;
  you are past the steep ways, past the narrow part.   132

See there the sun that shines upon your brow,
  the sweet new grass, the flowers, the fruited vines
  which spring up without need of seed or plow.   135

Until those eyes come gladdened which in pain
  moved me to come to you and lead your way,
  sit there at ease or wander through the plain.   138

Expect no more of me in word or deed:
  here your will is upright, free, and whole,
  and you would be in error not to heed   141

whatever your own impulse prompts you to:
  lord of yourself I crown and mitre you."

Notes

1–4. *As the day stands*: Meaning of this passage: It is shortly before sunset of the third day on the Mountain. Dante's details here are the reverse of those given at the opening of II, which see. *the land where his Maker's blood was shed*: Jerusalem. *the Ebro*: For Spain.

6. *God's glad Angel*: The Angel of Chastity. He is standing on the narrow rocky path outside the wall of fire.

8. *Beati mundo corde*: "Blessed are the pure in heart [for they shall see God]." (*Matthew*, v, 8.)

10–12. THE WALL OF FLAMES. It is, of course, the fire in which the Lustful are purified. It is also the legendary wall of fire that surrounded the Earthly Paradise. Note that all souls must pass through that fire. The readiest interpretation of that fact is that every soul must endure some purification before it can approach God (theoretically, a soul could climb Purgatory and endure no pain but this). Since no man's soul is perfect in its love, moreover, it must endure the fire that purifies impure love. Additionally, the allegorical intent may be that no man is entirely free of Lust. Having reached the Earthly Paradise, the soul has reached the Perfection of the Active Life. Below, its motion has been *toward* perfection. Now, after a few final rituals, the soul *becomes* perfect, and therefore changeless.

16. *I lean forward over my clasped hands*: Dante's hands must be clasped a bit below the waist. It is an odd posture, but it is also oddly Dantean.

17–18. *bodies I once saw burned*: Dante must mean as a witness at an execution. Burnings at the stake generally took place in public squares. They were a rather common spectacle. Dante's sentence of exile, it is relevant to note, decreed that he was to be burned if taken on Florentine territory.

23. Geryon: The Monster of Fraud. See *Inferno*, XVII, 1 ff., note.

37–39. *Pyramus . . . Thisbe*: Famous tragic lovers of Babylon. Ovid (*Metamorphoses*, IV, 55–166) tells their story. At a tryst by a mulberry (which in those days bore white fruit) Thisbe was frightened by a lion and ran off, dropping her veil. The lion, his jaws bloody from a recent kill, tore at the veil, staining it with blood. Pyramus, arriving later, saw the stained veil, concluded that Thisbe was dead, and stabbed himself. Thisbe, returning, found him and cried to him to open his eyes for his Thisbe. At that name Pyramus opened his eyes, looked at her, and died, Thisbe, invoking the tree to darken in their memory, thereupon stabbed herself. (*Cf.* Shakespeare's *Romeo and Juliet*.) The mulberry roots drank their blood and the fruit turned red ever after.

40. *my hard paralysis melted*: Note how Dante describes his emotions throughout this passage. He is afraid, to be sure. But the fear is of his human body and habit. His soul yearns forward, but his body will not obey until Reason has overcome mortal habit.

58. *a light*: This is the Angel Guardian of the Earthly Paradise. He corresponds to the Angel guarding the Gate. At every other ascent in Purgatory, Dante has met one angel. Here, he meets two, one on either side of the fire. It is the song of this Angel that has guided the Poets through the flames. In all probability, too, it is this Angel that strikes away the final *P* from Dante's brow (or perhaps it was consumed in the fire). It is unlikely that the Final P was removed by the Angel of Chastity, since the Poets had not yet been through the fire, *i.e.*, had not really crossed all of the Cornice.

60. *Venite benedicti patris mei*: "Come ye blessèd of my Father." (*Matthew*, xxv, 34.)

68. *my shadow*: Virgil and Statius, of course, cast none.

94. *At the hour . . . when Venus, first returning*: Venus is in the sign of Pisces, which immediately precedes Aries, in which sign the sun now is. It is, therefore, Venus Morningstar. Thus it is the hour before dawn, in which the truth is dreamed.

97–108. DANTE'S DREAM. Leah and Rachel were, respectively, the first- and second-born daughters of Laban and the first and second wives of Jacob. Many authors before Dante had interpreted them as representing the Active and the Contemplative Life of the Soul. Leah's white hands (*le belle mani*) symbolize the Active Life, as Rachel's eyes (lines 104–108) symbolize the Contemplative Life.

Since it is the truth Dante is dreaming, these figures must foreshadow others, as the eagle of his earlier dream (IX, 19 ff.) represented Lucia. Thus Leah prefigures Matilda, who will appear soon, and Rachel prefigures Beatrice, who will appear soon thereafter. But just as the eagle is not to be confused with Lucia, so Leah and Rachel are not to be narrowly identified with Matilda and Beatrice except as allegorical dream equivalents, for Matilda and Beatrice may very well be taken, as part of their total allegory, to represent the Active and the Contemplative Life of the Soul.

127. ff. *"My son,"* he said: These are Virgil's last words, for the Poets have now reached the extreme limit of Reason's (and Art's) competence. Virgil continues

awhile with Dante into the Earthly Paradise (walking, one should note, behind rather than ahead of Dante) but he has no more to say. A little later in fact (XXIX, 55–57) when Dante turns to Virgil out of old habit as if for an explanation of the strange and marvelous sights he comes on, he receives in answer only a look as full of awe as his own. And later yet (XXX, 43 ff.), when Dante turns from Beatrice to look for him, Virgil has vanished.

For Virgil has now performed all that he had promised at their first meeting (*Inferno*, I, 88 ff.), and Dante's soul is now free to obey its every impulse, for it now contains nothing but Good.

143. *I crown and mitre you*: Crown as king of your physical self and mitre (as a bishop) as lord of your soul. Dante has not, by much, achieved the full lordship of his soul, but he has achieved as much as Virgil (Reason) can confer upon him. A bishop's mitre, though it confers great authority, does not confer final authority. And a king, for that matter, may still be subject to an emperor, as he certainly would be, in Dante's view, to God.

Canto XXVIII

It is the morning of the Wednesday after Easter, Dante's fourth day on the Mountain, and having been crowned Lord of Himself by Virgil, Dante now takes the lead for the first time, wandering at his leisure into *The Sacred Wood* of the Earthly Paradise until his way is blocked by the waters of *Lethe.*

His feet stopped, Dante sends his eyes on to wander that Wood and there suddenly appears to him a solitary lady singing and gathering flowers. She is *Matilda,* who symbolizes *The Active Life of the Soul.*

In reply to Dante's entreaty, Matilda approaches to the other bank of the river. So standing, three paces across from him, she offers to answer all that Dante wishes to ask. Dante replies that he is in some confusion about the sources of the wind and the water of the Earthly Paradise. Matilda promises to dispel the mists from his understanding and proceeds to explain in great detail *The Natural Phenomena of The Earthly Paradise,* which is to say, the source of the wind, the vegetation, and the water. She further explains the special powers of the water of *Lethe* and of *Eunoë* and concludes with some remarks on the errors of the ancient poets in the location of the Earthly Paradise. At her last words, Dante turns to his two ancient poets to see how they are taking her remarks. Finding them smiling, he turns back once more to Matilda.

> Eager now to explore in and about
>   the luxuriant holy forest evergreen
>   that softened the new light, I started out,   3

> without delaying longer, from the stair
>   and took my lingering way into the plain
>   on ground that breathed a fragrance to the air.   6

> With no least variation in itself
>   and with no greater force than a mild wind,
>   the sweet air stroked my face on that sweet shelf,   9

> and at its touch the trembling branches swayed,
>   all bending toward that quarter into which
>   the holy mountain cast its morning shade;   12

> yet not so far back that in any part
>   of that sweet wood the small birds in the tops
>   had reason to stop practicing their art;   15

> but bursting with delight those singing throngs
>   within their green tents welcomed the new breeze
>   that murmured a sweet burden of their songs   18

> like that one hears gathering from bough to bough
>   of the pine wood there on Chiassi's shore
>   when Aeolus lets the Sirocco blow.   21

I had already come, slow bit by bit,
　so far into that ancient holy wood
　I could not see where I had entered it;　　　　24

when I came upon a stream that blocked my way.
　To my left it flowed, its wavelets bending back
　the grasses on its banks as if in play.　　　　27

The purest waters known to man would seem
　to have some taint of sediment within them
　compared to those, for though that holy stream　　30

flows darkly there, its surface never lit
　in its perpetual shade by any shaft
　of sun or moon, nothing could hide in it.　　　　33

My feet stopped, but my eyes pursued their way
　across that stream, to wander in delight
　the variousness of everblooming May.　　　　36

And suddenly—as rare sights sometimes do,
　the wonder of them driving from the mind
　all other thoughts—I saw come into view　　　39

a lady, all alone, who wandered there
　singing, and picking flowers from the profusion
　with which her path was painted everywhere.　　42

"Fair lady who—if outward looks and ways
　bear, as they ought, true witness to the heart—
　have surely sunned yourself in Love's own rays,　　45

be pleased," I said to her, "to draw as near
　the bank of this sweet river as need be
　for me to understand the song I hear.　　　　48

You make me see in my imagining
　Persephone as she appeared that day
　her mother lost a daughter; she, the Spring."　　51

As a dancer, keeping both feet on the ground
　and close together, hardly putting one
　before the other, spins herself around—　　　54

so did she turn to me upon the red
　and yellow flowerlets, virgin modesty
　making her lower her eyes and bow her head.　　57

And she did all I asked, for she came forward
　till I not only heard the melody
　of what she sang, but made out every word.　　60

And when she stood where the bright grasses are
　bathed and bent by the waves of the clear river,
　she raised her eyes—and gave my soul a star.　　63

I cannot think so glorious a ray
    shot out of Venus' eyes that time her son
    wounded her inadvertently in play.   66

There, on the other bank, smiling she stood
    and gathered to her arms more of the flowers
    that sprang up without seeds in that high wood.   69

The stream between us was three paces wide,
    but the Hellespont where Persian Xerxes crossed
    to leave a dire example to all pride,   72

in its raging between Sestos and Abydos,
    caused less hate in Leander than this in me,
    for not dividing so that I might cross.   75

"You are newcomers, and perhaps you find
    because I smile," she said, "here in this place
    chosen to be the nest of humankind,   78

some doubt that makes you wonder at the sight.
    To pierce such mists as gather on your thoughts
    the psalm, *Delectasti me*, will give you light.   81

And you in front who first entreated me,
    speak if you would know more. I came prepared
    to answer you as fully as need be."   84

"The way the wood hums and the waters flow,"
    I said then, "are at odds with the conclusions
    I drew from what I heard a while ago."   87

"I shall explain from what cause," she replied,
    "these things that have confused your mind proceed,
    and thus brush its obscuring mist aside.   90

That Highest Good which only Itself can please
    made man good, and for goodness, and It gave him
    this place as earnest of eternal peace.   93

But man defaulted. All too brief his stay.
    Defaulted, and exchanged for tears and toil
    his innocent first laughter and sweet play.   96

When vapors of the earth and water meet
    a storm is born, below there. Now these vapors
    reach up, as far as possible, toward heat.   99

To guard man from such warring elements
    this mountain soared so high that no earth vapor
    could rise above the gate of penitence.   102

Now since the air revolves in one conjoint
    and perfect circuit with The Primal Motion,
    unless its wheel is broken at some point;   105

here at this altitude, where it goes round
  in its pure state, it strikes the foliage
  which, being dense, is made to give off sound.   108

The stricken plant impregnates the pure air
  with its particular powers, which are then borne
  on the great wheel and scattered everywhere;   111

and the other earth, according to the powers
  of soil and climate in its various zones,
  conceives and bears its various fruits and flowers.   114

When this is understood there, no man need
  believe it strange when plants take root and spring
  out of the earth without apparent seed.   117

Know, too, the sacred soil on which you stand
  is bursting-full of species of all sorts,
  and bears fruits never picked by human hand.   120

The water you see here is from no source
  that needs replenishment from cloudy vapors,
  like streams that rise and fall: with constant force   123

it leaves a fountain that receives again,
  from God's Will, every drop that it pours forth
  to the two streams it sends across this plain.   126

On this side, it removes as it flows down
  all memory of sin; on that, it strengthens
  the memory of every good deed done.   129

It is called Lethe here: Eunoë there.
  And one must drink first this and then the other
  to feel its powers. No sweetness can compare   132

with the savor of these waters. And although
  you may at once, and with no more instruction,
  drink your soul's fill from the eternal flow,   135

let me bestow one thing more for good measure.
  Though I exceed my promise, I cannot think
  what I add now will meet with your displeasure.   138

Those ancients who made songs to celebrate
  man's Age of Gold, placed probably on Parnassus
  this perfect garden of his first pure state.   141

Here mankind lived its innocent first days.
  Here is the Eternal Spring and every fruit.
  This is the nectar that the poets praise."   144

She paused, I turned around to face my lords,
  the poets whose strains had honored ancient song,
  and saw they had received her final words   147

with smiles that lingered yet upon their faces;
then turned back to that lady of glad graces.

Notes

3. *softened the new light*: In its green shade. It is the morning of the Wednesday after Easter, the beginning of Dante's fourth day on the Mountain, and the last of his Divine Journey, for he will complete his tour of Heaven in less than a day. *I started out*: Note that for the first time it is Dante who leads the way in his new state as "king of himself."

11. *that quarter*: The West.

20. *the pine wood there on Chiassi's shore*: Chiassi (now Classe) was the seaport of Ravenna in 1300. It is now a desolate place left behind by the recession of the Adriatic.

21. *Aeolus*: In ancient mythology the god who kept the winds in his cave and controlled their blowing. *the Sirocco*: The South Wind, which in Italy is the wind from Africa.

36. *everblooming May*: See line 143. It is eternally springtime in the Earthly Paradise.

40. *a lady, all alone*: Matilda. She may be taken, as foreshadowed in Dante's dream of Leah and Rachel, to symbolize the Active Life of the Soul. She is the innocence that guides Dante through the Earthly Paradise to Beatrice. Thus, she is the intermediary between Human Reason and the various manifestations of Beatrice as Divine Love, Faith, the Contemplative Life of the Soul, and the Church Triumphant, among others.

There has been a great deal of speculation among commentators concerning her possible historical identity. Dante clearly treats her as someone he recognizes at once, for he does not ask her name. And later (XXXIII, 119) when her name is mentioned, he asks none of his usual questions about her identity.

Nevertheless there seems to be no point in trying to identify her with any historic person. The allegorical point may very well be that, having achieved the Earthly Paradise by his own active pursuit of the Good, Dante instantly recognizes the Active Life of the Soul. He has, moreover, just had a prophetic dream of her coming.

45. *sunned yourself in Love's own rays*: In the light of God.

50. *Persephone*: Daughter of Demeter (whose name signifies "Mother Earth"), the goddess of vegetation. One day, as Persephone was gathering flowers in a field, she was carried off to the lower world of Hades (with the consent of Zeus, her fathear). At the insistence of Demeter, Zeus sent Hermes to fetch her back. Persephone, however, had eaten a quarter of a fateful pomegranate and, in consequence, could only return for three quarters of each year, being forced to return to the lower world for the fourth quarter.

Thus Persephone represents the vegetative cycle, spending spring, summer, and fall with Demeter (as Mother Earth) but descending to the lower world (into the ground) for the winter. When she is in the lower world she rules beside her husband as the goddess of the dead, but she forever returns to her mother as the virgin daughter (spring). Matilda not only reminds Dante of Persephone, but of Persephone as she was in that original springtime before she was carried off to the lower world.

51. *she, the Spring*: The flowers fell from Persephones' arms when Hades abducted her. Dante certainly means "the Spring" as both those lost flowers, and as the unchanging springtime of the world's first innocence. The myth, of course, is obviously concerned with the idea of virgin innocence, and as obviously related to the Christian myth of the *Fall*.

65-66. *Venus'* . . . *her son*: Cupid was playing with his mother one day when one of the arrows in his quiver scratched her breast by accident and she was smitten with love of Adonis, the son of Myrrha by her own father (see *Inferno*, XXX, 38, and note). Ovid tells the story in *Metamorphoses*, X, 525 ff.

69. *that sprang up without seeds*: Here, in XVII, 115 ff., and below in 109–111, 114–117, and 118–119, Dante refers to seeds and to plants springing up without seed. At this point he seems quite clearly to intend, as suggested by *Genesis*, that the newly created earth brought forth of itself. At other times he seems to intend something like the distribution of plants by wind-borne seeds. I have not been able to satisfy myself on the exact nature of his theory on this point. Note that he does not deny that most earthly plants grow from seed, but declares that *some* plants spring up without apparent seed. He could mean that *new species* arise in consequence of wind-borne influences from the Earthly Paradise, thereafter reproducing themselves from their seed.

70. *three paces*: May symbolize the three steps to true repentance (contrition, confession, and the rendering of satisfaction), thereby repeating the motif of the three steps that lead to the Gate.

71. *Hellespont*: Now called the Dardanelles, the strait between Europe and Asia Minor. It is famous for its raging currents. *Xerxes*: Son of Darius, the Persian king. In 485 B.C. Xerxes crossed the Hellespont on a bridge of ships to invade Greece. Decisively defeated in a sea battle off Salamis, Xerxes fled back across the Hellespont undone, thus leaving to all posterity a dire example of the downfall of pride.

73-74. *Sestos and Abydos*: Cities on the Hellespont in, respectively, Greece and

Asia Minor. The Hellespont is about a mile wide between them. *Leander*: A young man of Abydos who fell in love with Hero, a priestess of Aphrodite at Sestos. Because of her position and of family opposition, they could not marry but decided to meet clandestinely every night. Leander swimming to her across the Hellespont, guided by a light from Hero's tower. One night the light blew out and Leander lost his direction, was carried off by the current, and drowned. The next morning Hero found his body washed ashore and threw herself into the current. The story of Hero and Leander has been told by countless poets, none of whom thought to provide him with a rowboat.

78. *the nest of humankind*: The Earthly Paradise is the Garden of Eden.

81. *Delectasti me*: Psalm XCII, "I will triumph in the works of Thy hands." Matilda's phrase is from verse 4: "For Thou, Lord, hast made me glad through Thy work" (*Quia delectasti me, Domine, in factura tua*). The light the psalm will give, of course, is the fact that Matilda smiles for sheer joy in God's works.

87. *what I heard a while ago*: In XXI, 40–57, Statius told Dante that no rain nor snow could fall, nor any variation in the weather occur above the Gate. Dante's confusion arises from the fact that he cannot see how to take the wind he feels, nor the waters he sees flowing, except as products of earthly weathers.

91. *That Highest Good, which only Itself can please*: Two ideas central to Dante's thinking are expressed in this phrasing.

The first is Dante's idea of purification. God is conceived as perfect goodness. As such, He can be pleased only by perfect goodness. In that estate He made man. And to that spiritual state man, since the Fall, must strive to return in order to regain God, who will take to Himself only the perfection He originally created.

The second, basic to all Dante's conception of the Earthly Paradise (and later of Heaven) is that perfection is unchangeable. God, being perfect, cannot change, since any change from perfection would necessarily be toward imperfection. It is the lot of fallen man that is beset by chance and change, he being imperfect. Thus the perfection of the fruit in the garden. And thus the perfect clearness of the waters, and the fact that they do not have their source in the chance changes of evaporation and condensation, but flow at a constant (unchanging) rate from the fountain of the Will of God.

97–99. *When vapors of the earth and water meet*: This is Dante's basic conception of the origin of storms in the clash of earthy (fiery) and watery vapors (see *Inferno*, XXIV, 145–147). *toward heat*: Toward the Sun. These vapors (evaporations) are produced by heat and seek, by natural affinity, to rise to the Sun that called them forth.

103–108. *Now since the air revolves in one conjoint . . .*: The earth is conceived as standing still while the atmosphere moves from East to West at the constant rate imparted to it, as to the heavenly spheres, by the Primum Mobile. On the earth's surface the air is deflected by many obstructions (surface turbulence) that make it flow in all directions, but at the altitude of the Earthly Paradise one experiences only the air's unperturbed original motion. This is the "mild wind" Dante felt (lines 8–9), as it is the wind that makes the whole wood murmur (lines 17–18).

109–120. (See also note to line 69.) The phrasing here seems to suggest that all earthly plants have their origins in "virtues" or "powers" (somehow distinct from seeds). They impart these virtues to the wind that bears them around the world as wind-borne gifts of Heaven. On earth, if soil and climate favor, these "virtues" cause new species to spring up (which then reproduce themselves from their own seeds). But since no earthly soil and climate is perfect (unchanging), no zone on earth can raise all plants, whereas in the Earthly Paradise *all* created plants may be found, including species unknown to mankind since the Fall.

130. *Lethe*: In classical mythology, a river of Hades from which the souls of the dead drink forgetfulness of their first existence. Dante, with his usual readiness to adapt ancient mythology to his own purposes, places it in the Earthly Paradise, and gives it the power (directly related to its original power) of washing from the souls who drink of it, every last memory of sin. Note, too, that Dante's Lethe (*Inferno*, XXXIV, 133) flows down to the bottom of Hell, bearing down to Satan, to be frozen into the filthy ice around him, the last lost vestiges of the sins of the saved.

Eunoë: Having adapted Lethe to his purpose, Dante invents as its complement Eunoë (the name meaning, literally, "good memory") and gives it the power to strengthen every memory of good deeds done. The powers of the two rivers will not operate, however, unless one drinks from them in the right order. So drinking from them is surely an allegory of the way to Heaven: one must first drink of Lethe (leave all evil behind) and then of Eunoë (reawaken and strengthen every good in the soul).

146–147. *the poets*: Virgil and Statius would be two of the poets to whom Matilda refers. Dante turns around to see how they have taken her remarks about their errors. Finding them smiling at the receipt of such enlightenment, Dante turns back to Matilda. Line 146 and some of the detail of line 148 are my own invention, forced by the requirements of form and rhyme. Dante says literally: "I turned completely round to my poets, and saw they had received her last explanation with smiles; then turned my face to the gracious lady."

Canto XXIX

The Heavenly Pageant

Chanting a blessing on those whose sins are forgiven, Matilda moves
upstream along one bank of Lethe, and Dante keeps pace with her on the
other side. A glorious light and a sweet melody grow on the air, filling
Dante with such rapture that he cries out against Eve's daring, through
which such joys were lost to mankind.

Soon thereafter he sees the approach of *The Heavenly Pageant*. It is led
by *Seven Golden Candelabra* that paint *A Seven-Striped Rainbow* on the
sky. Behind them come *Twenty-Four Elders* (the Books of the Old Testament), and behind them *Four Beasts* (the Four Gospels), who guard *A
Triumphal Chariot* (the Church), drawn by a *Griffon* (Christ). At the
right wheel of the Chariot dance *The Three Theological Virtues*; at its left
wheel, *The Four Cardinal Virtues*. This group is followed, in order, by
Two Elders representing Luke as the author of *Acts* and Paul as the author
of the fourteen epistles; by *Four Elders* representing James, Peter, John, and
Jude as authors of the four Catholic epistles; and finally by *A Single Elder*
representing John as the author of *Revelation*.

When the Chariot reaches a point directly across from Dante, a thunderclap resounds, and the entire pageant halts upon that signal.

> Her words done, she began her song again—
>   *Beati quorum tecta sunt peccata*—
>   as if in love when love is free of pain.   3
>
> As nymphs of old went wandering alone
>   through the deep-shaded woodlands, some pursuing,
>   and others seeking to evade, the Sun;   6
>
> so, then, she started up the riverside
>   and, on my own bank, I kept pace with her,
>   matching her little steps with shortened stride.   9
>
> Some fifty paces each we moved this way,
>   when both banks curved as one; and now I found
>   my face turned to the cradle of the day.   12
>
> Nor had we gone as far again, all told,
>   beyond the curve, when she turned to me, saying:
>   "Dear brother, look and listen." And behold!—   15
>
> through all that everlasting forest burst
>   an instantaneous flood of radiance.
>   I took it for a lightning-flash at first.   18

But lightning comes and goes. The light I saw
   not only stayed on but grew more resplendent.
   "What can this be?" I asked myself in awe.   21

And a sweet melody filled the bright air—
   so sweet that I reproached in righteous zeal
   Eve's fatal recklessness. How could she dare?—   24

one woman alone, made but a moment since—
   all heaven and earth obedient—to refuse
   the one veil willed by High Omnipotence;   27

beneath which, had she stayed God's acolyte,
   I should have known before then, and for longer
   those raptures of ineffable delight.   30

My soul hung tranced in joy beyond all measure
   and yearning for yet more, as I moved on
   through those first fruits of the eternal pleasure;   33

when, under the green boughs that spread before us
   the air became a blaze, and the sweet sound
   we had been hearing grew into a chorus.   36

O holy, holy, Virgins, if for you
   I ever suffered vigils, cold, or fasts,
   occasion spurs me now to claim my due.   39

Empty all Helicon! Now is the time!
   Urania, help me here with your full choir,
   to bring things scarce conceivable to rhyme!   42

I saw next, far ahead, what I believed
   were seven golden trees (at such a distance
   and in such light the eye can be deceived);   45

but in a while, when I had drawn so near
   that chance resemblances confused by distance
   no longer made false images appear,   48

that power that reaps for reason's mill could see
   that they were candelabra; and in the chant
   it heard that word *Hosanna!* ringing free.   51

Above the gold array flamed seven times seven
   candles more lucent than the mid-month moon
   at midnight in the calm of clearest heaven.   54

I turned about, amazed at what I saw,
   to my good Virgil, and he answered me
   in silence, with a look of equal awe.   57

I turned back then to those sublimities
   that were approaching at so slow a pace
   that new brides might outdistance them with ease.   60

The lady cried: "Why have you set your mind
  so fixedly upon those living lights
  that you do not observe what comes behind?" 63

Then I saw people walking like attendants
  behind their lords, and clothed in robes so white
  earth has no snow of such a pure resplendence. 66

Upon my left the polished river shone
  bright as a mirror, and when I looked in
  I saw my left side there, perfectly drawn. 69

And when I had moved close enough to be
  kept at a distance by no more than water,
  I halted my slow steps, better to see. 72

I saw the flames advance, leaving the air
  painted behind, as if by massive strokes,
  or by bright pennons they were trailing there; 75

thus, all the trailing heavens were aglow
  with seven bands of light of the same color
  as Delia's girdle or Apollo's bow. 78

Those bands stretched back further than I could see,
  and the distance separating side from side
  came to ten paces, as it seemed to me. 81

And there, advancing two by two beneath
  that seven-striped sky came four-and-twenty elders,
  each crowned in glory with a lily-wreath. 84

And all sang with one voice, triumphantly:
  "Blessèd art thou among the daughters of Adam!
  Blessèd thy beauty to eternity!" 87

And when those souls elect, as in a dream,
  had left behind the flowers and the new grass
  that shone before me, there across the stream, 90

as star follows on star in the serene
  of heaven's height, there came on at their backs
  four beasts, and these wore wreaths of living green. 93

Each had three pairs of wings, and every pair
  was full of eyes. Were Argus living yet,
  his eyes would be most like what I saw there. 96

I cannot spend my rhymes as liberally
  as I should like to in describing them,
  for, reader, other needs are pressing me: 99

but read Ezekiel where he sets forth
  how they appeared to him in a great storm
  of wind and cloud and fire out of the North; 102

and such as he recounts, such did I see;
except that in the number of their wings
John differs with him, and agrees with me.   105

Within the space they guarded there came on
a burnished two-wheeled chariot in triumph,
and harnessed to the neck of a great Griffon   108

whose wings, upraised into the bands of light,
inclosed the middle one so perfectly
they cut no part of those to left or right.   111

Higher than sight its wing-tips soared away.
Its bird-like parts were gold; and white the rest
with blood-red markings. Will it serve to say   114

Rome never saw such a caparison,
no, not for Africanus, nor yet Augustus?
The Sun's own would seem shabby by comparison;   117

yes, even the Sun's own chariot, which strayed
and was destroyed in fire by Jove's dark justice
that day the frightened Earth devoutly prayed.   120

Beside the right wheel, dancing in a gyre,
three maidens came. The first one was so red
she would be barely visible in fire.   123

The second looked as if both flesh and bone
were made of flawless emerald. The third
seemed a new snow no slightest wind has blown.   126

And now the white one led the dance, and now
the red: and from the song the red one sang
the others took their measure, fast or slow.   129

Beside the left wheel, dancing in a flame
of purple robes, and led by one who had
three eyes within her head, four glad nymphs came.   132

Behind these seven came on, side by side,
two elders, different in dress, but both
by the same massive bearing dignified.   135

One showed he was a follower of the art
of great Hippocrates, whom Nature made
to heal the creatures dearest to her heart.   138

The other, his counterpart, carried a blade
so sharp and bright that at the sight of it,
even across the stream, I was afraid.   141

Next I saw four who walked with humble mien.
And last of all, one who moved in a trance,
as if asleep but his face was firm and keen.   144

These seven were robed like the first twenty-four
in flowing robes of white, but, for their crowns,
it was not wreaths of lilies that they wore, 147

but roses and whatever blooms most red.
One would have sworn, seeing them at a distance,
that they were wearing flames about the head. 150

And when the chariot had reached the place
across from me, I heard a thunderclap
that seemed a signal to those souls in grace, 153

for there, in unison with the exalted
first flaming standards, all that pageant halted.

Notes

2. *Beati quorum tecta sunt peccata*: This is Dante's elision of Psalm XXXII, 1: "Blessed are they [whose transgression is forgiven] whose sins are covered."
11. *both banks curved as one*: Note the regularity (constancy, perfection) of the river's curve.
12. *the cradle of the day*: The East.
23–30. *so sweet that I reproached . . .*: For having thrown away the glory of the Earthly Paradise by refusing to endure the one veil (of ignorance) under which, had Eve been dutiful, Dante would have known his present bliss since birth (hence, "before then, and for longer").
33. *the eternal pleasure*: The joys of Heaven. The joys of the Earthly Paradise are the first fruits of the great harvest to come.
37–42. INVOCATION OF THE MUSES. Dante is about to describe the entrance of the Heavenly Pageant, a spectacle of such splendor that it is difficult to conceive, let alone put into rhyme. For his great effort, therefore, he summons all the Muses from Helicon, calling upon Urania to preside, since she is the Muse of Astronomy, hence of heavenly things. (Her name in Greek means, literally, "the heavenly one." *O holy, holy Virgins*: The Nine Muses. *with your full choir*: With all the other Muses.
43 ff. THE HEAVENLY PAGEANT. The Pageant Dante now describes is an allegory of the Church Triumphant in the form of a religious procession or a formal masque in which devout mummers present themselves in allegorical guises. The center of the Pageant is the Chariot of The Church Triumphant, guarded by the Four Gospels, and attended on the right by the Three Theological Graces and on the left by the Four Cardinal Virtues. The Chariot itself is drawn by the Griffon, who represents the twofold nature of Christ as Man-and-God. Before this central group walk twenty-four Elders representing the books of the Old Testament. Behind the central group walk seven Elders representing the books of the New Testament. The entire procession is led by seven enormous Candelabra whose candles trail a rainbow canopy across the sky representing the Seven Gifts of the Spirit under which the Church moves.
Dante has not presented any allegory of such formality up to this point, and some readers have thought the allegory of the Pageant stiff and lifeless. One should bear in mind, however, that Dante is beginning to deal, now, not with reason but with revelation, and that the increased formality of his allegory here is apt to its content, and apt again in its resemblance to the rituals of the Church whose triumph he is representing. Note too, as distinct from the rest of Dante's allegory, that these figures do not enter as themselves (St. John, for example, appears in three guises) but as heavenly beings made up to represent others.
43–51. *I saw next . . .*: Dante sees in the distance what he takes to be seven trees of gold. Drawing nearer, he sees they are, in reality, enormous candelabra. At that point, too, he is close enough to make out that the word being sung by the chorus (line 36) which was first heard as a distant melody (line 21) is "Hosanna!" *chance resemblances*: Of the bases of the candelabra to tree trunks. *that power that reaps for reason's mill*: The discernment of the senses through which reason draws the data of nature from which it derives its concepts.
50. THE SEVEN CANDELABRA. On the Mountain the Lord specified to Moses the exact form of the seven-branched candelabrum of pure gold which was to be an essential part of the tabernacle (*Exodus*, xxv, 31–37). In *Revelation*, i. 12, John had

a vision of seven candelabra and interpreted them as seven churches (i, 20). Later (iv, 5) he interprets them as the Seven Gifts of the Holy Spirit (wisdom, understanding, counsel, might, knowledge, piety, and fear of the Lord). As the Candelabra advance in the van of the procession, their candles paint the sky overhead with a seven-striped rainbow that represents these Gifts. Thus, the Candelabra may be taken as the light and glory of God from which issue the Seven Gifts of the Holy Spirit. The Church follows where the Candelabra lead.

51. *Hosanna!*: (Literally, "Save, we pray!") On Palm Sunday as Christ was about to enter Jerusalem, he was hailed at Bethphage on the Mount of Olives with the words "Hosannah to the son of David!" (*Mathew*, xxi, 9.) The chant is especially apt in that Christ, as the Griffon, is about to enter in triumph.

56. *my good Virgil*: A new and much more familiar form of address signifying Dante's new state. Dante has always referred to Virgil with titles of honor and superiority.

57. *a look of equal awe*: Allegorically: Dante, out of old habit, turns to Reason for an explanation, but finds that Reason itself is overawed. Virgil has already explained (XXVII, 129) that he has passed the limit of his understanding.

60. *new brides*: Walking back from the altar. Hence, at a very slow pace. But even that pace would easily outdistance this procession.

64. *I saw people walking*: These are the figures made up as four and twenty elders who represent the books of the Old Testament as counted by St. Jerome in his *Gallican Psalter* (the twelve minor prophets are counted as one book, and so are *Ezra-Nehemiah, I and II Kings, I and II Samuel,* and *I and II Chronicles*). Thus the elders represent all Revelation before Christ. They wear white robes and wreaths of lilies as symbols of the purity of their faith. John has a vision of them in *Revelation,* iv, 4-5, and explains them, there, as the Twelve Patriarchs and the Twelve Apostles. In his vision they wore crowns of gold. Their song (lines 86–87) is an adaptation of the words used by Gabriel and Elisabeth in addressing Mary at the time of the Annunciation. (*Luke,* i, 28, 42.)

78. *Delia's girdle*: The rainbow-colored halo round the moon. Delia was another name for Diana, the moon goddess. *Apollo's bow*: The rainbow. Apollo was, of course, the Sun.

79–81. *stretched back further than I could see*: Allegorically, the Gifts of the Holy Spirit stretch further back into time than any man can reckon. *ten paces*: May certainly be taken as the Ten Commandments in which the Seven Gifts of the Holy Spirit were revealed, and through which they may be enjoyed.

93–105. THE FOUR BEASTS. They represent the Four Gospels of Matthew, Mark, Luke, and John that follow immediately upon the Old Testament. Their wreaths of living green signify Hope. The wings may be taken as signifying the speed with which the Gospels spread through the world. The fact that there are three pairs of wings obviously suggests the Trinity, and the eyes may be taken as Omniscience which is able to see past, present, and future. That much stated, Dante refers the reader to *Ezekiel,* i, 4–14, for a detailed description, except that they are there described as having only four wings, and Dante follows John (*Revelation,* iv, 8) in giving them six.

95. *Argus*: Jove made love to Io. Juno, in wifely jealousy, turned Io into a cow and set Argus of the hundred eyes to watch her. Mercury, sent by Jove, caused Argus to fall into an enchanted sleep and cut his head off. Juno set Argus' eyes in the tail of the peacock. Dante makes the point that the peacock's eyes, bright as they are, are dead, whereas the eyes in the feathers of these beasts are alive.

106 ff. THE CHARIOT OF THE CHURCH TRIUMPHANT. Within the square guarded by the Four Gospel Beasts the Church is represented by a chariot so splendid that Rome never saw its equal, not even in the triumphs of Scipio Africanus or of Augustus. The very chariot of the Sun could not compare with it.

Its two wheels may best be taken as representing the Old and the New Testament. It is drawn by the Griffon that represents Christ, and it is flanked by the Theological Virtues and the Cardinal Virtues.

108 ff. THE GRIFFON. A mythical figure with the fore parts of an eagle and the hind parts of a lion, here meant to represent the dual role of Christ as God and Man, his birdlike part divine, his lionlike part animal, hence human, and the unity of the two a symbol of his incarnation as the Word. His upraised wings, their tips soaring higher than the sight of man can follow, extend into the seven-striped heaven and inclose the central stripe representing MIGHT as the central Gift of the Holy Spirit and as a symbol of His triumph. The Griffon's coloration is probably suggested by *Song of Solomon,* v, 10–11: "My beloved is white and ruddy, the chiefest among ten thousand. His head is as the most fine gold."

118–120. *the Sun's own chariot, which strayed . . .*: The Chariot of the Sun was driven by Apollo. One day Phaëthon, Apollo's son, tried to drive it, but could not manage the horses. The chariot swerved from its path, scorching the sky and threatening to destroy the Earth. In terror Earth prayed to Jove for deliverance, and Jove destroyed the chariot with a thunderbolt. The scar left on the sky by Phaëthon's course became the Milky Way.

121–129. THE THREE THEOLOGICAL VIRTUES. They are Caritas (Christian Love), Faith, and Hope. Caritas is so red she could scarcely be seen in a fire. Hope is green, and Faith pure white. They dance in a ring at the Chariot's right wheel, and Faith and Caritas take turns leading the dance, while Hope (who cannot move except as Faith and Caritas direct) follows. Note that it is Caritas ("And the greatest of these is Charity") that sings the song to which they dance.

130–132. THE FOUR CARDINAL (OR NATURAL) VIRTUES. They are Prudence, Justice, Fortitude, and Temperance. They are dressed in the Imperial Purple, for they represent the Classical Virtues. Prudence, who leads them in their dance, has three eyes symbolizing that it is her duty to look at and consider the past, the present, and the future. Note, too, that the Classical and the Theological Virtues *must* go together if the soul is to develop.

133 ff. THE SEVEN ELDERS. These represent the remaining books of the New Testament (aside from the Four Gospels). Note that it is the books, not the persons, that are represented, for John appears three times in this procession; first as the Gospel, next as the Epistles, and finally as *Revelation*. Thus the first two are *Acts* and the Fourteen Epistles. The next four are the Catholic Epistles. And the final single figure is *Revelation*. They wear wreaths of brightest red to signify the ardor of Caritas.

136–137. *One showed he was a follower of the art of great Hippocrates*: Luke, as the author of *Acts*. In *Colossians*, iv, 14, Paul describes him as "the beloved physician." He is the doctor of souls, as Hippocrates was the doctor of bodies.

139–141. *The other, his counterpart*: The figure is Paul. The sword he carries may symbolize his martyrdom by a sword, or more aptly "the sword of the Spirit, which is the word of God." (*Ephesians*, vi, 17.) Thus he is here the taker rather than the healer of lives, as presented in the Epistles.

154–155. *the exalted first flaming standards*: The candelabra that led the procession like pennons. *in unison*: The rear and the van of the procession stopped at the same instant.

Canto XXX

Virgil Vanishes

The procession halts and the Prophets turn to the chariot and sing "Come, my bride, from Lebanon." They are summoning *Beatrice*, who appears on the left side of the chariot, half-hidden from view by showers of blossoms poured from above by A *Hundred Angels*. Dante, stirred by the sight, turns to Virgil to express his overflowing emotions, and discovers that *Virgil Has Vanished*.

Because he bursts into tears at losing Virgil *Dante Is Reprimanded by Beatrice*. The Angel Choir overheard immediately breaks into a Psalm of Compassion, but Beatrice, still severe, answers by detailing Dante's offenses in not making proper use of his great gifts. It would violate the ordering of the Divine Decree, she argues, to let Dante drink the waters of Lethe, thereby washing all memory of sin from his soul, before he had shed the tears of a real repentance.

When the Septentrion of the First Heaven,
    which does not rise nor set, and which has never
    been veiled from sight by any mist but sin,   3

and which made every soul in that high court
    know its true course (just as the lower Seven
    direct the helmsman to his earthly port),   6

had stopped; the holy prophets, who till then
    had walked between the Griffon and those lights,
    turned to the car like souls who cry "Amen."   9

And one among them who seemed sent from Heaven
    clarioned: "*Veni, sponsa, de Libano,*"
    three times, with all the others joining in.   12

As, at the last trump every saint shall rise
    out of the grave, ready with voice new-fleshed
    to carol *Alleluliah* to the skies;   15

just so, above the chariot, at the voice
    of such an elder, rose a hundred Powers
    and Principals of the Eternal Joys,   18

all saying together: "*Benedictus qui venis*";
    then, scattering flowers about on every side:
    "*Manibus o date lilia plenis.*"   21

Time and again at day break I have seen
    the eastern sky glow with a wash of rose
    while all the rest hung limpid and serene,   24

and the Sun's face rise tempered from its rest
  so veiled by vapors that the naked eye
  could look at it for minutes undistressed.   27

Exactly so, within a cloud of flowers
  that rose like fountains from the angels' hands
  and fell about the chariot in showers,   30

a lady came in view: an olive crown
  wreathed her immaculate veil, her cloak was green,
  the colors of live flame played on her gown.   33

My soul—such years had passed since last it saw
  that lady and stood trembling in her presence,
  stupefied by the power of holy awe—   36

now, by some power that shone from her above
  the reach and witness of my mortal eyes,
  felt the full mastery of enduring love.   39

The instant I was smitten by the force,
  which had already once transfixed my soul
  before my boyhood years had run their course,   42

I turned left with the same assured belief
  that makes a child run to its mother's arms
  when it is frightened or has come to grief,   45

to say to Virgil: "There is not within me
  one drop of blood unstirred. I recognize
  the tokens of the ancient flame." But he,   48

he had taken his light from us. He had gone.
  Virgil had gone. Virgil, the gentle Father
  to whom I gave my soul for its salvation!   51

Not all that sight of Eden lost to view
  by our First Mother could hold back the tears
  that stained my cheeks so lately washed with dew.   54

"Dante, do not weep yet, though Virgil goes.
  Do not weep yet, for soon another wound
  shall make you weep far hotter tears than those!"   57

As an admiral takes his place at stern or bow
  to observe the handling of his other ships
  and spur all hands to do their best—so now,   60

on the chariot's left side, I saw appear
  when I turned back at the sound of my own name
  (which, necessarily is recorded here),   63

that lady who had been half-veiled from view
  by the flowers of the angel-revels. Now her eyes
  fixed me across the stream, piercing me through.   66

And though the veil she still wore, held in place
  by the wreathed flowers of wise Minerva's leaves,
  let me see only glimpses of her face,   69

her stern and regal bearing made me dread
  her next words, for she spoke as one who saves
  the heaviest charge till all the rest are read.   72

"Look at me well. I am she. I am Beatrice.
  How dared you make your way to this high mountain?
  Did you not know that here man lives in bliss?"   75

I lowered my head and looked down at the stream.
  But when I saw myself reflected there,
  I fixed my eyes upon the grass for shame.   78

I shrank as a wayward child in his distress
  shrinks from his mother's sternness, for the taste
  of love grown wrathful is a bitterness.   81

She paused. At once the angel chorus sang
  the blessèd psalm: *"In te, Domine, speravi."*
  As far as *"pedes meos"* their voices rang.   84

As on the spine of Italy the snow
  lies frozen hard among the living rafters
  in winter when the northeast tempests blow;   87

then, melting if so much as a breath stir
  from the land of shadowless noon, flows through itself
  like hot wax trickling down a lighted taper—   90

just so I froze, too cold for sighs or tears
  until I heard that choir whose notes are tuned
  to the eternal music of the spheres.   93

But when I heard the voice of their compassion
  plead for me more than if they had cried out:
  "Lady, why do you treat him in this fashion?"   96

the ice, which hard about my heart had pressed,
  turned into breath and water, and flowed out
  through eyes and throat in anguish from my breast.   99

Still standing at the chariot's left side,
  she turned to those compassionate essences
  whose song had sought to move her, and replied: 102

"You keep your vigil in the Eternal Day
  where neither night nor sleep obscures from you
  a single step the world takes on its way;   105

but I must speak with greater care that he
  who weeps on that far bank may understand
  and feel a grief to match his guilt. Not only   108

by the workings of the spheres that bring each seed
   to its fit end according to the stars
   that ride above it, but by gifts decreed 111

in the largesse of overflowing Grace,
   whose rain has such high vapors for its source
   our eyes cannot mount to their dwelling place; 114

this man, potentially, was so endowed
   from early youth that marvelous increase
   should have come forth from every good he sowed. 117

But richest soil the soonest will grow wild
   with bad seed and neglect. For a while I stayed him
   with glimpses of my face. Turning my mild 120

and youthful eyes into his very soul,
   I let him see their shining, and I led him
   by the straight way, his face to the right goal. 123

The instant I had come upon the sill
   of my second age and crossed and changed my life,
   he left me and let others shape his will. 126

When I rose from the flesh into the spirit,
   to greater beauty and to greater virtue,
   he found less pleasure in me and less merit. 129

He turned his steps aside from the True Way,
   pursuing the false images of good
   that promise what they never wholly pay. 132

Not all the inspiration I won by prayer
   and brought to him in dreams and meditations
   could call him back, so little did he care. 135

He fell so far from every hope of bliss
   that every means of saving him had failed
   except to let him see the damned. For this 138

I visited the portals of the dead
   and poured my tears and prayers before that spirit
   by whom his steps have, up to now, been led. 141

The seal Almighty God's decree has placed
   on the rounds of His creation would be broken
   were he to come past Lethe and to taste 144

the water that wipes out the guilty years
   without some scot of penitential tears!"

Notes

1. *the Septentrion of the First Heaven*: The Septentrion is the seven stars of the Big Dipper. Here Dante means the seven candelabra. They are the Septentrion of the First Heaven (the Empyrean) as distinct from the seven stars of the dipper which occur lower down in the Sphere of the Fixed Stars.

2. *which does not rise nor set*: The North Star does not rise or set north of the equator, but the Septentrion, revolving around the North Star, does go below the horizon in the lower latitudes. This Septentrion of the First Heaven, however, partaking of the perfection and constancy of Heaven, neither rises nor sets but is a constant light to mankind. So these unchanging lights guide the souls of man on high, as the "lower Seven" (line 5), in their less perfect way, guide the earthly helmsmen to their earthly ports.

7. *the holy prophets*: The twenty-four elders who represent the books of the Old Testament. (See XXIX. 64, note.)

10. *one among them*: *The Song of Solomon.*

11. *Veni, sponsa, de Libano*: "Come [with me] from Lebanon, my spouse." *Song of Solomon*, iv, 8. This cry, re-echoed by choirs of angels, summons Beatrice, who may be taken here as revelation, faith, divine love, hence as the bride of the spirit, to Dante (man's redeemed soul).

17–18. *a hundred Powers and Principals*: Angels.

19. *Benedictus qui venis*: "Blessed is he who cometh." (*Matthew*, xxi, 9.)

21. *Manibus o date lilia plenis*: "Oh, give lilies with full hands." These are the words of Anchises in honor of Marcellus. (*Aeneid*, VI, 883.) Thus they are not only apt to the occasion but their choice is a sweetly conceived last literary compliment to Virgil before he vanishes.

31. *a lady*: Beatrice. She is dressed in the colors of Faith (white), Hope (green), and Caritas (red).

34. *since last it saw*: Beatrice died in 1290. Thus Dante has passed ten years without sight of her.

36. *stupefied*: Dante describes the stupor of his soul at the sight of the living Beatrice in *La Vita Nuova*, XIV and XXIV. Then, however, it was mortal love; here it is eternal, and the effect accordingly greater.

54. *washed wtih dew*: By Virgil. I, 124.

55. *Dante*: This is the only point in the *Commedia* at which Dante mentions his own name. Its usage here suggests many allegorical possibilities. Central to all of them, however, must be the fact that Dante, in ending one life (of the mind) and beginning a new one (of faith) hears his name. The suggestion of a second baptism is inevitable. And just as a child being baptized is struck by the priest, so Beatrice is about to strike him with her tongue before he may proceed to the holy water.

64. *that lady*: There are thirty-four Cantos in the *Inferno* and this is the thirtieth of the *Purgatorio*, hence the sixty-fourth Canto of the *Commedia*. This is the sixty-fourth line of the sixty-fourth Canto. In Dante's numerology such correspondences are always meaningful. Six plus four equals ten and ten equals the sum of the square of trinity and unity. Obviously there can be no conclusive way of establishing intent in such a structure of mystic numbering, but it certainly is worth noting that the line begins with "that lady." The Italian text, in fact, begins with *vidi la donna*, i.e., I saw the lady [who represents the sum of the square of trinity plus unity?]. The lady, of course. is Beatrice.

68. *wise Minerva's leaves*: The olive crown.

80. *his mother's sternness*: Beatrice appears in the pageant as the figure of the Church Triumphant. The Church is the mother of the devout and though she is stern, as law decrees, her sternness is that of a loving mother.

83–84. *In te, Domine, speravi . . . pedes meos*: In mercy the angel chorus sings Psalm XXXI, 1–8, beginning "In thee, O Lord, do I put my trust" and continuing as far as "thou hast set my feet in a large room."

85–90. *the spine of Italy*: The Apennines, *the living rafters*: The trees, *the land of shadowless noon*: Africa. In equatorial regions the noonday sun is at the zenith over each point twice a year. Its rays then fall straight down and objects cast no shadows.

101. *compassionate essences*: The Angel chorus.

106. *greater care*: For his understanding that make for your intercession.

109–11. *the working of the spheres . . .*: The influence of the stars in their courses which incline men at birth to good or evil ends according to the astrological virtue of their conjunctions.

114. *our eyes*: Beatrice is still replying to the plea of the Angel choir. Hence "our eyes" must refer not to mortal eyes, but to the eyes of the blessed. Not even such more-than-human eyes may mount to the high place of those vapors, for that place is nothing less than the Supreme Height, since Grace flows from God Himself.

124–126. *my second age*: Beatrice's womanhood. When she had reached the full bloom of youth Dante turned from her and wrote to his *donna gentile*. Allegorically, he turned from divine "sciences" to an overreliance upon philosophy (the human "sciences"). For this sin he must suffer.

144–145. *were he to come past Lethe*: In passing Lethe and drinking its waters, the soul loses all memory of guilt. This, therefore, is Dante's last opportunity to do penance.

Canto XXXI

Beatrice · Matilda

Beatrice continues her reprimand, forcing Dante to confess his faults until
he swoons with grief and pain at the thought of his sin. He wakes to find
himself in Lethe, held in the arms of Matilda, who leads him to the other
side of the stream and there immerses him that he may drink the waters
that wipe out all memory of sin.

Matilda then leads him to *The Four Cardinal Virtues*, who dance about
him and lead him before *The Griffon* where he may look into *The Eyes of
Beatrice*. In them Dante sees, in a *First Beatific Vision*, the radiant reflection of the Griffon, who appears now in his human and now in his godly
nature.

The Three Theological Virtues now approach and beg that Dante may
behold *The Smile of Beatrice*. Beatrice removes her veil, and in a *Second
Beatific Vision*, Dante beholds the splendor of the unveiled shining of
Divine Love.

"You, there, who stand upon the other side—"
    (turning to me now, who had thought the edge
    of her discourse was sharp, the point) she cried   3

without pause in her flow of eloquence,
    "Speak up! Speak up! Is it true? To such a charge
    your own confession must give evidence."   6

I stood as if my spirit had turned numb:
    the organ of my speech moved, but my voice
    died in my throat before a word could come.   9

Briefly she paused, then cried impatiently:
    "What are you thinking? Speak up, for the waters
    have yet to purge sin from your memory."   12

Confusion joined to terror forced a broken
    "yes" from my throat, so weak that only one
    who read my lips would know that I had spoken.   15

As an arbalest will snap when string and bow
    are drawn too tight by the bowman, and the bolt
    will strike the target a diminished blow—   18

so did I shatter, strengthless and unstrung,
    under her charge, pouring out floods of tears,
    while my voice died in me on the way to my tongue.   21

And she: "Filled as you were with the desire
    I taught you for That Good beyond which nothing
    exists on earth to which man may aspire,   24

what yawning moats or what stretched chain-lengths lay
  across your path to force you to abandon
  all hope of pressing further on your way?   27

What increase or allurement seemed to show
  in the brows of others that you walked before them
  as a lover walks below his lady's window?"   30

My breath dragged from me in a bitter sigh,
  I barely found a voice to answer with;
  my lips had trouble forming a reply.   33

In tears I said: "The things of the world's day,
  false pleasures and enticements, turned my steps
  as soon as you had ceased to light my way."   36

And she: "Had you been silent, or denied
  what you confess, your guilt would still be known
  to Him from Whom no guilt may hope to hide.   39

But here, before our court, when souls upbraid
  themselves for their own guilt in true remorse,
  the grindstone is turned back against the blade.   42

In any case that you may know your crime
  truly and with true shame and so be stronger
  against the Siren's song another time,   45

control your tears and listen with your soul
  to learn how my departure from the flesh
  ought to have spurred you to the higher goal.   48

Nothing in Art of Nature could call forth
  such joy from you, as sight of that fair body
  which clothed me once and now sifts back to earth.   51

And if my dying turned that highest pleasure
  to very dust, what joy could still remain
  in mortal things for you to seek and treasure?   54

At the first blow you took from such vain things
  your every thought should have been raised to follow
  my flight above decay. Nor should your wings   57

have been weighed down by any joy below—
  love of a maid, or any other fleeting
  and useless thing—to wait a second blow.   60

The fledgling waits a second shaft, a third;
  but nets are spread and the arrow sped in vain
  in sight or hearing of the full-grown bird."   63

As a scolded child, tongue tied for shame, will stand
  and recognize his fault, and weep for it,
  bowing his head to a just reprimand,   66

so did I stand. And she said: "If to hear me
   grieves you, now raise your beard and let your eyes
   show you a greater cause for misery."   69

The blast that blows from Libya's hot sand,
   or the Alpine gale, overcomes less resistance
   uprooting oaks than I, at her command,   72

overcame then in lifting up my face;
   for when she had referred to it as my "beard"
   I sensed too well the venom of her phrase.   75

When I had raised my eyes with so much pain,
   I saw those Primal Beings, now at rest,
   who had strewn blossoms round her thick as rain;   78

and with my tear-blurred and uncertain vision
   I saw Her turned to face that beast which is
   one person in two natures without division.   81

Even veiled and across the river from me
   her face outshone its first-self by as much
   as she outshone all mortals formerly.   84

And the thorns of my repentance pricked me so
   that all the use and substance of the world
   I most had loved, now most appeared my foe.   87

Such guilty recognition gnawed my heart
   I swooned for pain; and what I then became
   she best knows who most gave me cause to smart.   90

When I returned to consciousness at last
   I found the lady who had walked alone
   bent over me. "Hold fast!" she said, "Hold fast!"   93

She had drawn me into the stream up to my throat,
   and pulling me behind her, she sped on
   over the water, light as any boat.   96

Nearing the sacred bank, I heard her say
   in tones so sweet I cannot call them back,
   much less describe them here: "*Asperges me.*"   99

Then the sweet lady took my head between
   her open arms, and embracing me, she dipped me
   and made me drink the waters that make clean.   102

Then raising me in my new purity
   she led me to the dance of the Four Maidens;
   each raised an arm and so joined hands above me. 105

"Here we are nymphs; stars are we in the skies.
   Ere Beatrice went to earth we were ordained
   her handmaids. We will lead you to her eyes;   108

but that your own may see what joyous light
  shines in them, yonder Three, who see more deeply,
  will sharpen and instruct your mortal sight."   111

Thus they sang, then led me to the Griffon.
  Behind him, Beatrice waited. And when I stood
  at the Griffon's breast, they said in unison: 114

"Look deep, look well, however your eyes may smart.
  We have led you now before those emeralds
  from which Love shot his arrows through your heart."   117

A thousand burning passions, every one
  hotter than any flame, held my eyes fixed
  to the lucent eyes she held fixed on the Griffon.   120

Like sunlight in a glass the twofold creature
  shone from the deep reflection of her eyes,
  now in the one, now in the other nature.   123

Judge, reader, if I found it passing strange
  to see the thing unaltered in itself
  yet in its image working change on change.   126

And while my soul in wonder and delight
  was savoring that food which in itself
  both satisfies and quickens appetite,   129

the other Three, whose bearing made it clear
  they were of higher rank, came toward me dancing
  to the measure of their own angelic air.   132

"Turn, Beatrice, oh turn the eyes of grace,"
  was their refrain, "upon your faithful one
  who comes so far to look upon your face.   135

Grant us this favor of your grace: reveal
  your mouth to him, and let his eyes behold
  the Second Beauty, which your veils conceal."   138

O splendor of the eternal living light!
  who that has drunk deep of Parnassus' waters,
  or grown pale in the shadow of its height,   141

would not, still, feel his burdened genius fail
  attempting to describe in any tongue
  how you appeared when you put by your veil   144

in that free air open to heaven and earth
whose harmony is your shining shadowed forth!

Notes

1. *the other side*: Of Lethe. But also the other side of the immortal life, i.e., still living.

2–3. *edge . . . point*: The image of the sword (of Justice) is carried over from lines 56–57 of the preceding Canto. It is continued in line 42, below. So far the sword has only cut, now it pierces.

11. *the waters*: Of Lethe.

16 ff. *arbalest . . . snap . . . diminished blow*: The figure is a bit confusing. Dante seems to say that the bolt (corresponding to an arrow) of a crossbow strikes the target with less force when the bow snaps. He does not stop to consider that the bolt may miss the target entirely. Nevertheless, the intent of his figure is clear enough.

25. *moats . . . chain-lengths*: These were, of course, defensive military measures. The moats guarded castles. The chains were strung to block roads, bridges, and gates. Both measures imply great labor forces. Thus the point of Beatrice's question: "What enormous forces blocked your way?" The block was, of course, within Dante himself.

42. *the grindstone is turned back against the blade*: Turning the grindstone away from the blade sharpens it. Turning it back against the blade dulls it. Thus Beatrice is saying that when a soul openly confesses in true repentance what could not in any case be hidden from God, the sword of Justice is blunted, *i.e.*, no longer cuts as deeply.

49–60. DANTE'S FOLLY. If the beauty of her earthly body was Dante's supreme joy and still decayed to mere dust, says Beatrice, how could Dante have placed his trust in any other earthly thing? *love of a maid*: Dante mentions another maiden in some of his songs but in an indefinite way. No specific reference can be attached to these words.

62. *nets*: Were sometimes used for trapping birds.

68–75. *your beard*: Beatrice means "your face," but the word choice is especially cutting. She has been accusing Dante of acting like a child or a fledgling bird. To refer to his beard, therefore, is a sarcastic way of reminding him that he is, presumably, a full-grown man. *a greater cause for misery*: The sight of her accompanied by the guilty knowledge that he had turned away from so much beauty and perfection.

80–81. *that beast which is one person in two natures*: The Griffon. He is the masque of Christ and represents His two aspects as man and God.

83. *first-self*: Her mortal self.

92. *the lady who had walked alone*: Matilda.

94. *She had drawn me into the stream*: Dante wakens to find Matilda bending over him. She has already pulled Dante into Lethe and he is in the water up to his throat, but Matilda walks *upon* the water. The fact that this particular miracle is attributed specifically to Christ cannot fail to suggest an allegorical meaning.

97. *the sacred bank*: The far bank, the other side. One bank of Lethe is nearer the world, the other nearer Heaven. The sacred bank, moreover, lies the other side of the absolution of Lethe's water. On the near side sin may still be said to exist; on the sacred side, even the memory of sin has been washed away. Contrast Beatrice's words in line 1.

99. *Asperges me: Asperges me hyssopo, et mundabor; lavabis me, et super nivem dealbabor.* ("Purge me with hyssop, and I shall be clean; wash me, and I shall be whiter than snow.") *Psalms* li, 7. These are the words the priest utters when he sprinkles holy water over the confessed sinner to absolve him. Matilda, that is to say, is performing the office of absolution. Her action, therefore, must be seen as being directly connected with Dante's confession and repentance, for nothing else could prepare him for absolution.

104. *the Four Maidens*: The Four Cardinal Virtues: Justice, Prudence, Fortitude, and Temperance. In their present manifestation they are nymphs. In another manifestation they are the four stars Dante saw above him when he arrived at the base of the mountain. (I, 23, note.) As the Cardinal Virtues (*i.e.*, the best man can achieve without the revelation of Christ's church) they cannot themselves bring the soul to the Second Vision (of Divine Love receiving the soul) but they can lead to the First Vision (of the Two Natures of Christ), and thence to the Three Theological Virtues, through which the Second Vision may be received.

Since Beatrice, in one of her present manifestations, represents the Authority of the Church, lines 104–105 must mean that the Four Cardinal Virtues were ordained to be the handmaidens of the Church even before it was founded, working in the virtuous pagans, and in all men, to prepare the way for the triumph of the Church.

110. *yonder Three*: The Theological Virtues: Faith, Hope, and Charity (*i.e., Caritas*).

116. *those emeralds*: The eyes of Beatrice. Dante may have intended to describe them as green (hazel) but more likely his choice of words here is meant only to signify "jewel bright." Green is, of course, the color of Hope, and an allegorical significance may be implied in that.

118–126. THE EYES OF BEATRICE. Led by the Four Cardinal Virtues, Dante takes his place before the Griffon and receives a first beatific vision of its nature, seeing now the lion (the human) and now the eagle (the divine); now one, now the other, constantly shifting, though the Griffon itself remains immovable (*i.e.*, constant, perfect). He does not, however, see the two natures as one. For that revelation he must wait till he reaches the top of Paradiso.

Note that Dante does not achieve his revelation by looking at the Griffon itself, but rather by looking at its reflection in the eyes of Beatrice (as the Church). Thus he achieves here the first fruits of Faith, seeing as much of the nature of God as is perceivable in the first life. The final revelation can happen only in Heaven, in the rapturous presence of God.

129. *both satisfies and quickens appetite*: "They that eat me shall yet be hungry, and they that drink me shall yet be thirsty." (*Ecclesiasticus*, xxiv, 21.)

138. *the Second Beauty*: The smile of Beatrice (Divine Love). Dante was led to the First Beauty by the Four Cardinal Virtues. Now the Three Theological Virtues, as higher beings, lead him to the second, and higher beauty, which is the joy of Divine Love in receiving the purified soul.

140. *Parnassus' waters*: The fountain of Castalia. To drink from it is to receive poetic gifts. To grow pale in the shadow of Parnassus signifies to labor at mastering the art of poetry. Note that Dante makes no effort to describe the smile of Divine Love, but only his rapture at beholding it.

145-146. *that free air*: Dante has earlier made the point that the Earthly Paradise possesses an atmosphere that is entirely unconstrained by earthly influences, but moves only in perfect harmony with the primal motion. That harmony is, however, no more than the shadow of the shining of Perfect Love.

Canto XXXII

Departure of the Heavenly Pageant · Transformation of the Chariot

Beatrice unveils and for the first time in ten years Dante looks upon her face. When he recovers from that blinding sight, Dante finds the Heavenly Pageant has wheeled about and is heading east. Dante and Statius follow the Chariot to *The Tree of Good and Evil*, which rises to vast heights but bears neither leaves nor flowers. The Griffon ties the pole of the Chariot to the Tree, and the Tree immediately breaks into leaf and flower. The Heavenly Pageant greets this wonder with a hymn unknown to mortals. Overpowered by the singing *Dante Sleeps*.

He awakens to find himself, as he believes at first, alone with Matilda. The Heavenly Pageant has, in fact, departed, but as Dante soon learns, Beatrice has remained behind to guard the chariot and the Seven Nymphs have remained to attend her. She is seated upon the ground, on the roots of the tree and under its shade.

Dante then witnesses an allegorical masque of *The Corruption of the Church Through Wealth*. First *An Eagle* (the Roman Empire) attacks the tree and the chariot. Then *A Fox* (heresy). Then the Eagle returns and covers the chariot with its feathers. Immediately *A Dragon* (Satan) rips at the chariot's foundation. The chariot then covers itself with the feathers (riches) and is converted into *A Monstrous Beast* on which rides *A Harlot* (the corrupted Papacy) attended by *A Giant* (the French Monarchy) that beats the harlot and drags the monster into the woods and out of sight.

My eyes were fixed with such intensity
   on quenching, at long last, their ten years' thirst
   that every sense but sight abandoned me.   3

Tranced by the holy smile that drew me there
   into the old nets, I forgot all else—
   my eyes wore blinders, and I could not care.   6

When suddenly my gaze was wrenched away
   and forced to turn left to those goddesses:
   "He stares too fixedly," I heard them say.   9

And as a man is blinded by the light
   when he has looked directly at the sun,
   just so I found that I had lost my sight.   12

When I could make out lesser (I mean, of course,
   "less sensible objects") as compared to the greater
   from which I had been called away by force,   15

I saw the legion of those souls in grace
   had turned right-wheel-about, and marched back now
   with the sun and the seven torches in its face.   18

As forward troops when they are giving ground
  turn under their shields, and their standards face about
  before the rest of the column has turned round—   21

just so the vanguard of that heavenly force
  had all gone by before the chariot
  had swung its pole around to the new course.   24

Then to their wheels the ladies turned together,
  and the Griffon once more pulled the sacred car,
  not ruffling so much as a single feather.   27

Statius and I followed across that park
  with the lady who had led me through the ford,
  behind the wheel that turned the lesser arc.   30

We marched across the sacred wood which she
  who heeded a forked tongue had left deserted,
  our steps timed by angelic melody.   33

We had moved on, I think, about as far
  as three good bowshots, end to end, might reach,
  when Beatrice descended from the car.   36

"Adam!" I heard all murmur, censuring him.
  Then they all formed a circle round a tree
  that bore no leaf nor flower on any limb.   39

It soared so high that even in woods like those
  the Indians know it would have seemed a wonder;
  and the crown spread out the more the more it rose.   42

"Blessèd art thou, Griffon, whose beak hath rent
  no morsel of the sweet wood of this tree,
  for it grips the belly with a raging torment!"   45

—So shouted all the others as they stood
  about the tree. And the two-natured being:
  "Thus is preserved the seed of every good!"   48

Then he drew up before the widowed mast
  the chariot's pole, and what came from the tree
  he gave it back, and tied the two stems fast.   51

As in the spring on earth, when the great light
  falls mingled with the rays of those sweet stars
  that follow Pisces into Heaven's height,   54

the trees begin to swell, then burgeon full,
  each one in its own hue, before the Sun
  harnesses his team beneath the Bull—   57

just so the boughs that had been bare before
  took color, turning something less than rose
  and more than violet as they bloomed once more.   60

The hymn I heard those blessèd souls sing then
is not sung here, nor did I understand it;
nor did I hear it through to the Amen.   63

Could I portray the eyes of Argus here,
lulled one by one by drowsy tales of Syrinx,
that time their pitiless watch cost him so dear,   66

as a painter paints his model, I would try
to show exactly how I fell asleep.
But who can image drowsiness? Not I.   69

Therefore, I pass to my waking, and declare
a radiance tore the veil of sleep; a voice
cried out: "Arise! What are you doing there?"   72

When they were shown the flowering of that Tree
that makes the angels hungry for Its fruit
and sets a feast in Heaven eternally,   75

Peter, John, and James, awe-stricken, fell
into a sleep from which they were recalled
by the same word that broke a greater spell;   78

and saw their company reduced, as both
Moses and Elijah vanished from them;
and saw the Master's robe change back to cloth.   81

Just so did I awaken from my dream
to find, bent over me, the compassionate lady
who had conducted me along the stream.   84

Fearful I cried out, "Beatrice! Where is she?"
And the lady: "She is seated on the roots
of the new foliage, as you can see,   87

encircled by the seven shining Graces.
The others mount to Heaven behind the Griffon,
intoning sweeter and profounder praises."   90

If she said more, her words were lost on me,
for now my eyes were fixed once more on Beatrice,
my senses closed to all that was not she.   93

She sat on the bare earth alone, left there
to guard the chariot that the Biformed Beast
had fastened to the tree with such great care.   96

A living cloister ringing her about,
the Seven Nymphs stood, holding in their hands
those candles no wind ever shall bllow out.   99

"Here briefly in this forest shall you dwell;
and evermore, with me, be of that Rome
in which Christ is a Roman. Hence, look well   102

there at the great car, and that you may be
   a light to the dark world, when you return
   set down exactly all that you shall see."   105

Thus Beatrice; and I, devoutly bent
   at the feet of her commands, turned mind and eye
   as she had willed, in all obedient.   108

No flash from densest clouds when the rains fall
   from the remotest reaches of the sky
   ever shot down as fast out of the squall   111

as did the bird of Jove that I saw break
   down through the tree, ripping the flowers, the leaves,
   even the bark, with its fierce claws and beak.   114

He struck the chariot a tremendous blow,
   at which it lurched like a storm-battered ship,
   now rolled to port, now starboard, to and fro.   117

Next came a fox, so gaunt and angular
   it seemed to know no fit food; and it pounced
   upon the cab of the triumphal car.   120

But threatening all its filthy sins with woe
   my lady sent it reeling back from there
   as fast as such a bag of bones could go.   123

Then, through the tree, I saw the bird descend
   once more into the car, and shed its plumes
   to feather it in gold from end to end.   126

And from the sky, as if a heart let slip
   all of its grief in one sound, a voice cried:
   "O what a load you bear, my little ship!"   129

Then, as I watched, I saw a fissure split
   the earth between the two wheels, and a dragon
   rise to the car and sink its tail in it.   132

Much as an angry wasp draws back its stinger,
   it drew its tail back, ripping the car's floor,
   and wandered off as if it meant to linger.   135

Like rich soil left to weeds, what then remained
   covered itself with feathers, which no doubt
   had been intended to burnish what they stained.   138

And both the wheels and the pole were overgrown,
   and all the car to the last part, and all
   in less time than the lips part for a moan.   141

So changed, the holy ark began to sprout
   heads from its various parts: three from the pole,
   one from each corner. Seven in all grew out.   144

The three were horned like oxen, but the four
were each armed with a single evil horn.
No one had seen the monster's like before.   147

Secure as a great fortress on a crag,
an ungirt harlot rode the beast, her eyes
darting with avarice. Beside that hag,   150

and ready to risk all to keep her his,
a giant strode erect, and as they passed,
from time to time the two exchanged a kiss.   153

But when she turned her hungry eyes on me,
her savage lover in a bestial rage
whipped her from head to foot unmercifully.   156
Then in a jealous fit the brute untied
the monster from the tree, and dragged it off
into the woods, far toward the other side,   159

until between me and the doxie queen
on her weird beast, he made the trees a screen.

Notes

1–9. DANTE'S RAPTURE ADMONISHED. Beatrice had died in 1290. Dante has not, therefore, seen her for ten years, and the sight of her unveiled face so draws him into the old nets (of love) that he loses track of all else until he is brought to his senses by overhearing the Three Maidens charge him with overdoing. For it is immoderate (*non è bello, i.e.,* it is not an Aristotelian mean of good conduct) to stare so intensely, even at the vision of eternal beauty, if in so doing a man loses sight of the other gifts of God. Bear in mind, too, that Dante is staring with his earthly memory of the other Beatrice. The Heavenly Beatrice has not yet been truly revealed to him. That revelation will take place in the next Canto.

16–18. The Heavenly Pageant came originally from the east. It passed Dante, executed a right-wheel-about, and is now returning, face to the east. Accordingly, it now has in its face the light of the sun as well as that of the candelabra.

20. *under their shields:* Troops turning in retreat within range of the enemy held their shields over their heads for protection.

22. *the vanguard of that heavenly force:* The twenty-four elders.

30. *the wheel that turned the lesser arc:* The right. In making a right turn, it would swing through the lesser arc. The poets, therefore, are walking behind the Three Theological Virtues.

36. *when Beatrice descended:* In this masque, Beatrice has entered in a chariot that represents the Church Triumphant. The procession is now moving to the tree that represents the Civil Authority of the Holy Roman Empire. Her descent in order to approach on foot signifies the humility the Church should display before civil authority, as commanded by Paul (*Romans,* xiii, 1): "Let every soul be subject unto the higher powers. For there is no power but of God: the powers that be are ordained of God." To this, as Dante's image of the ideal Church, contrast his lament for the evils that befell the Church when it grew rich and arrogant (*Inferno,* XIX, 109–111, and note), and the final allegory of the present Canto.

37–60. THE TREE OF GOOD AND EVIL. This passage contains an elaborate conception, difficult in itself, and made more difficult by much of Dante's phrasing in what is certainly his least attractive style.

The tree, to begin with, is instantly recognizable, by its resemblance to its offshoot on the ledge below, as the original Tree of Good and Evil. It is for this reason that all souls murmur against Adam at sight of it.

Then, in a second symbolism, the tree is made to represent the Holy Roman Empire, towering so high (and spreading wider as it soars) that no tree in the Indian forests (the comparison is from Virgil) could equal it. (The comparison to Indian forests implies, of course, the superiority of the Christian empire.) But though enormous, the tree is, by itself, barren.

When Christ (the Griffon) approaches the tree, all praise Him for not having eaten (peculiar diet) the sweet-tasting wood (the material riches of the Empire), for by His holy poverty in this world, He escaped the bellyache of corruption (with which the Church has been plagued ever since it grew rich). The Griffon replies that only so (in holy poverty) can the seed of goodness be preserved.

To understand the Griffon's next action, it is necessary to know that the true cross, according to legend, had been cut from the Tree of Good and Evil. The Griffon draws the Chariot (the Church) to the tree and binds fast to the tree "what came from it," *i.e.,* the pole of the chariot. Thus one may understand that the pole the Griffon has been pulling (and what draws the Church forward) is the true cross. This interpretation is disputed but does have the virtue of being coherent.

Now with the Church securely bound to the Empire by the true cross, the tree that had been barren breaks into bloom, turning (lines 59–60) something less than rose and more than violet (*i.e.,* the Imperial purple).

For good measure, Dante throws in a legendary reference and several astrological ones. Sense of lines 52–57: "As in the spring on earth when the great light falls mingled with the days of those sweet stars [of Aries, the sign in which the sun rides from March 21 to April 19] that follow Pisces [the zodiacal sign immediately preceding Aries] the trees begin to swell, then burgeon full . . . before the Sun [Apollo, the charioteer of the Sun] harnesses his team [to bear the Sun across the sky] beneath the Bull [Taurus, the sign the Sun enters on April 20]."

64–65. *Argus . . . Syrinx*: Argus (called Panoptes or "the all-seeing") had a hundred eyes all over his body. When Jupiter was smitten by Io, Juno changed the girl into a cow and sent Argus to keep watch over her. Jupiter, in his turn, sent Mercury to lull Argus to sleep either by the magic of his flute or, in the version Dante follows, by a kind of Arabian Nights series of tales about Syrinx, who was loved by Pan, and who was changed into a reed by her sisters to save her from Pan's pursuit. His watch cost him dear because Mercury, after lulling him to sleep, cut off his head. Juno set the eyes of her dead gamekeeper into the tail of the peacock, the bird sacred to her. (See XXIX, 95, note.)

70 ff. DANTE'S DREAM AND AWAKENING. The strains of the heavenly hymn lull Dante into a blissful sleep, which may be taken as symbolizing the serenity of the Kingdom. A radiance reaches through his closed eyes and he awakens to hear a voice cry "Arise!" This is the word with which Christ called Lazarus, among others, from the "greater spell" of death. Obviously, therefore, Dante's awakening symbolizes one more release from mortal error into eternal life. Opening his eyes, Dante finds Matilda bending over him. It was she who cried to him, and at first Dante thinks that all the others have left and that he is alone with her.

Dante then compares his experience to that of Peter, John, and James at the Transfiguration. "And after six days Jesus taketh with him Peter, and James, and John his brother, and bringeth them up into a high mountain apart, and he was transfigured before them: and his face did shine as the sun, and his garments became white as the light . . . they fell on their face, and were sore afraid. And Jesus came and touched them and said, Arise, and be not afraid. And lifting up their eyes, they saw no one, save Jesus only." (*Matthew,* xvii, 1–8.) And see also *Luke,* ix, 28–36, especially, "Now Peter and they that were with him were heavy with sleep: but when they were fully awake, they saw his glory, and the two men that stood with him."

Basing his account on these two passages, Dante adds his own allegory. The vision that is shown to the disciples becomes a vision of Christ as the Mystic Tree of Heaven (which is, of course, another aspect of the Tree of Good and Evil). The vision, however, is not of the fruit of the tree but of its flowers (line 73). It is, therefore, the vision of the flowering promise of Christ, from which will follow the fruit of eternal rejoicing. The vision is especially apt since, during Dante's sleep, Christ (the Griffon) has reascended to Heaven with most of the Heavenly Procession. There Dante shall follow him in the *Paradiso,* and there the fruit of felicity awaits.

73. *that Tree*: Christ.

81. *and saw the Master's robe change back to cloth*: I.e., back to its mortal state, as it was before the Transfiguration.

83. *the compassionate lady*: Matilda.

85. *Fearful*: Seeing only Matilda by him. Dante is afraid that Beatrice has left.

86–90. *She is seated on the roots of the new foliage*: As Christ, after his Transfiguration, resumed his earthly appearance, so Beatrice, having entered as the figure of revelation aboard the triumphal chariot, is now seated upon the ground.

Beatrice is seated on the ground and *under* the new foliage (that sprang from the touch of Christ–the Griffon). Let the tree in this aspect symbolize the Holy Roman Empire, and the roots Rome. The chariot, of course, represents the Church. It rests on the roots (Rome) and is tied to the tree (the Empire). Beatrice (Divine Love) is left on earth to guard the chariot under the protective shade of the tree, while the Griffon (Christ) ascends to Heaven followed by the rest of the Heavenly Train, which is singing a hymn that is sweeter and profounder than earth can understand.

Beatrice is left on earth encircled and attended by the Seven Nymphs (the Three Theological Virtues and the Four Cardinal Virtues).

109–111. Dante's meteorological figure here is based on the belief that the highest reaches of the sky are the domain of fire. The highest clouds, therefore, being closest to the sphere of fire would be especially subject to fiery influences and would give forth the most powerful lightning flashes.

112. *the bird of Jove:* The eagle. See *Ezekiel,* xvii, the Parable of the Eagles and the Cedar. There, the eagle represents the Babylonian persecution of the Jews. Here, Dante clearly enough intends its attack to symbolize the Roman persecution of the early Christians.

118. *a fox:* Is most usually taken to represent the heresies that threatened the early Church and that were repelled by the divine wisdom of the Church Fathers.

124–129. THE GIFT OF THE EAGLE. The Eagle of Imperial Rome returns and covers the car (the Church) with its feathers (riches) and a voice from Heaven cries out in grief. The grief is clearly for the evils that descended upon the Church when it grew rich. Dante must certainly have had the Donation of Constantine (see *Inferno,* XIX, 109–111, and note) in mind in the first feathering of the car. The second gift of the eagle would then symbolize the whole process whereby the temporal wealth of the Empire passed so largely into the hands of the Church.

131. *a dragon:* Satan.

135. *as if it meant to linger:* Having broken the floor of the car (the foundation of the Church, once it has been weakened by wealth), Satan would certainly not run away, but rather remain to see what other mischief he could do, wandering off only very slowly.

142–147. THE CAR TRANSFORMS ITSELF INTO A SEVEN-HEADED MONSTER. "And I saw a woman sitting upon a scarlet-colored beast full of the names of blasphemy, having seven heads and ten horns." (*Revelation,* xvii, 3.)

The Seven Heads have been interpreted in endless ingenious ways. Let them be taken as representing the Seven Deadly Sins. They thus took root in the Church as soon as it covered itself with wealth. The first three of the seven are Pride, Wrath, and Avarice. Being the worst sins, they sprout from the pole (*i.e.,* they come before the others). And since they represent offenses against both God and one's neighbors, they are represented as having two horns. The four lesser sins (Acedia, Envy, Gluttony, and Lust) offend God but not necessarily one's neighbors and they are, therefore, represented as having single horns. Thus the total of ten horns.

149–150. *an ungirt harlot:* She represents the Papacy as it existed under Boniface VIII and Clement V, the two popes Dante most charges with corruption. (See *Inferno,* XIX, and note to 77–79.) "Ungirt" (Dante uses *sciolta,* "untied, unbound") should be understood to imply both lewdness (immodesty of dress) and lack of restraint (knowing no bounds). *her eyes darting with avarice:* looking everywhere for plunder.

152. *a giant:* The French monarchy, and especially Philip the Fair (Philip IV, 1268–1314, crowned in 1285), who made the Papacy his puppet.

154. *But when she turned her hungry eyes on me:* The question here is why the giant beats the harlot for looking at Dante. Again, many answers have been suggested, but two seem most to the point.

If Dante is taken here as representing Italy, the whipping can only refer to Philip's humiliation of Boniface VIII (see Canto XX, 85–93, note), and the harlot's covetous glance at Dante-as-Italy would represent Boniface's intrigues with various rulers. It was these intrigues that put him most at odds with Philip.

On the other hand, Dante may be taken to represent the typical Christian who looks to the Church for guidance. The allegory would then be saying that every time the corrupt Church is stirred by a wish to return to its true pastoral mission, the French kings whip her and drag her back to sin.

158. *and dragged it off:* In 1304 Philip engineered the election of Clement V and transferred the Papal Seat (dragged it off) to Avignon.

Canto XXXIII

Dante's Purification Completed

The Seven Nymphs sing a hymn of sorrow for the grief of the Church, and
Beatrice answers with Christ's words announcing his resurrection. All then
move onward, Beatrice summoning Dante to her side as they walk on.
Beatrice begins her discourse with an obscurely worded prophecy of the
Deliverance of the Church. In much simpler language, she then utters her
Final Reproach to Dante for having so lost sight of the truth.
Just as she finishes, the train halts before *The Great Spring* from which
flow the waters of both Lethe and Eunoë. At Beatrice's command, the
Seven Nymphs lead Dante forward and he *Drinks the Waters of Eunoë*. By
drinking the waters of Lethe, Dante has already forgotten all sin and error;
now every good is strengthened in him. Thus is his *Final Purification* completed, and Dante rises "perfect, pure, and ready for the stars."

"*Deus, venerunt gentes*"—the Holy Seven,
   in alternating chorus through their tears,
   first three, then four, raised a sweet chant to Heaven;   3

and Beatrice, when she heard them mourn such loss
   sighed with a grief so deep that even Mary
   could not have changed more at the foot of the cross.   6

But when the other virgins in their choir
   fell still for her reply, she rose erect
   in holy zeal, and said, as if afire: 9

"*Modicum et non videbitis me;*
   et iterum, dearly beloved sisters,
   modicum, et vos videbitis me."   12

Then placing the Seven before her, she moved ahead
   with a nod to me, to the Lady, and to the Sage
   that had remained, to follow where she led.   15

So she strolled on, and she had not yet laid
   her tenth step on the sward, when she turned round
   and struck my eyes with her eyes as she said   18

with a serene tranquillity: "Draw near,
   that you may, if I wish to speak to you
   as we move on, be better placed to hear."   21

When I was, as I should be, at her side,
   she said: "Dear brother, why are you not moved
   to question me as we move on? —Tongue-tied,   24

like one who knows his station is beneath
    that of the presences in which he stands,
    and cannot drag his voice across his teeth,   27

so did I, with a voice almost choked through,
    manage to say: "My Lady, all my need
    and all that is my good is known to you."   30

And she to me: "My wish is that you break
    the grip of fear and shame, and from now on
    no longer speak like one but half awake.   33

The cart the dragon broke was, and is not;
    let him whose fault that is believe God's wrath
    will not be calmed by soup, however hot.   36

The eagle you saw shed its plumes back there
    to make the cart a monster and a prey,
    will not remain forever without heir;   39

for certain as my words, my eyes foresee,
    already nearing, the unstayable stars
    that bring the time in which, by God's decree,   42

five hundred, ten, and five shall be the sign
    of one who comes to hunt down and destroy
    the giant and his thievish concubine.   45

My prophecy, being obscure as those
    of Themis and the Sphinx, may fail to move you,
    since all such words hide what they should disclose;   48

but soon now, like an Oedipus reborn,
    events themselves shall solve the dark enigma,
    and without loss of either sheep or corn.   51

Note my words well, and when you give them breath,
    repeat them as I said them, to the living
    whose life is no more than a race toward death.   54

And when you come to write them down, make clear
    what you have seen of the Tree, now twice-despoiled
    since all-creating God first raised it here.   57

All those who rob or break those boughs commit
    a blasphemy-in-deed, offending God
    who sacred to Himself created it.   60

For just one bite, the First Soul's tears were spilt
    five thousand years and more, yearning for Him
    who suffered in His own flesh for that guilt.   63

Your wits must be asleep not to have known
    that a particular reason must account
    for its great height and its inverted crown.   66

Had not your idle thoughts been to your brain
 an Elsan water, and your pleasure in them
 a Pyramus to the mulberry's new stain,   69

those two facts surely should have made you see
 the justice of God's interdict shine forth
 as the moral meaning of the form of the Tree.   72

It is my wish—because I see your mind
 turned into stone, and like a stone, so darkened
 that the light of what I tell you strikes it blind—   75

that you bear back, if not in writing, then
 in outline, what I say, as pilgrims wreathe
 their staffs with palm to show where they have been."   78

And I to her: "As pressed wax will retain
 a faithful imprint of the signet ring,
 so is your seal imprinted on my brain.   81

But why do your desired words fly so high
 above my power to follow their intent
 that I see less and less the more I try?"   84

"They fly so high," she said, "that you may know
 what school you followed, and how far behind
 the truth I speak its feeble doctrines go;   87

and see that man's ways, even at his best,
 are far from God's as earth is from the heaven
 whose swiftest wheel turns above all the rest."   90

"But," I replied, "I have no recollection
 of ever having been estranged from you.
 Conscience does not accuse me of defection."   93

And she then with a smile: "If, as you say
 you lack that memory, then call to mind
 how you drank Lethe's waters here today.   96

As certainly as smoke betrays the fire,
 this new forgetfulness of your wish to stray
 betrays the sinfulness of that desire.   99

But I assure you that I shall select
 the simplest words that need be from now on
 to make things clear to your dull intellect."   102

Now with a brighter flame and slower pace
 the sun was holding its meridian height,
 which varies round the world from place to place,   105

when suddenly—as one who leads a line
 of travelers as their escort will stop short
 at a strange sight or an unusual sign—   108

so stopped the Seven at an edge of shade
 pale as a shadow cast by a cold peak
 on a cold stream deep in an Alpine glade.   111

And there ahead of them, in a single flow,
 Tigris and Euphrates seemed to rise
 and part as friends who linger as they go.   114

"O light and glory of mankind," I cried,
 "what is this flood that pours forth from one source
 and then parts from itself to either side?"   117

In answer to that prayer I heard the name
 "Matilda" and "ask her." Who spoke up then
 as one does who absolves himself of blame: 120

"This, and much more, I have this very day
 explained to him, and Lethe certainly
 could not have washed that memory away."   123

And Beatrice: "Perhaps a greater care,
 as often happens, dims his memory
 and his mind's eye. But see Eunoë there—   126

lead him, as is your custom, to the brim
 of that sweet stream, and with its holy waters
 revive the powers that faint and die in him."   129

Then as a sweet soul gladly shapes its own
 good will to the will of others, without protest,
 as soon as any sign has made it known,   132

so the sweet maid, taking me by the hand
 and saying in a modest voice to Statius,
 "Come you with him," obeyed the good command.   135

Reader, had I the space to write at will,
 I should, if only briefly, sing a praise
 of that sweet draught. Would I were drinking still!   138

But I have filled all of the pages planned
 for this, my second, canticle, and Art
 pulls at its iron bit with iron hand.   141

I came back from those holiest waters new,
 remade, reborn, like a sun-wakened tree
 that spreads new foliage to the Spring dew   144

in sweetest freshness, healed of Winter's scars;
 perfect, pure, and ready for the Stars.

Notes

1. *Deus, venerunt gentes*: Psalm LXXIX, the lamentation for the destruction of Jerusalem. "O God, the heathen are come into thine inheritance; thy holy temple have they defiled; they have laid Jerusalem on heaps." So have the later unbelievers despoiled and defiled the Church.

3. *first three, then four*: The Seven Nymphs sing the psalm antiphonally, the Three Theological Virtues singing first (they being higher in the scale of things), and then the Four Cardinal Virtues.

5-6. *even Mary could not have changed more*: The comparison is not a hyperbole. Beatrice, mourning for the crucifixion of the Church, would endure the same grief Mary suffered at the crucifixion of her son, Christ and the Church being one.

10-12. *Modicum et non videbitis me . . .* : "A little while and ye shall not see me; and again a little while, and ye shall see me [because I go to the Father]." (*John*, xvi, 16.)

These are Christ's words to his disciples, announcing his resurrection. Beatrice speaks them afire with her holy zeal in reply to the mournful psalm. She is saying, in effect, that the triumph of the True Faith shall be seen again. On one level her words may be taken to mean that the pure in heart shall rise above the corruption of the Church to see Christ again in Heaven. More likely, Dante meant that the Church shall be purged until Christ is once more truly visible in its workings.

14-15. *the Lady*: Matilda. *the Sage that had remained*: Statius. The other Sage, Virgil, has departed.

17. *her tenth step*: Every number mentioned by Dante invites allegorical conjecture, and many have taken the "ten" here to refer to the Ten Commandments. The interpretation seems doubtful, however, especially since the actual steps taken were not yet ten.

18. *struck my eyes with her eyes*: Dante takes this forceful way of emphasizing the power of her eyes. (The Lamps of Heaven?)

19. *serene tranquillity*: The Change in Beatrice is not a matter of feminine mood. When Dante still had upon himself a stain of neglect, Beatrice berated him for it. But he has now done fit penance and the stain has been removed, thereby removing all cause for anger.

22. *When I was, as I should be, at her side*: Dante's whole progress up to this time has been, as it should be the object of every soul, to stand beside Divine Love.

27. *and cannot drag his voice across his teeth*: It is characteristic of Dante that a certain pungency should creep into his phrasing even at such sublime moments.

31-33. *like one but half awake*: Dante has achieved purification, and all memory of sin has been washed from him by the waters of Lethe. He must yet drink of the waters of Eunoë, which will strengthen every good memory in him. Because he has not yet been so strengthened, he still speaks, partly, with the habituated fears and confusions of his former ways. It is these fears and confusions Beatrice is telling him to put by.

34-36. Beatrice now refers to the allegory that concluded Canto XXXII, assuring Dante, as in her answer to the psalm, that a dawn of righteousness is approaching. *was, and is not*: These are the words of John, *Revelation*, xvii, 8: "The beast thou sawest was, and is not." *soup*: In some parts of ancient Greece a murderer could protect himself from all vengeance if for nine successive days he ate soup on the grave of his victim. In Florence it became a custom to stand guard for nine days over the grave of a murdered man to see that no one ate soup upon it. The reference is a strange one, but Dante's intent is, clearly, that no such simple rite will ward off the vengeance of God.

37-39. *the eagle . . . will not remain forever without heir*: The eagle is, of course, the Roman Empire. The true heir of the Caesars, who will restore order and goodness, will come at last. Dante thought of Frederick II as the last real heir of the Caesars.

41. *the unstayable stars*: Nothing can stay the stars in their courses. Beatrice foresees propitious stars already near at hand. (God's wrath will not be stayed: cf. lines 35-36.)

43. *five hundred, ten, and five*: As Beatrice says in the next tercet, she is speaking in the veiled tongue of prophecy, and her words hide what they should disclose. Whatever the numerological significance Dante intended by the number, it cannot be identified. Since Dante could make himself clear enough when he wanted to, and since he goes on to have Beatrice say that her meaning is hidden, it follows, as a fair guess, that Dante deliberately kept his reference vague.

46-51. The basic sense of this passage is: "Though my way of speaking is obscure, events themselves will soon make clear my meaning." It is the mythological references that may confuse the modern reader. *Themis*: Daughter of Gaea (Earth) and Uranus (Heaven). She was the second wife of Zeus, and later, no longer as his wife, became his Goddess of Law and Order. She was noted for the obscurity of her oracles. *the Sphinx*: A monster with the head of an innocent maiden and the body of a savage beast. One of the oracles of Themis. She waited for travelers on a rock near Thebes and killed them when they failed to solve her famous riddle: "What walks on four legs in the morning, on two at noon, and on three at night?" *Oedipus*: The ill-fated King of Thebes answered properly that the riddle meant a man in the three stages of his life (for he crawls on all fours as an infant, walks on two legs in the middle of his life, and totters on two legs and a cane thereafter). The Sphinx was so enraged on hearing the right answer that she killed herself. (Dante's text reads not "Oedipus" but "the Naiads." The Naiads had no connection with the riddle. Dante's error follows a corrupt text of Ovid's *Metamorphoses*, VII, 759, which reads "Naiades"—the Naiads—for "Laiades"—son of Laius, *i.e.*, *Oedipus*.) *without loss of either sheep or corn*: Themis, to avenge her oracle, sent a monstrous beast to ravage the flocks and fields of Thebes.

52. *and when you give them breath*: This phrase is my own invention, forced upon the text by the, to me, clear nceessity to render line 54 with "death" as the rhyme. I hope the rendering will seem at least approximately Dantean: since the words thus far have been spoken only by Beatrice, a spirit, they have not yet been given breath, as they will be when Dant repeats them with his mortal voice.

56. *twice-despoiled*: Dante probably meant the Fall as the first despollment of the tree, and the corruption of the Church as the second.

59. *blasphemy-in-deed*: As distinct from blasphemy-in-word and blasphemy-in-thought.

61. *the First Soul's*: Adam's.

62. *five thousand years and more*: According to *Genesis*, v. 5, Adam lived 930 years on earth. According to *Paradiso*, XXVI, 118, he then waited in Limbo for 4,302 years. Dante follows, in this, the chronology of the ecclesiastical historian Eusebius, who set Christ's birth in the year 5200 since the Creation. Christ's death, therefore (and the Harrowing of Hell, for which see *Inferno*, IV, 53, note), would have occurred in the year 5232.

65. *particular reason*: The tree is enormously tall and broadens toward the crown (hence "inverted"). The "particular reason" for such a form must have been to make the fruit inaccessible to man. The story of *Genesis*, however, indicates that Eve certainly had no trouble getting her apple. It must follow that the tree has grown since *Genesis*. According to the chronology of Eusebius, the year 1300 would be the year 6500 since Creation—time enough for the knowledge of good and evil to show some substantial growth rings.

68-69. *an Elsan water*: The Elsa, a river of Tuscany, is so rich in lime that at some points along its course objects left in its waters will either petrify or become coated. So Dante's idle thoughts (seemingly flowing *around* his brain more than *through* it) have petrified his intellect, *a Pyramus to the mulberry's new stain*: The blood of Pyramus (and Thisbe) stained the mulberry red. (See XXVII, 37 ff., note.) So Dante's delight in his idle thoughts has stained his intellect. Lines 73-75, below, further explain Dante's meaning here.

72. *the moral meaning*: The form of the tree symbolizes its essential nature. Interpreted in the moral sense (as distinct, for example, from the allegorical narrative, or anagogical senses) the two main facts of the tree's form (its great height and inverted crown) express how far above and beyond man is the final understanding of Good and Evil. Hence the justice of God's interdict in forbidding man what lies beyond his grasp.

74. *turned into stone*: As if by Elsan waters. *so darkened*: As was the mulberry.

77-78. *as pilgrims wreathe their staffs with palm*: The palm grows in the Holy Land. Returning pilgrims wreathed their staffs with palm to prove they had been there.

86. *what school you followed*: The school of philosophy, whose error lies in placing its dependence on reason as an end, and which cannot, therefore, comprehend the mysteries of faith.

89-90. *the heaven whose swiftest wheel* . . . : The Primum Mobile, uppermost of the nine spheres. Since all the spheres turn together, the outermost must move most swiftly.

91-102. BEATRICE'S LAST REPROACH. Dante protests that he has no recollection of ever having been estranged from Beatrice, despite the fact that he had relied more heavily on human philosophy than on divine love. Beatrice, smiling, points out that he has just drunk the waters of Lethe, whose powers wipe away all memory of sin. Since they have wiped out the memory of his estrangement, it follows that the estrangement was sinful.

But Beatrice cannot mean that he sinned in following Virgil, for she herself sent him to Dante. Dante's sinful estrangement must have happened before he met Virgil. And since it was from the four beasts of worldliness that Virgil rescued Dante, setting him on the road to the mysteries of faith, worldliness (or the overexaltation of philosophy as his guide) must be the sin that estranged Dante from Beatrice. (See note to XXX, 124-126.)

103. *brighter flame and slower pace*: To an observer the sun seems brightest at its noon height and seems to move most slowly then. (Its slowness is an illusion, as is the speed with which it seems to set once it has touched the horizon, but its brightness can be accounted for by the fact that its rays travel a vertical, and hence shortest, course through the atmosphere at noon.)

105. *varies round the world from place to place*: In one sense, the sun is always at the meridian: it is always noon somewhere on the earth.

113. *Tigris and Euphrates*: The Tigris flows through Turkey and Iraq (ancient Chaldea) to join the Euphrates, which rises in Armenia and flows into the Persian Gulf. *Genesis*, ii, 10 ff., identifies the Euphrates as one of the four rivers of Eden, all of which rise from the same source. The rivers of Dante's Earthly Paradise are Lethe and Eunoë. They "seem to rise" as if they were Tigris and Euphrates rising from a single spring.

117. *parts from itself to either side*: The two rivers flow off in opposite directions, just as their powers, rising from one source, work in opposite ways to achieve one good.

122–123. *Lethe certainly could not have washed that memory away*: There being nothing sinful in it.

142–146. Dante ends each canticle with the word "stars," a fixed architectural device, and one that any rendition must preserve at whatever cost. Unfortunately for English renditions, the cost of forcing a rhyme for "stars" is great, and I have had to take considerable liberties. More closely rendered, these lines read: "I came back from that holiest wave [flood] made new like new trees renewed with new foliage, pure and prepared to mount to the stars."

The Paradiso

Canto I

The Invocation

The Sphere of Fire · The Music of the Spheres

Dante states his supreme theme as Paradise itself and invokes the aid not only of the Muses but of Apollo.

Dante and Beatrice are in *The Earthly Paradise*, the Sun is at the Vernal Equinox, it is noon at Purgatory and midnight at Jerusalem when Dante sees Beatrice turn her eyes to stare straight into the sun and reflexively imitates her gesture. At once it is as if a second sun had been created, its light dazzling his senses, and Dante feels the ineffable change of his mortal soul into Godliness.

These phenomena are more than his senses can grasp, and Beatrice must explain to him what he himself has not realized: that he and Beatrice are soaring toward the height of Heaven at an incalculable speed.

Thus Dante climaxes the master metaphor in which purification is equated to weightlessness. Having purged all dross from his soul he mounts effortlessly, without even being aware of it at first, to his natural goal in the Godhead. So they pass through *The Sphere of Fire*, and so Dante first hears *The Music of the Spheres*.

> The glory of Him who moves all things rays forth
>   through all the universe, and is reflected
>   from each thing in proportion to its worth.   3
>
> I have been in that Heaven of His most light,
>   and what I saw, those who descend from there
>   lack both the knowledge and the power to write.   6
>
> For as our intellect draws near its goal
>   it opens to such depths of understanding
>   as memory cannot plumb within the soul.   9
>
> Nevertheless, whatever portion time
>   still leaves me of the treasure of that kingdom
>   shall now become the subject of my rhyme.   12
>
> O good Apollo, for this last task, I pray
>   you make me such a vessel of your powers
>   as you deem worthy to be crowned with bay.   15
>
> One peak of cleft Parnassus heretofore
>   has served my need, now must I summon both
>   on entering the arena one time more.   18
>
> Enter my breast, I pray you, and there breathe
>   as high a strain as conquered Marsyas
>   that time you drew his body from its sheath.   21

395

O power divine, but lend to my high strain
  so much as will make clear even the shadow
  of that High Kingdom stamped upon my brain,   24

and you shall see me come to your dear grove
  to crown myself with those green leaves which you
  and my high theme shall make me worthy of.   27

So seldom are they gathered, Holy Sire,
  to crown an emperor's or a poet's triumph
  (oh fault and shame of mortal man's desire!)   30

that the glad Delphic god must surely find
  increase of joy in the Peneian frond
  when any man thirsts for it in his mind.   33

Great flames are kindled where the small sparks fly.
  So after me, perhaps, a better voice
  shall raise such prayers that Cyrrha will reply.   36

The lamp of the world rises to mortal view
  from various stations, but that point which joins
  four circles with three crosses, it soars through   39

to a happier course in happier conjunction
  wherein it warms and seals the wax of the world
  closer to its own nature and high function.   42

That glad conjunction had made it evening here
  and morning there; the south was all alight,
  while darkness rode the northern hemisphere;   45

when I saw Beatrice had turned left to raise
  her eyes up to the sun; no eagle ever
  stared at its shining with so fixed a gaze.   48

And as a ray descending from the sky
  gives rise to another, which climbs back again,
  as a pilgrim yearns for home; so through my eye   51

her action, like a ray into my mind,
  gave rise to mine: I stared into the sun
  so hard that here it would have left me blind;   54

but much is granted to our senses there,
  in that garden made to be man's proper place,
  that is not granted us when we are here.   57

I had to look away soon, and yet not
  so soon but what I saw him spark and blaze
  like new-tapped iron when it pours white-hot.   60

And suddenly, as it appeared to me,
  day was added to day, as if He who can
  had added a new sun to Heaven's glory.   63

Beatrice stared at the eternal spheres
   entranced, unmoving; and I looked away
   from the sun's height to fix my eyes on hers.   66

And as I looked, I felt begin within me
   what Glaucus felt eating the herb that made him
   a god among the others in the sea.   69

How speak trans-human change to human sense?
   Let the example speak until God's grace
   grants the pure spirit the experience.   72

Whether I rose in only the last created
   part of my being, O Love that rulest Heaven
   Thous knowest, by whose lamp I was translated.   75

When the Great Wheel that spins eternally
   in longing for Thee, captured my attention
   by that harmony attuned and heard by Thee,   78

I saw ablaze with sun from side to side
   a reach of Heaven: not all the rains and rivers
   of all of time coùld make a sea so wide.   81

That radiance and that new-heard melody
   fired me with such a yearning for their Cause
   as I had never felt before. And she   84

who saw my every thought as well as I,
   saw my perplexity; before I asked
   my question she had started her reply.   87

Thus she began: "You dull your own perceptions
   with false imaginings and do not grasp
   what would be clear but for your preconceptions.   90

You think you are still on earth: the lightning's spear
   never fled downward from its natural place
   as rapidly as you are rising there."   93

I grasped her brief and smiling words and shed
   my first perplexity, but found myself
   entangled in another, and I said: 96

"My mind, already recovered from the surprise
   of the great marvel you have just explained,
   is now amazed anew: how can I rise   99

in my gross body through such aery substance?"
   She sighed in pity and turned as might a mother
   to a delirious child. "The elements   102

of all things," she began, "whatever their mode,
   observe an inner order. It is this form
   that makes the universe resemble God.   105

In this the higher creatures see the hand
of the Eternal Worth, which is the goal
to which these norms conduce, being so planned.   108

All Being within this order, by the laws
of its own nature is impelled to find
its proper station round its Primal Cause.   111

Thus every nature moves across the tide
of the great sea of being to its own port,
each with its given instinct as its guide.   114

This instinct draws the fire about the moon.
It is the mover in the mortal heart.
It draws the earth together and makes it one.   117

Not only the brute creatures, but all those
possessed of intellect and love, this instinct
drives to their mark as a bow shoots forth its arrows.   120

The Providence that makes all hunger here
satisfies forever with its light
the heaven within which whirls the fastest sphere.   123

And to it now, as to a place foretold,
are we two soaring, driven by that bow
whose every arrow finds a mark of gold.   126

It is true that oftentimes the form of a thing
does not respond to the intent of the art,
the matter being deaf to summoning—   129

just so, the creature sometimes travels wide
of this true course, for even when so driven
it still retains the power to turn aside   132

(exactly as we may see the heavens' fire
plunge from a cloud) and its first impulse may
be twisted earthward by a false desire.   135

You should not, as I see it, marvel more
at your ascent than at a river's fall
from a high mountain to the valley floor.   138

If you, free as you are of every dross,
had settled and had come to rest below,
that would indeed have been as marvelous   141

as a still flame there in the mortal plain."
So saying, she turned her eyes to Heaven again.

Notes

1. *of Him who moves all things*: God as the unmoved mover. Since any change from perfection would have to be toward a lessening, God is changeless in Dante's conception. Himself changeless (unmoved), therefore, he imparts the creating motion to all things.

2–3. *reflected* . . . *in proportion to its worth*: The more perfect the thing, the more perfectly it will reflect God's perfect shining. The more clouded the glass, so to speak, the less its ability to reflect the light.

4. *that Heaven of His most light*: "that heaven that takes (i.e., "receives" and, by implication, "reflects again") the most of His light." The Empyrean.

5–12. *those who descend* . . . *lack*: Dante was not a mystic in the pure sense of the word, but all mystics have stressed the ineffability of the mystical experience. How does one convey any rapturous experience once the rapture is over? William James in his *Varieties of Religious Experience* offers a fine introductory discussion of this question, *as our intellect draws near its goal*: The goal of intellect is God.

13–36. THE INVOCATION. Herefore, Dante has invoked the Muses. Now he invokes Apollo himself as the God of Poetry, and as the father of the Muses. Note, too, that Apollo is identified with the Sun and that Dante has consistently used the Sun as a symbol for God.

15. *crowned with bay*: The laurel wreath awarded to poets and conquerors. See also line 29 and XXV, 1–12.

16. *one peak of cleft Parnassus*: Parnassus has two peaks: Nisa, which was sacred to the Muses; and Cyrrha, which was sacred to Apollo. Heretofore Nisa has been enough for Dante's need, but for this last canticle he must summon aid from both peaks (i.e., from all the Muses and from Apollo as well).

20–21. *Marsyas*: The satyr Marsyas challenged Apollo to a singing contest and was defeated. Ovid (*Metamorphoses*, VI, 382–400) recounts in gory detail how Apollo thereupon punished him by pulling him out of his skin leaving all the uncovered organs still functioning.

Note that in this godly sport the skin was not pulled off Marsyas but that Marsyas was pulled out of his skin. In citing this incident Dante may be praying that he himself, in a sense, be pulled out of himself (i.e., be made to outdo himself), however painfully. *its sheath*: its skin.

23–27. *make clear even the shadow*: Sense: "Lend me enough power to make clear so much as the shadow of the ineffable light, and your power and my lofty theme will win me a laurel crown." *your dear grove*: The grove in which grows the sacred laurel, or bay.

31. *the glad Delphic god*: Apollo.

32. *Peneian frond*: The laurel or bay, so called for Daphne, daughter of the river god Peneus. Cupid, to avenge a taunt, fired an arrow of love into Apollo and an arrow of aversion into Daphne. Fleeing from the inflamed Apollo, Daphne prayed to her father and was changed into a laurel tree.

36. *Cyrrha will reply*: Cyrrha, Apollo's sacred peak, is here taken for Apollo himself. If Apollo does not heed his prayer, Dante will at least show the way, and perhaps a better poet will come after him and have his prayer answered by Apollo, whereby Paradise will at last be well portrayed.

37–42. THE POSITION OF THE SUN AT THE VERNAL EQUINOX. Short of pages of diagrams, there is no way of explaining Dante's astronomical figure in detail. A quick gloss must do: *the lamp*: The Sun. *various stations*: various points on the celestial horizon from which the sun rises at various times of the year. *four circles with three crosses*: The four circles here intended are: (1) the celestial horizon, (2) the celestial equator, (3) the ecliptic, and (4) equinoxial colure. The equinoxial colure is the great circle drawn through both poles and the two equinoxial points (the solsticial colure, similarly, passes through both poles and the two solsticial points). Since the equinox occurs when the sun crosses the celestial equator, both equinoxial points must lie on the equator and the equinoxial colure must be at right angles to the celestial equator. The celestial equator is the infinite extension of the plane of the earth's equator into the celestial sphere.

When the sun is in the position shown in the diagram the time is sunrise of the vernal equinox and all four circles meet, each of the other three forming a cross with the celestial horizon. Astrologers took this to be a particularly auspicious conjunction. Its *happier course* (line 40) brings the brighter and longer days of summer. Its *happier conjunction* (line 40) with the stars of Aries bring it back to the sign of the first creation (*see Inferno*, I, 38–39, note). And certainly the fact that the diagram forms three crosses would weigh it with the good omens of both the cross and trinity. All would once more be in God's shaping hand. So the *wax of the world* (line 41) is warmed and sealed, in a first sense by the warmth of approaching summer, and in a clearly implicit spiritual sense by the favor of God's will upon His creation.

This complicated figure could hardly have failed to suggest, further, some reference to the Four Cardinal Virtues, the Three Theological Virtues, and to the approaching Sun as Divine Illumination, now drawing to the full summer of mankind—for bear in mind that the southern hemisphere, in Dante's geography, was all water: there would be no mankind for the Sun to shine upon in its southern summer.

43–44. *evening here and morning there*: At the time Dante returned from drinking the waters of Eunöe. It is now noon, for only at noon could the entire southern hem-

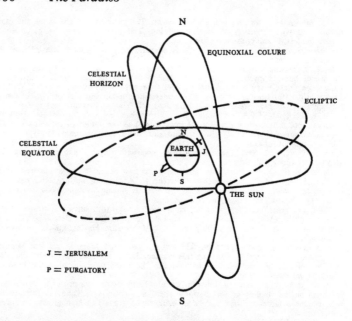

N

EQUINOXIAL COLURE

CELESTIAL
HORIZON

ECLIPTIC

CELESTIAL
EQUATOR

N

EARTH

J

P

S

THE SUN

J = JERUSALEM

P = PURGATORY

S

isphere be alight and the north dark—or so Dante must clearly intend, though I do not understand how that could be.

46. *had turned left*: Beatrice had been facing east with Eunöe before her. She now turns her eyes north to the sun.

47. *no eagle ever*: In the Middle Ages men believed that the eagle was able to stare directly into the sun.

49–54. *and as a ray*: Just as a descending ray of light strikes a reflecting surface and sends a reflected ray back upward, and at the same angle at which it struck the surface, so Beatrice's action in looking at the sun descends upon Dante like a ray from on high that enters through his eyes and strikes upward to his mind giving rise to a "reflected" action.

62. *day was added to day*: Dante perceives the increased brilliance of the light as if God had added a second sun to the sky, and he wonders at it. He does not yet know that the light has grown so much more brilliant because he is soaring through space toward the sun. He believes himself to be still in the Terrestrial Paradise.

Dante's device here, in showing himself as soaring toward God at enormous speed without, at first, realizing that he is soaring, is a superbly conceived climax to the whole theme of Purification as Gradual Weightlessness. In Hell all is gross and heavy. At the start of the Ascent of Purgatory, Dante almost drops from exhaustion. As he mounts and sin is stricken from him, he climbs ever more lightly. Now purified and perfected, he need not even think about mounting on high. His new nature draws effortlessly to God.

68. *Glaucus*: The fisherman Glaucus, noting how his catch revived and leaped into the sea after being laid upon a certain herb, ate some of it and was transformed into a god (Ovid, *Metamorphoses*, XIII, 898–968). Staring at Beatrice, Dante feels the beginning inside himself of that change that will make him, too, immortal.

73–75. *the last created part of my being*: The soul, which is created after the body. (See *Purgatorio*, XXV, 37–75.) *O Love that rulest Heaven*: God. *whose lamp*: Beatrice as the reflector of God's love.

76–78. *The Great Wheel etc.*: Dante says, literally: "The wheel that Thou, in being desired [i.e., loved] by it, makest eternal." The Great Wheel is the Primum Mobile, its motion deriving from the love of God. *captured my attention*: Indicates that Dante turned his eyes from Beatrice to look up again. *that harmony*: The Music of the Spheres.

80. *ablaze with sun*: Dante believed that the earth's atmosphere extended as high as the Sphere of the Moon. Beyond the Moon is another atmosphere of fire. This sphere of fire was believed to cause lightning. (See also line 115, "the fire about the moon".)

92. *natural place*: The Sphere of Fire. It summons all fire to itself. Conflicting forces of nature force the lightning downward, but the fiery elements dislocated under stress find their way back to their natural place. Dante still nas not realized that he and Beatrice are soaring toward Heaven at an incalculable speed.

93. *there*: To the Sphere of Fire.

104. *an inner order*: In relation to one another, and each in its relation to the total and to its final end, as fire to fire (see line 115). The end of man is God; therefore, the purified soul ascends naturally and inevitably to Him.

106. *the higher creatures*: The rational beings of creation: angels, heavenly spirits, and men.

108. *these norms*: The mode and form of lines 103–104.

123–124. *the heaven*: The Empyrean. *the fastest sphere*: The Primum Mobile. The Empyrean does not move and it is beyond space. It is eternal and perfect Love (therefore unchangeable) and holds within its constancy all of space, including the outermost and greatest sphere, the Primum Mobile.

125. *that bow*: The innate impulse of all creatures to seek their place in God.

127–135. The free will of creatures allows them, despite the innate order of all things, to yield to false pleasures and so to resist God's plan as the matter in which the artist works, being base and imperfect, may resist his intent to give it ideal form. One might argue against this figure that the artist in this case, being God, is omnipotent and could, at will, work in perfect matter. But to enter into such an argument would only be to bump heads on the question of fallible free will within an omnipotent creation—a question that has vexed Christian theology for millennia.

141. *that would indeed have been . . . marvelous*: Because then it would be going against the order of the universe. What is purified must ascend to God as inevitably as earthly waters must flow downhill.

Canto II

Warning to the Reader

THE FIRST SPHERE: THE MOON
Beatrice Explains the Markings on the Moon

Dante and Beatrice are soaring to *The Sphere of the Moon* at a speed
approaching that of light. Dante warns back the shallow reader: only those
who have eaten of the knowledge of God may hope to follow him into the
last reaches of his infinite voyage, for it will reveal such wonders as only
faith can grasp.

His warning concluded, he and Beatrice enter the Sphere of the Moon
and pass into the substances of the moon as light into water, as God incar-
nated himself into man, or as the saved soul reenters God, without disrup-
tion of the substance thus entered.

Still unenlightened by the ultimate revelation, Dante does not understand how there can appear on the diamond-smooth surface on the moon
(as he conceived it) those markings we know as *The Man in the Moon*,
and which the Italians knew as *Cain with His Bush of Thorns*.

Beatrice asks for his explanation, refutes it, and proceeds to explain the
truth of the moon's markings.

> O you who in your wish to hear these things
>   have followed thus far in your little skiffs
>   the wake of my great ship that sails and sings,   3
>
> turn back and make your way to your own coast.
>   Do not commit yourself to the main deep,
>   for, losing me, all may perhaps be lost.   6
>
> My course is set for an uncharted sea.
>   Minerva fills my sail. Apollo steers.
>   And nine new Muses point the Pole for me.   9
>
> You other few who have set yourselves to eat
>   the bread of angels, by which we live on earth,
>   but of which no man ever grew replete;   12
>
> you may well trust your keel to the salt track
>   and follow in the furrow of my wake
>   ahead of the parted waters that close back.   15
>
> Those heroes who sailed to Colchis, there to see
>   their glorious Jason turned into a plowman,
>   were not as filled with wonder as you will be.   18
>
> The connate and perpetual thirst we feel
>   for the God-like realm, bore us almost as swiftly
>   as the sight soars to see the heavens wheel.   21

Beatrice was looking upward and I at her
  when—in the time it takes a bolt to strike,
  fly, and be resting in the bowstring's blur—   24

I found myself in a place where a wondrous thing
  drew my entire attention; whereat she
  from whom I could not hide my mind's least yearning   27

turned and said, as much in joy as beauty:
  "To God, who has raised us now to the first star
  direct your thoughts in glad and grateful duty."   30

It seemed to me a cloud as luminous
  and dense and smoothly polished as a diamond
  struck by a ray of sun, enveloped us.   33

We were received into the elements
  of the eternal pearl as water takes
  light to itself, with no change in its substance.   36

If I were a body (nor need we in this case
  conceive how one dimension can bear another,
  which must be if two bodies fill one space)   39

the more should my desire burn like the sun
  to see that Essence in which one may see
  how human nature and God blend into one.   42

There we shall witness what we hold in faith,
  not told by reason but self-evident;
  as men perceive an axiom here on earth.   45

"My lady," I replied, "in every way
  my being can, I offer up my thanks
  to Him who raised me from the world of clay.   48

But tell me what dark traces in the grain
  of this bright body show themselves below
  and cause men to tell fables about Cain?"   51

She smiled a moment and then answered me:
  "If the reckoning of mortals fails to turn
  the lock to which your senses hold no key,   54

the arrows of wonder should not run you through:
  even when led by the evidence of the senses
  the wings of reason often do not fly true.   57

But what do *you* believe the cause to be?"
  And I: "That these variations we observe
  are caused by bodies of varying density."   60

And she: "You will certainly come to know your view
  is steeped in falsehood. If you listen well
  to the counter-arguments I shall offer you.   63

The eighth sphere shines with many lamps, and these
    may be observed to shine with various aspects,
    both in their qualities and quantities.   66

If rare or dense alone could have produced
    all this, one power would have to be in all,
    whether equally or variously diffused.   69

Diversity of powers can only spring
    from formal principles, and all but one
    would be excluded by your reasoning.   72

Now if rarity produced the marks you mention,
    then the matter of this planet must be transparent
    at certain points, due to its rarefaction;   75

or it must be arranged like fat and lean
    within a body, as, so to speak, a book
    alternates pages. But it may be seen   78

in an eclipse that the first cannot be true,
    for then the sun's light, as it does in striking
    rare matter of any sort, would pass right through.   81

Since it does not, we may then pass along
    to the second case, and if I prove it false,
    I shall have shown that your whole thought is wrong.   84

If this rare matter is not spread throughout
    the planet's mass, then there must be a limit
    at which the denser matter will turn about   87

the sun's rays, which, not being allowed to pass,
    will be reflected as light and color are
    from the leaded back of a clear looking glass.   90

Now you may argue, in Avicenna's track,
    that the ray seems darker in one place than in others
    since it is being reflected from further back.   93

From such an *instance* (if you will do your part)
    you may escape by experiment (that being
    the spring that feeds the rivers of man's art).   96

Take three clear mirrors. Let two be set out
    at an equal distance from you, and a third
    between them, but further back. Now turn about   99

to face them, and let someone set a light
    behind your back so that it strikes all three
    and is reflected from them to your sight.   102

Although the image from the greater distance
    is smaller than the others, you must note
    that all three shine back with an equal brilliance.   105

Now, as the power of the sun's rays will strip
    the wintry ground on which the snow has lain
    of the cold and color that held it in their grip,   108

so you, with mind stripped clean, shall I delight
   with such a radiance of the living truth
   that it will leap and tremble in your sight.   111

Within the heaven of peace beyond the sky
   there whirls a body from whose power arises
   the being of all things that within it lie.   114

The next sphere, that which is so richly lit,
   distributes this power to many essences
   distinct from itself, yet all contained within it.   117

The other spheres, in various degrees,
   dispose the special powers they have within
   to their own causes and effects. All these   120

great universal organs, as you now know,
   proceed from grade to grade. Each in its order
   takes power from above and does its work below.   123

Now then, note carefully how I move on
   through this pass to the truth you seek, for thus
   you shall learn how to hold the ford alone.   126

The motion and the power of the sacred gyres—
   as the hammer's art is from the smith—must flow
   from the Blessèd Movers. It is their power inspires.   129

And thus that Heaven made loveliest in its wheel
   by many lamps, from the deep mind that turns it
   takes the image and makes itself the seal.   132

And as the soul within your mortal clay
   is spread through different organs, each of which
   is shaped to its own end; in the same way   135

the high angelic Intelligence spreads its goodness
   diversified through all the many stars
   while yet revolving ever in its Öneness.   138

This varying power is variously infused
   throughout the precious body that it quickens,
   in which, like life in you, it is diffused.   141

Because of the glad nature from which it flows,
   this many-faceted power shines through that body
   as through the living eye the glad soul glows.   144

From this source only, not from rare and dense,
   comes that by which one light and another differs—
   the formal principle whose excellence,   147

conforming to its own purposes, makes appear
   those markings you observe as dark and clear.

Notes

3. *of my great ship*: See *Purgatorio*, I, 1-2. There Dante refers to "the little bark of my indwelling powers." For the present voyage nothing less than a great (God-inspired) ship will do.

7-9. No poet has ever undertaken any such subject as Dante now sings. Poetically, therefore, he is embarking on waters no man has ever sailed. Apollo will guide his helm by the rules of poetry, but it is Minerva, goddess of wisdom, who must fill his sails, and the Muses who must be his navigators. *nine new Muses*: Dante says, simply, *"nove Muse."* But *"nove"* may mean either *"nine'"* or *"new." the Pole*: Dante says "the Bears" (Ursa Major and Ursa Minor. The North Star is in Ursa Minor but its position in the sky is usually located by first identifying Ursa Major, the stars of Ursa Minor being dim.)

11. *the bread of angels*: The knowledge of God. It is by that, Dante says, that we are able to live, but no mortal man can grasp enough of it to become satisfied, the Divine Mystery being veiled from man.

13-15. The few who have sought the knowledge of God are described as having keels. Hence they sail in something more seaworthy than the little skiffs of the others. Those few may dare the voyage, but note how closely they must follow Dante—they must stay in the very furrow of his wake, ahead of the waters that flow back to close it. Clearly, Dante means that he must be followed with the most scrupulous attention if the truth of his poem is to be grasped.

16-17. *Those heroes*: The Argonauts. Jason led them to Colchis to get the Golden Fleece. The Colchian King offered to give Jason the fleece if he would subdue two fire-breathing brass-hooved bulls, yoke them, plow the field of Ares with them, sow the field with dragon's teeth, and then defeat the army of warriors that would spring up from the teeth.

19. *connate*: Dante says *"concreata."* The thirst for God is born in the instant the soul is formed.

20-21. *almost as swiftly as the eye*: Dante and Beatrice soar upward at almost the speed of light.

23-24. The bolt of a crossbow would leave the bowstring so rapidly that human sense could not measure the rate of change. Hence, the figure means "instantly." But Dante has deliberately reversed the motion, a daring hysteron-proteron. Prof. John Freccero cites it, in the best interpretation known to me, as an example of Dante's "retrospective technique." Bear in mind that Dante is looking backward at the world and sees earthly actions in reverse. See XXII, 109, for another such usage.

27. *drew my entire attention*: As noted in line 22, Dante's attention had been fixed on Beatrice.

29. *to the first star*: The "first star" is the Moon. Dante has reached the first sphere of the Ptolemaic system.

32. *dense and smoothly polished as a diamond*: Dante finds the surface of the Moon to be diamond-smooth and highly polished (the telescope that was to reveal the jagged surface had not yet been invented).

35. *the eternal pearl*: The Moon.

37-42. THE UNITY OF GOD AND MAN. Dante is dealing here in the mysteries of faith. On Earth two bodies, being conceived as solids, cannot occupy the same space ("one dimension cannot bear another"). Yet, as light is received by water with no change in its self-unity, so Dante enters into the substance of the Moon, and this miraculous unity with which he enters the Moon-substance without disrupting it, sends his mind soaring to the mystery of the incarnation of God, and to the ultimate reception of the good man into the ineffable Logos. *that Essence*: Christ as the Man-God.

44. *not told by reason*: Reason is only the handmaiden of faith. With his final purification in the Earthly Paradise, Dante passed beyond reason to the greater way of knowing. Virgil's last words to Dante were: "Lord of yourself I crown and miter you." With his subsequent purification Dante achieves the state in which every effort of the will and of the intellect cease. Yet the understanding grows, for now the soul perceives as self-evident what had seemed incomprehensible to mere reason.

49-51. *dark traces . . . Cain?* In Dante's Italy what we call the Man in the Moon was fabled to be Cain with a Bush of Thorns. Recall that Dante has just described the lunar surface as being diamond-smooth and polished: such a surface would not show dark traces.

52-57. Sense: No wonder men fable falsely when they have no sensory evidence on which to base their reasoning. Even in matters about which firm sensory evidence is available to them they do not always reason correctly.

64-66. *The eighth sphere*: The Sphere of the Fixed Stars. *lamps*: Stars. *qualities and quantities*: Coloration and intensity. The phrasing of Beatrice's disquisition is characteristically Scholastic: one can only repeat the admonition of the first six lines of the present Canto and hope the willing reader will accept the invitation of lines 10-18.

68. *power*: The influence of the stars upon the earth and upon the lives of men.

71. *formal principle*: Scholastic teaching distinguishes two principles in all bodies: the *material*, which is to say, the first matter, which is the same in all; and the *formal*, which is to say the substantial form that produces the various species and innate abilities of living forms. The *formal principle* is active; the *material principle*, passive. Dante's reasoning is false in that it would reduce all to a single principle.

73. ff. BEATRICE'S EXPLANATION OF THE MARKINGS OF THE MOON. In *Il Convivio*, II, 14, Dante had attributed these traces to differences in the density of the lunar matter, whereby the body reflected the light unequally. In this he followed Avicenna. (The reference to Avicenna in line 91 is not explicitly in the original text, but it is clearly implied.) Now, with Beatrice as his revelation, he refutes his earlier belief, having her first show that such a belief leads to impossible conclusions, and then having her assign the true cause to the special power diffused by the Primum Mobile. That power, though itself indivisible, dispenses itself with varying intensity according to the different bodies it permeates—as the soul, for example, permeates some parts of the body more intensely than it does others.

Beatrice's argument is a curious one, Scholastic, pragmatic, and mystical by turn. She begins by demonstrating that Dante's belief involves a true dilemma (an either/or) and proceeds to reduce either term to an absurdity, offering in evidence practical observations of an eclipse and an experiment she suggests to Dante. As noted above, she then explains the phenomenon by the mystic nature of the Primum Mobile.

93. *reflected*: Dante says *"rifratto"* (refracted). The physics of his time did not distinguish between reflection and refraction.

94. *instance*: A technical term (*"instanza"*) of Aristotelian and Scholastic logic signifying "counter-proposition." Dante's figure treats the *instance* as a trap from which one must escape with the aid of experiment.

96. *art*: Learning. See *Inferno*, XI, 97–105. In Dante "art" signifies the skills, the crafts, and all the methods by which man understands and wins control over nature. It is always distinct from the higher knowledge of faith.

97–105. THE EXPERIMENT. Dante assumes in this experiment that the heavenly bodies are highly reflective surfaces. Thus by shining a light into three mirrors, two equidistant from him and one further back, and noting (though the size of the remoter image is smaller) that the brightness of all three is equal, he seems to argue that light of equal intensity is equally brilliant from whatever distance it is reflected. The argument is ingenious but any reader interested in the rudiments of science will be able to offer his own refutation of the experiment when its conclusions are applied to heavenly bodies at astronomic distances as seen at varying angles through a varying atmosphere.

108–109. *cold and color*: Both the cold and the whiteness are removed from the ground. *so you, stripped in your mind*: So Dante, the cold and color of error stripped from his mind, will be flooded with the living light (like the fructifying light and heat of returning Spring) of the truth.

112. *the heaven of peace beyond the sky*: The Empyrean. I have had to take liberties here. A literal rendering would be: "within the heaven of the divine peace."

113. *a body*: The Primum Mobile. Since the Empyrean (which lies beyond) is beyond space, the sphere of the Primum Mobile contains all of the universe. Taking its power from the all-encompassing Godhead (The Empyrean), it gives rise to all being.

115. *the next sphere*: Of the Fixed Stars.

120. *to their own causes and effects*: Each sphere to those causes and effects influenced by its particular powers.

123. *takes power from above*: From God. *and does its work below*: Ultimately upon man (the influence of the heavens upon mortal lives) but intermediately some of the work of each sphere must be to transmit certain powers (undiminished) to the spheres below.

124–126. Beatrice, as ever, is acting as Dante's teacher. Here, in a military figure, she instructs him to take careful note of how her argument proceeds through the next point, that by her example Dante may learn how to defend the ford (the crossing to the truth) by himself.

127. *gyres*: Circlings.

129. *the Blessed Movers*: The Angels, Powers, Principalities, and Intelligences who influence each sphere.

130. *the Heaven made loveliest by many lamps*: The Sphere of the Fixed Stars.

131–132. *from the deep mind*: Of God. The Sphere of the Fixed Stars receives its power from God (through the Primum Mobile) and taking His image from above, makes itself the seal that impresses that image on the spheres below (as a seal impresses its given image upon wax).

135. *shaped to its own end*: As the eye to sight, the ear to sound, *etc.*

140. *the precious body*: Of the Sphere of the Fixed Stars, here compared to the human body, because its unity comprises so many varied organs.

142. *the glad nature*: Of God.

147. *formal principle*: (see also note to line 71.) The power of the Divine and Angelic Intelligence is the intrinsic and substantial cause which produces the effect of dark and clear according to the various ways in which it enters into conjunction with the stars.

Canto III

The Inconstant · *Piccarda, Constance*

As Dante is about to speak to Beatrice he sees the dim traceries of human faces and taking them to be reflections, he turns to see what souls are being so reflected. Beatrice, as ever, explains that these pallid images are the souls themselves. They are *The Inconstant*, the souls of those who registered holy vows in Heaven, but who broke or scanted them.

Among them *Piccarda Donati* identifies herself, and then identifies *The Empress Constance*. Both, according to Dante's beliefs, had taken vows as nuns but were forced to break them in order to contract a political marriage. Not all the souls about them need have failed in the same vows, however. Any failure to fulfill a holy vow (of holy orders, to go on a prilgrimage, to offer special services to God) might place the soul in this lowest class of the blessed.

Piccarda explains that every soul in Heaven rejoices in the entire will of God and cannot wish for a higher place, for to do so would be to come into conflict with the will of God. In the perfect harmony of bliss, everywhere in Heaven is Paradise.

> That sun that breathed love's fire into my youth
> had thus resolved for me, feature by feature—
> proving, disproving—the sweet face of truth.   3
>
> I, raising my eyes to her eyes to announce
> myself resolved of error, and well assured,
> was about to speak; but before I could pronounce   6
>
> my first word, there appeared to me a vision.
> It seized and held me so that I forgot
> to offer her my thanks and my confession.   9
>
> As in clear glass when it is polished bright,
> or in a still and limpid pool whose waters
> are not so deep that the bottom is lost from sight,   12
>
> a footnote of our lineaments will show,
> so pallid that our pupils could as soon
> make out a pearl upon a milk-white brow—   15
>
> so I saw many faces eager to speak,
> and fell to the error opposite the one
> that kindled love for a pool in the smitten Greek.   18
>
> And thinking the pale traces I saw there
> were reflected images, I turned around
> to face the source—but my eyes met empty air.   21
>
> I turned around again like one beguiled,
> and took my line of sight from my sweet guide
> whose sacred eyes grew radiant as she smiled.   24

"Are you surprised that I smile at this childish act
of reasoning?" she said, "since even now
you dare not trust your sense of the true fact,   27

but turn, as usual, back to vacancy?
These are true substances you see before you.
They are assigned here for inconstancy   30

to holy vows. Greet them. Heed what they say,
and so believe; for the True Light that fills them
permits no soul to wander from its ray."   33

So urged, I spoke to those pale spirits, turning
to one who seemed most eager, and began
like one whose mind goes almost blank with yearning.   36

"O well created soul, who in the sun
of the eternal life drinks in the sweetness
which, until tasted, is beyond conception;   39

great would be my joy would you confide
to my eager mind your earthly name and fate."
That soul with smiling eyes, at once replied: 42

"The love that fills us will no more permit
hindrance to a just wish than does that Love
that wills all of Its court to be like It.   45

I was a virgin sister there below,
and if you search your memory with care,
despite my greater beauty, you will know   48

I am Piccarda, and I am placed here
among these other souls of blessedness
to find my blessedness in the slowest sphere.   51

Our wishes, which can have no wish to be
but in the pleasure of the Holy Ghost,
rejoice in being formed to His decree.   54

And this low-seeming post which we are given
is ours because we broke, or, in some part,
slighted the vows we offered up to Heaven."   57

And I then: "Something inexpressibly
divine shines in your face, subliming you
beyond your image in my memory: 60

therefore I found you difficult to place;
but now, with the assistance of your words,
I find the memory easier to retrace.   63

But tell me, please: do you who are happy here
have any wish to rise to higher station,
to see more, or to make yourselves more dear?"   66

She smiled, as did the spirits at her side;
   then, turning to me with such joy she seemed
   to burn with the first fire of love, replied: 69

"Brother, the power of love, which is our bliss,
   calms all our will. What we desire, we have.
   There is in us no other thirst than this.   72

Were we to wish for any higher sphere,
   then our desires would not be in accord
   with the high will of Him who wills us here;   75

and if love is our whole being, and if you weigh
   love's nature well, then you will see that discord
   can have no place among these circles. Nay,   78

the essence of this blessèd state of being
   is to hold all our will within His will,
   whereby our wills are one and all-agreeing.   81

And so the posts we stand from sill to sill
   throughout this realm, please all the realm as much
   as they please Him who wills us to His will.   84

In His will is our peace. It is that sea
   to which all moves, all that Itself creates
   and Nature bears through all Eternity."   87

Then was it clear to me that everywhere
   in Heaven is Paradise, though the Perfect Grace
   does not rain down alike on all souls there.   90

But as at times when we have had our fill
   of one food and still hunger for another,
   we put this by with gratitude, while still   93

asking for that—just so I begged to know,
   by word and sign, through what warp she had not
   entirely passed the shuttle of her vow.   96

"The perfection of her life and her great worth
   enshrine a lady hereabove," she said
   "in whose rule some go cloaked and veiled on earth,   99

that till their death they may live day and night
   with that sweet Bridegroom who accepts of love
   all vows it makes that add to His delight.   102

As a girl, I fled the world to walk the way
   she walked, and closed myself into her habit,
   pledge to her sisterhood till my last day.   105

Then men came, men more used to hate than love.
   They tore me away by force from the sweet cloister.
   What my life then became is known above.   108

This other splendor who lets herself appear
here to my right to please you, shining full
of every blessedness that lights this sphere,   111

understands in herself all that I say.
She, too, was a nun. From her head as from mine
the shadow of the veil was ripped away.   114

Against her will and all propriety
she was forced back to the world. Yet even there
her heart was ever veiled in sanctity.   117

She is the radiance of the Empress Constance
who by the second blast of Swabia
conceived and bore its third and final puissance."   120

She finished, and at once began to sing
Ave Maria, and singing, sank from view
like a weight into deep water, plummeting   123

out of my sight, which followed while it could,
and then, having lost her, turned about once more
to the target of its greater wish and good,   126

and wholly gave itself to the delight
of the sweet vision of Beatrice. But she
flashed so radiantly upon my sight   129

that I, at first, was blinded, and thus was slow
to ask of her what I most wished to know.

Notes

1. *That sun*: Beatrice. It was she who first breathed love's fire into Dante's youth. (See also *Purgatorio*, XXX, 40–42 and *Paradiso*, XXX, 75.)

3. *proving*: Her views, the truth. *and disproving*: My views, error.

9. *my confession*: Of the error Dante now recognizes (concerning the markings of the moon).

13. *a footnote of our lineaments*: The figure seems oddly out of context but its intent is clear: Dante is suggesting that the image is related to the face as a footnote is related to the text.

15. *a pearl upon a milk-white brow*: The brow would have to be death-pale as marble, but perhaps Dante intends these spirits to be chalky-white.

16. THE INCONSTANT. All these spirits registered vows in Heaven and then either broke or slighted them. Both of those cited took vows as nuns and were then forced to break them against their own wishes. One must assume, however, that the same category would include not only monks and priests who similarly gave up holy orders, but all who offered up a vow of any sort and then failed to observe it strictly.

They are "assigned here" (line 30), which is to say they appear on the moon (the inconstant planet), but each has his throne in the Empyrean (see IV, 23). All the souls of the blessed, whatever their rank in Heaven, experience as much bliss as they are capable of and cannot wish for more. Within the divine order each seeks and finds its proper place.

18. *the smitten Greek*: Narcissus. His error was in taking a reflection (his own) to be a real face. Dante's opposite error is in taking real faces to be reflections.

32. *the True Light*: God.

33. *permits no soul to wander*: So Dante's phrasing, but it should be understood

that filled as these souls are by the True Light, their inability to stray from its ray (contrast Dante's situation in line 27) is not a prohibition but a choice of their own perfected volition. They are not capable of error.

44. *that Love*: God, as the essence of *Caritas*.

46. *virgin sister*: A nun.

49. *Piccarda*: Piccarda Donati was the daughter of Simone Donati (*Inferno*, XXV, 32) and sister of Forese (*Purgatorio*, XXIII, 48) and of the war-leader, Corso (*Purgatorio*, XXIV, 82ff.). Forese was Dante's friend. Dante was married to Gemma Donati, who also had a brother named Forese, but Piccarda's family was grander than Dante's in-laws.

Piccarda was already a nun and living in her convent when her brother Corso, needing to establish a political alliance, forced her to marry Rossellino della Tossa of Florence. Various commentators report that Piccarda sickened and soon died as a consequence of having been so forced against her will and vows.

52–54. THE BLISS OF THE BLESSED. Every soul in Heaven, whatever its station, is entirely happy because it is entirely identified with God's plan and has no joy but in being formed to His will. The essence of God is love, i.e., *caritas*, the love of others. With *caritas* as the essential mood of the *Paradiso*, no soul can help but rejoice in the joy of all about it. Contrast the state of things in the *Inferno*: the infernal souls have all refused to accept and to identify themselves with the Divine Love; each, therefore, is closed into itself, and no soul in Hell can derive any comfort from any other (see *Inferno*, V, note to line 102). Joy finds its increase exactly in being freely given to others. As Piccarda soon makes clear to Dante, that joy is expressed in Heaven in no way but in the complete identification with God's love.

63. *easier to retrace*: A desperate simplification of Dante's untranslatable *"m'è più latino"* (literally: "it is more Latin to me"). Learned men of Dante's time used Latin naturally and gracefully. Thus to make a thing "more Latin" was to facilitate it. An opposite form of a similar idiom is our still current "It's Greek to me."

66. *to make yourselves more dear*: To God.

69. *the first fire of love*: Could variously be taken to mean God, the Moon (the first lit sphere of the Universe, which is Love), or the bliss mortals feel in the fire of newly awakened love. On the narrative level the last seems most likely, but the other meanings could function along with it.

95–96. *warp . . . shuttle*: The vertical strings of a loom are the warp. Across them the shuttle draws the woof. Not to draw the shuttle entirely through is to leave the weaving unfinished, hence her vow unfulfilled.

98. *a lady*: Saint Clara of Assisi (1194–1253). Born Chiara Sciffi, she became a disciple of St. Francis and, under his influence, founded in 1212 an order of nuns. *hereabove*: Higher in Heaven. Probably in the Empyrean, but Dante does not mention her again.

101. *that sweet Bridegroom*: Christ. He is so-called several times in the New Testament.

102. *all vows . . . that add to His delight*: Only those vows that conform to His love are acceptable. A vow to perform a trivial or an evil action would have no standing.

109. *This other splendor*: The Empress Constance (1154–1198). As the last of the line of Norman kings who took southern Italy in the eleventh century, she was Empress of the Two Sicilies (Sicily and Naples). She married the Emperor Henry VI in 1185 and became the mother of Frederick II. Dante follows a legend, for which there was no basis in fact, that she had become a nun and was forced to leave her convent to marry Henry.

109. *lets herself appear*: Dante says, "who shows herself to you." Clearly, the souls in Paradise can make themselves visible or invisible at will (i.e., Heaven reveals itself of its own love). At the end of the conversation the whole company withdraws from sight.

119. THE THREE BLASTS OF SWABIA. These are the three great princes whose origins were in Swabia (in Germany). Frederick Barbarossa was the first. His son, Henry VI, was the second. To Henry, Constance bore the third, Frederick II.

Canto IV

Beatrice Discourses:

The True Seat of the Blessed · Plato's Error ·
Free Will · Recompense for Broken Vows

Piccarda has told Dante that she inhabits the sphere of the inconstant
Moon because she broke her vows against her will. Dante is torn by doubts
that could lead to heresy. Was Plato right in saying souls come from their
various stars preformed, and then return to them? If so, what of *Free Will?*
And if Heaven is Justice, how have these souls sinned in being forced
against their wills? And if Heaven is truth, what of the contradiction
between Piccarda's statements and Beatrice's?

Beatrice resolves all of Dante's doubts. When she has finished Dante asks
if men may offer *Other Recompense for Broken Vows.*

A man given free choice would starve to death
  between two equal equidistant foods,
  unable to get either to his teeth.   3

So would a lamb, in counterbalanced fear,
  tremble between two she-wolves and stand frozen.
  So would a hound stand still between two deer.   6

If I stood mute, then, tugged to either side,
  I neither blame myself, nor take my doubt—
  it being necessary—as cause for pride.   9

I did not speak, but on my face, at once,
  were written all my questions and my yearnings,
  far more distinctly than I could pronounce.   12

And Beatrice did as Daniel once had done
  when he raised Nebuchadnezzar from the wrath
  that made him act unjustly in Babylon.   15

"I see full well how equal wish and doubt
  tear you two ways," she said, "so that your zeal
  tangles upon itself and cannot breathe out.   18

You reason: "If the will that vowed stays true,
  how can another's violence take away
  from the full measure of bliss that is my due?"   21

And I see a second doubt perplex that thought
  because the souls you see seem to return
  to the stars from which they came, as Plato taught.   24

These are the question that bear down your will
  with equal force. Therefore, I shall treat first
  the one whose venom has more power to kill.   27

Choose the most God-like of the Seraphim—
   takes Moses, or Samuel, or take either John,
   or even Mary—not one is nearer Him,   30

nor holds his seat atop the blessèd spheres
   in any heaven apart from those you saw;
   nor has his being more or fewer years.   33

All add their beauty to the Highest Wheel,
   share the sweet life, and vary in it only
   by how much of the Eternal Breath they feel.   36

They showed themselves here not because this post
   has been assigned them, but to symbolize
   that they stand lowest in the Heavenly host.   39

So must one speak to mortal imperfection,
   which only from the *sensible* apprehends
   whatever it then makes fit for intellection.   42

Scripture in like manner condescends,
   describing God as having hands and feet
   as signs to men of what more it portends.   45

So Holy Church shows you in mortal guise
   the images of Gabriel and of Michael,
   and of the other who gave back Tobit's eyes.   48

For if Timaeus—as seems rather clear—
   spoke literally, what he says about souls
   is nothing like the truth shown to us here.   51

He says the soul finds its own star again,
   from which, as he imagines, nature chose it
   to give form to the flesh and live with men.   54

But it may be the words he uses hide
   a second meaning, which, if understood,
   reveals a principle no man may deride.   57

If he means that the blame or honor due
   the influence of each sphere returns to it,
   his arrow does hit something partly true.   60

This principle, misunderstood, once drove
   almost the whole world to attach to planets
   such names as Mars and Mercury and Jove.   63

The other doubt that agitates your mind
   is not as venemous, for not all its malice
   could drive you from my side to wander blind.   66

For mortal men to argue that they see
   injustice in our justice is in itself
   a proof of faith, not poisonous heresy.   69

But since the truth of this lies well within
the reach of your own powers, I shall explain it,
just as you wish.—If violence, to begin,   72

occurs when those who suffer its abuse
contribute nothing to what forces them,
then these souls have no claim to that excuse.   75

For the will, if it will not, cannot be spent,
but does as nature does within a flame
a thousand or ten thousand winds have bent.   78

If it yield of itself, even in the least,
then it assists the violence—as did these
who could have gone back to their holy feast.   81

If their whole will had joined in their desire—
as whole will upheld Lawrence on the grill,
and Mucius with his hand thrust in the fire,   84

just so, it would have forced them to return
to their true way the instant they were free.
But such pure will is too rare, we must learn!   87

If you have gleaned them diligently, then
these words forever destroy the argument
that would have plagued your mind time and again.   90

But now another pass opens before you,
so strait and tortuous that without my help
you would tire along the way and not win through.   93

I made you understand beyond all doubt
that these souls cannot lie, for they exist
in the First Truth and cannot wander out.   96

Later you heard Piccarda say that she
who stood beside her kept her love of the veil;
and it seems that what she said contradicts me.   99

Time and again, my brother, men have run
from danger by a path they would not choose,
and on it done what ought not to be done.   102

So, bending to his father's prayer, did he
who took his mother's life. Alcmaeon I mean,
who sought his piety in impiety.   105

Now weigh within your own intelligence
how will and violence interact, so joining
that no excuse can wipe out the offense.   108

Absolute will does not will its own harm,
but fearing worse may come if it resists,
consents the more, the greater its alarm.   111

Thus when Piccarda spoke as she did to you,
   she meant the absolute will; and I, the other.
   So both of us spoke only what was true."   114

—Such was the flowing of that stream so blest
   it flows down from the Fountain of All Truth.
   Such was the power that laid my doubts to rest.   117

"Beloved of the First Love! O holy soul!"
   I said then, "You whose words flow over me,
   and with their warmth quicken and make me whole,   120

There is not depth enough within my love
   to offer you due thanks, but may the One
   who sees and can, answer for me above.   123

Man's mind, I know, cannot win through the mist
   unless it is illumined by that Truth
   beyond which truth has nowhere to exist.   126

In That, once it has reached it, it can rest
   like a beast within its den. And reach it can;
   else were all longing vain, and vain the test.   129

Like a new tendril yearning from man's will
   doubt sprouts to the foot of truth. It is that in us
   that drives us to the summit from hill to hill.   132

By this am I encouraged, by this bidden,
   my lady, in all reverence, to ask
   your guidance to a truth that still lies hidden: 135

can such as these who put away their veils
   so compensate by other good works done
   that they be not found wanting on your scales?"   138

Beatrice looked at me, and her glad eyes,
   afire with their divinity, shot forth
   such sparks of love that my poor faculties   141

gave up the reins. And with my eyes cast down
I stood entranced, my senses all but flown.

Notes

1–9. DANTE'S DOUBT. The phrasing of this passage is difficult. Nor am I sure I have found the right rendering of all the grammatical ambiguities. The intent, on the other hand, is clear. Piccarda's account of herself has raised questions that, as we shall see, tear Dante's understanding in two directions at once. Beatrice, as usual, senses his self-division and resolves all in the conversation that follows.

The difficulty of the phrasing is caused by the interplay of the ideas "free choice" and "necessity." Dante follows Aquinas in this: if the choices offered to a man are entirely equal, no choice can be made and the man cannot act. Thus Dante takes neither blame nor praise for his indecisive doubts since he was unable to choose between them.

13. *as Daniel had done*: Nebuchadnezzar, King of Babylon, condemned all his diviners to death because they could not interpret a dream he had forgotten. Daniel first

divined the dream and then interpreted it, calming the fury of the king. (*Daniel*, II, 1–45.)

19. *if the will that vowed stays true*: Dante is thinking of what Piccarda said. If her will to keep her vows never faltered, how can the fact that her brother's violence forced her to act against her will alter her just reward for the purity of her intentions (which, seemingly, should have earned her a higher place in Heaven).

24. *as Plato taught*: As Dante rendered the *Timaeus*, Plato taught that souls existed in the stars before they entered human bodies (Wordsworth's "Ode on the Intimations of Immortality" is a well-known treatment of this theme) and returned, at the body's death, to the same stars from which they had come. Such a doctrine, however, denies free will, the soul being pre-created to a fixed place in Heaven's order. And yet the souls of the Inconstant seem to return to the inconstant Moon. Thus one thought negates the other, leaving Dante's mind ensnared between the two.

27. *whose venom has more power to kill*: The doctrine within which lurks the greater danger of self-destroying heresy.

28–63. THE PLACE IN HEAVEN OF THE BLEST. Every soul in heaven is equally a part of God. As Beatrice goes on to explain, all have their seats in the Empyrean. The various spheres in which *they appear to Dante* only symbolize the degree of their beatitude. It is necessary to use such symbols because the limited comprehension of mankind could not begin to grasp the truth in any other way. Thus, the Bible speaks of God as if he had a manlike body when he is in fact Essence. Beatrice's point is that every soul is equally in God. All have their place in one Heaven, all are eternal. They vary only in the degree of their beatitude, which is determined by their own ability to absorb the infinity of God's bliss.

36. *the Eternal Breath*: Recall from *Genesis* that it was God's breath that quickened the dust to life. The Eternal Breath, therefore, is the gift of life, and the difference in the beatitude of the blessed must be in the degree to which they are quickened to their Eternal life. The pallor of those moon-souls, as contrasted to the blinding radiance of those who appear higher, may also, perhaps, be taken as a measure of how much of the Eternal Breath is in them.

48. *the other*: Raphael, the third archangel. He cured Tobit of blindness (*Tobit*, XI, 2–17).

54. *to give form*: (The rest of this line, though implicit in Dante, is my own rhyme-forced addition.) The soul, in Scholastic teaching, is the *formative power*. (See *Purgatorio*, XXV, 40–42, note.) The body is simply the matter upon which it works to impress its form.

61–63. *this principle*: That souls come down from the stars (or spheres, or planets) and return to them. *almost the whole world*: The exception was the Jews. All others imagined multiple gods (Mars, Mercury, and Jove, for example) whose names they attached to the planets. *Jove*: For Jupiter.

64–69. *the other doubt*: Of the justice of placing Piccarda and Constance among the Inconstant when they were forced to break their vows against their will. This doubt is not as venemous because it does not lead to heresy. The Council of Constantinople (540 A.D.) had denounced the doctrine of the *Timaeus* as heretical. But the church had not pronounced infallibly on the matter of Dante's second doubt. That second doubt, therefore, might lead Dante into error but not into heresy. It could not, therefore, drive him from Beatrice (Revealed Truth) to wander blind outside the church. *proof of faith*: To doubt a particular manifestation of divine justice implies a belief in its existence.

77. *as nature does within a flame*: The flame, that is to say, rises again.

81. *their holy feast*: Their convents and their vows.

83. *Lawrence*: In 258, during the reign of Valerius, St. Lawrence, then deacon of Rome, was ordered by the Roman Prefect to send him the treasure of the church. Lawrence sent him the poor and the oppressed, declaring that they were the one treasure. He was thereupon martyred. After many other tortures, he was roasted on a grill, but remained steadfast under torture. Jacobus de Voragine (*The Golden Legend*) reports him as saying to his torturer: "Thou hast roasted the one side, tyrant, now turn the other and eat."

84. *Mucius*: Mucius Scaevola, a young man of ancient Rome. He vowed to kill Porsenna and let his right hand be consumed by fire when its thrust missed the mark. Note that, as in the Whips and Reins of the Purgatory, Dante presents both a sacred and a classical example.

94. *I made you understand*: See III, 31–33.

96. *the First Truth*: God.

97–98. *she who stood beside her*: Constance.

105. *his piety*: To his father. *impiety*: To his mother. For Alcmaeon see *Purgatorio*, XII, 49–51 and note.

106–114. The central idea of this passage is the difference between the Absolute and Conditioned Will. The Absolute Will is incapable of willing evil. The Conditioned Will, when coerced by violence, interacts with it and consents to a lesser harm in order to escape a greater. All that Piccarda said was true of the Absolute Will, but all that Beatrice has said is true of the Conditioned Will.

113–115. *that stream*: Stands for both Beatrice and her discourse, *the Fountain of All Truth*: God. Dante's figure also expounds Beatrice's allegorical function as Revealed Truth (which flows from God, the Fountain of All Truth, and calms all doubt from the souls of those to whom it descends).

127. *In That*: In the truth of God, within which the soul may rest as instinctively as does a beast within its den.

Canto V

Beatrice explains the *Sanctity of the Vow, its Relation to Free Will, The Limited Range Within Which Vows May Be Altered*, and the *Dangers of Evil Vows*.

When she has finished, she and Dante soar to the *Second Sphere*. There a host of radiant souls gathers to dance homage around Beatrice and Dante. These are the *Seekers of Honor*, souls who were active in their pursuit of the good, but who were motivated in their pursuit by a desire for personal honor, a good enough motive, but the least of all good motives.

One soul among them addresses Dante with particular joy. In Canto VI this soul identifies itself as the radiance that in mortal life was the *Emperor Justinian*.

"If, in the warmth of love, I manifest
 more of my radiance than the world can see,
 rendering your eyes unequal to the test,   3

do not be amazed. These are the radiancies
 of the perfected vision that sees the good
 and step by step moves nearer what it sees.   6

Well do I see how the Eternal Ray,
 which, once seen, kindles love forevermore,
 already shines on you. If on your way   9

some other thing seduce your love, my brother,
 it can only be a trace, misunderstood,
 of this, which you see shining through the other.   12

You ask if there is any compensation
 the soul may offer for its unkept vows
 that will secure it against litigation."   15

So Beatrice, alight from Heaven's Source,
 began this canto; and without a pause,
 continued thus her heavenly discourse: 18

"Of all creation's bounty realized,
 God's greatest gift, the gift in which mankind
 is most like Him, the gift by Him most prized,   21

is the freedom he bestowed upon the will.
 All his intelligent creatures, and they alone,
 were so endowed, and so endowed are still.   24

From this your reasoning should make evident
 the value of a vow that is so joined
 that God gives His consent when you consent.   27

When, therefore, God and man have sealed the pact,
the man divests himself of that great treasure
of which I speak—and by his own free act.   30

What can you offer, then, to make amends?
How can you make good use of what is His?
Would you employ extortion to good ends?   33

This much will make the main point clear to you.
But since the church grants dispensations in this,
whereby what I have said may seem untrue;   36

you must yet sit at table, for the food
you have just taken is crusty; without help
you will not soon digest it to your good.   39

Open your mind to what I shall explain,
then close around it, for it is no learning
to understand what one does not retain.   42

The essence of this sacrificial act
lies, first, in *what* one does, and, second, in *how*—
the *matter* and the *manner* of the pact.   45

This second part cannot be set aside
except by full performance; on this point
what I said earlier stands unqualified.   48

Thus it was mandatory to sacrifice
among the Jews, though the offering itself
might vary, or a substitute might suffice.   51

The other—what I have called the *matter*—may
be of the sort for which a substitution
will serve without offending in any way.   54

But let no man by his own judgment or whim
take on himself that burden unless the keys
of gold and silver have been turned for him.   57

And let him think no change a worthy one
unless what he takes up contains in it,
at least as six does four, what he puts down.   60

There are, however, things whose weight and worth
tip every scale, and for these there can be
no recompense by anything on earth.   63

Let no man make his vow a sporting thing.
Be true and do not make a squint-eyed choice
as Jephthah did in his first offering.   66

He had better have cried, 'I had no right to speak!'
than, keeping his vow, do worse. And in like case
will you find that chief war leader, the great Greek   69

whose Iphigenia wept her loveliness,
    and made both fools and wise men share her tears
    hearing of such dark rites and her distress.   72

Be slower to move, Christians, be grave, serene.
    Do not be like a feather in the wind,
    nor think that every water washes clean.   75

You have the Testaments, both old and new,
    and the shepherd of the church to be your guide;
    and this is all you need to lead you true.   78

If cunning greed comes promising remission,
    be men, not mad sheep, lest the Jew among you
    find cause to point his finger in derision.   81

Do not be like the lamb that strays away
    from its mother's milk and, simple and capricious,
    fights battles with itself in silly play!"   84

—Thus Beatrice to me, just as I write.
    Then she turned, full of yearning, to that part
    where the world is quickened most by the True Light.   87

Her silence, her transfigured face ablaze
    made me fall still although my eager mind
    was teeming with new questions I wished to raise.   90

And like an arrow driven with such might
    it strikes its mark before the string is still,
    we soared to the second kingdom of the light.   93

My lady glowed with such a joyous essence
    giving herself to the light of that new sky
    that the planet shone more brightly with her presence.   96

And if the star changed then and laughed with bliss,
    what did I do, who in my very nature
    was made to be transformed through all that is?   99

As in a fish pond that is calm and clear
    fish swim to what falls in from the outside,
    believing it to be their food, so, here,   102

I saw at least a thousand splendors move
    toward us, and from each one I heard the cry:
    "Here is what gives increase to our love!"   105

And as those glories came to where we were
    each shade made visible in the radiance
    that each gave off, the joy that filled it there.   108

Imagine, reader, that I had started so
    and not gone on—think what an anguished famine
    would then oppress your hungry will to know.   111

So may you, of yourself, be able to see
　how much I longed to know their names and nature
　the instant they had shown themselves to me. 　114

—"O well born soul, permitted by God's grace
　to see the thrones of the Eternal Triumph
　while still embattled in the mortal trace, 　117

the lamp that shines through all the vaults of Heaven
　is lit in us; if, therefore, you seek light
　on any point, ask and it shall be given." 　120

—So spoke one of those pious entities.
　And my lady said: "Speak. Speak with full assurance.
　And credit them as you would deities!" 　123

"I do indeed see that you make your nest
　in your own light, and beam it through your eyes
　that dazzles when you smile, o spirit blest. 　126

But I know not who you are, nor why you are
　assigned here, to this sphere that hides itself
　from men's eyes in the rays of another star." 　129

These were my words, my face turned to the light
　that had just spoken; at which it made itself
　far more resplendent yet upon my sight. 　132

Just as the sun, when its rays have broken through
　a screen of heavy vapors, will itself
　conceal itself in too much light—just so, 　135

in its excess of joy that sacred soul
　hid itself from my sight in its own ray,
　and so concealed within its aureole, 　138

it answered me, unfolding many things,
　the manner of which the following canto sings.

Notes

9-12. *some other thing*: The light of God, once seen, kindles eternal love and no soul so kindled can stray from it. Since Dante's soul has already been so kindled, the only possible error remaining to him is that he could mistakenly believe he sees the light of God in some lessor object and so be seduced by that lesser thing, not because his love is lacking, but because his understanding is.

15. *litigation*: At the bar of judgment.

16-18. An odd tercet. In it Dante pauses only to say Beatrice did not pause but spoke and went on speaking. A literal rendering (I have had to take liberties) would be: "So Beatrice began this canto; and, like a man who does not interrupt his discourse, continued her sacred process [of reasoning and explication] as follows:".

19-33. THE SANCTITY OF HOLY VOWS. Dante has asked if a man may not, by other good works, made amends for an unfulfilled vow. Beatrice replies that God's greatest gift to man is his free will, and that a vow is a direct compact with God wherein man, of his free will, offers that freedom back to God. Once God accepts, the man's will is no longer free for it has been given to God. How then is man free to will what is good, his will and freedom now belonging to God? To assert a free will that is no longer his is to seek to embezzle his way to the good.

23. *All his intelligent creatures*: Angels and men.

43. *this sacrificial act*: It need not, of course, be restricted to the vows taken for religious purposes. One might, for example, vow to fast, or to go on a pilgrimage, or to give some or all of his goods to the poor, or to live in a specified way.

49-57. *Thus it was mandatory*: The law of the Jews absolutely required them to offer sacrifices to the Lord (the *substance* of the covenant) but allowed them some latitude in what might be sacrificed (the *manner*). The manner of the vow may be changed if its substance is kept, but the change must not be arbitrary (for man, having given away his will, may not choose at his own pleasure), and no man should make such a change without having submitted his case to church authority (whereby the gold and silver keys of papal authority are turned for him).

58–60. Sense of this tercet: Let no man think it worthy (even with church authority) to change the substance of his vow to a lesser thing. Rather, the new substance should be greater than the former at least as six is to four. It is always well to look for a special significance in Dante's use of numbers, but I know of none here. He seems to be using six-to-four simply as a reasonable ratio of increase.

61–62. *things whose weight and worth tip every scale:* A vow of chastity would involve such a thing, virginity being irreplaceable. A vow of a lifetime of service would, similarly, involve what is irreplaceable. By contrast, a man who vowed to make a gift of money to charity every year of his life, and who then loses all his money, might satisfy his vow by substituting labor, or even, if he grows infirm, prayer. Were he, on the other hand, to steal in order to keep his money vow, that would be an evil thing.

66. *Jephthah:* King of Israel. He fought the Ammonites and vowed that if he were victorious he would offer up to God the first thing he saw coming out of the door of his house. The first thing he saw was his daughter and he sacrificed her (*Judges,* XI).

67. *have cried, 'I had no right to speak!'* No right to speak such a vow. In so crying he would have renounced the vow, and better so, says Dante, than to do worse in the act of keeping it.

69–70. *the great Greek whose Iphigenia:* Agamemnon. Iphigenia was his daughter. Dante follows the legend in which Agamemnon vowed before the birth of Iphigenia that he would sacrifice to Artemis the loveliest creature the year brought forth. Rather than sacrifice Iphigenia, he did not keep his vow. Years later, however, when the Greek ships were becalmed at Aulis, the other Greek leaders, especially Menelaus, blamed their distress on the unkept vow and Agamemnon was finally persuaded to send for Iphigenia and to sacrifice her.

79. *cunning greed:* The greed of those who offer dispensations and other holy offices for money. To Dante such practices were damnable simony.

80. *lest the Jew among you:* The Jew could then point his finger in derision because his law was incorruptible in the matter of sacrifices.

86–87. To avoid a volume of scholarly disputation, let these lines be taken to mean that Beatrice turned to both the Sun (it was at the equator) and the Empyrean (thus toward the "True Light" in both senses) and that she and Dante ascended in the same way as before. In an instant, then, they soar to Mercury, their arrival signified by the increase in Beatrice's radiance.

94. *glowed with such a joyous essence:* Both the joy and the light are greater because she is now nearer God and has more of His essence breathed into her.

97–99. *the star:* Mercury. Dante regularly refers to planets as stars. Sense of these lines: "If the star could be so changed (being material), how could I not change, who was created with soul as my essence, hence born to be transformed through all there is, from dust to Godliness."

100 ff. THOSE WHO SOUGHT HONOR BUSILY (THE PERSONALLY AMBITIOUS). The souls in the sphere of Mercury worked, in their earthly lives, for honor and glory. On seeing the newcomers they burst into joyous revels (as in their heart's wish they had sought themselves to be honored by such revels? each giving what is most nearly of himself?). These souls sought the good actively and for good reason, but, in a sense, *for the least of all good reasons.* The light they give forth is so bright that they are often lost to Dante's sight in their own radiance—a double felicity, first, as it describes the essence of their natures, and, second, because Mercury is so near the Sun that it is often hard to see because it is swallowed into the Sun's glow.

107–108. *each shade made visible, in the radiance:* The counterplay of "shade" and "radiance" seems to imply that the lineaments of these souls were traced upon the radiance that enclosed them.

114. *the instant they had shown themselves to me:* Note here and hereafter how regularly Dante speaks of the Paradisal souls as showing themselves rather than as being seen by him. (Cf. III, 109.) It is the nature of what belongs to Heaven to reveal itself of its own love and volition rather than to be apprehended by mortal means. There is also, of course, the fact that these souls are here only as symbolic manifestations, their real seat being in the Empyrean (IV, 28–63 and note).

117. *while still embattled:* Dante says, literally, "before your time in the militia is left behind." The essential point is that Heaven is the Eternal Triumph of which mortal life (for man) is the battle. Cf. the common phrase, "the church militant."

128–129. *this sphere that hides itself from men's eyes in the rays of another star:* The other star is the Sun. As noted above (note to 100 ff.) Mercury is often lost in the Sun's aura.

Canto VI

The Spirit Identifies Itself as the soul of *The Emperor Justinian* and proceeds to recount its life on earth, its conversion by *Agapetus*, and its subsequent dedication to *The Codification of the Law*.
It proceeds next to a *Discourse on the History of the Roman Eagle*. It concludes by identifying the spirit of *Romeo da Villanova* as one among the souls of the Second Heaven.

"Once Constantine had turned the eagle's wing
    against the course of Heaven, which it had followed
    behind the new son of the Latian king,   3

two hundred years and more, as mankind knows,
    God's bird stayed on at Europe's furthest edge,
    close to the mountains out of which it rose.   6

And there, his wings spread over land and sea,
    he ruled the world, passing from hand to hand;
    and so, through many changes, came to me.   9

Caesar I was, Justinian I am.
    By the will of the First Love, which I now feel,
    I pruned the law of waste, excess, and sham.   12

Before my work absorbed my whole intent
    I knew Christ in one nature only, not two;
    and so believing, I was well content.   15

But Agapetus, blessèd of the Lord,
    he, the supreme shepherd pure in faith,
    showed me the true way by his holy word.   18

Him I believed, and in my present view
    I see the truth as clearly as you see
    how a contradiction is both false and true.   21

As soon as I came to walk in the True Faith's way
    God's grace moved all my heart to my great work;
    and to it I gave myself without delay.   24

To my Belisarius I left my spear
    and God's right hand so moved his that the omen
    for me to rest from war was more than clear.   27

Of the two things you asked about before
    this puts a period to my first reply.
    But this much said impels me to say more   30

that you may see with how much right men go
   against the sacred standard when they plot
   its subornation or its overthrow.   33

You know what heroes bled to consecrate
   its holy destiny from that first hour
   when Pallas died to give it its first state.   36

You know that for two centuries then its home
   was Alba, till the time came when the three
   fought with the three and carried it to Rome. 39

What it did then from the Sabine's day of woe
   to good Lucretia's, under the seven kings
   who plundered the neighboring lands, you also know, 42

and how it led the Chosen Romans forward
   against the powers of Brennus, and of Pyrrhus,
   and of many a rival state and warring lord. 45

Thence the fame of Torquatus, curly Quintius,
   and the Decii and Fabii. How gladly
   I bring it myrrh to keep it glorious.   48

It dashed to earth the hot Arabian pride
   that followed Hannibal through the rocky Alps,
   from which, you, Po, sweet river, rise and glide. 51

Under it triumphed at an early age
   Scipio and Pompey. Against the mountain
   that looked down on your birth it screamed its rage. 54

Then as that age dawned in which Heaven planned
   the whole world to its harmony, Caesar came,
   and by the will of Rome, took it in hand. 57

What it did then from the Var to the Rhine is known
   to Isère, Arar, Seine, and every valley
   from which the waters of the Rhone flow down. 60

And what it did when it had taken flight
   from Ravenna and across the Rubicon
   no tongue may hope to speak nor pen to write. 63

It turned and led the cohorts into Spain;
   then to Dyrrachium; and then struck Pharsalus
   so hard that even the hot Nile felt the pain. 66

Antandros and the Simoïs, where it first saw light,
   it saw again, and Hector's grave, and then—
   woe to Ptolemy—sprang again to flight. 69

Like a thunderbolt it struck at Juba next;
   then turned once more and swooped down on your West
   and heard again the Pompeian trumpet vexed. 72

For what it did above its next great chief
  Brutus and Cassius wail in Cocytus;
  and Modena and Perugia came to grief.   75

For that, the tears still choke the wretched wraith
  of Cleopatra, who running to escape it,
  took from the asp her black and sudden death.   78

With him it traveled far as the Red Sea;
  and with him brought the world such peace that Janus
  was sealed up in his temple with lock and key.   81

But what this sign that moves my present theme
  had done before, all it was meant to do
  through the mortal realm it conquered—all must seem   84

dim shadows of poor things, if it be scanned
  with a clear eye and pure and honest heart,
  as it appears in the third Caesar's hand;   87

for the Living Justice whose breath I here breathe in
  gave it the glory, while in that same hand,
  of avenging His just wrath at Adam's sin.   90

Now ponder the double marvel I unfold:
  later, under Titus, it *avenged*
  the vengeance taken for that crime of old!   93

And when the sharp tooth of the Lombard bit
  the Holy Church, victorious Charlemagne,
  under those same wings, came and rescued it.   96

Now are you truly able to judge those
  whom I accused above, and their wrongdoing,
  which is the cause of all your present woes.   99

One speeds the golden lilies on to force
  the public standard; and one seizes it
  for private gain—and who knows which is worse?   102

Let them scheme, the Ghibellines, let them plot and weave
  under some other standard, for all who use
  this bird iniquitously find cause to grieve!   105

Nor let the new Charles think his Guelphs will be
  its overthrow, but let him fear the talons
  that have ripped the mane from fiercer lions than he.   108

Many a father's sinfulness has sealed
  his children's doom: let him not think his lilies
  will take the place of God's bird on His shield.   111

—This little star embellishes its crown
  with the light of those good spirits who were zealous
  in order to win honor and renown;   114

and when desire leans to such things, being bent
from the true good, the rays of the true Love
thrust upward with less force for the ascent;   117

but in the balance of our reward and due
is part of our delight, because we see
no shade of difference between the two.   120

By this means the True Judge sweetens our will,
so moving us that in all eternity
nothing can twist our beings to any ill.   123

Unequal voices make sweet tones down there.
Just so, in our life, these unequal stations
make a sweet harmony from sphere to sphere.   126

Within this pearl shines, too, the radiance
of Romeo, whose good and beautiful works
were answered by ingratitude and bad chance.   129

But the Provençals who worked his overthrow
have no last laugh: he walks an evil road
who finds his loss in the good that others do.   132

Four daughters had Count Raymond, each the wife
of a Christian king, thanks to this Romeo,
a humble man, a pilgrim in his life.   135

Envy and calumny so moved Raymond then
that he demanded accounting of this just soul
whose management had returned him twelve for ten.   138

For this he wandered, aged, poor, and bent,
into the world again; and could the world
know what was in his heart that road he went   141

begging his life by crusts from door to door,
much as it praises him now, it would praise him more.

Notes

General Note: THE FIGURE OF JUSTINIAN. The glowing spirit identifies itself
as the soul of Justinian (482–565) who became Emperor of Rome in 527.
     He emerges, in his own account, as a luminous and magnanimous spirit. A Chris-
tian, he subscribed to the Monophysitic Heresy, which accepted the divine nature of
Christ but rejected his incarnation in mortal flesh. From this heresy he was converted
by Agapetus (Pope from 535–536). As soon as he was converted, God's grace moved
him to his great task of codifying the Roman Law, and to that work he gave himself
wholly, leaving the conduct of his armies (which he had led with great success) to
his general, Belisarius. So Dante sees him.
     Another reading of history might have suggested several pits of Hell that might
have claimed Justinian. Dante seems not to have known of the tyrannies of Justinian's reign, nor that the Justinian codification was the work of Tribonius, undertaken
by him on Imperial command.
     Whatever one's reading of history, one should note as part of Dante's structure
that in *Inferno* VI he summarizes the condition of Florence, in *Purgatorio* VI the
state of Italy, and here in *Paradiso* VI, the history of the Roman Empire.
     1–3. *turned the eagle's wing*: The Imperial Eagle, standard and symbol of Rome.

In 330 Constantine moved the seat of Empire to Byzantium. Thus the Roman eagle flew east "against the course of Heaven," which turns from east to west, but also against the will of heaven, for Dante believed God had decreed Rome to be the seat of His church and the Roman Empire to be its earthly arm.

He also believed that Constantine moved the seat of empire to Byzantium in order to give Rome to the church. This gift was the "Donation of Constantine" (see *Inferno*, XIX, 109–111, note) whereby the church (as Dante believed) grew rich and corrupt, hence, once more "against the course of Heaven."

The "new son of the Latian king" was Aeneas. He came from Troy (*with the course of heaven*), married Lavinia, daughter of the Latian king, and founded the line of the Roman Empire.

4. *two hundred years and more*: Byzantium became the imperial seat in 330. Justinian became emperor in 527. Thus the eagle had stayed at Europe's furthest edge for 197 years before it came to Justinian's hand. Some commentators argue that Dante meant the period from 330 to Justinian's military conquests in the east in 536. Such a reading brings the period to 206 years, justifying Dante's "two hundred years and more." It seems simpler, however, to assume that Dante made a mistake in his dates.

6. *close to the mountains out of which it rose*: The Trojan mountains. They are not far from Byzantium on a continental scale.

10–12. *Caesar I was*: On earth. But now only the name given him at the baptismal font is valid. *which now I feel*: May be taken to mean "now I am in Heaven" but the primary interpretation must be "now since my conversion."

19–20. *as closely as you see, etc.*: As a first principle of logic, a statement that contradicts itself contains both truth and falsehood. Of two contradictory terms only one can be true and the other must be false. Dante uses it here as an example of what is self-evidently true to human intellect. In Justinian's present state (informed by divine revelation) the duality of Christ's nature is as clear to him as is the nature of a logical contradiction to mortal intellect. (See also II, 45.)

25. *Belisarius*: Justinian's famous general was born 505, died 565. His successful campaigns against the Ostrogoths restored most of the Empire's authority over Italy. Dante seems not to have known that Justinian, in 562, in one of the endless intrigues of the Byzantine court, stripped "his" Belisarius of rank and had him imprisoned—an arrangement that became nearly standard as the Roman soldier's pension plan.

31–33. DENUNCIATION OF THE GUELPHS AND GHIBELLINES. Dante has asked to know (V, 126–127) the spirit's identity and why he was in the Sphere of Mercury. Lines 1–27 answer Dante's first question, but the nature of that reply moves Justinian to add a denunciation of both the Guelphs and Ghibellines for opposing the true purpose of the Holy Roman Empire, whose history (and divine right) he then recounts. *with how much right*: None at all. *the sacred standard*: The Imperial Eagle. *when they plot its subornation*: The Ghibellines; they sought to suborn imperial authority to their own ends. *or its overthrow*: The Guelphs; they sought to end imperial authority and leave matters in the hands of local lords.

36. *Pallas*: Son of Evander, a Greek who had founded a kingdom on the present site of Rome. Evander joined Aeneas in fighting Turnus, king of the Rutulians. In the fighting Pallas was killed by Turnus. As a result of his victory, Aeneas acquired a kingdom that included the hereditary rights of Pallas. Thus Pallas died to give the eagle its first kingly state. Or so at least runs the Virgilian version followed by Dante.

THE HISTORY OF THE ROMAN EAGLE

37–39. Following his victory over Turnus, Aeneas established his seat at Lavinium. His son, Ascanius, moved it from there to Alba Longa, called the Mother of Rome. There the eagle remained until the seventh century B.C. the Curiatii (the three heroes of Alba) were vanquished by the three Horatii of Rome.

40–42. Expelled from Alba, Romulus established a base in Rome on the Palatine and recruited a band of raiders who carried out the raid on the Sabines (the often-painted Rape of the Sabine Women) in order to get wives. From this robber settlement grew the kingdom of Rome. Through a succession of seven kings it raided and looted its neighbors until Sextus, son of Tarquinius Superbus (the last of the Roman kings), violated Lucretia. When she died as a result of his attack, the people rose in anger, overthrew the king, and founded the Republic of Rome, in 510 B.C.

43–45. During the Republic, the Eagle was carried to many triumphs by Chosen Romans. Condensing almost three full centuries of history into nine lines, Dante cites the defeat of Brennus and his Gauls (circa 390 B.C.) and of Pyrrhus and his Greek invaders (280 B.C.).

46–48. From the Republican victories was born the fame of Torquatus (Titus Manlius Torquatus) who defeated (among others) the Gauls. In these battles one of the

Fabii also distinguished himself. As did Lucius Quintius, called Cincinnatus because of an unruly lock of hair (from Latin *cincinnus*, a curl). The story of how he left the plow to become dictator of Rome and to conquer the Aquians in 485 B.C. is well known to schoolboys. Three generations of the Decii died in battle from 340 to 280 B.C., the last of these engagements being the defeat of the Greeks under Pyrrhus. And in 218 B.C. Quintus Fabius Maximus, the most notable of the Fabii, defeated Hannibal (see below).

Justinian recites these names and says he rejoices in anointing their fame with myrrh. (Myrrh was used by the ancients in embalming, as a means of preserving the body.) Note that Justinian, though on earth he was ambitious for his own glory, now rejoices in citing the glory of others.

49–51. It (the Eagle) defeated Hannibal in 218 B.C. Dante follows the custom of his times in referring to all inhabitants of north Africa as Arabs. The Po, here apostrophized, rises in the Alps.

52–54. Bracketing Scipio and Pompey, Justinian leaps from 218 to 81 B.C. In 218 Scipio Africanus, then seventeen, saved his father's life in battle against Hannibal at Ticinus. At twenty he defeated Hannibal's forces in Spain. And at thirty-three, by his successful invasion of Africa, brought about the destruction of Hannibal and of Carthage.

Pompey's first great victory (over Marius in 81 B.C.) occurred when he was twenty-five.

"The mountain that overlooked your [Dante's] birth" is Fiesole, and at Fiesole, according to Roman legend, the Eagle of the Republic overthrew Catiline.

55–60. These two tercets refer to the coming of Julius Caesar (born 102 or 100 B.C.; assassinated March 15, 44 B.C.) and to the Gallic Wars. In Dante's view of the Empire as the seat God had chosen for His church, Caesar was serving Heaven's plan in laying the foundation of Empire, for the Empire would bring the whole world into the harmony that would arise from unification under a single imperial rule.

Lines 58–60 describe the territory of the Gallic Wars (58–50 B.C.).

61–66. The Rubicon flows between Ravenna and Rimini. In Caesar's time it marked the boundary line between Italy and Gaul. In crossing it (January 11, 49 B.C.), Caesar left his province without permission of the senate, thus precipitating civil war.

64–66. Before the year was out Caesar struck Ilerda in Spain, defeating Pompey's lieutenants. (Note that in this case the eagle is striking against the eagle, for Pompey's cohorts also carried the Roman standard.) In the next year Caesar laid siege to Pompey in Dyrrachium (modern Durres in Albania), broke off, and then engaged Pompey again at Pharsalus in Thessaly (August 9, 48 B.C.), this time winning a great victory. *even the Nile felt the pain*: Because Pompey fled to Egypt and was killed there by Ptolemy.

67–69. Antandros is a coastal town near Troy. The Simoïs is a nearby river. Aeneas sailed from Antandros when he brought the eagle to Italy. After Pompey's death, Caesar visited Troy. Thus the Eagle saw its homeland again. From Troy ("Woe to Ptolemy") Caesar moved to Egypt, defeated Ptolemy, and gave Egypt to Cleopatra.

70–72. Led by Caesar, the Eagle next overthrew Juba, king of Numidia (46 B.C.) under whom fourteen republican legions had formed. In the next year he struck again at Spain ("on your West") where Pompey's two sons had gathered a new army.

73–78. Augustus, Caesar's nephew, was "its next great chief." After Caesar's murder led by Cassius and Brutus, Augustus became the standard-bearer. He defeated Marc Antony at Modena in 43 B.C., then formed an alliance with him, and the two together finished Brutus and Cassius at Philippi in 42 B.C. In 41 B.C. Augustus defeated Marc Antony's brother Lucius at Perugia. And in 31 B.C. Augustus defeated Marc Antony at Actium. Antony committed suicide soon after his defeat, and Cleopatra did the same when she heard the news.

79–81. *him*: Augustus. *far as the Red Sea*: The limit of the Empire. Augustus was now undisputed ruler of all Rome and the Empire was at peace. *Janus*: The gates of his temple were always open in time of war. Now they were closed (as they had been only twice before) to indicate peace throughout the Empire. Thus the serene time was set for the birth of Christ, the Prince of Peace.

85–90. Tiberius was the third Caesar. The great glory given the eagle in his reign was the Crucifixion, for thereby the sin of Adam was wiped clean and the gates of Heaven were opened to redeemed mankind.

91–93. Under Titus, the fourth Caesar, Jerusalem was taken in a bloody conquest which Dante saw as a vengeance taken for a just vengeance. His argument would probably run that it was just to exact vengeance for Adam's sin and that God sent His only begotten son to mankind for that purpose. Yet, in exacting a vengeance upon the man, the Jews also offended the god, and it is just that they be made to suffer for that crime against God. Such would seem to be the basis for the prejudice against the Jew, and many vexed questions are, of course, involved: If God decreed the Crucifixion, had the Jews any choice? Are they more guilty than Pilate who simply washed his hands and let his soldiers drive the nails? What is free will in confrontation with a preordained act of God's will? Such questions must be referred to a quality of revelation unknown to footnotes.

94–96. Justinian now leaps ahead over six centuries. Desiderius, an eighth-century king of the Lombards, rose against the church but was overthrown by Charlemagne in 774 A.D. Charlemagne, as Emperor of the Holy Roman Empire, was still bearing the eagle standard.

97–98. *those whom I accused above*: The Guelphs and Ghibellines. See lines 31 ff.

100–102. *one speeds the golden lilies on to force the public standard*: The Guelphs. They urge the Lilies of France against the Eagle. *one seizes it for private gain*: The Ghibellines. They seek to pervert the Imperial standard to their own ends.

106. *the new Charles*: Charles II (The Lame) of Anjou, King of Naples and leader of the Guelphs.

109–111. *father's sinfulness . . . children's doom*: Justinian is pronouncing what may be a general sentiment, but he must certainly intend some reference to the woes that befell the house of Anjou, as Charles Martel (son of Charles the Lame) will amplify in VIII, 40–84.

112–114. Justinian has now answered Dante's first question (concerning his identity) and completed his additional remarks. He now addresses the second question (as to why he is in the Sphere of Mercury and what sort of spirits are with him). He identifies this sphere as the manifest realm of the personally ambitious.

115–120. Dante's phrasing is especially dense in these lines and I have had to take more than usual liberties in order to bring it to rhyme. His point here may be stated as follows: "We of this sphere worked for the Good but did so in seeking honor for ourselves rather than for the one true motive, which is the love of God. When desire is so bent from the true good, it follows that the upward thrust toward God is lesser for being bent aside. Therefore we are low in Heaven. Yet part of our joy is in knowing that our station is well chosen, our reward being exactly equal to our merit."

121–123. *By this means*: By letting us recognize how exactly our present state corresponds to the merit we showed in our lives.

124. *down there*: On earth.

128. *Romeo*: Romeo da Villanova. He was born circa 1170 and became prime minister and chamberlain of Raymond Berenger IV, Count of Provence from 1209 to 1245. Dante follows the legend that Romeo, passing through Provence on his way back from a pilgrimage, attached himself to Raymond's court and soon achieved high station by his wise management of Raymond's affairs. Among his triumphs, Romeo negotiated the marriages of Raymond's four daughters, each to a king. Later the local nobles, envious of Romeo's position, accused him of mismanaging the treasury. When Raymond demanded an accounting, Romeo pointed to the increase in the treasury, and picking up his pilgrim's staff once more, left the court to wander as he had come.

131. *have no last laugh*: The nobles of Provence have committed the sin of envy and must suffer for it. They also have no last laugh in that Provence lost a good manager of the realm.

Canto VII

Justinian and his companions break into a *Hymn to the God of Battles* and, dancing, disappear into the distance. Dante, torn by doubt, longs to ask how a just vengeance may justly be avenged, but dares not speak. Beatrice, sensing his confusion, answers his question before he can ask it.

She explains the *Double Nature of the Crucifixion*, and why the Jews, though blameless in the crucifixion of the man, were still guilty of sacrilege against the God. She then explains why God chose this means of redemption, and why that choice was *The Greatest Act of All Eternity*.

She then explains the difference between *Direct and Indirect Creation* and concludes by proving *Why the Resurrection of the Flesh Is Certain*.

"*Osanna sanctus Deus Sabaoth*
superillustrans claritate tua
felices ignes horum malachoth!" 3

—So, giving itself to its own harmony,
the substance of that being, over which
two lights were joined as one, appeared to me. 6

And all those souls joined in a holy dance,
and then, like shooting sparks, gone instantly,
they disappeared behind the veil of distance. 9

I stood, torn by my doubts, "Speak up. Speak up,"
I said inside myself. "Ask the sweet lady
who slakes your every thirst from the sweet cup." 12

But the awe that holds my being in its sway
even at the sound of BEA or of TRICE
kept my head bent as if I dozed away. 15

But she soon soothed my warring doubt and dread,
for with a smile whose ray could have rejoiced
the soul of a man tied to the stake, she said: 18

"I know by my infallible insight
you do not understand how a just vengeance
can justly be avenged. To set you right 21

I shall resolve your mind's ambivalence.
Listen and learn, for what I shall now say
will be a gift of lofty consequence. 24

Because he would not, for his own good, take
God's bit and rein, the man who was not born,
damning himself, damned mankind for his sake. 27

Therefore, for many centuries, men lay
in their sick error, till the Word of God
chose to descend into the mortal clay.   30

There, moved by His Eternal Love alone,
he joined in His own person that other nature
that had wandered from its Maker and been cast down.   33

Now heed my reasoning: so joined again
to its First Cause, this nature (as it had been
at its creation) was good and without stain.   36

But by its own action, when it turned its face
from the road of truth that was its road of life,
it was driven from the garden of God's grace.   39

If the agony on the cross, considering this,
was a punishment of the nature thus assumed,
no verdict ever bit with greater justice;   42

Just so, no crime to match this can be cited
when we consider the Person who endured it
in whom that other nature was united.   45

Thus, various sequels flow from one event:
God and the Jews concurred in the same death;
for it the earth shook and the heavens were rent.   48

You should no longer find it hard to see
what is meant in saying that just vengeance taken
was afterwards avenged by just decree.   51

I see now that your mind, thought upon thought,
is all entangled, and that it awaits
most eagerly the untying of the knot.   54

You think: 'I grasp the truth of what I hear.
But why God chose this means for our redemption—
this and no other—I cannot make clear.'   57

No one may grasp the hidden meaning of
this edict, brother, till his inborn senses
have been made whole in the sweet fire of love.   60

Truly, therefore, since so many sight,
and so few hit, this target, I shall now
explain exactly why this means was right.   63

That Good, which from Itself spurns every trace
of envy, in Itself sends out such sparks
as manifest the everlasting grace.   66

Whatever is uttered by Its direct expression
thereafter is eternal; His seal once stamped,
nothing can ever wipe out the impression.   69

Whatever is poured directly from Its spring
  is wholly free; so made, it is not subject
  to the power of any secondary thing.   72

The Sacred Fire that rays through all creation
  burns with most joy in what is most like It;
  the more alike, the greater Its elation.   75

All of these attributes endow the nature
  of humankind; and if it fail in one,
  it cannot help but lose its noble stature.   78

Sin is the one power that can take away
  its freedom and its likeness to True Good,
  whereby it shines less brightly in Its ray.   81

Its innate worth, so lost, it can regain
  only by pouring back what guilt has spilled,
  repaying evil pleasure with just pain.   84

Your nature, when it took sin to its seed,
  sinned totally. It lost this innate worth,
  and it lost Paradise by the same deed.   87

Nor could they be regained (if you heed my words
  with scrupulous attention) by any road
  that does not lead to one of these two fords: 90

either that God, by courtesy alone,
  forgive his sin; or that the man himself,
  by his own penitence and pain, atone.   93

Now fix your eye, unmoving, on the abyss
  of the Eternal Wisdom, and your mind
  on every word I say concerning this!   96

Limited man, by subsequent obedience,
  could never make amends; he could not go
  as low in his humility as once,   99

rebellious, he had sought to rise in pride.
  Thus was he shut from every means himself
  to meet God's claim that He be satisfied.   102

Thus it was up to God, to Him alone
  in His own ways—by one or both, I say—
  to give man back his whole life and perfection.   105

But since a deed done is more prized the more
  it manifests within itself the mark
  of the loving heart and goodness of the doer,   108

the Everlasting Love, whose seal is plain
  on all the wax of the world, was pleased to move
  in all His ways to raise you up again.   111

There was not, nor will be, from the first day
   to the last night, an act so glorious
   and so magnificent, on either way.   114

For God, in giving Himself that man might be
   able to raise himself, gave even more
   than if he had forgiven him in mercy.   117

All other means would have been short, I say,
   of perfect justice, but that God's own Son
   humbled Himself to take on mortal clay.   120

And now, that every wish be granted you,
   I turn back to explain a certain passage,
   that you may understand it as I do.   123

You say: 'I see the water, I see the fire,
   the air, the earth; and all their combinations
   last but a little while and then expire.   126

Yet all these were creations! Ought not they—
   if what you said of them before is true—
   to be forever proof against decay?'   129

Of angels and this pure kingdom of the soul
   in which you are, it may be said they sprang
   full-formed from their creation, their beings whole.   132

But the elements, and all things generated
   by their various compoundings, take their form
   from powers that had themselves to be created.   135

Created was the matter they contain.
   Created, too, was the informing power
   of the stars that circle them in Heaven's main.   138

From the given potencies of these elements
   the rays and motions of the sacred lamps
   draw forth the souls of all brutes and all plants.   141

But the Supreme Beneficence inspires
   your life directly, filling it with love
   of what has made it, so that it desires   144

that love forever.—And from this you may
   infer the sure proof of your resurrection,
   if you once more consider in what way   147

man's flesh was given being like no other
   when He made our first father and first mother."

Notes

1–3. The hymn sung by these spirits as they depart is addressed to the God of triumphant armies (the God, as Dante believed, who led the Roman Eagle) and is compounded of Hebrew and Latin, the two languages of Heaven (though *malachoth* —"kingdoms"—should properly be *mamlachoth*) and may be rendered: "Hosannah, holy God of Sabaoth [of the armies], lighting from above with Your luster the blessed fires of these kingdoms!" The blessed fires (*felices ignes*) are the souls of heaven.

4–6. *its own harmony*: The harmony of the blessed voices. *two lights*: May stand, perhaps, for Justinian's double glory as Emperor and Lawgiver. *appeared to me*: Note, throughout the *Paradiso*, how Dante's phrasing suggests not that he saw the things of Heaven with his own senses, but that they were manifested to him by the blessed spirits as an act of love.

10 ff. DANTE'S DOUBT. Dante is torn between his thirst to know and his reluctance to ask. The question that fills him is "How can a just revenge be justly punished?" As usual, Beatrice (and her action in all such cases is certainly an allegory of her character as Divine Revelation) knows his wish before he can speak it and grants it before he can ask.

13–15. Intent of these lines: "But, as ever, the awe that overcomes my being if I hear so much as part of her name, made me unable to raise my head to speak and I kept it bent down like the head of a man who is dozing off while in an upright position."

25–51. THE CRUCIFIXION. Beatrice argues that the death of Christ was just because he had taken upon Himself both the nature and guilt of mankind. His expiation was just because the sin of His human nature was great. But since He was also a God, the pain inflicted upon His divinity was a sacrilege and demanded punishment. So ran the Scholastic argument Dante follows here.

26. *the man who was not born*: Adam.

29. *the Word of God*: Christ.

31–33. *Eternal Love*: The Holy Ghost. *His own person*: Christ, the Son. *that other nature*: Man. *Maker*: God the Father.

40. *considering this*: Considering what I have just said of the guilt of human nature and of the fact that Christ willingly assumed that guilt in His own person.

48. *earth shook . . . heavens were rent*: See *Matthew*, XXVII, 11–15.

66. *Grace*: Dante says "beauty." The Scartazzini-Vandelli commentary offers the following interpretation of this tercet: "The Divine Goodness, which rejects from Itself every trace of envy, being in Itself a single ardent flame, scintillates so that it shoots forth from Itself, like sparks, part of its Eternal Beauty, and by these (sparks) makes beautiful Its creatures. One must say *part* (of Itself) because a finite creature is not capable of the Infinite."

67–72. Dante is distinguishing here between "direct" (Godly) and "secondary" (angelic and human) creation. What God creates directly is eternal because nothing can wipe out the impression of His seal, and it is free because secondary creations have no power upon it. The point is further made in lines 130–144 below.

76. *all of these attributes*: The three Godly gifts are named above: immortality (lines 67–69), freedom (lines 70–72), and resemblance to God (lines 73–75). It follows that to lose any one these attributes is to fall from the first-created nobility (Adam's original state).

81. *it shines less brightly in Its ray*: Since God's fire rays forth most brightly in that which is most like God, and since sin makes man less like God, sin makes man shine less brightly in God's ray.

85–86. *seed . . . totally*: The seed is Adam. By his sin, all mankind fell from its first innate worth and lost Paradise.

97. *Limited man*: Man is limited by his mortal means. Within them, no depth of humility to which he could descend could be proportionate to the height he had sought in his rebellious sin. For man's sin was in seeking to become God, and there is no equivalent depth to which he could sink in recompense, for in sinning he had already damned himself to Hell.

104–105. *by one* (way): Mercy. *or both*: Mercy and Justice. Since man could not save himself, God could have forgiven him outright as an act of mercy. Or he could have created a man so perfect that he was capable of just expiation (that would have been the way of Justice). But in giving Himself through His own Son, He chose the double way that was both divine mercy and human justice. In the tercets that immediately follow Dante celebrates this choice as the supreme act of all eternity. *his whole life and perfection*: Because through Christ's redemption he could once more be received into Heaven and the whole life from which Adam's sin had excluded him.

114. *on either way*: On the way of mercy or on the way of justice.

122. *explain a certain passage*: Lines 67 ff. There Beatrice had explained that whatever God utters as His direct expression is eternal.

124–125. *water . . . fire . . . air . . . earth*: These were believed to be the four elements of which all things were compounded. Hence, they and their combinations make up all the material creation. These elements (seen as phenomena of the matter they contain, the matter itself being directly created) are the effects of certain directly created powers in nature, not as direct effects of God. As secondary effects, therefore, they are corruptible, whereas the soul of man, a direct creation, is eternal.

135. *powers that had themselves to be created*: Angels. God, of course, is the one power that did not Itself have to be created.

139–141. The four elements that give form to all matter (the matter being itself God-created and eternal but itself formless) derive their potencies from fixed (and first created) principles of nature which are ruled by angels. The stars in their courses then work upon these potencies and draw from them the sensitive and vegetative souls of beasts and plants (but not man's soul, which is God-created).

145–149. THE PROOF OF THE RESURRECTION OF THE FLESH. "From this," says Beatrice—from the principle declared in lines 67-68 that everything directly created by God is eternal, and from the fact that Adam and Eve were directly created by God—"you may infer the sure proof of your resurrection." There seems to be no explanation of Beatrice's reason for saying "your" (rather than "the" or "our") resurrection. As a codescendant of Adam and Eve, she must herself expect the resurrection of her flesh on Judgment Day.

Canto VIII

THE THIRD SPHERE: VENUS   *The Amorous: Charles Martel*

Dante and Beatrice reach the *Sphere of Venice, the Third Heaven.* Instantly, a band of souls that had been dancing in the Empyrean descends to the travelers. These are the souls of the *Amorous.* As we learn in Canto IX, many of them, perhaps all, were so full of the influence of Venus that they were in danger of being lost to carnality. Through the love of God, however, their passion was converted from physical love to true *caritas,* and thus do they rejoice in Heaven.

Their spokesman is *Charles Martel of Anjou.* He identifies himself and prophesies dark days for the Kingdom of Naples because of the meanness of King Robert, his brother. Dante asks how it is that mean sons can be born of great fathers, and Charles answers with a *Discourse on the Diversity of Natural Talents,* a diversity he assigns to the influence of the stars, as God provided them for man's own good as a social being, for only by diversity of gifts can society function. God had planned all these variations to a harmonious end. It is mankind, by forcing men into situations not in harmony with their talents, that strays from God's plan.

The world, to its own jeopardy, once thought
    that Venus, rolling in the third epicycle,
    rayed down love-madness, leaving men distraught.　　3

Therefore the ancients, in their ignorance,
    did honor not to her alone, but offered
    the smokes of sacrifice and votive chants　　6

to Dione and to Cupid, her mother and son,
    and claimed that he had sat on Dido's lap
    when she was smitten by love's blinding passion.　　9

From her with whom my song began just now
    they took the name of the star that woos the Sun,
    now shining at its nape, now at its brow.　　12

I reached it unaware of my ascent,
    but my lady made me certain I was there
    because I saw her grow more radiant.　　15

And as a spark is visible in the fire,
    and as two voices may be told apart
    if one stays firm and one goes lower and higher;　　18

so I saw lights circling within that light
    at various speeds, each, I suppose, proportioned
    to its eternal vision of delight.　　21

No blast from cold clouds ever shot below,
    whether visible or not, so rapidly
    but what it would have seemed delayed and slow　　24

to one who had seen those holy lights draw nigh
to where we were, leaving the dance begun
among the Seraphim in Heaven on high.   27

And from the first who came, in purest strain
"Hosannah" rang; so pure that, ever since,
my soul has yearned to hear that sound again.   30

Then one of them came forward and spoke thus:
"We are ready, all of us, and await your pleasure
that you make take from us what makes you joyous.   33

In one thirst and one spiraling and one sphere
we turn with those High Principalities
to whom you once cried from the world down there: 36

'O *you whose intellects turn the third great wheel!'*
So full of love are we that, for your pleasure,
it will be no less bliss to pause a while."   39

I raised my eyes to the holy radiance
that was my lady, and only after she
had given them her comfort and assurance,   42

did I turn to the radiance that had made
such promises. "Who are you?" were my words,
my voice filled with the love it left unsaid.   45

Ah, how it swelled and grew even more bright,
taking increase of bliss from my few words,
and adding new delight to its delight.   48

So changed, it said: "My life there among men
was soon concluded; had it lasted longer
great evils yet to be would not have been.   51

The ecstasy that is my heavenly boon
conceals me: I am wrapped within its aura
as a silkworm is enclosed in a cocoon.   54

You loved me much, and you had reason to,
for had I stayed below, you would have seen
more than the green leaves of my love for you.   57

The left bank of the land washed by the Rhone
after its waters mingle with the Sorgue's
waited, in due course, to become my own;   60

as did that horn of Italy that lies
south of the Tronto and Verde, within which
Bari, Gaeta, and Catona rise.   63

Already on my brow there shone the crown
of the land the Danube bathes when it has left
its German banks. And though not yet my own,   66

beautiful Sicily, the darkened coast
between the Capes of Faro and Passero,
there on the gulf that Eurus lashes most,   69

(not dimmed by Typhoeus, as mythology
would have men think, but by its rising sulfur)
would yet have looked to have its kings, through me,   72

from Charles and Rudolph, but that the bitter breath
of a populace subjected to misrule
cried out through all Palermo's streets 'Death! Death!'   75

And could Robert have foreseen how tyranny
will drive men mad, he would have fled in fear
from Catalonia's greedy poverty.   78

For some provision surely must be made,
by him or by another, lest on his ship,
already heavy laden, more be laid.   81

His nature, born to avarice from the loins
of a liberal sire, would have required lieutenants
who cared for more than filling chests with coins."   84

—"Sire, I hold dearer this felicity
that fills me when you speak, believing it
as visible to you as it is to me,   87

there where every good begins and ends.
And this, too, I hold dear—that you discern it
in looking on Him from whom all love descends.   90

You have given me joy. Now it is in your power
to give me light. For your words leave me in doubt:
how, if the seed is sweet, may the fruit be sour?"   93

Thus I. And he: "Could I make you recognize
one truth of what you ask, then what is now
behind your back, would be before your eyes.   96

The Good by which this kingdom you now climb
is turned and gladdened, makes its foresight shine
as powers of these great bodies to all time.   99

Not only does that Perfect Mind provide
for the diversities of every nature
but for their good and harmony beside.   102

And thus whatever arrow takes its arc
from this bow flies to a determined end,
it being aimed unerringly to its mark.   105

Else would these heavens you now move across
give rise to their effect in such a way
that there would be not harmony, but chaos.   108

This cannot be unless the intellects
that move these stars are flawed, and flawed the first,
which, having made them, gave them such defects.   111

—Should I expound this further?" he said to me.
And I: "There is no need, for now I know
nature cannot fall short of what must be."   114

And he: "Would man be worse off than he is,
there on earth, without a social order?"
"Yes!" I replied. "Nor need I proof of this."   117

"And can that be, unless men there below
lived variously to serve their various functions?
Your master, if he knows, answers you 'no.' "   120

So point by point that radiant soul disputes.
Now he concludes: "Your various aptitudes,
it follows, therefore, must have various roots.   123

So one man is born Xerxes, another Solon;
one Melchizedek, and another he
who, flying through the air, lost his own son.   126

That ever-revolving nature whose seal is pressed
into our mortal wax does its work well,
but takes no heed of where it comes to rest.   129

So Esau parted from Jacob in the seed;
and Romulus was born of such humble stock
that Mars became his father, as men agreed.   132

Begotten and begetter, but for the force
of overruling providence, the son's nature
would always follow in the father's course.   135

—And now what was behind shines out before.
But to make you understand how much you please me,
I would wrap you in one corollary more: 138

what Nature gives a man Fortune must nourish
concordantly, or nature, like any seed
out of its proper climate, cannot flourish.   141

If the world below would learn to heed the plan
of nature's firm foundation, and build on that,
it then would have the best from every man.   144

But into holy orders you deflect
the man born to strap on a sword and shield;
and make a king of one whose intellect   147

is given to writing sermons. And in this way
your footprints leave the road and go astray."

Notes

1. *to its own jeopardy*: Because in so believing it risked the wrath that has often descended upon the idolatrous.

2. *epicycle*: Not to be confused with "sphere." The epicycle of Venus turns around the center line of the Third Sphere. Thus the planet keeps appearing in various positions around the sun, "now shining at its nape" (behind it, hence Venus as evening star), "now at its brow" (before it, hence Venus as morning star) as Dante says in line 12 below. In line 96 this epicyclic motion becomes allegorically significant. In line 135 this image theme is brought to rest. This sweetly managed development is a fine example of Dante's way with imagery.

3. *rayed down love-madness*: The rays of Venus, the pagans believed, drove men and women mad with love.

7. *Dione*: One legend has it that Venus was the daughter of Dione and Zeus. *Cupid*: He has many mythological manifestations. Dante is here taking him as the son of Venus by Mars or, more probably, by Mercury.

8-9. *had sat on Dido's lap*: When she was smitten by love for Aeneas, the passion that led to her death. (See *Inferno*, V, 61, 86). Line 9 is my own rhyme-forced addition and does not occur in Dante.

10. *her*: Venus.

11-12. *that woos the Sun*: The apparent motion of Venus is from one side of the Sun to the other. See note to line 2, above.

19 ff. THE AMOROUS. These lights are the souls of the Amorous; not the pagan distortion of love-madness, but the Christian and divine radiance of *caritas*. Like all the souls of Heaven, they manifest themselves (at will) in their appropriate sphere, but they have their true place in the Empyrean among the Seraphim. They have been dancing there in their eternal joy when they become aware of Dante and Beatrice and, in a passion of *caritas,* descend to them at inconceivable speeds, still dancing and singing *Hosannah*.

22-24. *blast from cold clouds, etc*: Hot dry vapors colliding with cold wet clouds were believed to discharge visible or invisible blasts of wind at great speeds. Lightning was believed to be a blast of wind moving so fast that the friction of its motion caused it to ignite. But even such a rate of descent would have seemed laggard as compared to the descent of these souls when they see Dante and Beatrice. *below*: In earth's atmosphere.

31. *Then one of them*: Charles Martel (see below). He explains that all the souls of this sphere dance in perpetual bliss in the Empyrean, but that they are all so full of love and so eager to give joy to others, that to pause from bliss a while in order to give joy to others will seem no less bliss.

34. *In one thirst*: For God's love. *and one spiraling*: In one eternal circling of God's throne. *and one sphere*: In a round with the angels and powers of this third Heaven.

35-37. *those High Principalities*: The third heaven, we are to understand, is moved by Principalities (angels of a certain rank), or so Dante himself once addressed them in the words here quoted (from the *Convivio*). In IX, 61, however (see note), that function is assigned to Thrones. For the orders of angels see XXVIII.

40-84. CHARLES MARTEL. Born 1271, the first son of Charles II (The Lame) of Anjou. Crowned King of Hungary (though in title only) 1290. Died 1295. His conversation indicates that he and Dante had met on earth, probably when Charles visited Florence in 1294, and that Charles had intended to be Dante's royal patron. This Charles Martel must not be confused with the better known Charles Martel (Charles the Hammer), King of the Franks, who lived circa 688-741. The following dates may offer some useful points of reference in the maze of intrigue that marked the Kingdom of the Two Sicilies:

1268 Charles I of Anjou (French) defeats Conradin (German) at Tagliacozzo. (See *Inferno*, XXVIII, 17.)

1271 Charles Martel (grandson of Charles I) born.

1282 The Sicilian Vespers (Easter Day) in which most of the French (rulers of Sicily) were massacred in a popular uprising. In October of the same year Peter III of Aragon (Spanish) invaded Sicily and captured Messina, last French strongpoint. The House of Anjou is not totally driven from Sicily but retains the Kingdom of Naples (it and Sicily being the "Two Sicilies"). Soon after Peter's invasion, Pope Martin IV, anxious to defend the temporal rights of the Church in Sicily, declares a crusade against Aragon.

1284 Charles II (the Lame), father of Charles Martel, is captured in the Bay of Naples by the forces of Peter III of Aragon, and is held for ransom in Spain.

1286 Charles I dies while Charles II is still captive, and Charles Martel becomes regent at age 15.

1288 Charles II is released and takes over the rule of Naples. (Robert, Lodovico, and John, younger brothers of Charles Martel . . . are surrendered to Peter of Aragon as hostages for Charles' ransom, and they remain in Spain until 1295.)

1290 Charles Martel becomes titular King of Hungary.

1295 Charles Martel dies (before his father).

The warfare that followed the Sicilian Vespers continued for thirty years, spurred constantly by the Vatican, and involved not only the powers of Anjou and of Aragon, but of Valois and of Sicily, and of the Papal States, in various shifting alliances.

In lines 50–51, Charles points out that he died young, but declares that had he lived longer he might have averted the great evils of this long warfare by establishing harmony among the contesting forces. As becomes heavenly souls, Charles is a bit of an optimist: the intrigues of the various Popes who ruled from 1282 to 1303, and of their various secular allies, could hardly have been combed smooth by a stripling, but Charles seems to have had generous intentions toward Dante, and Dante repays him even more generously.

43. *the radiance that had made*: Charles. In line 33 he had promised to give Dante what would make him joyous.

48. *adding new delight to its delight*: Love of others is the delight and radiance of these souls. The thought of being able to give pleasure to Dante by answering his question makes the light of loving bliss swell and burn even more brightly.

51. *yet to be*: Charles is talking, of course, as of 1300. There were yet to be more than two years of war before the defeat of Charles of Valois in Sicily and the peace of 1303.

54. The silkworm in its cocoon was a common symbol of transfiguring rebirth. Note that the Sphere of Venus is the last in which the souls suggest any trace of human form or lineaments. The spirits higher up appear only as flames, until, in the Empyrean, something like their human forms reappears but mystically transfigured.

57. *more than the green leaves*: Charles stayed in Florence for three weeks on his visit of 1294, was warmly received by the Florentines, and responded warmly. Dante seems to have struck up a friendship with Charles and seems to have been promised Charles's love and patronage. Had Charles lived, Dante would have seen more than the promise (the green leaves) of Charle's love; he would have seen the fruit of it (active patronage).

58–60. *The left bank, etc.* The land so marked was Provence. Charles I (King of Naples and brother of the King of France) acquired it by marriage. It thus became attached to the crown of Naples, was passed on to Charles II, and would have passed on to Charles Martel as the firstborn heir.

61. *that horn of Italy*: The territory so described was the former Kingdom of Naples, to which Charles was also heir. The Tronto and the Verde (now called the Garigliano) draw a nearly complete line across Italy. Together they were the main boundary between the Papal States to the north and the Kingdom of Naples to the south.

64–66. The Danube rises in Germany and flows east through Hungary. Charles Martel had the glow of the Hungarian crown on his brow, but the throne was occupied by Andreas III of Venice. Charles was King in title only. In 1310 Charles Robert, son of Charles Martel, became King of Hungary in fact as well as in title.

66–75. *And though not yet my own*: The passage is in Dante's denser style and complicated by the strange parenthesis about Typhoeus, a Titan associated with the fires and smokes of the earth's interior. He rose against Zeus, who (in the legend Dante follows) hurled him deep into the earth and piled Aetna upon him. Dante, in his paradisal freedom from the errors of mythology, explains that the smoke shrouds of Sicily are caused not by Typhoeus but by the burning sulfur of volcanoes.

The parenthesis understood, the gist of the rest of the passage is that Charles Martel, but for the overthrow of the French in the Sicilian Vespers, would have ruled Sicily and so continued in his sons the bloodlines of Anjou (on his side) and of Rudolph of Hapsburg (on his wife's side). *Faro*: Cape Faro, the northeast tip of Sicily. *Passero*: Cape Passero, the southeast tip. Dante calls them Pelorus and Pachynus. *Eurus*: The east wind. *the bitter breath . . . Palermo's streets*: The Sicilian Vespers. *misrule*: Of Charles I of Anjou.

76–78. *Robert*: Became King of Naples in 1309. He was one of the younger brothers of Charles Martel who remained in Spain from 1288 to 1295 as hostages for Charles II. In Catalonia, Robert made friends among the Spanish, who later became powerful in his government of Naples and who, in the greed of their poverty, oppressed the people. Charles is prophesying that Robert, a weak man, will reap a bad harvest from the seeds of misrule he has sown.

80. *on his ship*: Charles Martel may mean the "ship" of Robert's soul, already wallowing under the load of Catalonian avarice he has permitted, and which may damn him too; or he may mean the "ship" of state of abused Naples, once destined to be his own kingdom.

85–90. The sense of this difficult passage depends on the reader's awareness of "there where every good begins and ends." I believe "there" is best understood as "the Empyrean" (the true seat of these souls whose manifestations appear in the various heavens). With "there" so understood, the passage may be paraphrased: "Because I believe this felicity I feel is as clear to you up 'there' as it is to me, it is the dearer to me. And it is also dear to me that you discern my felicity (up 'there') by looking directly upon God (to whom my joy is known) rather than by looking merely into my heart."

93 ff. THE VARIATIONS OF PERSONAL ENDOWMENT. Dante asks how sweet seed can bear sour fruit, i.e., how a noble father can beget a mean son. Charles explains the central truth whereby what is now behind Dante's back (hence, unseen) will reveal itself to his eyes.

Obviously it would not be just for one family or bloodline to inherit all the high qualities of mankind, as would be the case if the sons of great fathers always inherited greatness. God does not will it so.

Yet such would be the case were the qualities of the father (the active *mael* principle as discussed in *Purgatorio*, XXV, 37 ff.) transmitted to the children without any external force affecting the transmission. That external force is the influence of the stars bearing on the hour of the individual's birth in order to serve God's just and harmonious ends. For God created man as a social being, and since society requires many different talents, God assigns to the spheres the power to generate this necessary diversity.

99. *these great bodies*: The heavenly bodies. Their influences on mankind are powers granted them by God's providence. (Note that Dante uses "providence" always in the sense of "pre-vision," i.e., foresight.)

109–111. The argument here is *reductio ad absurdum*. The heavenly bodies could produce chaos instead of harmony only if the Intelligences that move each sphere were imperfect, and if the First Intelligence (God) were also imperfect, having created defective agents. Since these things cannot be, the argument is false, and one must conclude that only harmony can flow from the order of God's creation, all things interplaying to His ordained ends.

114. *nature cannot fall short of what must be*: The universe, having been created and predestined to God's sure purpose, cannot do less than He predestined it to do.

117. *Nor need I proof of this*: Charles has just presented proofs of reason to support the truth of universal harmony. Dante is saying that on this point of the good of society to mankind he needs no such proofs, his own intellect being sufficient. In *De Monarchia* Dante discussed the nature of man as a civic being.

120. *Your master*: Aristotle. In the *Ethics* and elsewhere he expounds the various offices men in society must serve for the good of all.

120–123. The soul of Charles Martel has carried the disputation forward by deduction. Now it concludes: the various (and necessary) endowments required of social man could not follow from the single genetic source of the active (father) principle (which would reproduce itself without change) but must arise from various roots (the shifting influences of the heavenly bodies).

124–126. *Xerxes*: The Persian King. He is the type of the warleader. *Solon*: Athenian lawgiver of the seventh century B.C., the type of the legislator. *Melchizedek*: As in *Genesis*, XIV, 18, "he was the priest of the most high God," hence, the type of the spiritual leader. *he who, flying . . . lost his own son*: Daedalus, the type of the artisan and mechanic.

127–129. *That ever-revolving nature*: The power of the ever-turning spheres. This nature (this rank of nature) impresses its influence upon mortals as a seal is pressed into wax, thus effecting its generalized purposes (the distribution of various gifts to mankind) but without regard to where its gift lodges.

130–132. *Esau . . . Jacob*: Though twins, they were markedly different in character. "In the seed" is crucial here: Dante seems to imply that their genetic inheritance was identical. If so, only the diverse influence of the stars could have affected their differences. *Romulus*: His father was so humble that men were able to say he was born of Mars (as they could not have said had his father been sufficiently well known to have been remembered).

139–141. If a man's natural abilities (from his genetic inheritance and from the influences of the stars) sort well with the conditions into which he is born (as determined by Fortune, the agent of divine foresight), then the man prospers. But if his abilities and his fortune are not so sorted, then, like a seed planted in an unsuitable climate, his gift cannot achieve its full growth.

145–148. *into holy orders*: Charles's general sense is clear enough here but he probably intends an additional reference to his younger brother Lodovico who became Bishop of Toulouse. *and make a king of one*: Here, in addition to the general sense, Charles certainly intends a reference to his brother Robert, who paid little attention to his duties as King of Naples, and who composed a number of ornate sermons and other discourses.

Canto IX

THE THIRD SPHERE: VENUS *The Amorous: Cunizza, Folquet, Rahab*

Cunizza da Romano next appears, lamenting the woes that have befallen her native Venetia and prophesying great grief to her countrymen for pursuing false fame on earth. Cunizza has begun her remarks by pointing out a soul who rejoices beside her in Heaven as one who pursued good ends. When she finishes speaking that soul identifies itself as *Folquet*, once *Bishop of Marseilles.* Folquet narrates his life and indicates that, like Cunizza, his amorous nature first led him to carnality but later filled him with passion for the True Love of God. Folquet then answers Dante's questions about the *Nature of the Third Heaven*, identifies *Rahab*, the Whore of Jericho, as the first soul to ascend to that sphere, and concludes with a *Denunciation of Boniface VIII* for neglecting the Holy Land and all things spiritual, and a further *Denunciation of Florence* as a corrupt state and as the source of Papal corruption. A just vengeance, he prophesies, will not be long delayed.

Fair Clemence, when your Charles, in speaking thus
    had shone his light into my mind, he told me
    of the schemes and frauds that would attack his house. 3

But he said to me: "Say nothing. Let the years
    turn as they must." And so I can say only
    that they who wrong you shall find cause for tears. 6

Now to the Sun, the all-sufficing good,
    the eternal being of that sacred lamp
    had turned itself again to be renewed. 9

O souls deceived! ill-born impieties
    who turn your hearts away from the True Love
    and fix your eyes on empty vanities! 12

—And lo! another of those splendors now
    draws near me, and his wish to give me pleasure
    shows in the brightening of his outward glow. 15

The eyes of Beatrice, which, as before
    were fixed on me, saw all my wish and gave it
    the assurance of their dear consent once more. 18

"O blessed spirit, be pleased to let me find
    my joy at once," I said. "Make clear to me
    that you are a true mirror of my mind!" 21

Thereat the unknown spirit of that light,
    who had been singing in its depths, now spoke,
    like one whose whole delight is to delight. 24

"In that part of the sinful land men know
   as the Italy which lies between Rialto
   and the springs from which the Brenta and Piave flow,   **27**

there stands a hill of no imposing height;
   down from it years ago there came a firebrand
   who laid waste all that region like a blight.   **30**

One root gave birth to both of us. My name
   was Cunizza, of Romano, and I shine here
   because this star conquered me with its flame.   **33**

Yet gladly I embrace the fate that so
   arranged my lot, and I rejoice in it,
   although it may seem hard to the crowd below.   **36**

This bright and precious jewel of our sky,
   whose ray shines here beside me, left great fame
   behind him on the earth; nor will it die   **39**

before this centenary is five times told.
   Now ask yourself if man should seek that good
   that lives in name after the flesh is cold.   **42**

The rabble that today spills through the land
   bound by the Tagliamento and the Adige
   think little of that, nor, though war's bloody hand   **45**

rips them, do they repent. But Paduan blood,
   having shunned its duty, shall soon stain the water
   that bathes Vicenza and drains into mud.   **48**

And there rules one who yet holds high his head,
   there where the Sile and the Cagnano join,
   for whom the net already has been spread.   **51**

And Feltro shall yet weep the treachery
   of its foul priest; no man yet entered Malta
   for a crime as infamous as his shall be.   **54**

Great would that ewer be that could hold at once
   the blood Ferrara will spill, and tired the man
   who set himself to weigh it ounce by ounce;   **57**

—all this the generous priest will freely give
   to prove his party loyalty; but then
   such gifts conform to how those people live.   **60**

On high are mirrors (you say 'Thrones') and these
   reflect God's judgment to us; so enlightened,
   we have thought it well to speak these prophecies."   **63**

Here she fell still and, turning, made it clear
   she was drawn to other things, joining once more
   the wheel of souls that dance through that third sphere.   **66**

That other Bliss, he I had heard her say
    was precious to her, now showed himself to me
    like a fine ruby struck by the sun's ray.   69

Up there, joy makes those souls add light to light,
    as here it makes us laugh, while down below
    souls darken as they grieve through Hell's long night.   72

"God sees all, and your insight, blessèd being,
    makes itself one with His," I said, "and thus
    no thought or wish may hide beyond your seeing.   75

Why does your voice, then, which forever sings
    Heaven's delight as one with those Blest Flames
    who wrap themselves about with their six wings,   78

not grant my wish? Had I the intuition
    with which to read your wish as you read mine,
    I should not be still waiting for *your* question!"   81

"The greatest basin to which earth's waters flow
    —aside from the sea that girdles all the land—"
    his voice began when I had spoken so,   84

"extends so far against the course of the sun,
    between opposing shores, that at its zenith
    the sun must cross what first was its horizon.   87

I first saw light on that sea's shore between
    the Ebro and that river whose short course
    parts Tuscan from Genoese—the Magra, I mean.   90

Sunrise and sunset are about the same
    for Bougiah and my city, whose blood flowed
    to warm its harbor's waters when Caesar came.   93

My name—to such as knew it on the earth
    was Folquet; here eternally my ray
    marks all this sphere, as its ray marked my birth.   96

Dido did not burn hotter with love's rage,
    when she offended both Sichaeus and Creusa,
    than I, before my locks grew thin with age.   99

Nor she of Rhodopè who felt the smart
    of Demophoön's deception, nor Hercules
    when he had sealed Iole in his heart.   102

But none repents here; joy is all our being:
    not at the sin—that never comes to mind—
    but in the All-Ordering and All-Foreseeing.   105

Here all our thoughts are fixed upon the Love
    that beautifies creation, and here we learn
    how world below is moved by world above.   108

But that you may take with you from this sphere
full knowledge of all it makes you wish to know,
I must speak on a little further here.   111

You wish to know who is within this blaze
you see in all its splendor here beside me,
like purest water lit by the sun's rays.   114

Know, then, that in it Rahab finds her good;
and that, one with our choir, she seals upon it
the highest order of beatitude.   117

Of all Christ's harvest, her soul was the one
first summoned by this Heaven, on which the shadow
the earth casts rests the point of its long cone.   120

It was fitting in every way that she should thus
adorn one of these heavens as a palm
of the high victory two palms won for us,   123

for she it was who helped win the first glory
of Joshua's victory in the Holy Land
(which seems to have slipped from the Pope's memory).   126

Your Florence—which was planted by the One
who first turned on his Maker, and whose envy
has given men such cause for lamentation—   129

brings forth and spreads the accursed flower of gold
that changes the shepherd into a ravening wolf
by whom the sheep are scattered from the fold.   132

And so the Gospels and Great Doctors lie
neglected, and the Decretals alone
are studied, as their margins testify.   135

So Pope and Cardinal heed no other things.
Their thoughts do not go out to Nazareth
where the blessèd Gabriel opened wide his wings.   138

But the Vatican, and the other chosen parts
of Holy Rome that have been, from the first,
the cemetery of those faithful hearts   141

that followed Peter and were his soldiery,
shall soon be free of this adultery."

Notes

1–6. THE PROPHECY OF CHARLES MARTEL. On the death of Charles Martel (1295) the throne of Naples passed to his son Caroberto, but in 1309 Robert the Wise (younger brother of Charles and, therefore, Caroberto's uncle) usurped the throne. Thus the direct line of Charles Martel lost the crown of Naples. Robert and his followers, however, will yet have cause to weep in the disastrous consequences of their deceptions and of the suffering inflicted upon Robert's subjects by his Spanish lieutenants. Dante does not specify what will cause their tears, but the subsequent history of the Kingdom of Naples left generous provision for any amount of mourning.

There is no wholly satisfactory identification of the Clemence Dante here addresses. Charles' wife was named Clemence, but she died in 1295, and Dante's words seem clearly addressed to a living person. Charles' mother was also called Clemence, and she lived until 1323, but she was customarily known as Maria of Hungary, the daughter of Rudolph I of Hapsburg. And Charles had a daughter named Clemence, but if Dante intended the daughter, it seems odd to refer to the father as "her Charles."

8. *the eternal being*: Charles.

13. *another of those splendors*: Cunizza da Romano (*circa* 1198-*circa* 1279), younger daughter of Ezzolino II, Count of Onora, and the cruelest of the Ghibelline tyrants. He is in Hell with the Violent against their Neighbors (*Inferno*, XII, 110).

Cunizza was known as an outgoing woman, her tendencies attested by the fact that she had various lovers as well as three husbands. Sordello was one among her lovers (*Purgatorio*, VI, 58 ff.). Among other bad choices, she willed her estate to Alessandro and Napoleone, Counts of Mangone, two of the worst sinners in Hell (*Inferno*, XXXII, 41–60). There seems to be no way of knowing why Dante put her in Paradise. He must have credited her with a true contrition in her later years, and certainly he might have been moved to show that even a great sinner could find heaven's grace through repentance, but at best she would have been scheduled for more than twenty-one years in Purgatory. Her case may have been helped by the fact that in 1265 she manumitted a number of slaves who had been in bondage to her father and brothers.

15. *outward glow*: Dante regularly conceives the spirits of heaven as having an inner and an outer glow, of which only the outer is visible to him.

16. *as before*: As when Dante, with his eyes, asked of Beatrice's eyes their permission to talk to Charles Martel (VIII, 40–42).

19–21. Dante knows by now that the heavenly spirits know his thoughts without need for him to speak them, and that knowledge fills him with the expectation of joy. He asks Cunizza to give him that joy without delay, by demonstrating that she can address his unspoken thoughts.

22. *the unknown spirit*: Cunizza has not yet identified herself to Dante.

26–27. *Rialto*: The principal island of Venice, here taken for all of Venice. *the Brenta and Piave*: These rivers have their sources in the mountains north and northwest of Florence. The area so defined is la Marca Trivigiana whose principal city is Treviso.

29. *a firebrand*: Ezzolino (or Azzolino), Cunizza's brother.

33. The flame of Venus is, of course, love.

34–36. *the fate that so arranged my lot*: Cunizza's amorous nature was the force of fate that shaped her lot. The crowd below (mortal men) may think it painful for her to recall her natural amorousness and the loose life to which it led her. Yet that same fire of passion, properly directed to the love of God, was also the source of her blessedness.

37 ff. *This bright and precious jewel*: Folquet of Marseilles, a troubadour poet who became a Cistercian monk, and who was Bishop of Toulouse from 1205 to 1231. He was a leader (as he informs Dante in lines 123–142) in the atrocious crusade against the Albigensians. The fame he left on earth was written darkly enough in Albigensian blood, but Cunizza (and, through her, Dante) seems here to honor him as one who inveighed against the false passions of the people of Marca Trivigiana, exhorting them to seek the pure and lasting fame of an honored memory.

40. *this centenary*: The year 1300 was a Jubilee year (see *Inferno*, XVIII, 28–33, note). Dante is probably saying that five more centenaries will pass before Folquet's fame dies.

43–48. CUNIZZA'S PROPHECY. The Tagliamento and Adige are rivers. The land they bound is, approximately, the present Venetia. The Bacchiglione flows through this land a bit south of its center, passes by Vicenza and then Padua, and empties into the swamps behind Venice ("drains into the mud"). Dante's text can be variously interpreted but points clearly enough to the defeat of the Paduans outside Vicenza in 1314 by Dante's great patron, Can Grande della Scala. The duty the Paduans shunned was, in general, the observance of justice but, specifically, their allegiance to the empire as represented by Can Grande, the reigning Ghibelline.

49–51. Rizzardo da Cammino, Lord of Treviso ("where the Sile and Cagnano join"), was treacherously murdered in 1312 while playing chess. He was the son of "the good Gherardo" (*Purgatorio*, XVI, 124 and 138), the son-in-law of Judge Nin (*Purgatorio*, VIII, 53 ff.), and the husband of "my Giovanna" (*Purgatorio*, VIII, 71).

52–60. The Malta here referred to was a papal prison near Lake Bolsena. The worst of its criminals had yet to commit a crime as foul as the one that would be committed by Alessandro Novella, Bishop of Feltro, who accepted a group of Ghibelline refugees from Ferrara as his guests, and then (in July of 1314) turned them over to Pino della Tosa, one of the Spanish agents of Robert of Naples, to be beheaded. Thus the Bishop fell to his place in Ptolemea among those who were treacherous against their guests. (Sinner in that category, bear in mind, did not await their death to begin their damnation, but fell instantly into the ice of Cocytus, their earthly bodies being assumed by fiends.)

The blood of the Ferrarans would fill a great urn, but this generous priest (an irony) will give it gladly in duty to his party (Guelph), and be it said (another and a savage irony) such gifts of blood will suit the way the people of Marca Trivigiana live.

61. *Thrones*: There is no established creed concerning the hierarchy of the angels but Dante sets forth their orders. Cunizza's words indicate that Dante conceives the informing spirits of Venus (and probably of each of the spheres) to be Thrones. See also VIII, 35–37, note.

62–63. *so enlightened*: It is in the full illumination of God's judgment and wisdom that Cunizza has thought well to utter her prophecy. Clearly, however, she is the spokesman for all the spirits of this sphere.

64–66. To understand these lines, one should refer to VIII, 16–27 and 34–36, in which Dante describes how these souls dance their eternal delight in God.

67. *That other bliss*: Folquet. Dante does not yet know who he is, except as Cunizza referred to him in line 37 as "this bright and precious jewel."

70–71. *Up there*: In Heaven. *as here*: On earth.

73–81. Since the Heavenly Soul is one with God, it shares God's omniscience and no thought or wish may hide from it. Folquet, therefore, knows instantly what Dante is yearning to ask. Why then does he not speak at once? Had Dante the gut of Paradisal omniscience, he declares, he would not have waited so long to gratify whatever wish Folquet may have. Dante's wish, of course, is to know the spirit's identity. *those Blest Flames . . . six wings*: The Seraphim. "Each one had six wings; with twain he covered his face, and with twain he covered his feet, and with twain he did fly" (*Isaiah*, VI, 2).

82–87. *the greatest basin . . . aside from the sea that girdles all*: The Mediterranean. Folquet conceives it as if he were standing in Spain; hence it extends against the course of the sun, from west to east. In common with most of his contemporaries Dante believed that the Mediterranean extended through 90° of latitude (it actually covers 42°): thus the sun at Zenith over Jerusalem would have Gibraltar as its horizon, and moving west, would be at zenith over what was at first its horizon.

88–92. *the Ebro*: The Spanish river. *the Magra*: Runs south into the Mediterranean for a bit over 40 miles (its short course) between Tuscany and Liguria (whose capital city is Genoa). Marseilles lies about halfway between the two rivers and is in almost the same latitude as Bougiah (or Bougie) in Algeria (5° E.). Thus the two cities would have the sun rise and set at almost the same time.

92–93. *blood flowed . . . when Caesar came*: In 49 B.C., when Caesar left Brutus to defeat the forces of Pompey at Marseilles while he himself "swooped down on Spain." (*Purgatorio* XVIII, 102).

94. *to such as knew it*: Cunizza introduced (the unidentified) Folquet (38–39) as one who "left great fame behind him." Folquet is careful to speak of himself in far more modest terms.

95–96. *my ray marks all this sphere*: Folquet is now one with God. His radiance, therefore, is impressed upon Venus (influencing it) as powerfully as the influence of Venus impressed itself upon him at his birth.

97–99. *Dido*: See *Inferno*, V, 61–62, and note. Having conceived so violent a passion for Aeneas that she killed herself when he left, she wronged both Sichaeus, her dead husband, and Creusa, Aeneas's dead wife.

100–102. *she of Rhodopè . . . Demophoön*: Phyllis, daughter of King Sithon of Thrace (wherein rises Mount Rhodopè) was to marry Demophoön. When he did not arrive on the wedding day, she hanged herself and was changed into an almond tree. Demophoön (Ovid, *Heroides*, 2) narrates how the bridegroom arrived only after a painful delay only to find that Phyllis had gone out on a limb.

101–102. *Hercules . . . Iole*: See *Inferno*, XII, 67, note. Folquet's three references are all to mythic figures who died painfully for love.

104. *not at the sin—that never comes to mind*: When the purified soul reaches the Terrestrial Paradise it is bathed in the waters of Lethe and the very memory of sin is taken from it (*Purgatorio*, XXXI, 91–102). Yet both Cunizza (30–36) and Folquet make the point that they do not regret their amorous natures, which once led them into carnality, because the same impulse later led them to the True Love. (See also *Purgatorio*, XXXIII, 91–102, and note.) There Dante, newly washed in Lethe, forgets that he was ever estranged from Beatrice, and she proves the sinfulness of his estrangement by the very fact that Lethe washed its memory from him.

One might argue that the pure soul forgets sin in what might be called the active sense, recalling its existence only in a passive and conceptual way that has no power upon it. After every subtlety, however, there remains an unresolvable contradiction in Dante's handling of this point, and the contradiction arises directly from the narrator's necessity. In whatever way these souls are conceived, Dante has to give them something to talk about, and the narrator has never existed who can sustain a conversation about mankind without bringing sin into it.

109–112. Folquet is mind-reading here, as directed to in lines 73–81. He has satisfied Dante's unspoken question about his identity and his place in Heaven. He now continues by answering Dante's next unspoken question. Note that he does not promise to explain the total mysteries of the Third Heaven but only to satisfy all the questions that arise in Dante's mind (which is yet incapable of of conceiving the ultimate mystery).

115. *Rahab*: When Joshua sent spies before him into Jericho, Rahab, a harlot of that city, hid them from the king's men and helped them to escape. Thus she helped the people of Israel to regain the promised land, and immediately following the crucifixion her soul (which must have been in Limbo) was summoned by the Third Heaven, the first of its elected.

119–120. *shadow . . . rests the point of its long cone*: Some scholars of Dante's time believed that the cone of the earth's shadow came to a point in the third sphere.

121–126. *as a palm*: As a trophy. *two palms*: Of Christ when he was nailed to the cross. It is fitting that Rahab should be the heavenly trophy of Christ's victory for she had helped Israel win its promised land. It is a pity, Dante has Folquet say, that the Pope cares so little for the Holy Land (he had done nothing to reestablish Christianity there after Acre, the last Christian stronghold, fell to the Saracens in 1291).

127. *the One*: Satan was, of course, the first to turn on God, and it was Mars who founded Florence (*Inferno*, XIII, 143–150) but Dante's invective has a firm foundation in those church fathers who held that Mars and all the pagan gods were fiends.

130–132. *the accursed flower of gold*: The Florentine florin, a gold coin stamped with a lily. Dante's figure of a tree that bears magically evil flowers begins with "planted" in line 127. The power of gold transforms the shepherd (the Church, the Papacy in general, and Boniface VIII in particular) so that he preys on the sheep he should lead and guard.

132–135. *Great Doctors*: The Church Fathers, givers of doctrine. *the Decretals*: The volumes of canon law. Gregory IX ordered the compilation of the first five volumes in 1234 and Boniface VIII had a sixth added. The margins of the Decretals testify (by being worn and covered with annotations) how seriously they were studied, for they covered the temporal rights and privileges of the Church's vast power and wealth, and a knowledge of canon law could make a shyster's fortune.

138. *where . . . Gabriel opened wide his wings*: At the Annunciation.

Canto X

Doctors of the Church

The First Garland of Souls: Aquinas

Dante revels in the joy of God's creation and especially in the art shown by the placement of *The Equinoctial Point*. So rejoicing, he enters the *Sphere of the Sun*, unaware of his approach until he has arrived.

A *Garland of Twelve Souls* immediately surrounds him and Beatrice, the glory of each soul shining so brilliantly that it is visible even against the background of the Sun itself. These are *Twelve Doctors of the Church*, philosophers and theologians whose writings have guided the church in creed and canon law. Their spokesman, appropriately, is *Thomas Aquinas*. He identifies the souls in order around the ring.

When Aquinas has finished, the souls dance around Dante and Beatrice, raising their voices in harmonies unknown except to Heaven itself.

Contemplating His Son with that Third Essence
　　of Love breathed forth forever by Them both,
　　the omnipotent and ineffable First Presence　　　　3

created all that moves in mind and space
　　with such perfection that to look upon it
　　is to be seized by love of the Maker's grace.　　　6

Therefore, reader, raise your eyes across
　　the starry sphere. Turn with me to that point
　　at which one motion and another cross,　　　　　9

and there begin to savor your delight
　　in the Creator's art, which he so loves
　　that it is fixed forever in His sight.　　　　　12

Note how the wheel on which the planets ride
　　branches from there obliquely: only thus
　　may the earth that calls to them be satisfied.　15

For if these two great motions never crossed,
　　the influence of the heavens would be weakened
　　and most of its power upon the earth be lost.　18

For if its deviation were to be
　　increased or lessened, much would then be wanting,
　　both north and south, from the earth's harmony.　21

Stay on at table, reader, and meditate
　　upon this foretaste if you wish to dine
　　on joy itself before it is too late.　　　　　24

I set out food, but you yourself must feed!
  For the great matters I record demand
  all my attention and I must proceed.   27

Nature's majestic minister, the Sun,
  who writes the will of Heaven on the earth
  and with his light measures the hours that run,   30

now in conjunction (as I have implied)
  with Aries, rode those spirals whose course brings him
  ever earlier from the eastern side.   33

And I was with the Sun; but no more aware
  of my ascent than a man is of a thought
  that comes to mind, until he finds it there.   36

It is Beatrice, she it is who leads our climb
  from good to better, so instantaneously
  that her action does not spread itself through time.   39

How radiant in its essence that must be
  which in the Sun (where I now was) shows forth
  not by its color but its radiancy.   42

Though genius, art, and usage stored my mind,
  I still could not make visible what I saw;
  but yet may you believe and seek to find!   45

And if our powers fall short of such a height,
  why should that be surprising, since the sun
  is as much as any eye has known of light?   48

Such, there, was the fourth family of splendors
  of the High Father who fills their souls with bliss,
  showing them how He breathes forth and engenders.   51

"Give thanks!" my lady said. "With all devotion
  give thanks to the Sun of Angels, by whose grace
  you have been lifted to this physical one!"   54

The heart of mortal never could so move
  to its devotion, nor so willingly
  offer itself to God in thankful love,   57

as mine did when these words had passed her lips.
  So wholly did I give my love to Him
  that she sank to oblivion in eclipse.   60

Nothing displeased, she laughed so that the blaze
  of her glad eyes pierced my mind's singleness
  and once again divided it several ways.   63

Splendors of living and transcendent light
  circle us now and make a glowing crown,
  sweeter in voice than radiant in sight.   66

Latona's daughter sometimes seems to us
  so banded when the vaporous air weaves round her
  the thread that makes her girdle luminous.   69

In Heaven's courts, from which height I have come,
  are many gems so precious and so lovely
  that they cannot be taken from the kingdom.   72

Of such those splendors sang. Who does not grow
  wings that will fly him there, must learn these things
  from the tidings of the tongueless here below.   75

When, so singing, those Sun-surpassing souls
  had three times turned their blazing circuit round us,
  like stars that circle close to the fixed poles,   78

they stood like dancers still caught in the pleasure
  of the last round, who pause in place and listen
  till they have caught the beat of the new measure.   81

And from within its blaze I heard one start:
  "Since the ray of grace from which true love is kindled—
  and then by loving, in the loving heart,   84

grows and multiplies—among all men
  so shines on you to lead you up these stairs
  that none descend except to climb again;   87

whoever refused your soul, it being thirsty,
  wine from his flask, would be no freer to act
  than water blocked from flowing to the sea.   90

You wish to know what flowering plants are woven
  into this garland that looks lovingly
  on the lovely lady who strengthens you for Heaven.   93

I was a lamb among the holy flock
  Dominic leads to where all plenty is,
  unless the lamb itself stray to bare rock.   96

This spirit on my right, once of Cologne,
  was my teacher and brother. Albert was his name,
  and Thomas, of Aquinas, was my own.   99

If you wish, similarly, to know the rest
  let your eyes follow where my words shall lead
  circling through all this garland of the blest.   102

The next flame springs from the glad smile of Gratian
  who so assisted one court and the other
  that in him Heaven found good cause for elation.   105

The next to adorn our chorus of the glad
  was the good Peter who, like the poor widow,
  offered to Holy Church all that he had.   108

The fifth light, and the loveliest here, shines forth
  from so magnificent a love that men
  hunger for any news of it on earth;   111

within it is that mind to which were shone
  such depths of wisdom that, if truth be true,
  no mortal ever rose to equal this one.   114

See next the taper whose flame, when formerly
  it burned in mortal flesh, saw most profoundly
  the nature of angels and their ministry.   117

Within the lesser lamp next on my right
  shines the defender of the Christian Age
  whose treatise led Augustine toward the light.   120

Now if your mind has followed on my praise
  from light to light, you are already eager
  to know what spirit shines in the eighth blaze.   123

In it, for having seen the sum of good,
  there sings a soul that showed the world's deceit
  to any who would heed. The bones and blood   126

from which it was cruelly driven have their tomb
  down there in Cieldauro: to this peace
  it came from exile and from martyrdom.   129

See next the flames breathed forth by Isidore,
  by Bede, and by that Richard whose 'Contemplations'
  saw all that a mere man can see, and more.   132

The next, from whom your eyes return to me,
  is the glory of a soul in whose grave thoughts
  death seemed to be arriving all too slowly: 135

it is the flame, eternally elated,
  of Siger, who along the Street of Straws
  syllogized truths for which he would be hated."   138

Then as a clock tower calls us from above
  when the Bride of God rises to sing her matins
  to the Sweet Spouse, that she may earn his love,   141

with one part pulling and another thrusting,
  tin-tin, so glad a chime the faithful soul
  swells with the joy of love almost to bursting—   144

just so, I saw that wheel of glories start
  and chime from voice to voice in harmonies
  so sweetly joined, so true from part to part   147

that none can know the like till he go free
  where joy begets itself eternally.

Notes

1–3. The idea of Trinity will hardly be contained in a footnote, but note the essence of Dante's doctrine. The Father is the Creator. The Son is Wisdom—the Word of God. Together, they eternally breathe forth the Third Essence of Love, the Holy Ghost. Note, therefore, that it is forever being born.

7–27. THE PERFECTION OF THE CREATION. Dante summons the reader to ponder the perfection of God's creation as exemplified by the point of the vernal equinox. It is at this point that the Sun's ecliptic crosses the celestial equator into the northern hemisphere. The two great circles intersect at an angle of 23° 27'.

These two circles are the "one motion and another." (The Sun is now at the vernal equinox.) The apparent equatorial (or diurnal) motion is from east to west. The apparent order in which the signs of the Zodiac appear along the ecliptic is from west to east. It follows, therefore, that the influences of the planets, following the zodiacal path, vary from north to south of the equator (see below, note to 32–33), striking the earth variously but in a fixed progression that is part of God's inscrutable plan. Were the courses of the equator and the ecliptic to run parallel, or were the angles between them to change, the influences of the spheres would be weakened, and earth that stands ever in need of those influences ("earth that calls on them") would lose the full good of their powers.

This is the mystical foretaste Dante offers the reader, bidding him to stay at table and feed himself (i.e., study God's ways) while Dante pursues his demanding theme.

31. *as I have implied*: In lines 8–9 ff., where he said the sun was at the vernal equinox, at which point it must be in Aries.

32–33. *those spirals*: The path of the Sun seems to be a spiral (as may be noted when it is drawn on a globe) from the Tropic of Capricorn (the southern limit of the sun's motion) to the Tropic of Cancer (the northern limit). These Tropics are the latitudes 23° 27' south and north respectively (the same angle at which the ecliptic crosses the equator). As the apparent spiral of the sun's course brings it toward the Tropic of Cancer, we see it rise earlier every day.

43–45. *Though genius, art, and usage stored my mind*: None of these resources of human understanding (reason) can make visible what faith alone can find.

48. *as much as any eye has known of light*: Dante (following Aristotle) sets the sun as the maximum of light the human eye can see and, therefore, the human mind can imagine. The sun-surpassing radiance of Heaven is, therefore, beyond human imagination.

49. *the fourth family*: The Fourth Sphere of the Blest.

51. *how He breathes forth and engenders*: Once more of the mystery of the Trinity. Through all Eternity God is conceived as creating the Son, in union with whom He eternally breathes forth the Holy Ghost.

52–54. *the Sun of Angels*: God. *this physical one*: The sun. As the sun lights man, so God lights the angels.

55–63. Note the allegorical possibilities. At the bidding of Beatrice (Revealed Truth) the man turns his mind so utterly to God that he forgets her until her joy in his absorption draws him back from single-minded devotion to an awareness of other (and necessarily lesser) things.

64. *transcendent*: Transcending the light of the sun.

67. *Latona's daughter*: The Moon. See *Purgatorio*, XX, 130–132, note. In vaporous air the moon seems girdled with light. Dante's figure conceives the vapors as weaving the thread (of light) that makes her glowing girdle.

72. *that they cannot be taken from the kingdom*: In one sense, no description can take the idea of them from heaven to mortal imagination. In a second, they are treasures Heaven reserves to itself because man is unworthy and incapable of them.

74–75. *must learn . . . from the tidings of the tongueless*: i.e., not at all. Every human tongue is mute to speak the treasures of Heaven. One must go there himself (i.e., undertake the purification that leads to celestial sensibilities).

82–87. The speaker is Aquinas (see 97–99, note) and he has just announced nothing less than Dante's salvation.

89–90. *no freer to act than water*: Would not be acting according to his nature. The nature of the Celestial Soul is *caritas* and only an impediment outside itself can prevent it from giving love freely.

91–92. *what flowering plants*: What souls. *are woven into this garland*: Are in this company of souls that wreathe Beatrice round.

95. *Dominic*: St. Dominic, founder of the Dominican Order. He will be discussed at length in XII, 34ff.

97–99. *Thomas Aquinas*: Aquinas (1227–1274), known as the "Doctor Angelicus," was author of the "Summa Theologica" (a principal source of Dante's learning), founder of Thomistic philosophy, and perhaps the most learned of Catholic theologians. He was not canonized until 1323, two years after Dante's death. Dante, therefore, was writing of Thomas, not of St. Thomas. As befits the modes of Heaven,

Thomas does not mention his own name till he has identified the spirit on his right, a brother Dominican and his teacher. *Albert*: Albertus Magnus (circa 1200–1280), the "Doctor Universalis" who, with Aquinas, reestablished Aristotelian learning in Western thought. He was teaching in Cologne in 1248 when Aquinas went there to be his student. Albertus was canonized and proclaimed a Doctor of the Church in 1931.

100. *to know the rest*: Of the encircling souls.

103. *Gratian*: Or Gratianus. Twelfth-century scholar. It is for his "Decretum Gratiani" that Aquinas credits him with correlating and harmonizing civil and ecclesiastical law (the "one court and another").

107. *the good Peter*: Petrus Lombardus. Born early in the twelfth century, Bishop of Paris 1159, died 1160. Called "Magister Sententiarum" because of his "Sententiarum Libri IV," a compilation of scriptures and texts of the church fathers. In a sense, he did for doctrine what Gratianus did for canon law, and Dante typically puts the two side by side. *like the poor widow*: In his preface to "Sententiarum" Peter modestly compares himself to the poor widow in *Luke*, XXI, 1–4 who gave her two mites (all she had) to the treasury of the church.

109–114. *The fifth light*: Solomon, *so magnificent a love*: As expressed in the "Song of Songs" which was thought to be the wedding hymn of the Church and God. *men hunger for any news*: Of Solomon's final fate. *I Kings*, XI, 1–9 records the sins of Solomon's age and theologians of Dante's time debated whether he had been saved or damned. *if truth be true*: If Scripture (which is truth) be true. Hence: it certainly is true. *no mortal ever rose to equal this one*: Dante says, literally, "no second [equal] has risen." Adam, of course, knew God directly, and Christ was man-and-God. Both, therefore, surpassed Solomon. But Christ may be said to have descended and Adam to have issued from God, whereby they did not "rise." Whether or not Dante had these thoughts in mind, his words echo *I Kings* III, 12: "that there was none like thee before thee, neither after thee shall any arrive like unto thee." The exact phrasing of this line is important for it will be referred to several times in the next three Cantos.

115. *whose flame*: The soul of Dionysus the Areopagite, converted by St. Paul (*Acts*, XVII, 34) and wrongly believed in Dante's time to be the author of "The Celestial Hierarchy."

119. *the defender of the Christian Age*: Dante may intend here Paulus Orosius, fifth-century Spanish priest whose *Historiarum Adversus Paganos* defended the effect of Christianity upon the Roman Empire. Or he may intend Marius Victorinus, fourth-century Roman, who became a Christian theologian, and whose example was believed to have contributed to the conversion of St. Augustine.

123. *what spirit shines in the eighth blaze*: Boethius. Anicius Manlius Severinus Boethius was born in Rome circa 470, studied in Greece, became consul of Theodoric the Ostrogoth in 510, later to be imprisoned by Theodoric in Pavia on charges of treason and magic, and executed in 524. His "De Consolatione Philosophiae," written in prison, is a work of pagan dignity that defends the joys of the good life without reference to any eternal reward. Despite its essential paganism, its influence upon the Middle Ages (and upon Dante) was enormous, among other reasons, as a source of late classical learning. In time the death of Boethius came to be thought of as a martyrdom. His remains were formally moved to a tomb in Pavia's Cieldauro (Church of St. Peter) in the eighth century, and though never canonized, he grew to be locally revered as St. Severinus.

130. *Isidore*: Of Seville (circa 560–636). Became Archbishop of Seville circa 600. Canonized St. Isidore, 1598. Designated a Doctor of the Church, 1722. His major work, "Etymolcgiae," was highly prized as an encyclopedia of medieval learning.

131. *Bede*: The Venerable Bede (circa 673–735). English Bible scholar and historian. The title of Venerable (the three orders of holiness are venerable, blessed, and saint, in mounting order) was conferred in the ninth century. Pope Leo declared him a Doctor of the Church in 1899.

131. *Richard*: Richard of St. Victor. Twelfth-century English mystic and theologian. Birthdate unknown; died circa 1173. He was called the Great Contemplater after one of his treatises, "De Contemplatione."

133. *from whom your eyes return to me*: Thus completing the round of the twelve doctors.

135. *death seemed to be arriving all too slowly*: In his eagerness to be done with the vanity of this world and to begin the eternal life.

137. *Siger*: Siger of Brabant. Born circa 1226. An outstanding Averroist philosopher, he taught philosophy at the University of Paris (which was then on *la rue de Feurre* or Street of Straws) and was cited for heresy in 1277 before the Grand Inquisitor of France (hence, "the truths for which he would be hated"). He fled to Orvieto to appeal his case to the Papal Court but was stabbed to death (circa 1283) by his secretary, probably in a mad fit.

140–141. *the Bride of God*: The Church. *the Sweet Spouse*: Christ.

Canto XI

Doctors of the Church

*The First Garland of Souls: Aquinas · Praise of St. Francis ·
Degeneracy of Dominicans*

The spirits complete their song and their joyous dance and once more
gather around Dante and Beatrice.

Aquinas reads Dante's mind and speaks to make clear several points
about which Dante was in doubt. He explains that Providence sent two
equal princes to guide the Church, St. Dominic, the wise law-giver, being
one, and St. Francis, the ardent soul, being the other. Aquinas was himself
a Dominican. To demonstrate the harmony of Heaven's gift and the unity
of the Dominicans and Franciscans, Aquinas proceeds to pronounce a *Praise
of the Life of St. Francis*. His account finished, he returns to the theme of
the unity of the Dominicans and Franciscans, and proceeds to illustrate it
further by himself lamenting the *Degeneracy of the Dominican Order*.

O senseless strivings of the mortal round!
  how worthless is that exercise of reason
  that makes you beat your wings into the ground!   3

One man was giving himself to law, and one
  to aphorisms; one sought sinecures,
  and one to rule by force or sly persuasion;   6

one planned his business, one his robberies;
  one, tangled in the pleasure of the flesh,
  wore himself out, and one lounged at his ease;   9

while I, of all such vanities relieved
  and high in Heaven with my Beatrice,
  arose to glory, gloriously received.   12

—When each had danced his circuit and come back
  to the same point of the circle, all stood still,
  like votive candles glowing in a rack.   15

And I saw the splendor of the blazing ray
  that had already spoken to me, smile,
  and smiling, quicken; and I heard it say: 18

"Just as I take my shining from on high,
  so, as I look into the Primal Source,
  I see which way your thoughts have turned, and why.   21

You are uncertain, and would have me find
  open and level words in which to speak
  what I expressed too steeply for your mind   24

when I said 'leads to where all plenty is,'
and 'no mortal ever rose to equal this one.'
And it is well to be exact in this.   27

The Providence that governs all mankind
with wisdom so profound that any creature
who seeks to plumb it might as well be blind,   30

in order that the Bride seek her glad good
in the Sweet Groom who, crying from on high,
took her in marriage with His blessèd blood,   33

sent her two Princes, one on either side
that she might be secure within herself,
and thereby be more faithfully His Bride.   36

One, in his love, shone like the seraphim.
The other, in his wisdom, walked the earth
bathed in the splendor of the cherubim.   39

I shall speak of only one, though to extol
one or the other is to speak of both
in that their works led to a single goal.   42

Between the Tupino and the little race
sprung from the hill blessèd Ubaldo chose,
a fertile slope spreads up the mountain's face.   45

Perugia breathes its heat and cold from there
through Porta Sole, and Nocera and Gualdo
behind it mourn the heavy yoke they bear.   48

From it, at that point where the mountainside
grows least abrupt, a sun rose to the world
as this one does at times from Ganges' tide.   51

Therefore, let no man speaking of that place
call it *Ascesi*—'I have risen'—but rather,
Oriente—so to speak with proper grace.   54

Nor was he yet far distant from his birth
when the first comfort of his glorious powers
began to make its warmth felt on the earth: 57

a boy yet, for that lady who, like death
knocks on no door that opens to her gladly,
he had to battle his own father's wrath.   60

With all his soul he married her before
the diocesan court *et coram patre*;
and day by day he grew to love her more.   63

Bereft of her First Groom, she had had to stand
more than eleven centuries, scorned, obscure;
and, till he came, no man had asked her hand: 66

none, at the news that she had stood beside
  the bed of Amyclas and heard, unruffled,
  the voice by which the world was terrified;   69

and none, at word of her fierce constancy,
  so great, that even when Mary stayed below,
  she climbed the Cross to share Christ's agony.   72

But lest I seem obscure, speaking this way,
  take Francis and Poverty to be those lovers.
  That, in plain words, is what I meant to say.   75

Their harmony and tender exultation
  gave rise in love, and awe, and tender glances
  to holy thoughts in blissful meditation.   78

The venerable Bernard, seeing them so,
  kicked off his shoes, and toward so great a peace
  ran, and running, seemed to go too slow.   81

O wealth unknown! O plenitude untried!
  Egidius went unshod. Unshod, Sylvester
  followed the groom. For so it pleased the bride!   84

Thenceforth this father and this happy lord
  moved with his wife and with his family,
  already bound round by the humble cord.   87

He did not grieve because he had been born
  the son of Bernardone; he did not care
  that he went in rags, a figure of passing scorn.   90

He went with regal dignity to reveal
  his stern intentions to Pope Innocent,
  from whom his order first received the seal.   93

Then as more souls began to follow him
  in poverty—whose wonder-working life
  were better sung among the seraphim—   96

Honorius, moved by the Eternal Breath,
  placed on the holy will of this chief shepherd
  a second crown and everflowering wreath.   99

Then, with a martyr's passion, he went forth
  and in the presence of the haughty Sultan
  he preached Christ and his brotherhood on earth;   102

but when he found none there would take Christ's pardon,
  rather than waste his labors, he turned back
  to pick the fruit of the Italian garden.   105

On the crag between Tiber and Arno then, in tears
  of love and joy, he took Christ's final seal,
  the holy wounds of which he wore two years.   108

When God, whose loving will had sent him forward
to work such good, was pleased to call him back
to where the humble soul has its reward,   111

he, to his brothers, as to rightful heirs
commended his dearest Lady and he bade them
to love her faithfully for all their years.   114

Then from her bosom, that dear soul of grace
willed its return to its own blessèd kingdom;
and wished its flesh no other resting place.   117

Think now what manner of man was fit to be
his fellow helmsman, holding Peter's ship
straight to its course across the dangerous sea.   120

Such was our patriarch. Hence, all who rise
and follow his command will fill the hold,
as you can see, with fruits of paradise.   123

But his flock has grown so greedy for the taste
of new food that it cannot help but be
far scattered as it wanders through the waste.   126

The more his vagabond and distant sheep
wander from him, the less milk they bring back
when they return to the fold. A few do keep   129

close to the shepherd, knowing what wolf howls
in the dark around them, but they are so few
it would take little cloth to make their cowls.   132

Now, if my words have not seemed choked and blind,
if you have listened to me and taken heed,
and if you will recall them to your mind,   135

your wish will have been satisfied in part,
for you will see how the good plant is broken,
and what rebuke my words meant to impart   138

when I referred, a while back in our talk,
to 'where all plenty is' and to 'bare rock.' "

Notes

15. *rack*: Dante says "candellier," which may be taken to mean candlestick, but
equally to mean the candle-racks that hold votive candles in churches. The image of
the souls as twelve votive candles in a circular rack is certainly apter than that of
twelve candles in separate candlesticks.

25–26. *lead to . . . all plenty*: X, 95. *no mortal ever*: X, 114.

28–42. INTRODUCTION TO THE LIFE OF ST. FRANCIS. Compare the words
of Bonaventura in introducing the life of St. Dominic, XII, 31–45.

31. *the Bride*: The Church.

32. *crying from on high*: *Matthew*, XXVII. 46, 50; *Mark*, XV, 34, 37; *Luke*,
XXIII, 46; and *John*, XIX, 26–30; all record Christ's dying cries upon the cross.

34. *two Princes, one on either side*: St. Dominic and St. Francis. Dominic, on one
side (line 39 equates his wisdom with the cherubic), by his wisdom and doctrinal

clarity made the church secure within itself by helping to defend it against error and heresy. Francis, on the other (line 37 ascribes to him seraphic ardor of love), set the example that made her more faithfully the bride of Christ.

43–51. ASSISI AND THE BIRTH OF ST. FRANCIS. The passage, in Dante's characteristic topophiliac style, is full of local allusions, not all of them relevant to St. Francis, but all describing the situation of Assisi, his birthplace. Perugia stands to the east of the upper Tiber. The Tiber at this point runs approximately north to south. Mt. Subasio, a long and many spurred crest, runs roughly parallel to the Tiber on the west. Assisi is on the side of Subasio, and it was from Assisi that the sun of St. Francis rose to the world, as "this one" (the actual sun in which Dante and Aquinas are standing) rises from the Ganges. The upper Ganges crosses the Tropic of Cancer, the line of the summer solstice. When the sun rises from the Ganges, therefore, it is at its brightest.

the Tupino: Skirts Mt. Subasio on the south and flows roughly west into the Tiber. *the little race*: The Chiascio [KYAH-show] flows south along the length of Subasio and empties into the Tupino below Assisi. *blessèd Ubaldo*: St. Ubaldo (1084–1160), Bishop of Gubbio from 1129. He chose a hill near Gubbio as a hermitage in which to end his days, but died before he could retire there. *Porta Sole*: Perugia's west gate. It faces Mt. Subasio. In summer its slopes reflect the sun's ray through Porta Sole; in winter, covered with snow, they send the cold wind. *Nocera* [NAW-tcheh-ra], *Gualdo* [GWAHL-doe]: Towns on the other side of (behind) Subasio. Their heavy yoke may be their subjugation by Perugia, or Dante may have meant by it the taxes imposed by Robert of Naples and his Spanish brigands.

51–54. It is such passages that certify the failures of all translation. *Ascesi*, which can mean "I have risen," was a common name for Assisi in Dante's day. *Oriente*, of course, is the point at which the sun rises. Let no man, therefore, call Assisi "I have risen" (i.e., a man has risen), but let him call it, rather, the dawning east of the world (a sun has risen).

55 ff. *yet far distant*: While he was still young. The phrasing continues the figure of the new-risen sun.

Francis, born Bernardone, was the son of a relatively prosperous baker and, early in life, assisted his father. In a skirmish between Assisi and Perugia he was taken prisoner and later released. On his return to Assisi (he was then twenty-four) he abandoned all worldly affairs and gave himself entirely to religious works.

a boy yet: Here, as in line 55, Aquinas is overdoing it a bit: twenty-four is a bit old for being a boy yet. *that lady*: Poverty. *his own father's wrath*: In 1207 (Francis was then twenty-five) he sold one of his father's horses along with a load of bread and gave the money to a church. In a rage, his father forced the church to return the money, called Francis before the Bishop of Assisi, and there demanded that he renounce his right to inherit. Francis not only agreed gladly but removed his clothes and gave them back to his father saying, "Until this hour I called you my father on earth; from this hour I can say in full truth 'our Father which art in Heaven.'"

he married: In his "Hymn to Poverty" Francis himself celebrated his union to Poverty as a marriage. He had married her before the diocesan court of Assisi, *et coram patre* (before the court, i.e., in the legal presence of, his father). The marriage was solemnized by his renunciation of all possessions.

64–66. *her First Groom*: Christ. *he*: St. Francis.

68. *Amyclas*: Lucan reported (see also *Convivio*, IV, 13) how the fisherman Amyclas lay at his ease on a bed of seaweed before Caesar himself, being so poor that he had nothing to fear from any man. Not even this report of the serenity Mistress Poverty could bring to a man, and not even the fact that she outdid even Mary in constancy, climbing the very cross with Christ, had moved any man to seek her in marriage.

79. *Bernard*: Bernard di Quintavalle, a wealthy neighbor, became the first disciple of Francis, kicking off his shoes to go barefoot in imitation of the master.

82–84. *unknown*: To men. Holy Poverty is the wealth none recognize, the plenitude none try. *Egidius . . . Sylvester*: The third and fourth disciples of Francis. Peter, the second disciple, seems not to have been known to Dante. *the groom*: Francis. *the bride*: Poverty.

87. *the humble cord*: Now a symbol of the Franciscans but then in general use by the poor as a makeshift belt.

88. *grieve*: At his humble origins.

93. *his order first received the seal*: In 1210. But Innocent III thought the proposed rule of the order so harsh that he granted only provisional approval.

96. *among the seraphim*: In the Empyrean, rather than in this Fourth Heaven.

97–99. *Honorius . . . second crown*: In 1223, Pope Honorius III gave his fully solemnized approval of the Franciscan Order.

100–105. In 1219, St. Francis and eleven of his followers made a missionary pilgrimage to Greece and Egypt. Dante, whose facts are not entirely accurate, may have meant that pilgrimage; or he may have meant Francis's projected journey to convert the Moors (1214–1215) when Francis fell ill in southern Spain and had to give up his plans.

106–108. In 1224, on a crag of Mt. Alvernia (on the summit of which the Franciscans have reared a commemorative chapel), St. Francis received the stigmata in a rapturous vision of Christ. He wore the wound two years before his death in 1226, at the age of (probably) forty-four.

109–117. The central reference here is to Dame Poverty. *her bosom*: The bare ground of Poverty. *no other resting place*: Than in the bare ground.

119. *his fellow helmsman*: St. Dominic. *Peter's ship*: The Church.

121–132. THE DEGENERACY OF THE DOMINICANS IN DANTE'S TIME. Aquinas was a Dominican. As a master touch to symbolize the harmony of Heaven and the unity of Franciscans and Dominicans, Dante puts into the mouth of a Dominican the praise of the life of St. Francis. That praise ended, he chooses the Dominican to lament the degeneracy of the order. In XII, Dante will have the Franciscan, St. Bonaventure, praise the life of St. Dominic and lament the degeneracy of the Franciscans.

122. *his command*: The rule of the Dominicans. *will fill his hold*: With the treasures of Paradise. Dante is carrying forward the helmsman metaphor of lines 118–120, though the ship is now commanded by a patriarch. Typically, the figure changes at once to a shepherd-and-flock metaphor.

136. *in part*: In X, 95–96, in identifying himself as a Dominican, Aquinas said the Dominican rule "leads to where all plenty is" unless the lamb itself stray to "bare rock." In lines 25–26, above, he refers to these words and also to his earlier statements (X, 114) about Solomon's wisdom (that "no mortal ever rose to equal this one"). What he has now finished saying about the degeneracy of the Dominicans will satisfy part of Dante's wish (about "plenty" and "bare rock"). The other part of his wish (about "no mortal ever rose to equal this one") will be satisfied later.

137. *the good plant*: Of the Dominican rule strictly observed.

Canto XII

Doctors of the Church
                            The Second Garland of Souls: Bonaventure ·
                            Praise of St. Dominic · Degeneracy of Franciscans

As soon as Aquinas has finished speaking the wheel of souls begins to turn, and before it has completed its first revolution it is surrounded by a *Second Garland of Twelve Souls.*

The spokesman of this second company is *St. Bonaventure.* In the harmonious balances of Heaven the Dominican Aquinas had spoken the praise of the life of St. Francis. In the same outgoing motion of love the Franciscan Bonaventure now speaks the *Praise of the Life of St. Dominic.* And as Aquinas had concluded by lamenting the degeneracy of the Dominican Order, so Bonaventure concludes his account with a *Lament for the Degeneracy of the Franciscan Order.* He then identifies the other souls in his Garland.

So spoke the blessèd flame and said no more;
  and at its final word the holy millstone
  began revolving round us as before.   3

And had not finished its first revolution
  before a second wheel had formed around it,
  matching it tone for tone, motion for motion.   6

As a reflection is to the source of light,
  such is the best our sirens and muses sing
  to the chanting of those sheaths of pure delight.   9

As through thin clouds or mists twin rainbows bend
  parallel arcs and equal coloring
  when Juno calls her handmaid to attend—   12

the outer band born of the inner one,
  like the voice of that wandering nymph of love consumed,
  as vapors are consumed, by the summer sun—   15

whereby all men may know what God made plain
  in the pledge he gave to Noah that the waters
  of the great deluge would not come again—   18

just so, those semipiternal roses wove
  their turning garland round us, and the outer
  answered the inner with the voice of love.   21

And when the exalted festival and dance
  of love and rapture, sweet song to sweet song,
  and radiance to flashing radiance,   24

had in a single instant fallen still
  with one accord—as our two eyes make one,
  being moved to open and close by a single will—   27

from one of those new splendors a voice came;
and as the North Star draws a needle's point,
so was my soul drawn to that glorious flame.   30

Thus he began: "The love that makes me shine
moves me to speak now of that other leader
through whom so much good has been said of mine.   33

When one is mentioned the other ought to be;
for they were militant in the same cause
and so should shine in one light and one glory.   36

The troops of Christ, rearmed at such great cost,
were struggling on behind the Holy Standard,
fearful, and few, and laggard, and half lost,   39

when the Emperor who reigns eternally—
of His own grace and not for their own merit—
took thought of his imperiled soldiery;   42

and, as you have heard say, He sent His bride
two champions by whose teachings and example
the scattered companies were reunified.   45

In the land to which the West wind, soft and glad,
returned each Spring to open the new leaves
with which, soon, all of Europe will be clad,   48

at no great distance from the beat and bite
of those same waves behind which, in its course,
the sun, at times, hides from all mortal sight,   51

a fortunate village lies in the protection
of the great shield on which two lions are,
one subjugating and one in subjection.   54

Within its walls was born the ardent one,
true lover and true knight of the Christian faith;
bread to his followers, to his foes a stone.   57

His mind from the instant it began to be,
swelled with such powers that in his mother's womb
he made her capable of prophecy.   60

And when he and his Lady Faith before
the holy font had married and endowed
each other with new gifts of holy power,   63

the lady who had spoken for him there
saw, in a dream, the wonder-working fruit
that he and his inheritors would bear.   66

To speak him as he was, a power from Heaven
was moved to give him the possessive form
of His name unto Whom he was wholly given.   69

Dominicus he was called. Let him be known
  as the good husbandman chosen by Christ
  to help Him in the garden He had sown.   72

A fitting squire and messenger of Christ
  he was, for his first love was poverty,
  and such was the first counsel given by Christ.   75

Often his nurse found him in meditation
  at night on the bare floor, awake and silent,
  as if he were saying, 'This is my vocation.'   78

O Felix his father in true 'felicity!'
  O mother truly Joan, 'whom God has graced!'
  —if the names can be translated literally!   81

Not as men toil today for wealth and fame,
  in the manner of the Ostian and Taddeo,
  but for love of the true manna, he soon became   84

a mighty doctor, and began to go
  his rounds of that great vineyard where the vine,
  if left untended, pales and cannot grow.   87

Before that Seat where once the poor were fed
  and tended (now, through no fault of its own,
  but by its degenerate occupant, corrupted)   90

he did not ask the right to keep as pay
  three out of every six, nor a benifice,
  nor *decimas quae sunt pauperum Dei*;   93

but license in the sick world there below
  to battle for that seed from which are sprung
  the four and twenty plants that ring you now.   96

Then, will and doctrine joined, and in the light
  of apostolic office, he burst forth,
  like a torrent from a mountain vein, to smite   99

the stumps and undergrowths of heresy.
  And where the thickets were least passable,
  there his assault bore down most heavily.   102

And from him many rivulets sprang to birth
  by which the Catholic orchard is so watered
  that its little trees spring greener from the earth.   105

If such was the one wheel of the great car
  in which the Church rode to defend herself
  and win in open field her civil war,   108

you cannot fail to see with a clear mind
  the excellence of that other, about whom,
  before I joined you, Thomas was so kind.   111

But the track its great circumference cut of old
   is so abandoned that the casks are empty,
   and where there once was crust, now there is mold.   114

His family, that formerly used to go
   in his very footsteps, is so turned around
   that it prints toe on heel, and heel on toe.   117

Soon shall we see the harvest of these years
   of lazy cultivation, and hear the darnel,
   the storehouse shut against it, shed its tears.   120

Search our book leaf by leaf and you will see,
   I have no doubt, written upon some page:
   'I am today all that I used to be.'   123

But not at Casal' nor Acquasparta—there
   they come to keep our rule, and in the keeping
   one loosens it, one tightens it like a snare.   126

I am the life of Bonaventure, on earth
   of Bagnoregio, who in great offices
   always put back the things of lesser worth.   129

Illuminato and Augustine are here,
   two of the first-come of the barefoot poor.
   For the cord they wore God holds them ever dear.   132

The prior Hugo is here, and the deathless glow
   of Peter Mangiadore, and Peter of Spain
   whose light still shines in twelve small books below.   135

And the prophet Nathan, and the eternal part
   of Chrysostom, and Anselm, and that Donatus
   who gladly turned his hand to the first art.   138

Rabanus is also here; and here beside me
   shines the Calabrian abbot Joachim
   whose soul was given the power of prophecy.   141

The ardent courtesy of my holy brother
   and his apt praise of one great paladin
   moved me to say this much about the other   144

in emulous and loving eulogy;
   and so moved all these of my company."

Notes

2. *the holy millstone*: The wheel of souls, called a millstone here perhaps to suggest the ponderous turning of God's will (cf. the expression "the mills of the Gods") but also to describe their motion, for a millstone moves slowly when it starts to turn, and this wheel of souls had not completed its first revolution before it was surrounded by another wheel.

5. *a second wheel*: Of twelve more splendors. In the heavenly hierarchy these are probably a grade inferior to the souls of the first wheel (line 13: "the outer band

born of the inner one"). The inner band, moreover, revolves nearer the center of the sun (Divine Illumination). Lines 10–18 certainly suggest that the two wheels are complementary to one another. The total of twenty-four may suggest a reference to the books of the Old Testament. (See *Purgatorio*, XXIX, 64, note.)

10–18. The compounding of metaphors in this passage is characteristically Dantean. The twin rainbows were said to occur when Juno called her handmaiden (Iris) to attend her. Iris (the Rainbow) was the messenger of the Gods as well as being especially associated with Juno. Thus, when she attends her mistress she presents herself in a double splendor. Line 13 is based on Dante's belief that the outer band of a twin rainbow is a reflection of the inner band. This reflection is like the voice of Echo, an outer reflection of the inner (first) sound. Echo was the wandering nymph who wasted away for love of Narcissus (consumed by the fire of love as vapors are consumed by the Sun) until the gods changed her to a stone. The figure then shifts from classical mythology to the Bible, referring to *Genesis*, IX, 8–17, in which God made a pact with Noah and his sons, promising that the Deluge would not be repeated, and hung the rainbow in the sky as token of His pledge.

28. *one of those new splendors*: St. Bonaventure. A Franciscan, he eulogizes St. Dominic and laments the decay of the Franciscan order, just as Aquinas, a Dominican, has eulogized St. Francis and lamented the decay of the Dominican order. Later, Bonaventure will identify the other souls of his circle (lines 130 ff.).

St. Bonaventure (1221–1274) was born Giovanni di Fidanza at Bagnoregio (now Bagnorea) near Lake Bolsena. He was a scholar saint and a leading theologian. He became Minister General of the Franciscan Order in 1257 and was created Cardinal Bishop of Albano in 1273. Much of his scholarship was carried out in France, where he died during the sessions of the second Council of Lyons. He was canonized in 1482 by Sixtus IV and pronounced sixth (Doctor Seraphicus) among the Doctors of the Church by Sixtus V in 1587.

31–45. INTRODUCTION TO THE LIFE OF ST. DOMINIC. Compare the words of Aquinas in introducing the Life of St. Francis (X, 28–42).

32. *that other leader*: St. Dominic.

33. *through whom*: The phrasing is obscure. Dante probably means that the earlier praise of St. Francis (Bonaventure's leader) is due to Dominic because his rule taught Aquinas such loving praises.

37–39. *rearmed*: By the blood of martyrs when persecution had all but scattered it. *the Holy Standard*: The Cross.

43. *as you have heard said*: In XI, 32 ff. *His bride*: The Church.

46–51. The land here referred to is Spain. In the sea beyond it, according to Dante's geography, the sun hides from all mortal sight when it is midnight in Jerusalem. For Dante, all of the earth's land area consisted of an arc of 180° from India to Spain with Jerusalem at the center, the other 180° of the earth's circumference being water. Thus, when the sun was at its furthest point from Jerusalem it shone only upon the watery wastes, hidden from the eyes of mortals.

52–54. *a fortunate village*: Calahorra, birthplace of St. Dominic, lies on the Ebro about 60 miles due south of the Bay of Biscay where it washes the westernmost point of the Spanish-French border. *the great shield*: Of the house of Castile. It is quartered and contains on one side a castle above a lion and on the other a lion above a castle, thus one lion is subjugating the castle and the other is being subjugated by it.

55 ff. LIFE OF ST. DOMINIC (1170–1221). Not all of the deaths Dante offers in his account of St. Dominic have a historic base. Dominic may have been born of an ancient family named Guzman, but little is known of his origins. He was an austere but undeviating man of mercy and with whole faith in pure doctrine. Beginning as an Augustinian, Dominic sought to overcome the heresies of the Albigensians, partly in defense of the pure faith and partly to save them from the terrors of the crusade that eventually destroyed them in a hideous blood bath. He founded the Dominican Order with the special purpose of saving the Albigensians from destruction in this world and damnation in the next. In 1215 he won provisional papal approval of his order from Innocent III, and, in 1216, full confirmation by Honorius III. He died in Bologna in 1221 and was canonized in 1234. Unlike Francis, who dreaded learning as a corruptive force and praised the holy ignorance of the rude and simple mind, Dominic labored for purity of doctrine and founded his order for missionary scholars who were to go forth and preach the pure faith. Thus the Founding principles of the two great orders were in many senses opposed and yet complementary.

The notes that follow comment on Dante's version of the life of St. Dominic, not on the historical record:

58–60. The mind and soul form at the instant of conception and take on the gifts assigned by the influences of the spheres. While still in the womb, Dominic was said to be so gifted that his mother foresaw the Dominican Order in a dream of giving birth to a black and white dog. Black and white are the Dominican colors, and *"Domini canes"* translates "hounds of the Lord."

61–66. Dominic married the faith at the Baptismal font, each bringing the other a dowry of strength and of holy purpose. Following his baptism, his godmother is supposed to have dreamed that he had a star on his forehead, a sign that he would bring God's light to man.

67–75. "Dominic" is the possessive form of Latin *"Domine"* (the Lord). Note the triple use of "Christ" to rhyme with itself. Dante has not so rhymed before in the "Comedy." He will again in XIV, XIX, and XXXII. He will not rhyme "Christ" with any other word because none is fit to be joined with that holy name. In a *tenzone* against Forese (who appears in *Purgatorio,* XXIII) the younger Dante had once made use of what he probably came to think of as a sacrilegious rhyme on "Christ." This later device may be his way of making amends.

75–81. As noted above, little is known about Dominic's parents. The details of their names, like the tales of Dominic's prenatal powers, are the stuff of pious folk tales.

82–87. *the Ostian:* Enrico di Susa, who became Bishop of Ostia in 1271. *Taddeo:* Probably Taddeo d'Alderotto, a Florentine physician born circa 1215. The first was a successful scholar of canon law, the second of medicine. Both acquired money and fame as a result of their secular studies. Dominic, on the other hand, studied only for the true manna of spiritual knowledge in order that he might labor in the vineyard (the Church) in which the vines wither and grow pale if they are neglected.

88–96. Because of a decree against the founding of new Orders, Dominic had to plead for many years before he could win approval from the papal seat which is now (i.e., as of 1300) corrupted by Boniface VIII. Dominic did not ask permission to dispense church wealth (withholding two or three of every six coins for himself), nor for a benefice, nor for *decimas quae sunt pauperum Dei* (the tithes that belong to God's poor). He asked only for license to combat heresy, and thus to defend the seed of the true faith from which are sprung, as plants of the everlasting tree, the twenty-four doctors that surround Dante as Bonaventure speaks.

97–102. The reference here is to Dominic's years of labor against the Albigensian heresy. He joined a mission for that purpose as early as 1203. In 1206 he opened in France a mission house dedicated to saving Albigensian women from their heresy. In 1208 Innocent III declared a crusade against the Albigensian plain-folk (they were anti-church and among other major points of doctrine, denied the Resurrection). In seven years of savage warfare and massacres the Albigensians were wiped out. Thus, when Dominic was allowed in 1215 to found his Order of Preaching Friars, he had already been laboring for at least twelve years to wipe out heresy, not by the sword, but by winning the heretics back to the faith through his preachments.

106–111. *If such was the one . . . the excellence of that other:* Since the car (the chariot) must have two equal wheels if it is to work properly, the excellence of the one wheel (Dominic) testifies to the excellence of the other (Francis), about whom Aquinas spoke in XI.

122 ff. LAMENT FOR THE DECLINE OF THE FRANCISCAN ORDER. Bonaventure now laments the decline of his Franciscans as Aquinas earlier lamented the decline of the Dominicans. The core of this metaphor has changed from the chariot of the war to the two-wheeled cart in which peasants haul grapes from the vineyard. The circumference of this great wheel (the Franciscan order) no longer turns in its former track, going back and forth from the vineyard to the winery. Hence the grapes (souls? good works?) are not brought in, and in the barrels (salvation? rectitude? the church?) where once there used to gather the crust of sediment left by good wine, there is now only the mold that forms in empty barrels.

117. *toe on heel, and heel on toe:* Instead of walking, as the first disciples did, in the footsteps of St. Francis, the decayed Franciscans walk backward in them, leaving their toe prints on the heel of the true tracks, and their heel prints on the toes; hence, walking in the other direction.

118–120. *the harvest . . . of lazy cultivation:* Bonaventure's moral point and its symmetrical response to Aquinas's lament for the decline of the Dominican Order are clear enough, but historically, the original rule of St. Francis was so harsh that it was, in effect, banned by the church. Its severity had, in fact, caused a schism within the order even before the death of St. Francis. One group sought to modify the rule of absolute poverty. The other (the Zealots or Spiritual Franciscans from whom stemmed the Penitentes) insisted on the rule to the point of open conflict with church authority. In 1318, in fact, four of the Spirituals were burned for heresy when they refused to modify the original rule of St. Francis.

There is an odd irony in the history of the Franciscans. The piety, fervor, and absolute poverty of the early monks made its impression upon a pious people, who began to make rich gifts to the order. Inevitably, an administrator had to appear, and so the monks of poverty had to acquire stewards and accountants. St. Bonaventure sought to resolve this conflict by teaching that all the property given to the friars was the property of the church but was held for their use (*usus pauperis*) in their life and work.

This schism was the lazy cultivation that made a bad harvest inevitable. Given the nature of Bonaventure's teaching, the bad harvest (the darnel) would be those Franciscans who risked excommunication by insisting, against direct papal orders, on the unmitigated rule (though he would, of course, include those Franciscans who observed the modified rule too slackly. Darnel or rye grass or black caraway springs up among the cultivated grains. Its hard seeds, ground up with the edible grains and so eaten as bread, can cause nervous disorders. It (the damned souls?) must be weeded out carefully (by good cultivation) and kept out of the good grain, the storehouse (the order? the church? heaven?) shut against it.

121–123. *our books*: Used figuratively for the Franciscan Order. *some page*: Some brother, some member of the Order.

124–126. *Casal*: The Franciscan monastery as Casale in Monferato. Ubertino di Casale (1259–1338) was general of the chapter and, favoring the Sprituals, so tightened the rule that he was forced to leave the Order. *Acquasparta*: In Todi. From this monastery Matteo d'Acquasparta rose to be general of the Order in 1287 and cardinal in 1288. Under him the Franciscan rule was substantially relaxed.

THE SOULS OF THE SECOND GARLAND:

130. *Illuminato and Augustino*: Two of the early brothers. Illuminato accompanied St. Francis on his mission to the East. Augustino joined the order in 1210.

133. *The prior Hugo*: Hugo of St. Victor (1096?–1141). Born in Saxony, he went to the monastery of St. Victor in Paris in 1115, where he taught philosophy and theology. In 1133 he was made prior and given charge of all studies.

134. *Peter Mangiadore*: Of Troyes (1110–1179?), Dean of the Cathedral of Troyes, 1147–1164. His *Historia Scholastica* was long the standard work on Bible history. *Peter of Spain*: Became John XXI in 1276, died in 1277. He was born in Lisbon circa 1226. Among the twelve books here referred to was his well-known summary of logical principles, *Summulae logicales*.

136. *the prophet Nathan*: See *II Samuel*, XII. Nathan spoke out against the sins of King David.

137. *Chrysostom*: The name in Greek means "Golden Mouth," a tribute to his oratorical power. He was John of Antioch (344?–407), Metropolitan of Constantinople. Like Nathan, he denounced the sins of the ruler. He was exiled for his pains by the Empress Eudoxia. *Anselm*: Born in Aosta, Lombardy, circa 1033. As Archbishop of Canterbury (from 1093) he fought the king on the question of the recognition of the Pope. Forced into exile in 1103, he returned to Canterbury in 1107, and died there in 1109. *Donatus*: Lived in Rome about the middle of the fourth century. He wrote commentaries on Terence and Virgil (the latter of which may have been what recommended him to Dante for his place here) and a book on grammar that was widely used in Dante's time. Grammar is "the first art" (first of the seven liberal arts that make up the trivium and quadrivium of the classical curriculum).

139. *Rabanus*: Rabanus Maurus (776?–856). Became Archbishop of Mainz in 847. Bible scholar, poet, and author of *De clericorum institutione*, a manual for clerics.

140. *Joachim*: Of Fiore (1132?–1202). A Cistercian mystic whose doctrines were especially popular among the Spiritual Franciscans who opposed Bonaventure. There is no historic evidence of his prophetic gift, and some of his preachments were specifically condemned by the Lateran Council in 1215 and by Alexander IV in 1256.

142–144. *my holy brother*: St. Thomas. *one great paladin*: St. Francis. *the other*: St. Dominic. The paladins were the twelve great champions who surrounded Charlemagne.

Canto XIII

THE FOURTH SPHERE: THE SUN *The Intellect of the Faith:*
Theologians and Doctors of the Church: Aquinas

The Twenty-Four blessèd spirits, moved by the concluding words of Bonaventure, manifest themselves as a mystical constellation while ringing forth a
hymn of praise that fills all Heaven.

When the hymn has been sung Aquinas speaks again. He has read
Dante's mind and addresses its perplexity, explaining *Why None Ever Rose
to Equal Solomon's Wisdom.* He concludes with a *Warning Against Hasty
Judgment.*

If you would understand what I now write
  of what I saw next in that Heaven, imagine
  (and hold the image rock-fast in your sight)   3

the fifteen brightest stars the heavens wear
  in their living crown, stars of so clear a ray
  it pierces even the mist-thickened air;   6

imagine that Wain that on our heaven's breast
  lies night and day, because the tiller's tu.ning
  causes no part of it to sink to rest;   9

imagine the bright mouth of the horn one sees
  flower from the axle star, around which spins
  the first wheel—and imagine all of these   12

forming two constellations, each a wreath
  (like that the daughter of King Minos made
  when through her limbs she felt the chill of death)   15

and imagine, last, that one wreath has its rays
  inside the other, and that both are turning
  around one center but in opposite ways.   18

So might you dimly guess (if mankind could)
  what actual stars, joined in their double dance,
  circled around the point on which I stood;   21

though such experiences outrun our knowing
  as the motion of the first and fastest heaven
  outruns the low Chiana's sluggish flowing.   24

There they sang no Bacchic chant nor Paean,
  but Three Persons in One Divine Nature
  and It and human nature in One Person.   27

The song and circling dance ran through their measure,
and now those holy lights waited on us,
turning rejoiced from pleasure to new pleasure.   30

The silence of these numina was broken
by the same lamp from which the glorious life
of God's beloved pauper had been spoken.   33

It said: "Since one sheaf has been thrashed my brother,
and the good grain of it has been put by,
sweet love invites me now to thrash the other.   36

Into that breast, you think, from which was carved
the rib that went to form the lovely cheek
for whose bad palate all mankind was starved,   39

and into that the lance pierced when it made
such restitution for the past and future
that every guilt of mankind was outweighed,   42

as much of wisdom's light, to the last ray,
as human nature can contain, He breathed
by whose power they were clad in mortal clay.   45

And, therefore, you were puzzled when I came
to the fifth light and said no mortal ever
had matched the wisdom sheathed within its flame.   48

Now open your eyes to what I shall say here
and see your thought and my words form one truth,
like the center and circumference of a sphere.   51

All things that die and all that cannot die
are the reflected splendor of the Form
our Father's love brings forth beyond the sky.   54

For the Living Light that streams forth from the Source
in such a way that it is never parted
from Him, nor from the Love whose mystic force   57

joins them in Trinity, lets its grace ray down,
as if reflected, through nine subsistant natures
that sempiternally remain as one.   60

From thing to thing to the last least potencies
the ray comes down, until it is so scattered
it brings forth only brief contingencies;   63

and these contingencies, I would have you see,
are those *generated things* the moving heavens
bring forth from seeds or not, as the case may be.   66

The wax of these things, and the powers that press
and shape it, vary; thus the Ideal seal
shines through them sometimes more and sometimes less.   69

So trees of the same species may bring forth
    fruit that is better or worse; so men are born
    different in native talent and native worth.   72

Were the wax most ready and free of every dross,
    and were the heavens in their supreme conjunction,
    the light of the seal would shine through without loss: 75

but nature scants that light in all it makes,
    working in much the manner of a painter
    who knows the true art, but whose brush hand shakes.   78

But if the Fervent Love move the Pure Ray
    of the First Power to wield the seal directly,
    the thing so stamped is perfect in every way.   81

So once a quickening of the dust of earth
    issued the form of the animal perfection;
    so once the Virgin Womb quickened toward birth.   84

Therefore I say that I am one with you
    in the opinion that mankind was never,
    nor will be, what it once was in those two.   87

Having said this much, I must yet go on
    or you would ask: 'How then can it be said,
    no mortal ever rose to equal this one?'   90

But to make clear what yet seems not to be,
    think who he was, and what it was that moved him
    to answer when God said, 'What shall I give thee?'   93

I speak these words that you may understand
    he was a king, and asked the Lord for wisdom
    in governing his people and his land,   96

and not to know the number and degree
    of our motor-angels, nor if a premised 'may'
    can ever conclude, in logic, 'this must be,'   99

nor if there is prime motion, nor if in the space
    of a semicircle a non-right triangle
    may be drawn with the diameter as its base.   102

Hence you may see that when I spoke before
    of unmatched wisdom, it was on royal prudence
    that the drawn arrow of my intention bore.   105

Note well that I said 'rose' when I spoke of it.
    Thus you will see I spoke only of kings,
    of whom there are many, though so few are fit.   108

Such were my words, and taken in this light
    they are consistent with all that you believe
    of our first father and of our Best Delight.   111

And lead weights to your feet may my words be,
    that you move slowly, like a weary man,
    to the 'yes' and 'no' of what you do not see.   114

For he is a fool, and low among his kind,
    who answers yea or nay without reflection,
    nor does it matter on which road he runs blind.   117

Opinions too soon formed often deflect
    man's thinking from the truth into gross error,
    in which his pride then binds his intellect.   120

It is worse than vain for men to leave the shore
    and fish for truth unless they know the art;
    for they return worse off than they were before.   123

Of this, Parmenides and Melissus bear
    their witness to all men, along with Bryson,
    and others who set out without knowing where;   126

so Arius, Sabellius, and their schools
    who were to Scripture like a mirroring sword,
    distorting the straight faces to mislead fools.   129

Men should not be too smug in their own reason;
    only a foolish man will walk his field
    and count his ears too early in the season;   132

for I have seen a briar through winter's snows
    rattle its tough and menacing bare stems,
    and then, in season, open its pale rose;   135

and I have seen a ship cross all the main,
    true to its course and swift, and then go down
    just as it entered its home port again.   138

Let Tom and Jane not think, because they see
    one man is picking pockets and another
    is offering all his goods to charity,   141

that they can judge their neighbors with God's eyes:
    for the pious man may fall, and the thief may rise."

Notes

1–24. THE DANCE OF THE TWO GARLANDS. The passage, though in Dante's most elliptical style, presents the basically simple image of the two garlands of souls transformed into twin constellations in the form of two concentric wheels revolving in opposite directions around the point on which Dante is standing.

To envision the glory of the twenty-four stars (twelve and twelve), the reader is invited to pick the fifteen brightest stars from anywhere in heaven (4–6), to add to them the seven stars of the Big Dipper (7–9), and to add the two bright stars from the mouth of the Little Dipper (10–12).

All these are to be imagined as forming into the two circles, each like the Corona Borealis, which, according to legend, was made from the bridal wreath of Ariadne (daughter of King Minos) when, abandoned by Theseus, she is found by Dionysus and is taken to heaven to become his wife (13–15).

Put all these imaginings together and you may glimpse perhaps a shadow of the actual experience, for such things surpass mortal understanding by as much as the speed of the Primum Mobile surpasses the flow of the Chiana, a Tuscan river that, in Dante's time, wound sluggishly through swamplands that have since been drained (19–24).

8. *the tiller*: The Pole. It turns all the stars. Those of the Big Dipper, however, are so close to it that they never set, but lie night and day at the Celestial North Pole ("our heaven's breast").

25. *Paean*: Specifically a hymn to Apollo, though used generally for any pagan hymn.

30. *pleasure to new pleasure*: From the pleasure of praising God to the pleasure of serving Him in an act of *caritas*.

31. *numina*: A numen (pl. numina) is a divine spirit or a god conceived as a person.

32. *the same lamp*: St. Thomas Aquinas.

33. *God's beloved pauper*: St. Francis.

34–36. At the end of XI, Thomas had finished explaining his use of "where all plenty is." He paused in XII for Bonaventure to give the counterpoint to his Franciscan eulogy and Dominican lament. That first sheaf of understanding, then, has been thrashed (the grains of truth extracted from the straw). Now he is moved by love to thrash the second sheaf, separating from Dante's error (the straw) the truth about the widsom of Solomon, and of Aquinas's earlier words (X, 114) "no mortal ever rose to equal this one."

38. *the lovely cheek*: Cheek, in conjunction with rib and breast, results in a somewhat anatomically strewn figure of speech, but is meant to stand here as a synecdoche for Eve, the part standing for the whole, while specifically referring to the part of her that contained the sinful palate.

40. *and into that*: That breast (of Christ).

47. *the fifth light*: Solomon. (See X, 109–114).

48 ff. THE WISDOM OF SOLOMON. Aquinas proceeds to explain why "no mortal man ever rose to equal this one" in wisdom, for Aquinas's statement had perplexed Dante, who had immediately concluded (as we shall see) that Aquinas was implying that Solomon was wiser than Christ and than Adam, though that could not be.

Aquinas parses the question in meticulous Scholastic detail in order to clear Dante's misconception, explaining, in essence, that though Adam and Christ-the-man were wiser than Solomon, containing more of the light of God, they were *direct* creations of God, whereas Solomon was a *secondary* creation, arising from Nature. Thus, Solomon sprang from the earth ("rose"), whereas Adam and Christ-the-man sprang directly from God and were apart from mortal creation.

53. *Form*: The Platonic Form. Idea.

55–58. *the Living Light*: The Son, as the Wisdom of mankind. *the Source*: The Father as Creator. *the love*: The Holy Ghost.

59–60. *nine subsistant natures*: The nine orders of angels that attend the heavenly spheres.

61–63. *thing*: Actuality. (It. *atto*.) The Scholastic term for "that which actually exists." *potency*: That which does not exist but that has the power of coming into being. *contingency*: What could exist (what could have actuality) but does not.

66. *from seeds or not*: See *Purgatorio*, XXVIII, 69, and 109–120, and note, for Dante's theory of wind-sown generative "virtues."

67–69. *the wax*: The matter that is available for the formation of contingencies. The term is used here metaphorically. It is not part of Scholastic terminology, *the powers that press*: The influences of the heavens. "Press" continues the "seal-in-wax" metaphor. *the ideal Seal*: A metaphoric equivalent of the Ideal Form of Plato, here, the Divine Concept. It is perfect and unchangeable but, descending through the constant changes of the Spheres to the flux of matter, it is transmitted and received in a necessarily diminished way. Thus the Divine Idea shines through all things, and through some more than through others, but never perfectly.

79–81. The rendering of the original lines is much disputed, but their general sense is clear. Secondary creation, as Aquinas has explained, is never entirely perfect. Direct creation, on the other hand, is necessarily so. In lines 52–60 Aquinas explained direct creation as the ray of the Father and of the Son conjoined in Trinity. Here the force of the periphrasis is to cite all the Trinity in One, the Fervent Love being the Holy Ghost, the Pure Ray being the Son, and the First Power being the Father.

83. *the animal perfection*: The perfection of animal existence (as contrasted, perhaps, to angelic existence). In its ideal form this perfection was embodied in Adam and in Christ-the-man, as direct creations.

86. *in the opinion*: Which Aquinas has read in Dante's mind.

88. *those two*: Adam and Christ-the-man.

90. *this one*: Solomon.

91. *but to make clear what yet seems not to be*: Aquinas knows everything that

passes in Dante's mind. Thus, he not only instructs but knows instantly how much of the instruction has registered; the perfect, if supernatural, teacher.

93. *'What shall I give thee?'*: After Solomon went to Gideon and offered up a thousand burnt offerings, the Lord appeared in a dream and asked what gift he would choose. Solomon asked for the wisdom with which to rule his people. *I Kings,* III 4–14.

97–102. THE WISDOM SOLOMON DID NOT SEEK. Aquinas cites a number of propositions that engaged medieval learning. *motor-angels*: The angels that moved the spheres. How many they were, and of what degree (e.g., Principalities or Thrones) provided the subject of many disputations. *may . . . this must be*: Any qualification of the premise must, logically, be reflected in the conclusion. The premise "x may be" can never lead to the conclusion "x must be," but logicians kept trying in ingenious ways to derive a "must be" from a "may be." *if there is prime motion*: Prime motion would be uncaused motion. The learned question here would be whether or not such motion can exist. *semicircle . . . non-right angle*: Euclid demonstrated that any triangle whose base is the diameter of a circle and whose apex is on the circumference of that circle must be a right triangle. Medieval mathematicians, however, tried to theorize a non-right triangle to these specifications.

Hence, all these examples are of the wisdom required for playing abstract and learned games, as opposed to the wisdom Solomon sought in order to deal justly with God's people.

Earlier in his life, Dante himself had sometimes been drawn to metaphysical hairsplitting. Here he is renouncing all such, as he had earlier renounced his overreliance on natural philosophy, in order to seek the greater truths of faith.

103–108. The reference here is, once again, to X, 109–114: "No mortal ever rose to equal this one." Aquinas is explaining that the "arrow of his intention" was sighted only upon the qualities of royal prudence. It was in that order of wisdom (and not, for example, in metaphysical speculation) that Solomon was unequaled.

And that specific intent, Aquinas adds, Dante may see for himself if he will recall that Aquinas had said "rose" to equal. That usage could apply only to kings, one gathers, since only kings may be said to "rise" above the masses of mankind. In another sense, neither Christ-the-man and Adam, being direct creations, could have "risen."

Such fine-spun parsing of a construction that could have had several meanings may leave the modern reader uneasy and lead him to miss the point. Dante conceives these spirits as direct participants in God's omniscience and infallibility. Their every word, therefore, is exactly chosen and must be studied meticulously.

It is not their words that lack clarity but Dante's understanding that lacks vision. Their very use of language, for that matter, is a concession to Dante, akin to their willingness to manifest themselves to him, not as they ultimately are, but in the closest approximation that Dante can grasp. Since their knowledge is a direct ray from God, their understanding is reflected from one to the other, through God, with no need of words.

111. *our first father*: Adam. *our Best Delight*: Christ.

112 ff. AQUINAS REPROACHES DANTE. Dante had jumped to a conclusion. Because he failed to understand what Aquinas had said, he concluded that Aquinas had contradicted the truth in speaking of Solomon. Now that the contradiction has been resolved, Aquinas warns him not to be in a hurry to decide "yes" or "no" in matters that surpass his understanding.

117. *on which road*: Whether the road of affirmation or of denial.

123. *worse off*: Because they will have left their ignorance only to fall into error.

124–126. THE FOOLISH PHILOSOPHERS. All three of the philosophers here mentioned were refuted by Aristotle in the *Organon* (*Sophistici Elenchi*, I, 10) and that is probably all Dante knew of them. Parmenides taught that all things come from and return to the Sun. Melissus, a disciple of Parmenides, taught that there is no motion in the universe but only an appearance of motion. Bryson labored devotedly and at great length to square the circle.

127–129. THE HERETICAL PHILOSOPHERS. Arius, an Alexandrian priest (died in 336) taught that the Son, having been created by the Father, could not be one with Him. Sabellius advanced the Monarchian heresy that there is no real distinction between Father and Son and that the Trinity was merely a succession of modes in which a single person appears. Little is known about him except that he was probably born in Libya and that he died about 265.

139–143. *Tom and Jane*: Anyone in general. (Dante says: *"donna Berta or ser Martino."*) It is easy for people in general, observing that one man acts sinfully and another piously, to conclude that the sinful man will be damned and the pious one saved. But that could be a hasty judgment. No man should let himself believe that he can foresee another's fate with the eyes of Divine Omniscience. The pious man may fall from grace (as even Solomon turned to idolatry in his old age and risked damnation) or a thief may repent and win his seat in heaven.

Canto XIV

Thomas Aquinas has finished speaking. Now, anticipating the wish Dante
has not yet realized is his own, Beatrice begs the double circle of Philosophers and Theologians to explain to Dante the state in which the blessèd
will find themselves after the *Resurrection of the Flesh*. The radiant spirit
of *Solomon* answers.

As Solomon finishes his discourse and the souls about him cry "Amen!"
Dante becomes aware of a *Third Circle of Souls*, higher and more radiant
even than the first two. Its radiance dawns slowly and indistinctly at first,
and then suddenly bursts upon him. Only then does he realize that he and
Beatrice have been ascending and that he has entered the *Fifth Sphere*,
Mars. The souls he had seen in the third great circle are those of the *Warriors of God*. There Dante beholds, shining through the Sphere of Mars (in
about the way the rays of a star sapphire shine within the stone), the
Vision of Christ on the Cross.

"The water in a round vessel moves about
    from center to rim if it is struck from within,
    from rim to center if it is struck from without."   3

—Such was the thought that suddenly occurred
    to my rapt mind when the immortal ray
    of Thomas had pronounced its final word,   6

occasioned by the likeness to the flow
    of his speech and my lady's, she being moved
    to speak when he had done, beginning so: 9

"There is another need this man must find
    the holy root of, though he does not speak it,
    nor know, as yet, he has the thought in mind.   12

Explain to him if the radiance he sees flower
    about your beings will remain forever
    exactly as it shines forth in this hour;   15

and if it will remain so, then explain
    how your restored eyes can endure such brilliance
    when your beings have grown visible again."   18

As dancers in a country reel flush brighter
    as they spin faster, moved by joy of joy,
    their voices higher, and all their gestures lighter—   21

so at my lady's prompt and humble plea
   the sacred circles showed yet greater joy
   in their dance and in their heavenly harmony.   24

Those who mourn, here, that we must die to gain
   the life up there, have never visualized
   that soul-refreshing and eternal rain.   27

That One and Two and Three that is eternal,
   eternally reigning in Three and Two and One,
   uncircumscribed, and circumscribing all,   30

was praised in three great paeans by each spirit
   of those two rings, and in such melody
   as would do fitting honor to any merit.   33

And I heard, then, from the most glorious ray
   of the inner circle, a voice as sweetly low
   as the angel's must have sounded to Mary, say: 36

"Long as the feast of Paradise shall be,
   so long shall our love's bliss shine forth from us
   and clothe us in these radiant robes you see.   39

Each robe reflects love's ardor shining forth;
   the ardor, the vision; the vision shines down to us
   as each is granted grace beyond his worth.   42

When our flesh, made glorious at the Judgment Seat,
   dresses us once again, then shall our persons
   become more pleasing in being more complete.   45

Thereby shall we have increase of the light
   Supreme Love grants, unearned, to make us fit
   to hold His glory ever in our sight.   48

Thereby, it follows, the vision shall increase;
   increase the ardor that the vision kindles;
   increase the ray its inner fires release.   51

But as a coal, in giving off its fire,
   outshines it by its living incandescence,
   its form remaining visible and entire;   54

so shall this radiance that wraps us round
   be outshone in appearance by the flesh
   that lies this long day through beneath the ground;   57

nor will it be overborne by so much light;
   for the organs of the body shall be strengthened
   in all that shall give increase of delight."   60

And "Amen!" cried the souls of either chain
   with such prompt zeal as to make evident
   how much they yearned to wear their flesh again;   63

perhaps less for themselves than for the love
  of mothers, fathers, and those each soul held dear
  before it became an eternal flame above.   66

And lo! all round me, equal in all its parts,
  a splendor dawned above the splendor there
  like a horizon when the new day starts.   69

And as, at the first coming on of night,
  new presences appear across the sky,
  seeming to be, and not to be, in sight;   72

so did I start to see Existences
  I had not seen before, forming a ring
  around the other two circumferences.   75

Oh sparkling essence of the Holy Ghost!
  How instantly it blazed before my eyes,
  defeating them with glory, their function lost!   78

But Beatrice let herself appear to me
  so glad in beauty, that the vision must lie
  with those whose glory outdoes memory.   81

From her I drew again the power of sight,
  and looked up, and I saw myself translated,
  with her alone, to the next estate of light.   84

I was made aware that I had risen higher
  by the enkindled ardor of the red star
  that glowed, I thought, with more than usual fire.   87

With all my heart, and in the tongue which is
  one in all men, I offered God my soul
  as a burnt offering for this new bliss.   90

Nor had the flame of sacrifice in my breast
  burned out, when a good omen let me know
  my prayer had been received by the Most Blest;   93

for with such splendor, in such a ruby glow,
  within two rays, there shone so great a glory
  I cried, "O Helios that arrays them so!"   96

As, pole to pole, the arch of the Milky Way
  so glows, pricked out by greater and lesser stars,
  that sages stare, not knowing what to say—   99

so constellated, deep within that Sphere,
  the two rays formed into the holy sign
  a circle's quadrant lines describe. And here   102

memory outruns my powers. How shall I write
  that from that cross there glowed a vision of Christ?
  What metaphor is worthy of that sight?   105

But whoso takes his cross and follows Christ
    will pardon me what I leave here unsaid
    when *he* sees that great dawn that rays forth Christ.   108

From arm to arm, from root to crown of that tree,
    bright lamps were moving, crossing and rejoining.
    And when they met they glowed more brilliantly.   111

So, here on earth, across a slant of light
    that parts the air within the sheltering shade
    man's arts and crafts contrive, our mortal sight   114

observes bright particles of matter ranging
    up, down, aslant; darting or eddying;
    longer and shorter; but forever changing.   117

And as a viol and a harp in a harmony
    of many strings, make only a sweet tinkle
    to one who has not studied melody;   120

so from that choir of glories I heard swell
    so sweet a melody that I stood tranced,
    though what hymn they were singing, I could not tell.   123

That it was raised in lofty praise was clear,
    for I heard "Arise" and "Conquer"—but as one
    may hear, not understanding, and still hear.   126

My soul was so enraptured by those strains
    of purest song, that nothing until then
    had bound my being to it in such sweet chains.   129

My saying so may seem too bold at best,
    since I had not yet turned to those dear eyes
    in which my every yearning found its rest.   132

But think how the living seals of every beauty
    grow stronger toward their heights, and though I had not
    turned to those others yet in love and duty,   135

reason may yet dismiss the charge I bring
    against myself in order to dismiss it;
    and see the holy truth of what I sing;   138

for my sacred pleasure in those sacred eyes
    can only become purer as we rise.

Notes

1-9. Dante and Beatrice are standing in the center of a double circle of souls that forms, so to speak, a rim around them. The rim suggests to Dante the flow of ripples in a round basin filled with water. If the basin is struck from the outside, the ripples flow toward the center, growing smaller. In Dante's fancy, the sound of Thomas's voice had flowed in this way, from rim to center. Now Thomas falls still and Beatrice speaks from the center, her voice seeming to flow outward like ripples from the center to the rim.

10–18. *another need*: To know the truth of the resurrection of the flesh. Dante has not spoken this thought. He does not yet know, in fact, that it is forming in his mind, but Beatrice knows he is about to think to ask how it will be after the Day of Judgment if these souls retain their superhuman radiance after they have resumed their bodies (grown visible again). How will their restored human eyes be able to bear such radiance both within and without?

22. *prompt*: Beatrice entered her plea in Dante's behalf even before he knew it was what he wished. It hardly seems possible to be prompter.

27. *rain*: Of light.

35. *a voice*: Solomon.

36. *as the angel's must have sounded*: At the Annunciation.

40. *robe*: In which each spirit is clad.

40–42. As ever in Dante, many degrees of being exist within each category. The brilliance in which these souls are robed is in proportion to (reflects) the degree of ardor (of *caritas*) that burns in each. That intensity, in turn, reflects the intensity of each soul's beatific vision. And the vision is granted to each soul by God's grace, in proportion to the worth of the individual soul. But that grace is more than even such great souls as these can merit: it is God's gift to man beyond man's merit.

67–81. THE THIRD RING OF SOULS. There is no way of assigning an exact symbolism to this third ring of souls, though three of anything is a natural unity in Dante. The third circle appears above the other two and outshines even their glory. The third circle appears dimly and slowly at first, then bursts upon Dante's vision just as he and Beatrice soar into the next higher heaven (of Mars). The third circle is also identified as the "sparkling essence of the Holy Ghost" (line 76). It is reasonable, then, to think of the earlier two circles of Philosophers and Theologians as being identified with the Father and the Son, the law and the wisdom of the Trinity, surmounted and encompassed by its ardor. So interpreted, the shining of the third circle becomes a first view of the souls of the Sphere of Mars, the heaven of God's warriors; and the two spheres (of the Sun and of Mars) combine into a symbolism of the Trinity.

82–84. *from her*: Divine Revelation restores Dante's vision. *translated*: The ascent, despite the slow dawning of the vision of the Third Circle of Souls, is here presented as being instantaneous. *with her alone*: With Beatrice, leaving the spirits of the Fourth Heaven behind. *to the next estate*: The Fifth Heaven, the Sphere of Mars.

88–90. Dante waits for no prompting from Beatrice but offers his soul in thanks to God, offers it as wholly as if it were a burnt offering sent aloft in the consuming fire (ardor of soul) of sacrifice. *the tongue which is one in all men*: The tongue of true prayer. Men may phrase it in different languages, but its essence is always the same.

94 ff. THE VISION OF CHRIST ON THE CROSS. Embedded in the Sphere of Mars (much like the rays of a star sapphire but with a magnitude on the order of the Milky Way) a cross forms on the Heaven of Mars, and in a ruby glow (the redness of Mars and the blood of Christ's sacrifice are both indicated here), Christ himself shines forth.

96. *Helios*: Greek for "sun" and specific to Apollo. Dante is praising God for the glory in which he arrays His vision.

100. *that sphere*: Mars.

102. *a circle's quadrant lines*: A quadrant is one fourth of a circle. The lines that describe the four quadrants form a cross within a ring.

103–108. *Christ . . . Christ . . . Christ*: Dante never rhymes "Christ" with anything but itself, no word being worthy of being so paired.

109. *that tree*: The Cross.

111. *And when they met they glowed more brilliantly*: The lights Dante sees are souls. Their radiance is the flame of *caritas* within them. Whenever two or more meet there their love of one another flares the brighter.

112–117. THE FIGURE OF MOTES IN A RAY OF SUN. Having begun his figure on a galactic scale, Dante shifts to the scale of earthly particles dancing in a ray of sun that strikes across a darkened room. The shift is dramatic and the figure of motes in sunlight not only apt in itself but apt again to set the scale of the galactic vision, the souls, in their enormous dimension, being so far from Dante that they are seen as motes.

127–140. DANTE'S RAPTURE. Hitherto, Dante has found his bliss in Beatrice, and it has been to her eyes that he has turned as each new vision awed him. Here, however, he is so enraptured by the vision of the cross and by the power of the music that he has not turned to Beatrice. He has even declared that nothing in all that has gone before has filled him with such bliss.

Shall he then be accused of ignoring Beatrice? Of neglecting her, his ardor cooled? He brings the charge against himself only that he may dismiss it. His joy in her can only become purer and more intense as they ascend to the heights of the glorious mystery.

In one allegorical sense, of course, there is the perfect beauty, beyond even Divine

Revelation, of the thing revealed. The Heavenly Soul, subsumed into the body of God, becomes its own revelation. In that sense, even Beatrice must be outgrown, as Virgil was, though the comparison is questionable, the one relation being finite and the other infinite. Beatrice cannot be outgrown: she has her place in God, as Dante is aspiring to his. When she does leave him at the height of Heaven, it is to reassume her throne in God. She does not disappear but takes her place, and as Dante grows closer to God he grows closer to Beatrice. Thus, to look away from Beatrice toward God is to turn the more closely to Beatrice.

131. *those dear eyes*: Of Beatrice.

133–135. *living seals*: The Heavens. Their influences stamp themselves, as a signet does in wax, upon the souls of men. *those others*: The eyes of Beatrice.

Canto XV

The Warriors of God · Cacciaguida

The souls of the great cross stop their singing in order to encourage Dante
to speak, and one among them descends to the foot of the cross like a
shooting star, glowing with joy at the sight of Dante. It is, as Dante will
discover, *Cacciaguida,* Dante's own great-great-grandfather.

Cacciaguida addresses Dante as "Blood of mine," and though he already
knows Dante's thoughts, he begs his descendant to speak them for the joy
of hearing his voice.

Dante does as he is bid, and Cacciaguida, in answer to Dante's request,
identifies himself, gives an *Account of Ancient Florence,* and explains how
he followed *Conrad* in the Crusades, *Became a Knight,* and died in battle
passing from *Martyrdom to Bliss.*

Good will, in which there cannot fail to be
　　the outgoing love of right (just as we find
　　self-seeking love in all iniquity),　　　　　　　　　3

stopped the sweet trembling harp, and let fall still
　　the blessèd viol, upon whose many strings
　　the Hand of Heaven plays Its sacred will.　　　　　6

How shall those beings not heed a righteous prayer
　　when, to encourage me to speak my wish,
　　they stopped with one accord, and waited there?　　9

Justly they mourn in their eternal wasting
　　who, in their love for what does not endure,
　　stripped off the hope of this love everlasting.　　12

As through the pure sky of a peaceful night
　　there streaks from time to time a sudden fire,
　　and eyes that had been still move at the sight,　　15

as if they saw a star changing its post
　　(except that none is gone from where it started,
　　and blazed its little while, and soon was lost)—　　18

so, in a trail of fire across the air,
　　from the right arm to the foot of the great cross,
　　a star streaked from the constellation there.　　21

Nor did that gemstone leave its diadem.
　　Like fire behind an alabaster screen,
　　it crossed those radiant ranks, still one with them.　　24

Just so did the shade of ancient Ilium
　　(if we may trust our greatest muse) go forth
　　to greet Aeneas in Elysium.　　　　　　　　　27

"*O sanguis meus, o superinfusa*
gratia Dei, sicut tibi, cui
bis unquam coeli ianua reclusa?"   30

So spoke that radiance as I stared wide-eyed.
  Then I turned my eyes back to my blessèd lady,
  and between those two souls I stood stupefied,   33

for such a fire of love burned in her eyes
  that mine, I thought, had touched the final depth
  both of my Grace and of my Paradise.   36

Then, radiating bliss in sight and sound,
  the spirit added to his opening words
  others I could not grasp: they were too profound. 39

Nor did the spirit's words elude my mind
  by his own choice. Rather, his thoughts took place
  above the highest target of mankind.   42

And when the bow recovered from the effect
  of its own ardor, and its words arced down
  nearer the target of our intellect,   45

the first on which my straining powers could feed
  were: "Praised be Thou, O Triune Unity
  which showeth me such favor in my seed!"   48

Continuing: "The sight of you assuages
  a long dear hunger that grew within this lamp
  from which I speak, as I perused the pages   51

of the Great Book where neither black nor white
  can ever change. I give thanks to this spirit
  whose love gave you the wings for this high flight. 54

You believe that what you think rays forth to me
  from the Primal Intellect, as five and six,
  if understood, ray forth from unity.   57

And for that reason you do not inquire
  who I may be, nor why I am more joyous
  than the other spirits of this joyous choir.   60

And you are right: for here in Paradise
  greatest and least alike gaze in that Mirror
  where thoughts outsoar themselves before they rise. 63

But, that the Sacred Love in which I wake
  to the eternal vision, and which fills me
  with a sweet thirst, you may the sooner slake,   66

let your own voice, assured, frank, and elated
  sound forth your will, sound forth your soul's desire,
  to which my answer is already fated!"   69

I turned to Beatrice and while I still
   sought words, she heard, and smiled such glad assent
   the joy of it gave wings to my glad will.   72

Thus I began: "When the First Equipoise
   shone forth to you, love and the power to speak love
   became in each of you an equal voice;   75

because the Sun that warmed and lighted you
   contains its heat and light so equally
   that though we seek analogies, none will do.   78

But mortal utterance and mortal feelings—
   for reasons that are evident to you—
   have no such equal feathers to their wings.   81

I, then, being mortal, in the perturbation
   of my unequal powers, with heart alone
   give thanks for your paternal salutation.   84

I do indeed beseech you, holy flame,
   and living topaz of this diadem,
   that you assuage my hunger to know your name."   87

"O leaf of mine, which even to foresee
   has filled me with delight, I was your root."
   —So he began in answer to my plea.   90

And then: "The first to take your present surname
   (whose soul has crawled the first round of the mountain
   a century and more), he who became   93

father of your grandfather, was my son.
   You would do well, by offering up good works,
   to shorten his long striving at his stone.   96

Florence, within her ancient walls secure—
   from them she still hears *tierce* and *nones* ring down—
   lived in sweet peace, her sons sober and pure.   99

No golden chains nor crowns weighed down her spirit,
   nor women in tooled sandals and studded belts
   more to be admired than the wearer's merit.   102

A father, in those days, was not terrified
   by the birth of a daughter, for marriage and marriage portion
   had not escaped all bounds on either side.   105

No mansions then stood uninhabited.
   No Sardanapalus had yet arrived
   to show what may be done in hall and bed.   108

Montemario had not yet been outshone
   by your Uccellatoio, which having passed it
   in the race up, shall pass it going down.   111

Bellincion Berti, with whom I was acquainted,
went belted in leather and bone; and his good wife
came from the mirror with her face unpainted.   114

I have seen the lords of Vecchio and of Nerli
content to wear plain leather, and their wives
working the spindle and distaff late and early.   117

Fortunate they! And blest their circumstance!
Each sure of her own burial place; none yet
deserted in her bed because of France.   120

One watched the cradle, babbling soft and low
to soothe her child in the sweet idiom
that is the first delight new parents know.   123

Another, spinning in her simple home,
would tell old tales to children gathered round her,
of Troy, and of Fiesole, and of Rome.   126

A Cornelia or Cincinnatus would amaze
a modern Florentine as a Cianghella
or a Lapo would have startled men in those days.   129

To so serene, so fair a townsman's life,
to a citizenry so wedded in good faith,
to such sweet dwelling, free of vice and strife,   132

Mary gave me—called in the pain of birth—
and in your ancient Baptistry I became
a Christian—and Cacciaguida, there on earth.   135

Moronto and Eliseo my brothers were.
My wife came from the valley of the Po.
The surname you now bear drives from her.   138

I served with Conrad in the Holy Land,
and my valor so advanced me in his favor
that I was knighted in his noble band.   141

With him I raised my sword against the might
of the evil creed whose followers take from you—
because your shepherds sin—what is yours by right.   144

There, by that shameless and iniquitous horde,
I was divested of the flesh and weight
of the deceitful world, too much adored   147

by many souls whose best hope it destroys;
and came from martyrdom to my present joys.

Notes

4–6. Dante does not say "harp" and "viol" but "lyre" and "strings." I take him to
be referring to XIV, 117, and repeat the phrasing of that line to reinforce the reference. In any case, it is the spirits themselves who are the instruments, and it is God's

Will (the Hand of Heaven) that plays upon them. Now, however, as an act of heavenly *caritas*, they have foregone the bliss of their singing and wait silently to be the more readily at Dante's service.

7–12. Since *caritas* is the essence of Heaven, it is the joy of the blessèd to hear and to grant righteous prayers. It is fitting, therefore, that the damned mourn forever, having deliberately cast from themselves, for the sake of temporal satisfactions, the everlasting love that would have received them with such eager joy.

22–24. The soul whose glory Dante sees flashing like a falling star is compared first to a gem on a ribbon or diadem, and then to a fire moving behind an alabaster screen. The soul does not leave the blessèd company, but moves through it, so rapidly and so brightly that it seems to be a falling star. Dante is standing at the foot of the great cross. Thus, the spirit approaches him from within it, remaining inside the cross, but at the point closest to Dante.

25–27. *Ancient Ilium*: Anchises, i.e., "the ancient king of Ilium." *Aeneid*, VI, 684 ff., narrates the meeting of Anchises and Aeneas in the Elysian Fields. *Muse*: For "poet." Virgil.

28–30. "O blood of mine! O ever abundant grace of God poured over you! To whom was the gate of Heaven ever thrown open twice, as it is to you?" *twice*: Now, while Dante is still in the flesh, and again after his death. St. Paul was borne up in a dream to the Third Heaven, but Dante has come in the flesh. The speaker is Cacciaguida (cah-cha-GWEE-da), Dante's great-great-grandfather. The details of Cacciaguida's life are best presented piecemeal, in the notes of the conversation that follows. Note, however, that Cacciaguida lived in the middle and later twelfth century when the spoken language was still basically Latin. The reference to Virgil and to the *Aeneid* makes it doubly felicitous that he begin his remarks in Latin.

31–36. Dante is astonished by the fact that this new soul addresses him as "Blood of mine!" He turns to Beatrice (Revelation) and sees her eyes light with such bliss that he believes he has experienced the final joy of Heaven. Beatrice, of course, is radiant with her foreknowledge of Dante's pleasure when he learns the identity of the new soul.

37–39. *in sight and sound*: By the sight of his radiance and by the quality of his voice. *added to his opening words*: some commentators have taken this phrasing to signify that Cacciaguida continued in Latin. He may have done so but that can hardly be Dante's point, for Latin would have posed no problem of understanding. There is, rather, a much richer point to be made. Cacciaguida left the earth about a century before this meeting. His long absorption into the Divine Intellect has given him infinite insights and has made natural to him modes of thought beyond mortal understanding. He must learn, therefore, to adjust his speech to Dante's understanding, and he begins by overshooting it.

What he has been absorbed into is, of course, omniscience, and omniscience, one might argue logically enough, would have no need to learn by trial and error. Yet, as a touch of characterization, his first inability to speak on Dante's level is masterful.

42. *target*: Not only does his thought exist at a higher level than any arrow of human thought could reach, but higher even than man could think of placing the target.

48. *seed*: Line of descent.

52. *the Great Book*: Of fate. *black nor white*: To alter the black would be to change what is written. To alter the white would be to add to or subtract from what is written. If neither can be changed, no least change is possible.

53. *this spirit*: Beatrice.

55. Dante is asserting, as a principle of mathematics, that all numbers (Five or Six, for example) derive from One. So all knowledge derives from the Primal Thought, which is unity.

62. *the greatest and least alike*: All souls in Paradise brim full of the most bliss they can achieve or conceive, and all are united in the body of God. Yet, as everywhere in Dante, degrees of difference are meticulously observed. Perhaps this state of things will seem contradictory to human reason, but we are here dealing with revelation. And certainly one can accept the premise that God's grace, while giving to each its fill, gives one soul a greater capacity than another.

63. *where thoughts outsoar themselves before they rise*: I have had to yield to a rhyme-forced metaphor. Dante's text, rendered literally, would read: "In which, before you think it, your thought outspreads itself."

64–69. Cacciaguida knows Dante's wish and what the answer will be, but has a sweet thirst to hear Dante's voice: an understandable grandfatherly sentiment.

73–87. DANTE'S REPLY TO CACCIAGUIDA. Cacciaguida has asked that Dante speak in his "own voice, assured, frank, and elated." In one sense, then, he has asked the poet Dante to rejoice Heaven with the power of poetry. Dante replies with a passage so superbly balanced that the temptation to cite it as an example of Dante's highest style is counterbalanced only by the fact that he achieves such heights so regularly.

The First Equipoise: God, in whom all attributes co-exist equally, as light and heat co-exist in the sun. When the spirits of the Blessèd are subsumed into the body of God, they, too, share this fullness of equal powers. Thus, their feelings of love and their ability to express those feelings are equal to one another in their fullness. Mortal man's powers of feeling, on the other hand, outrun his powers of utterance. In the perturbation of his unequal powers, therefore, Dante can give thanks only with his heart. Thus, hearing Cacciaguida address him as *"sanguis meus"* (his "paternal salutation") he is more deeply moved than he has power to express.

88–89. *"O leaf of mine . . . I was your root"*: Dante seems not to have known his lineage prior to Cacciaguida, who therefore describes himself as the root of the family tree of which Dante is the present leaf. The metaphoric tree can foresee little continuity from a leaf, and certainly "branch of mine" might have promised more for the future. In "leaf," Dante may have meant to express his transcience and smallness as compared to Cacciaguida's eternal glory. *foresee*: Dante uses *"aspettando"* (awaiting). But since Heavenly souls can foresee what they wait for—and rhyme demanding—I have thought this rendering reasonable.

91–96. *present surname*: The surname Alighieri (then Aldighiero) is thus identified as having originated with Cacciaguida's son. The name occurs in a Florentine document of 1189. This Aldighiero (father of Bellincione, who fathered Dante's father) was still alive in 1201 though his date of death is not known. "A century and more," therefore, is a bit too long. *first round of the mountain*: Of Purgatory. The ledge of the Proud. Pride may have been a hereditary failing of the Alighieri, or Dante may be further recognizing his own weakness. (Cf. *Purgatorio*, XIII, 133–138.)

97. *her ancient walls*: The original Roman walls. In 1173 a new ring of walls was completed, and others were added in 1284.

98. *from them . . . tierce and nones*: The church called La Badia was built on the old Roman walls. This church rang all the canonical hours (including *tierce* and *nones*).

103–105. In Dante's time, Florentine girls were married in childhood, before they were ten in some cases, and with such enormous dowries that it was said a man with one daughter was impoverished and a man with two ruined. *on either side*: The marriage custom escaped all bounds of moderation, on one side because the girls were too young, and on the other because the dowry demands were too great.

106. *no mansions then stood uninhabited*: Mansions might be empty because wealthy Florentines kept great suites and halls for ostentatious display, rather than to live in; or because dissolute living had destroyed ancestral fortunes and hereditary palaces had to be closed for lack of maintenance; or because the owners (like Dante) had been forced into exile. Dante probably intends all of these reasons, for all are part of the degeneracy he has Cacciaguida lament.

107–108. *Sardanapalus*: King of Assyria from 667 to 626 B.C. He is cited as the type of the luxurious and libertine debauché of the harem. *in hall and bed*: i.e., "indoors" (by way of debauchery and of riotously expensive display).

109–111. *Montemario*: (Mon-teh-MAHR-i-o): A hill with a commanding view of Rome. *Uccellatoio* (Oo-tchell-ah-TOY-oh): A hill with a similar view of Florence. The splendor of the view from the Uccellatoio had not yet outdone the view from Montemario, but just as Florence is rising faster than Rome, so will she plunge to ruin faster.

112–113. *Bellincion Berti*: A nobleman of some importance, honorary citizen of Florence, and father of "the good Gualdrada" (see *Inferno*, XVI, 38, note). *belted in leather and bone*: i.e., simply—a leather belt with a bone clasp rather than ornamented stuff with a jeweled clasp.

115. *Vecchio* (Veh-kyo): *Nerli* (NEHR-lee): Both were Guelph lords of Caccuagui-da's time and leading citizens of Florence.

119. *sure of her own burial place*: As Dante was not, having been exiled. As, by implication, few later Florentines could be, since any of them might find himself banished.

120. *because of France*: In both of two possible senses. Florentine bankers and merchants often traveled to France, hence they were often out of town. But in France, too, they learned vices for which they abandoned their wives even when they were back in Florence.

122. *the sweet idiom*: Baby talk.

127–129. Dante is contrasting a man and woman of decayed Florence to a man and woman of republican Rome. *Cornelia*: Daughter of Scipio Africanus and mother of the Roman paragons, the Gracchii. Dante saw her in Limbo (*Inferno*, IV 128). *Cincinnatus*: See VI, 46–48, note. *Cianghella*: (Chan-GHELL-ah) A Florentine woman married to a lord of Imola. She died about 1330, having acquired a reputation for a sharp tongue, a haughty extravagance, and an easy bed. *Lapo*: Lapo Saltorello. A Florentine poet and lawyer noted for his extravagant living. He and Dante were banished in the same decree of March 10, 1302.

133–134. *Mary . . . called in the pain of birth*: Sense: Cacciaguida's mother, in the throes of her birth pains, cried out a plea to the Virgin Mary, who thereupon granted him life and sweet dwelling in ancient Florence. *Baptistry*: Of San Giovanni. See *Inferno*, XIX, 17–18, and note.

136–138. There is no historic record of any of the persons here mentioned.

139. *Conrad*: Dante says "the Emperor Conrad." (Conrad III, reigned 1137–1152.) He went crusading in 1147 and was defeated at Damascus. He never visited Florence, however, whereas Conrad II (reigned 1024–1039) knew Florence well. Conrad II crusaded against the Saracens in Calabria. Dante has probably run the two Conrads into one.

143–144. *the evil creed*: Islam. *because your shepherds sin*: See *Inferno*, XXVII, 82 ff. Because of bad popes (such as Boniface VIII) the Holy Land, which Dante held to be rightfully Christian, was left to Islam. In Dante's view, a proper pope would have called for a crusade and hacked it free of un-Godly hands.

149. *from martyrdom to my present joys*: To call a death in battle a "martyrdom" may be stretching the meaning of the word. In any case, Cacciaguida, having died fighting for the faith—for God—seems to have mounted directly to his place in Heaven. (Cf. the Islamic belief that true believers who die in battle mount instantly to heavenly bliss.)

Canto XVI

The Warriors of God: Cacciaguida

Dante thrills with pleasure on learning that his ancestor had been elevated to knighthood, and feeling the power of pride of ancestry even in Heaven, in which there is no temptation to evil, he has a new insight into the family pride in which mortals glory. Moved by pride, Dante addresses Cacciaguida with the formal *"voi,"* an affectation at which Beatrice, half amused, admonishes him with a smile.

Dante then asks Cacciaguida for details of his birth and ancestry and of *The History of Early Florence*. Cacciaguida, as if to warn Dante away from pride of ancestry, dismisses the question of his birth and of his forebears as a matter best passed over in silence, and proceeds to a detailed account of the lords and people of Florence in the days when her bloodlines and traditions had not been diluted by the arrival of new families. It is to this "mongrelization" of the Florentines that Cacciaguida attributes all the subsequent degeneracy of Florence.

> O trivial pride of ours in noble blood!
> 　　that in possessing you men are possessed,
> 　　down here, where souls grow sick and lose their good,　　3
>
> will never again amaze me, for there, too,
> 　　where appetite is never drawn to evil—
> 　　in Heaven, I say—my own soul gloried in you!　　6
>
> You are a mantle that soon shrinks and tears.
> 　　Unless new cloth is added day by day,
> 　　time will go round you, snipping with its shears!　　9
>
> I spoke again, addressing him with that *"voi"*
> 　　whose usage first began among the Romans—
> 　　and which their own descendants least employ—　　12
>
> at which my Lady, who stood apart, though near,
> 　　and smiling, seemed to me like her who coughed
> 　　at the first recorded fault of Guinevere.　　15
>
> "You are my father," I started in reply.
> 　　"You give me confidence to speak out boldly.
> 　　You so uplift me, I am more than I.　　18
>
> So many streams of happiness flow down
> 　　into my mind that it grows self-delighting
> 　　at being able to bear it and not drown.　　21
>
> Tell me, then, dear source of my own blood,
> 　　who were your own forefathers? when were you born?
> 　　and what transpired in Florence in your boyhood?　　24

Tell me of St. John's sheepfold in those days.
How many souls were then within the flock,
and which of them was worthy of high place?"   27

As glowing coals fanned by a breath of air
burst into flames, so did I see that light
increase its radiance when it heard my prayer.   30

And as its light gave off a livelier ray,
so, in a sweeter and a softer voice—
though not in the idiom we use today—   33

it said: "From the day when *Ave* sounded forth
to that in which my mother, now a saint,
being heavy laden with me, gave me birth,   36

this flame had come back to its Leo again
to kindle itself anew beneath his paws
five hundred times plus fifty plus twenty plus ten.   39

My ancestors and I were born in the place
where the last quarter of the course begins
for those who take part in your annual race.   42

Of my fathers, be content with what you have heard.
Of who they were and whence they came to Florence
silence is far more fitting than any word.   45

Of men who could bear arms there were counted then,
between Mars and the Baptist, the fifth part
of what may be mustered there from living men.   48

But the citizenry, now mongrelized by the blood
of Campi, of Certaldo, and of Figghine,
was pure then, down to the humblest planer of wood.   51

Oh how much better to have been neighbors of these
of whom I speak, and to have Trespiano
and Galuzzo still fixed as your boundaries,   54

than to have swallowed them and to bear the stink
of the yokel of Aguglione, and of Signa's boor
who still has eyes to swindle and hoodwink.   57

Had the world's most despicable crew not shown
a hard stepmother's face and greed to Caesar
but been a loving mother, one who is known   60

as a Florentine, and who trades in goods and debt,
would be back in Simifonti, where his grandsire
once gypsied in the streets for what he could get.   63

Montemurlo would still be owned by its own counts,
the Cerchi would be in the parish of Acone,
and in Valdigreve, still, the Bondelmounts.   66

It has always been a fact that confusion of blood
    has been a source of evil to city-states,
    just as our bodies are harmed by too much food;   69

and that a bull gone blind will fall before
    a blind lamb does. And that one sword may cut
    better than five has been proved in many a war.   72

If you will think of Luni and Urbisaglia,
    how they have passed away, and how, behind them,
    are dying now Chiusi and Sinigaglia,   75

it should not be too hard to comprehend,
    or strange to hear, that families dwindle out,
    when even cities come at last to an end.   78

All mankind's institutions, of every sort,
    have their own death, though in what long endures
    it is hidden from you, your own lives being short.   81

And as the circling of the lunar sphere
    covers and bares the shore with never a pause,
    so Fortune alters Florence year by year.   84

It should not, therefore, seem too wondrous strange
    to hear me speak of the good Florentines
    whose fame is veiled behind time's endless change.   87

I knew the Ughi, the Catellini, the line
    of the Greci, Filippi, Ormanni, and Alberichi—
    illustrious citizens, even in decline.   90

I knew those of Sannella, and those of the Bow,
    and the Soldanieri, Ardinghi, and Bostichi;
    as grand as they were ancient, there below.   93

Not far from the portal that now bears the weight
    of such a cargo of new iniquity
    as soon, now, will destroy the ship of state,   96

once lived the Ravignani, from whom came
    Count Guido Guerra, and whoever else
    has since borne Bellincione's noble name.   99

The della Pressa were already furnished
    with knowledge of how to rule, and Galigaio
    had his gold hilt and pommel already burnished.   102

Great already were the lands of the vair,
    Sacchetti, Guiochi, Fifanti, Barucci, and Galli
    and of those who blush now for the stave affair.   105

The trunk that bore the many-branched Calfucci
    had grown already great; already called
    to the curule were Sizii and Arrigucci.   108

How great I have seen them who are now undone
   by their own pride! And even the balls of gold—
   in all great deeds of Florence, how they shone!   111

So shone the fathers of that gang we see
   in the bishop's palace when your See falls vacant,
   fattening themselves as a consistory.   114

That overweening and presumptuous tribe—
   a dragon to all who run from it, a lamb
   to any who stand and show a tooth or bribe—   117

were coming up, though still so parvenu
   Donato was hardly pleased when his father-in-law
   made him a relative of such a crew.   120

The Caponsacchi had come down by then
   from Fiesole to market; the Infangati
   and Giudi were established as good townsmen.   123

And here's an astonishing fact, though little known:
   in ancient times a gate of the inner wall
   was named for those of the Pera, now all gone.   126

All those whose various quarterings display
   the staves of the great baron whose name and worth
   are kept alive every St. Thomas' Day   129

owe him the rank and privilege they enjoy,
   though one who binds those arms with a gold fringe
   makes common cause today with the hoi polloi.   132

Gualterotti and Importuni were then well known.
   And Borgo would still be a peaceful place
   had it not acquired new neighbors from Montebuon'.   135

The line from which was born your grief and strife
   because of the righteous anger that ruined you,
   and put an end to all your happier life,   138

was honored in itself and its allies.
   O Buondelmonti, what ill you did in fleeing
   its nuptials to find comfort in other ties!   141

Many would still be happy whom we now pity,
   had God seen fit to let the Ema drown you
   on the first day you started for the city.   144

But it was fitting that to the broken stone
   that guards the bridge, Florence should offer a victim
   to mark the last day's peace she has ever known.   147

With such as these, and others, my first life's years
   saw Florence live and prosper in such peace
   that she had, then, no reason to shed tears.   150

With such as these I saw there in my past
so valiant and so just a populace
that none had ever seized the ensign's mast   153

and hung the lily on it upside down.
Nor was the red dye of division known."

Notes

1. *in noble blood*: Pride of birth into a family with patents of nobility.

6. *my own soul gloried in you*: On hearing that Cacciaguida had been knighted by (whichever) Conrad. The point is curiously made. Despite the statements of many of Dante's commentators, who were probably working backward from Dante's own claim rather than from any historical record, there is no recorded evidence either that Cacciaguida had been knighted, or even that he had served in the crusades. Dante may be following a family legend, or he may be inventing his own claim to nobility, the latter an oddly uncelestial act of pride. Dante, in any case, hastens to disclaim any real merit in the possession of noble ancestry unless the descendants labor to maintain the family's true nobility of soul.

10–12. *voi*: The second person plural. It seems to have come into use as the deferential form of address to a single person in about the third century A.D., but Dante is following the popular belief of his time that it was first used in addressing Caesar when he assumed all the high offices of the Republic and so became, in effect, many personages in one. English does not distinguish between *"tu"* (you-singular) and *"voi"* (you-plural) except perhaps in the dialect of the southern states where "you" (singular) and "you-all" (plural) is standard. *least employ*: The modern Romans, always a mannerless lot, made the least use of this polite or deferential form. The "you" that begins each of the three sentences in lines 16–18 is this *"voi."*

13–15. Beatrice notes Dante's foible in using the *"voi"* form and admonishes him with a half-amused smile that reminds him of the wife of Mallehaut (see *Inferno*, V, 124–134, and notes) who coughed when she first saw Guinevere with Launcelot.

25. *St. John's sheepfold*: Florence. John the Baptist was its patron saint.

34. *Ave*: Hail. The first word spoken to Mary by the Angel of the Annunciation.

37–39. *this flame*: Mars. *its Leo*: Astrologers asserted various special connections between Mars and Leo. Both were classified as "hot and dry." And Leo is the constellation of the Lion, the warlike and heraldic beast perhaps closest to the god of war.

39. THE DATE OF CACCIAGUIDA'S BIRTH. The Annunciation took place on March 25. Scartazzini cites a text of Dante's time that sets the Martian year at 686.94 days. That figure multiplied by 580 and divided by the 365.2466 days of the earth year (as Scartazzini asserts, my mathematics floundering in his wake) yields as a birthdate January 25, 1091. Even Scartazzini does not complicate his computations by entering a correction for various calendar reforms. In any case, Cacciaguida is thought to have died when he was about 56.

40–42. The annual race was run in Florence on June 24, the Feast of St. John. "Quarter" here signifies "quarter of a town," as in "Latin Quarter." Scholars disagree as to the course of the race and the exact quarter Dante had in mind. Porta San Piero is generally favored by the commentators.

43. *Of my fathers*: This much in answer to Dante's first question, and also as a rebuke to Dante for his pride of ancestry, but note, too, that this answer covers Dante's own ignorance of his remoter ancestry.

47. *between Mars and the Baptist*: To be between Mars and the Baptist signifies, in effect, to be in Florence, the statue of Mars on the Ponte Vecchio and the Baptistry of St. John marking two of the limits of Florence in Cacciaguida's time. In 1300 Florence had a population of about 70,000, of which (according to a doubtful estimate by Scartazzini) about 30,000 were able to bear arms.

50. *of Campi, of Certaldo* (tchehr-TAHL-doh) *and of Figghine* (fee-GHEE-neh): All are nearby places a self-righteous Florentine would think of as the backwoods. Florence was on the main highway of invasion from the north. Inevitably, therefore, many tribal strains were joined in its people. Dante is seldom temperate in his views of outsiders.

52–57. *those of whom I speak*: In line 50. *Trespiano*: A crossroads village now at the edge of Florence, but in Cacciaguida's time an hour's walk away on the road to Bologna. *Galuzzo*: A village at about the same distance on the road to Siena. *the yokel of Aguglione* (ah-goo-LYOW-neh): Baldo d'Aguglione. His family name traces to a "backwoods" castle in Val di Pesa, but he became a power in Florence. He was probably involved in the swindles Dante cites in *Purgatorio*, XII, 100–105. On September 3, 1311 he issued a decree recalling a number of Florentine exiles but left Dante's name off the list, whereby, of course, he put himself on Dante's list to be registered as a stink in Heaven. *Signa's boor:* Fazio dei Morubaldini of Signa (SEE-nyah), a hamlet near Florence. Fazio was a lawyer of Dante's time with a considerable reputation as a grafter, swindler, and barrator.

58–59. *crew:* The clergy. *Caesar:* Here as a symbol of temporal government. Sense: Had the church been a loving mother in temporal affairs.

60. *one who is known:* Dante may have had a specific person in mind but many Florentines, old-line and parvenu, traded as merchants and pawnbrokers. Dante seems to charge all such evil commerce to the influx of new families that resulted from the political scheming of the church.

62. *Simifonti:* A castle and town in Valdessa captured by Florence in 1202.

64. *Montemurlo:* A castle beteeen Pistoia and Prata. It formerly belonged to the counts Guidi (see *Inferno*, XXX, 76–77). In 1254, unable to defend the castle against the Pistoians, the counts sold it to Florence.

65. *the Cerchi* (TCHEHR-kee); *Acone* (ah-CON-eh): is in Val di Sieve. In Dante's time, the Cerchi had become leaders of the White Party in Dante's own soi-disant ancestral quarter of Porta San Piero.

66. *Valdigreve:* South of Florence where the Buondelmonti had a castle called Montebuoni. In 1135 the castle was taken from them by the Florentines and they were forced to move into Florence, where they became powerful in Borgo Sant' Apostolo.

67. *confusion of blood:* The admixture of new blood lines to those of an old established population.

73–75. Cacciaguida is citing examples of Dead or enfeebled cities; the first two are already dead, the second two are dying. *Luni:* An ancient city on the Magra at the northern boundary of Tuscany, already a ruin in Dante's time. *Urbisaglia* (oor-bee-SAH-lyah): In the March of Ancona; not quite dead in Dante's time. *Chiusi* (KYOO-zee); Ancient Clusium. In Val di Chiana. *Sinigaglia* (see-nee-GAH-lyah): On the coast north of Ancona. Both were ravaged by malaria in Dante's time, but both have survived their prophesied extinction.

84. *so Fortune alters Florence:* Now raising her on the flood, now letting her down on the ebb. Fortune, of course, is Dame Fortune.

88–90. *Ughi* (OO-ghee), *etc.:* Cacciaguida lists six solid old families of the first half of the eleventh century and says they were illustrious even in their decline. In 1300 these families had finished declining and were extinct, at least as influential voices in Florentine affairs.

91. *those of the Bow:* The family dell' Arca. They and the other four families here cited were numerous and powerful in Cacciaguida's time. In Dante's time the dell' Arca clan was extinct; the Soldanieri, a Ghibelline clan, still existed but had been banished; and the descendants of the other three clans had lost power and social standing.

94. *the portal:* Of San Piero, where the Cerchi ruled in Dante's time (see line 65) showing the destruction of Florence.

97–99. *Ravignani . . . Count Guido Guerra . . . Bellincione:* Bellincione (bell-een-TCHOE-neh) Berti dei Ravignani (rah-vee-NYAH-nee) was praised in XV, 112–114. Count Guido Guerra VI was praised in *Inferno*, XVI, 37–39, though he is damned among the sodomites. He was a great grandson of Bellincione, who was the father of Good Gualdrada. Through another daughter, his name descended to many members of the Adimari family (see Filippo Argenti, *Inferno*, VIII, 32, note, and note to line 119 below).

100. *della Pressa:* An emergent family (in Cacciaguida's time) who had been elected to govern some of the nearby territories of Florence. Their descendants were charged with betraying the Florentines at Montaperti (for which see *Inferno*, X, 86, and note to 32–51).

101. *Galigaio* (gal-ee-GUY-oh): A noble family of Porta San Piero, here said to have been already of the knighthood ("gold hilt and pommel") in Cacciaguida's time, but reduced to the rank and file by 1300.

103. *vair:* A fur, usually of a small squirrel. Represented in heraldry by rows of little bells. It appeared on the arms of the Pigli (PEE-lyee), a family of Porta San Pancrazio.

104. A continuation of the early eleventh-century Florentine social register.

105. *those who blush now for the stave affair:* The Chiaramontesi of Porta San Piero. See *Purgatorio*, XII, 100–105, note.

106. *Calfucci* (kahl-FOO-tchee): Were collateral with the Donati. Dante's wife, Gemma, was a Donati.

108. *the curule:* A chair in which only the highest officers of Rome might sit. Here used to indicate highest rank. *Sizii* (see-TZEE-yee) *and Arrigucci* (ah-ree-GOO-tchee): Neither family was extinct by Dante's time, but the first was nearly so, and the second much reduced.

110. *balls of gold*: From the arms of the Lamberti. Mosca, one of this line, is in the Bolgia of the Sowers of Discord (*Inferno*, XXVIII, 106, and note).

112. *so shone the fathers of that gang we see*: As the Lamberti once shone in every great deed of Florence so shone (in evil deeds) the Visdomini and the Tosinghi, hereditary patrons and defenders of the episcopal see and palace. Whenever the see fell vacant, they were in charge of episcopal affairs until a new bishop was elected. Dante here accuses them of forming themselves into a private consistory in order to fatten themselves on the resources of the see.

115. *That . . . tribe*: The Adimari. Dante had special reasons for disliking them. When Dante was banished, Boccaccio Adimari took over his forfeited estates and resisted every effort to rescind the decree of banishment.

119. *Donato . . . his father-in-law*: Bellincione married the good Gualdrada to Umbertino Donati of the family of the Counts Guidi. He then married another daughter to the upstart Adimari, thus relating the two families. The Donati refused to acknowledge kinship.

121-123. *Caponsacchi . . . Giudi . . . Infangati*: Three Ghibelline families, once well established, but much diminished by Dante's time. Is it only coincidence that these three names mean, at root, Head-in-a-sack, Judases (or Jews), and Covered-with-mud? Could Dante be suggesting that these Johnny-come-latelies were as outlandish as their names in comparison with the old-line Florentines?

125. *the inner wall*: The first (Roman) wall of the city. Cacciaguida is saying that Dante would know the long-vanished della Pera family was an ancient one, but not that it traced back to the very founding of Florence.

127-132. Hugh of Brandenburg, known in Italy as Ugo il Grande, marchese di Toscano, was the Imperial Vicar of Tuscany. Thus he was the voice of Imperial authority and order (see note to *Purgatorio*, VI, 100) and Tuscany's chief Ghibelline. His arms bore seven staves, which are variously reproduced in the arms of "all those" families he raised to knighthood and greatness (among them the Giandotti, Pulci, della Bella, and Neri). He died on St. Thomas' Day, 1006, and it is still part of the festival of St. Thomas to offer solemn prayer to Ugo in the Abbey he built in Florence. *though one who binds those arms*: Giano (DJAH-no) della Bella. He was exiled in 1295 and was no longer making common cause with the hoi polloi. But Dante, though he had to become a Guelph once there were no more Ghibellines in Florence, still has his only political hope in the party of the Emperor and will not miss a chance to condemn the great Ghibelline families that identified themselves with the cause of vulgar independence.

133. *Gualterotti and Importuni*: Guelph families of Borgo Santo Apostolo, great in Cacciaguida's time, but common workingmen in Dante's.

136. *new neighbors from Montebuon'*: The Buondelmonti. Cacciaguida goes on to describe the grief and disorder they brought to Florence. Their houses were next to those of the Gualterotti and Importuni.

136-138. *The line*: Of the Amidei. A great family related to the Lamberti and allied to many noble families of Florence. Despite the fact that it was of much higher rank, it betrothed one of its daughters to Buondelmonte dei Buondelmonti, who broke off the nuptials in order to marry a daughter of the Donati. The Amidei, in "righteous anger" at this affront by a man of lower rank, held a council of war. It was at this council that Mosca dei Lamberti (*Inferno*, XXVIII, 106, and note) declared, "A thing done has an end." As a result Buondelmonti was murdered at the foot of the statue of Mars in 1215. As a result of that murder Florence, previously united, became divided into Guelph and Ghibelline factions, and was plunged into civil war, thereby ending its "happier life."

143. *the Ema*: A river bounding the lands from which the Buondelmonti were dispossessed before they came to Florence.

145-147. *the broken stone*: The mutilated statue of Mars. It is fitting, says Cacciaguida in bitter irony, that Florence should mark its return to the rule of Mars by offering up the blood of a victim at the foot of the mutilated statue of its first pagan patron.

153-154. Cacciaguida means that the Florentines had never been defeated in war. It was a custom to mock the vanquished by flying their captured flags upside down on the mast. The lily was, of course, the emblem of France.

155. The ancient standard of Florence bore a white lily on a red field. In 1251 the Guelphs changed their standard to a red lily on a white field, the Ghibellines preserving the original. Thus there were two Florentine standards and division had dyed the lily red. The "red dye," of course, is also the blood spilled in war.

Canto XVII

The Warriors of God: Cacciaguida

Beatrice and Cacciaguida already know what question is burning in Dante's mind, but Beatrice nevertheless urges him to speak it, that by practicing Heavenly discourse he be better able to speak to men when he returns to Earth. So urged, Dante asks Cacciaguida to make clear the recurring *Dark Prophecies of Dante's Future*.

Cacciaguida details *Dante's Coming Banishment from Florence*, identifies the patrons Dante will find, and assures Dante of his future fame. He warns Dante not to become bitter in adversity assuring him that the Divine Comedy, once it becomes known, will outlive the proudest of the Florentines and bring shame to their evil memories for ages to come.

> Like him who went to Clymene to learn
>   if what he had heard was true, and who makes fathers
>   unwilling to yield to their sons at every turn—   3
>
> such was I, and such was I taken to be
>   by Beatrice and by the holy lamp
>   that, earlier, had changed its place for me.   6
>
> Therefore my lady: "Speak. And let the fire
>   of your consuming wish come forth," she said,
>   "well marked by the inner stamp of your desire;   9
>
> not that we learn more by what you say,
>   but that you better learn to speak your thirst,
>   that men may sooner quench it on your way."   12
>
> "Dear root of my existence, you who soar
>   so high that, as men grasp how a triangle
>   may contain one obtuse angle and no more,   15
>
> you grasp contingent things before they find
>   essential being, for you can see that focus
>   where all time is time-present in God's mind.   18
>
> While I was yet with Virgil, there below,
>   climbing the mountain where the soul is healed,
>   and sinking through the dead world of its woe,   21
>
> dark words of some dark future circumstance
>   were said to me; whereby my soul is set
>   four-square against the hammering of chance: 24
>
> and, therefore, my desire will be content
>   with knowing what misfortune is approaching;
>   for the arrow we see coming is half spent."   27

—Such were the words of my reply, addressed
  to the light that had spoken earlier; and with them
  as Beatrice wished, my own wish was confessed.   30

Not in dark oracles like those that glued
  the foolish like limed birds, before the Lamb
  that takes our sins away suffered the rood;   33

but in clear words and the punctilious style
  of ordered thought, that father-love replied,
  concealed in and revealed by his own smile: 36

"*Contingency*, whose action is confined
  to the few pages of the world of matter,
  is fully drawn in the Eternal Mind;   39

but it no more derives *necessity*..
  from being so drawn, than a ship dropping down river
  derives its motion from a watcher's eye.   42

As a sweet organ-harmony strikes the ear,
  so, from the Primal Mind, my eyes receive
  a vision of your future drawing near.   45

As Hippolytus left Athens, forced to roam
  by his two-faced and merciless stepmother,
  just so shall you leave Florence, friends, and home.   48

So is it willed, so does it already unfold,
  so will it soon be done by him who plots it
  there where Christ is daily bought and sold.   51

The public cry, as usual, will blame you
  of the offended party, but the vengeance
  truth will demand will yet show what is true.   54

All that you held most dear you will put by
  and leave behind you; and this is the arrow
  the longbow of your exile first lets fly.   57

You will come to learn.how bitter as salt and stone
  is the bread of others, how hard the way that goes
  up and down stairs that never are your own.   60

And what will press down on your shoulders most
  will be the foul and foolish company
  you will fall into on that barren coast.   63

Ingrate and godless, mad in heart and head
  will they become against you, but soon thereafter
  it will be they, not you, whose cheeks turn red.   66

Their bestiality will be made known
  by what they do; while your fame shines the brighter
  for having become a party of your own.   69

Your first inn and first refuge you shall owe
  to the great Lombard whose escutcheon bears
  the sacred bird above, the ladder below.   72

In such regard and honor shall he hold you,
  that in the act of granting and requesting,
  what others do late, shall be first between you two.   75

With him you will see another, born of this star
  and so stamped by the iron of its virtues
  that he shall be renowned for deeds of war.   78

The world has not yet noticed him: these spheres
  in their eternal course above his youth
  have turned about him now only nine years.   81

Before the Gascon sets his low intrigue
  to snare high Henry, men will start to speak
  of his disregard of money and fatigue.   84

The knowledge of his magnanimities
  will spread so far that men will hear of it
  out of the mouths of his very enemies.   87

Look you to him and his great works. The fate
  of many shall be altered by his deeds,
  the rich and poor exchanging their estate.   90

And write this in your mind but remain silent
  concerning it . . ."—and he said things about him
  to astonish even those who shall be present.   93

Then added: "Son, these are the annotations
  to what was told you. These are the snares that hide
  behind a few turns of the constellations.   96

But do not hate your neighbors: your future stretches
  far beyond the reach of what they do
  and far beyond the punishment of wretches."   99

—When, by his silence, that blessèd soul made clear
  that he had finished passing his dark shuttle
  across the threads I had combed for him there,   102

I then, as one who has not understood
  longs for the guidance of a soul that sees,
  and straightway wills, and wholly loves the good: 105

"Father, I do indeed see time's attacks
  hard spurred against me to strike such a blow
  as shall fall most on him who is most lax.   108

And it is well I arm myself with foresight.
  Thus, if the dearest place is taken from me,
  I shall not lose all place by what I write.   111

Down through that world of endless bitter sighs,
and on the mountain from whose flowering crown
I was uplifted by my lady's eyes,   114

and then through Heaven from ray to living ray,
I have learned much that would, were it retold,
offend the taste of many alive today.   117

Yet if, half friend to truth, I mute my rhymes,
I am afraid I shall not live for those
who will think of these days as 'the ancient times.' "   120

The light in which my heaven-found treasure shone
smiled brighter in its rapture, coruscating
like a gold mirror in a ray of sun;   123

then answered me: "A conscience overcast
by its own shame, or another's, may indeed
be moved to think your words a bitter blast.   126

Nevertheless, abjure all lies, but match
your verses to the vision in fullest truth;
and if their hides are scabby, let them scratch!   129

For if your voice is bitter when first tested
upon the palate, it shall yet become
a living nutriment when it is digested.   132

This cry you raise shall strike as does the wind
hardest at highest peaks—and this shall argue
no little for your honor, as you will find.   135

Therefore you have been shown—here in these spheres,
there on the mount, and in the valley of woe—
those souls whose names most ring in mortal ears;   138

for the feelings of a listener do not mark
examples of things unknown, nor place their trust
in instances whose roots hide in the dark;   141

nor will men be persuaded to give ear
to arguments whose force is not made clear."

Notes

1-3. *him who went to Clymene*: Phaeton, son of Clymene and Apollo. Epaphus had told him Apollo was not his father and the boy had run to his mother to be reassured. Phaeton makes all fathers chary of yielding too readily to their sons by his example in persuading Apollo to let him drive the chariot of the Sun. Apollo consented but Phaeton was not strong enough to control the horses. They bolted and the Sun was about to burn Earth and sky when Zeus stopped the chariot with a thunderbolt, killing Phaeton. Thus the reluctance Phaeton teaches fathers is for the good of the sons.

6. *changed its place*: In descending to the foot of the cross.

7-12. The mixed metaphor with which Beatrice opens is once again based on the impress of a signet in wax. Here the fire is the wax and inner desire the signet. She and Cacciaguida (and all the heavenly souls) already know Dante's mind and their knowledge of it cannot be increased by his speaking, but by encouraging him to discourse on a heavenly level, Beatrice is preparing him the better to speak his soul's need when he returns to earth, in order that men may be moved to the good he urges.

13–18. Sense of this passage: "You grasp the future as easily as men grasp a problem in geometry, for your sight is fixed upon God's mind, in which all time is one and present." *root*: Dante uses "*piota*," which may mean "root, soil around a root, sod, turf, or sole of the foot."

16. *contingent things*: Contingency, in Scholastic terminology, is "that which could or could not exist." Contingency is dependent upon the action of *necessity* (that which must necessarily exist). Contingent being is possible, finite, and secondary. Necessary being is certain, infinite, and primary.

29. *to the light*: To Cacciaguida.

31–32. *that glued the foolish like limed birds*: Bird-lime, a highly viscous substance, is spread on boughs and used to trap birds much as flies are trapped on fly paper. Dante compares the sayings of pagan oracles to that lime, in which the pagan world let itself be trapped before the Lamb of Christ suffered to set men free of such traps.

36. *his own smile*: "Smile" is used here for "gladness of spirit"—a regular usage in the *Paradiso*. That gladness is revealed to Dante by the brightening of the flame that hides Cacciaguida from Dante's view. Thus he is both concealed in and revealed by the brighter shining of his bliss.

37–42. Divine foreknowledge of *contingency* does not confer *necessity* because man is given free will. The nature of free will within the workings of omniscient prevision is a point of faith and must be referred to the mysteries rather than to reason.

46. *Hippolytus*: Son of Theseus and the Amazon Antiope. He rejected the advances of his stepmother, Phaedra, and she, accusing him of what she herself wanted, turned Theseus against him. Theseus not only drove him from home but called on Poseidon for vengeance and Poseidon sent a bull from the sea to kill Hippolytus as he was driving his chariot along the shore. Ovid tells the story in *Metamorphoses*, XV, 487 ff. Through Cacciaguida, Dante is, of course, protesting that the charges brought against him were as false and self-seeking as Phaedra's against Hippolytus.

Dante, as a high official of Florence and a leader of the Whites, was charged, vaguely and inconclusively, with grafting. The "Anonimo Fiorentino," a nearly contemporary fourteenth-century commentary, says that part of the charge brought against Dante was his "opposition to the Holy Mother Church," which in this case is, clearly enough, another way of saying "opposition to the politics of Pope Boniface VIII."

50–51. *him who plots it*: Boniface VIII, if not in person and with Dante specifically in mind, then through his corrupt agents and evil policies. *where Christ is daily bought and sold*: Rome, i.e., the Vatican.

52–53. *you of the offended party*: Both Dante and his party, the Whites.

53–54. *the vengeance truth will demand*: Truth will take its vengeance by punishing those who are guilty. In so doing, it will bear witness to what is true. Throughout this passage (from line 46) Boniface VIII is compared to Phaedra. (See *Inferno*, XII, 12–18, and note.) For the force of the comparison it is well to bear in mind that Phaedra was born of a foul beast (the Minotaur) and a queen so lecherous that she crept into a wooden cow in order to be taken by the bull. Phaedra later committed suicide, overcome by her guilt, her death clearing the name of Hippolytus. Hippolytus, curiously enough, survived a shift of legend and appears in Catholic hagiography as St. Hippolytus or St. Hippolyte.

62. *the foul and foolish company*: Dante seems to be alluding to his own party, the Whites. As a fallen leader, he seems to feel his party has betrayed him. In any case there seems to be nothing to hope for from political parties. In line 69 Cacciaguida praises him for having become his own party of one.

63. *that barren coast*: Of exile.

65–66. *soon thereafter . . . cheeks turn red*: The same sort of machinations that led to Dante's banishment led Florence into foolish wars and bloody internal disorders that left the Florentines with more than enough reasons for blushing. The Whites in particular suffered many humiliations and bloody defeats.

69. *A party of your own*: In 1266, the Ghibellines were driven forever from Florence (see *Inferno*, X, 32–51, note). The Guelphs, thereupon, divided into Whites and Blacks, and Dante became a member of the Whites' ruling council. At the end of 1301 the Blacks elected a new *podestà*, and on January 27, 1302, while Dante was on a mission to Rome, the Blacks published a decree fining him 5,000 florins and banishing him for two years. On March 10, not having appeared to pay his fine, Dante was banished permanently, and sentenced to death if he returned. In 1303, the Whites, joined now with the remnants of the Ghibellines, were gathering forces for an assault on Florence, and Dante was their ambassador at the court of Bartolomeo della Scala, Lord of Verona. At that time Boniface VIII died, and was succeeded by Benedict XI, who sent a cardinal to Florence to negotiate a settlement. With that hope in view, Dante remained affiliated with the Whites. The Blacks, however, resisted all

negotiation, and the Whites prepared an attack that was repulsed with heavy losses at La Lastra, above Florence, July 20, 1304. Dante seems to have felt that the internal bickerings of the Whites had caused the carnage, and it was probably after La Lastra that he withdrew, damning Blacks and Whites together, to become a one-man party of his own.

71 ff. THE SCALIGERI (DELLA SCALA). The ancient noble family of the Scaligeri (its German branch was named Scaliger) ruled over Verona and later acquired the office of Imperial Vicar of Tuscany. Alberto died in 1301 and was succeeded, in order, by his three sons: Bartolomeo, died 1304; Alboino, died 1311; Francesco (Can Grande), who shared power with Alboino beginning in 1308, became sole lord of Verona in 1311, and died in 1329. (Dante died in 1321.) Francesco was Dante's great patron and the lord on whom Dante based some of his hope of peace and order in Italy. (See *Inferno*, I, 95, and note.) *the great Lombard*: Francesco. *the sacred bird*: The eagle. The arms of the Scaligeri displayed a ladder (*scala*) below an eagle.

73–75. Others ask first and give later. But between Bartolomeo and Dante (as, note, among the souls of Heaven) the giving shall be first and any request (of service from the other) shall come late, the service having already been freely offered.

76. *another*: Can Grande. He won no particular renown as a warrior. "Of war" (line 78) does not occur in Dante. It is my own rhyme-forced addition. Yet to be stamped by the influence of Mars, praised by one of the warriors of God, and to be hailed, as Dante may have intended, as the Greyhound that shall hunt down and destroy evil, can only be appropriate to a warrior, even when the war record is missing. Perhaps Dante was still hoping ahead from the time of (as distinct from time "in") the writing, for Can Grande was then in power.

81. *nine years*: Earth years. Cacciaguida does not say nine "times." Nine Martian years would equal about seventeen earth years and Can Grande was nine years old on March 9, 1300. (Note that March is "Mars month.")

82–83. *the Gascon . . . high Henry*: The Gascon is Clement V (see *Inferno*, XIX, 77–79, and note. Also *Purgatorio*, XXXII, 149–150). He succeeded Boniface VIII to the Papal throne in 1305, and to the baptismal font of Hell in 1314. Henry VII of Luxembourg, Emperor 1308–1313 (see *Purgatorio*, VII, 96, and note), was the main prop of Dante's hopes for a general peace and for the end of his exile. Clement invited him to Rome with fair promises but threatened to excommunicate him in 1312. "Before," therefore (line 82), means "before 1312." By that time Can Grande was twenty-one, had been joint lord of Verona for four years, and sole lord for one. *men will start to speak*: Dante says, literally, "sparks of his virtue will appear."

92–93. *him*: Can Grande. *those who shall be present*: To bear witness to the astonishing things Cacciaguida prophesies to Dante while enjoining him not to repeat them.

96. *a few turns*: Probably intended as daily rather than annual revolutions. At the Easter season of 1300 Dante was less than two years from his banishment.

108. *on him who is most lax*: Who has least foreseen and forearmed himself.

110. *the dearest place*: Florence.

112. *that world*: Hell.

113. *flowering crown*: The Earthly Paradise.

Canto XVIII

Beatrice comforts Dante, who is pondering the bitter and the sweet of Cacciaguida's prophecy, then instructs him to turn back to Cacciaguida, who proceeds to name among the souls who form the Cross of Mars *The Great Warriors of God*. They flash like shooting stars along the arms of the cross. Finished, Cacciaguida reascends to his original place in the right arm and the whole choir resumes its hymn.

Dante turns back to Beatrice, sees her grow yet more beautiful, and knows they have made the *Ascent to the Sixth Sphere*. He sees the pale glow of Jupiter replace the red glow of Mars and in that silvery sheen he sees *The Vision of Earthly Justice*, a spectacular arrangement of lights that spell out a message, letter by letter, and then form as an *Eagle* (The Empire) ornamented by glowing lilies (France).

Moved by this vision of Justice, Dante prays that these souls of Heavenly Justice will visit their wrath upon the corrupt Pope, who, like a money-changer in the temple, denies the sacraments of God's people by excommunication and interdiction, in order to sell back to them what is rightfully theirs. So, for the love of money does the successor of Peter and Paul betray holy office.

Now that holy mirror rejoiced alone,
    rapt in its own reflections; and I tasted
    the bitterness and sweetness of my own.   3

My guide to God said: "Turn your thoughts along
    a happier course. Remember I dwell near
    the One who lifts the weight of every wrong."   6

I turned to the loving sound of my soul's aid,
    and the love my eyes beheld in her sacred eyes
    I leave unsaid—not only am I afraid   9

my powers of speech fail, but my memory
    cannot return so far above itself
    unless Another's grace be moved to guide me.   12

This much of what I felt I can report—
    that as I looked at her my will was freed
    of every other wish of any sort,   15

for the Eternal Bliss that rayed down whole
    into my Beatrice, shone back from her face
    and its reflection there gladdened my soul.   18

And with a smile so radiant that my eyes
  were overcome, she said then: "Turn and listen:
  not in my eyes alone is Paradise."   21

As, here on earth, the face sometimes reveals
  the wish within, if it is wished so strongly
  that all the soul is gripped by what it feels—   24

so, in the flaming of the holy ray
  to which I turned, I read the inner will,
  and knew that it had something more to say.   27

It spoke thus: "In this fifth limb of the tree
  whose life is from its crown, and bears forever,
  and never sheds a leaf, I would have you see   30

elected spirits who, in the world's use,
  before they came to Heaven, were so renowned
  their great worth would make greater every Muse.   33

Look at the arms of the cross. As the swift flame
  within a flame does, so, within that choir,
  shall flash the splendor of each soul I name."   36

I saw along the cross a streak of light
  as he pronounced the name of Joshua:
  nor did the saying reach me before the sight.   39

And at the name of the great Maccabee
  I saw another, spinning; and the string
  that whirled that top was its own ecstasy.   42

And just as hunters follow their falcons' flights,
  so, at the names of Charlemagne and Roland,
  my rapt attention followed two more lights.   45

Then William of Orange, and then Rinoard
  drew my eyes after them along that cross.
  And then the good duke Godfrey, and Robert Guiscard.   48

Then, moving once more through those lights, the light
  that had come down to greet me, let me hear
  its art among the choir of Heaven's height.   51

I turned to my right to learn from Beatrice,
  whether by word or sign, what I should do,
  and I beheld her eyes shine with such bliss,   54

with such serenity, that she surpassed
  the vision of every other accustomed beauty
  in which she had shone, including even the last.   57

And as a man, perceiving day by day
  an increase of delight in doing good,
  begins to sense his soul is gaining way—   60

so, seeing that Miracle surpass the mark
   of former beauty, I sensed that I was turning,
   together with Heaven, through a greater arc.   63

And such a change as fair-skinned ladies show
   in a short space of time, when from their faces
   they lift the weight of shame that made them glow—   66

such change grew on my eyes when I perceived
   the pure white radiance of the temperate star—
   the sixth sphere—into which I was received.   69

Within that jovial face of Paradise
   I saw the sparkling of the love that dwelt there
   forming our means of speech before my eyes.   72

As birds arisen from a marshy plain
   almost as if rejoicing in their forage
   form, now a cluster, now a long-drawn skein—   75

so, there, within their sheaths of living light,
   blest beings soared and sang and joined their rays,
   and *D*, then *I*, then *L* formed on my sight.   78

First they sang and moved to their own song;
   then having formed themselves into a letter,
   they stopped their song and flight, though not for long.   81

O holy Pegasean who consecrates
   the power of genius, giving it long life,
   as it, through you, gives life to cities and states—   84

so fill me with your light, that as it shines
   I may show forth their image as I conceive it:
   let your own power appear in these few lines!   87

In five times seven vowels and consonants
   they showed themselves, and I grasped every part
   as if those lights had given it utterance.   90

The first words of that message as it passed
   before me were *DILIGITE IUSTITIAM.*
   QUI IUDICATIS TERRAM were the last.   93

Then, in the fifth word, at the final *M*
   they stayed aligned, and silvery Jupiter
   seemed to be washed in a gold glow around them.   96

More lights descended then and took their place
   on top of the *M*, and sang, as I believe,
   a hymn to the Good that draws them to Its grace.   99

Then—just as burning logs, when poked, let fly
   a fountain of innumerable sparks
   (from which fools used to think to prophesy)—   102

more than a thousand of those lights arose,
   some to a greater height, some to a lesser,
   each to the place the Sun that lit it chose.   105

And as each took its place in that still choir
   I saw the head and shoulders of an eagle
   appear in the fixed pattern of that fire.   108

The One who paints there needs no guide's behest.
   He is Himself the guide. From Him derives
   the skill and essential form that builds a nest.   111

The other sparks, at first content to twine
   in the form of golden lilies round the M
   now moved a bit, completing the design.   114

O lovely star, how rich a diadem
   shown forth to let me understand our justice
   flows to us from the heaven you begem.   117

Therefore I pray the mind that initiated
   your power and motion, to observe the source
   of the smoke by which your ray is vitiated;   120

that it be moved to anger once again
   against the buyers and sellers in the temple
   whose walls were built of blood and martyr's pain.   123

O soldiery of Heaven to whose array
   my mind returns, pray for all those on earth
   who follow bad example and go astray.   126

In earlier eras wars were carried on
   by swords; now, by denying this man or that
   the bread the Heavenly Father denies to none.   129

But you who scribble only to scratch out,
   remember that Peter and Paul, who died for the vineyard
   you trample, still defend the good you flout.   132

Well may you say: "My heart's wish is so set
   on the image of the saint who lived alone
   and who was forced to give his head in forfeit,   135

as if it were a favor at a 'ball—
   what do I care for the Fisherman or old Paul!"

Notes

1–3. *that holy mirror*: Cacciaguida. The image is of the blest soul as a mirror and reflector of God's ray. (Cf. XIV, 40–42.) *the bitterness*: Of the prophesied exile and of the triumph of his enemies. *the sweetness*: Of prophesied poetic fame.

4–6. Beatrice tells Dante to put away the bitter part of his thoughts (of revenge). She reminds him that she is close to God whose justice rights all wrongs, and that she will always be there as his protector. Her allegorical function as Divine Revelation is, of course, especially relevant here.

12. *Another's*: God's.

13–18. The vision of God's eternal bliss, rayed directly into Beatrice's eyes, and so reflected to Dante, fills his soul entirely and drives from it all thoughts of seeking revenge for the wrongs done him.

17. *face*: As he often does, Dante uses *aspetto* ("face") to mean "eyes."

25. *the holy ray*: Cacciaguida.

34. *Look at the arms of the cross*: Cacciaguida is speaking from within the base of the cross. He wants Dante to look up to the arms.

38 ff. THE GREAT WARRIORS OF GOD. Joshua, succeeding Moses, led Israel into the promised land. Judas Maccabaeus freed Israel from the Syrian tyranny. Charlemagne, in driving the Moors out of Europe, restored the Empire and freed the Spanish church. Roland (Orlando in Italian) was the nephew of Charlemagne and his greatest knight. (See *Inferno*, XXXI, 17, note.) William of Orange, hero of various medieval French romances, was the ideal of the Christian knight and was said to have died a monk. Rinoardo Rainouart served under William as his chief lieutenant. He was reputed to have been a convert from paganism and to have died in holy orders but he, like William, is largely a legendary figure. Godfrey or Gottfried of Bouillon was the leader of the first crusade and became the first Christian king of Jerusalem. He died in 1100. Robert Guiscard, son of Tancred d'Hauteville, a Norman war leader, joined with his brothers in 1046 to war against the Saracens in southern Italy, becoming duke of Puglia and of Calabria. He died in 1085.

39. *nor did the saying reach me before the sight*: I.e., the naming and the flashing of these souls take place in the same instant.

49–63. THE ASCENT TO JUPITER. As usual the transition to the next sphere is rapid. Cacciaguida returns to his place in the right arm of the cross and joins with the choir when it resumes its singing. (Cf. XV, 7–12, and note.) Beatrice becomes still more beautiful and still more radiant and Dante senses that he has entered the next Heaven.

57. *including even the last*: The phrasing is unusual but unusually exact. Beatrice grows more beautiful and more radiant with each new ascent. Now, entering the sixth Heaven, her new beauty exceeds not only her accustomed beauty, but even its own last manifestation (see lines 7–12) which Dante lacked power to describe.

61. *that Miracle*: Beatrice.

63. *through a greater arc*: It is unlikely that such a change of motion would register on merely human senses, but each ascending sphere must, necessarily, revolve through a greater arc than the last, being farther from the center.

64–69. Dante has just passed from the redness of Mars to the whiteness of Jupiter, and in about the time it takes a fair-skinned lady to grow pale again when she recovers from a blush of shame, his eyes adjust to the new radiance. Whatever Dante understood of the ability of ladies to recover from a sense of shame, his intent is clear, and the mood of the image is appropriate if the reader will visualize one of those quick flushes of innocence and maiden modesty much admired in the courtly tradition, though rare in ours.

68. *the temperate star*: Ptolemy described Jupiter as a temperate mean between hot Mars and cold Saturn. Appropriately, it serves as the Heaven of the wise and just— souls who were the models of proportioned and temperate being.

70. *jovial*: The other name of Jupiter is, of course, Jove. Dante is punning, intending both "Jove" and "jovial."

72. *our means of speech*: The alphabet.

70 ff. DANTE'S VISION OF THE WISE AND JUST. Dante's conception here was unprecedented in his times, but the modern reader can grasp it easily by conceiving the vision as a huge moving electric sign of the sort called "spectaculars." The lights of the sign are the radiances of the spirits themselves. Those lights first spell out a message, one letter at a time. The last word of the message is then transformed into an eagle, which is then ornamented by further recombinations of the lights. In the Canto that follows the eagle will move its beak and speak, and then, taking flight, circle around Dante.

78–99. THE ALPHABET MESSAGE. The message formed by the lights, beginning with the letters *D*, and *I*, and *L* running to thirty-five letters, is: *DILIGITE IUSTI-TIAM QUI IUDICATIS TERRAM*—"Love righteousness, ye that are judges of the earth."

82. *Pegasean*: The Muses drink from the spring called Hippocrene that sprang from the earth where Pegasus struck it with his hoof. The nine Muses together may properly be called Pegaseans. Dante uses the singular form, perhaps to invoke the Muses generally.

88–90. *five times seven*: The thirty-five letters of the spelled-out message. *they*: The souls within their sheaths of light. *as if those lights had given it utterance*: I do not know why hearing a letter spoken should make it "graspable" than seeing it flash across the sky, but Dante, a primitive art critic at best, was always filled with awe by the sort of visual representation that seemed to make the viewer hear what he was seeing. (Cf. *Purgatorio*, X, 52–60.)

95–96. *silvery Jupiter*: Jupiter was reputed to have a silvery sheen that set it apart from other white stars. The souls, however, are encased in sheaths of golden light.

102. *prophesy*: By asking a question (for example, "How many years shall I live?"), then poking the fire, and counting the sparks to get an answer.

104–105. *greater . . . lesser . . . to the place the Sun that lit it chose*: See once more XIV, 40–42. It is the Sun (God) who decrees the pattern of the eagle, assigning to each soul its place in the pattern according to the amount of grace It rays forth to each.

109–11. The general meaning of this passage is clear enough: God is the creator whose creation is guided by no other, Himself being the guide. The last line, however, is in Dante's densest style. "Essential form" is a Scholastic term equivalent to "form" in the Platonic sense. "Nest," I think, must be taken as a lovely symbol of the way in which God's art fills His creation. Birds, though they know nothing about architecture, draw from God the skill (the virtue) that enables them to build intricate and beautiful nests. So, by extension, are all the arts of this world derived from the guidance of the Unguided.

112. *The other sparks*: "Innumerable sparks" shot up from the vision and "more than a thousand of them" rose to form the head and shoulders of the eagle. The other sparks first wove lilies around the *M*; then, moving a little, completed the body of the eagle by filling out the body of the original *M*. If the letter is visualized in the rounded form common in medieval manuscripts and much like our lower case "m," and if the head and shoulders of an eagle are drawn in above the "m," it takes little imagination to visualize how the "m" could form the eagle's body. In the figure below, the dotted lines suggest the manner of the change.

113. *lilies*: Could not fail to suggest the French monarchy, as the Eagle could not fail to suggest the Empire. Dante may very well mean that, were wisdom and justice to rule, France should adorn the Empire in union with it instead of following its own divisive course.

115–117. *O lovely star*: Jupiter. Earthly justice is an effect of its influence upon men. It is the ideal of earthly justice the souls have been expressing in their flashing message and in the symbolism of the eagle and of the lilies.

122. *the temple*: The Church. Dante, at sight of the Imperial Eagle of justice, is moved to inveigh against papal avarice and corruption. "*M*," as various commentators have pointed out, is the first letter of *Monarchia*. In *De Monarchia*, I, 11, Dante had argued: "Justice is possible only under a [good] monarchy." If this inference from the *M* is valid (and Dante was, in fact, much given to such devices) we are once more on the theme of a spiritual church within a strong temporal empire as the one hope of Europe.

123. *blood*: If the original text reads "sangue." Some texts read *"segni"* ("signs," of which the English rendering would be "signs/portents/miracles/prophecies").

126. *bad example*: Of papal corruption.

128–129. *now, by denying . . . the bread*: The bread of God's grace, particularly as received through the sacraments. By denying the sacraments through excommunications and interdictions, the papacy wages war against peace and justice, forcing men and states to buy back the sacraments that should rightfully be theirs.

130. *you*: Dante uses the singular form *"tu."* He must, therefore, be referring to a single evil pope. If he is speaking as of 1300 that pope would, of course, be Boniface

VIII. *scribble only to scratch out*: Instead of preparing bulls that will clarify God's intent to all time, the evil popes merely scribble excommunications, interdictions, and denials of justice in order to cancel them again for a fee.

134. *the image of the saint*: John the Baptist. But in a bitter irony, Dante portrays the corrupt popes as having their hearts set not on the saint but on his image, for it was stamped on the Florentine gold florin. Thus their love of St. John is the love of money. *who lived alone*: In the desert. (See *Luke*, I, 80.)

135–136. *his head in forfeit . . . favor at a ball*: The daughter of Herodias so pleased Herod with her dancing that he offered her "whatsoever she would ask." She asked for the head of John the Baptist on a charger, and against his own inclination Herod kept his word (*Matthew*, XIV, 1–11. *Mark*, VI, 21–28).

137. *the Fisherman*: St. Peter. Used here as a familiar and contemptuous term. *old Paul*: St. Paul. Again the form of address shows lack of respect.

Canto XIX

THE SIXTH SPHERE: JUPITER

The Just and Temperate Rules · The Eagle

The Eagle made up of the many souls of the Just and Temperate Rulers moves its beak and speaks as if it were a single entity, announcing that it is the chosen symbol of *Divine Justice.* Dante is afire to understand the nature of the Divine Justice and begs the Eagle to explain it, but he is told that the infinity of God's excellence must forever exceed his creation, and that none may fathom His will, whereby it is presumptuous of any creature to question the Divine Justice. Man must be content with the guidance of Scripture and with the sure knowledge that God is perfect, good, and just.

Dante had once pondered the justice of virtuous pagans. The Eagle tells him it is not for him to sit in judgment on God's intent. It affirms that except as he believes in Christ no soul may ascend to Heaven, yet it adds that the virtuous pagan shall sit nearer Christ than many another who takes Christ's name in vain.

The Eagle concludes with a *Denunciation of the Bestialized Kings of Christendom* in 1300.

Before me, its great wings outspread, now shone
   the image of the eagle those bright souls
   had given form to in glad unison.   3

Each seemed a little ruby in the sky,
   and the sun's ray struck each in such a way
   the light reflected straight into my eye.   6

What I must now call back from memory
   no voice has ever spoken, nor ink written.
   Nor has its like been known to fantasy.   9

For I saw and heard the beak move and declare
   in its own voice the pronouns "I" and "mine"
   when "we" and "ours" were what conceived it there.   12

"For being just and pious in my time,"
   it said, "I am exalted here in glory
   to which, by wish alone, no one may climb;   15

and leave behind me, there upon the earth,
   a memory honored even by evildoers,
   though they shun the good example it sets forth."   18

Just as the glow of many living coals
   issues a single heat, so from that image
   one sound declared the love of many souls.   21

At which I cried: "O everlasting blooms
   of the eternal bliss, who make one seeming
   upon my sense of all your many perfumes—   24

my soul has hungered long: breathe forth at last
the words that will appease it. There on earth
there is no food with which to break its fast.   27

I know that if God's justice has constructed
its holy mirror in some other realm,
your kingdom's view of it is not obstructed.   30

You know how eagerly I wait to hear;
you know the what and wherefore of the doubt
I have hungered to resolve for many a year."   33

Much as a falcon freed of hood and jess
stretches its head and neck and beats its wings,
preening itself to show its readiness—   36

so moved the emblem that was all compounded
of praises of God's grace; and from it, then,
a hymn they know who dwell in bliss resounded.   39

Then it began to speak: "The One who wheeled
the compass round the limits of the world,
and spread there what is hidden and what revealed,   42

could not so stamp his power and quality
into his work but what the creating Word
would still exceed creation infinitely.   45

And this explains why the first Prideful Power,
highest of creatures, because he would not wait
the power of the ripening sun, fell green and sour.   48

And thus we see that every lesser creature
is much too small a vessel to hold the Good
that has no end; Itself is Its one measure.   51

Therefore, you understand, our way of seeing,
which must be only one ray of the Mind
that permeates all matter and all being,   54

cannot, by its very nature, be so clear
but what its Author's eye sees far beyond
the furthest limits that to us appear.   57

In the eternal justice, consequently,
the understanding granted to mankind
is lost as the eye is within the sea: 60

it can make out the bottom near the shore
but not on the main deep; and still it is there,
though at a depth your eye cannot explore.   63

There is no light but from that ever fresh
and cloudless Halcyon; all else is darkness,
the shadow and the poison of the flesh.   66

By now, much that was hidden from your view
by the living Justice of which you used to ask
so many questions, has been shown to you.　69

For you used to say, 'A man is born in sight
of Indus' water, and there is none there
to speak of Christ, and none to read or write.　72

And all he wills and does, we must concede,
as far as human reason sees, is good;
and he does not sin either in word or deed.　75

He dies unbaptized and cannot receive
the saving faith. What justice is it damns him?
Is it his fault that he does not believe?'　78

—But who are you to take the judgment seat
and pass on things a thousand miles away,
who cannot see the ground before your feet?　81

The man who would split hairs with me could find
no end of grounds for questioning, had he not
the Scriptures over him to guide his mind.　84

O earthbound animals! minds gross as wood!
Itself good in Itself, the Primal Will
does not move from Itself, the Supreme Good!　87

Only what sorts with It is just. It sways
toward no created good, but of Itself
creates all Good by sending forth Its rays."　90

As a stork that has fed its young flies round and round
above the nest, and as the chick it fed
raises its head to stare at it, still nest-bound—　93

so did that blessèd image circle there,
its great wings moved in flight by many wills,
and so did I lift up my head and stare.　96

Circling, it sang; then said: "As what I sing
surpasses your understanding, so God's justice
surpasses the power of mortal reasoning."　99

Those blazing glories of the Holy Ghost
stopped, still formed in the sign that spread the honor
of Rome across the world, to its last coast,　102

grew still, then said: "To this high empery
none ever rose but through belief in Christ,
either before or after his agony.　105

But see how many now cry out 'Christ! Christ!'
who shall be farther from him at the Judgment
than many who, on earth, did not know Christ.　108

Such Christians shall the Ethopian scorn
  when the two bands are formed to right and left,
  one blest to all eternity, one forlorn.   111

What shall the Persians say to your kings there
  when the Great Book is opened and they see
  the sum of their depravities laid bare?   114

There shall be seen among the works of Albert,
  that deed the moving pen will soon record
  by which Bohemia shall become a desert.   117

There shall be seen the Seine's grief for the sin
  of that debaser of the currency
  whose death is waiting for him in a pig's skin.   120

There shall be seen the pride whose greed confounds
  the mad Scot and the foolish Englishman
  who cannot stay within their proper bounds.   123

There, the debaucheries and the vain show
  of the Spaniard and the Bohemian who knew
  nothing of valor, and chose not to know.   126

And there, the cripple of Jerusalem:
  a 1 put down to mark the good he did,
  and then, to mark his villainies, an *M*.   129

There, the baseness and the greedy rage
  of the watchdog who patrols the burning island
  on which Anchises closed his long old age;   132

and to make clear how paltry is his case,
  his entry will be signs and abbreviations
  that the record may say much in little space. 135

And there the filthy deeds shall be set down
  of his uncle and his brother, each of whom
  cuckolded a great family and a crown.   138

There shall be marked for all men to behold
  Norway's king and Portugal's; and Rascia's,
  who lost most when he saw Venetian gold.   141

Oh happy Hungary, had she suffered all
  without more griefs ahead! Happy Navarre
  were she to make her peaks a fortress wall!   144

And every Navarrese may well believe
  the omen of Nicosìa and Famagosto
  whose citizens have present cause to grieve   147

the way their beast, too small for the main pack,
keeps to one side but hunts on the same track."

Notes

10–12. The eagle, though composed of many souls, speaks as a single entity, so symbolizing the unity of these souls in God.

15. *by wish alone*: No soul may earn such glory by its own merit, but only by the gift of God's grace. (See XIV, 42.)

18. *it*: The memory of those who lived in justice and piety.

25. *breathe forth*: I.e., speak, but phrased in this way in order to continue the figure of flowers breathing forth their perfumes.

26–27. *on earth . . . no food*: Mortal understanding cannot satisfy Dante's hunger to know the nature of God's justice.

28–33. DANTE'S QUESTION ON THE NATURE OF DIVINE JUSTICE. The question is best understood by referring to IX, 61–63. "On high are mirrors (you say 'Thrones') and these reflect God's judgment to us." "On high" as spoken by Cunizza in the sphere of Venus could mean "in Jupiter" or somewhere higher. Whatever the rendering of this point, Dante is asking for nothing less than an explanation of the nature of God's Justice. In reply, he is given many particulars by the way, but the sum of it is that God's Justice is inscrutable and that the question is unanswerable. Not even these enormously elevated souls can know the full answer.

40–45. THE INFINITY OF GOD'S EXCELLENCE. Great as is God's creation, the Word (*Logos*, the creating source) cannot create what it does not Itself infinitely exceed.

46. *the first Prideful Power*: Satan. He was first among all created things, yet (as above) infintely below his creator. His sin of pride was in wishing to equal God (instead of ripening and growing more perfect in His light) and therefore he fell green and sour.

52. *our*: Some texts read "your," but such a reading would imply that only mortals are inferior to God, whereas the eagle's point is that all parts of His creation (including the angels and the souls of the blest) are infinitely inferior to God. In line 59 the eagle does speak of what would be "your world" (mankind). There it has changed the grounds of the discussion and is explicating the difference between heavenly and mortal understanding—a second infinity of difference that does not invalidate the first.

65. *Halcyon*: God. His revelation is the one light. By comparison, the light of the intellect is a darkness and leads to error (the shadow) and to sin (the poison) of the flesh.

68–69. *of which you used to ask so many questions*: About the nature of divine justice. See lines 25–33.

80. *a thousand miles away*: Is not intended as a map measurement but as a general way of saying "a great distance." From God, as one may understand. From the man by Indus' water. And from both.

82. *with me*: With the eagle, as the heavenly symbol of God's justice. There would be endless grounds for doubts and fine arguments had not Scripture set forth all a man need know about Divine Justice.

91–96. A double long-tail simile: as the stork did, so did the image; as the chick did, so did Dante.

95. *by many wills*: By the conjoined wills of all the gemlike souls that make up the image of the eagle.

97–99. The harmonies and the language of the hymn are beyond Dante's powers of comprehension. He, like a fledgling stork, gapes up at what is beyond him. And so is it with his grasp of Divine Justice.

101. *stopped*: Their circling.

102–105. Note how adroitly this pause serves to mute the effective but no longer needed image of the mother stork circling its chick, and to sound in its place the majesty of the eagle.

105. *before*: By belief in the promised Messiah. *after*: By belief in the risen Christ. It is by allowing a place in Heaven to what may be called the "Messianic Christians" that Dante can seat such souls as Solomon's in Heaven.

106–108. As before Dante rhymes the name of Christ only with itself.

108. *the many who did not know Christ*: So in part to answer Dante's doubts about the virtuous Hindu. All the Virtuous Pagans, to be sure, will be closer to Christ in Limbo than those professing Christians who damned themselves. But since Dante has allowed one pagan (Virgil) to ascend to the Earthly Paradise, it is perhaps his understanding that the Virtuous Pagans will be settled there after the Judgment. Higher, as the eagle has declared in line 104, they cannot go, though in *Purgatorio*, I, 74–75, Cato of Utica is marked for special blessing in the resurrection.

109. *Ethiopian*: Used as a generic term for all pagans.

110. *when the two bands*: At the seat of Judgment when the sheep and the goats are set to Christ's right and left hand.

112. *Persians*: Another generic term for pagans.

115. *Albert*: Albert I, Emperor from 1298 to 1308. He is the "German Albert" of *Purgatorio*, VI, 97 ff. He invaded Bohemia in 1304. As of 1300, therefore, the pen must wait four years before it moves to record his deed.

118–120. *the Seine*: For France, generally. *that debaser of the currency*: Philip the Fair (*v. Purgatorio*, VII, 109, and note; and XX, 85–93, and note). He debased the coinage to finance his wars and brought misery to France. Dante, it is well to remember, punished counterfeiters (*Inferno*, XXX) not out of love of money, but because a sound coinage was an essential principle of social order. *death . . . in a pig's skin*: In 1314, in the course of a royal hunt, a wild boar ran under Philip's horse. Philip was thrown and died soon after of his injuries. Dante certainly relishes such a way of bringing down the mighty and evil.

121–123. *greed*: For more land. *Scot . . . Englishman*: The Scottish and English kings in their endless border wars.

124–126. *the Spaniard*: Probably Ferdinand IV. *the Bohemian*: Probably Wenceslaus IV (*v. Purgatorio*, VII, 102, note). With or without specific identification, Dante's general point is clear.

127–129. *cripple of Jerusalem*: Charles II of Anjou, known as Charles the Lame. (*v.* VIII, 82, note; *Purgatorio*, VII, 124–129, and *Purgatorio*, XX, 79, note.) He was King of Jerusalem only by the act of giving himself that title. In the Book of Judgment his virtues will be marked by the number 1 and his villainies by the letter *M* (a thousand).

131–132. *the watchdog*: Frederick II of Sicily (*v. Purgatorio*, III, 115). *burning island*: Sicily. *on which Anchises*: He died at Drepanum, modern Trapani.

133. *paltry*: So paltry a man could not be allowed much space in the book of the Recording Angel, but his life was so evil that his sins will have to be written down in signs and abbreviations in order to squeeze them all in.

137–138. *his uncle and his brother*: King James of Majorca, brother of James I of Aragon; and James II of Aragon, son of James I. Each disgraced the crown he wore; both disgraced the house of Aragon. *cuckolded*: They disgraced their family and their kingdom from within, as a wife does when she cuckolds her husband.

140. *Norway's king*: In 1300, Hacon VII. *Portugal's*: Dionysus. *Rascia's*: Orosius II. Rascia was part of Serbia. Orosius seems to have altered the metal content of Venetian money on a substantial scale. *lost most*: His falsifying of the currency would slate him for a meeting with Master Adam in Hell (*v. Inferno*, XXX).

142. *Hungary*: Andrew III, a good king, ruled in 1300. Hungary had endured many ruinous wars. If only her sufferings were all behind her, as of course they are not.

143–144. *Navarre*: The ancient kingdom of what is now southern France and northern Spain. Joanna of Navarre married Philip the Fair of France in 1284 but remained sole ruler of Navarre. After her death in 1304, her son Louis inherited Navarre, and when his father died in 1314, he became Louis X, king of France and Navarre. So Navarre passed under French rule, the bitterness of which they were to learn in full. Hence, they would have been happier had they armed the mountains around them (the Pyrenees) as fortress walls for keeping out the French.

145–149. *Nicosìa and Famagosta*: The two principal cities of Cyprus. *Their beast*: Henry II of the French house of Lusignan was king of Cyprus in 1300, a man given to debaucheries for which the people paid dearly. Every Navarrese would have done well in 1300 to have taken him as an example of French rule and of what Navarre would suffer when it passed under the French crown. *the main pack*: Of the bestialized kings of Christendom. Henry is too small a beast to run in the main pack but he runs along to one side of it on the track of the same bestialities.

Canto XX

The Just and Temperate Rulers · The Eagle

The eagle pauses briefly and the spirits of the blest sing a hymn, not as one symbolic entity, but each in its own voice. The hymn ended, the Eagle resumes speaking in its single voice, and identifies as the chief souls of this sphere those lusters that compose its eye. In order they are: *David, Trajan, Hezekiah, Constantine, William of Sicily,* and *Ripheus.*

Dante is astonished to find Trajan and Ripheus in Heaven, both of whom he had thought to be pagans, but the Eagle explains how by the special grace of God Ripheus was converted by a vision of Christ a millennium before His descent into the flesh, and Trajan was returned from Limbo to his mortal body long enough to undergo conversion to Christ and to allow his soul to mount to Heaven.

So once again for Dante's doubts about the virtuous Hindu and God's justice, for who can say how many more God has so chosen to his grace? The Eagle concludes with a praise of God's predestined justice, rejoicing even in the limitation of its own knowledge, resting in the assurance that the unknown consequences of God's will cannot fail to be good.

When the sun, from which the whole world takes its light,
    sinks from our hemisphere and the day fades
    from every reach of land, and it is night;   3

the sky, which earlier it alone had lit,
    suddenly changes mode and reappears
    in many lights that take their light from it.   6

I thought of just that change across night's sill
    when that emblem of the world and of its leaders
    had finished speaking through its sacred bill;   9

for all those living lights now shone on me
    more brightly than before, and began singing
    a praise too sweet to hold in memory.   12

O heavenly love in smiling glory wreathed,
    how ardently you sounded from those flutes
    through which none but the holiest impulse breathed.   15

When then those precious gems of purest ray
    with which the lamp of the sixth heaven shone
    let their last angel-harmony fade away,   18

I seemed to hear a great flume take its course
    from stone to stone, and murmur down its mountain
    as if to show the abundance of its source.   21

And as the sound emerging from a lute
   is tempered at its neck; and as the breath
   takes form around the openings of a flute—   24

just so, allowing no delay to follow,
   the murmur of the eagle seemed to climb
   inside its neck, as if the neck were hollow.   27

There it was given voice, and through the bill
   the voice emerged as words my heart awaited.
   And on my heart those words are written still.   30

"Look closely now into that part of me
   that in earth's eagles can endure the Sun."
   the emblem said, "—the part with which I see.   33

Of all the fires with which I draw my form
   those rays that make the eye shine in my head
   are the chief souls of all this blessèd swarm.   36

The soul that makes the pupil luminous
   was the sweet psalmist of the Holy Ghost
   who bore the ark of God from house to house: 39

now, insofar as he himself gave birth
   to his own psalms, he is repayed in bliss,
   and by that bliss he knows what they are worth.   42

Of the five that form my eyebrow's arc, the one
   whose glory shines the closest to my beak
   consoled the widow who had lost her son;   45

now he understands what price men pay
   who do not follow Christ, for though he learns
   the sweet life, he has known the bitter way.   48

The next in line on the circumference
   of the same upper arch of which I speak,
   delayed his own death by true penitence;   51

now he knows that when a worthy prayer
   delays today's event until tomorrow,
   the eternal judgment is not altered there.   54

The third, to give the Shepherd sovereignty,
   (with good intentions though they bore bad fruit)
   removed to Greece, bearing the laws and me;   57

now he knows the evil that began
   in his good action does not harm his soul
   although it has destroyed the world of man.   60

And him you see upon the arc beneath
   was William of that land that mourns the life
   of Charles and Frederick, as it mourns his death;   63

now he knows how heaven's heart inclines
to love a just king, as he makes apparent
by the radiance with which his being shines.   66

Who would believe in the erring world down there
that Ripheus the Trojan would be sixth
among the sacred lusters of this sphere?   69

Now he knows grace divine to depths of bliss
the world's poor understanding cannot grasp.
Even *his* eye cannot plumb that abyss."   72

Like a lark that soars in rapture to the sky,
first singing, and then silent, satisfied
by the last sweetness of its soul's own cry—   75

such seemed that seal of the Eternal Bliss
that stamped it there, the First Will at whose will
whatever is becomes just what it is.   78

And though my eagerness to know shone clear
as colors shining through a clearest glass,
I could not bear to wait in silence there;   81

but from my tongue burst out "How can this be?"
forced by the weight of my own inner doubt.
—At which those lights flashed in new revelry.   84

And soon then, not to keep me in suspense,
the blessèd emblem answered me, its eye
flashing a yet more glorious radiance.   87

"I see that you believe these things are true
because I say them. Yet, you do not see how.
Thus, though believed, their truth is hidden from you. 90

You are like one who knows the name of a thing
whose quiddity, until it is explained
by someone else, defies his understanding.   93

By every living hope and ardent love
that bends the Eternal Will—by these alone
the Kingdom of Heaven suffers itself to move.   96

Not as men bend beneath a conqueror's will.
It bends because it wishes to be bent.
Conquered, its own benificence conquers still.   99

You marvel at the first and the fifth gem
here on my brow, finding this realm of angels
and gift of Christ made beautiful by them.   102

They did not leave their bodies, as you believe,
as pagans but as Christians, in firm faith
in the pierced feet one grieved and one would grieve. 105

One rose again from Hell—from whose dead slope
    none may return to Love—into the flesh;
    and that was the reward of living hope;   108

of living hope, whose power of love made good
    the prayers he raised to God to bring him back
    to life again, that his will might be renewed.   111

And so the glorious soul for whom he prayed,
    back in the flesh from which it soon departed,
    believed in Him who has the power to aid.   114

Believing, he burst forth with such a fire
    of the true love, that at his second death
    he was worthy of a seat in this glad choir.   117

The other, by that grace whose blessings rise
    out of so deep a spring that no one ever
    has plumbed its sources with created eyes,   120

gave all his love to justice, there on earth,
    and God, by grace on grace, let him foresee
    a vision of our redemption shining forth.   123

So he believed in Christ, and all his days
    shunning the poisonous stink of pagan creeds,
    he warned the obstinant to change their ways.   126

More than a thousand years before the grace
    of baptism was known, those maids you saw
    at the right wheel, stood for him in its place.   129

Predestination! Oh how deep your source
    is rooted past the reach of every vision
    that cannot plumb the whole of the First Cause!   132

Mortals, be slow to judge! Not even we
    who look on God in Heaven know, as yet,
    how many He will choose for ecstasy.   135

And sweet it is to lack this knowledge still,
    for in this good is our own good refined,
    willing whatever God Himself may will."   138

In these words the blest emblem of that sphere
    gave me these gentle curatives of love
    which which my clouded vision was made clear.   141

And as the skillful harpist, string by string,
    makes every cord attend on a good singer,
    adding a greater pleasure to the singing;   144

so, I recall, that as it spoke to me
    these paradisal words, the holy lights
    of Trajan and Ripheus in sweet harmony,   147

as if they blinked their eyes with one accord,
made their flames pulse in time with every word.

Notes

1–12. THE DAY AND NIGHT IMAGE AND THE HEAVENLY EAGLE. The metaphor is subtle but its essence simple. The symbolic eagle (as a unity projected by many blessèd wills) stops speaking through its bill as a single entity and a hymn rings forth not from the eagle, but from the many lustrous beings who compose it. Each of these beings is now giving voice to its joy not through the symbol but from itself.

This change Dante compares to the twin faces of the heavens: by day there is the one direct light of the Sun (a unity, as with the Eagle); by night there is the shining of many heavenly bodies, all of which (according to Dante's astronomy) glow not from within themselves but by reflecting the light of the Sun (as these souls glow by reflecting God's ray).

our hemisphere: The land mass of the world, all of it north of the equator, and all contained in an arc of 180° from India to Spain. Thus, when the sun is 90° west of Spain it lights only the waters on the other side of the earth and all the land mass is dark.

31. *that part*: The eye. The Eagle is once again speaking as a unified entity. The ancients believed that the eagle could look straight into the sun. Note that only one eye is mentioned. The symbolic eagle must be conceived as appearing in heraldic profile, despite the fact that it flew a circle around Dante's head in the previous canto.

38. *the sweet psalmist*: David. See *Inferno*, IV, 58.

40–42. The first thought here, a simple one, is that the measure of his present bliss (the reward being proportionate to the act) lets David know the true worth of his psalms. That thought is complicated by the parenthetical "insofar, *etc.*" Since the Holy Ghost moved in David, Dante seems to be saying, some of his psalms sprang from It, and his present bliss cannot be repayment to him for an act of the Holy Ghost. As Dante pointed out in VI, 118–120, part of the delight of each heavenly soul consists in knowing that his bliss is exactly equal to his merits.

43. *the one*: Trajan. See *Purgatorio*, X, 70–90.

48. *he has known the bitter way*: Trajan had been long in Limbo. See note to 106 ff., below.

49–54. Hezekiah, offering a true repentance on his death bed, was allowed to live for fifteen more years (*II Kings*, XX, 1–11; *II Chron.*, XXXII, 24–26; *Isaiah*, XXXVIII, 1–7). *now he knows*: To what extent prayer may vary the preordained divine plan without altering it. These lines are best understood by referring to *Purgatorio*, VI, 28–51. Few readers will have remembered the point Dante left open in those lines, but Dante seems never to forget. To read him is to experience mind in extraordinary order.

55–60. The Emperor Constantine. With the purest of intentions (so Dante's version of it) Constantine ceded the Western Empire to the Church (the Shepherd) and moved his seat of Empire to Greece, bearing with him Roman law and "me" (the Roman Eagle). See *Purgatorio*, XXXII, 124–129; *Inferno*, XIX, 109–111, and notes.

Constantine earns in Heaven that the evil consequences of a good action (or the good consequences of an evil action) do not change the nature of the original action —a point made by Aquinas in his *Summa*.

62. *William*: William II (the Good), king of the Two Sicilies from 1166 to 1189. He was the last of the house of Tancred. In Dante's time, the kingdom of Naples passed to Charles the Lame (XIX, 127) and the Kingdom of Sicily to Frederick II (XIX, 131). Sicily mourns its present evil as it mourns the passing of its happiness with the death of William.

65. *as he makes apparent*: The degree of brilliance flashed forth by each soul is the measure of its relative bliss. William, by shining more brightly than most there, shows that he is more blest than most.

68. *Ripheus*: Virgil mentioned him once (*Aeneid*, II, 426 ff.) as the one most just man among the Trojans and as the one who most loved the right. No more is known of him, and Dante is thus free (see below) to invent a pre-Christian conversion for him. *sixth*: Dante says "fifth" among those who make up the eyebrow. Beginning with David as the eyeball, such a count would rank Ripheus sixth among the souls of this sphere; and, rhyme dictating, I have so rendered the passage.

89. *see how*: See how these things can be true.

92. *quiddity*: I.e., "thingness" or "whatness." In Scholastic terminology: "that which causes a thing to be what it is."

94–99. These paradoxes are, of course, the language of the mystery: God is unmovable but God is love and as love moves Him, He yields gladly to it, conquering by His act of love.

102. *and gift of Christ*: Not in Dante's text but necessary for the line and clearly implicit in what the Eagle is saying. Trajan and Ripheus, having been pagans, would not have had the gift of Christ's redemption. It is for this reason that Dante marvels at finding them in Heaven.

103–105. Ripheus and Trajan, as the Eagle will explain, did not "leave their bodies" as pagans but as Christians and firm believers, one (Trajan) in the pierced feet (the Crucifixion) that had already taken place; the other (Ripheus) in the Crucifixion yet to come.

106–117. THE RESURRECTION AND CONVERSION OF TRAJAN. Dante follows a legend that Gregory I (Pope from 590 to 604 and later St. Gregory) prayed so ardently for the salvation of Trajan that God's voice replied "I grant pardon to Trajan." Since God so granted, it was, of course, predestined that he should so grant. Trajan, therefore, could never have been truly damned, for no prayer can help the damned. But since none may go from Hell to Heaven (with the exception of those souls Christ took with him in the Harrowing of Hell), it was necessary to restore Trajan to the flesh long enough to permit his conversion to Christ.

108. *living hope*: Of Gregory.

120. *created eyes*: Nothing God has created can plumb the mystery of its creator. Compare lines 130–132 below.

121–129. THE CONVERSION OF RIPHEUS. Unhampered by any historical record, Dante creates a legend of Ripheus as a Christian before the fact. Granted a vision of Christ to come, he believed utterly and was saved. In place of baptism (over a thousand years before baptism came into being) the three maids who stood at the right wheel of the Chariot of the Church in the Pageant of the Terrestrial Paradise (i.e., the Three Theological Virtues) stood as his godmothers in some equivalent ritual. (*V. Purgatorio*, XXIX, 121 ff.)

132. *that cannot plumb*: As, certainly, no human vision can. As even the chosen souls of Heaven cannot.

135. *how many He will choose*: Had Dante cared to, he could have made a rather accurate guess as to God's intention when he reached the Empyrean. In XXX, 128–132, he tells us that few seats are left open in Paradise (Judgment Day will take place when the last throne of Heaven is filled). And in XXXII, 25–27, he has St. Bernard point out the empty thrones, the number of which Dante might reasonably have guessed, though had he done so he would have found himself prophesying the end of the world within fairly tight limits, a prophecy Dante wisely chose not to utter. Poetry is, among other things, the art of knowing what to leave out.

Canto XXI

THE SEVENTH SPHERE: SATURN

The Contemplative: Peter Damiano

Beatrice and Dante enter the Sphere of Saturn. *Beatrice Does Not Smile* in her new bliss to announce their arrival, for her radiance would then be such that Dante's mortal senses would be consumed, as Semele was consumed by the Godhead of Jupiter. Rather, Beatrice announces that they are there and commands Dante to look into the crystalline substance of that Heaven for the vision he will see of the *Souls of the Contemplative.*

Dante turns and beholds a vision of a *Golden Ladder* on which countless Splendors arise and descend wheeling like birds in flight. That host of the blessèd descends only as far as a given rung, but one radiance among them draws closer to Dante and indicates by its radiance that it is eager to bring him joy. It is the soul of *Peter Damiano*, a Doctor of the Church, renowned for a severely ascetic life even in high church office. Peter Damiano explains to Dante that *The Mystery of Predestination* is beyond the reach of all but God, and that men should not presume to grasp it. He concludes with a *Denunciation of Papal Corruption*, and at his words, all the souls of Saturn fly down to form a ring around him and thunder forth *Heaven's Righteous Indignation* at evildoers. So loud is their cry that Dante cannot make out their words, his senses reeling at that thunderclap of sound.

My eyes were fixed once more on my lady's face;
    and with my eyes, my soul, from which all thought,
    except of her, had fled without a trace.   6

She did not smile. "Were I to smile," she said,
    "You would be turned to ash, as Semele was
    when she saw Jupiter in his full Godhead;   3

because my beauty, which, as it goes higher
    from step to step of the eternal palace,
    burns, as you know, with ever brighter fire;   9

and if it is not tempered in its brightening,
    its radiance would consume your mortal powers
    as a bough is shattered by a bolt of lightning.   12

We have soared to the Seventh Splendor, which is now
    beneath the Lion's blazing breast, and rays
    its influence, joined with his, to the world below.   15

Now make your eyes the mirror of the vision
    this mirror will reveal to you, and fix
    your mind behind your eyes in strict attention."   18

Could any man conceive what blessèd pasture
 my eyes found in her face when I turned away,
 at her command, to find another nurture—   21

then would he know with what a rush of bliss
 I obeyed my heavenly escort, balancing
 one side and the other, that joy against this.   24

Within the crystal that bears round the world
 the name of its great king in that golden age
 when evil's flag had not yet been unfurled,   27

like polished gold ablaze in full sunlight,
 I saw a ladder rise so far above me
 it soared beyond the reaches of my sight.   30

And I saw so many splendors make their way
 down its bright rungs, I thought that every lamp
 in all of heaven was pouring forth its ray.   33

As grackles flock together at first light,
 obeying a natural impulse to move as one
 to warm their night-chilled feathers in glad flight;   36

after which, some go off and do not come back,
 others return to the points from which they came,
 and others stay with the flock in its wheeling track;   39

—just such an impulse seemed to work among
 those sparkling essences, for they flocked together
 the instant they had reached a certain rung.   42

One that came nearest where we stood below
 then made itself so bright I said to myself:
 "I well know with what love for me you glow!"   45

But she from whom I await the how and when
 of my speech and silence, was still; and despite my
                                        yearning
 I knew it was well to ask no questions then.   48

She saw in the vision of Him who sees all things
 what silence held my eager tongue in check,
 and said to me: "Give your soul's impulse wings!"   51

"O blessèd being hidden in the ray
 of your own bliss," I said in reverence,
 "I am not worthy, but for her sake, I pray,   54

who gives me leave to question, let me know
 why you, of all this sacred company,
 have placed yourself so near me, here below;   57

and tell me why, when every lower sphere
 sounds the sweet symphony of Paradise
 in adoration, there is no music here."   60

"Your sight is mortal. Is not your hearing, too?"
he said. "Our song is still for the same reason
Beatrice holds back her smile—for love of you. 63

Only that I might make your spirit gladder
by what I say and by the light that robes me,
have I come so far down the sacred ladder. 66

Nor was it greater love that spurred me: here
as much—and more—love burns in every soul,
as the flaming of these radiances makes clear. 69

But the high love that makes us prompt to serve
the Judge who rules the world, decrees the fate
of every soul among us, as you observe." 72

"O sacred lamp," I said, "I understand
that in this court glad love follows the will
of Eternal Providence, needing no command; 75

but the further point I cannot grasp is this:
why, among all these blisses with whom you dwell,
were you alone predestined to this office?" 78

Before I finished speaking, that lamp of grace
like a millstone at full speed, making an axle
of its own center, began to spin in place. 81

And then the Love within the lamp replied:
"I feel the ray of God's light focused on me.
It strikes down through the ray in which I hide. 84

Its power, joined to my own, so elevates
my soul above itself, that I behold
the Primal Source from which it emanates. 87

My bliss flames only as that ray shines down.
As much of glory as I am given to see
my flame gives back in glory of its own. 90

But in all Heaven, the essence most aglow,
the Seraph that has God in closest view,
could not explain what you have asked to know. 93

The truth of this is hidden so far down
in the abyss of the Eternal Law,
it is cut off from all created vision. 96

Report what I have said when you are back
in the mortal world, that no man may presume
to move his feet down so profound a track. 99

On earth the mind is smoke; here, it is fire.
How can it do there what it cannot do
even when taken into heaven's choir?" 102

I left that question, his own words having thus
  prescribed me from it; and, so limited,
  was content to ask him humbly who he was.   105

"Not far from your own birthplace, row on row
  between Italy's two shores, peaks rise so high
  that on them thunder sounds from far below.   108

A humpback ridge called Catria rises there.
  Beneath it stands a holy hermitage
  once given entirely to meditation and prayer."   111

So, for the third time now, that soul of grace
  began to speak, continuing: "I became
  so rooted in God's service in that place,   114

I lived on lenten olive-food alone
  and bore both heat and cold indifferently,
  rejoicing ever more in contemplation.   117

Once that cloister sent here, sphere on sphere,
  harvests of souls. Now all its works are vain
  as, soon now, righteous punishment shall make clear. 120

I was Peter Damiano there, and became
  Peter the Sinner by the Adriatic
  in the abbey sacred to Our Lady's name.   123

Little was left me of my mortal course
  when I was chosen and summoned to wear the hat
  that seems forever to pass from bad to worse.   126

Cephas, and the great ark of the Holy Ghost
  once came among mankind barefoot and gaunt,
  eating by chance, with charity as their host.   129

But now your pastors are so bloated and vain
  they go propped on either side, with a man before
  and another coming behind to bear the train.   132

They cover even their mounts with the cloaks they wear
  so that two beasts move under a single hide.
  O Heavenly Patience, how long will you forebear!" 135

As he spoke these words, I saw more ardors yearning
  downward in circling flight, from rung to rung;
  and grow more radiant with every turning.   138

Round him they came to rest, and all burst forth
  in unison of love: a cry so loud
  the like of it has not been heard on earth.   141

Nor could I understand it, for the peal
of that ominous thunder made my senses reel.

Notes

5. *as Semele was*: Semele loved Jupiter (Zeus) and Juno (Hera) tricked the girl into begging Jupiter to show himself to her in the full splendor of his godhead (as the other gods saw him). Semele was consumed to ash by that radiance. (See Ovid, *Metamorphoses*, III, 253 ff., and *Inferno*, XXX, 1–2, note.)

13–15. *the Seventh Splendor*: The Seventh Heaven (Saturn). Once again the arrival is instantaneous. For the reasons given, Beatrice does not manifest the new bliss by smiling, but simply announces that they have arrived. *the Lion*: The Constellation Leo. Dante describes Saturn as being in conjunction with Leo, as in fact it was in parts of March and April of 1300. Thus the influence of Leo is mixed with that of Saturn.

17. *this mirror*: The Sphere of Saturn. All the spheres are, in one sense, crystalline reflectors of God's light. In another sense, of course, they let the light through undiminished, but such differenecs are of the mystery. Dante uses the same figure for the sun in *Purgatorio*, IV, 62.

19–24. A graciously turned devotion. The thought is complex yet sweetly balanced. Sense: "Could the reader begin to imagine how sweet it was to feast my eyes (like lambs in blessèd pasture) on the beatitude of Beatrice's face, then he might understand how sweet it was to obey even her command to turn away from such bliss to find another."

25–27. *the crystal*: The Sphere of Saturn. It bears around the world the name ot Saturn, who was the world's king in the Golden Age of man before sin had appeared among mankind.

28–42. THE VISION OF THE HEAVENLY LADDER. "And he dreamed, and beheld a ladder set up on earth, and the top of it reached to heaven: and behold the angels of God ascending and descending on it." So *Genesis*, XXVIII, 12, describes Jacob's ladder. Here, however, Dante adapts it to his own purposes, placing it within the crystal of the Sphere of Saturn, describing it as being made of blazing gold (to signify the worth of the contemplative soul? as the height of the ladder signifies that soul's ascent to the top of heaven?).

The normal course of the contemplative soul would, of course, be to ascend rather than to descend the ladder. Love, however, remains a first principle, and to welcome Dante and Beatrice in purest love, these souls descend joyously, though forever rising again, to return to their natural height of bliss.

42–45. *a certain rung*: Dante offers no further specifications. The rung seems simply to fix a point below which these souls (whose natural impulse is to rise) choose not to descend at first, though one spirit does draw closer (as, later, all do). This first spirit indicates, by the increase of its radiance, the love it feels for Dante, and its readiness to offer him any service, though protesting that its love is no greater than that of any other soul of this host.

43. *And one*: St. Peter Damiano (1007–1072), as he will later identify himself. He was never officially canonized though he was venerated in Ravenna. He was, however, officially pronounced a Doctor of the Church. His many writings enjoin strict monastic rules and mortification of the flesh.

Born in Ravenna, he became a Benedictine and entered the Camadolese house at Fonte Avellana in 1035, became Prior about 1043, and Cardinal-Bishop of Ostia in 1057 or 1058, accepting his elevation, as all reports agree, against his own inclination, and continuing in every high office a life of monastic severity.

46–51. Beatrice's allegorical role as Divine Revelation is especially relevant here. Looking into the vision of all-seeing God, she sees Dante's yearning and gives him permission to speak to the waiting soul.

52–60. DANTE'S QUESTIONS. With Beatrice's permission, Dante asks the spirit, first, why it was chosen to come closer than the others, and, second, why there is no heavenly harmony to be heard in this Sphere, since all the Spheres below ring with joyous singing. The second question, being the more important, is answered first (lines 61–63), and then the first (lines 64–72).

67–69. The reply may, perhaps, best be taken as an example of heavenly modesty. At the same time, however, it is partly a statement of fact: all souls in heaven are glorious with love (as the radiances about the poet make clear), and since Peter Damiano is not the foremost soul in Heaven, there are those whose souls will shine more brightly than does his.

70–72. These lines are, in effect, Dante's way of introducing the theme of predestination, which will be discussed later. If the language is difficult, the difficulty lies not in the language itself but in the fact that the concept is unusual and necessarily abstruse. Peter Damiano explains that he descended farther than the other souls because he was predestined to by the will of God. In so saying, he makes clear that every action of all these souls, as each goes up and down the ladder, is similarly predestined. Every heavenly soul, in the grace of love that is granted to it, is a glad servant of the Divine will that assigns the fate of each.

And here, certainly, is the extension of what Virgil foresaw dimly in *Purgatorio*, XXVII, 140–143, in telling Dante he was free to follow his own inner impulse. "Here," Virgil says, "your will is upright, free, and whole." At the Paradisal level, however, glorified by revelation, Dante makes it clear that it is not a matter of the individual will but of joyous identification with the service for which God has predestined each soul. (*Cf.* III, 85: "In His will is our peace." See also XX, 130 ff.)

74. *this court*: The court of Heaven.

75. *Eternal Providence*: It may be well, in this discussion of predestination, to remind some readers that "providence" derives from Latin *pro*, before, and *videre*, to see. Note also that the heavenly souls need not be commanded to follow God's foreseeing and predestined will: this glad love suffices to move them in concord with God.

79–81. *Before I finished speaking*: Before the last three words of line 78. It is at the sound of the word "predestination" that the soul of Peter Damiano begins to spin for joy. Dante does not specifically say that it went on spinning as it talked, but he does describe the soul as beginning to spin, and he does not say that it stopped. The spinning seems an aptly Dantean way to indicate great joy. The soul, moreover, goes into a trance in which it has a direct vision of God; and the spinning might well serve as an established symbol of the trancelike state (cf. "whirling dervish"). There is also the thematic precedent of the grackles in whirling flight, whereby the act of spinning becomes a motif of this canto. Allegorically, too, it may be said that the contemplative soul revolves around its own center (which is, of course, love).

For all these reasons, I think the soul of Peter Damiano should be visualized as spinning on through the rest of the canto, whirled round and round in a glorious vision of God.

82–90. PETER DAMIANO'S VISION OF GOD. Speaking in a trance of bliss, spinning for joy in the rapture of its vision, yet moved by heavenly Love to share its joy with Dante, the soul explains that it is experiencing a vision of God, who focuses His ray into the ray in which the soul hides. (Dante says "in which I embowel myself," i.e., embody myself, and I have been unable to render this felicity.) As has been explained in XIV, 40–42, this is God's grant of grace, and the soul shines brighter to the extent that grace enables it to reflect God's ray.

96. *created vision*: The vision of which any created thing is capable. Only God's uncreated vision can plumb the mystery of predestination. And if the truth is beyond the highest soul in Heaven—as Peter Damiano goes on to say—how can the feeble mind of man think to reach to it? For this reason, he charges Dante, upon his return to the world, to warn men away from presuming to know the unknowable (for such a presumption would involve the sin of pride).

99. *to move his feet*: As a hunter does.

104–105. *so limited, was content*: The question of the soul's identity is not a trivial one. In due observance of fit proportion, however, it has to be recognized as a lesser matter than the abysmal mystery of predestination.

109. *Catria*: Lies between Gubbio and Pergola. Below it (the "holy hermitage") stands the monastery of Santa Croce di Fonte Avellana of the Camaldolese rule (established at Camaldoli about 1012 by St. Romualdo). This rule minimized the community organization of the monastery but established a particularly severe rule for the individual monks.

115–116. *lenten olive-food*: Olive oil being common in Italy, and butter and lard (like all animal products) being expensive, and therefore luxurious, lenten food (*"cibi di liquor di'ulivi"*) was prepared in nothing but olive oil. Here we should probably understand a diet of simple crusts dipped in olive oil. Even at that, Peter Damiano seems to be suggesting that he ate high on the ecclesiastical hog: Rohrbacher's "Ecclesiastical History" (cited by Scartazzini) gives the diet of the order as plain bread and water for four days of each week, with a few greens added on other days, and with such feasting regularly interrupted by days of fasting. *both heat and cold*: The rule required the monks to go barefoot.

120. *as . . . righteous punishment shall make clear*: As everyone in Heaven seems to do, Peter mourns for the good old days when Fonte Avellana sent whole harvests of monks to heaven (and particularly, one may infer, to Saturn, which is the kingdom of the contemplative). Now, however, the saintly rule has been corrupted, and since God's justice will not long tolerate such a state of affairs, that corruption shall be made manifest by the punishment God shall, soon now, send down upon it.

121–123. This tercet has been a scholar's battleground and reputations have fought and died over the question of its proper punctuation and of its relevance to the historical record, such as it is. Civilian readers need only know that Peter went by both names, adopting the second as an act of piety (he had adopted the first in gratitude to his brother, who had made possible his education), and that he went to Ravenna ("by the Adriatic") as a papal emissary. He lived there for two years in the monastery of Santa Maria Pomposa.

124. *little was left me of my mortal course*: Peter became a cardinal in 1057 or 1058. He died in 1072.

125-126. *the hat*: Of a cardinal. In passing from one wearer to another, it seems forever to go from a bad man to a worse—another lament for the corruption of the times.

127. *Cephas*: The name Christ gave to Simon, who became Peter. The word means "rock" in Hebrew, as *"pietra"* does in Italian, "Pietro" being the masculine form of the word used as a man's name. Cf. "founded on a rock." *the great ark of the Holy Ghost*: St. Paul.

130. *pastors*: Can only mean "popes" here—those who fill the offices once held by the pastors Peter and Paul. The parish priests of Dante's time may have eaten better than did Peter Damiano, but they did not move about without a great retinue, a warder out in front to clear the way, servants and officials on either side to press back the throng, and a trainbearer following to carry the trailing skirts of their opulent robes.

136-138. *yearning . . . and grew more radiant*: So moved by their renewed joy in the justice of Peter Damiano's denunciation; for their love of what is good and their righteous indignation at what is evil are a conjoined impulse in them. They proceed to cry out like thunder against the evils Peter Damiano has condemned, their cry so loud that Dante's senses reel at the thunderous sound and are unable to make out the words of the cry. Heaven has no other voice in which to speak of evil. Such, on the Paradisal level, is righteous indignation. Cf. *Inferno*, VIII, 43 and note.

Canto XXII

THE SEVENTH SPHERE: SATURN
The Contemplative: St. Benedict

ASCENT TO THE SPHERE OF THE FIXED STARS

THE EIGHTH SPHERE: THE FIXED STARS
Dante Looks Back at the Universe Below

Dante's senses still reeling, he turns to Beatrice, who reassures him and prophesies that he will live to see *God's Vengeance Descend on the Corruptors of the Church*. She then calls his attention to the other souls of this sphere. Looking up, Dante sees *A Hundred Radiant Globes*, one of which draws near and identifies itself as the heavenly splendor that had been *St. Benedict*.

Benedict explains that the Golden Ladder, like the contemplative life, soars to the summit of God's glory, and he laments that so few of his Benedictine monks remain eager to put the world behind them and begin the ascent, for they are lost in the degeneracy of bad days. Yet God has worked greater wonders than would be required to restore the purity of the church.

So saying, Benedict is gathered into his heavenly choir of radiances, and the whole company ascends to the top of the sky and out of sight.

Beatrice then makes a sign and Dante feels himself making the *Ascent to the Eighth Sphere, The Sphere of the Fixed Stars*. But before the souls of that Sphere are revealed to him, Beatrice bids him look back to see how far she has raised him. Dante looks down through the Seven Spheres in their glory, seeing all the heavens at a glance, and the earth as an insignificant speck far below. Then turning from it as from a puny thing, he turns his eyes back to the eyes of Beatrice.

> My senses reeled, and as a child in doubt
>   runs always to the one it trusts the most,
>   I turned to my guide, still shaken by that shout;   3
>
> and she, like a mother, ever prompt to calm
>   her pale and breathless son with kindly words,
>   the sound of which is his accustomed balm,   6
>
> said: "Do you not know you are in the skies
>   of Heaven itself? that all is holy here?
>   that all things spring from love in Paradise?   9
>
> Their one cry shakes your sense: you can now see
>   what would have happened to you had they sung,
>   or had I smiled in my new ecstasy.   12
>
> Had you understood the prayer within their cry
>   you would know now what vengeance they called down,
>   though you shall witness it before you die.   15

The sword of Heaven is not too soon dyed red,
nor yet too late—except as its vengeance seems
to those who wait for it in hope or dread.   18

But look now to the others. Turn as I say
and you shall see among this company
many great souls of the Eternal Ray."   21

I did as she commanded. Before my eyes
a hundred shining globes entwined their beams,
soul adding grace to soul in Paradise.   24

I stood there between longing and diffidence
and fought my longing back, afraid to speak
for fear my questioning might give offense.   27

And the largest and most glowing globe among
the wreath of pearls came forward of its own prompting
to grant the wish I had not given tongue.   30

These words came from within it: "Could you see,
as I do, with what love our spirits burn
to give you joy, your tongue would have been free.   33

To cause you no delay on the high track
to the great goal, I shall address myself
to none but the single question you hold back.   36

The summit of that mountain on whose side
Cassino lies, once served an ill-inclined
and misted people in their pagan pride.   39

And I am he who first bore to that slope
the holy name of Him who came on earth
to bring mankind the truth that is our hope.   42

Such grace shone down on me that men gave heed
through all that countryside and were won over
from the seductions of that impious creed.   45

These other souls were all contemplatives,
fired by that warmth of soul that summons up
the holy flowers and fruits of blessèd lives.   48

Here is Romualdus, and Maccarius, too.
Here are my brothers who kept within the cloister
and, never straying, kept hearts sound and true."   51

And I to him: "The love you have made clear
in speaking as you have, and the good intent
I see in all the glories of this sphere,   54

have opened all my confidence: it grows
and spreads wide on your warmth, rejoicing in it
as does, in the Sun's heat, a full-blown rose.   57

I therefore beg you, Father: can I rise
  to such a height of grace that I may see
  your unveiled image with my mortal eyes?"   60

And he then: "Brother, this shall be made known
  in the last sphere. Your wish will be answered there
  where every other is, including my own.   63

There, every wish is perfect, ripe, and whole.
  For there, and there alone, is every part
  where it has always been; for it has no pole,   66

not being in space. It is to that very height
  the golden ladder mounts; and thus you see
  why it outsoars the last reach of your sight.   69

The patriarch Jacob saw it, saw it mount
  to lean on that very sill, that time he dreamed it
  covered with angels beyond all mortal count.   72

To climb it now, however, none makes haste
  to lift his feet from earth. My rule lives on
  only to fill the parchments it lays waste.   75

The walls that were retreats in their good hour
  are dens for beasts now; what were holy cowls
  are gunny sacks stuffed full of evil flour.   78

But even compound usury strikes less
  against God's will and pleasure, than does that fruit
  whose poison fills the hearts of monks with madness. 81

For all the goods of the Church, tithes and donations,
  are for the poor of God, not to make fat
  the families of monks—and worse relations.   84

The flesh of mortals is so weak down there
  that a good beginning is not reason enough
  to think the seedling tree will live to bear.   87

Peter began with neither silver nor gold;
  I, with prayer and fasting. And Brother Francis
  in humble poverty gathered souls to his fold.   90

And if you look at the origins of each one,
  then look again at what it has become,
  you will see that what was white has changed to dun. 93

Yet Jordan flowing backward, and the sea
  parting as God willed, were more wondrous sights
  than God's help to His stricken church would be."   96

So did he speak; then faded from my eye
  into his company, which closed about him,
  and then, like a whirlwind, spun away on high.   99

And my sweet lady with a simple sign
   raised me along that ladder after them,
   conquering my nature with her power divine.   102

There never was known down here, where everything
   rises or falls as natural law determines,
   a speed to equal the motion of my wing.   105

Reader, so may I hope once more to stand
   in that holy Triumph, for which I weep my sins
   and beat my breast—you could not draw your hand   108

out of a tongue of flame and thrust it back
   sooner than I sighted and had entered
   the sign that follows Taurus on Heaven's track.   111

O glorious constellation! O lamp imbued
   with great powers, to whose influence I ascribe
   all my genius, however it may be viewed!   114

When I drew my first breath of Tuscan air
   the Sun, the father of all mortal life,
   was rising in your rays and setting there.   117

And then when I was granted Heaven's grace
   to enter the great wheel that gives you motion,
   I was led upward through your zone of space.   120

To you devoutly now my prayer is sped:
   make my soul worthy of the call it hears
   to the great passage that still lies ahead!   123

"You are so near the final health of man
   you will do well to go clear-eyed and keen
   into that good," my Beatrice began.   126

"Therefore, before you enter further here
   look down and see how vast a universe
   I have put beneath your feet, bright sphere on sphere.   129

Thus may you come in the fullness of delight
   to the Triumphant Court that comes in joy
   through the round ether to your mortal sight."   132

My eyes went back through the seven spheres below,
   and I saw this globe, so small, so lost in space,
   I had to smile at such a sorry show.   135

Who thinks it the least pebble in the skies
   I most approve. Only the mind that turns
   to other things may truly be called wise.   138

I saw Latona's daughter glowing there
   without that shadow that had once misled me
   to think her matter was part dense, part rare.   141

My eyes looked on your son, Hyperion,
    nor did they falter. And wheeling close around him,
    I saw the motion of Maia and Dione.   144

Next I saw how Jupiter mediates
    between his father and son, and I understood
    why the motion of one and the other vacillates.   147

And all the seven, in a single view,
    showed me their masses, their velocities,
    and the distances between each in its purlieu.   150

And turning there with the eternal Twins,
    I saw the dusty little threshing ground
    that makes us ravenous for our mad sins,   153

saw it from mountain crest to lowest shore.
Then I turned my eyes to Beauty's eyes once more.

Notes

13–15. *the prayer within their cry*: Dante heard the sound of the cry, but not the prayer within it (what the words said). We may now understand that these souls called on God to show His wrath at the corruption of the Church, and perhaps of the papacy in particular. What retribution Dante will witness before he dies is not specified. History suggests the capture of Boniface VIII at Alagna by the mercenaries of Philip the Fair under William de Nogaret as one possible vengeance (v. *Purgatorio*, XX, 85–93 and note). Or it may suggest Philip's maneuver in 1304 whereby Clement V was elected Pope and the papacy removed to Avignon (v. *Purgatorio*, XXXII, 158 and note). But neither event can be taken as a large-scale visitation of God's wrath, and neither, certainly, ended papal corruption. Beatrice's prophecy is best taken, I believe, as simply one more way of denouncing the corrupt. Dante would, of course, have welcomed such a visitation of God's wrath, but he clearly has no specific event in mind.

16–18. Beatrice is making the point that God's vengeance is always taken at the proper and inevitable moment, never too soon, and never too late, though to the wicked (who wait for it with dread) it seems always to come too soon, and to the pious (who wait for it with hope for the downfall of evil) it seems always to come too late.

19. *the others*: Dante's attention has been fixed on St. Peter Damiano. Now Beatrice directs his attention to the other great spirits of this sphere.

28–29. *the largest and most glowing globe*: Contains the spirit of St. Benedict (480–543). There is some historic uncertainty about his life, the recorded facts having been subject to pious increment. He was born at Nursia in Umbria and went to Rome for his education. There, appalled by the wickedness of the Romans, he left the world about the year 500 and lived in a cave on Mount Subiaco, his rigid asceticism and holiness drawing disciples to him, though he seems never to have been ordained. About 525 he moved with his followers to Monte Cassino and there, after destroying a temple to Apollo, founded the great central monastery of the Benedictine order on the rule he had already established for his followers on Subiaco. He died at Monte Cassino on March 21, his feast day, and was buried in the same grave with his sister, Ste. Scholastica.

33. *your tongue would have been free*: To ask the questions Dante held back from speaking.

34–36. St. Benedict's exact point in this passage will be clear if one recalls that many of the heavenly spirits have answered not only the questions Dante had spoken or framed in his mind, but others, too, though he had not yet thought to think them. To speed Dante on his way, St. Benedict will answer only the one question Dante has clearly in mind.

38. *once served*: By having upon its peak a temple of Apollo. Especially in the outlying districts, paganism survived well into the Middle Ages. St. Benedict is saying that he was the first to bring Christianity to the mountain people on and around Cassino.

45. *that impious creed*: The cult of Apollo.

49. *Romualdus*: St. Romualdo (956–1027), founder of the Camaldolese Order (*v.* note to XXI, 109). *Maccarius*: Probably St. Maccarius of Alexandria (died 404) a disciple of St. Anthony. He lived in the desert between the Nile and the Red Sea and was reputed to have been the leader of 5000 eremites. Dante may have had in mind Maccarius the Egyptian (circa 301–391) also a disciple of St. Anthony. Or Dante may have thought of the two as one person.

55–57. A literal rendering of these lines might read: ["These things] have caused my confidence to dilate just as the sun does a rose, which, when opened, becomes as great as it had the power to become."

60. *unveiled image*: The image in which the soul would appear were Dante's eyes not blinded by the radiance that veils it.

61. *Brother*: Dante has addressed him as "Father" out of respect, but all the souls in Heaven are brothers and sisters of the one Father, and above honorary titles.

62. *in the last sphere*: In the Empyrean. There (*v.* XXXII, 35) St. Benedict does appear to Dante among the glories of the mystic rose.

63. *including my own*: My own wish to content you in your wish. St. Benedict does not imply that every wish finds fulfillment in the presence of God, but rather that "this good" and "every other" do.

64–69. Only the mystery of revelation will make clear, and only to the elected soul, these mysteries of God's love. In one sense, we may gather from the vocabulary of exaltation, all good is from God, and since no part of good has ever left Him, every part of every good wish, in being returned to God's presence, is back where it always has been. For God is also ubiquitous, His presence limited by no boundary, since it is not a dimension of space.

It is to the crown of that sublimity that exists beyond dimension that the Golden Ladder mounts, outsoaring the reach of any soul's (physical or spiritual) sight.

70–72. The vision of Jacob's ladder is described in *Genesis*, XXVIII, 12 ff.

73–75. Another sounding of the theme of latter-day degeneracy, St. Benedict's rule for the contemplative was designed to raise the soul toward Heaven (as if climbing the ladder). Now, however, none of his monks is in any hurry to forego the pleasures of the earth, and so the Benedictine rule lives on as a waste of the parchments on which it is copied, since none observe it.

78–84. Once the clerics sought God in prayer, meditation, and acts of charity. Then all the possessions of the church were held in trust for the poor, to be distributed to them at need. Now, however, the fruit of avarice has poisoned the hearts of clerics, and the wealth that should be used to help God's poor is used by the monks themselves to swell the purse and position of their families, or for worse relations (the latter probably signifying that corrupt monks kept mistresses and bad companions in luxurious establishments).

86–87. Dante says, literally: "A good beginning is not enough [to certify the interval] from the birth of the oak to the harvest of acorns."

91. *each one*: Of the three folds founded by the three great saints.

94–96. *Jordan . . . the sea parting*: Most commentators read these lines as a statement of hope: "The same will that caused the Jordan to flow backward and the Red Sea to divide, could will the lesser miracle of restoring purity to the church." Others read it in the opposite sense: "It would be more wondrous to see Jordan flow backward and the sea divide than to see the church restored to purity." Especially in view of the fact that Beatrice has promised Dante that he would live to see God's vengeance on the corruptors of the Church, the more hopeful interpretation seems to be the more likely.

98. *his company*: The other souls of the Contemplative. Their choir closes about him (an allegory of the unity of the souls of Heaven?) and instantly ascends to the top of the sky.

100–111. ASCENT FROM SATURN TO THE SPHERE OF THE FIXED STARS. Once again the ascent is instantaneous. Beatrice, by a simple sign, raises Dante to the next sphere, her power overcoming his nature. On one level his "nature" is his mortal weight, which is here uplifted despite the forces of gravity. On another, it is the human soul, gross and imperfect in itself, yet able by the power of Divine Revelation to soar toward God.

103. *down here*: On earth, and within the operations of earth's natural laws, from which Dante has escaped.

105. *my wing*: To signify "my flight." But note that Dante says "wing" rather than "wings." He may have intended an allegorical point. The soul, while still earthbound, may seek to soar with reason as one wing and with faith as the other. In Heaven, however, the ascent is accomplished by the single wing of faith, that power of the soul that brings it to the transcendent recognition of God.

108. *beat my breast*: In penitence.

108–109. *draw your hand . . . and thrust it back*: The sequence of this action is deliberately reversed in another hysteron-proteron. See note to II, 23–24.

111. *the sign that follows Taurus*: Gemini. *Heaven's track*: The Zodiac.

112–123. INVOCATION OF GEMINI. Dante's invocation is spoken not in the *persona* of the pilgrim en route, but in that of the poet at his desk, looking back to his great journey.

Gemini, Dante lets us know, is the zodiacal sign under which he was born (lines 115–117) and whose influence determined his poetic genius (lines 112–114). In 1265 the Sun entered the sign of Gemini on May 18 and passed from it on June 17. (The exact date of Dante's birth is not known, but these dates set firm limits for it.) It is allegorically felicitous certainly that Dante, in ascending to (being born into) the Sphere of the Fixed Stars, should pass through his natal constellation.

124. *the final health of man*: God.

134. *this globe*: The Earth.

139. *Latona's daughter*: The Moon (as Diana, sister of Apollo, the Sun, both children of Latona).

140–141. *without that shadow*: See II, 46 ff. Dante is looking now at the face of the moon we call the dark side and which is never visible from Earth. The sun that lights it, moreover, must be between it and Dante, probably to one side, though it would be nothing now for His Heaven-heightened vision to see through the sun. As the next tercet indicates, Dante was at least able to look directly into the sun.

142. *your son, Hyperion*: The Sun as the son of Hyperion, himself the son of Uranus and Terra.

144. *Maia and Dione*: Here stand for Mercury and Venus. Maia was one of the seven sisters of the Pleiades and the mother of Mercury. Dione was the mother of Venus. I do not know why Dante takes the mothers for the children here.

145–147. *Jupiter . . . his father and son*: Jupiter was the son of Saturn and the father of Mars. The temperate planet, Jupiter, lies between the excessively hot planet Mars and the excessively cold planet Saturn. Such are the terms of Dante's astrology. Dante does not explain how this theory of a temperate mean between fire and ice allows him to understand the eccentricities of the orbits of Mars and Saturn—perhaps he conceives Jupiter as a moderating force that attracts the planets on its either side. Whatever the theory, the observable fact is that these planets, as seen from Earth, do wander all over the star chart; their orbits swing sometimes close to the sun and sometimes away, and they rise sometimes before it and sometimes after it. But Dante's reference here is all the more confusing in that all the planets wander in this way.

150. *purlieu*: Dante uses the word "*riparo*" (the place to which one repairs in the same sense that astrologers speak of "the house" of Mars or of some other planet. Hence Dante must mean the orbit of each considered as the place that is particularly its own.

151. *the eternal Twins*: Gemini.

152. *the dusty little threshing ground*: The Earth, so described as an insignificant and busy flat patch of dust as compared to the glory and serenity of the Heavens.

153. *Beauty's eyes*: The eyes of Beatrice, which are the eyes of Heaven.

Canto XXIII

The Triumph of Christ · *The Virgin Mary* · *The Apostles* ·
The Angel Gabriel · *St. Peter*

Beatrice stares expectantly toward that part of the sky where the Sun is at
its highest point, and Dante, moved by the joy of her expectation, follows
her look. Almost at once there descends from the highest Heaven the
radiant substance of the *Vision of Christ Triumphant* as it rays forth on
the garden of all those souls who have been redeemed through Christ. The
splendor too much for his senses, *Dante Swoons*. He is recalled to himself
by Beatrice and discovers that, newly strengthened as he has been by the
vision of Christ, he is able to look upon her smile of bliss.

Beatrice urges him to look at the Garden of Christ's Triumph, upon the
Rose of the *Virgin Mary* and the Lilies of the *Apostles*. Christ, taking
mercy on Dante's feeble powers, has withdrawn from direct view and now
rays down from above.

Dante fixes his eyes on the brightest splendor (the Virgin Mary) and
sees a crown of flame descend to summon her back to the Empyrean. It is
the *Angel Gabriel*. So summoned, Mary ascends to where her son is, and
the flames of the souls yearn higher toward her. There, among the souls
that remain below, Dante identifies *St. Peter*.

As a bird in its sweet canopy of green
    covers the nest of its beloved young
    through all the night when nothing can be seen;   3

but eager for the loved, lit face of things,
    and to go hunting for its fledglings' food
    in toil so glad that, laboring, she sings;   6

anticipates the day on an open bough
    and in a fire of love awaits the sun,
    her eyes fixed eagerly on the pre-dawn glow—   9

just so my lady waited—erect, intense—
    all her attention toward that part of heaven
    beneath which the sun's daily pace relents: 12

and I, observing her blissful expectation,
    became like one who yearns for more than he has,
    feeding his hope with sweet anticipation.   15

But the interval between *when* and *when* was slight—
    the *when* of my waiting, I say, and the *when* of seeing
    the sky began to swell with a new light.   18

And Beatrice said: "Before you now appears
    the militia of Christ's triumph, and all the fruit
    harvested from the turning of the spheres."   21

I saw her face before me, so imbued
  with holy fire, her eyes so bright with bliss
  that I pass on, leaving them unconstrued.   24

As Trivia in the full moon's sweet serene
  smiles on high among the eternal nymphs
  whose light paints every part of Heaven's scene;   27

I saw, above a thousand thousand lights,
  one Sun that lit them all, as our own Sun
  lights all the bodies we see in Heaven's heights;   30

and through that living light I saw revealed
  the Radiant Substance, blazing forth so bright
  my vision dazzled and my senses reeled.   33

Oh my Beatrice, sweet and loving guide!
  "What blinds you," she said to me, "is the very power
  nothing withstands, and from which none may hide.   36

This is the intellect and the sceptered might
  that opened the golden road, from Earth to Heaven,
  for which mankind had yearned in its long night."   39

Fire sometimes spreads so wide that it shoots forth
  from a cloud that can no longer hold it in,
  and against its nature, hurtles down to earth.   42

That feast of bliss had swollen my mind so
  that it broke its bounds and leapt out of itself.
  And what it then became, it does not know.   45

"Open your eyes and turn them full on me!
  You have seen things whose power has made you able
  to bear the bright smile of my ecstasy!"   48

As one whose sense have been stricken blind
  by a forgotten vision comes to himself
  and racks his wits to call it back to mind—   51

such was I at that summons, my spirit moved
  to a thankfulness that shall live on forever
  within the book where what is past is proved.   54

If there should sound now all the the tongues of song
  Polyhymnia with her eight sisters nourished,
  giving their sweetest milk to make them strong,   57

they could not help me, singing thus, to show
  a thousandth part of my lady's sacred smile,
  nor with what glory it made her features glow.   60

Just so, that Heaven may be figured forth,
  my consecrated poem must make a leap,
  as a traveler leaps a crevice there on earth.   63

My theme is massive, mortal shoulders frail
  for such a weight. What thoughtful man will blame me
  for trembling under it for fear I fail?   66

The seas my ardent prow is plowing here
  are no place for small craft, nor for a helmsman
  who will draw back from toil or cringe in fear.   69

"Why are you so enamored of my face
  you do not turn your eyes to see the garden
  that flowers there in the radiance of Christ's grace?   72

The Rose in which the Word became incarnate
  is there. There are the lilies by whose odor
  men found the road that evermore runs straight."   75

Thus Beatrice. And I, prompt to her guidance
  in fullest eagerness, raised my feeble lids
  once more to battle with that radiance.   78

At times when the sun, through broken clouds, has rayed
  one perfect beam, I have seen a field of flowers
  blazing in glory, my own eyes still in shade: 81

just so, I saw a host of hosts made bright
  by rays of splendor striking from above,
  but could not see the source of that pure light.   84

O Majesty that seals them in such glory!
  you raised yourself on high, withdrawing there
  in order that my feeble eyes might see!   87

The name of that Sweet Flower to which I pray
  morning and night, seized all my soul and moved it
  to fix my eyes upon the brightest ray;   90

and when both my eyes had been allowed to know
  the luster and magnitude of that chosen star
  that triumphs there as it triumphed here below,   93

from Heaven's height a torch of glory came,
  shaped like a ring or wreath, and spinning round her,
  it wound and crowned her in its living flame.   96

The sweetest strain that ever swelled aloud
  to draw the soul into itself down here,
  would be as thunder from a shattered cloud,   99

compared to the melody that then aspired
  from the bright lyre that crowned the purest gem
  by which the brightest heaven is ensapphired.   102

"I am the Angelic Love that wheels around
  the lofty ecstasy breathed from the womb
  in which the hostel of Our Wish was found;   105

so shall I wheel, Lady of Heaven, till
   you follow your great Son to the highest sphere
   and, by your presence, make it holier still."   108

Thus the encircling melody of that flame
   revealed itself; and all the other lamps
   within that garden rang out Mary's name.   111

The royal mantle whose folds are spread abroad
   round all the spheres, and that most burns and quickens
   being nearest to the breath and ways of God,   114

turned its inner shore at such a height
   above the point at which I then was standing
   that I could not yet bring it into sight.   117

I could not, therefore, with my mortal eyes
   follow the flight of that crowned flame that soared
   to join her son in the highest Paradise.   120

And as a newly suckled infant yearns
   after its mother with its upraised arms,
   expressing so the love with which it burns;   123

each of the splendors of that company
   extended its flame on high in such a way
   as made its love of Mary plain to me.   126

Then they remained there, still within my sight,
   singing *"Regina coeli"* in tones so sweet
   the memory still fills me with delight.   129

Oh what treasures cram and overflow
   those richest coffers of the eternal grace
   who sowed such good seed in the world below!   132

Here is true life and relish of the treasure
   their tears laid up in the Babylonian exile,
   in which Christ left man gold beyond all measure.   135

Here sits in triumph under the lofty Son
   of God and the Virgin Mary in His triumph,
   and in the company of everyone   138

crowned from the New or the Old Consistory,
   the soul that holds the great keys to such glory.

Notes

1–15. THE EAGERNESS OF BEATRICE. Beatrice is awaiting the vision of the Triumph of Christ. Dante does not know what expected delight has filled her with such bliss, but seeing her so tranced in expectation, he, too, begins to yearn for what has not yet been revealed.

The poet expresses this feeling of intense and joyous anticipation in a memorable long-tail simile of a mother bird that has spent the night covering its young, held there by love and by the night that keeps her from the joyous labors of hunting their food. Before the light of day, the mother bird is already out of the leaf-canopy, poised on an open bough to await the new dawn, and to begin her love's labors at the first possible instant.

Beatrice is compared to that mother bird. (Thematically, this expectation of a great new rebirth of the light must certainly be related to the fact that Dante is in Gemini, his zodiacal birth sign.) Dante, as if he were her fledgling, is fired by the contagion of Beatrice's blissful expectation.

This memorable figure marks the transition to the upper Heaven, for Dante and Beatrice are now beyond the planetary spheres, in the sphere of the Fixed Stars, and beyond them lies only the Empyrean itself, which is the total presence of God.

12. *the sun's daily pace relents*: At meridian the Sun seems to slow its pace. Beatrice is looking toward that part of heaven where the Sun (Divine Illumination) is at its noon height. It is all but inevitable that the vision of the Triumph of Christ should come from that portion of the sky.

16. *when*: Dante uses "when" (*quando*) as it is used in Scholastic terminology, meaning "time of" or "duration."

20-21. *all the fruit harvested from the turning of the spheres*: The first-created angels of Heaven did, of course, share in Christ's triumph, but they were not part of its harvest, which consisted of the redemption of the souls of men. Once the soul had entered into that triumph (mounted to Heaven), it would manifest itself in one of the spheres, though it was in essence in the choir of the Empyrean. Thus the militia of Christ must contain all the souls of glory whose manifestations populate the spheres of Heaven (including now the Sphere of the Fixed Stars).

In another sense "harvested from the turning of the spheres" intends the shaping influences of the spheres upon the souls of men, disposing them to the good that gains their triumph. And, of course, the phrase also intends "harvested from time" (i.e., distinct from the angels, who were never temporal).

24. *unconstrued*: In Scholastic terminology "to construe" meant "to express the true essense of a thing."

25-26. *Trivia*: Diana, the Moon, in her manifestation as a nymph. *eternal nymphs*: The stars. See *Purgatorio*, XXXI, 106.

30. *lights all the bodies*: Lights all stars (which are supposed, as the moon does, to send forth only the reflection of the sun's light).

32. *the Radiant Substance*: Of Christ.

33. *my vision dazzled*: Only a moment ago (XXII, 142-143) Dante had looked straight into the Sun without discomfort. At the vision of the radiance of Christ, however, Dante's senses reel, and in a moment he will swoon. The art of juxtaposing details in a way that constantly gives scale to an all-containing system of values is one of the marvels of Dante's genius.

35. *the very power*: Of Christ.

40. *fire*: Lightning.

42. *against its nature*: The nature of fire is to ascend toward the Sphere of Fire (v. I, 115, and *Purgatorio*, XXXII, 109 ff.). Contrary to its nature (which is to rise to God), Dante's spirit swoons and falls.

43. *That feast of bliss*: The vision of the Triumph of Christ.

46-48. See XXI, 4 ff. and 62 ff. There Beatrice had to hold back her smile of ecstasy because it would have destroyed Dante, whose sense could not have contained it. Now, allegorically, having sustained the vision of the Triumph of Christ and looked upon His Radiant Substance, Dante's eyes have been prepared for the full glory of Beatrice (Divine Revelation).

56-57. *Polyhymnia*: The Muse of sacred songs. (Her name means "many-hymned.") She and her eight sisters were the fountainhead of all song and all poetry. *their sweetest milk*: The Muses gave suck to the poets, thereby transmitting to them the powers of song. How these virgin sisters maintained their milk supply is one more item to be filed among the sacred mysteries.

61. *Just so*: Just as it is impossible to describe to mortal sensibilities the glory of the smile of Beatrice (an allegory of revelation), so must the poem that would describe Heaven leap over such matters as human understanding cannot fathom.

67-69. Cf. the opening lines of Canto II.

73-75. *The Rose*: The Virgin Mary. *the Word*: Logos. *the lilies*: Primarily, perhaps, the Apostles, but also the total of all souls that share in the Triumph of Christ, their example forever showing the straight way to others. *whose odor*: Cf. the common pious phrase, "odor of sanctity."

77. *lids*: Rather than eyes. Dante has just swooned at the radiance of Christ. Now, obedient to the command of Beatrice, he turns to look again, but with his eyes lidded, his mortal senses bracing themselves to bear the ineffable radiance (cf., too, his admonition in line 69. Only the spirit that will risk all may dare the glories of Heaven).

79-87. The figure is based on the common phenomenon of seeing a ray of sun light a field of flowers while one is standing in the shadow of covering cloud. So the rays of Christ's glory strike down to illuminate the souls of the redeemed, Christ, of his infinite mercy, having withdrawn from Dante's sight, for it could not have borne the full glory of His shining. Lines 85–87 may certainly be pondered as a possible allegory of the resurrection of Christ.

85. *seals*: The seal here would be the ray; the flowers, the wax that takes the impress of the light and shines forth as marked by the light.

88 ff. THE VISION OF THE VIRGIN MARY. Beatrice (line 73) has told Dante that Mary was among the radiances he saw before him. When Dante finally manages to fix his eyes on the splendor before him (the radiance of Christ having withdrawn mercifully) he makes out the brightest star in that host of splendors. As he watches, a crown of flame descends from the Empyrean and encircles her. This new radiance is God's messenger, Gabriel, the Angel of the Annunciation. *Sweet Flower, brightest ray*: The Virgin Mary. *had been allowed to know*: As always in Paradise, it is not Dante's will that discerns the vision (though he wills it utterly) but the souls that reveal themselves to him.

101–102. *gem . . . ensapphired*: The original is *zaffiro . . . s'inzaffira*. Dante must have chosen the sapphire as the gem of purest blue, the color of Heaven. *purest gem*: The Virgin Mary. *the bright lyre*: The Angel Gabriel. *the brightest heaven*: The Sphere of the Fixed Stars.

105. *Our Wish*: Christ. The womb of Mary was the hostel in which the Word found lodging in mortal flesh.

107. *the highest sphere*: The Empyrean.

110. *revealed itself*: Dante says literally, "impressed its seal," the equivalent of writing its signature, i.e., "identified itself."

112–114. *the royal mantle*: The Primum Mobile. *most burns*: With ardent joy. *and quickens*: Being the outer sphere whose revolutions control the turning of all those it encloses, it turns faster than any of the others.

115. *its inner shore*: The spheres of course, have depth. Could Dante's vision have reached to see the Primum Mobile it would have seen only its inner surface, here called a shore.

120. *to join her son*: As Gabriel had prayed her to do.

128. *Regina coeli*: Queen of Heaven.

133–135. Both the text and the interpretation of the original are disputed. I have settled for what seems to be the most direct rendering, taking "the Babylonian exile" to signify the soul's time on earth. Heaven, then, would be the longed-for Jerusalem. In their exile, in steadfast faith and holy tears, these souls laid up the heavenly treasure they now enjoy, as Christ left it to all men.

139. *Old and New Consistory*: The Old and the New Testament.

140. *the soul that holds the keys*: St. Peter.

Canto XXIV

The Triumph of Christ · St. Peter · The Examination of Faith

Christ and Mary having ascended to the Empyrean, St. Peter remains as
the chief soul of the Garden of Christ's Triumph. Beatrice addresses the
souls in Dante's behalf, and they, in their joy, form into a dazzling *Vertical
Wheel of Spinning Radiances.*

Beatrice then begs St. Peter to conduct an *Examination of Dante's Faith.*
St. Peter thereupon questions Dante on the *Nature of Faith, The Possession of Faith, The Sources of Faith, The Proof of the Truth of Faith,
Man's Means of Knowing that the Miracles of Faith Actually Took Place,*
and finally on *The Content of Christian Faith.*

Dante answers eagerly, as would a willing candidate being examined by
his learned master. The examination concluded, St. Peter shows his pleasure
by dancing three times around Dante.

"O spirits of that chosen company
    that feeds on the Lamb of God, the flesh of which
    satisfies hunger to all eternity—   3

if by God's grace this man is given a foretaste
    of what falls from your table, before death
    takes him from time and lays his body waste,   6

consider the boundless thirst with which he burns;
    bedew him from your plenty. You drink forever
    the waters of that spring for which he yearns!"   9

So spoke Beatrice, and those blissful souls,
    flaming as bright as comets, formed themselves
    into a sphere revolving on fixed poles.   12

As the wheels within a clockwork synchronize
    so that the innermost, when looked at closely
    seems to be standing, while the outermost flies;   15

just so those rings of dancers whirled to show
    and let me understand their state of bliss,
    all joining in the round, some fast, some slow.   18

From one I saw, the loveliest of them all,
    there grew a radiance of such blessedness
    that it outshone the hosts of the celestial.   21

Three times it danced round Beatrice to a strain
    so heavenly that I have not the power
    so much as to imagine it again.   24

Therefore my pen leaps and I do not write;
    not words nor fantasy can paint the truth:
    the folds of heaven's draperies are too bright.   27

"O sacred sister whose prayer is so devout,
the ardor of your love enters my bliss
within that lovely sphere and calls me out."   30

—When it had come to rest, that Fire of Love
directed its breath to my lady and spoke these words
exactly as I have set them down above.   33

And she: "Eternal Light of the great priest
to whom Our Lord brought down and gave the keys
to the sublimities of this joyous feast;   36

at your own pleasure, whatever it may be,
test this man on the greater and lesser points
of the faith in which you once walked on the sea.   39

If love and hope and faith are truly his
you will discover it, for your eyes are turned
where you can see the image of all that is.   42

But since this realm is peopled from the seed
of the true faith, he will the better praise it,
could he discuss with you the perfect creed."   45

As a bachelor arms himself for disquisition
in silence till the master sets the terms
for defending, not deciding, the proposition;   48

so did I arm myself for the expression
of every proof, preparing while she spoke
for such an examiner, and such profession.   51

"Speak, good Christian, manifest your worth:
what is faith?"—At which I raised my eyes
to the light from which these words had been breathed forth: 54

then turned to look at Beatrice, and she
urged me with her eyes to let the waters
of the spring that welled within my soul pour free.   57

"May the Grace that grants the grace of this confession
to the captain of the first rank," I began,
"grant that my thoughts may find worthy expression!"   60

Continuing: "Father, as it was set down
by the pen of your dear brother, who, with you,
set Rome on the road that leads to glory's crown,   63

faith is the *substance* of what we hope to see
and the *argument* for what we have not seen.
This is its *quiddity*, as it seems to me."   66

Next I heard: "This is, in fact, the essence.
But do you understand why he classifies it
first with substances, then with *argument*?"   69

And I in answer: "The profundities
  that here reveal themselves so liberally
  are so concealed, down there, from mortal eyes   72

they exist in belief alone. On belief the structure
  of high hope rises. It is *substant*, therefore,
  or 'standing under' by its very nature.   75

Starting with this belief, it is evident,
  we must reason without further visible proofs.
  And so it partakes, by nature, of *argument*."   78

I heard: "If all that mortal man may know
  through mortal teaching were as firmly grasped,
  sophists would find no listeners there below."   81

Such was the breath from that Love's Ecstasy,
  continuing then: "You have assayed this coinage,
  its weight and metal content, accurately;   84

now tell me if you have it in your possession."
  And I then: "Yes. I have. So bright, so round,
  usage has worn down none of its impression."   87

After these words the breath once more resounded
  from the light that shone before me: "This dear gem
  on which all good and power of good are founded—   90

whence comes it to you?" And I, "The shower of gold
  of the Holy Ghost, which pours down endlessly
  over the sacred Scrolls, both New and Old,   93

reasons it to such logical certainty
  that, by comparison, all other reasoning
  can only seem confused and dull to me."   96

And I heard: "These propositions, the Old and New
  that move you to this conclusion, for what reason
  do you accept them as divinely true?"   99

And I: "The proof that shows the truth to me
  is in the works that followed. Never has nature
  heated and forged such iron in its smithy."   102

And I was answered: "Tell me how you know
  there were such works. What seeks to prove itself—
  it only and nothing more—swears it was so."   105

"If the whole world became Christian without the aid
  of the miraculous, that is a miracle
  a hundred times greater than the rest," I said,   108

"for poor and hungry, by faith alone upborne,
  you entered the field and sowed there the good plant
  that was a vine once, and is now a thorn."   111

This said, that high and holy choir let ring
    "*Te Deum laudamus!*" sounding through the spheres
    such melody as the souls of heaven sing.   114

And that Baron, who, examining my belief
    from branch to branch, had drawn me out already
    to where we were approaching the last leaf,   117

began again: "The grace whose loving good
    had pledged itself to your mind, has moved your mouth,
    up to this point, to open as it should.   120

I approve what has emerged thus far, but now
    it is time you should explain *what* you believe,
    and from what source it comes to you, and how."   123

"O holy Father, spirit that now can see
    what faith once held so firmly that you were prompter
    than younger feet to the tomb in Galilee,"   126

my answer ran, "you wish me to expound
    the *form* of my own promptness to believe,
    and you ask what reasons for it I have found.   129

And I reply: I believe in one God, loved,
    desired by all creation, sole, eternal
    who moves the turning Heavens, Himself unmoved.   132

And for this faith I have the evidences
    not only of physics and of metaphysics,
    but of the truth that rains down on my senses   135

through Moses, the prophets, the psalms, through the Evangel,
    and through you and what you wrote when the Ardent Spirit
    made you the foster father of God's People.   138

And I believe in three Persons; this Trinity,
    an essence Triune and Single, in whose being
    is and *are* conjoin to eternity.   141

That this profound and sacred nature is real
    the teachings of the evangels, in many places,
    have stamped on the wax of my mind like a living seal.   144

This is the beginning, the spark shot free
    that gnaws and widens into living flame,
    and, like a star in Heaven, shines in me."   147

As a master who is pleased by what he hears
    embraces his servant as soon as he has spoken,
    rejoicing in the happy news he bears;   150

so, that glorious apostolic blaze
    at whose command I had spoken heard me out,
    and blessing me in a glad chant of praise,   153

danced three times round me there in the eighth great rim,
    such pleasure had my speaking given him.

Notes

1-9. PRAYER OF BEATRICE TO THE TRIUMPHANT HOSTS. Now that Christ and Mary have returned to highest heaven, the triumphant spirits are gathered around St. Peter (an allegory of Peter's role as Christ's vicar following the Resurrection). As usual, Beatrice asks the spirits to grant Dante's still unspoken wish. The tone of her prayer is clear enough, but its ellipses and metaphoric shifts require some agility of the reader:

What Dante is burning for is, of course, the revelation on which these spirits feed, forever replete (the Feast of the Lamb of God). God's grace has given him a foretaste of that feast while he is yet in the flesh: not, so to speak, a seat at Heaven's table but some of the scraps from it.

In recognition of the immensity and worthiness of Dante's wish, therefore, Beatrice asks these spirits to bless his thirst to know ("bedew him from your plenty"). Dew as a blessing and a refreshment is a well-established metaphor. Beatrice carries it a step further (relating it to the scraps of Heaven's table) by pointing out that the elect drink forever (their thirst forever sated) the waters of that Font (the Presence of God) for which the man thirsts (who would be gratified by so much as a drop from the waters of that illimitable spring).

10-18. It is a little difficult to visualize the dance of the triumphant souls. Dante says they formed into a sphere with fixed poles and compares them to clockwork. But Dante often uses "sphere" and "wheel" interchangeably. It is reasonable, therefore, to visualize the souls as forming into a great wheel of substantial depth (perhaps another millstone) that revolves around a fixed axis ("fixed poles"). The image of clockwork suggests (and the action of the next two cantos verifies) that the wheel is above Dante and broadside to him.

Within that vertical wheel the souls dance in circles to express the joy they feel in being able to give joy to Dante and Beatrice. So rapidly do they spin their circles that they appear only as wheels of light. Like clockwork–i.e., many motions contained within one master motion–the individual wheels spin at various rates. Since the speed with which each soul circles indicates the degree of bliss it feels, and knowing Dante's inclination to set things forth in exact gradations, it seems well to think of each wheel as being produced by the circling of a single soul rather than by a group of souls dancing in a ring.

19. *one . . . the loveliest of them all*: The radiance of St. Peter.

22. *three times*: It would be all but impossible for Dante to use the number three without intending the Trinity.

23-24. *my imagination fails*: Dante is not only unable to express, but he cannot even reimagine the blessèd beauty of Peter's song.

25. *my pen leaps*: Cf. **XXIII, 62.**

27. *the folds of Heaven's draperies are too bright*: To indicate the folds of a drapery, a painter must shadow the recesses of the cloth while highlighting the raised surfaces. But the inner radiance of heavenly things is such that the folds shine as bright as the surfaces, or, perhaps, Dante means to say more brightly.

Or in another, or in a complementary sense: A painter can depict the folds of draperies only when subtleties of color are available to him, and human speech and human imagination are too gross to portray the subtleties of Heaven.

31. *that Fire of Love*: St. Peter. Note that he has already descended from the great wheel, so prompt are the souls of Heaven to give joy.

39. See *Matthew*, XIV, 28 ff.

44. *he will the better praise it*: To men, on his return to Earth.

46. *bachelor*: As in "bachelor of arts," i.e., a candidate for a learned degree.

48. *for defending, not deciding*: The candidate marshals and evaluates the evidence which he submits to the master. Only the master decides. The relation is essentially that of lawyer and judge.

51. *such an examiner*: St. Peter. *and such a profession*: Of the Christian faith.

52-147. THE EXAMINATION OF FAITH. It may seem a spectacular action for Dante to be examined on his catechism by St. Peter himself (in the next two cantos he is further examined by St. James as the Apostle of Hope and by St. John as the Apostle of Love), yet, properly understood, the conception is a sublime one. For in a final sense every man of the faith must answer to nothing less than the Apostolic Creed, making himself worthy to be examined by the true source. As, allegorically, all values must be derived from the supreme test of values.

The examination is divided into six part:

52-81. WHAT IS FAITH? The anonymous *Epistle to the Hebrews* (which Dante attributes to St. Paul) provides the source of the first answer (XI, 1) "Now faith is the substance of things hoped for, the evidence of things not seen."

substance: In Scholastic terminology "what exists in itself." But Aquinas had set forth that "No quality is a substance; but faith is a quality." Faith, therefore, could not be a substance. Dante circumvents this difficulty, perhaps more ingeniously than persuasively, by rendering the *"substantia"* of *Hebrews* as "that which stands under" (*sub* and *stare*).

argument: The means whereby the intellect reaches toward the inherent truth of things. It is necessary but limited, as reason is limited.

quiddity: See XX, 92. The companion term "quality" signifies the likeness of a thing to something else, "quiddity" signifying the way in which a thing is like itself.

59. *captain of the first rank*: St. Peter. Dante calls him "*l'alto primipilo*," literally, "the chief fighter in the first rank" according to the classifications of the Roman army. Such is St. Peter's rank in the militia of Christ.

62. *of your dear brother*: St. Paul.

79–81. *through mortal teaching*: As distinct from Heavenly revelation. Could all men grasp that much as firmly as Dante has done, the fine spun arguments of the sophists would find no audience on earth, for none would pay attention to them.

82–87. THE POSSESSION OF FAITH. *Such was the breath of that love's ecstasy*: Below this height of Heaven Dante had been content with such phrases as "so spoke that radiance." But the conversations of high Heaven will not answer to the terms that describe human discourse. Dante is conversing not with a man but with a breath that issues from a radiance. *this coinage*: The golden coinage of faith by which man purchases Heaven. *weight*: Faith as argument. *content*: Faith as substance.

Peter then asks if Dante has faith: "Have you this coinage in your purse?" (I could find no rhyme for "purse" and had to settle for "in your possession.") Dante affirms that he does indeed have it, so bright (clear) and so round (not worn down by usage nor clipped or shaved by subterfuge) that he is left in no doubt of the mint impression (i.e., there is no uncertainty about his faith).

89–96. THE SOURCES OF FAITH. Dante affirms that his faith comes to him from the word of God as set forth in the Testaments ("the Sacred Scrolls, both New and Old"). *this dear gem*: Faith.

97–102. THE PROOF OF THE TRUTH OF FAITH. Dante affirms that he knows the divine truth of Scripture by the proof of the works (the miracles) that followed from them. *these propositions*: The Testaments. A metaphoric extension of the preceding terminology of logic. *works that followed*: Miracles. Nothing in nature (here conceived as a smithy) could bring such works into being.

103–114. HOW DO WE KNOW THE MIRACLES DESCRIBED IN THE OLD AND NEW TESTAMENTS ACTUALLY OCCURRED? Scripture, says St. Peter, seeks to prove itself as the word of God by asserting the existence of miracles. But if one has not actually observed a miracle, he has only Scripture's own word for it. How then can he be sure of the truth of miracles?

With the sort of ingenuity that characterizes Scholastic argument at times, Dante delivers his final and (to him) most telling argument: had the miracles reported by Scripture not taken place, one would have to assert an even greater miracle to explain how Christianity had spread through "the whole world" without divine intercession. St. Augustine had used the same argument as proof of the truth of Scripture. At Dante's words the redeemed souls break into a hymn of praise.

what seeks to prove itself: Scripture. *field*: Battlefield. As God's Captain of the first rank Peter entered the field of pagan Rome and sowed there the good seed of faith. *that was a vine . . . now a thorn*: Another denunciation of papal corruption. Peter had planted the Lord's vineyard (the Church) but corruption has left only a barren thicket choked by thorns.

115–147. IN WHAT DOES A CHRISTIAN HAVE FAITH? "That Baron" (St. Peter) asks in *what* Dante believes and from what source he derives it and how he derives it. Dante affirms his belief in a single triune and everlasting God, and declares that he is persuaded to believe by physical, metaphysical, and scriptural proofs.

124–125. *now can see what faith once held so firmly*: The Triumph of Christ, a matter of faith during his mortal life, a fact forever before his eyes in Heaven.

125–126. *you were prompter than younger feet*: See *John*, XX, 3–10. St. John was the first to approach the tomb of Christ, but Peter was the first to enter it and the first to believe in the resurrection. The greater promptness indicates the greater zeal, and thus the greater triumph of the heavenly soul.

128. *form*: In Scholastic terminology, the same as the Platonic Form, the idea of the thing, which is independent of particular instances, as, for example, the "form" of Justice would exist noumenally, if only in God's mind, even if no single instance of Justice could be found on earth. Contingency is that which comes into being as an instance of form, the form itself being eternal.

130–132. THE ATTRIBUTES OF GOD. *loved, desired*: See I, 77. *sole*: Not plural as believed by the pagans and by various heretical sects. *eternal*: Without beginning or end, contrary to the heresy that ascribed a beginning to God and, hence, duration. *moves . . . Himself unmoved*: against the heresy that God was moved (affected) by things, Dante asserts his unchangeability, for God is perfect and any change (motion) in Him would have to be away from perfection.

136–138. *Moses, the prophets, the psalms*: I.e., the Old Testament. *the Evangel and through you*: The New Testament, commonly divided into the Evangelical and Apostolic books. *you*: The Italian is the plural form *"voi."* The reference, therefore, is to all the apostles. *people*: In mercy's heavenly name, the reader is requested to avert his eyes as he passes this rhyme.

143. *the teachings of the evangels in many places*: Among various New Testament passages that assert the Unity of the Trinity, see *Matthew* XXVIII, 19, and *John* V, 19ff.

154. *danced three times round me*: Dante implies no proud boast in being so honored by St. Peter. Peter would rejoice in the same way over any soul that has shone Dante's zeal and faith.

Canto XXV

St. James · The Examination of Hope · St. John the Apostle

Dante, blessed by St. John himself as a reward for his labors and his hope, declares that if his poem may serve to soften his sentence of exile from Florence, he will return to his baptismal font at San Giovanni and there place on his own head the poet's laurel wreath. Such is one of the great hopes of his poem, and on that note *St. James,* the Apostle of Hope, shows himself.

Beatrice begs James to conduct the *Examination of Hope* and she herself, in answer to the first question, testifies to Dante's *Possession of Hope.* Dante then replies on *The Nature of Hope,* on the *Content of His Hope,* and on the *Sources of Hope.*

The examination triumphantly concluded, a cry in praise of the grace of hope rings through Paradise, and thereupon *St. John the Apostle* appears. Dante stares into John's radiance hoping to see the lineaments of his mortal body. The voice of John, the Apostle of Love (*caritas*) calls to him that what he seeks is not there, and when Dante looks away he discovers he has been *Blinded by the Radiance of Love.*

If ever it comes to pass that the sacred song,
    to which both heaven and earth so set their hand
    that I grew lean with laboring years long,   3

wins over the cruelty that exiles me
    from the sweet sheepfold where I slept, a lamb,
    and to the raiding wolves an enemy;   6

with a changed voice and with my fleece full grown
    I shall return to my baptismal font,
    a poet, and there assume the laurel crown;   9

for there I entered the faith that lets us grow
    into God's recognition; and for that faith
    Peter, as I have said, circled my brow.   12

Thereafter another radiance came forth
    from the same sphere out of whose joy had come
    the first flower of Christ's vicarage on earth.   15

And my lady, filled with ecstasy and aglow,
    cried to me: "Look! Look there! It is the baron
    for whom men throng to Galicia there below!"   18

At times, on earth, I have seen a mating dove
    alight by another, and each turn to each,
    circling and murmuring to express their love;   21

exactly so, within the eighth great sphere,
    one glorious great lord greeted the other,
    praising the diet that regales them there.   24

Those glories, having greeted and been greeted,
turned and stood before me, still and silent,
so bright I turned my eyes away defeated.   27

And Beatrice said, smiling her blessedness:
"Illustrious being in whose chronicle
is written our celestial court's largesse,   30

let hope, I pray, be sounded at this height.
How often you personified that grace
when Jesus gave His chosen three more light!   33

"Lift up your head, look up and do not fear,
for all that rises from the mortal world
must ripen in our rays from sphere to sphere."   36

So spoke the second flame to comfort me;
and I raised my eyes to the mountains that before
had borne them down by their weight of majesty.   39

"Since of His grace Our Lord and Emperor calls
and bids you come while still in mortal flesh
among His counts in His most secret halls;   42

that you, the truth of this great court made clear,
may make the stronger, in yourself and others,
the hope that makes men love the good down there,   45

say what it is, what power helped you to climb,
and how you bear its flowering in your mind."
—So spoke the second flame a second time.   48

And that devout sweet spirit that had led
the feathers of my wings in that high flight
anticipated my reply, and said: 51

"Church Militant, as is written in the Sun
whose ray lights all our hosts, does not possess
a single child richer in hope—not one.   54

It was for that he was allowed to come
from Egypt to behold Jerusalem
before his warring years had reached their sum.   57

The other two points—raised not that you may know
but that he may report how great a pleasure
hope is to you, when he returns below—   60

I leave to him. They will not be difficult.
Nor will the truth seem boastful. Let him answer
and may God's grace appear in the result."   63

As a pupil who is eager to reply
to his professor, knowing his subject well,
and quick to show his excellence—such was I.   66

"Hope," I said, "is the certain expectation
of future glory. It is the blessèd fruit
of grace divine and the good a man has done.   69

From many stars this light descends to me,
but it was first distilled into my heart
by the ultimate singer of Ultimate Majesty.   72

'Let them hope in Thee,' sang the God-praising poet,
'whoso doth know Thy name!' And who can feel
a faith as firm as mine is and not know it?   75

And your epistle sent down once again
a fresh dew on his dew, till I was full
and overflowed to others your sweet rain."   78

While I was speaking thus a luminescence
trembled within the bosom of that flame,
sudden and bright as lightning's incandescence.   81

"Love that still burns in me," I heard it breathe,
"for that grace that followed even to the palm,
and till I left the field for happy death,   84

moves me to speak further: you know the true
and lasting joy she brings: gladden me, therefore,
by telling me what Hope holds forth to you."   87

And I: "From scripture, new and old, descends
the symbol, and the symbol points me to it.
All those whom God has chosen as His friends—   90

as Isaiah testifies—they shall be dressed
in double raiment in their native land;
and that land is this sweet life with the blest.   93

And your brother, where he writes so ardently
of the white robes, sets forth this revelation
in great detail for all of us to see."   96

As soon as I had spoken there rang clear
from overhead, "Let them hope in Thee, O Lord!"
and the response rang back from all that sphere.   99

At once within that choir there blazed a ray
so bright that if the Crab had such a star
one month of winter would be a single day.   102

And as a joyous maid will rise and go
to join the dance, in honor of the bride
and not for any reasons of vain show,   105

so did that radiant splendor, there above,
go to the two who danced a joyous reel
in fit expression of their burning love.   108

It joined them in the words and melody;
and like a bride, immovable and silent,
my lady kept her eyes fixed on their glory.   111

"This is he who lies upon the breast
of Our Pelican; and this is He elected
from off the cross to make the great behest."   114

So spoke my lady, nor, her pose unbroken,
did she once let her rapt attention stray,
either before or after she had spoken.   117

As one who stares, squinting against the light,
to see the Sun enter a partial eclipse,
and in the act of looking loses his sight—   120

so did I stare at the last flame from that sphere
until a voice said, "Why do you blind yourself
trying to see what has no true place here?   123

My body is earth in earth where it shall be
one with the rest until our numbers grow
to fill the quota of eternity.   126

Only the Two Lamps that are most aglow
rose to their blessèd cloister doubly clad.
Explain this to your world when you go below."   129

And when these words were said the flaming wreath
broke off the dancing and the sweet accord
in which it had combined its three-part breath,   132

as oars that have been striking through the sea
pause all together when a whistle sounds
to signal rest or some emergency.   135

Ah, what a surge of feeling swept my mind
when I turned away an instant from such splendor
to look at Beatrice, only to find   138

I could not see her with my dazzled eyes,
though I stood near her and in Paradise!

Notes

1–12. DANTE'S HOPE. Dante has just been examined on his Faith, the first of the Christian Graces. Now he will be examined on Hope, the second. As a first sounding of the theme of Hope, perhaps to demonstrate that hope is ever green within him, he declares his dream of returning to Florence and of being crowned with a laurel wreath (baptized as a poet) at the font of "his beautiful San Giovanni" at which he was baptized into the faith, for the possession of which St. Peter so honored him at the end of the last canto.

3. *that I grew lean*: With the labor of writing his great poem.

5–6. *the sweet sheepfold*: Florence. *the wolves*: The leaders of Florentine politics.

7. *with a changed voice*: He will return not as a singer of love songs, as he began, but as the master singer of God's universal scheme. And not as a baby but as a man. *and with my fleece full grown*: Continues the lamb image of line 5.

13. *Thereafter*: After St. Peter had three times circled Dante's brow.

14. *the same sphere*: Not from the Sphere of the Fixed Stars, the Eighth Heaven, in which Dante, Beatrice, and these souls are, but from the sphere of light the souls had formed for joy when Beatrice uttered her prayer (XXIV, 12).

17–18. *the baron . . . Galicia*: The second of the barons of Christ is St. James. His tomb is in Santiago di Compostela in Galicia, Spain, and was a shrine to which many pilgrimages were made in the Middle Ages.

23. *one glorious great lord*: St. Peter. *the other*: St. James.

24. *the diet that regales them there*: The love of others, *caritas*.

29–33. *in whose chronicle . . . largesse*: i.e., "whose writings tell of the generosity and benevolence of the court of Heaven." See *Epistle of James*, I, 5, 17. Dante seems to have confused two St. Jameses into one. The *Epistle of James* is generally attributed to the James called "the Lord's brother" in *Gal.*, I, 19 (see also *Acts*, XV, 13) not to James the Apostle whose shrine is in Compostela. *let hope be sounded at this height*: St. James was particularly associated with the grace of hope. In Heaven, however, there is nothing to hope for, all having been achieved. *his chosen three*: Matthew (XVII, 1 ff.), *Mark* (IX, 2), and *Luke* (VIII, 51, and IX, 28) all cite the special trust Jesus placed in Peter, James, and John ("gave his chosen three more light"). Medieval commentators on Scripture cited them as the three pillars of the church and had them representing the Christian Graces, Peter representing Faith; James, Hope; and John, Charity (*caritas*).

34–36. *do not fear*: Dante is afraid the splendor will blind him. St. James, as a first example of hope, perhaps, reassures him; these rays do not destroy but strengthen, preparing Dante's developing soul for the vision of God. "Sphere to sphere" is a rhyme-forced addition, not in the text but implicit.

37. *second flame*: St. James.

38. *mountains*: Peter and James. So called to indicate their stature among the blessèd. (See *Psalms*, LXXXVI, 1, CXX, 1, and *Matthew*, V, 14.)

48. *So spoke*: This, of course, is Dante's way of saying that St. James had spoken lines 34–36, that Dante had obeyed him (lines 37–39), and that St. James had then continued (lines 40–47).

49. *that devout sweet spirit*: Beatrice.

49–63. THE EXAMINATION OF HOPE. In lines 46–47, St. James has put three questions to Dante, the last of which asks if Dante possesses the Grace of Hope. Before Dante can speak, Beatrice answers for him that no man in the church possesses more, for how else could he have ascended to Heaven itself? Were Dante to speak the greatness of his hope, however, his words might seem immodest. It is for this reason that she (Divine Revelation) speaks for him.

The other two questions are "What is Hope?" and "What are its sources?" On these points she will let Dante speak, not that James (who already knows) needs his reply, but to let Dante say it out in order that he may return to Earth with a full accounting in terms mortal reason can grasp.

52. *the Sun*: God. Dante's hope is known to God, therefore, to all the blessèd.

56–57. *Egypt*: The mortal life, earthly bondage. *Jerusalem*: Heaven, deliverance. *warring years*: Dante's mortal years in the church militant.

58. *not that you may know*: Since he knows already, informed by the ray of God.

59–60. *how great a pleasure hope is to you*: As the special patron of the grace he himself no longer needs.

67–69. THE NATURE OF HOPE. These lines are Dante's answer to "say what it is" (line 45).

70–78. THE SOURCES OF HOPE. Dante offers no physical or metaphysical proofs. Hope arises in man as a direct revelation, its light coming "from many stars" (many sacred writings), the first of them, for him, being the Psalms and the second St. James' own epistle. *ultimate singer of Ultimate Majesty . . . the God-praising poet*: David. *"Let them hope in thee . . ." Psalms*, IX, 11.

83–84. *that grace*: Hope. *the palm*: Martyrdom. *left the field*: Abandoned the warfare of the church militant for the bliss of the church triumphant, i.e., heaven.

86. *her*: Hope.

88–96. THE PROMISE (OR OBJECT) OF HOPE. The one hope that matters is, of course, the hope of Heaven. *the symbol*: Of the blessings to which hope leads. *it*: Hope. Sense: The scriptures show the good that awaits those who hope in God, and the good so symbolized points me to hope.

91–92. *Isaiah testifies*: See *Isaiah*, LXI, 7. *double raiment*: The glory in which Dante sees the souls clad plus the glory of the resurrected flesh after the Day of Judgment.

94–96. *your brother*: St. John. *where he writes . . . white robes*: *Apocal.*, VII.

97–102. Dante has affirmed the promise of hope offered by the revelations of Scripture, particularly of Isaiah in the Old Testament and of John in the New. As soon as he has spoken, the words of the Ninth Psalm ring out from far above and all the whirling spheres chorus the response. Then, from among them, there grows a splendor that outshines all others there. It is the soul of St. John, the apostle of love, and brightest of the chosen three as Love (*caritas*) is the greatest of the Christian Graces.

100. *a ray*: St. John.

101–102. *so bright*: That if the Crab (the constellation which is the zodiacal sign for December and January) contained a star as bright, that winter month would be one long day, the light of such a star replacing the light of the sun during the night hours.

113. *Our Pelican*: One of the medieval epithets for Christ. The pelican was believed to nourish its young by striking its breast until it bled and then giving them its blood. Another legend ran that the pelican performed in this way when it found its young dead, reviving them with its blood.

113–114. *chosen from off the cross*: Chosen by Christ while He was on the cross to remain behind and be a son to Mary (*John*, XIX, 26–27).

118–135. THE LEGEND OF ST. JOHN. *John*, XXI, 20–23, provided the basis for the medieval legend that St. John had been translated to heaven body and soul. Here, Dante sets out to correct that misinterpretation of scripture.

He starts with a long-tail simile of a man who has heard there will be a partial eclipse of the sun and who, therefore, allows himself to look directly at it and becomes blind in trying to see what he cannot bear. The eclipse here would, of course, be the darkening of the soul's radiance when the physical body moves in front of it.

As Dante is staring, the voice of St. John asks why he is blinding himself in the useless effort to see what is not there (see *I Corinthians*, XV, 50). St. John's mortal body, as he tells Dante, is in the earth. Only Jesus and Mary ascended to heaven in their physical bodies. (Some readers will recall that Enoch and Elijah were translated to heaven in their physical bodies, but Dante is obviously following the legend that they were borne only as high as the Terrestrial Paradise.)

125. *one with the rest*: One among all other mortal bodies left in the earth and indistinguishable from them until the resurrection.

125–126. *until our number . . . quota of eternity*: Clearly, Dante believes that God has ordained salvation for some exact number of souls and that the Judgment will follow when the last elected soul has been gathered to Heaven.

127–128. *the Two Lamps that are most aglow*: Christ and Mary. *doubly clad*: In body and soul.

130–135. In the usual order of his long-tail similes, Dante puts the likeness first and then compares to it the thing that is like it. Here he reverses that usual order, first describing the action, and then comparing it.

136. DANTE SUFFERS TEMPORARY BLINDNESS. Turning from the splendors before him to speak to Beatrice, Dante discovers that he cannot see her! I take St. John's remarks at the beginning of the next canto as the key to this allegory on the progress of the soul. God is beyond our mortal senses. The true vision can come, therefore, only when the senses are enlarged, having been shattered in the blaze of revelation and replaced by a new perception. As St. John says in line 12 of the next canto, Beatrice (Divine Revelation) has the power to heal. Not only will she remove Dante's blindness but he will see the better for it.

Canto XXVI

THE EIGHTH SPHERE: THE FIXED STARS
Examination of Love (Caritas) · *Adam*

John assures Dante that Beatrice will restore his sight. Dante expresses his willingness to await her will since he knows her to be Love. John, thereupon, begins the *Examination of Love*, asking Dante to explain how he came into the *Possession of Love*, and what drove him to seek it. He then asks Dante to describe the *Intensity of Love* and to discuss the *Sources of Love*.

Dante concludes with a praise of God as the source of Love. At his words all Heaven responds with a paean, and immediately *Dante's Vision Is Restored*.

There appears before him a fourth great splendor which Beatrice identifies as the soul of *Adam*. Dante begs Adam to speak, and learns from him the *Date of Adam's Creation, How Long Adam Remained in Eden, The Cause of God's Wrath*, and *What Language Adam Spoke in His Time on Earth*.

While I stood thus confounded, my light shed,
   out of the dazzling flame that had consumed it
   I heard a breath that called to me, and said: 3

"Until your eyes once more regain their sense
   of the sight you lost in me, it will be well
   for discourse to provide a recompense.   6

Speak, therefore, starting with the thing that most
   summons your soul to it, and be assured
   your sight is only dazzled and not lost;   9

for she who guides you through this holy land
   has, in a single turning of her eyes,
   the power that lay in Ananias' hand."   12

"As she wills, late or soon, let remedy
   come to my eyes," I said, "the gate through which
   she brought the fire that ever burns in me.   15

The Good that is this cloister's happiness
   is the Alpha and Omega of the scripture
   love reads to me with light and heavy stress."   18

The same voice that had soothed my fear away
   when I found suddenly that I could not see
   called me back to the question. I heard it say: 21

"Surely a finer sieve must sift this through.
   You must explain what made you draw your bow
   at this exalted target—what and who."   24

And I: "By the arguments of philosophy
   and by authority that descends from here
   such Love has clearly stamped its seal upon me.   27

For the Good, to the extent imperfect sense
   grasps its goodness, kindles love; the brighter
   the more we understand its excellence.   30

To the Essence then in which lies such perfection
   that every good thing not immediate to It
   is nothing more than Its own ray's reflection—   33

to It, above all else, the mind must move
   once it has seen the truth that is the proof
   and argument that so compels man's love.   36

That truth he first made evident to me
   whose proofs set forth the First Cause and First Love
   of every sempiternal entity.   39

It was proved by the True Maker's voice sent forth
   to Moses when It said, meaning Itself,
   'I shall cause you to see a vision of all worth.'   42

And proved by you in the high proclamation
   that cries to earth the secrets of this heaven
   more clearly than any other revelation."   45

And I heard: "As human reason and Holy Writ
   in harmony have urged you, keep for God
   the first, most sovereign passion of your spirit.   48

But tell me if you feel yet other ties
   bind you to Him. Say with how many teeth
   this love consumes you." So in Paradise   51

Christ's Eagle spoke his sacred purpose whole,
   concealing nothing; rather, urging me
   to make a full profession of my soul.   54

I therefore: "All those teeth with power enough
   to turn the heart of any man to God
   have joined in my heart, turning it to Love.   57

The existence of the world, and my own, too;
   the death He took on Himself that I might live;
   and what all believers hope for as I do—   60

these and the living knowledge mentioned before
   have saved me from the ocean of false love
   and placed me by the true, safe on the shore.   63

The leaves that green the Eternal Garden's grove
   I love to the degree that each receives
   the dew and ray of His all flowering love."   66

The instant I fell still, my love professed,
    all Heaven rang with "Holy! Holy! Holy!"
    my lady joining with the other blest.   69

As bright light shatters sleep, the man being bid
    to waken by the visual spirit running
    to meet the radiance piercing lid by lid,   72

and the man so roused does not know what he sees,
    his wits confounded by the sudden waking,
    till he once more regains his faculties;   75

so from my eyes, my lady's eyes, whose ray
    was visible from a thousand miles and more,
    drove every last impediment away;   78

in consequence of which I found my sight
    was clearer than before, and half astonished,
    I questioned her about a fourth great light   81

near us, and she: "In that ray's Paradise
    the first soul from the hand of the First Power
    turns ever to its maker its glad eyes."   84

As a bough that bends its crown to the wind's course,
    and then, after the blow, rises again
    uplifted by its own internal force;   87

so did I as she spoke, all tremulous;
    then calmed again, assured by a desire
    to speak that burned in me, beginning thus: 90

"O first and only fruit earth ever saw
    spring forth full ripe; O primal sire, to whom
    all brides are equally daughters and daughters-in-law;   93

speak, I beg, devoutly as I may.
    You know my wish. To hear you speak the sooner
    I leave unsaid what there is no need to say."   96

An animal, were it covered with a shawl
    and moved beneath it, would reveal its motion
    by the way in which the cloth would rise and fall;   99

in the same way, that first soul let me see
    through the motion of its covering, with what joy
    it moved in Heaven to bring joy to me.   102

Then breathed forth: "Without any need to hear
    what you would say, I know your wish more surely
    than you know what you take to be most clear.   105

I see it in the True Mirror, Itself the perfect
    reflector of all things in Its creation,
    which nothing in creation can reflect.   108

You wish to know how many years it is
   since God created me in the high garden
   where she prepared you for these stairs to bliss;   111

and how long my eyes enjoyed the good they prized;
   and the true reason for the great rejection;
   and the tongue I spoke, which I myself devised.   114

Know, my son, that eating from the tree
   was not itself the cause of such long exile,
   but only the violation of God's decree.   117

Longing to join this company, my shade
   counted four thousand three hundred and two suns
   where your lady summoned Virgil to your aid.   120

And circling all its signs, I saw it go
   nine hundred and thirty times around its track
   during the time I was a man below.   123

The tongue I spoke had vanished utterly
   long before Nimrod's people turned their hands
   to the work beyond their capability,   126

for nothing of the mind is beyond change:
   man's inclination answers to the stars
   and ranges as the starry courses range.   129

That man should speak is nature's own behest;
   but that you speak in this way or in that
   nature lets you decide as you think best.   132

Till I went down to the agony of Hell
   the Supreme Good whose rays send down the joy
   that wraps me here was known on earth as *EL*;   135

and then was known as *JAH*; and it must be so,
   for the usage of mankind is like a leaf
   that falls from the branch to let another grow.   138

On the peak that rises highest, my total stay,
   in innocence and later in disgrace,
   was from the first bright hour of my first day,   141

to the hour after the sixth, at which the sun
   changed quadrant, being then at meridian."

Notes

12. *the power . . . Ananias' hand*: Ananias cured the blindness of St. Paul by the laying on of hands. *Acts.* IX, 10 ff.

16–18. The gist of this passage is that the love of Beatrice (Revelation) is identical with the love of God. Beyond that gist, almost every commentator has his own interpretation. "The Good" is clearly God, the joy of heaven's cloister, and the Alpha and Omega of all scripture. But is scripture to be taken as specifically Holy Scripture, as all that Christian Love has been able to read of God's intent, or as both together? And is "light and heavy stress" to be taken poetically to signify "both accented and unaccented feet" (i.e., reading every last syllable), or to signify "both the more and the less important messages," or (again) some combination of the two?

19–66. THE EXAMINATION ON LOVE. In lines 4–9 St. John had called on Dante to discourse on love (the love of God, Christian love, *caritas*) assuring him in lines 10–12 that Beatrice (Divine Revelation) would restore his sight. Dante replies that he will await her pleasure since it was through his eyes that she first brought him the fire of love with which he burns. He then adds the generalized and elusive comment of lines 16–18. Now St. John calls Dante to a more searching examination and a more detailed answer. So to the first question of the examination proper: by whose hand (by what means) was the bow of his intention aimed at such a target as love?

26. *from here*: Heaven. The authority from Heaven is Scripture.

26–63. THE SOURCES OF LOVE. Dante answers that the knowledge of God's goodness inevitably leads to love and that the sources of that knowledge are, jointly, human reason and divine revelation. St. John, however, presses Dante to speak of the intensity of love and of his other promptings to it. So pressed, Dante cites the existence of the world as the creation of Divine Love, his own existence, the death Jesus took upon Himself, and the hope that is common to all faith.

37. *That truth*: That God is the Supreme Good and Supreme Love. *he*: Possibly Plato. "The Symposium" identifies love as the first of all the eternal essences. But more likely Aristotle who argued a single God of Love as the first principle of creation, the "unmoved mover" of "The Metaphysics" which is "the object of desire."

40–42. See Exodus, XXXIII, 19.

43–45. "I am Alpha and Omega, the beginning and the ending, saith the Lord which is, and which was, and which is to come, the Almighty" (*Revelation*, I, 8).

50–57. *teeth*: Urgings, promptings. It is not by accident that the Apostle of Love uses such a figure and that Dante repeats it. A softer figure would detract from the ardor necessary to the love of God, about which there can be nothing bland.

52. *Christ's Eagle*: St. John.

61. *the living knowledge mentioned before*: That God is the Supreme Good.

63. *by the true*: By the sea of true love. Cf. *Inferno*, I, 91 ff.

64–66. The Eternal Gardener is, of course, God; His grove, the world; its leaves, mankind. Heretofore Dante has discussed only Love of God. Here he adds Love of Others. Men are worthy of love to the extent each is loved by God. (Cf. *Inferno*, XX, 26–30, where Virgil scolds Dante for the impiety of pitying those whom God has justly damned.)

70–72. In simplest gloss: "As a bright light wakes a sleeping man." But how does the light reach the man's consciousness when he is asleep? Dante follows medieval authorities, Albertus Magnus among them, who posited a "visual spirit," an essence of man's nervous system which rises to respond to the light penetrating the layers of the eyelid and eye. Albertus Magnus theorized that this visual spirit rose from the vapors of certain delicate foods.

78. *drove every last impediment away*: The power of Beatrice's thousand-mile ray having penetrated the lids (of blindness) that covered Dante's eyes after the dazzling vision of St. John, rouses Dante's visual spirit and he is able to see again, more clearly than before. The figure will seem strange to present-day physiologists but the moral is clear: only as one loses his mortal senses can he endure the enlargement of revelation.

83. *the first soul*: Adam.

91. *only*: Eve might be thought to be such a fruit but Dante must have thought of her as part of Adam. *Genesis*, II, 22–24 would have given him ample scriptural authority for such a view.

97–102. Not Dante's most felicitous figure. It hardly honors the First Father to be compared to an animal under a cloth, the cloth representing his enshrouding radiance. Adam, moreover, is *in* not *under* the radiance. Yet the figure does convey a sense of how things are perceived in Heaven.

109–114. Dante's first wish is to know the date of Adam's creation. (*the exalted garden*: The Terrestrial Paradise. *she*: Beatrice.) His second is to know how long Adam remained there. His third, to know the exact cause of God's wrath. His fourth, to know what language Adam invented for himself.

Adam answers not in the order in which he finds these questions in Dante's mind, but in the order of their importance (a fine subtlety in portraying the heavenly souls) beginning with Original Sin.

118–120. *this company*: Of elected souls. *suns*: Annual, not daily. Were daily suns intended the time would amount to less than twelve years. And any possible ambiguity is resolved in line 121 where Adam speaks of the sun turning through all the signs of the zodiac. *where your lady summoned Virgil*: Limbo.

121–123. *all its signs*: Of the Zodiac. *nine hundred and thirty*: Adam's age at death is so given in *Genesis*, V, 5. *below*: on earth.

124–132. In *De vulgari eloquentia,* I, 6, Dante had claimed that Adam's original language was used by all of mankind up to the time Nimrod and his people were stricken at the Tower of Babel; and that it was still spoken threafter by the Hebrews. As a mortal theorist, Dante was speculating there, as he is here. As the master builder of his own great metaphor, however, this touch in which revelation cancels the earlier error of human reason, is a superb detail. *answer to the stars:* To the influence of the stars. What we call the stars do not vary notably in their courses, but the moon and the planets (stars to Dante) wander all over the face of the heavens causing ever shifting conjunctions.

133–138. *EL . . . JAH*: Dante has Adam speak these syllables as *"J"* and *"EL,"* the *"J"* being a form of *"Y."* In that order *"Y"* or *"Yeh"* or *"Jah"* followed by *"EL"* may suggest some primitive form of JAHVEH or JAHVEL. Such an interpretation is conjectural, however, and I have transposed the two syllables for rhyme purposes.

139–143. Adam declares that his whole sojourn in the Terrestrial Paradise was six hours (and perhaps part of the seventh). His time was from the dawn on the day of his creation, to the hour that follows the sixth. The total circuit of the sun is 360°, which divides into four quadrants of 90° or six hours. Assuming the time of Adam's creation to be at the vernal equinox, when day and night are each twelve hours long, the first hour of light would be from six to seven A.M., the end of the sixth would be at noon, and the hour after the sixth would be from noon to one P.M. Adam says "from the first hour . . . to the hour after the sixth." He does not say how far into that hour he remained, but it would be native to Dante's mind and style to intend Adam's expulsion to fall exactly at high noon. Half an allegorical day is about as long as any man can stay innocent.

Canto XXVII

Denunciation of Papal Corruption

ASCENT TO THE PRIMUM MOBILE

St. Peter grows red with righteous indignation and utters a *Denunciation of Papal Corruption*. All Heaven darkens at the thought of such evil. Peter's charge, of course, is that the papacy has become acquisitive, political, and therefore bloody. Having so catalogued the crimes of the bad popes, Peter specifically charges Dante to repeat among mankind the wrath that was spoken in Heaven.

The triumphant court soars away and Dante is left with Beatrice who tells him to look down. Dante finds he is standing above a point midway between Jerusalem and Spain, and having seen earth (and all its vaunted pomps) as an insignificant mote in space, Dante once more turns his thoughts upward as Beatrice leads him in the *Ascent to the Primum Mobile*, discoursing en route on the *Nature of Time* (which has its source in the Primum Mobile). The *Time of Earth's Corruption*, Beatrice tells Dante, is drawing to a close.

"Glory to the Father, the Son, and the Holy Ghost"—
a strain so sweet that I grew drunk with it
rang from the full choir of the heavenly host.   3

I seemed to see the universe alight
with a single smile; and thus my drunkenness
came on me through my hearing and my sight.   6

O joy! O blessedness no tongue can speak!
O life conjoint of perfect love and peace!
O sure wealth that has nothing more to seek!   9

The four great torches were still burning there,
and the one that had descended to me first
began to outshine all else in that sphere.   12

As Jupiter might appear if it and Mars
were birds and could exchange their glowing plumes—
such it became among the other stars.   15

The Providence that assigns to Heaven's band
the offices and services of each,
had imposed silence there on every hand   18

when I heard: "You need not wonder that I change hue,
for as I utter what I have to say
you shall see all these beings change theirs, too.   21

The usurper of the throne given to me,
to me, to me, there on the earth that now
before the Son of God stands vacant, he   24

560

has made a sewer of my sepulcher, a flow
    of blood and stink at which the treacherous one
    who fell from here may chuckle there below." 27

With the same color I have seen clouds turn
    when opposite the rising or setting sun,
    I saw the sweet face of all heaven burn. 30

And as a modest lady whose pure bearing
    is self-secure, may blush at another's failings,
    though they be only mentioned in her hearing; 33

so Beatrice changed complexion at a breath,
    and such eclipse came over heaven then
    as when Supreme Might suffered mankind's death. 36

Then he continued speaking as before,
    his voice so changed, so charged with indignation
    that his appearance could not darken more: 39

"The bride of Christ was not suckled of old
    on blood of mine, of Linus, and of Cletus
    to be reared as an instrument for grabbing gold. 42

It was to win this life of blessedness
    Sixtus, and Pius, and Calixtus, and Urban
    let flow the blood and tears of their distress. 45

We never meant that men of Christian life
    should sit part on the right, part on the left
    of our successors, steeled for bloody strife. 48

Nor that the keys consigned into my hand
    should fly as emblems from a flag unfurled
    against the baptized in a Christian land. 51

Nor that my head should, in a later age,
    seal privilege sold to liars. The very thought
    has often made me burn with holy rage! 54

From here in every pasture, fold, and hill
    we see wolves dressed as shepherds. O hand of God,
    mankind's defender, why do you yet lie still? 57

Gascons and Cahorsines are crouched to drink
    our very blood. Oh excellent beginning,
    to what foulest conclusion will you sink? 60

Yet the high Providence that stood with Rome
    and Scipio for the glory of the world
    will once again, and soon, be seen to come. 63

You, son, who must yet bear around earth's track
    your mortal weight, open your mouth down there:
    do not hold back what I have not held back!" 66

Just as the frozen vaporings sift down
  out of our earthly atmosphere when the horn
  of heaven's Goat is burnished by the Sun;   69

Just so, up there, I saw the ether glow
  with a rising snow of the triumphant vapors
  who had remained a while with us below.   72

My eyes followed their traces toward the height,
  followed until the airy medium
  closed its vast distance on my upward sight;   75

at which my lady, seeing me absolved
  from service to the height, said: "Now look down
  and see how far the heavens have revolved."   78

I looked down once again. Since the last time,
  I had been borne, I saw, a length of arc
  equal to half the span of the first clime;   81

so that I saw past Cadiz the mad route
  Ulysses took; and almost to the shore
  from which Europa rode the godly brute.   84

And yet more of this little threshing floor
  would have been visible but, below my foot,
  the sun was ahead of me by a sign and more.   87

My mind, which ever found its Paradise
  in thinking of my lady, now more than ever
  burned with desire to look into her eyes.   90

If nature or art ever contrived a lure
  to catch the eye and thus possess the mind,
  whether in living flesh or portraiture,   93

all charms united could not move a pace
  toward the divine delight with which I glowed
  when I looked once more on her smiling face.   96

In one look then I felt my spirit given
  a power that plucked it out of Leda's nest
  and sent it soaring to the swiftest heaven.   99

From its upper and lower limits to its center
  it is so uniform, I cannot say
  what point my lady chose for me to enter.   102

But she, knowing what yearning burned in me,
  began thus—with so rapturous a smile
  God seemed to shine forth from her ecstasy: 105

"The order of the universe, whose nature
  holds firm the center and spins all else around it,
  takes from this heaven its first point of departure. 108

This heaven does not exist in any place
   but in God's mind, where burns the love that turns it
   and the power that rains to it from all of space.   111

Light and Love contain it in one band
   as it does all the rest; and such containment
   only the Cunctitenant can understand.   114

Its own motion unfactored, all things derive
   their motions from this heaven as precisely
   as ten is factored into two and five.   117

So may you understand how time's taproot
   is hidden in this sphere's urn, while in the others
   we see its spreading foliage and its fruit.   120

O Greed that has drawn down all Adam's blood
   so deep into its dark that none has strength
   to raise his eyes above its evil flood!   123

The will of man comes well to its first flower,
   but then the rain that sets in endlessly
   blights the good fruit and leaves it green and sour.   126

Faith and innocence are found nowhere
   except in little children; and both have fled
   before their cheeks have sprouted a first hair.   129

Still young enough to lisp, one fasts and prays;
   then, his tongue freed, devours all sorts of food
   even in Lent, even on fasting days.   132

Another will love his mother and behave
   while yet a lisper, who, with his freed speech
   will be impatient to see her in her grave.   135

So the fair daughter of Him who leaves us night
   and brings us morning, changes her complexion,
   and her white skin turns black in Heaven's sight.   138

Consider, if you marvel at what I say,
   how there is none to govern on the earth,
   whereby the human family goes astray.   141

But before January falls in spring
   because of that odd day in each hundred years
   that all neglect down there, these spheres shall ring   144

so loud with portents of a season's turn
   that the long awaited storm will sweep the fleet,
   blowing the bows around to dead astern   147

and set the true course straight. Then all shall see
   first blossom turn to good fruit on the tree."

Notes

10–11. *the four great torches*: Peter, James, John, and Adam. *the one that had descended to me first*: Peter.

13–15. Jupiter (white) and Mars (red) are conceived here as two firebirds who partially exchange their glowing plumage. The point is that the aura of St. Peter, without losing its essential white brilliance, begins to glow with a redder (more martial) light. The change indicates a change of mood: a fiercer St. Peter is about to denounce the corruption of the Papacy by his evil successors.

17. *offices*: Empowering appointments. Cf. "office of the mass." *services*: The times each is called upon to perform his offices. Since all is preordained by God, each slightest action is from God's will.

21. *change theirs*: Change their hues.

22. *the usurper*: Boniface VIII.

25. *my sepulcher*: Rome as the seat of papal authority. According to tradition, Peter was buried there.

26. *the treacherous one*: Satan.

35–36. "Now from the sixth hour there was darkness over all the land until the ninth hour." *Matthew*, XXVII, 45. See also *Mark*, XV, 33, and *Luke*, XXIII, 44–45. The apostles report the eclipse as darkness and Dante treats it as a reddening. It seems unlikely it was so dark a red as to suggest night shadow. Perhaps Dante saw that flush of righteous indignation as showing like night on earth, but blush-red as seen from heaven's height.

37–39. The quality of the reaction invites a speculation: men work themselves into moods and are carried away by them at times, but heavenly beings express instant recognition and total justice; they register instantly, therefore, the exactly right reaction to things.

41–44. All these here named were early bishops of Rome, Peter's first successor being traditionally believed to be Linus, and his successor, Cletus (Anacletus). The others followed at various intervals: Sixtus 117-circa 127, Pius 142-circa 149, Calixtus 217–222, and Urban 222–230. Not all were martyred, as line 45 would seem to suggest, but all suffered in the flesh and in the spirit for the sins of mankind.

47–48. *part on the right, part on the left*: To indicate any warring parties of Christians, the bloody divisions of Dante's time being first the Guelphs and Ghibellines, and then the Black and the White Guelphs, those divisions often incited or abetted by the corrupt Popes for purposes of their own politics.

49–51. *keys*: The papal keys, emblems of the Pope's authority were used on the banner of the Vatican States, which had often been carried into battle against Christians—a bloody perversion, in Dante's view, of the papal mission.

52–53. *my head . . . a seal*: The papal seal, stamped on many documents whose intent was venial, bore the purported likeness of St. Peter.

58. *Gascons and Cahorsines*: Clement V was from Gascony; John XXII from Cahors. Both filled the Papal Court with greedy favorites from their native lands. And both, of course, were guilty of the further sin of being French in Italy.

61–63. God's foreseeing provision, as Dante would have understood it, must have helped Scipio overthrow Hannibal, else Rome would not have remained the glory of the world and could not have become the proper seat of holy church.

64–66. This charge, laid upon him by St. Peter himself, is, of course, Dante's ultimate license to denounce papal corruption. Effectively enough, the very charge is itself the ultimate denunciation.

67–75. All the souls who remained below when Mary ascended now rise to the Empyrean like a reverse snowfall. The figure Dante chooses for their ascent is not his most felicitous in that the snow image cannot suggest either the radiance of the souls nor the necessary speed of their ascent. *when the horn of heaven's Goat is burnished by the Sun*: The sun is in Capricorn (heaven's Goat) at about mid-January, hence at the time when "frozen vaporings" come down as snow.

79 ff. The last (and first) time Dante looked down was as he entered the Sphere of the Fixed Stars (XXII, 127 ff.). Now, as he is about to leave this Sphere, he looks down again and sees he has revolved through 90°. He has, therefore, been in this heaven six hours, one quarter of a daily turn. 90° is the amount of arc equal to half the span of the first clime. Geographers of Dante's time divided the northern hemisphere into seven habitable "climes" or "climates" running parallel to the equator. The southern hemisphere, of course, was taken to be water, the Mount of Purgatory excepted, and the northern landmass was taken to spread 180° from Spain to India.

The earthly point above which Dante is passing is about midway between Jerusalem and Spain. He can see the eastern shore of the Mediterranean and westward beyond Spain into the Atlantic. It would be allegorically pleasant to be able to say he was over Rome at this moment before ascending into the last sphere, and Dante may well have had that thought in mind, but nothing in the text permits more than a guess.

82–84. *past Cadiz*: The Atlantic. *the mad route Ulysses took*: See *Inferno*, XXVI, 90 ff. *the shore from which Europa*: Phoenicia on the eastern coast of the Mediterranean. Zeus appeared to Europa there as a bull and, taking her on his back, bore her to Crete. "Godly brute" is rhyme-forced: Dante says, literally, "the shore on which Europa became a sweet burden."

85–87. *threshing floor*: The Earth. (See XXII, 127 ff.) *more . . . would have been visible*: Dante's view is cut off by darkness because the Sun is ahead of him in Aries. He is in Gemini. The sign of Taurus lies between. A zodiacal sign covers 30°. The sun, therefore, is something more than two hours ahead of him and perhaps as much as four (if it is in the middle of Aries and he in the middle of Gemini). Part of the world below Dante must, therefore, lie in shadow.

98. *Leda's nest*: Gemini, the sign of the twins, Castor and Pollux. Zeus appeared to Leda as a swan and, according to the most common legend, she bore him Castor and Pollux. "Nest" is a *jeu d'esprit* derived from Zeus's traveling costume when he called on Leda.

100–102. ENTRANCE INTO THE PRIMUM MOBILE. Dante knew he entered the Eighth Sphere at the point of heaven marked by Gemini (XXII, 152). The Ninth Sphere, however, is so uniform that he can make out no point of reference. Beatrice, of course, knows his confusion and hastens to explain to him the nature of the Ninth Sphere.

103. *what yearning*: To understand the nature of the new sphere.

106–108. The firmly held center is the Earth. In the nature of the Ptolemaic universe, whose originating motion is the Primum Mobile, all else is made to revolve around that center.

114. *the Cunctitenant*: God, the all-containing. He contains the Primum Mobile as it contains all else.

115–117. Ten is precisely determined as the product of the factors two and five. The Primum Mobile, itself unfactorable (i.e., defined and limited by nothing), imparts the factors that determine every other motion, setting the speed, regularity, and deviation of every other heavenly motion.

118–120. Time is measured by the motion of the heavenly bodies, but the source of time, like the root of a tree, is hidden in the urn (flowerpot) of the Primum Mobile, while the heavenly bodies show forth in the other spheres as the foliage and fruit of the hidden cause. *So may you understand*: By what I say.

131. *his tongue freed*: When he has grown out of his childish lisp.

132. I have translated what I take to be Dante's intent rather than his words. Dante says simply "in whatever moon," meaning both "in whatever month" (including Lent) and "at whatever time of the month" (including Fridays and other stated days of fasting).

136–138. Few of Dante's tercets are open to so many interpretations. I follow Scartazzini-Vandelli in reading the passage as a denunciation of the corruption of the church, the fair daughter of the Sun (it being always, in Dante, a symbol of God). The Sun, arriving, brings morning and, departing, leaves night. The fair daughter, once immaculately white (the color of innocence) and still apparently so in mortal manifestation shows black (corrupt and evil) in the sight of Heaven.

271-A

140. *none to govern*: The Church being corrupt and the Emperor having abandoned Italy.

143. *that odd day in each hundred years*: The calendar as reformed under Julius Caesar fixed the year at 365 days and 6 hours, introducing an error of about 13 minutes, approximately one hundredth of a day. In each century, therefore, the calendar would move the months a day forward into the advancing season. In a millennium, January would have moved ten days nearer the spring. In 1582, the Gregorian calendar (developed under Pope Gregory XIII) substantially corrected this error.

Canto XXVIII

THE NINTH SPHERE: THE PRIMUM MOBILE   *The Angel Hierarchy*

Dante turns from Beatrice and beholds a vision of *God As a Non-Dimensional Point of Light* ringed by *Nine Glowing Spheres* representing the *Angel Hierarchy.*

Dante is puzzled because the vision seems to reverse the order of the Universe, the highest rank of the angels being at the center and represented by the smallest sphere. Beatrice explains the mystery to Dante's satisfaction, if not to the reader's, and goes on to catalogue the *Orders of the Angels.*

When she whose powers imparadise my mind
    had so denounced and laid bare the whole truth
    of the present state of miserable mankind;   3

just as a man before a glass can see
    a torch that burns behind him, and know it is there
    before he has seen or thought of it directly;   6

and turns to see if what the glass has shown
    is really there; and finds, as closely matched
    as words to music, the fact to its reflection;   9

just so, as I recall, did I first stare
    into the heaven of those precious eyes
    in which, to trap me, Love had set his snare;   12

then turned, and turning felt my senses reel
    as my own were struck by what shines in that heaven
    when we look closely at its turning wheel.   15

I saw a Point that radiated light
    of such intensity that the eye it strikes
    must close or ever after lose its sight.   18

The star that seems the smallest, seen from here,
    would seem a moon, were it placed next to this,
    as often we see star by star appear.   21

And at about the distance that a halo
    surrounds a heavenly radiance that paints it
    on the densest mist that will yet let it show;   24

so close around the Point, a ring of fire
    spun faster than the fastest of the spheres
    circles creation in its endless gyre.   27

Another surrounded this, and was surrounded
    by a third, the third by a fourth, the fourth
    by a fifth, and by a sixth the fifth, in turn, was bounded.   30

The seventh followed, already spread so wide
   that were Juno's messenger to be made complete
   she could not stretch her arc from side to side.   33

And so the eighth and the ninth, and each ring spun
   with an ever slower motion as its number
   placed it the further out from the first one,   36

which gave forth the most brilliant incandescence
   because, I think, being nearest the Scintilla,
   it drew the fullest share of the true essence.   39

I was on tenterhooks, as my lady saw.
   To ease my mind she said: "From that one Point
   are hung the heavens and all nature's law.   42

Look at the closest ring: I would have you know
   it spins so fast by virtue of Love's fire,
   the ray of which pierces it through and through."   45

And I to her: "Were the ordering we find
   in the universe like that of these bright wheels,
   what I have seen would satisfy my mind.   48

But in the sensible universe one can see
   the motions of the spheres become more godlike
   the nearer they are to the periphery.   51

If there is food for my soul's appetite
   in this most glorious and angelic temple
   whose only boundaries are love and light,   54

you must explain why it has been so planned
   that the form and the exemplum are at odds;
   for by myself I cannot understand."   57

"It is small wonder such a knot defies
   your fingers, for since none has ever tried it,
   the coils have set together like a vise."   60

So spoke my lady, going on to say:
   "If you would understand, grasp what I tell you,
   and around it give your mind's best powers full play.   63

The physical spheres are graduated in size
   according to the power that infuses each
   and fixes it to its station in the skies.   66

The greater good intends a greater grace.
   A greater body can hold more of good
   if all its parts are perfect, as in this case.   69

This sphere, then, that spins with it as it goes
   all of the universe, must correspond
   to the angel sphere that most loves and most knows.   72

If you will measure not by what appears
   but by the power inherent in these beings
   that manifest themselves to you as spheres,   75

you will observe a marvelous correspondence
   of greater power to larger, and lesser to smaller,
   between each Heaven and its Intelligence."   78

As the airy hemisphere serenes and glows,
   cloudless and blue into its furthest reach,
   when from his gentler cheek Boreas blows,   81

purging and dissolving with that breeze
   the turbulent vapors, so that heaven smiles
   with the beauty of its every diocese;   84

so was it in my mind, once I was given
   my lady's clear reply; and I saw the truth
   shining before me like a star in heaven.   87

And at her last word every angel sphere
   began to sparkle as iron, when it is melted
   in a crucible, is seen to do down here.   90

And every spark spun with its spinning ring:
   and they were numberless as the sum of grain
   on the last square of the chessboard of the king.   93

From choir to choir their hymn of praise rang free
   to the Fixed Point that holds them in fixed place,
   as ever was, as evermore shall be.   96

And she who felt uncertainty bedim
   my dazzled mind explained: "The first two circles
   have shown you the Seraphim and Cherubim.   99

Being led, they chase the reins in their eagerness
   to resemble the Point the more, and they can the more
   the more they look upon Its blessedness.   102

The beings in the next bright wheel you see
   are titled Thrones of the Eternal Aspect;
   and they complete the first great trinity.   105

And know that all these raptures are fulfilled
   to the degree that each can penetrate
   the Truth in which all questioning is stilled.   108

Hence one may see that the most blest condition
   is based on the act of seeing, not of love,
   love being the act that follows recognition.   111

They see as they are worthy. They are made
   to their degrees by grace and their own good will.
   And so their ranks proceed from grade to grade.   114

The second trinity that blossoms here
  in this eternal springtime of delight
  whose leaves nocturnal Aries does not sear,   117

warble 'Hosannah!' everlastingly,
  and their three melodies sound the three degrees
  of blessedness that form this trinity.   120

These are the divinities therein found:
  Dominations first, then Virtues, then, in order,
  the ranks of Powers within the widest round.   123

In the next two dances of this exhaltation
  whirl Principalities first, then the Archangels.
  The last contains the Angelic jubilation.   126

All fix their eyes on high and as their sight
  ascends their power descends to all below.
  So are all drawn, as all draw, to God's height.   129

Dionysius gave himself to contemplation
  of these same orders with such holy zeal
  that he named and ranked them just as I have done.   132

Gregory, later, differed with his conclusions.
  But hardly had he wakened in this heaven
  then he was moved to laugh at his own delusions.   135

And if a truth so hidden was made clear
  by one still in the weight of mortal dust,
  you need not wonder: one who saw it here   138

returned and told him this: this and much more
  of the bright truth these circles hold in store."

Notes

1–21. The figure is based on *Psalms*, XIX, 1: "The heavens are telling the glory of God and the firmament proclaims his handiwork." Wherever we look in the Primum Mobile, Dante tells us in lines 13–15, we see the glory of God.

He proceeds to describe this glory as a vision of God and the Hierarchies of the Angels. (What David saw dimly from Earth, Dante sees in detail at heaven's height.)

But first the image is approached by seeing it reflected in the heaven of Beatrice's eyes (revelation) to which Dante's soul is ever drawn by love. From the revelation of Love (a heaven in itself), Dante turns to the glory itself, to find the fact in exact accord with the reflection.

It is an elaborate and sublimely conceived figure, and will certainly do as an example of Dante's fully let out paradisal style, of the high range of his rhetoric as opposed to some of the deliberate coarsening of style he found necessary in treating the Inferno.

6. *directly*: Not reflected.

14. *my own*: His own eyes. *that heaven*: The Primum Mobile.

16. *a Point*: The term is used in its strict mathematical sense to symbolize God as an immaterial and non-spatial essence.

19. *from here*: From Earth.

26. *the fastest of the spheres*: The Primum Mobile.

32. *Juno's messenger*: Iris, the rainbow. As Juno's messenger, the rainbow is conceived as descending from heaven to earth; at most, therefore, as a quarter of a circle. Were the rainbow to be extended to a full 180° across the sky, the distance it

could span at its greatest spread could not equal the circumference of the seventh ring.

21–36. THE HIERARCHY OF ANGELS. They surround God as the heavenly spheres surround the Earth, but their motions, contrary to those of the heavenly spheres, are greater as they lie closer to the center. Opposition (paradox) is a natural part of the language of mysticism. These spheres seem at first to be a sort of counter-universe. But note that the principle of both "universes" remains the same, for in either system, the spheres have greater motion and greater "virtue" as their placement draws nearer to God. In lines 52–57 below, Dante begs Beatrice to explain the mystery of this seeming paradox and in 58–78 Beatrice resolves Dante's uncertainties, going on then (97–129) to set forth the nine orders of the angelic beings grouped in three trinities: First Trinity: Seraphim, Cherubim, Thrones; Second Trinity; Dominations, Virtues, Powers; Third Trinity: Principalities, Archangels, Angels.

36. *the first one*: The first ring. Not to be confused with The Point.

37. *which*: The first ring.

38. *the Scintilla*: God. The Point.

50. *more godlike*: Possessed of greater powers as indicated by greater speed and greater brilliance.

56. *the form*: Platonic form, the essential, unchanging noumenal concept of which any exemplum is an instance.

59. *since none has tried it*: Small wonder. Since Dante is the first to have reached this height of Heaven and to have returned from it, Dante is the first to state the problem.

58–60. BEATRICE'S REPLY. The gist of Beatrice's reply is that Dante is to observe a marvelous correspondence between each of the physical spheres and its assigned Angel Intelligence. Yet the juxtaposition of these two, so to speak, mirror images, speaks a masterful conception. God conceived as the center of the Angel Hierarchy and God conceived as the circumference of the physical universe, are not two but one, twin manifestations of one creative force; and the interplay of these two images is powerfully relevant to Dante's belief that physical and spiritual law co-exist and interplay as twin manifestations of one will. God is the radiating center of all spiritual energy and He is simultaneously the all-containing bound and limit of physical creation.

Yet, aside from the magnificence of Dante's conception here, there remain problems of interpretation in Beatrice's reply. If the largest physical sphere corresponds to the smallest angelic sphere, what then of the assertion that a larger body contains more good than a smaller one, if both are perfect? Dante, even as a pilgrim awaiting instruction, must have grasped that the greater power results from closer proximity to God: the whole journey of the *Comedy* is scaled to that proximity. It is odd that Beatrice, having mentioned so much else, does not mention proximity to God as the essence of the mystery.

In accepting the beauty of Beatrice's revelation, Dante certainly implies that we must ponder these points. Perhaps the central clue is in lines 73–75: Dante does not see the Angel Hierarchy as it is but as it manifests itself to him in the form of nine spheres. Seen from all lower levels, these spheres are contained in God and surrounded by Him, for God is Allness. Seen in this nonphysical manifestation at the height of Heaven, the spheres surround Him, for God is nondimensional essence.

65. *the power*: The "virtue" of each, its power to influence the course of what lies below it. The power, of course, descends to each as a ray from God, more powerfully to the nearer spheres, but in each the amount of power is infused through all parts of the sphere equally.

70. *this sphere*: The Primum Mobile, the source of all motion in the physical universe. As the most powerful of the spheres and as the one closest to God, it corresponds to the inner ring of the Angel Hierarchy, the Seraphim.

78. *Intelligence*: The Angel Intelligence of each sphere.

82. *Boreas*: The North Wind. When he blows straight out of his mouth the wind is from the north, which in Italy is from the Alps. Italians call that wind *"il tramontano,"* and think of it as the stormy source of bitter winter cold. When Boreas blows from his left cheek, the resultant northeaster (*"il grecale"*) is thought of as a source of storms and of cloudy skies. But when he blows from the right (the gentler) cheek, Italians experience "il maestrale," the sky-clearing wind from the northwest.

84. *every angel sphere*: The rings of the Angel Hierarchy. They react to the perfection of Beatrice's answer with a sparkling shower of joy.

91. *is worked*: Dante says only "iron that boils." But molten iron does not shoot sparks in the quantity Dante suggests unless it is hammered or poured. *spun with its spinning ring*: On earth, sparks tend to fly away from their sources. Here they stay in place, keeping pace with the rotation of the heavenly ring. The sparks may be taken as the individual angel intelligences within each ring; the added brightness of each, as evidence of the increase of its joy.

92–93. *the chessboard of the king*: The legend is still common and variously told.

In one form, the inventor of chess offered the game to the king, who was so pleased with it that he ordered the inventor to name his own reward. The inventor asked that a single grain of wheat be placed on the first square of the board, two on the second, four on the third, and so on until the 64th increment was reached. The king, no mathematician, agreed gladly. It must have been at about the twelfth square (1,080,576 grains, if my figuring is sound) that the king began to learn the power of mathematics and that the number of grains would mount by the 64th square to something more than 18,000,000,000,000,000,000.

99. *have shown you*: As ever in Heaven, Dante does not see through the power of his own senses; rather, visions are manifested to him out of *caritas*. These symbolic visions cannot be taken as the thing itself, for the mystery of heavenly being is beyond Dante; as, in one sense, it is beyond all but God. Dante is offered symbolic representations at a level he can begin to grasp with the aid of Beatrice (Revelation).

100-102. *Being led, they chase the reins*: The figure should become clear if one thinks of the opposite condition of drawing back from the reins. The Angel Intelligences are all eagerness to pursue what leads them ever faster. *to resemble the Point, etc.*: To make themselves more godlike. Pride, the first of sins, it must be noted, springs from man's desire to be himself God. The Angel Intelligences yearn toward God in love (as it is man's charge to make himself over in God's image), not in rebellion, as Satan was moved.

102-105. Dante, ever a symbolic numerologist, divides the nine ranks into three trinities. Each rank, likely, expresses an aspect of God. The first two ranks of the first trinity may well be taken as being entirely beyond human understanding. Of the Thrones he has already spoken in IX, 61-62: "On high are mirrors (you say 'Thrones') and these reflect God's judgment to us." Thus the Thrones would seem to be God's aspect as Supreme Justice.

106. *all these raptures*: All the angelic beings of all the nine ranks, not simply those of the first trinity.

108. *the Truth in which all questioning is stilled*: God.

116-117. *springtime . . . nocturnal Aries*: In spring the sun is in Aries and its stars are not visible in the day sky. In autumn the sun has moved to the opposite sign (Libra) and the stars of Aries are visible at night. Thus nocturnal Aries may be said to be the sign under which the plants that blossomed in spring turn to seared leaves.

118. *warble*: The idea of "warbling" Hosannah may seem odd and yet it is native to the language Dante has invented for his *Paradiso*. The angel beings sing their praises with an ecstasy akin to the nisus of birds. The word Dante uses is *"sverna"* (*svernare*—literally, "to unwinter," and by extension, "to sound the glad spring song of birds").

121-123. *therein*: Within the second trinity. *the widest round*: The third of the second trinity.

124. *dancers*: Ranks, orders. Called dances to denote exhaltation.

130. *Dionysius*: St. Dionysius, the Areopagite. A Greek mystic of the first century A.D. His conversion by St. Paul is recorded in *Acts*, XVII, 34. To him was attributed the thesis *De coelesti hierarchia*, from which Dante draws the details for his Angel Hierarchy.

133. *Gregory*: St. Gregory (*circa* 540-604), called "the Great." Pope from 590. Among many other writings he revised Dionysius' treatise on the angel hierarchies. As Beatrice tells it, he had hardly awakened in heaven before he saw how wrong he had been, whereupon he was moved to laugh at his own delusions. His error, to be sure, was a harmless mistake; not a heresy, nor in any way sinful.

138. *one who saw it here*: St. Paul (*II Corinthians*, XII, 2 ff.) tells of his ascent to the third heaven "whether in the body or out of the body I do not know." Dante's presumption here is that Paul told Dionysius what he had seen in heaven, and thus the accuracy of Dionysius' description (though if he were merely reporting what he had been told by Paul, he need hardly have given himself to such zealous contemplation as Beatrice ascribes to him in 130-132).

140. *hold in store*: A rhyme-forced addition. Dante says simply "of the truth of those circles." Since that truth is the revelation that awaits the pious soul, I hope I may argue that "hold in store" is implicit.

Canto XXIX

The Angel Hierarchy

Beatrice, gazing on God, sees Dante's unspoken questions and explains to him *God's Intent in Willing the Creation, The Eternity of God,* and the *Simultaneity of Creation.*

She proceeds then to explain the *Time from the Creation to the Revolt of the Angels, How the Loving Angels Began Their Blissful Art,* and that *Grace Is Received According to the Ardor of Love.*

She then *Denounces Foolish Teachings,* and concludes by pointing out *The Infinity and The Distinction of the Angels.*

When Latona's twins, one setting in the sign
   of Aries and the other rising in Libra,
   are belted by the same horizon's line;   3

as long then as the zenith's fulcrum bears
   their perfect balance, till one and the other leave
   their common belt and change their hemispheres,   6

so long did Beatrice, smiling her delight,
   stay silent, her eyes fixed on the Fixed Point
   whose power had overcome me at first sight.   9

Then she began: "I do not ask, I say
   what you most wish to hear, for I have seen it
   where time and space are focused in one ray.   12

Not to increase Its good—no mil nor dram
   can add to true perfection, but that reflections
   of his reflection might declare 'I am'—   15

in His eternity, beyond time, above
   all other comprehension, as it pleased Him,
   new loves were born of the Eternal Love.   18

Nor did He lie asleep before the Word
   sounded above these waters; 'before' and 'after'
   did not exist until His voice was heard.   21

Pure essence, and pure matter, and the two
   joined into one were shot forth without flaw,
   like three bright arrows from a three-string bow.   24

And as in glass, in amber, or in crystal
   a ray shines so that nothing intervenes
   between its coming and being, which is total;   27

so the threefold effect rayed from its Sire
   into created being, without beginning
   and without interval, instantly entire.   30

Order was the co-created fact
  of every essence; and at the peak of all,
  these angel loves created as pure act.   33

Pure potential held the lowest ground;
  between, potential-and-act were tied together
  so tight they nevermore shall be unbound.   36

Hieronymus wrote to you of the long span
  of centuries in which such beings existed
  before the other world was made for man;   39

but the Scribes of the Holy Ghost clearly declare
  the true account in many passages,
  as you will see if you will read with care.   42

It can, in part, be grasped by intellection,
  which cannot grant such powers could long exist
  apart from the functioning of their perfection.   45

This much will answer where, and when, and how
  the angels were created; and so are quenched
  the first three flames of your desire to know.   48

Nor could you count to ten and ten before
  some of those angels fell from Heaven to roil
  the bedrock of the elemental core.   51

The rest remained here and around their Cause
  began the art you see, moved by such bliss
  that their glad revolutions never pause.   54

It was accursèd pride for which they fell,
  the pride of that dark principal you saw
  crushed by the world's whole weight in deepest Hell.   57

These you see here were humble, undemanding,
  and prompt in their acknowledgment of the Good
  that made them capable of such understanding;   60

whereby their vision was exalted higher
  by illuminating grace and their own merit,
  in which their wills are changeless and entire.   63

Now hear this and, beyond all doubt, believe it:
  the good of grace is in exact proportion
  to the ardor of love that opens to receive it.   66

And now, if you have heeded what I said,
  you should be able to observe this college
  and gather much more without further aid.   69

But since your earthly schoolmen argue still
  that the angelic nature is composed
  of understanding, memory, and will,   72

I will say this much more to help you see
    the truth that is confounded there below
    by the equivocations of sophistry: 75

these beings, since their first bliss in the sight
    of God's face, in which all things are revealed,
    have never turned their eyes from their delight.   78

No angel's eye, it follows, can be caught
    by a new object; hence, they have no need
    of memory, as does divided thought.   81

So men, awake but dreaming, dare to claim,
    believing it or not, they speak the truth—
    though the hypocrite's is the greater sin and shame. 84

You mortals do not walk a single way
    in your philosophies, but let the thought
    of being acclaimed as wise lead you astray.   87

Yet heaven bears even this with less offense
    than it must feel when it sees Holy Writ
    neglected, or perverted of all sense.   90

They do not count what blood and agony
    planted it in the world, nor Heaven's pleasure
    in those who search it in humility.   93

Each man, to show off, strains at some absurd
    invented truth; and it is these the preachers
    make sermons of; and the Gospel is not heard.   96

One says the moon reversed its course to throw
    a shadow on the sun during Christ's passion
    so that its light might not shine down below;   99

others say that the sun itself withdrew
    and, therefore, that the Indian and the Spaniard
    shared the eclipse in common with the Jew.   102

These fables pour from pulpits in such torrents,
    spewing to right and left, that in a year
    they outnumber the Lapi and Bindi in all Florence.   105

Therefore the ignorant sheep turn home at night
    from having fed on wind. Nor does the fact
    that the pastor sees no harm done set things right.   108

Christ did not say to His first congregation:
    'Go and preach twaddle to the waiting world.'
    He gave them, rather, holy truth's foundation.   111

That, and that only, was the truth revealed
    by those who fought and died to plant the faith.
    They made the Gospel both their sword and shield.   114

Now preachers make the congregation roar
  with quips and quirks and so it laugh enough,
  their hoods swell, and they ask for nothing more.   117

But in their tippets there nests such a bird
  that the people, could they see it, would soon know
  what faith to place in pardons thus conferred.   120

Because of these such folly fills the earth
  that, asking neither proof nor testimonials,
  men chase whatever promise is held forth.   123

On such St. Anthony's pig feeds on, unstinted,
  and others yet more swinish feast and guzzle
  and pay their way with money never minted.   126

But we have strayed. Therefore before we climb
  turn your attention back to the straight path
  that we may fit our journey to our time.   129

So many beings are ranked within this nature
  that the number of their hosts cannot be said
  nor even imagined by a mortal creature.   132

Read well what Daniel saw at heaven's height.
  You will soon see that when he speaks of 'thousands'
  every finite number is lost from sight.   135

To all, the Primal Light sends down Its ray.
  And every splendor into which it enters
  receives that radiance in its own way.   138

Therefore, since the act of loving grows
  from the act of recognition, the bliss of love
  blazes in some of these, and in some it glows.   141

Consider then how lofty and how wide
  is the excellence of the Eternal Worth
  which in so many mirrors can divide   144

its power and majesty forevermore,
Itself remaining One, as It was before."

Notes

1-9. Latona (or Leto) was, according to early legend, the wife of Zeus before he married Hera. Later legend has her as his mistress. In any case she bore him Apollo (the Sun) and Diana, or Artemis (the Moon).

At the vernal equinox the sun sets in Aries as the moon rises in the opposite sign of Libra. For a moment, with the zenith as the fulcrum of these sky-wide scales, they are perfectly balanced and wear the line of the horizon as a common belt. Then, each changing hemisphere—one dropping below the horizon, the other rising above it —the balance is broken.

The language of astronomy, legend, and the zodiac is not as immediate to us as it was to Dante and the figure may seem strained, yet it does describe Beatrice's brief pause with tonal embellishments sweetly appropriate to the Paradisal elevation.

Gist of this passage: "Beatrice looked up a moment in silence."

12. *where time and space focus into one ray*: God, ubiquitous and eternal.

13-15. A much disputed passage. (Where I have used "reflected" Dante used *"splendore,"* but Dante always used the verb *"splendare"* or the noun *"splendore"* to mean reflected rather than direct light.) God, being perfect, cannot add to His own good, already having all. It was not for self-increase that He created other beings, but that His ray of love, reflected to His created beings, might permit those reflections to say "I am," *i.e.,* to share in the joy of existence.

18. *new loves:* The angels.

19-21. The question would be: "Where was God and what did He do before the Creation?" The answer: "He was Himself, sufficient, perfect, and eternal." *Before* and *after* are conditions of time, and God, as stated in line 16, is beyond time.

21-24. THE SIMULTANEITY OF CREATION. All created things came into being in the same instant, projected perfectly from God's perfect will.

There were, in fact, three-string crossbows in Dante's time. The figure, therefore, has precedent, but the numerological significances of trinity are always apt and may be read into the figure at will.

Pure essence: Immaterial intelligences. The angels. *pure matter:* The physical materials of the universe and the lower animals. *the two joined into one:* Creatures composed of both soul and physical matter. Mankind.

31-36. The Creation is an act of love imposed upon formless chaos. It was, therefore, inherently orderly. All the essences of that instant creation emerged in fixed ranks within the order of creation. The angels rank highest because (see XXVIII, 127-129) they have the power to influence what lies below them, having been created as pure act. At the bottom rank stands man, the material intelligence that exists as pure potential, as the receiver of divine influences he cannot influence. In between, the heavens were created as both act and potential, subject to influences from above, and able to influence what lies below.

37. *Hieronymus:* St. Hieronymus, also known as St. Jerome (c. 342-420), was one of the first great biblical scholars. *wrote to you:* "To you," of course, is the equivalent of "to mankind." In one of his epistles he asserted the precreation of the angels, a doctrine opposed to the one Beatrice is expounding.

40. *the Scribes of the Holy Ghost:* The writers of scripture. All of them were said to have been "entered" (*i.e.,* inspired by) the Holy Ghost.

42-45. Dante must not be understood to imply that the angels, whose pure act or function is to move toward God, would cease to exist if they were denied the exercise of their perfection. Rather, they are eternal, which is to say they cannot cease to exist; and, as even man's intellect may understand, for such perfect action and existence to be expended on nothing would be chaos and a denial of the orderliness of creation. Since that order cannot be denied, the angels cannot be denied their perfect function.

51. *the elemental core:* Earth. Its elements are earth, air, fire, and water. Earth is, of course, the bedrock of the material universe; its core, Hell; and Hell's core, Satan. Beatrice informs Dante that Satan and his rebellious crew plunged to Earth (roiling the elemental core in the splash that raised the Mount of Purgatory, and roiling it since by their very existence) within a twenty-count of the Creation. The inherent orderliness of creation—a force for setting things instantly in their right ranking—could not tolerate the presence of perverted angels in Heaven for more than an instant.

At the end of Canto XXVI, Adam told Dante that his stay in the Terrestrial Paradise was less than seven hours. Beatrice has already asserted the simultaneity of the Creation. Since Satan was in the Garden and tempting Eve for some time before the Fall, he could not, in any case, have remained long in Heaven.

53. *this art:* Of circling around God, their cause. The art of the angels is to receive God's ray from above and to spread its influence below.

56. *that dark Principal:* Satan.

61-66. Dante intends a distinction here between illuminating grace and consuming grace. He is following Aquinas (*Summa theologica* I, 62, 4). Illuminating grace is God's gift to the soul, which may then, through zealous love, earn the consuming grace of the direct vision of God. The power of illuminating grace is, in fact, directly measurable by the ardor of love with which the soul receives it.

67-69. Beatrice tells Dante he is now prepared to look about this heaven and to observe its nature without further help from her. Characteristically, however (was Dante indulging a gentle and tender humor on the narrative level?), she talks on to the end of the canto.

81. *divided thought:* Human intelligence, lacking absolute content and concentration, must categorize, dividing its attention, which is to say, putting some things out of mind at times to be summoned back later by memory. The intelligence of angels, on the contrary, is eternally aware of all knowledge and memory and, therefore, irrelevant to it.

83. *believing it or not:* None has the truth, but some are only deluded, whereas others, ambitious for reputation and gifts, preach as truth what they do not them-

selves believe. These latter, as hypocrites and falsifiers, are clearly more sinful than those who are merely misled.

97–102. An eclipse of the sun by the moon would throw only a limited cone of shadow, whereas were the sun itself to withdraw, the whole earth (from Spain to India) would be dark. Recent commentators have disputed the text of this passage. As I have done throughout, I follow the reading established by Scartazzini-Vandelli.

104. *spewed to right and left*: In the manner of demagogic oratory.

105. *the Lapi and Bindi*: Lapo and Bindo were, and are, common Florentine surnames. An equivalent reading in American terms might be: "they outnumber the Joneses and Smiths in the phonebook."

111. *holy truth's foundation*: "For no other foundation can one lay than that which is laid, which is Jesus Christ." *I Corinthians* III, 11.

117. *their hoods swell*: With pride in their clownish performances. "Hoods" here for "heads."

118. *in their tippets*: The tippet is the long hanging point of a monk's hood or sleeves. Mendicant friars stuffed their tippets with all sorts of dubious religious articles and trade goods to be sold to pious simpletons along with unauthorized indulgences. Thus did they do the devil's work, and so the bird that nests in their tippets is the devil himself.

122. *testimonials*: Documents bearing papal or episcopal seals as authority to sell indulgences. Genuine documents of this sort did exist, but false documents seemed to work equally well upon the gullible.

124–126. St. Anthony the Eremite (251–356) was usually depicted with a pig (representing the devil) rooting at his feet. In Florence, pigs belonging to the various monastery herds were called St. Anthony's cows, rooting in gardens, and even in houses, with no interference from the superstitious and pious folk. On such credulity, St. Anthony's pigs (these swinish mountebank monks) feed, and with them others yet (concubines, cronies, relatives) who eat and drink their fill, paying with fantastic and worthless promises (money never minted).

127–129. To digress from a subject is, metaphorically, to wander from the straight path. The straight path of this sphere is toward the study of the angelic nature. Having strayed from it, Beatrice and Dante must now hurry if they are to complete their set course in the time remaining to them before they ascend to the Empyrean.

130. *this nature*: The angelic nature.

Canto XXX

THE EMPYREAN *Praise of Beatrice's Beauty* · *The River of Light* ·
The Mystic Rose · *The Throne of Henry VII* ·
Denunciation of Evil Popes

The great theme is drawing to a close. Here in the Empyrean, Beatrice is at
last at home, her beauty made perfect, and Dante utters a lofty *Praise of
Beatrice*.

Beatrice promises Dante a *Vision of Both Hosts of Paradise*. He is
blinded by a new radiance, hears a voice announce that he shall be given
new powers, and immediately he sees a *Vision of a River of Light*. As in
the Terrestrial Paradise, he is commanded to drink. No sooner is his face
submerged in the water than the vision grows circular and re-forms as a
Vision of the Mystic Rose.

> When, as may be, the sun's noon heat is shed
> six thousand miles away, while, where we are,
> earth's shadow makes an almost level bed; 3
>
> when, at our zenith, the sky begins to show
> such changes that a star or two begins
> to fade from the eyes of watchers here below; 6
>
> and as the sun's most radiant serving maid
> comes nearer yet, and heaven puts out its lamps
> one by one, till the loveliest, too, must fade— 9
>
> just so that Triumph that forever races
> around the blinding ray of the fixed Point
> that seems embraced by what Itself embraces, 12
>
> faded from sight, degree by slow degree;
> at which I turned my eyes from the lost vision
> to Beatrice, as love commanded me. 15
>
> If all that I have said of her below
> were gathered now into a single paean,
> that would be scant praise of her beauty now. 18
>
> The beauty I saw there transcends all measure
> of mortal minds. I think only her Maker
> can wholly comprehend so great a treasure. 21
>
> Here I concede defeat. No poet known,
> comic or tragic, challenged by his theme
> to show his power, was ever more outdone. 24
>
> As feeblest eyes, struck by the sun, go blind,
> so the remembrance of my lady's smile
> strikes every recognition from my mind. 27

From the first day I looked upon her face
  in this life, to this present sight of her,
  my song has followed her to sing her praise. 30

But here I must no longer even try
  to walk behind her beauty. Every artist,
  his utmost done, must put his brushes by. 33

So do I leave her to a clarion
  of greater note than mine, which starts to draw
  its long and arduous theme to a conclusion. 36

She, like a guide who has his goal in sight
  began to speak again: "We have ascended
  from the greatest sphere to the heaven of pure light. 39

Light of the intellect, which is love unending;
  love of the true good, which is wholly bliss;
  bliss beyond bliss, all other joys transcending; 42

here shall you see both hosts of Paradise,
  one of them in the aspect you shall see
  when you return the day all bodies rise." 45

As a flash of lightning striking on our sight
  destroys our visual spirits, so that the eye
  cannot make out even a brighter light; 48

just so, an aureole burst all about me,
  swathing me so completely in its veil
  that I was closed in light and could not see. 51

"The Love that keeps this Heaven ever the same
  greets all who enter with such salutation,
  and thus prepares the candle for His flame." 54

No sooner had these few words penetrated
  my hearing than I felt my powers increase
  beyond themselves; transcendant and elated, 57

my eyes were lit with such new-given sight
  that they were fit to look without distress
  on any radiance, however bright. 60

I saw a light that was a river flowing
  light within light between enameled banks
  painted with blossoms of miraculous spring; 63

and from the river as it glowed and rolled
  live sparks shot forth to settle on the flowers.
  They seemed like rubies set in bands of gold; 66

and then, as if the fragrance overthrew
  their senses, they dove back into the river;
  and as one dove in there, out another flew. 69

"The flame of high desire that makes you yearn
    for greater knowledge of these things you see
    pleases me more the more I see it burn.   72

But only this same water satisfies
    such thirst as yours. You must bend down and drink."
    —So spoke the sun and pole-star of my eyes.   75

And added: "The river and the jewels you see
    dart in and out of it, and the smiling flowers
    are dim foretastes of their reality.   78

Not that these fruits are in their natures tart
    and unformed, but that you still lack the vision
    of such high things. The defect is on your part."   81

No babe in arms that ever wakened hungry
    from having slept too long could turn its face
    to its dear mother's milk more eagerly   84

than I bent down to drink in Paradise
    of the sweet stream that flows its grace to us,
    so to make better mirrors of our eyes.   87

No sooner were my eyes' eaves sweetly drowned
    in that bright stream to drink, than it appeared
    to widen and change form till it was round.   90

I have seen masqueraders here below
    shed the disguises that had hidden them
    and show their true appearances. Just so,   93

the sparks and spring flowers changed before my eyes
    into a greater festival, and I saw
    the vision of both courts of Paradise.   96

O splendor of God eternal through which I saw
    the supreme triumph of the one true kingdom,
    grant me the power to speak forth what I saw!   99

There in Heaven, a lamp shines in whose light
    the Creator is made visible to His creature,
    whose one peace lies in having Him in sight.   102

That lamp forms an enormous circle, such
    that its circumference, fitted to the Sun
    as a bright belt, would be too large by much.   105

It is made up entirely of the reflection
    of rays that strike the top of the first-moved sphere,
    imparting to it all its power and motion.   108

And as a slope shines in the looking glass
    of a lake below it, as if to see itself
    in its time of brightest flower and greenest grass;   111

so, tier on tier, mounting within that light,
there glowed, reflected in more than a thousand circles,
all those who had won return to Heaven's height.   114

And if so vast a nimbus can be bound
within its lowest tier, what then must be
the measure of this rose at its topmost round?   117

Nor were my eyes confounded by that sea
and altitude of space, but took in all,
both number and quality, of that ecstasy.   120

There, far and near cause neither loss nor gain,
for where God rules directly, without agents,
the laws that govern nature do not pertain.   123

Into the gold of the rose that blooms eternal,
rank on rank, in incenses of praise
it sends up to the Sun forever vernal—   126

I, yearning to speak and silent—Beatrice drew me,
and said: "Now see how many are in the convent
of the white robes. Behold our far-flung city.   129

And see the benches—every one a throne—
how every rank of them is filled so full
that few are wanted before all is done.   132

That great throne with the crown already set
above it draws your eyes. To it shall come—
before your own call to this nuptial banquet—   135

the soul, already anointed, of Henry the Great,
who will come to Italy to bring law and order
before the time is ripe to set things straight.   138

Tranced in blind greed, your ever deepening curse,
you have become as mindless as an infant
who screams with hunger, yet pushes away his nurse.   141

The prefect of the holy court will be
a man who will profess his cause in public
while working to defeat it secretly.   144

But after that God will not long permit
his simony, he shall be stuffed away
where Simon Magus, headfirst in the pit,   147

pays for his guilt. There, paying for his own,
he shall force the guilt of Alagna further down."

Notes

1–15. ASCENT TO THE EMPYREAN. Heretofore the glories of the heavens have
shone like stars in glorious night. In the Empyrean, God (the Sun) shines forever in
the fullness of His glorious day, obscuring all other heavenly bodies except as they

reflect His light. The ascent into the Empyrean, therefore, is a dawning, and Dante's figure for it is based on an earthly dawn.

When the sun is at its noon height over India (about 6000 miles away) dawn is just beginning in Italy and the Earth's shadow is almost a level line (level bed) out into space (i.e., nearly perpendicular to a line dropped from the zenith). Then the stars directly overhead begin to fade, the dimmest first, then the brighter. Then as dawn (Aurora, the serving maid of Apollo, the Sun) draws nearer, all the stars go out, even the loveliest and brightest.

Just so nine rings of the three trinities of Angelic beings fade as Dante and Beatrice ascend into the first dawning of the direct vision of God. Obviously the dimmer outer rings would fade first, then the others in order.

12. *embraced by what Itself embraces*: The Angel Rings seem to contain God within their rounds, whereas it is God who contains them and all else.

22-23. THE BEAUTY OF BEATRICE. As Dante ascended each new heaven and became more able to perceive, Beatrice grew more beautiful (was able to reveal more of herself to his senses). Now fully disclosed in the direct light of the Empyrean she surpasses conception: only God can realize her full beauty.

On another level it is only natural that Dante stand inarticulate before the full beauty of Divine Revelation. What religious man could think himself equal to describing the entire beauty of Revelation? (Such inarticulateness is all the more effective when it overtakes a man who boasted of his powers in *Inferno*, IV, 100-102, XXV, 91-99, XXXII, 7-9, and in *Paradiso*, II, 1-18.)

35-36. *to a clarion of greater note than mine*: Does Dante mean that a greater poet will follow to sing the full beauty of Beatrice? He has just said that only God can fully realize her beauty.

I think it is no accident that Dante says "clarion" rather than "lyre." The Day of Judgment will be announced by a clarion call, and on that day the souls of all mortals may look upon Beatrice in her full beauty. Dante's "clarion" must occupy itself with drawing its long and arduous theme to a conclusion.

39. *the greatest sphere*: The Primum Mobile. *heaven of pure light*: The Empyrean.

43. *both hosts of Paradise*: The Angels and the Blessèd.

44. *one of them*: The Blessèd. Those who once wore mortal bodies which shall be returned to them on Judgment Day. Within the Mystic Rose Dante does see the radiances of the Blessèd with their lineaments etched upon them. He is offered this sight as a special dispensation in a climactic act of *caritas*.

47. *visual spirits*: See XXVI, 70-72.

52. *The Love*: God. *that keeps his Heaven ever the same*: All the other heavens rotate in constant change. The Empyrean, reflecting God's unchanging and unchangeable perfection, is always the same.

54. *and thus prepares the candle for His flame*: Dante has several times been blinded by the light that prepared him for better vision. Here the candle of his soul is put out by the splendor of the Empyrean to be relit by the light of God Himself.

60-66. As Dante makes clear in line 95 below, the sparks are Angels and the flowers, the Blessèd. The river may be taken as the endless flowering of God's grace. Some religious commentators suggest that the two banks represent the Church. As verified by lines 76-78 below, the rubies of line 66 should be taken to be Angels and the bands of gold as the Blessèd.

77. *jewels*: Dante says "topazes" and the topaz was believed to have the power of reflecting things without distortion, certainly a relevant suggestion in context, though "topazes" here does not accord with "rubies" in line 66.

82 ff. *no babe in arms*: "Except ye be converted and become as little children, ye shall not enter into the kingdom of heaven" (*Matthew*, XVIII, 3).

87. *better mirrors*: The better to reflect God.

88-89. *my eyes' eaves*: His eyelashes. Dante has, of course, plunged his face into the river. It may seem odd to say that he drank with his eyes, but note that this is a river of light, and that it is to wash the last mortal weakness from his eyes that Dante is drinking. See also the common idiom: "My eyes drank in the sight of it."

95-97-99. *I saw*: Now and then in the *Paradiso* Dante says "I saw." More often he uses some such phrase as "there appeared to me" or "it manifested itself." Such phrasing is deliberate. "I saw" implies an action of the speaker's own powers. Heaven, however, is a gift of grace: Dante does not see it through his own powers; rather it manifests itself to him as an act of love, and does so not in its true essence but in manifestations graspable by Dante's mortal mind.

Here, however, Dante uses "I saw" as one of his rare triple rhymings on the same word. In Dante an unusual device always indicates unusual stress. It occurs, moreover, at one of the great climaxes of the poem.

For Dante has just experienced the first direct revelation of God. Until he drank from the stream he could not see things with the spontaneous intuition of heavenly souls, who partake directly of the mind of God. Now he, too, has achieved the beginnings of Paradisal power. This is the true rebirth, the spiritual enlargement to which the entire journey has been directed. And soon now, as Virgil left him below, Beatrice will leave him to take her throne among the hosts of the Blessèd, though in a larger sense she will be with him forever, both her soul and Dante's being contained in God.

108. *power*: Virtue. The ability to influence what lies below it. *motion*: Its own rapid revolution.

112 ff. THE MYSTIC ROSE. As ever in Paradise, the heavenly beings manifest themselves to Dante at the highest level he is capable of grasping at each point of his development. At every stage they have sent their manifestations down to him as an act of love. They themselves remain forever in the direct presence of God.

Now, his vision at last approaching perfection, Dante sees them in their supreme heavenly state, ranked tier on tier in a huge stadium that gives forth the appearance of an enormous white rose basking in the eternal springtime of the direct light of God. Note, however, that he sees the rose not directly (even at this point he is not yet ready) but as a vision reflected in the sea of God's light.

For purposes of placing Dante in relation to it, the Rose may be thought of as an immense, truncated, inverted, floating cone marked off in many tiers. The tier first reflected to Dante from that sea of light is the bottom one, the upper tiers being only partially visible at this point. The nimbus of the bottom tier (lines 115–116) is far greater than the circumference of the Sun (lines 104–105).

114. *those who had won return*: The loyal angels, having never left, would not have won return.

116–117. *what then must be its measure*: There are more than a thousand tiers. If the lowest is greater by far than the circumference of the Sun, what must be the dimensions of its upper ring, a thousand steps up from such magnitude?

118–123. On earth we see near things in detail and far things indistinctly. The laws of nature, however, are God's agencies and have no force where God rules without intermediaries. So, despite the galactic dimensions of the rose, Dante sees all in minute detail, not only each being in that multitude, but the quality of each one's ecstasy.

124 ff. *Into the gold of the rose*: The central corona of the rose, from which the petals grow, is always golden, or so it was in Dante's time, though some modern hybrids no longer have a golden center. *Beatrice drew me*: If the Mystic Rose is conceived as a vast circular stadium Dante and Beatrice are now in the center of the arena looking up at the tiers.

132. *few are wanted before all is done*: As with so many other revelationists, Dante believes God will not long endure the evils of mankind and that the trump of Judgment will soon sound.

136. *Henry*: Henry VII of Luxemburg, Emperor 1308–1313. He was not, strictly speaking, referred to as Henry the Great, but I have been forced to call him that for purposes of rhyme. See *Purgatorio*, VII, 96, note, and for the background of Henry's attempt at order in Italy see *Purgatorio*, VI, 100, note. In the *Purgatorio* Dante says Henry came too late. Here he says he came before the time was ripe. In either case the result was the same and Dante attributes Henry's failure to the evil designs of the bad popes Beatrice now goes on to denounce before the full court of Heaven. It is certainly relevant, here, to note that Dante placed his one hope of returning to Florence on the outcome of Henry's efforts to settle the hatreds of Italian politics.

138. *already anointed*: As Holy Roman Emperor.

140. *you*: You Italians.

142. *The prefect*: The pope. *The holy court*: Rome, the Vatican. Here Dante intends Clement V, who worked to defeat Henry's policy, though he professed to support it.

143–144. I have found it necessary to translate the intent rather than the phrasing of Dante's lines here. Literally rendered, they would read: "Who will not walk with him the same road openly and covertly," a strange figure that has Clement walking beside Henry on two separate roads at the same time.

145. *God will not long permit*: Clement died eight months after Henry, on April 20, 1314.

147. *where Simon Magus, headfirst in the pit*: With the Simoniacs in the Third Bolgia of the Eighth Circle (*Inferno*, XIX). There the sinners are stuffed head-first into a tubelike baptismal font, their feet kicking the air, their soles aflame. As each replaces his successor in selling holy office, the earlier tenant is shoved down into some undescribed lower pit, sealed from the eyes of all.

149. *the guilt of Alagna*: Boniface VIII. He was born at Alagna (or, variantly, Anagna).

Canto XXXI

THE EMPYREAN *The Mystic Rose · The Angel Host ·
Beatrice Leaves Dante · St. Bernard*

The second soldiery of the Church Triumphant is the *Angel Host* and
Dante now receives a vision of them as a *Swarm of Bees* in eternal transit
between God and the Rose.

Dante turns from that rapturous vision to speak to Beatrice and finds in
her place a reverend elder. It is *St. Bernard,* who will serve as Dante's guide
to the ultimate vision of God. Bernard shows Dante his *Last Vision of Beatrice,* who has resumed her throne among the blessèd. Across the vastness
of Paradise, Dante sends his soul's prayer of thanks to her. *Beatrice Smiles*
down at Dante a last time, then turns her eyes forever to the Eternal Fountain of God.

Bernard, the most faithful of the worshippers of the Virgin, promises
Dante the final vision of God through the Virgin's intercession. Accordingly, he instructs Dante to raise his eyes to her throne. Dante obeys and
burns with bliss at the vision of her splendor.

Then, in the form of a white rose, the host
   of the sacred soldiery appeared to me,
   all those whom Christ in his own blood espoused.   3

But the other host (who soar, singing and seeing
   His glory, who to will them to his love
   made them so many in such blissful being,   6

like a swarm of bees who in one motion dive
   into the flowers, and in the next return
   the sweetness of their labors to the hive)   9

flew ceaselessly to the many-petaled rose
   and ceaselessly returned into that light
   in which their ceaseless love has its repose.   12

Like living flame their faces seemed to glow.
   Their wings were gold. And all their bodies shone
   more dazzling white than any earthly snow.   15

On entering the great flower they spread about them,
   from tier to tier, the ardor and the peace
   they had acquired in flying close to Him.   18

Nor did so great a multitude in flight
   between the white rose and what lies above it
   block in the least the glory of that light;   21

for throughout all the universe God's ray
   enters all things according to their merit,
   and nothing has the power to block its way.   24

This realm of ancient bliss shone, soul on soul,
with new and ancient beings, and every eye
and every love was fixed upon one goal.   27

O Threefold Light which, blazoned in one star,
can so content their vision with your shining,
look down upon us in the storm we are!   30

If the barbarians (coming from that zone
above which Helice travels every day
wheeling in heaven with her belovèd son)   33

looking at Rome, were stupefied to see
her works in those days when the Lateran
outshone all else built by humanity;   36

what did I feel on reaching such a goal
from human to blest, from time to eternity,
from Florence to a people just and whole—   39

by what amazement was I overcome?
Between my stupor and my new-found joy
my bliss was to hear nothing and be dumb.   42

And as a pilgrim at the shrine of his vow
stares, feels himself reborn, and thinks already
how he may later describe it—just so now   45

I stood and let my eyes go wandering out
into that radiance from rank to rank,
now up, now down, now sweeping round about.   48

I saw faces that compelled love's charity
lit by Another's lamp and their own smiles,
and gestures graced by every dignity.   51

Without having fixed on any part, my eyes
already had taken in and understood
the form and general plan of Paradise: 54

and—my desire rekindled—I wheeled about
to question my sweet lady on certain matters
concerning which my mind was still in doubt.   57

One thing I expected; another greeted me:
I thought to find Beatrice there; I found instead
an elder in the robes of those in glory.   60

His eyes and cheeks were bathed in the holy glow
of loving bliss; his gestures, pious grace.
He seemed a tender father standing so.   63

"She—where is she?" I cried in sudden dread.
"To lead you to the goal of all your wish
Beatrice called me from my place," he said;   66

"And if you raise your eyes you still may find her
in the third circle down from the highest rank
upon the throne her merit has assigned her."   69

Without reply I looked up to that height
and saw her draw an aureole round herself
as she reflected the Eternal Light.   72

No mortal eye, though plunged to the last bounds
of the deepest sea, has ever been so far
from the topmost heaven to which the thunder sounds   75

as I was then from Beatrice; but there
the distance did not matter, for her image
reached me unblurred by any atmosphere.   78

"O lady in whom my hope shall ever soar
and who for my salvation suffered even
to set your feet upon Hell's broken floor;   81

through your power and your excellence alone
have I recognized the goodness and the grace
inherent in the things I have been shown.   84

You have led me from my bondage and set me free
by all those roads, by all those loving means
that lay within your power and charity.   87

Grant me your magnificence that my soul,
which you have healed, may please you when it slips
the bonds of flesh and rises to its goal."   90

Such was my prayer, and she—far up a mountain,
as it appeared to me—looked down and smiled.
Then she turned back to the Eternal Fountain.   93

And the holy Elder said: "I have been sent
by prayer and sacred love to help you reach
the perfect consummation of your ascent.   96

Look round this garden, therefore, that you may
by gazing at its radiance, be prepared
to lift your eyes up to the Trinal Ray.   99

The Queen of Heaven, for whom in whole devotion
I burn with love, will grant us every grace
because I am Bernard, her faithful one."   102

As a stranger from afar—a Croat, if you will—
comes to see our Veronica, and awed
by its ancient fame, can never look his fill,   105

but says to himself as long as it is displayed:
"My Lord, Jesus Christ, true God, and is this then
the likeness of thy living flesh portrayed?"—   108

just so did I gaze on the living love
of him who in this world, through contemplation,
tasted the peace which ever dwells above.   111

"Dear son of Grace," he said, "you cannot know
this state of bliss while you yet keep your eyes
fixed only on those things that lie below;   114

rather, let your eyes mount to the last round
where you shall see the Queen to whom this realm
is subject and devoted, throned and crowned."   117

I looked up: by as much as the horizon
to eastward in the glory of full dawn
outshines the point at which the sun went down;   120

by so much did one region on the height
to which I raised my eyes out of the valley
outshine the rays of every other light.   123

And as the sky is brightest in that region
where we on earth expect to see the shaft
of the chariot so badly steered by Phaeton,   126

while to one side and the other it grows dim—
just so that peaceful oriflamme lit the center
and faded equally along either rim.   129

And in the center, great wings spread apart,
more than a thousand festive angels shone,
each one distinct in radiance and in art.   132

I saw there, smiling at this song and sport,
she whose beauty entered like a bliss
into the eyes of all that sainted court.   135

And even could my speech match my conception,
yet I would not dare make the least attempt
to draw her delectation and perfection.   138

Bernard, seeing my eyes so fixed and burning
with passion on his passion, turned his own
up to that height with so much love and yearning   141

that the example of his ardor sent
new fire through me, making my gaze more ardent.

Notes

1–2. In **XXX**, 43, Beatrice promised that Dante would see both hosts of Paradise.
The first host is of the sacred soldiery, those who were once mortal and who were
redeemed by Christ. They are seated upon the thrones of the Mystic Rose in which
are gathered eternally the essences of all those heavenly souls that manifested themselves to Dante in the various spheres below, moved by *caritas* to reveal themselves
to Dante at the various levels of his developing understanding. How these souls could
be eternally within the Rose while yet manifesting themselves to Dante in the various

spheres is, of course, one of the mysteries to be grasped only by revelation. The essential point is that as Dante becomes better able to see; the vision of Heaven unfolds to him ever more clearly and ever more profoundly.

The second soldiery is of the angels who never left heaven. They soar above the Rose like Heavenly bees, in constant motion between the Rose and the radiance of God. Unlike earthly bees, however, it is from God, the mystical hive of grace, that they bring the sweetness to the flower, bearing back to God, of course, the bliss of the souls of Heaven. (See lines 16–18).

The first host is more emphatically centered on the aspect of God as the Son; the second, on the aspect of God as the Father.

13. See the vision of God and Heaven in *Ezekiel*, I, 14 ff.

14. See the similar vision in *Daniel*, X, 4 ff.

22–24. God illuminates all things in the exact degree that each is worthy of illumination (which is to say, able to receive it), and nothing may block from any other thing the light it is in condition to receive. No soul, that is to say, can receive less of God than it is able to contain at any given stage of its development.

27. *one goal*: God.

32. *Helice*: The nymph Helice (I am afraid the reader will have to Anglicize her name as HEL-ees) attracted Zeus and was turned into a bear by jealous Hera. Zeus translated his nymph to heaven as Ursa Major, the constellation of the Great Bear which contains the Big Dipper. Arcas, her son by Zeus, was translated to Ursa Minor, within which he forms the Little Dipper.

The two dippers, being near the pole, are always above the horizon in the northland, the zone from which the barbarians came.

35. *the Lateran*: The Lateran is today a section of old Rome. Here Dante uses it to signify Rome in general.

39. *from Florence to a people just and whole*: This is Dante's last mention of Florence. Note that Florence has not improved but that on the universal scale it has become too insignificant for the sort of denunciation he once heaped upon it.

42. *my bliss was to hear nothing and be dumb*: At such a moment of ecstasy Dante wants neither to speak nor to hear others speak, but only to stand rapt before the glory of such revelation.

Note that Dante believes he is standing next to Beatrice. "To hear nothing" must mean he does not even wish to hear her speak. On the personal level, such a feeling might seem an affront to his lady; yet there is no affront: even she, as she herself would insist, must be silent before the greater vision. The figure of Beatrice is a complex symbol. To simplify matters for the beginning reader of Dante, I have taken her allegorically in simplest terms as Divine Revelation. So taking her, Dante's seeming rejection of her blends harmoniously with the total of his vision, for if Beatrice is Divine Revelation (an agent of God), Dante is now near God Himself (that which Revelation is meant to reveal).

43. *shrine of his vow*: It was a custom of the pious, as thanks for an answered prayer, to win forgiveness of sins, or as a testimony of faith, to vow a journey to a stated shrine or temple. Such pilgrimages were often dangerous. Travel was rare in the Middle Ages, and the pilgrim returned from far shrines was much sought after for the hopefully miraculous, and in any case rare, news he brought back. How could Dante, having traveled to the Infinite Summit, fail to think ahead to the way he would speak his vision to mankind?

58. *One thing I expected; another greeted me*: Dante expected to see Beatrice. He sees instead St. Bernard. As Virgil, his service done, vanished at the top of Purgatory, so now Beatrice has left Dante, though not to vanish but to resume her throne among the blessèd. In the next passage Dante will look up and see her there.

60. *an elder*: St. Bernard (1090–1153), the famous Abbot of Clairvaux, a contemplative mystic and author. Under him the Cistercian Order (a branch of the Benedictines with a stricter rule than the original order) flourished and spread. All Cistercian monasteries are especially dedicated to the Virgin, and St. Bernard is particularly identified with her worship.

66. *Beatrice called me from my place*: In succeeding Beatrice, Bernard clearly becomes the allegorical figure of Contemplation, and so a progress of the soul: From Human Reason or Aesthetic Wisdom the soul mounts to Revelation at which time the final bliss becomes Contemplation of God as He reveals Himself.

Bernard, himself one of the most famous contemplatives of the church, has a second function. The ultimate revelation must come as a special grace and grace can be granted in answer to the prayers of the worthy. The worthiest being in the Mystic Rose is the Virgin and Bernard as her special servitor will pray to her that she pray God to grant Dante's most ardent wish.

68. *the third circle down*: In the Mysitc Rose (see diagram in XXXII) Mary sits in the topmost tier, Eve directly below her, Rachel (the Contemplative Life) below Eve. Beatrice sits to the right of Rachel. In Dante, of course, every mention of three must suggest trinity, but the reader is left to decide for himself the significance of the Mary-Eve-Rachel trinity.

73–75. To what altitude the sound of thunder reaches through the atmosphere and how far that would be from the bottom of the deepest sea are questions a scientist might perhaps determine. For Dante the upper height would be the top of the atmosphere and he would have understood that upper limit as being close to the moon. Whatever the specifications, the poetic force of the passage powerfully suggests vast dimensions.

81. *to set your feet upon Hell's broken floor:* As she did when she descended to Limbo (as, of course, a manifestation) to summon Virgil.

103. *a Croat:* Probably used here in a generic sense to signify the native of any far off Christian land, but Croatia, aside from lying at one of the outer limits of Christianity, was also known for the ardor of its religious belief.

104. *our Veronica:* From *vera icon,* the true image. Certainly the most famous relic in St. Peter's, the Veronica was the handkerchief of the faithful follower ever after known as St. Veronica. She gave it to Jesus to wipe the blood from his face on the road to Calvary, and what was believed to be the true likeness of Jesus was believed to have appeared on what was believed to be the cloth in what was believed to be His own blood.

110–111. According to legend, Bernard was rewarded for his holiness by being permitted a vision of Heaven's blessedness while he was yet on earth.

112–117. The way to perfect consummation is ever upward toward God. Dante has been staring at Bernard, awed by that vision of holiness. In modesty and as an act of loving guidance, Bernard tells him to prepare his eyes for the ultimate vision by looking up to Mary on her throne.

118–123. The comparison is not, as careless readers sometimes take it to be, between a dawn and a sunset (whose brightnesses would be approximately equal) but between the eastern and western horizons at dawn. Bright as Heaven is, Mary outshines it as the east outshines the west at daybreak.

124–129. The shaft of the chariot of the Sun would project ahead of the horses. It would, therefore, be the first point of light of the new dawn, that moment when light glows on the eastern rim while the horizon to north and south is still dark. Thus Mary not only outshines all heaven as the east at daybreak outshines the west, but even at the uppermost tier of the blessèd, those radiances at either side of her are dim by comparison.

132. *art:* Motion. No two angel beings are exactly equal in their brightness, nor in the speed of their flight. These festive angels are, of course, another manifestation of the Angel Hierarchy. At this height of heaven and revelation, it should not seem contradictory for them to revolve forever around God while they forever circle Mary. The two circlings are clearly meant to be one. Heaven, moreover, reveals itself in one manifestation after another of the truth only God can entirely grasp.

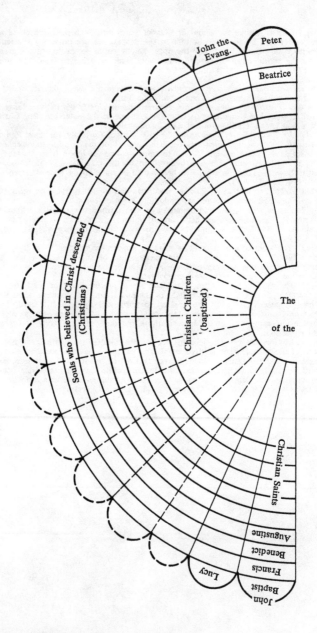

THE MYSTIC ROSE (after Gardner)
No specific number of petals or of tiers should be under-

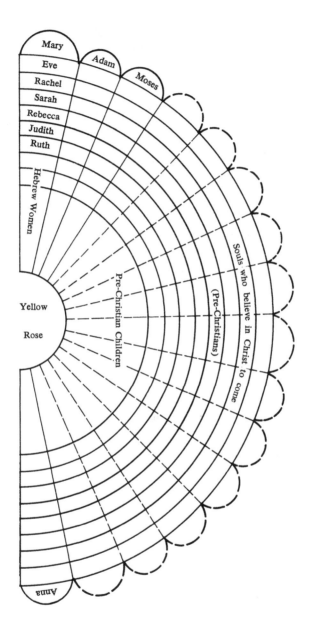

Mary
Eve
Rachel
Sarah
Rebecca
Judith
Ruth

Hebrew Women

Adam

Moses

Yellow

Rose

Pre-Christian Children

(Pre-Christians)

Souls who believe in Christ to come

Anna

stood. The dotted lines indicate the parts of the rose
which Dante does not describe in detail.

Canto XXXII

St. Bernard · The Virgin Mary ·
The Thrones of the Blessèd

His eyes fixed blissfully on the vision of the Virgin Mary, Bernard recites
the orders of the Mystic Rose, identifying the thrones of the most blessèd.

Mary's Throne is on the topmost tier of the Heavenly Stadium. Directly
across from it rises the *Throne of John the Baptist.* From her throne to the
central arena (The Yellow of the Rose) descends a *Line of Christian
Saints.* These two radii form a diameter that divides the stadium. On one
side are throned *Those Who Believe in Christ to Come;* on the other,
Those Who Believed in Christ Descended. The lower half of the Rose contains, on one side, the *Pre-Christian Children Saved by Love,* and on the
other, the *Christian Children Saved by Baptism.*

Through all these explanations, Bernard has kept his eyes fixed in adoration upon the Virgin. Having finished his preliminary instruction of Dante,
Bernard now calls on him to join in a *Prayer to the Virgin.*

> Still rapt in contemplation, the sainted seer
> assumed the vacant office of instruction,
> beginning with these words I still can hear: 3
>
> "The wound that Mary healed with balm so sweet
> was first dealt and then deepened by that being
> who sits in such great beauty at her feet. 6
>
> Below her, in the circle sanctified
> by the third rank of loves, Rachel is throned
> with Beatrice, as you see, there at her side. 9
>
> Sarah and Rebecca and Judith and she
> who was the great-grandmother of the singer
> who for his sins cried, 'Lord, have mercy on me!'— 12
>
> as I go down the great ranks tier by tier,
> naming them for you in descending order,
> petal by petal, you shall see them clear. 15
>
> And down from the seventh, continuing from those
> in the first six tiers, a line of Hebrew women
> forms a part in the tresses of the rose. 18
>
> Arranged to form a wall thus, they divide
> all ranks according to the view of Christ
> that marked the faith of those on either side. 21
>
> On this side, where the flower is in full bloom
> to its last petal, are arranged all those
> whose faith was founded upon Christ to Come; 24

on that, where the half circles show the unblended
    gaps of empty seats, are seated those
    whose living faith was fixed on Christ Descended.   27

And as, on this side, the resplendent throne
    of Heaven's Lady, with the thrones below it,
    establishes the line of that division;   30

so, facing hers, does the throned blessedness
    of the Great John who, ever holy, bore
    the desert, martyrdom, and Hell's distress;   33

and under him, forming that line are found
    Francis, Benedict, Augustine, and others
    descending to this center round by round.   36

Now marvel at all-foreseeing profundity:
    this garden shall be complete when the two aspects
    of the one faith have filled it equally.   39

And know that below that tier that cuts the two
    dividing walls at their centerpoint, no being
    has won his seat of glory by his own virtue,   42

but by another's, under strict condition;
    for all of these were spirits loosed from flesh
    before they had matured to true volition.   45

You can yourself make out their infant graces:
    you need no more than listen to their treble
    and look attentively into their faces.   48

You do not speak now: many doubts confound you.
    Therefore, to set you free I shall untie
    the cords in which your subtle thoughts have bound you.   51

Infinite order rules in this domain.
    Mere accidence can no more enter in
    than hunger can, or thirst, or grief, or pain.   54

All you see here is fixed by the decree
    of the eternal law, and is so made
    that the ring goes on the finger perfectly.   57

These, it follows, who had so short a pause
    in the lower life are not ranked higher or lower
    among themselves without sufficient cause.   60

The king in whom this realm abides unchanging
    in so much love and bliss that none dares will
    increase of joy, creating and arranging   63

the minds of all in the glad Paradise
    of His own sight, grants them degrees of grace
    as He sees fit. Here let the effect suffice.   66

Holy Scripture clearly and expressly
  notes this effect upon those twins who fought
  while still within their mother. So we see   69

how the Supreme light fittingly makes fair
  its aureole by granting them their graces
  according to the color of their hair.   72

Thus through no merit of their works and days
  they are assigned their varying degrees
  by variance only in original grace.   75

In the first centuries of man's creation
  their innocence and the true faith of their parents
  was all they needed to achieve salvation.   78

When the first age of man had run its course,
  then circumcision was required of males,
  to give their innocent wings sufficient force.   81

But when the age of grace came to mankind
  then, unless perfectly baptized in Christ,
  such innocents went down among the blind.   84

Look now on her who most resembles Christ,
  for only the great glory of her shining
  can purify your eyes to look on Christ."   87

I saw such joy rain down upon that face—
  borne to it by those blest Intelligences
  created thus to span those heights of space—   90

that through all else on the long road I trod
  nothing had held my soul so fixed in awe,
  nor shown me such resemblances to God.   93

The self-same Love that to her first descended
  singing "*Ave Maria, gratia plena*"
  stood before her with its wings extended.   96

Thus rang the holy chant to Heaven's Queen
  and all the blessèd court joined in the song,
  and singing, every face grew more serene.   99

"O holy Father who endures for me
  the loss of being far from the sweet place
  where fate has raised your throne eternally,   102

who is that angel who with such desire
  gazes into the eyes of our sweet Queen,
  so rapt in love he seems to be afire?"   105

Thus did I seek instruction from that Great One
  who drew the beauty of his light from Mary
  as the morning star drew beauty from the sun.   108

And he: "As much as angel or soul can know
  of exultation, gallantry, and poise
  there is in him; and we would have it so,   111

for it was he who brought the victory
  to Mary when the Son of God had willed
  to bear the weight of human misery.   114

But let your eyes go where my words point out
  among this court, and note the mighty peers
  of the empire of the just and the devout.   117

Those two whose bliss it is to sit so close
  to the radiance of the Empress of All Joy
  are the two eternal roots of this our rose: 120

The one just to the left of her blessedness
  is the father whose unruly appetite
  left man the taste for so much bitterness;   123

and on her right, that ancient one you see
  is the father of Holy Church to whom Christ gave
  the twin keys to this flower of timeless beauty.   126

And that one who in his prophetic sight
  foretold the evil days of the Sweet Bride
  won by the spear and nails, sits on his right.   129

While by the other father and first man
  sits the great leader to whom manna fell
  to feed an ingrate and rebellious clan.   132

Across the circle from Peter, behold Anna.
  She feels such bliss in looking at her daughter
  she does not move her eyes to sing 'Hosanna!'   135

And opposite the father of us all
  sits Lucy, who first urged your lady to you
  when you were blindly bent toward your own fall.   138

But the time allowed for this dream vision flies.
  As a tailor must cut the gown from what cloth is given,
  just so must we move on, turning our eyes   141

to the Primal Love, that as your powers advance
  with looking toward him, you may penetrate
  as deep as may be through His radiance.   144

But lest you should fall backward when you flare
  your mortal wings, intending to mount higher,
  remember grace must be acquired through prayer.   147

Therefore I will pray that blessèd one
  who has the power to aid you in your need.
  See that you follow me with such devotion   150

your heart adheres to every word I say."
And with those words the saint began to pray.

Notes

1–3. *Still rapt in contemplation*: Of the Virgin. His eyes have not left her. Nor do they turn again to Dante. Following his own preachment in XXXI, 112–117, he keeps his eyes on high. The text permits the assumption that Bernard turns his eyes from the Virgin to look at the various parts of the Mystic Rose as he identifies them, later, for Dante. Certainly, however, Bernard could identify every detail of the Rose without having to look at it, and every quality of Dante's mind and style would be better honored by thinking of Bernard as staring adoringly on the Virgin throughout. *the vacant office of instruction*: Formerly held by Beatrice. *I still can hear*: A rhyme-forced addition, not in Dante's text.

4–6. Mary, Mother of God, sits in the uppermost tier. At her feet in the second tier sits Eve, Mother of Man. *the wound*: Original sin. *balm so sweet*: Jesus. *opened*: The first fault, Eve's disobedience. *driven deeper*: Her seduction of Adam, thus spreading sin to all mankind. *in such great beauty*: Eve, having been created directly by God, was perfect in her beauty.

8–9. *Rachel . . . Beatrice at her side*: See *Inferno*, II, 102: "Where I was sitting with the ancient Rachel." Rachel, the younger wife of Jacob, symbolizes the contemplative life, as her sister Leah, also Jacob's wife, symbolizes the active life. In relation to Bernard she may be taken allegorically to be Contemplation and he to be the Contemplative Soul.

10–12. *Sarah*: Wife of Abraham. *Hebrews*, XI, 11–14, cites her as the mother (by miraculous fertility in her old age) of the Jews who foresaw Christ's coming and believed in him. *Rebecca*: Wife of Isaac. *Judith*: She killed Holofernes and freed the Jews. *and she*: Ruth, great-grandmother of David. *that singer*: David. *who for his sins*: His lust for Bathsheba, wife of Uriah. In order to marry Bathsheba, David sent Uriah to his death in the first line of battle. David's lament is in *Psalm L*.

Thus, the first descending rank, down tier by tier from Mary, is made up of Hebrew women, mothers of the children of God.

18. *part . . . tresses*: As if the rose were a head of hair and that vertical row of Hebrew women formed a part in it. In the next line the part becomes a wall.

22. *in full bloom*: That half of the rose-stadium that holds the pre-Christian believers would naturally be completely filled. On the other side there are thrones waiting for those who have yet to win salvation through Christ Descended. Dante, in fact, is laboring to earn one of them for himself. The Day of Judgment will be upon mankind when the last throne is filled, for Heaven will then be complete.

32–33. *the Great John*: The Baptist. He denounced Herod Antipos and was beheaded two years before the Crucifixion. He had to wait in Limbo for two years, therefore, till Christ came for him at the Resurrection. For the Harrowing of Hell, see *Inferno*, IV, 53, note.

40 ff. *below that tier*: The lower half of the rose-stadium contains the blessèd infants, the souls of those who died before they had achieved the true volition of reason and faith. They could not, therefore, win salvation by their own merit. *but by another's, under strict condition*: The necessary qualification for election is belief in Christ. These souls were too young at death to have formed their faith. Salvation is granted them not directly through belief in Christ but through the faith and prayers of their parents, relatives, and others of the faithful who interceded for them.

49. *many doubts*: The infants are ranked in tiers that indicate degrees of heavenly merit. But if they were saved through no merit of their own, how can one be more worthy than the other? Such is Dante's doubt, which Bernard goes on to set at rest by telling him, in essence, that God knows what He is doing.

58–59. *These . . . who had so short a pause*: The infants paused only briefly in the mortal life.

62. *dares*: I have no explanation of Dante's word choice here. "Not to dare" cannot fail to suggest intimidation. But in Paradise there can be no daring: every soul is in bliss exactly to the degree it is capable of bliss, and its capacity keeps increasing as it looks upon God. To dare (*ausare*, or in modern Italian, *osare*) must be taken as an impurity from the mortal vocabulary (in the sense of "even to think of") and not strictly of the heavenly tongue.

66. *the effect*: The cause is buried in God's mind. The effect must speak for itself.

67–72. The reference here is to Jacob and Esau. According to Genesis, XXV, 21 ff., they were at odds while still in their mother's womb. (Cf. the legend of Polyneices and Eteocles, twin sons of Oedipus and Jocasta.) Dante follows St. Paul (*Romans*, IX, 11–13) in interpreting the division between Jacob and Esau as a working of God's unfathomable will. "Even as it is written, Jacob I loved, but Esau I hated." Man can note the will of God in such matters ("the effect") but cannot plumb its causes. *according to the color of their hair*: For what may seem to be superficial reasons. Esau (*Genesis*, XXV, 25) was red-headed.

81. *sufficient force*: To mount to Heaven.

84. *among the blind*: Among the souls of Hell. Such infants were assigned to Limbo.

85. *on her who most resembles Christ*: The Virgin Mary.

88–99. THE GLORY OF THE VIRGIN. As Bernard directs, Dante fixes his attention on Mary and beholds her blazing in a splendor that rains down upon her in a host of angel beings. These fly from God to the Rose and back again like bees between the hive and the flower, with the difference that these bees bring the rain of light to the flower and are themselves the glorious rain.

88. *that face*: Mary's.

94. *the same Love*: The archangel Gabriel, the Angel of the Annunciation. Dante seems to conceive of Gabriel suspended in air before her, repeating the blissful chant of the Annunciation as he had first hymned it in Nazareth.

112. *the victory*: (Dante says "the palm.") Of God's election. Some commentators gloss it as Mary's triumph over all other Jewish women, all of whom would have been eager to bear the promised Messiah; and possibly so, but to be chosen by God would be triumph enough itself, and any thought of outshining the ladies of the neighborhood would be trivial by comparison.

118–126. *Those two*: Adam and St. Peter. Adam as Father of Mankind, Peter as Father of the Church. Note that Peter has the place of honor on the right.

127. *that one*: St. John the Evangelist. His *Apocalypse* was received as the prophetic book in which the entire history of the Church is foretold. He sits on Peter's right.

131. *that leader*: Moses. As the second great figure of the Old Testament he sits to the left of Adam.

133–135. *Anna*: Ste. Anna, Ste. Anne, mother of the Virgin. Her position directly across the circle from Peter's puts her to the right of John the Baptist. *does not move her eyes to sing 'Hosanna!'*: Like all the other heavenly beings, she constantly sings the praise of God. All others, naturally enough, look up as they sing. She, however, is so filled with bliss by the sight of Mary that she does not turn her eyes from her blessèd daughter. She praises God while looking at Mary. This detail can be interpreted in many ways, but all of them, of course, must center on the special position of Mary in Catholic doctrine and feeling.

136–138. *Lucy*: See *Inferno*, II, 97–100. It was she who first sent Beatrice to rescue Dante from the Dark Wood of Error. She sits opposite Adam. She would, accordingly, be to the left of John the Baptist.

139–141. The time granted for Dante's vision is limited. As a tailor must cut the gown from what cloth he is given, so Dante must get on with it, making what he can of his experience in the time allotted him.

142–144. In the act of looking at God man is given the power to see Him. Such is the gift of grace, and to the extent that grace is given, a man may see more or less deeply into God's glory.

148. *that blessed one*: Mary.

Canto XXXIII

St. Bernard · Prayer to the Virgin ·
The Vision of God

St. Bernard offers a lofty *Prayer to the Virgin*, asking her to intercede in
Dante's behalf, and in answer Dante feels his soul swell with new power
and grow calm in rapture as his eyes are permitted the Direct Vision of
God.

There can be no measure of how long the vision endures. It passes, and
Dante is once more mortal and fallible. Raised by God's presence, he had
looked into the Mystery and had begun to understand its power and majesty. Returned to himself, there is no power in him capable of speaking the
truth of what he saw. Yet the impress of the truth is stamped upon his
soul, which he now knows will return to be one with God's Love.

"Virgin Mother, daughter of thy son;
　　humble beyond all creatures and more exalted;
　　predestined turning point of God's intention;　　　　3

thy merit so ennobled human nature
　　that its divine Creator did not scorn
　　to make Himself the creature of His creature.　　　　6

The Love that was rekindled in Thy womb
　　sends forth the warmth of the eternal peace
　　within whose ray this flower has come to bloom.　　　　9

Here, to us, thou art the noon and scope
　　of Love revealed; and among mortal men,
　　the living fountain of eternal hope.　　　　12

Lady, thou art so near God's reckonings
　　that who seeks grace and does not first seek thee
　　would have his wish fly upward without wings.　　　　15

Not only does thy sweet benignity
　　flow out to all who beg, but oftentimes
　　thy charity arrives before the plea.　　　　18

In thee is pity, in thee munificence,
　　in thee the tenderest heart, in thee unites
　　all that creation knows of excellence!　　　　21

Now comes this man who from the final pit
　　of the universe up to this height has seen,
　　one by one, the three lives of the spirit.　　　　24

He prays to thee in fervent supplication
　　for grace and strength, that he may raise his eyes
　　to the all-healing final revelation.　　　　27

And I, who never more desired to see
    the vision myself than I do that he may see It,
    add my own prayer, and pray that it may be   30

enough to move you to dispel the trace
    of every mortal shadow by thy prayers
    and let him see revealed the Sum of Grace.   33

I pray thee further, all-persuading Queen,
    keep whole the natural bent of his affections
    and of his powers after his eyes have seen.   36

Protect him from the stirrings of man's clay;
    see how Beatrice and the blessèd host
    clasp reverent hands to join me as I pray."   39

The eyes that God reveres and loves the best
    glowed on the speaker, making clear the joy
    with which true prayer is heard by the most blest.   42

Those eyes turned then to the Eternal Ray,
    through which, we must indeed believe, the eyes
    of others do not find such ready way.   45

And I, who neared the goal of all my nature,
    felt my soul, at the climax of its yearning,
    suddenly, as it ought, grow calm with rapture.   48

Bernard then, smiling sweetly, gestured to me
    to look up, but I had already become
    within myself all he would have me be.   51

Little by little as my vision grew
    it penetrated further through the aura
    of the high lamp which in Itself is true.   54

What then I saw is more than tongue can say.
    Our human speech is dark before the vision.
    The ravished memory swoons and falls away.   57

As one who sees in dreams and wakes to find
    the emotional impression of his vision
    still powerful while its parts fade from his mind—   60

just such am I, having lost nearly all
    the vision itself, while in my heart I feel
    the sweetness of it yet distill and fall.   63

So, in the sun, the footprints fade from snow.
    On the wild wind that bore the tumbling leaves
    the Sybil's oracles were scattered so.   66

O Light Supreme who doth Thyself withdraw
    so far above man's mortal understanding,
    lend me again some glimpse of what I saw;   69

make Thou my tongue so eloquent it may
    of all Thy glory speak a single clue
    to those who follow me in the world's day;   72

for by returning to my memory
    somewhat, and somewhat sounding in these verses,
    Thou shalt show man more of Thy victory.   75

So dazzling was the splendor of that Ray,
    that I must certainly have lost my senses
    had I, but for an instant, turned away.   78

And so it was, as I recall, I could
    the better bear to look, until at last
    my vision made one with the Eternal Good.   81

Oh grace abounding that had made me fit
    to fix my eyes on the eternal light
    until my vision was consumed in it!   84

I saw within Its depth how It conceives
    all things in a single volume bound by Love,
    of which the universe is the scattered leaves;   87

substance, accident, and their relation
    so fused that all I say could do no more
    than yield a glimpse of that bright revelation.   90

I think I saw the universal form
    that binds these things, for as I speak these words
    I feel my joy swell and my spirits warm.   93

Twenty-five centuries since Neptune saw
    the Argo's keel have not moved all mankind,
    recalling that adventure, to such awe   96

as I felt in an instant. My tranced being
    stared fixed and motionless upon that vision,
    ever more fervent to see in the act of seeing.   99

Experiencing that Radiance, the spirit
    is so indrawn it is impossible
    even to think of ever turning from It.   102

For the good which is the will's ultimate object
    is all subsumed in It; and, being removed,
    all is defective which in It is perfect.   105

Now in my recollection of the rest
    I have less power to speak than any infant
    wetting its tongue yet at its mother's breast;   108

and not because that Living Radiance bore
    more than one semblance, for It is unchanging
    and is forever as it was before;   111

rather, as I grew worthier to see,
    the more I looked, the more unchanging semblance
    appeared to change with every change in me.   114

Within the depthless deep and clear existence
    of that abyss of light three circles shown—
    three in color, one in circumference: 117

the second from the first, rainbow from rainbow;
    the third, an exhalation of pure fire
    equally breathed forth by the other two.   120

But oh how much my words miss my conception,
    which is itself so far from what I saw
    that to call it feeble would be rank deception!   123

O Light Eternal fixed in Itself alone,
    by Itself alone understood, which from Itself
    loves and glows, self-knowing and self-known;   126

that second aureole which shone forth in Thee,
    conceived as a reflection of the first—
    or which appeared so to my scrutiny—   129

seemed in Itself of Its own coloration
    to be painted with man's image. I fixed my eyes
    on that alone in rapturous contemplation.   132

Like a geometer wholly dedicated
    to squaring the circle, but who cannot find,
    think as he may, the principle indicated—   135

so did I study the supernal face.
    I yearned to know just how our image merges
    into that circle, and how it there finds place;   138

but mine were not the wings for such a flight.
    Yet, as I wished, the truth I wished for came
    cleaving my mind in a great flash of light.   141

Here my powers rest from their high fantasy,
    but already I could feel my being turned—
    instinct and intellect balanced equally   144

as in a wheel whose motion nothing jars—
    by the Love that moves the Sun and the other stars.

Notes

1-39. ST. BERNARD'S PRAYER TO THE VIRGIN MARY. No reader who has come this far will need a lengthy gloss of Bernard's prayer. It can certainly be taken as a summarizing statement of the special place of Mary in Catholic faith. For the rest only a few turns of phrase need underlining. 3. *predestined turning point of God's intention*: All-foreseeing God built his whole scheme for mankind with Mary as its pivot, for through her He would become man. 7. *The Love that was rekindled in thy womb*: God. In a sense he withdrew from man when Adam and Eve sinned.

In Mary He returned and Himself became man. 35. *keep whole the natural bent of his affections*: Bernard is asking Mary to protect Dante lest the intensity of the vision overpower his faculties. 37. *Protect him from the stirrings of man's clay*: Protect him from the stirrings of base human impulse, especially from pride, for Dante is about to receive a grace never before granted to any man and the thought of such glory might well move a mere mortal to an hybris that would turn glory to sinfulness.

40. *the eyes*: Of Mary.

50. *but I had already become*: i.e., "But I had already fixed my entire attention upon the vision of God." But if so, how could Dante have seen Bernard's smile and geature? Eager students like to believe they catch Dante in a contradiction here. Let them bear in mind that Dante is looking directly at God, as do the souls of Heaven, who thereby acquire—insofar as they are able to contain it—God's own knowledge. As a first stirring of that heavenly power, therefore, Dante is sharing God's knowledge of St. Bernard.

54. *which in Itself is true*: The light of God is the one light whose source is Itself. All others are a reflection of this.

65–66. *tumbling leaves . . . oracles*: The Cumean Sybil (Virgil describes her in *Aeneid*, III, 441 ff.) wrote her oracles on leaves, one letter to a leaf, then sent her message scattering on the wind. Presumably, the truth was all contained in that strew, could one only gather all the leaves and put the letters in the right order.

76–81. How can a light be so dazzling that the beholder would swoon if he looked away for an instant? Would it not be, rather, in looking at, not away from, the overpowering vision that the viewer's senses would be overcome? So it would be on earth. But now Dante, with the help of all heaven's prayers, is in the presence of God and strengthened by all he sees. It is by being so strengthened that he can see yet more. So the passage becomes a parable of grace. Stylistically it once more illustrates Dante's genius: even at this height of concept, the poet can still summon and invent new perceptions, subtlety exfoliating from subtlety.

The simultaneous metaphoric statement, of course, is that no man can lose his good in the vision of God, but only in looking away from it.

85–87. The idea here is Platonic: the essence of all things (form) exists in the mind of God. All other things exist as exempla.

88. *substance*: Matter, all that exists in itself. *accident*: All that exists as a phase of matter.

92. *these things*: Substance and accident.

109–114. In the presence of God the soul grows ever more capable of perceiving God. Thus, the worthy soul's experience of God is a constant expansion of awareness. God appears to change as He is better seen. Being perfect, He is changeless within himself, for any change would be away from perfection.

130–144. The central metaphor of the entire *Comedy* is the image of God and the final triumphant inGodding of the elected soul returning to its Maker. On the mystery of that image, the metaphoric symphony of the *Comedy* comes to rest.

In the second aspect of Trinal-unity, in the circle reflected from the first, Dante thinks he sees the image of mankind woven into the very substance and coloration of God. He turns the entire attention of his soul to that mystery, as a geometer might seek to shut out every other thought and dedicate himself to squaring the circle. In *Il Convivio*, II, 14, Dante asserted that the circle could not be squared, but that impossibility had not yet been firmly demonstrated in Dante's time and mathematicians still worked at the problem. Note, however, that Dante assumes the impossibility of squaring the circle as a weak mortal example of mortal impossibility. How much more impossible, he implies, to resolve the mystery of God, study as man will.

The mystery remains beyond Dante's mortal power. Yet, there in Heaven, in a moment of grace, God revealed the truth to him in a flash of light—revealed it, that is, to the God-enlarged power of Dante's emparadised soul. On Dante's return to the mortal life, the details of that revelation vanished from his mind but the force of the revelation survives in its power on Dante's feelings.

So ends the vision of the *Comedy*, and yet the vision endures, for ever since that revelation, Dante tells us, he feels his soul turning ever as one with the perfect motion of God's love.